ISBN 978-1-333-76433-3
PIBN 10545014

1 MONTH OF
FREE
READING

at

www.ForgottenBooks.com

By purchasing this book you are eligible for one month membership to ForgottenBooks.com, giving you unlimited access to our entire collection of over 700,000 titles via our web site and mobile apps.

To claim your free month visit:

www.forgottenbooks.com/free545014

English
Français
Deutsche
Italiano
Español
Português

www.forgottenbooks.com

Mythology Photography **Fiction**
Fishing Christianity **Art** Cooking
Essays Buddhism Freemasonry
Medicine **Biology** Music **Ancient**
Egypt Evolution Carpentry Physics
Dance Geology **Mathematics** Fitness
Shakespeare **Folklore** Yoga Marketing
Confidence Immortality Biographies
Poetry **Psychology** Witchcraft
Electronics Chemistry History **Law**
Accounting **Philosophy** Anthropology
Alchemy Drama Quantum Mechanics
Atheism Sexual Health **Ancient History**
Entrepreneurship Languages Sport
Paleontology Needlework Islam
Metaphysics Investment Archaeology
Parenting Statistics Criminology
Motivational

THE

APPROACHING END OF THE AGE

VIEWED IN THE LIGHT OF

HISTORY, PROPHECY, AND SCIENCE.

BY

H. GRATTAN GUINNESS.

Ἀμήν ἔρχου, κύριε Ἰησοῦ.

FIFTH EDITION.

London:

HODDER AND STOUGHTON,

27, PATERNOSTER ROW.

—

MDCCCLXXX.

BUTLER & TANNER,
THE SELWOOD PRINTING WORKS.
FROME, AND LONDON.

PREFACE TO THE FIRST EDITION.

THE volume now presented to the Christian public, consists as will be observed, of four parts : the first is commended to the candid consideration of those who have not yet received the truth of *the premillennial advent of our Lord Jesus Christ*, the second and third take that truth as proved and granted, and address themselves especially to those who, holding pre-millennial views, are still looking for the manifestation of Antichrist, prior to the visible advent of Christ, those who adopt a literal interpretation of the Apocalyptic prophecies, including their chronological features—in other words, to the *futurist* school of prophetic interpreters. The fourth and last part, which consists of *an investigation into the system of times and seasons presented in the word and works of God*, contains not a few original observations and discoveries, which, if the author mistakes not, throw fresh light on the whole subject of Scripture prophecy, and which he thinks will be found of interest to all students of the prophetic word, as well as, he trusts, to all lovers of the Bible. Perhaps, he cannot better introduce the book to the reader, than by giving a brief outline of its history.

Imbued by education with the ordinary view, that a gradual improvement in the present state of things was to be expected till all the world should be converted, and a spiritual kingdom of God be universally established on earth, and that no return of Christ was to be looked for till the day of judgment at the end of the world,—the author no sooner began to study the Scriptures independently than he perceived, that this view obliged him to interpret in a forced and non-natural manner a vast variety of apparently clear and simple passages, both in the Old and New Testaments. Unable to rest satisfied with doing this, he was led to read a variety of works, both for and against premillennial views, especially that most able treatise ever penned *against* them, entitled " Christ's Second Coming, will it be Premillennial ? " by Dr. David Brown, of Aberdeen. Unable to reach any decision satisfactory to himself by this study of prophetic works, the author nearly twenty years ago laid them all aside, and very carefully and critically read through the entire Bible, marking, studying and considering every passage bearing on the subject, with a view to collect the full testimony of the Word of God respecting it. This plan he would earnestly commend to those who may be in doubt as to the truth on this fundamental point. It completely set his own mind at rest, and his views have never been shaken since. That a premillennial advent of Christ is clearly predicted in the Word of God, the writer never afterwards doubted, or hesitated to preach ; but the pressing claims of incessant evangelistic labours for many years, forbad his looking further into prophetic subjects.

A fuller acquaintance, acquired by personal observation, with the condition of the Greek and other professing Christian

Churches of Syria, Egypt, and Turkey, and of the effects of Mohammedan rule in the East, and also with the Papal system as developed in France and Spain, and with the Continental infidelity to which it has given rise, subsequently led the author to a careful study of the history of the Mohammedan and Papal powers, and of the prophecies of Scripture believed by many to relate to them. This resulted in a deep conviction that THOSE POWERS OCCUPY IN THE WORD OF GOD, AS PROMINENT A PLACE AS THEY HAVE ACTUALLY HELD IN THE HISTORY OF THE CHURCH.

The remarkable events of the years 1866–70, especially the outbreak of the Franco-German war, which put a stop to evangelistic efforts which the author had been for some time making in Paris, led him not only still further to consider the question of modern fulfilment of prophecy, but to prepare a work on the subject, which he intended to have published under the title of "Foretold and Fulfilled." This work advocated the Protestant or historic system of interpreting the symbolic prophecies of Daniel and the Apocalypse, and in doing so had necessarily to consider the question which lies at the base of the different views of unfulfilled prophecy taken by Christians — *the true meaning of the chronological statements contained in symbolic prophecy,* i.e., whether they are *literal* or whether they are *figurative.* In studying the masterly and exhaustive treatise of the Rev. T. R. Birks on this subject,[*]

---

[*] "First Elements of Sacred Prophecy, including an examination of several recent Expositions, and of the Year-day Theory," by the Rev. T. R. Birks, Fellow of Trinity College, Cambridge.

the author was deeply interested in a statement made on the authority of a Swiss astronomer, M. De Cheseaux, that **the** leading prophetic periods of Scripture are demonstrably *celestial cycles;* that is, periods *as definitely marked off as such* by celestial revolutions, as are our ordinary years or days. This led him to examine the nature of these eveles, and to investigate the connection between astronomic facts and Scripture chronology, and thus to the discovery that the *epacts* of the prophetic periods of Scripture form a remarkable septiform series.

Practical duties of a pressing nature connected with the foundation of the author's EAST LONDON INSTITUTE FOR HOME AND FOREIGN MISSIONS,* prevented the completion of the intended volume, and the papers connected with *the astronomic measures of the prophetic times* lay by for some years in the hands of the Rev. T. R. Birks of Cambridge.

But in 1876–7, when the long impending Eastern question came once more to the front, and attention was, by the tragic and eventful scenes transpiring in European Turkey, again directed to evident cotemporaneous fulfilments of prophecy, the author was strongly impressed with the duty of giving **to** his brethren without further delay, any light which God might have given him on this sacred and deeply interesting theme; of adding his contribution, however small, towards the understanding of the prophetic word, and in spite of many difficulties he has made leisure, during the last eighteen months, to complete his researches into the subject, and prepare the present volume for the press.

---

* See Appendix C.

In order to secure correctness in his astronomic statements, the author submitted a considerable portion of the fourth part of this work to the criticisms of Professor Adams of Cambridge, whose discovery of the planet Neptune by pure mathematical calculation, has long given him a position of the very highest eminence, as an authority in astronomic science. Professor Adams was kind enough to allow the author to read to him many (though not quite all) of his statements on " the connection of Times and Seasons natural and revealed," and he also verified some of M. De Cheseaux's calculations with reference to the cyclical character of the prophetic Times. Finding M. De Cheseaux's work in the British Museum, the author had it carefully copied for his own use, and subsequently sent it to Professor Adams that he might examine a point about which he had expressed some doubt, relative to the times of the equinoxes and of the summer solstice in the year of Daniel's vision 552 B.C.

The following letter from Professor Adams shows M. De Cheseaux to have been slightly in error on this point,—error easily accounted for by the want, in his day, of such accurate data as more modern science supplies—but which does not in the least affect his conclusions as to the cyclical character of the prophetic Times :—

OBSERVATORY, CAMBRIDGE, March 18, 1878.

MY DEAR SIR,

I received the copy of De Cheseaux safely, and I ought ere this to have sent you the result of my examination into the correctness of his statements. Pray pardon the delay, which has been caused by my having been so busy. I have calculated very approximately the times of the equinoxes and solstices for the year B.C. 552, which is that given by De Cheseaux as the year of Daniel's vision, and I find the following results, expressed in mean time at Jerusalem, reckoned from midnight.

				d.	h.	m.
Vernal equinox	...	March	...	27	8	2
Summer solstice	...	June	...	29	11	39
Autumnal equinox	...	Sept.	...	29	11	51
Winter solstice		Dec.		27	0	17

Hence the summer solstice and the autumnal equinox take place not far from noon at Jerusalem, but the vernal equinox takes place about four hours before noon. De Cheseaux's error appears to arise chiefly from his having supposed that the excentricity of the earth's orbit was the same in the time of Daniel as in his own time, whereas it was very sensibly greater. I have added the time of the winter solstice also, though it is not required for your purpose. . . . . The fact is that the change of excentricity and place of the apse of the orbit of any planet, is a compound phenomenon, due to the combined action of all the other planets, and therefore the final result is got by compounding together several variable quantities, which have quite different and indeed incommensurable periods. I will return your copy of De Cheseaux, which is quite beautifully done, immediately, either by post or railway, as I have done with it.

I remain, dear sir,

Yours very truly,

J. C. ADAMS.

As his letter did not reach the author in time to allow of his adding Professor Adams's correction to M. De Cheseaux's statement quoted on p. 404 of this work, he inserts it here.* The modern solar and lunar tables employed by Professor Adams, also showed some slight errors in M. De Cheseaux's calculations, amounting to *about an hour* in the period of 1040 years (referred to on p. 403) but in nowise invalidating the claim of that period to be considered *a cycle harmonizing the*

---

* The statement referred to has been omitted in this edition.

lunar month with the solar year, or the cyclical character of the associated prophetic periods of 1260 and 2300 years, of which it is the difference.

The author has also to acknowledge his indebtedness to the kind and valued criticisms of his friends, the Rev. Henry Brooke of Dovercourt, and Philip Henry Gosse, Esq., F.R.S., of Torquay, who saw portions of the prophetic parts of this work while it was passing through the press. Their accurate acquaintance with the prophetic Scriptures, and deep reverence for the Word of God, gave the suggestions they made a special value in this principal branch of the subject dealt with.

There remains to the author the grateful task of acknowledging the *very considerable help* he has had in writing and revising this volume from the practised pen of his beloved wife, for many years the sharer of his toils in various efforts to spread in different lands the knowledge of saving or of sanctifying Truth. The part which—in spite of much wearying labour by day and often by night, as Honorary Secretary of the EAST LONDON INSTITUTE FOR HOME AND FOREIGN MISSIONS —she has cheerfully taken in the task of preparing this work —however others may regard the result—will endear it to him while memory endures.

And now the author commends this work to the candour of the Christian Reader, and above all to the blessing of God! He alone knows how earnestly and incessantly the enlightenings of his own Holy Spirit have been sought, in the course of its preparation, how often the heartfelt prayer, " O send out thy light and thy truth, let them lead me," has gone up amid the studies of which it is the result. The Bible has been the main field explored, in the conviction, "in thy light we shall see light;" and in giving to the Church of Christ, the light on this high and holy subject, which has, he humbly believes, been granted in response to much prayer, he desires to ascribe to the only wise God, the giver of understanding, all glory, and honour, and praise. Of all his good gifts, knowledge, true knowledge of Him, of his works, of his word, and of his ways, is one of the best; and we are commanded to *grow* in such knowledge.

If this work lead his brethren in the ministry to an increased study of the Prophetic Scriptures, the author will feel richly rewarded, whether his own conclusions be received or not. He is conscious that his researches into the Divine system of times and seasons *have gone but a little way into the subject,* but his hope is that they may serve to indicate to abler minds and pens, a vein of ore which will richly repay working.

To one feature of the investigation he begs to call special attention. IT DEALS NOT WITH THEORIES BUT WITH FACTS: it consists **not** of *speculations* about the future, which are altogether foreign to it, and in which the writer has not the least inclination to indulge; it consists in a collection of facts, and of inferences drawn from those facts. The author has endeavoured to deal with the question, What are the *facts* of the world's history and chronology? What are the *facts* as to the nature, the objects, and the fulfilment of Scripture prophecy? What are the ascertained *facts* as to the plan of Providence? What are the *facts* as to the system of Times and Seasons in

Nature—the periodicity of vital phenomena, and the majestic revolutions of the worlds whose movements control the entire progress of terrestrial time? What are the links of connection between these facts? What are the laws which control them? What is the chronological system to which these chronological elements belong? The answers to these questions have been sought with care, and patient reflection. The inductive method has been followed throughout; the *facts* of revelation and the *facts* of nature, have been collected and compared; a broad basis has been thus constructed; and the conclusions reached have been limited, as far as possible, to *legitimate inferences from the facts considered.* The author claims that a candid consideration of the fourth part of this volume should prevent its ever being confounded with a class of writings which properly fail to command the attention of sober-minded Christian students. A wide distinction exists and should be recognised between *students and expositors of the Word and Works of God,* who humbly, soberly, and reverently searching into the facts of Nature and Scripture, of providence and of prophecy, reach conclusions which sanctified common sense can approve,—and *speculators,* who running away with isolated and mysterious expressions, indulge in imaginations of their own, and become *prophets,* instead of students of Divine prophecy. No employment of human intelligence is nobler, than an adoring inves- . tigation of the revealed purposes of God, "which things the angels desire to look into," while few are so puerile, as a presumptuous pretence of predicting the future, apart from such cautious and careful study of Divine revelation.

In conclusion, the author would strongly deprecate the false and foolish popular notion, that all study of prophecy is unpractical—a notion too often propagated by passing, but mischievously-influential allusions to the subject, from pulpit, platform, and press, made by those who know little either of it, or of its effects. It ought to be a sufficient rebuke to the levity that hazards such an assertion, or admits such an idea, to recall the facts, that one-third of the Bible consists of prophecy; and that our Lord and Master said, " Search the Scriptures," not a portion of them. The apostle Peter expressly tells us that we *do well to take heed* to the " more sure word of prophecy," as to a light shining in a dark place until the day dawn and the day star arise. Is it unpractical to make use of a good lantern on a pitch-dark night, in traversing a dangerous road? or is it not rather unpractical and unreasonable to attempt to dispense with it? And further, a special and emphatic blessing is attached to this study in the closing book of the Bible : " Blessed is he that readeth, and they that hear the words of this prophecy, and keep the things that are written therein, for the time is at hand."

It is a reflection of the gravest kind on the wisdom of God, to suppose that the study of a branch of truth to which He has in his word accorded singular prominence, should have an injurious tendency, or be devoid of a directly sanctifying effect : and moreover it is a conclusion completely at variance with all the facts of history and experience. Enoch was a student of prophecy; and of prophecy that is to this day unfulfilled, and Enoch was the saintliest of men, an eminently holy and practical preacher, who walked with God three hundred years, and was not, for God took him, and before his translation he had this testimony, that he pleased God. Noah was a student of unfulfilled prophecy, and Scripture presents no more practical preacher of righteousness than he was. All the holy prophets were students, and diligent students, too, of their own and of each other's predictions, and *especially of their chronological predictions.* "The prophets inquired and searched diligently, searching what or *what manner of time* the Spirit of Christ which was in them did signify, when it testified beforehand the sufferings of Christ, and the glories that should follow" (1 Pet. i. 10, 11). Daniel was a student of unfulfilled prophecy, yet he was not only a practical statesman, but a man of singular holiness, classed with Noah and Job as one of the *most* righteous of men.

There is everything in the nature of the study to make those who pursue it both practical and holy. It imbues the mind with the counsels and judgment of God about the affairs and events of earth; it reveals what *shall be*, and thereby lessens the inordinate power of that which *is now*, bringing the spirit under the influence of things unseen and eternal, and thereby weakening that of things seen and temporal. It affords to hope much needed food, lacking which we must languish and grow feeble; and to faith and love peculiar stimulus and enjoyment. Without an intelligent acquaintance with the teaching of the prophetic word, no man of God is or can be thoroughly furnished to all good works, for it is part of the "all

Scripture " given by inspiration, and profitable for the purpose of rendering him so.

Perhaps one reason for the prevailing neglect of prophetic expositions and preaching will be found on reflection, to lie, *not* in the fact that it is *un*practical, but rather in the fact that it is so *peculiarly practical*, that few have the boldness and courage to face the ridicule, opposition, and contempt it is sure to incur in the world. Jeremiah lived on the eve and in the crisis of a day of judgment on the apostate professing people of God. He was commissioned to deliver prophetic discourses full of denunciations of coming judgment, and of *chronological state-ments of its proximity and duration.* We know what Jere-miah's lot was, and few are prepared to play *his* sad and thank-less rôle in society !

So far from the study and exposition of the prophetic word being profitless and vain, we believe it is impossible to esti-mate the loss sustained by the Church, or the injury done to the world, by the very general and unjustifiable neglect of it. Is it not so that where one prophetic discourse is delivered, ten thousand doctrinal and practical sermons are preached? *By what authority do we thus shelve a line of truth to which divine wisdom has given such prominence in Scripture?* Is it not our duty to declare " *the whole counsel of God* " ? Those who have carefully looked into this subject, solemnly and with good ground believe, that the " word " we are commanded to " preach " is full of evidence that the long predicted and long delayed judgments on the Papal and Mohammedan powers, which are not only already begun, but are fast accomplishing before our eyes, are to issue, and that speedily, in such a burning of "Babylon the Great," as will light up all Christendom with its lurid glow,—the immediate precursor, if it be not the accompaniment, of the glorious advent of the King of kings. With all earnestness and sobriety of mind they assure their brethren that it is their deep conviction that *this is the testimony of sacred Scripture;* yet multitudes of Christian teachers, without even taking the trouble of examining into the subject, still preach the contrary, or imply it in their preaching; not from well-grounded conviction of its truth, but from educational prejudice, or mere force of habit. Is this right? Ought not every minister of the word to study for himself the teachings of Scripture, until he is satisfied that he has attained the truth on this momentous theme?

For if we are right—if there be unequivocal proof in the inspired volume, proof that no previous generation of Christians was in a position to appreciate as we are, that the day of Christ is at hand—that the time for evangelising the nations, and gathering in the church of the first-born is speedily to expire—that the long day of grace to the Gentiles is all but over, and that apostate Christendom, so long spared by the goodness of God, is soon to be cut off by his righteous severity—that the mystery of God is all but finished, and his manifested rule about to be inaugurated—that the great closing Armageddon conflict is at hand, and the complete overthrow of the confederated hosts of evil—*if* we be right in believing that scarcely a single prophecy in the whole Bible, relating to events prior to the second advent of Christ remains unfulfilled

—*if we be right*,—then surely every pulpit in England should be ringing with timely testimony to these truths,—surely these solemn and most momentous facts ought not, in the preaching of any of God's faithful witnesses throughout the world, to be· passed by in silence. And who that has not *studied* the subject can be in a position to say that we are *not* right— that these things are not so?

May such·a spirit as the Bereans had of old, be granted to the Christians of this generation, that they may diligently search the " more sure word of prophecy," and draw directly from that sacred fountain *the Truth as to the fast approaching future*, which God has graciously revealed ; and may this volume, through his blessing, prove in such researches, helpful to not a few.

East London Institute for
　　Home and Foreign Missions,
　　　　Harley House, Bow, E.
Mar. 21st, 1878.

PREFACE TO THE SECOND EDITION.

—◇◇◇—

THE author has been glad to see, by the sale of the first edition of two thousand copies of this work within eight months of its publication, that the important subject of which it treats is increasingly attracting the attention of students of Scripture. In preparing the book for a second edition, he has spared no pains in order to render it as accurate and as reliable as possible.

The present edition has been carefully corrected throughout, and all the astronomic calculations have been verified by a professional mathematician employed in one of the government astronomical offices.

A considerable amount of astronomic detail, which is of interest only to students, has been thrown into an appendix, in order to relieve and simplify the latter part of the work, and to adapt it for general readers.

Much additional matter, of a chronologic and historic character, has been introduced, and several fresh discoveries, of no small importance to the whole subject, are embodied in this edition. As the result of further research, the truth as to the Divine system of times and seasons has become more clear to the author's own mind, and it is, he trusts, more clearly presented now than previously.   *b*

There is added in an appendix a complete CALENDAR OF THE TIMES OF THE GENTILES, showing, in unbroken sequence, the main events from the beginning of the Babylonian monarchy (B.C. 747) to the present day. This calendar gives the names of the various monarchs of different dynasties, who have succeeded each other in the headship of the four great empires symbolised by the fourfold image of Daniel, together with their B.C. and A.D. dates, and the leading events of the history. It commences, as will be observed, with the era of Nabonassar, or date of the accession of the first king of Babylon. This date is determined with certainty and exactitude by a series of astronomic observations recorded by Ptolemy, and is therefore one of the best ascertained dates of remote antiquity. Prophetic students have long been divided in opinion as to the point from which the great " seven times " of prophecy should be dated. All agree that the *terminus a quo* must lie somewhere in the rise of the Babylonian monarchy, but there is difference of judgment as to the exact point. This calendar shows the remarkable fact—never, we believe, observed before—that from the *day of the accession of Nabonassar, the first king of Babylon, to the day of the fall of Romulus Augustulus, the last emperor of Rome, there elapsed an interval of precisely* 1260 *lunar years.* That the entire duration of the four great Pagan Gentile empires (prior to the tenfold division of the last) should thus measure, *precisely* " time, times and a half," seems to indicate that the era of Nabonassar should be regarded as, at any rate, an initial starting-point for the " Times of the Gentiles," though the overthrow of the throne of Judah by Nebuchadnezzar is un-doubtedly the full and final commencement of this great dis-pensational period. This remarkable fact indicates also that the *lunar* measurement of time must not be overlooked in researches as to the fulfilment of chronologic prophecy. Hence the distance of each event from the starting-point is, in the calendar, given not only in solar but also in lunar years. Like the great "week," whose chronicle it presents, this calendar is divided into two parts. The first gives the history of the 1260 years just mentioned, from the beginning of the Babylonian to the end of the Roman empire; and the second traces that of the 1260 years which have elapsed between the era of the rise and that of the fall of the Papal and Mohammedan powers. The latter not only gives the chronologic distance of each event from the era of Nabonassar—the commencement of the *whole* "seven times"—but also from the rise of the apostasies —the commencement of their second half. The Papal chrono-logy is given in solar, and the Mohammedan in lunar years, the Mohammedan calendar being lunar.

The chronology followed in the earlier part of the calendar is that of the Canon of Ptolemy, as verified by astronomical researches, and elaborately set forth in Clinton's "Fasti Hellenici." The chronology of the Roman empire, as far as the reign of Heraclius, is drawn from Clinton's "Fasti Romani"; intermediate and subsequent dates are taken from Blair's Chronological Tables, and its useful rearrangement in Rosse's Dictionary of Dates, compared with various chrono-logical works, ancient and modern. The chronology of recent

European history is given from Haydn's Dictionary of Dates, while that of the most recent and current events is taken from the annual register of the *Times* newspaper.

There is also added in an appendix a careful investigation into the subject of the " seventy weeks " of Dan. ix., a chronological prophecy of the first importance, as being the only one in Scripture indicating the period of the first advent of Christ, and one whose fulfilment is an unanswerable argument for the truth of Christianity.

The author sends forth this second edition with a deeper conviction than ever that there is ample and satisfactory evidence that we are indeed living in the closing years of this dispensation—the time of the end ; and with a stronger desire than ever that this solemn fact may be more widely perceived and acknowledged by the Church of God, in order to the increase of practical holiness, of joyful hope, and of earnest activity in the work of the Lord.

April 25th, 1879.

PREFACE TO THE FIFTH EDITION.

I N sending forth a fifth edition of this work within two years of its first publication, we thankfully record the fact, of which we have abundant evidence, that it has found acceptance with a large number of earnest Christians, of students of God's word, of ministers of the gospel, of saints who love the hope of their Lord's appearing. From Christians of various denominations and ranks in society, and of different nationalities, letters have been received expressing substantial and hearty agreement with the views it unfolds, and stating that spiritual blessing has been experienced in its perusal. For this, then, we give thanks to God, the alone Giver of every good and perfect gift, and rejoice that our labour has not been expended upon it in vain. I say we, for I associate with myself in this my beloved wife, my fellow-labourer in the gospel, whose valuable aid rendered in the preparation of this book made it our joint work, and constitutes its success our joint reward.

Very little alteration has been made in this edition; a few slight errors found in the fourth edition have been corrected, and a footnote has been added on page 78, containing Dean Alford's striking and valuable testimony to the correct interpretation of Revelation xx., as establishing the literality of the first resurrection, and the premillennial character of the Second Advent.

May grace be given to all who look for the speedy coming of our Lord to prove they do so by their spirit, their labours, and their lives! "What manner of persons ought we to be in all holy conversation and godliness?" How should we reflect upon a dark world the glow of the coming sunrise! How should we abound in our labours for the Lord, and that "*so much the more*" as we more clearly "see the day" "approaching"?

H. GRATTAN GUINNESS.

HARLEY HOUSE, BOW, E.,
February, 1880.

TABLE OF CONTENTS.

---◆---

Part I.

PROGRESSIVE REVELATION.

CHAPTER I.

CHAPTER II.

CHAPTER III.

Part II.

PROGRESSIVE INTERPRETATION.

CHAPTER I.

Part III.

FORETOLD AND FULFILLED.

CHAPTER I.

BABYLON THE GREAT.

CHAPTER II.

THE MAN OF SIN, OR ANTICHRIST.

Part IV.

INQUIRY INTO THE DIVINE SYSTEM OF TIMES AND SEASONS, NATURAL AND REVEALED.

SECTION I.

SOLAR AND LUNAR DOMINION, CAUSAL AND CHRONOLOGICAL.

CHAPTER I.

CHAPTER II.

SOLI-LUNAR DOMINION IN THE ORGANIC WORLD.

SECTION II.

THE LAW OF COMPLETION IN WEEKS.

CHAPTER I.

THE WEEK IN RELATION TO THE PERIODICITY OF VITAL PHENOMENA.

CONTENTS OF APPENDICES.

———◆———

APPENDIX A.

APPENDIX B.

APPENDIX C.

"The natural and moral constitution and government of the world are so connected, as to make up together but one scheme: and it is highly probable, that the first is formed and carried on merely in subserviency to the latter; as the vegetable world is for the animal, and organized bodies for minds. But the thing intended here, is, without inquiring how far the administration of the natural world is subordinate to that of the moral, only to observe the credibility, that one should be analogous or similar to the other; that therefore every act of Divine justice and goodness, may be supposed to look much beyond itself, and its immediate object; may have some reference to other parts of God's moral administration, and to a general moral plan: and that *every circumstance* of this his moral government, may be adjusted beforehand with a view to *the whole of it.* Thus for example: the determined length of time, and the degrees and ways, in which virtue is to remain in a state of warfare and discipline, and in which wickedness is permitted to have its progress; the times appointed for the execution of justice; the appointed instruments of it; the kind of rewards and punishments, and the manners of their distribution; all particular instances of Divine justice and goodness, and every circumstance of them, may have such respects to each other, as to make up all together, a whole, connected and related in all its parts: a scheme or system, which is as properly one as the natural world is, and of the like kind."

Bp. Butler.

PART I.

PROGRESSIVE REVELATION.

CHAPTER I.

GOD'S REVELATION OF HIMSELF TO MAN HAS BEEN A PRO-
GRESSIVE ONE.—TRUTH IN GENERAL HAS BEEN REVEALED
PROGRESSIVELY.—PROPHECY, THE DIVINE HISTORY OF THE
FUTURE, CONSISTS OF A SERIES OF PROGRESSIVE REVELA-
TIONS.—PRACTICAL RESULTS OF THE COMPREHENSION AND
APPLICATION OF THIS PRINCIPLE.

GOD has been pleased to make three great revelations
of Himself to man: his Works; his Word; and his
Son, and these revelations have been *progressive* in character.
Nature, the Law, the Gospel; a silent material universe, an
inspired Book, a living God-man; these are the three great
steps that have led from the death and darkness of sin to that
knowledge of the true God which is eternal life.

A fourth revelation of God, fuller and more perfect than
any, is yet to come. The only begotten Son, who is in the
bosom of the Father, who is the brightness of his glory and
the express image of his person, who "declared Him"
when He came the first time in grace and humiliation, will declare Him yet more fully when He comes a second time in
righteousness and in glory. Then the earth will be filled with
the knowledge of the Lord, as the waters cover the sea.

Each of these revelations is *in itself progressive*. The earth
and all that is therein, attained perfection by six distinct stages,

during the six days of creation. The angels followed with adoring wonder the fresh unfoldings of Divine wisdom, goodness, and power, presented in the gradual formation of this great globe, and in its myriad mysteries of vegetable and animal life, though to human eyes nature was presented perfect and complete. But human eyes could see at first the surface of things alone ; every advance in true science, enabling men to penetrate more deeply into the hidden wisdom of the work of God, has been a *progressive* revelation. And we have only begun, even now, to understand the glory of God, manifested in the universe. To us, more than to our ancestors, the heavens declare the glory of God, and the earth showeth his handi-work ; and to our children they will do so even more.

The Word of God is also a *progressive* revelation, and so has been the Providence recorded in that Word.

The Bible is composed of sixty-three separate books, written by forty various authors, during a period of 1600 years. The sacred writings develop a revelation which was continually unfolding itself through all those years ; and close with a book bearing the divinely given title of " The Revelation of Jesus Christ."

The third revelation of God, that afforded by the person and work of our blessed Lord Jesus Christ, was also *progressive.* The mere fact of his birth and existence in the midst of a world of sinners, was in itself an evidence of God's love to a guilty race. Each word He spoke, each act He performed, each day He lived, unfolded more and more of God. They who saw Him saw the Father, for He was his express image ; and not until He, the Maker and Judge of all, was exposed on the cursed tree, not till from his riven side flowed the water and the blood, not till He bowed his head and gave up the ghost, never till then, was the heart of God fully unveiled ; " hereby *perceive* we the love of God."

And it will be the same in the future ; for since finite man is destined through boundless mercy to an eternal advance in the knowledge of the infinite God, that knowledge must needs be vouchsafed in *progressive* revelations, adapted to man's ability to receive them. And herein will lie one of the joys of heaven, to be ever learning more of Him, who is the Truth, and from Him, of all things.

No student of Scripture can fail to be struck with the progressive character of its teachings. On no one subject was full information given at the beginning; all was revealed in germ only, and in the lapse of ages unfolded by degrees. Take, for instance, the doctrine of the Trinity: in the beginning God taught the unity of his nature, and the other truth that in the one God there are three persons, was only intimated; suggested by certain forms of expression, as the use of a plural noun with a singular verb, which occurs several hundred times, as in Gen. i. 1, Ps. lviii. 11. There were besides expressions, the accurate harmony of which with this truth, we who understand it can appreciate, but which were not revelations to those who were ignorant of it. Such for example is the divinely prescribed threefold form of benediction in Numbers; and such the seraphs' threefold ascription of praise in Isaiah, followed by the Lord Jehovah's question, "Who will go for *us*?" The later prophets assume the doctrine as true (Isa. xlviii. 16, Isa. ix. 6); but the New Testament alone reveals it fully.

Or take again the law of love; man's first duty towards his brother man. To the antediluvian world no law on the subject was given. To Noah, murder, the worst expression of hatred, was forbidden; through Moses the *doing* of any ill to the neighbour was prohibited, either in his person, his property, his reputation or his domestic interests. By the Lord Jesus the *feeling* of any enmity was forbidden; and not only so but positive love, even to the laying down of life itself for the brother, commanded. What an advance is the conception of love embodied in 1 Corinthians xiii. on that derived from Sinai, or even from the sermon on the mount.

Our present object is to trace this progress in connection with the prophecies of Scripture, and more especially with those of the New Testament.

I. *The prophetic teachings of Scripture consist of a series of progressive revelations.*

Its earliest predictions of any future event, have the character of outlines, later ones fill in the sketch, and the final ones present the finished picture. It is first the bud, next the half opened blossom, and lastly the flower in full bloom.

There was progress in the *amount of truth revealed*, as well as in the fulness of revelation on each point. The little stream-let of prophecy which sprang up in Eden and trickled down through the antediluvian ages, swelled by continual accessions, till it rushed a flowing Jordan through Israel's tribes, grew into a mighty Euphrates during the Babylonish captivity, and opened out into a vast delta around Patmos, whence its waters glide calmly into the ocean of eternity.

Adam heard one brief enigmatical prediction from the voice of God Himself. Noah sketched, in three inspired sentences, the great features of human history. In the curse on Canaan was contained in embryo the iniquity of the seven nations and their conquest by Joshua; the priority of blessing granted to Shem, similarly contained the subsequent choice of his descendant Abraham to be the heir of the world and father of the faithful. In the promise of enlargement given to Japheth, was contained the spiritual enlargement which took place when the Gentiles were received into the new covenant, and the physical en-largement accomplished in comparatively recent days by the European colonization of America, and conquest of India, both "tents of Shem." This prophecy spanned the stream of time with a few gigantic arches; carrying us over from the vineyard of Noah to the Anglo-Saxon empires of our own day.

The patriarchs learned from God many additional particulars as to the future: to Abraham was revealed the history of the descendants of his two sons, Ishmael and Isaac; the four hun-dred years' affliction of his posterity; the blessing of all nations through his seed, etc. Abraham, Jacob, and Moses, all saw Christ's day and were glad; Isaiah and Jeremiah revealed not only the proximate judgments and deliverances of Israel, but also incarnation and atonement. The visions of Daniel present not only a comprehensive but an orderly and consecutive prophetic narrative, of leading events, from his own day to the end of all things, a miniature universal history. The fall of Belshazzar; the rise of Cyrus, his conquests, the greatness of his empire; his successors, Cambyses, Smerdis, and Darius; the character, power, and conduct of Xerxes; the marvellous exploits of Alexander the Great, his sudden death, and the division of his empire; the reigns of the Ptolemies and Seleucidæ; the character and conquests of the Roman empire; the destruction of Jerusalem by Titus; the decay and division of the Roman empire; the rise of the Papacy and its career; its cruel persecutions of God's saints: all this and much more is foretold by the man greatly beloved.

The "burdens" of the later prophets concern Syria, Egypt, Edom, Tyre, Sidon, Moab, Philistia, Kedar, Elam, Babylon, Gog and Magog, besides Judah and Ephraim. Enoch's prophecy is comprised in one verse, and touches only one theme. Isaiah's has sixty-six chapters, and touches on an immense variety of topics. From our Lord and his apostles flowed additional revelations, which opened up subjects previously veiled in mystery, and cast a flood of light on every important feature of the present and of the future. Thus the volume of prophecy grew in bulk and in scope, with the ever increasing number of individuals and of nations, and with the consequent complexity and importance of the events to be announced by inspiration.

Further, the prophecies of *any one event* have also a distinctly progressive character; they increase both in fulness and in clearness as the period of fulfilment approaches. A guide, conducting a traveller to Chamounix, before starting from Geneva points out the glittering white mountain on the horizon as the goal of the day's journey, and adds a few general indications of the route. When the city and its suburbs are left behind the guide ceases perhaps to speak much of Mont Blanc, tells rather of the height of the Salève round which the road winds ; from some eminence he points out the towns and villages which dot the widespread plain beyond, and which must presently be passed; traces the windings of the Arve, speaks of Bonneville and Sallenches as marking stages of the journey, but allows the magnificent terminus of their wanderings to occupy for the time a comparatively secondary place, minor but nearer objects taking up his attention. At a later period of the day, when the glorious vision of the ever nearing mountain breaks afresh upon the traveller at Sallenches, the guide pours forth clear and copious descriptions of its various parts ; other things are forgotten now, they press on ; again the nearer hills shut out the mountain summit, but the guide tells how each turn of the last picturesque and winding valley will reveal some new view of it. When it reappears the traveller is startled by the nearer magnificence of the monarch of the Alps, it rivets his eye, it absorbs his attention ; the guide enters into minute particulars, describes the different "aiguilles" and summits of the mountain, so that as he approaches them one by one, the traveller recognises them. And now Chamounix and the glaciers come in sight, and the traveller finds as might have been expected, that what appeared, when fifty miles off, a simple outline of uniform white, breaks up into a series of jagged peaks, with awful shadows and frozen seas lying in deep valleys between ; that the one mountain is in reality half a dozen, and that what appeared at a distance merely a feature of the wide horizon, has developed into a vast and intricate region, in which he may wander for weeks without exploring it all. Yet, as he gazes up at the great summit, he realizes, that it is the very same mountain he first beheld from Geneva.

Thus, from the fall onwards, the *triumphs of the Cross* have been the great theme of prophecy. Even in Eden the main character and grand result of human history were foretold. Enmity was to subsist between Satan and men, with all its fruits of conflict and suffering; ultimately, the serpent's head was to be bruised, the author of evil destroyed, but the victory was to be dearly bought, for the woman's seed by whom it should be gained, should have his heel bruised in the battle. Here is the Bible in embryo, the sum of all history and prophecy in a germ. But what a mysterious enigma it was, what a slight shadowy outline, what a vague though blessed prospect! Still it was a light shining in a dark place; its beams were feeble, but to the eye of faith it was the one glimmer that irradiated the intense gloom of the future. But what desires it must have left unsatisfied, what questions unanswered! How long was this sore conflict to last? By what means were the vanquished to become the victors? Little could Adam and Eve know on these points; the one bright hope, like a glittering mountain top, defined their horizon; its form was rendered indistinct by the mists of ignorance; but it riveted their gaze, for the rest of that horizon was blank, and nought but travail and sorrow and labour in an accursed earth, lay between them and this hope.

To the view of Enoch, the seventh from Adam, this single future became dual. This first prophet, announced not only blessing, but judgment to come. He saw mankind divided into two classes, the saints and the ungodly (Jude 14); and he foretold a coming of the Lord with the *former* to execute judgment on the *latter*. Here was an advance: the previously revealed conflict reappears, and the previously revealed victory; but there shine out the additional truths that the conflict would not be between man and Satan alone, but between men and God, and that its termination would be effected only, by a coming of the Lord Himself to earth. In the sanctifying power of this truth Enoch walked in holy separation from the ungodly, and in holy fellowship with God, for three hundred years, and " before his translation he had this testimony that he pleased God."

To the patriarchs it was revealed that in their line should arise the promised Seed of the woman, in whom all the families of the earth should be blessed. Jacob's dying prophecy designated the very tribe in which He should appear, and threw some light on his character and work.   To Moses it was made known that the promised Deliverer should be a prophet, and David foretold that He should be a king and the manner of his kingdom (Psalm lxxii.).   The promise of his coming grew continually brighter and clearer ; but as yet it appeared only *one*, a glorious advent of a royal and triumphant Deliverer.   What the bruising of the heel should be, was still hidden in obscurity : the double nature of Christ, his true character and work, his rejection, suffering and death, had not yet been predicted ; they had been shadowed forth, it is true, in typical actions and ordinances ; but these were not understood even by the actors in them.

In a wondrous historic prefiguration Abraham and Isaac, all unconsciously to themselves, had symbolised the great truth that the Father would give the Son to be the sacrifice ; not knowing what he said, Isaac uttered the great question of all ages : " Behold the fire and the wood ; but where is the Lamb for the burnt offering ? " and Abraham gave the prophetic reply : " My son, God will provide Himself a Lamb."   But types like this, and like that of Joseph's rejection by his brethren, and exaltation to Egypt's throne, were not *revelations* to the then existing generations of men, although we in the light of the antitype can see them to have had a hidden meaning.   Nor was the paschal lamb in Egypt, nor the complex system of sacrifices inaugurated by Moses, any revelation of the victim character of Christ.   David in the Psalms wrote of his sufferings as well as his glories, but so little were these passages understood, that our Lord and his apostles had to expound them even in their day.

But when David had fallen asleep, and Solomon's typical reign was over, when declension and decay set in, and Israel's kingdom was on the wane, when a dark night of captivity and dispersion was approaching, then revelations multiplied. The star that had so long shone in the prophetic heaven, and been regarded as one round orb, was seen to be a binary star.   The objects and results of the first coming of Christ were announced, in such a way as to distinguish it from his second coming, yet not so clearly but that difficulties still left room for misconception. Many particulars and details were also added ; He was to spring out of the stem of Jesse, to be a virgin's son, and to bear the name Emmanuel ; his name moreover was to be called The Mighty God, the Everlasting Father, the Prince of Peace ; and there was to be no end of the increase of his government. The character of his kingdom was more fully described, and the fact revealed, that Gentiles as well as Jews, should share in its blessings. And strange new strains began to mingle in the music of the prophetic harp as Isaiah touched its strings, mournful tones which told of suffering and rejection, of oppression and bruises and wounds, to be inflicted on the coming One. He was to be a holy sinbearer, a silent sufferer, a slaughtered lamb ; He was to pour out his soul unto death ; He was to have a grave ; He was to be a substitute, a sin offering, an intercessor ; and only through experiences such as these to be " satisfied " and exalted, " and divide the spoil with the great." And Daniel, in full harmony, announced that Messiah should be cut off but not for Himself, and that his coming instead of bringing rest and glory to Israel, would be followed by trouble, war, and desolation. By degrees it thus became evident, that a long stretch of previously concealed valley, lay between the double summit of the mighty mountain, the hope of the coming and kingdom of Christ. Micah foretold that He should come out of Bethlehem, Zechariah that his feet should stand on the mount of Olives ; but who suspected that at least 1800 years were to elapse between the two events ? The exact period when He should come and be cut off was foretold, though in symbolic style ; and in the same style, a glimpse was given of the interval to elapse, before He came again to be " King over all the earth." Vast progress had been made when Malachi, closing the volume of Old Testament prophecy, spoke of the Lord coming suddenly to his temple, and the Sun of righteousness rising with healing in his wings. How amazingly more full and correct were the anticipations of Simeon and Anna than those of Adam and Eve ! The earlier saints could only cast a wondering gaze abroad over the earth, and up and down through unknown ages ; the later—knew the country, the city, the very building *in* which, and the very date *at* which, the Consolation of Israel should appear ; and when at last the aged saint held in his arms the long promised woman's Seed, he spoke of salvation, and of peace in believing, and of a sword that must pierce the heart of the virgin mother, proving that the mystery of the bruised heel was no dark one to his heart. But yet the consummation was not come, the serpent's head was all unbruised, his power seemed mightier than ever. The goal receded as it was approached ; the kingdom of Christ was come, but it was only in a mystery. Once more the light of prophecy streams forth, the interval is filled in with copious details by our Lord and his apostles. The King is to go into a far country and to return ; the mystery not made known in other ages is revealed by the Spirit, that the Gentiles should be fellow-heirs and partakers in the promises ; multitudinous features of the future are delineated by the pen of inspiration ; but the one grand old hope, the coming of Jesus Christ to rule, and reign, and judge, and destroy the devil and his works, still rises paramount to all the rest. Finally, in the Apocalypse the last stretch of country is laid open to view, each milestone of this closing stage of the journey may be as it were distinguished and counted, the mists have cleared away, the intervening hills and valleys have taken their proper places, and as each rapid revolution of our globe brings us almost consciously nearer to "that blessed hope," we gaze with ever growing admiration at its vastness, at its glories, at its unutterable height, at its awful shadows ; until as we see the old serpent, and death and hades, cast for ever into the lake of fire, and the New Jerusalem descend out of heaven, that the tabernacle of God may be evermore with men, we exclaim : "It is done ; the woman's seed hath bruised the serpent's head !"

Thus again, the prophecies respecting the resurrection of

the dead, and the future judgment, are few and dark in the Old Testament. Job anticipated resurrection personally, and Daniel speaks of a resurrection of part of the dead. But we have only to contrast these and similar hints, with the clear and copious predictions of 1 Corinthians xv. and 1 Thessalonians iv., in order to be convinced of the progressive character of revelation on this subject. It is Christ who has brought life and immortality *to light* through the gospel.

Thus again, the past and future restorations of Israel, so often blended in one prophecy in the Old Testament, are broadly distinguished in the New, and the hidden mystery of the calling of the Gentiles is interposed between them. Compare for instance Jeremiah xxx., xxxi., with Romans xi. : "the mystery of Christ . . . in other ages was not made known unto the sons of men, as it is now revealed unto his holy apostles and prophets by the Spirit, that the Gentiles should be fellow-heirs, and of the same body, and partakers of his promise in Christ by the gospel" (Eph. iii. 3–7). These words are an emphatic assertion of the principle of progressive revelation in prophecy.

II. *The prophecies of the New Testament have this progressive character, and divide themselves into five series of predictions, each series in the succession, being in advance of the preceding one.* There are :

1. The prophecies annunciatory of Christ, by the angels, by Zacharias, by Mary, by Elizabeth, by Simeon, and by John the Baptist.

2. The earlier prophecies of Christ Himself on earth.

3. The later prophecies of Christ : Matthew xxii.—xxv., Mark xiii., Luke xxi., John xiv.—xvi.

4. The prophetic teachings of the Holy Ghost through the apostles, contained in the Acts and in the epistles.

5. The Apocalypse, or final revelation of Christ from heaven· "the Revelation of Jesus Christ, which God gave to Him, to show unto his servants the things which must shortly come to pass."

The *first series* declared in general the character of Christ's person and the grand objects and results of his mission ; but they are silent as to all else.

The *second series*, or early prophecies of Christ Himself, in Matthew vii. and xiii., Mark iv., reveal *the mysteries of the kingdom of heaven*, its foundation and gradual development, its twofold character and its final issues.   That this was an advance on all previous revelations may be gathered from the words of our Lord in Matthew xiii. : " Blessed are your ears. for they hear; for verily I say unto you that many prophets and righteous men have desired to hear those things which ye hear, and *have not heard them.*"

The later prophecies of our Lord on earth, consist almost entirely of new revelations.   These embrace, the rejection of the Jews on account of their unbelief, the destruction of their city and temple, their dispersion among all nations, the treading down of Jerusalem by the Gentiles, the persecution of the Christian church, the world wide preaching of the gospel, and his own second coming, with the signs and events atending it; also his own approaching sufferings and departure to the Father, and his return to receive his people to Himself, with the coming and mission of the Holy Ghost during the interval of his absence.   Much as all this was in advance of the Lord's previous prophecies, He added, after making these revelations : " I have yet many things to say unto you, but ye cannot bear them now; howbeit, when He the Spirit of truth is come, He will guide you into all truth ; and He will show you things to come."   After all therefore that *had* been revealed concerning the future, very much still remained to be made known, and was to be made known by the teaching of the Holy Ghost.

Here is another distinct announcement of the principle of progressive revelation in prophecy.

With the expectations thus awakened we glance next at

The prophetic teachings of the Holy Ghost through the apostles. Examining the epistles in their chronological order, we find the two earliest, those to the church at Thessalonica, filled with the subject of the Lord's second coming and revealing much fresh truth in connection with it. It is to be accompanied by the transformation of living saints, the resurrection of dead saints, and their joint rapture to meet the Lord in the air; the manner of his return, and (negatively) the time of it, are announced. Copious and detailed descriptions of the apostasy to be developed in the Christian church are given, as also the history of the man of sin, in whose career that apostasy was to culminate; his Satanic origin, his lying wonders and unrighteous deceptions, his consumption by the spirit of the Lord's mouth, and his destruction by the brightness of his coming, are all foretold for the first time. ·

One or two years later, Paul wrote his first letter to the Corinthian church, in which revelations are made fuller than any previous ones, on the subject of resurrection; its principles, its manner, the nature of the bodies in which the saints will rise, the instantaneous transformation of the living to be effected at the sounding of the last trumpet, all these were newly revealed features. "Behold, I show you *a mystery:* we shall not all sleep, but we shall all be changed, in a moment, in the twinkling of an eye, at the last trump."

But, more important still, the *order* of this resurrection of the saints with respect to other events is mentioned: "Christ the firstfruits, afterward they that are Christ's at his coming. Then cometh the end." The resurrection of saints was to be subsequent to Christ's resurrection, prior to the end; but how long subsequent to the one, or how long prior to the other, is not here revealed.

About a year after, in his epistle to the Romans, the apostle clears up the mystery of Israel's future, and answers the questions whether God had cast off his ancient people, whether they had stumbled that they should fall. He reveals that their judicial rejection was but for a time; that it should terminate when the fulness of the Gentiles was brought in; and that then all Israel should be saved, and the Deliverer return to Zion

He thus "vindicates the ways of God to man," and shows that his gifts and calling, are without repentance.

Peter wrote his first epistle about ten years later; but though he speaks of the revelation of Jesus Christ, and the appearing of the Chief Shepherd, he added little to the sum of what was already known on these topics. But in his second epistle, written about the year 68, he unfolds the final doom of the heavens and the earth that are now; that they are to be burned up, the elements to melt with fervent heat and to be succeeded by a new heaven and a new earth wherein righteousness should dwell. He mentions also some particulars of the approaching apostasy, a subject on which Paul in his two letters to Timothy dwells more fully. Both apostles paint a dark picture of the "last days;" foretell scoffers, apostates, hypocrites, false teachers seduced by evil spirits to teach doctrines of devils, a form of godliness without power; and they speak also of their own near departure.

Then finally, thirty years later than the writings of the other apostles, and closing the inspired volume commenced by Moses 1600 years before, we find *the revelation made by Christ in glory to John.* It is the latest gift of a glorified Saviour to his suffering church, and is entirely different in manner, scope, and style from all that precedes it. It is all but wholly devoted to prophetic truth; it contains a full and orderly prophecy of the events that were to transpire to the end of time; it unveils new scenes, and its dark sayings are full of glorious light. It is evident that the prophetic matter of this book, was unrevealed previous to the death and crucifixion of Christ; for it is represented as contained in a seven-sealed book, written within and on the back side. A strong angel cries with a loud voice, "Who is worthy to open the book, and to loose the seven seals thereof?" and none is found worthy save the "*Lamb as it had been slain,*" who is in the midst of the throne. *He* comes and takes the book out of the right hand of Him that sits on the throne, and *He opens* its seven seals.

The descriptions contained in this book of the sufferings of the faithful church under persecution ; of the sins of Babylon the great ; of the judgment to be poured upon it ; of the advent of Christ and of the first resurrection ; of the millennial reign of Christ (barely mentioned elsewhere in the New Testament) ; of the universal revolt at its close ; of the judgments which follow ; of the New Jerusalem ; of the new heavens and the new earth ; and of the eternal state—have no parallel in the whole compass of Scripture.

Being written subsequently to the destruction of Jerusalem and the dispersion of the Jews, the Apocalypse omits reference to these events treated by earlier prophecies; and, being addressed to the Christian church, it omits much found elsewhere, that is exclusively Jewish. But as regards all that was future to it, and of importance to the church of God, it presents a consecutive series of visions, combining and connecting the separate revelations previously made, and adding much never before revealed.

III. From these facts the following inferences may be deduced.

1. *God does not reveal all the future at any one time*, but gradually, as the knowledge of it may be needed and can be received.

2. *We must not expect earlier prophecies to be equally comprehensive with later ones*, nor endeavour to construct from the gospels and epistles alone, the perfect map of coming events. By its position as the last and fullest prophecy of the Bible, the Apocalypse is in advance of all other revelations, and a correct knowledge of the future is impossible apart from the study of it. No difficulties therefore, arising from its symbolic style or apparent obscurity, should lead us to dispense with its teachings. The testimony of later prophecies should never be in the slightest degree distorted, nor anything subtracted from their fulness, in order to bring them into harmony with earlier ones ; but, on the contrary, their copious details and more comprehensive teachings, must be added to all pre-

vious revelations, and then allowed to modify the impressions we have received from earlier and more elementary predictions.

3. We must not therefore reject any particular prophetic truth because it is found " only in Revelation," but receive the teachings of this final prophecy on its inspired authority *alone,* when they are unconfirmed by other Scripture.

4. The Apocalypse being written for the church militant, for the dispensation to which we belong, and the days in which we live, is indispensable to the man of God who would now be thoroughly furnished to all good works. No portion of it should be considered as unimportant, or treated as superfluous. " Blessed is he that readeth and they that hear the words of this prophecy, and keep those things that are written therein, for the time is at hand." " If any man shall add unto these things, God shall add unto him the plagues that are written in this book ; and if any man shall take away from the words of the book of this prophecy, God shall take away his part out of the book of life, and out of the holy city, and from the things that are written in this book " (chap. xxii. 18, 19).

5. The Apocalypse, as a precious and principal light, shining in a dark place, until the day dawn and the Day Star arise, should be allowed to cast its rich and final rays back over all the prophecies on the subjects of which it treats, in the volume which it closes ; and its consecutive visions should be employed to bind together in their proper order, the separate links of such earlier predictions.

CHAPTER II.

IN the light of this principle of Progressive Revelation, let us now consider the most interesting and momentous question in connection with the future. the *relative period* of the return of our blessed Lord and Master.

Before examining the revelations of the Apocalypse on this subject, we will briefly glance at the general testimony of Scripture with respect to it; first that of the Old Testament, and then that of the New.

It is impossible that those who " love his appearing" should be indifferent as to the *season* of their Lord's return. Even the prophets searched diligently what manner of *time* the Spirit of Christ which was in them did signify, when it testified beforehand, the sufferings of Christ and the glories that should follow. With much more reason, *we*, who in his sufferings see our salvation, and in his glory our own eternal portion, *we*, who are espoused as a chaste virgin to Christ, and have his parting promise, "I will come again and receive you to Myself," may inquire diligently, and long to know, *when* we may hope to see Him as He is, and be for ever with our Lord. The more we long for an event itself, the more anxious we are to ascertain the probable period of its occurrence. It argues little love to the Lord if we do not ardently desire his return; and it argues little desire for his return. if we never search the Scriptures, prayerfully seeking to learn from them when we may expect it. It is true we are to let patience have her perfect work; but our patience should be "the patience of hope," not the patience of careless indifference; and hope will always suggest the inquiry, how long?

"How long, O Lord our Saviour, wilt Thou remain away?
Our hearts are growing weary, that Thou dost absent stay.
Oh when shall come the moment, when, brighter far than morn,
The sunshine of Thy glory, shall on Thy people dawn?"

It is true that ever since apostolic days it has been the bounden duty of the church to be ever watchful, ever waiting, for the return of God's Son from heaven. The teaching of Christ Himself and of his apostles, led the early generations of Christians in a very real sense, to expect the speedy return of their Lord. They took his promise "Lo, I come quickly," to mean quickly according to human calculations; we have learned by experience that it meant "quickly," counting a thousand years as one day ; and unless we have something more explicit than this by which to shape *our* expectations, we, Christians of the nineteenth century, would have little indeed to sustain *our* hope. A promise which has already extended over 1800 years might well extend over 1800 more, and the epiphany for which we wait be still ages distant.

But Scripture contains more than general *promises* on this subject ; it contains many specific, orderly, and even chronological *prophecies*. We have full and explicit inspired predictions by which to shape our expectations, and these numerous and detailed prophetic statements, do not leave us like shipwrecked sailors on a dark night, on a wild and stormy sea, deprived of chart and compass and ignorant of their bearings. If we will use them aright, they place us rather in the position of a weary crew, at the end of a long and dangerous voyage, exploring by the morning twilight, the chart on which their track has been marked down, noting the thousands of miles they have sailed, recognising each high land and island they have passed on their course, and all the lights and beacons long since left behind, cheering each other as they observe that the faithful chart, whose accuracy their long experience has demonstrated, *shows but two or three waymarks ahead,*—waymarks absolutely coming into sight,—and rejoicing in hope of a speedy entrance into a peaceful port.

But here we are met with an objection. Those who search and study the prophetic word are often rebuked by the quotation, " of that day and that hour knoweth no man." Now though some students of prophecy have degenerated into prophets, and have required to be reminded of these words, yet it is a mistake to suppose that they forbid investigation, or render hopeless beforehand, any well grounded and intelligent conclusions, as to the period of our Lord's return. The day and the hour of this great event have not assuredly been revealed, but its place on the general chart of human history, has as certainly not been concealed.

The analogy of the Old Testament would lead us to expect that dates would be given by which some approximation to a knowledge of the period of Christ's second coming, might, towards the close of the dispensation, be made. For however dark earlier generations of Israel may have been, as to the time of his *first* coming, those who lived during the five centuries immediately preceding it, had the light of distinct chronological prophecy, to sustain their hopes, and guide their expectations. Though Daniel's prediction of the " seventy weeks " was expressed in symbolic language, and perhaps not understood by the generation to whom it was first given, yet as a matter of history, we know that it was correctly interpreted by later generations, that it formed a national opinion as to the probable period of the appearance of Messiah the Prince, and that it taught the faithful, like Simeon and Anna, to be waiting for the consolation of Israel. Is it not likely that the later generations of the Christian church, which is indwelt by the Spirit of truth, of whom Christ expressly said " He shall show you things to come" should have as clear or clearer light, as to the period of the *second* advent?—light, *not as to its day or hour, not as to its month or year*, but as to its period, and especially as to its chronological *relation*, to other future events. From the fact that the Lord Jesus, as the New Testament abundantly proves, wished his disciples in all ages to be kept constant in love, and vigilant in holiness, by means of the *continual* expectation of his return, we may be sure beforehand, that the period of that event, will not be clearly revealed *in plain words*, either in the Old Testament or the New. Any revelation on the subject, will be sure to be characterized, by a marked and *intentional obscurity*, and to be of such a character as that only "the wise shall understand" it. On the other hand, as the second advent must bear to other great future events, the relation either of antecedent or subsequent, (even if not of cause or of effect,) its position *relatively to them*, must be more or less clearly indicated.

For if there exist in Scripture, an orderly chronological prophecy of future events, containing a prediction of the second coming of Christ, as one link in the chain, *its place*, in reference to all the other events, must of course be clear. And if such a prophecy contain *no* direct mention of the second advent, yet if it contain a mention of events, which, from other scriptures we know to *synchronize* with that advent, (such as the resurrection of saints, or the destruction of antichrist and his armies,) the *relative* position of the advent will still be clear.

Such prophecies exist ; they are given for our study ; and with the Holy Ghost as our guide we may confidently expect to learn from them with certainty, the *general order* of the great incidents, of the fast approaching end of the age. And not only so, but we may also expect, to be able to gather from such prophecies, read in the light of the whole revelation of God, an *approximate* knowledge of the actual period of the coming of the Lord. Of this we are not, we cannot be, intended to remain in ignorance, for it is with regard to prophetic chronology that it is expressly said, "the wise shall understand."

Let us seek then to ascertain, first from Old Testament prophecy, secondly from the more advanced teachings of the New Testament, and lastly from the final testimony of the Apocalypse, *the relative period* of our Lord's return ; and, as far as it is revealed, its *actual* point, in the course of the ages of human history.

The second advent of Christ could not have been distinctly

predicted in the Old Testament *as a second;* that would have involved a premature revelation of Messiah's rejection by Israel, of his death and re-ascension into heaven, and of the present dispensation of grace to the Gentiles. Prophecies so clear as either to *procure* or *prevent* their own fulfilment, were never delivered by Divine inspiration. The two comings of Christ, at that time both future, and having one and the same object—to redeem and restore humanity and to destroy the works of the devil—are seen as one, in early prophetic vision.

A coming of Christ is, however, extensively and clearly predicted in the Old Testament, of a character essentially different from his past coming, and which is to be accompanied by events of transcendent importance, none of which took place in connection with his first advent. It is therefore *a future coming*, and in relation to the first it is a *second*. He *did* come in humiliation as a gracious Saviour ; He *will* come in glory as a righteous Judge and King. In other words, without the expression being used, the second coming of Christ is foretold and described in places too numerous to mention, in the law, in the prophets, and in the psalms.

The Old Testament also largely prophesies, another great future event ; it plainly teaches that before this world's history is wound up, before time gives place to eternity, an age is to occur, which is to be earth's sabbath, man's jubilee, Christ's reign : the antitype of all sabbaths from Eden onward, the antitype of Israel's jubilees, the antitype of Solomon's glorious reign of prosperity and peace. Certain Scripture statements and analogies, (apart from the Apocalypse,) lead us to suppose that the duration of this period will be 1,000 years, whence it is commonly called THE MILLENNIUM.

By the mouth of all his holy prophets since the world began God has announced these "times of refreshing." The Lord Jesus when on earth alluded to this period and presented it as an object of hope to his people. "Ye who have followed Me," He said on one occasion in reply to a question from Peter, "in the regeneration, when the Son of man shall sit on the throne of his glory, ye also shall sit upon twelve thrones, judging the twelve tribes of Israel;" to Nathanael He said, "Hereafter ye shall see heaven opened, and the angels of God ascending and descending on the Son of man." This age is called "the dispensation of the fulness of times," in which God "will gather together in one all things in Christ" (Eph. i. 10), in which every knee shall bow to Jesus, and every tongue confess Him Lord, to the glory of God the Father (Phil. ii. 10). It is the oft foretold, oft promised kingdom of the Son of man; *not* God's reign over the world in providence; that has existed from the beginning, and could never therefore be the object either of prophecy or of promise; not Christ's present reign in the hearts of his people; not the present period at all, for Satan is at present usurping the throne of this world as king and God; two thirds of mankind still worship *him* in worshipping idols, and are his obedient slaves and miserable victims; the greater part of the other third worship and obey him indirectly, in serving sin; and even Christ's people, the little flock who own Him as Lord, fail to obey Him perfectly.

If Christ be king now, where is his honour? How does the dread majesty of his throne assert itself? He endures with much longsuffering all manner of rebellion; He allows his authority to be insulted, and his name blasphemed. He avenges not his own elect, who cry day and night unto Him; He permits the oppressor to triumph, and the wicked to prosper in the earth. These things shall not be in the day of his kingdom. Ps. lxxii. presents the manner of that kingdom. Its features are righteousness and judgment, flowing from Himself as fountain head, and from all subordinate rulers as his ministers; the poor and needy delivered, and their oppressors crushed; complete and universal submission of all kings and nations to Christ; abundant peace and eternal praise. Clearly this kingdom is *not come yet,* and clearly therefore it is *yet to come.* It is true that numerous passages speak of this present dispensation as in a certain sense the kingdom of God; but the expression also designates a still future period, altogether distinct from the present in its character. *This* is the kingdom of God in a mystery, *that* will be the kingdom of God in manifest power and glory.

And let it be remarked, this kingdom is no part of the eternal state which shall ensue when "the former things are passed away." It is the kingdom of the *Son*, the kingdom in which Christ as *Son of man* is supreme ; but in the eternal state the Son shall have delivered up the kingdom to God, even the Father, and shall Himself be subject, that God may be all in all (1 Cor. xv. 28). Now the period during which the Son *possesses* the kingdom, and the period which *dates from his delivering it up*, cannot be the same.

Again, the dispensation in question, though blessed and glorious beyond all that have preceded it, is yet governmentally and nationally imperfect ; mankind will be still divided into nations (Zech. xiv. 16), speak divers languages (Dan. vii. 14), be distinguished as Jews and Gentiles, and as governors and governed (Ps. lxxii.); whereas in the eternal state all will be under the sole and immediate government of God.

And further, it is a period which, though characterized in the main by righteousness, life and bliss, will yet be marred by sin, death and judgment ; men will still be mortal, and judgment will follow every transgression (Isa. lxv. ; Zech. xiv.), while in the eternal state there will be no more sin, no more death, no more curse (Rev. xxi. .

During this reign of Christ, He will have dominion from sea to sea, and from the river to the ends of the earth (Ps. lxxii. 8); but in the eternal state there will be "no more sea." In short the former will be a kingdom characterized by the gradual and progressive subjugation of all things to Christ, in which " the last enemy that shall be destroyed is death," while the eternal state *dates from* death's destruction, and in it insubjection is unknown.

This glorious age, is then a distinct one, which is to *follow* the present period, and to *precede* the new heavens and the new earth, in which the tabernacle of God shall be for evermore with men.

We have therefore a great future event, and a glorious future age, clearly predicted in Scripture, and it is a deeply momentous question which of the two is to come first. Is the millennial sabbath to be introduced by the coming of Christ, or to be followed by it? Ought the church to be expecting the millennium, or expecting her Lord first? Is the Divine programme of the future, first the millennium and then the advent, or first the advent and then the millennium?

It is strange that many children of God are content to leave this great question an open one, and to continue in willing ignorance on the subject. And it is doubly strange that too many who ought, as teachers of the truth, boldly to declare the whole counsel of God, should be content to promulgate through the entire course of their ministry, views which they hold from education and from habit, rather than as the result of research, and of strong conviction that they are *the truth*, views which they would be at a loss to sustain by solid scriptural argument. They never perhaps preach on prophecy at all, but they constantly make use of forms of expression, and quote Scripture in connections, which tacitly and very effectually teach error. They thus endorse the vaguely held traditional creed, that death is the certain prospect before each individual, and that as regards the church at large and the world, the present state of things will continue to improve gradually, until it merges into that blessed period of righteousness and peace, in which "the knowledge of the Lord shall cover the earth, as the waters cover the sea." This is a serious evil; scriptures misquoted are an efficient means of conveying unscriptural views. Multitudes of persons who have never studied the Bible on this subject, or received any direct instruction on it, have nevertheless, from this practice on the part of their teachers, imbibed views directly contrary to the truth.

And the views thus thoughtlessly imparted, and thoughtlessly received, are yet firmly held ; for mental habits are strong. That which we have always heard and supposed to be true, that which most people appear to hold as true, assumes the authority of ascertained truth in the mind, and the moment it is attacked, prejudice rises in arms to defend it. The consequence is, that notwithstanding the late large and rapid increase in the number of those who look for the coming of Christ as their own individual hope, and as the next great event in the history of the church and of the world, the majority of professing Christians, and especially those who have little or no leisure for reading and study, still retain the opposite view, look for death personally, and expect the coming of Christ to take place, only at the end of the world. Yet that coming is the grand motive uniformly presented in the New Testament to love, to obedience, to holiness, to spirituality of mind, to works of mercy, to watchfulness, to patience, to moderation and sobriety, to diligence, and to all other Christian graces.* "That blessed hope" is essential to the production of the Christian character in its perfection. What consolation it affords in bereavement and affliction! What holy restraint it is calculated to exercise, in prosperity and joy, and what an incentive it supplies to exertion in the Christian work and warfare!

And who is to blame that its power is so little felt by Christians in general? How shall they hear without a teacher? If their ministers never directly teach them the truth on this point, by expounding to them the numerous passages bearing on it in the New Testament, but leave them in ignorance or lead them indirectly into error, will the Great Shepherd of the sheep hold such under shepherds guiltless? Earnestly would we entreat all our brethren in the ministry, to *"preach the word"* on this great subject, *to give it in their ministry, the prominence it has in their Bibles;* to bring it in, whenever and wherever Scripture brings it in, and that is in connection with almost every topic of Christian privilege and duty.

---

* 1 Thess. iii. 13 ; Col. iii. 4, 5 ; Titus ii. 11–13 ; I John ii. 28, iii. 2, 3 ; Phil. iii. 20, 21 ; Matt. xvi. 27 ; Rev. xxii. 12 ; Matt. xxv. 13 ; Luke xii. 35, xviii. 7 ; James v. 7, 8 ; 1 Pet. i. 13 ; Matt. xxiv. 46 ; 1 Pet. v. 1–4.

It is vain to urge that the uncertainty of life and the possible nearness of death, are motives as powerful as the coming of Christ. Death can never be an object of hope to a Christian, nor a source of consolation ; God never intended it to be such ; it has lost its sting indeed to a believer, but it remains and must ever remain, a painful, humbling, afflictive, repulsive prospect ; salvation itself imparts no lustre to death. It must be so ; "it is sin's great conquest, and Satan's chief work, the fulness of sorrow and affliction, the triumph of corruption, the fulfilment of the curse. Oh it is a strange delusion of Satan to have made the capital curse of God eclipse the capital promise of God ! Satan's consummated kingdom over the body to take that place in our thoughts, which Christ's consummated kingdom in the body and spirit, even the resurrection, was meant to take."

Nor is it believers only who suffer from the habitual omission of a cardinal doctrine of Scripture in the teaching they hear from the pulpit. Who shall estimate the injustice done thereby to unbelievers? *The coming of the Lord draweth nigh!* Why is not the fact, the (for them) *awful* fact, proclaimed aloud in their hearing, and applied with all the earnestness of love, to arouse the sleeper from his dream, to destroy the delusions of the false professor, to unmask the hypocrite to himself, to warn the wicked from his way? The coming of the Lord draweth nigh ; to them who know not God and obey not the gospel of our Lord Jesus Christ, that coming must bring everlasting destruction ; on them it must fall as a fiery vengeance. Should they not be faithfully forewarned of their danger? Should they have the right to reproach their teachers that they sounded not the trumpet though they saw the sword approaching? What saith the Lord? "If the watchman see the sword come, and blow not the trumpet, and the people be not warned ; if the sword come and take any person from among them, he is taken away in his iniquity, but his blood will I require at the watchman's hand" (Ezck. xxxiii. 6).

Let sinners be startled by the announcement " THE JUDGE

STANDETH AT THE DOOR," and not soothed by the sound, of a softly approaching millennium. Let them be warned of the speedy dawn of a day of retribution, and not led to conclude it, at least a thousand years distant. If the preachers of the word will fling carelessly aside, one of the best weapons in the armoury of truth, can they wonder that their work is not as effective as it might be? If they would fain see conversions numerous as in apostolic days, let them preach the apostolic preaching, in which not only the *past*, but the *future* advent of Christ, had a grand and prominent place.

The two prophets of the Old Testament who furnish the most conclusive evidence on this subject are Daniel and Zechariah. The former, a royal captive from 'Judæa, was a pure and faithful witness for God in the corrupt, gentile court of Nebuchadnezzar king of Babylon, during the time of the Babylonish captivity of Israel. There is something singularly magnificent and massive in this prophet's interpretation of Nebuchadnezzar's divinely sent dream. Unencumbered by detail, the grand outline of this fundamental and far-reaching prophecy, is sketched with the few but firm and telling touches of a master hand ; like the blue vault of heaven, " majestic in its own simplicity," and embracing in one vast span the whole extent and circumference of earth, it seems to arch in the entire future of the world, with celestial ease and stability.

It starts from the time then present, and terminates on the verge of eternity. Its language is intelligible, and indeed can scarcely be misunderstood. Brief and condensed in the extreme, it lights only on the salient points, the mountain tops as it were, of human history ; but in so doing it must of course light on its *most* elevated and important summit, the glorious epiphany of the great God and our Saviour Jesus Christ. *Whereabouts* in the chain does it place that summit? This is the point on which we now seek its testimony. Let the reader ponder it and reply.

THE VISION OF NEBUCHADNEZZAR, KING OF BABYLON, TO
WHOM GOD HAD GIVEN UNIVERSAL DOMINION.

1. Thou, O king, sawest and behold a great image.
2. His head was of fine gold ;
3. His breast and his arms of silver ;
4. His belly and his thighs of brass ;
5. His legs of iron, and his feet part of iron and part of clay.

6. A stone was cut out without hands ;
7. *It smote the image on his feet ;*
8. It brake in pieces the iron, the clay, the brass, the silver, and the gold ;
9. It became a great mountain ;
10. *It filled the whole earth.*

THE INTERPRETATION.

1. Thou art this head of gold ;
2. After thee shall arise another kingdom ;
3. And a third kingdom of brass ;
4. And the fourth kingdom shall be strong as iron ;
5. That kingdom shall be divided ;

6. In the days of these kings,
7. *The God of heaven shall set up a kingdom ;*
8. It shall never be destroyed,
9. It shall consume all these kingdoms
10. *It shall stand for ever*

The dream is certain and the interpretation thereof is sure.

A succession of four similar universal earthly empires is foretold, and that they are to be followed by a fifth, the empire of the stone. The first four would be established and ruled by men, the last by "the God of heaven." The first four would be destroyed, the last would destroy them. The first four would be smitten and broken in pieces, the last would never be destroyed. The first four would form one great *image ;* the last would become a great *mountain*, and fill the whole earth. The first four would be consumed and carried away; the last would stand for ever.

By the universal consent of the church of all ages, and of all sections, the first four are allowed to be the Babylonian, the Persian, the Grecian, and the Roman empires; and the last the still future kingdom of the Son of man. The internal scriptural and historical evidence in favour of this interpretation, is so overwhelming, and the agreement of all students and commentators, of the early church, of the Greek and Roman Catholic churches, and of all Protestant churches, so complete, that the few who have of late years ventured to call it in question, must be regarded as rash, unsafe, presumptuous guides, who would destroy the very basis of all sound and solid interpretation of Scripture prophecy. It were superfluous to argue the point in a work like this; those who require it can easily find abundant evidence, and that of a most convincing character and edifying nature.*

We take it for granted therefore that this vision presents us with a brief historic outline, of the four great empires which have in succession held universal sway. It presents the last of the four, in two successive stages, first as legs of pure iron, secondly as ten toes composed of a mixture of iron and clay; representing under these emblems, first the Roman empire in its undivided imperial strength, and secondly the same empire in its divided condition.

During this last stage of the last empire, occurs a supernatural and tremendous revolution. All the previous changes had followed each other in the ordinary and natural course, and the kingdoms were in some senses a continuation of each other, for the great image is one. But now a kingdom that is no part of the image, that owns a supernatural origin, smites the image, grinds it to powder, takes its place, blots it out of

---

* See Birks' "Elements of Prophecy"

existence, and fills the whole earth. This fall of the stone cut out without hands, must symbolise something immensely more important and fundamental, than any political change the world has ever seen. Tremendous critical revolutions, such as the overthrow of Babylon by Cyrus, and of Persia's power by Alexander the Great, have in this prophecy been portrayed simply by the quiet change from one metal to another, in the parts of an unbroken image. What then is the great event symbolised by the *falling of the stone*, which puts an end to the image altogether, and precedes the establishment on earth of the kingdom of the God of heaven?

Is it, as some assert, the first advent of Christ, to establish Christianity? Impossible! for the stone falls *on the feet* of the image. The first advent took place in the time of the undivided imperial iron strength of the Roman empire, not after its decay and division into many kingdoms. Christianity had already been established for centuries, as the religion of the Roman empire, before the state of things symbolised by the ten toes of iron and clay arose.

Besides, the destruction of the image is attributed to the *fall* of the stone, *not* to its gradual expansion into a great mountain which fills the whole earth. Now Christianity did not destroy all earthly monarchy, at the time of its advent, or in its early ages. On the contrary! Its Founder suffered under Pontius Pilate the Roman governor, and his apostles were martyred by Nero and Domitian. Nothing whatever answering to the crushing, destructive fall of the stone took place at that time. The development of the stone into a mountain does not *begin* till the image *has been* "broken to pieces together, and become like the chaff of the summer threshing-floor." Now the gradual growth of Christianity has been taking place while the image still stands, and cannot therefore be the thing intended by this striking symbol. Besides this, the spiritual kingdom of God now established in the hearts of men, is in no respect similar to the great universal earthly empires which form the four first of this series. It is not of the world; it employs not the sword of conquest; it does not embrace as its subjects all within a certain territory; it is invisible, spiritual, heavenly. The empire of the stone is a fifth analogous to the other four, though of supernatural origin, wider extent, and longer duration; it is the universal empire of earth ruled directly by the God of heaven.

What then must be the transcendent event symbolised by the *falling* from above, with destructive force, on the feet of the image, (or final form of earthly monarchy,) of a stone cut out without hands? What can it be but the second coming of Christ with all his saints, to execute judgment on the ungodly, and to reign in righteousness and glory?

The symbol employed, a stone cut out without hands, is a most appropriate emblem of Christ and his church; that church which, as other scriptures show, is to be associated with him in the work of judgment. A stone cut out without hands is a miracle; Christ in his birth, in his resurrection, was such; and we his people are even now, "born not of the will of man, or of the will of the flesh, but of God" as to our spiritual natures, and our bodies are to be in the resurrection "quickened by his Spirit which dwelleth in us." Many other emblems present Christ and his people as one. They form one vine, one body, one temple; so here, one stone. Our Lord applies this emblem to Himself, in a way that seems almost an allusion to this prophecy : "whosoever shall fall on this stone shall be broken, but on whomsoever it shall fall it will grind him to powder." Peter applies it to the saints, "ye also as living stones." And Paul speaks of believers under the same figure as "builded together for an habitation of God through the Spirit." For more than 1800 years this mystic stone has been in process of cutting out. When "the trumpet shall sound and the dead shall be raised incorruptible, and we shall be changed," the separation will be complete, and the stone will *fall* on the feet of the image; that is, the Lord will come "with ten thousands of his saints, to execute judgment upon all." Earthly polities will then crumble for ever into dust ; empires, monarchies, and republics alike, will become as the chaff of the summer threshing-floor ; "the Lord shall be king over all the earth," and alone exalted in that day.

Here then we have the first distinct answer to our inquiry, as to the relative position of the second advent.

On the authority of this prophecy alone we may boldly assert, that it is destined to occur at the close of the present divided state of the Roman empire, and prior to the establishment of the millennial reign of Christ. And moreover, as the parts of the image bear a certain proportion to each other, we have some data by which to form an approximation to its actual period ; for the tenfold division of the Roman empire having already existed twelve or thirteen centuries, a strong presumption arises that its close must be at hand.

We turn now to the second great prophecy of Daniel in the seventh chapter of his book. The following are the leading points of the vision and of the interpretation respectively.

Daniel's Vision of the Four Great Beasts.

1. Four great beasts came up from the sea, diverse one from another.

2. The first like a lion, another like a bear, another like a leopard.

3. A fourth beast, dreadful. and terrible, and strong exceedingly.

4. It was diverse from all the beasts that were before it, and it had ten horns.

5. There came up among them another little horn.

6. In this horn were eyes like the eves of a man, and a mouth speaking great things.

7. The same horn made war with the saints and prevailed against them.

8. Until the Ancient of Days came, and

9. Judgment was given to the saints of the Most High ; and

10. The time came that the saints possessed the *kingdom.*

THE INTERPRETATION.

1. These great beasts which are four, are four kingdoms.

2. The fourth beast shall be the fourth kingdom upon earth.

3. The ten horns are ten kings (or kingdoms) that shall arise.

4. Another shall arise after them, diverse from the first (ten).

5. And he shall speak great words against the Most High.

6. He shall wear out the saints of the Most High;

7. They shall be given into his hand, until a time, and times, and the dividing of time.

8. BUT THE JUDGMENT SHALL SIT, and they shall take away his dominion.

9. The kingdom shall be given to the people of the saints of the Most High;

10. Whose kingdom is an everlasting kingdom.

Nebuchadnezzar beheld the former vision, and Daniel interpreted; now the prophet beholds, and an angel interprets.

The subject is in both visions in the main the same; but the second has many additional features. The four great empires of earth, appear under strangely contrasted symbols, to the king and to the prophet.

In the former case a worldly idolater looked up, and beheld a great fourfold image of earthly dominion; it was terrible, yet attractive to him in its brilliancy. In the latter case a man of God looked down, and beheld four great beasts, terrible only in their fierce brutality.

Power is a dazzling object of ambition; dominion has a fascinating attraction for men; but the humblest saint of God can afford to look down on earthly glory, as from a lofty elevation, in the calm consciousness of undeniable and immeasurable superiority. Four great beasts: that was all the earth produced to the eye of the holy Daniel!

D

The divinely selected symbols have an evident allusion to the two leading characteristics that have marked the four great Gentile empires, in contrast to the Jewish theocracy, and in still darker contrast to the coming kingdom of Christ. *Image worship* and *inhuman cruelty*, idolatry and persecution, have been their characteristics. The image embodies the one thought, the wild beast the other. Nebuchadnezzar made an image, probably *of* the image he had seen, and demanded for it world-wide worship, persecuting even to the fiery furnace, those who refused to bow down to it; and Daniel experienced the wild beast character of the second great empire, when condemned to the lions' den for his piety toward God.

That the four empires symbolised in this vision are the *same* four previously symbolised in the image can hardly be questioned. "The number is the same, four in each. The starting point is the same, for each was given while Babylon was the ruling power. The issue is the same, for both are immediately followed by the visible kingdom of Christ. The order is the same, for the kingdoms in the first vision, as all admit, are *successive*; and in the other there are no less than seven or eight clauses which denote a *succession* in time. There is the same gradation, for the noblest metal and the noblest animal take the lead in each series. Further, the kingdoms in each vision are described as occupying the whole space, till the dominion of the saints of God . . . The first empire is that of BABYLON, for to the king of BABYLON it was said, 'thou art this head of gold.' If we require the names of the two next kingdoms, the angel Gabriel continues the message of the prophet : 'The ram having two horns are the kings of MEDIA and PERSIA . . . the rough goat is the king of GRECIA.' If we ask the name and character of the fourth empire the evangelist supplies the answer, 'there went out a decree from CÆSAR AUGUSTUS that all the world should be taxed'; 'if we let Him alone, all men will believe on Him, and the ROMANS will come and take away both our place and nation.' Four supreme and ruling kingdoms, and four only, are announced *by name* in the word of God, from the time of Daniel to the close of the sacred canon." *

The main difference is that the latter prophecy, like a tele-scope of higher power, presents an enlarged and more detailed view, especially of the fourth empire. The image showed that it had two distinct stages : one pure iron, unmixed and undi-vided ; the other iron and clay mixed, the metallic parts divided. In this fourth beast we discern a new element, *the dominion of the little horn ;* and we thereby learn the moral reason for the judgment, which, in both visions alike, falls on the fourth em-pire in its last state. In connection with this last vision, the coming of Christ to judge is expressed in a clearer form, and the share which his people shall have in his reign. But the evidence it affords as to the *relative period* of the second advent, is in unison with that of the earlier vision. It places it at the end of the last phase of the fourth empire, and determines its *immediate* object to be the execution of judgment, and its *ulti-mate* object, the establishment on earth of the everlasting king-dom of the Most High, in which dominion shall be given to the saints. It thus announces that the coming of Christ, will be *prior* to his reign over the earth, in company with his saints , and it furnishes more accurate data also as to the actual period of the second advent. This latter however cannot be adduced in the present stage of our inquiry, since it is con-nected with two points of disputed interpretation, the considera-tion of which must be adjourned to the second part of this work. For the same reason the evidence of Daniel's last visions must here be presented but very imperfectly, and with-out any attempt to enter into detail.

We observe merely that the very comprehensive, (and con-sequently complicated,) prophecy of the " things noted in the Scripture of truth " (Dan. xi.), announces one unbroken series of wars, revolutions, persecutions, apostasies, disasters, and de-solations, as occupying the whole scene of vision, until Daniel's

---

* Birks' " First Two Visions," p. 20.

people should be delivered, and many of the dead arise (Dan. xii. 1-3). Now these two events, the deliverance of Israel from their great tribulation, and the resurrection of the just, are invariably associated in the prophecies with the personal coming of Christ (Zech. xiv. 5; 1 Thess. iv., 1 Cor. xv.). Therefore, though Daniel does not mention a second advent of Christ, for reasons before alluded to, yet he marks its place in this series, by the position assigned to the events which synchronize with it. Thus a third time he places it, at the close of the four great empires, or of the times of the Gentiles, at the close of Israel's dispersion and tribulation, and prior to the commencement of that kingdom, in which "they that be wise shall shine as the brightness of the firmament, and they that turn many to righteousness, as the stars for ever and ever," —*at the close of the fourth empire and before the millennial reign.*

The reign of Christ on earth is distinctly predicted in Zechariah xiv. 9, and many of its peculiar features are mentioned in verses which follow. This is an orderly and detailed prophecy, of the events that shall usher in that reign; and we have a definite statement, that foremost among those events, "*the Lord my God shall come, and all the saints with thee:* . . . and the Lord shall be king over all the earth; in that day there shall be one Lord, and his name one." In other words, we have in this prophecy a clear declaration that the advent will *precede* the millennial reign.

Again it is written "when the Lord shall build up Zion He shall appear in his glory." The building up of Zion, that is the restoration and conversion of Israel, must of course precede the millennial reign of Christ, over Israel and the earth, since it is inconceivable that Israel's dispersed and desolate condition, could continue during its course. A glorious epiphany of the Son of God, is to accompany according to this prophecy, the building up of Zion,—a premillennial event. The second advent of Christ, therefore takes place *before* the millennium.

The history of Israel is a typical history, prefiguring alike in its broad outline and in its minor features the history of the church. What is the general outline of that history? Is it a gradual and steady progress from bad to good, and from good to better, culminating at last in something very good and glorious? Nay, but the very reverse! It is a downward progress, a succession of backslidings and apostasies, from the days of Solomon to the Babylonish captivity, and from the restoration to the fall of Jerusalem under Titus, and the final judgment and dispersion of the ancient people of God. Now there would be no analogy, but a most marked and marvellous contrast between the type and the antitype, if the history of the church were to be a gradual *rise* from the state of things we now have, into a millennial condition of blessedness, purity, and peace. It would do violence not only to the analogy which exists between these two dispensations, but to the general moral analogy of *all* God's dispensations. Without exception hitherto *every* dispensation has ended in apostasy and judgment. Eden ended thus; the antediluvian world ended thus; the theocracy of Israel ended thus; the kingdom of Israel ended thus; the ministry of the prophets ended thus; the ministry of Christ in person ended thus; the ministry of the Spirit by the apostles ended thus, in the full and final rejection of Israel and in the giving of the kingdom of God to the Gentiles. *So far* the Gentile church has pursued a precisely similar course, and trodden the downward road of apostasy; and can it be believed, that the last stage of her course is to afford a total contrast to all previous analogies, and culminate in a millennium of moral perfection and physical glory? No! "when the Son of man cometh shall He find faith on the earth"? that is the question.

When we turn to the pages of the New Testament the conclusions to which these ancient prophecies have led us are in the fullest way confirmed.

There are in the New Testament, apart from the Apocalypse, about a hundred passages, in which the second coming of Christ is more or less fully presented. About half of these afford no clear information on the subject we are considering, though indirect premillennial arguments might be drawn from most of them. About twenty passages teach· with various degrees of explicitness, that the coming of Christ will precede "the times of the restitution of all things"; and there are four or five, which at first sight appear to favour an opposite view, but which on closer examination are found to harmonize with the rest. We will briefly review the leading passages of these two latter classes.

The most cursory survey of them as a whole, however, suggests two strong *prima facie* arguments in favour of the premillennial view. It is a remarkable fact, that while in these scriptures, *the return of the Lord Jesus* is everywhere prominent, the truth of a millennium to come is scarcely asserted. It is assumed as an acknowledged hope in one or two places, and alluded to in a few others; it is implied in some of our Lord's parables, but nowhere distinctly predicted, nowhere described, or presented as an object of hope. What is the natural inference? That no millennium is to occur? No! but that something else is to occur before it; and that the intervening event is the one, which the Holy Ghost would keep before the eye of the church, that intervening event being the glorious epiphany of the great God and our Saviour Jesus Christ.

For, supposing for a moment that a thousand years of righteousness and rest, purity and peace, *were* designed in the counsels of God, to succeed this age of sin and strife and suffering, *before* the oft promised return of the Lord Jesus, how unaccountable, how incredible that so little should be said about it! Supposing it were to occur on the other hand *after* that return, and consequent upon it, how perfectly natural, that in prophecies designed to comfort and guide the church during the interval of Christ's absence, it should be scarcely mentioned. Its character had been described in the Old Testament, and was well understood by Jewish Christians and by the early church. They expected its commencement indeed, in connection with Christ's first coming: "wilt Thou at this time restore again the kingdom to Israel?" and would never have entertained the thought, that it could occur during his absence. The events that should transpire during that absence, and the return that should introduce the kingdom, were therefore naturally the great subject matter of the prophecies of Christ and his apostles ; the subsequent millennial reign, taken as it were for granted, occupied a very subordinate place. The silence of the Lord Himself, and of the whole New Testament about the millennium, can be explained on no other supposition.

The period of the millennial reign is long ; its character is glorious, its events gigantic, its sphere universal; it will be no less than the subjugation of the entire world to Christ, the putting down of " *all* rule, and *all* authority and power," by the Son of God. If all this *be* to take place *prior* to his second coming, how impossible that He should overlook or omit it, in all his great prophetic descriptions of the entire course of the present dispensation.

In Matthew xxiv. Christ describes his second personal advent and the great events which shall precede it. He reveals the course of this evil age, and its close. He foretells wars, famines, pestilences, earthquakes, persecutions, false prophets, iniquities, apostasies, the preaching of the gospel "as a witness" to all nations, false signs and wonders, desolations, woes, including the great tribulation, and then He adds, "*Immediately after* the tribulation of those days shall the sun be darkened, and the moon shall not give her light, and the stars shall fall from heaven, and the powers of the heavens shall be shaken ; and then shall appear the sign of the Son of man in heaven, and then shall all the tribes of the earth mourn, and they shall see *the Son of man coming in the clouds of heaven, with power and great glory*, and He shall send his angels with a great sound of a trumpet, and they shall gather together his elect from the four winds, from one end of heaven to the other."

That these words describe his personal advent in glory is certain, and equally certain is it, that this comprehensive prophecy, contains no allusion to a millennium of blessedness and peace. Can this be reconciled with the view that our Lord expected that golden age previous to his coming? The same thing may be said of the series of prophetic parables in Matthew xiii. They certainly describe his second personal advent, and as certainly portray the leading features of the age which shall end with that event ; but they speak of no millen· nium. They describe exactly what we see around us, exactly what we know has characterized the past eighteen hundred years, a partial spread of truth, a vast upgrowth of apostasy and corruption in the professing church, a gathering out of the great sea of humanity a mingled mass of good and bad ; but no subjugation of the entire world to Christ, no signs of righteousness from shore to shore. If any one asserts that the parable of the leaven foretells a universality of godliness in this dispensation, let him reflect, that in order to give his assertion any value he must first *prove* that the "leaven" means good and not evil (a disputed point),* and secondly, that the "three measures of meal" means the entire human race, and not a definite part of it : *neither of which can be proved.* This is a parable without an inspired interpretation ; men can do no more than surmise its meaning ; such surmises should *accord*, not *clash*, with clearer revelations, and with the Lord's own interpretation of the parable of the tares and the wheat.

The same thing may be said of all the prophetic passages in the epistles of Paul : take for example that in the Second Epistle to the Thessalonians. He first describes the second coming of Christ with his mighty angels in flaming fire, to be glorified in his saints, and to take vengeance on the wicked. He then foretells THE great antecedent to that coming. What is it? A millennium of righteousness? No! a mystery of iniquity, the rise of the son of perdition, the manifestation of the man of sin, the fearful reign of Antichrist. Had *he* expected a long day of millennial light before Christ's return, how could he have foretold nothing, but a long night of spiritual darkness ?

To Peter, Paul, Jude, and John, the future of this dispensation was overshadowed with portentous gloom. They gaze

---

* Indeed, it may be remarked that in every other place in Scripture where "leaven" is spoken of, it clearly signifies *evil*.

with sorrowing hearts into its dark depths; they warn the church of approaching apostasy, and nerve it to meet coming persecution, encouraging it to hope for relief from both, *only* at the coming of the Lord (2 Thess. i. 7). Had *they* foreseen the Christian dispensation gradually developing into universal brightness, how would the blessed prospect have chased their sorrow and lit their countenances with smiles of gladness! But no! their looks brighten only, as they turn from the present dispensation to its close, and catch a glimpse of the rising of the Sun of Righteousness, "looking for that blessed hope and the glorious appearing of the great God and our Saviour Jesus Christ." If then the apostles expected no millennium before the second advent of Christ, why should we?

The second argument suggested by a glance at the general tenour of these prophecies is stronger, for it is positive rather than negative. The Lord and his apostles not only do *not* foretell a millennium of blessedness before the second coming, but they *do* foretell a series of events which could not co-exist with such a millennium. They predict a succession of wars, famines, plagues, earthquakes, persecutions, apostasies, and corruptions, the working of a mystery of iniquity, which culminates in the manifestation of the man of sin. Can these *coexist* with a millennium, whose characteristics are the absence of war, peace to the ends of the earth, universal prosperity of the righteous, times of refreshing, the subjugation of all kings to the "King of kings," the putting down of all rule and authority and power, the subjugation of his enemies beneath his feet, the triumphant reign of his saints, the filling of the world with the knowledge of the Lord, as the waters cover the sea? If the *former* series of events are to characterize the entire course of this dispensation, which is clearly the teaching of Scripture, *the latter cannot;* they mutually exclude each other. There can therefore be no millennium before Christ comes.

There are a number of passages in which the duty of constant watchfulness, is urged on the church. Take that in Luke xii. as a specimen. The Master bids us be like men that wait for their lord, pronounces a blessing on such as shall be found "*watching*," speaks of the uncertainty as to the time of his coming, whether it should be in the second, or in the third watch, uses the illustration of the thief, and adds, "be ye therefore ready also, for the Son of man cometh at an hour when ye think not."

Now, though it may be difficult, to watch and wait for an event, the time of whose occurrence is altogether uncertain, and may be very distant, yet it is not impossible. But it *is* impossible to watch and wait for an event which we *know* cannot occur during our lifetime, nor during that of our children, nor for many, many, subsequent generations. The millennium has not commenced yet ; we know it is to run a long course of a thousand years. If we know it is to precede our Master's return, how can *we* be, like men that wait for their Lord ? The thing is impossible, and Christ never commanded an impossibility ; therefore we must expect the millennium *after* his coming and not *before*. The early church with one consent placed the millennium revealed by St. John, *after the advent*, and felt it consequently no hindrance to their obedience to the Lord's command, "be ye ready also." An interval nearly twice as long, has it is true actually elapsed, and was of course foreknown to our Lord. But it was not *revealed*, and though a portion of it is prophetically announced, it is announced in such symbolic language as to secure its not being understood, until the understanding of it would be no hindrance to watchfulness. The Lord Jesus knew that fifty or sixty generations of men would live and die ere He would come again ; and He wished each one, to pass the time of its sojourning here, under the hallowing and cheering influence of " that blessed hope." He cannot consequently have *revealed* anything, that would justify the conclusion, "my Lord delayeth his coming." The thousand years of blessedness that He did reveal in the Apocalypse, through John, must consequently be subsequent to his return.

The apostle Paul twice uses the expression " we who are alive and remain, unto the coming of the Lord "; whether we regard these words, simply as the natural utterance of his own feelings, or as dictated by the Holy Ghost, they bear equally strong testimony to the fact, that the coming of Christ, and not the millennium, is the event for which Christians should look and wait. Taken as the language of Paul merely, they show how thoroughly imbued *he* was with the expectation that the then living generation of saints, his own cotemporaries, might witness the second advent. Clearly he expected no millennium first, unless he also expected to live beyond the age of Methuselah! And why after the lapse of eighteen hundred years, should we regard the coming of the Lord as more distant from us, than he did from him? Taking these words as an inspired expression, placed by the Holy Ghost in the lips of each successive generation of Christians, they are still more conclusive. It is a Divine warrant to all, to expect what Paul expected. The sorrowing mourners around each successive sleeper in Jesus, are to take up the glad strain, " *we* who are alive and remain, shall be caught up together with them in the clouds, to meet the Lord in the air, and so shall we ever be with the Lord." The hope was never to lie in abeyance, never to be out of date ; but to be ever glowing, bright and warm, in living hearts. Therefore the Holy Ghost cannot have *revealed* a millennium, before the second coming of Christ; for such a revelation must render the hope of that coming dim and distant, and comparatively powerless, for the purposes of consolation to which it is here applied All the Christians that have yet lived, would have been unable to use the words of Paul; and since the millennium has not begun yet, thirty or forty generations more, must be equally incapable of adopting the language ; only those in fact who shall live in the tenth and last century of the millennium, could do so.

Again the apostle Paul (Rom. viii. 18) uses two remarkable expressions, " the sufferings of this present time " and " the glory which shall be revealed in us." They respectively apply to *this dispensation,* and to the *millennial age.* He speaks of this present time as a period of suffering, not only to the sons of

God, but to the whole creation, which is under the bondage of corruption and subject to death. He speaks of that future age as a time of the manifestation of the sons of God, a time of "glorious liberty." He says that the whole creation groans and travails in pain together, and that we ourselves, in like manner groan within ourselves, while awaiting that period. He defines *the point* at which the transition from the one state to the other will take place, the point at which the millennium will commence, the point for which we wait. It is "*the redemption of our* BODY" that is *the resurrection.* But the resurrection will not come till Christ comes, we know these two events synchronize even to the twinkling of an eye. Therefore *the millennium will not come till Christ comes,* and *Christ will come before the millennium.* This conclusion can only be avoided by asserting, that during the millennium, the saints and the whole creation will be groaning and travailing in pain together, and with "earnest expectation" awaiting a better state of things.

In 2 Thessalonians ii. 8, in speaking of the destruction of the man of sin, the apostle declares that it will be effected by the brightness of Christ's coming, the ἐπιφανεία τῆς παρουσίας. Either therefore the man of sin, the great enemy of Christ, will live and reign throughout the millennium, which is incredible, or Christ will come before the millennium and destroy him.

The loving words of our Lord, "Ye now therefore have sorrow, but I will see you again and your heart shall rejoice," though they may have found a fulfilment, in the joy that filled the disciples' hearts, when they saw the Lord after his resurrection, have yet a prophetic bearing on the effect of his future coming. They harmonize with all the scriptures which represent the church as an espoused bride awaiting an absent bridegroom, and teach us that for the church that loves her absent Lord, joy can come only with his return. Either then prolonged sorrow, deep unsatisfied yearnings of soul, a painful sense of loneliness and bereavement, are consistent with millennial bliss; or else there can be no millennium for the church, till after the coming of Christ.

The millennium will be a peculiar period, unlike any period that has as yet been known on earth. If it were immediately to precede the coming of Christ, it would surely have been mentioned among the signs of that great event which we are exhorted to note. But it is never so mentioned ; *it is never mentioned at all in connection with an advent following it.* In no one single passage of Scripture can the two events be found in this order ; nor can a single text be produced in which the second advent of Christ is spoken of, *in connection with a preceding millennium.* We must therefore conclude that the millennium is to *follow* the coming of Christ.*

Having thus reviewed some of the general teachings of Scripture, both in the Old and New Testaments, concerning the relative period of the second advent, we now turn to the final prophecy of the Bible, in the expectation of finding there, fuller and clearer light on the subject. The conclusion we have reached is abundantly confirmed by the *general tenour* of the Apocalypse, and by the *direct evidence* of its closing visions.

This book presents the church as exposed to tribulation, and having need of patience, as bearing a painful and danger-ous testimony to Christ, and as enduring temptation and per-secution, right up to the time of the advent. Its author was in his own person, a representative of the church in these respects. " I John, who also am your brother, and companion in tribulation, and in the kingdom and patience of Jesus Christ, was in the isle that is called Patmos, for the word of God, and for the testimony of Jesus Christ." Never in the whole course of the book do we see the saints exalted and reigning, until after the second advent. The sweet picture of heavenly glory in chap. vii., occurs in unbroken sequence after a succession of war, famines, plagues, martyr deaths, and political convulsions. No period of holiness and peace on earth is mentioned as inter-vening. The seven trumpets announce an uninterrupted series of judgments, up to the moment when it is said " the kingdoms

---

* The order of the visions in Rev. xx. is no exception to this rule, as shown in the following pages.

of this world are become the kingdom of our Lord and of his Christ, and He shall reign for ever and ever" (xi. 15). The trumpets clearly represent, not millennial blessings, but providential judgment; they leave no room for a millennium before the coming of Christ. But any remains of doubt ought to be dispelled by the closing visions of this book. There, bright, clear, full, and harmonious with every previous prediction, stands out on almost the last page of inspiration, a grand and detailed *description* of the *epiphany* of Christ. It is a symbolic description it is true, for the revelation in which it occurs is a symbolic prophecy, but its symbols, interpreted by other scriptures, can hardly be mistaken; they serve rather as the steps of a ladder, to enable the mind to mount to the majesty of the theme. And there too, immediately succeeding it, stands out a second prophecy of THE REIGN of Christ and his saints, symbolic too, yet simple in its symbolism, and with even its simple symbols explained to make them simpler. As we look into these last unveilings of the counsel of God about the future, once more we ask the question, what is the prospect before us? A thousand years of bliss on earth, and then our Lord from heaven? or our Lord from heaven first, and then a thousand years of bliss? We remember as we await the reply, that it is the last testimony we can have, till the event itself give an answer, the last prophetic utterance of the Holy Ghost on the subject.

The Vision of the Advent of the King of Kings.

And I saw heaven opened,
And behold a white horse;
He that sat on him was called Faithful and True ·
In righteousness He doth judge and make war:
His eyes were as a flame of fire;
On his head were many crowns:
He had a name written that no man knew but He Himself
He was clothed with a vesture dipped in blood;
His name was called the WORD OF GOD.

And the armies which were in heaven followed Him,
>Upon white horses ;
Clothed in fine linen white and clean ;
Out of his mouth goeth a sharp sword ;
That with it He should smite the nations ;
And He shall rule them with a rod of iron.
He treadeth the winepress of the fierceness and wrath of
>Almighty God,
He hath on his vesture and on his thigh, a name written,
>KING OF KINGS AND LORD OF LORDS.

Rev. xix.

Every clause of this magnificent vision, determines the rider on the white horse to be Jesus Christ and none other. Heaven was opened to give Him exit ; a door *in* heaven had been previously opened for John to gaze on its hidden mysteries ; now heaven itself opens, and its armies follow their great Captain. He bears a fourfold name ; He is called Faithful and True ; who can He be but " Jesus Christ the faithful and true witness " ? He has also *a name that no man knows* but He Himself ; who can He be but the Son, whom " no man knoweth but the Father," the one, who of old said to Manoah, " Why askest thou thus after my name, seeing it is *secret ?* " His name is called " the Word of God " ; who can He be but He who in the beginning was with God and was God ? And on his vesture and on his thigh, are emblazoned the unmistakable words, " *King of kings and Lord of lords.* "

He comes to do a threefold work, each part of which belongs to Christ and to Christ alone, as other scriptures abundantly prove. " *In righteousness He doth judge and* make war " against the Beast and his armies (ver. 20). Who can He be but the Lord who shall consume that wicked son of perdition and man of sin, with the spirit of his mouth and the brightness of his coming ? (1 Thess. ii. 8.)

" He shall *rule the nations with a rod of iron.*" Who can He be but the only begotten Son of God, to whom are addressed the words of the second Psalm, " ask of Me and I shall give Thee the heathen for thine inheritance, and the uttermost parts of the earth for thy possession. Thou shalt break them with a rod of iron " ?

" *He treadeth the winepress* of the fierceness and wrath of Almighty God." Who can He be, but the glorious One, mighty to save, who says " I will tread down the people in mine anger," and " trample them in my fury " (Isa. lxiii.) ? His vesture dipped in blood identifies Him with this red-apparelled Conqueror and solitary Saviour.

" His eyes are as a flame of fire," as were the eyes of the one like unto the Son of man, seen by John in the first vision of this book. Who can He be but that God who is of purer eyes than to behold evil, and cannot look on iniquity? that God who searches the heart and tries the reins, and from whom no secrets are hid? " *On his head were many crowns,*" for " dominion and glory and a kingdom are given Him, that all nations and languages should serve Him." Who can He be but that Son of man who is also the Ancient of days, Israel's long looked for Messiah, earth's oft desired King, the King of righteousness, the King of Salem, which is the King of peace? On his head were many diadems : the royal crown, the victor's crown, the priestly crown, the nuptial crown, all befit his blessed brow; and on it rest the many diadems which recently adorned the bestial horns, united now on the head of Him who has vanquished them all. Who can He be but the One to whom every knee shall bow, and every tongue confess, the One who has received a name above every name? He is followed, not by angelic hosts, but by the saintly armies of heaven ; who can He be but the one, of whom Enoch prophesied, " the Lord cometh, with ten thousands of his saints "; the one of whom Zechariah wrote, " The Lord my God shall come, and all the saints with thee " ; the One who shall be glorified in his saints, and admired in all them that believe, in that day ?

And this vision can be a vision of nothing else but a *personal* advent of Christ. It cannot be a vision of a *spiritual* coming, every clause forbids the thought. For *such* a coming, it needs not that heaven should be opened ; for *such* a coming it needs not attendant armies of saintly warriors. The coming of the Lord *with ten thousands of his saints* has been regarded even from antediluvian ages, as his personal appearance to execute judgment on the ungodly.

It cannot be a vision of a *providential coming;* the previous chapters of this book, afford illustrations of the kind of Divine interference in the affairs of earth, which is intended by this expression. In the opening of the seven-sealed book, in the scattering of the coals of fire on the earth, in the sounding of the seven trumpets, Christ is seen acting providentially. But He is seen *in heaven;* thence He directs his various angelic and other agencies, for his *providence* needs not his personal *presence* on earth. " The heavens do rule " in providence *on behalf* of the saints, not *in conjunction* with them, whether man perceive it or not. If this vision represent merely a providential coming, to what end the opened heaven, and the forth issuing armies, following the King of kings ? No where is it promised or prophesied, that the saints shall share with Christ his present *providential* government; but it *is* promised that they shall share his future work of judging and ruling the world.

But further ; if it were a figurative, spiritual, or providential coming that is here represented, its character and its objects must needs be in harmony with those of all the spiritual and providential comings with which we are acquainted. In other words, if the coming here prefigured be an event belonging in any sense to this dispensation, it should harmonize with the known actions and operations of Christ during this dispensation. It does not do this; it is on the contrary in abrupt and violent contrast to them. The line of action here ascribed to the Lord Jesus, and the line of action which we know Him to have been pursuing ever since incarnation, are so antagonistic, as to preclude their characterizing one and the same dispensation. In the *vision,* " in righteousness He doth judge ; "

in *this age,* in grace He refuses to judge, saying "I came not to judge "; "man, who made Me a judge over you?" "I judge no man "; "neither do I condemn thee." In the vision, in righteousness He makes war; in this age, in grace He makes peace: He came to bring peace on earth, "He is our peace," "He is the Prince of peace." In the vision, "out of his mouth goeth a sharp sword, that with it He should smite the nations"; in this dispensation we are not smitten, but renewed by the word of God, which liveth and abideth for ever; the gospel does not smite the nations but quickens and blesses them. In the vision, "He ruleth the nations with a rod of iron "; in this age Christ does not ostensibly "rule *the nations*" at all, for Satan is the God of this world; but if He did, He would rule them in grace and by love, even as He rules his church, and not by the iron rod, of inflexible righteousness; He spares the nations, He is kind to the unthankful and unworthy, his longsuffering is salvation. In the vision, "He treadeth the winepress of the fierceness and wrath of Almighty God," that is, He executes the holy indignation of God against sinners. In this dispensation, He manifests the *love* of God to a guilty world, He receives gifts even for the rebellious, He beseeches sinners to be reconciled to God. Who would ever think of describing Christ's present actions in the words of this vision? The coming here prefigured, cannot then be an event of this age at all, it is the inauguration of a future age.

But it is argued this vision cannot prefigure a literal personal advent, its symbolic language proves that a figurative one only is intended. This is virtually to assert that a prophecy of the second advent of Christ is impossible in the Apocalypse; for it is throughout a book of symbols, it is written in the language of symbols, if it contain a prophetic vision of the second advent, it must therefore be expected to be a symbolic vision. Now seeing the second advent is the one climax to which everything in the book tends, can we suppose, that there exists in it no description of the great event itself? Impossible! *This then must be it, for there is no other.*

There is nothing in the nature of symbolic language to preclude its being used in describing literal events. The language of symbols is in this respect, on a par with any other language. The Egyptian hieroglyphics formed a symbolic language, but are the events of Egyptian history narrated and preserved in that language therefore figurative? on the contrary, plain, substantial, literal, history is *recorded* in those hieroglyphics, and plain, substantial, literal, events may in like manner be *predicted* in hieroglyphic or symbolic prophecy. Now a literal personal advent could not be predicted more clearly in the language of symbols than it is here.

Besides which, the judgment scene immediately succeeding, requires this vision to be a real *personal* advent. Scripture is ever harmonious with itself, elsewhere we find the work of judgment is committed by the Father to the Son, and that the Son executes it personally, not by proxy; He does not delegate the task to others, though He employs the assistance of saints and angels. The husbandman who sowed the seed, comes himself to put in the sickle, when the harvest is ripe; the lord of the vineyard comes himself to tread the winepress; so here. In former parts of the Apocalypse angels had been extensively employed. But now the Lord of hosts prepares Himself for the final battle, and comes personally to inaugurate by the judgment of the living,—the destruction of the antichristian hosts,—that great day of judgment, and day of the Lord, which lasts a thousand years, and ends with the final assize of the great white throne.

In short, a personal advent of Christ, is the theme, the main theme, of the whole Bible. The past advent did not accomplish the full results predicted; since *it* became *history*, a second advent has been the dominant note in every prophetic strain, and in the Apocalypse it becomes more prominent than ever. From the "behold He cometh with clouds" of the first chapter, to the "behold I come quickly" of the last, this theme prevades the book. The Apocalypse is a grand drama, the epiphany is its climax. " Hold fast till I come," is Christ's own word to Smyrna ; " behold I come quickly," his encouragement to Philadelphia ; the redeemed in heaven, rejoice in the prospect, " we shall reign on the earth." On the sounding ·of the seventh trumpet, the elders fall down in worship before God, because the moment is at last come, when He is to take his great power and reign on earth. Under the sixth vial the Lord repeats the warning note, " behold I come as a thief " ; and the Apocalypse, yea the Bible itself, ends with the same promise, " surely I come quickly."

" Now the present vision is the passage, and the only passage, where such a glorious advent of our Lord is distinctly described. Till then He is seen in spirit, as the Lamb in the heavenly places, as the priest at the heavenly altar, as the mighty angel, the mysterious messenger of the covenant, while the hour of mystery still continues, and still repeats the warning '*behold I come.*' Here in the vision heaven is opened, and *He is seen to come,* in manifest glory as the Word of God. After this He is spoken of as already come. In the very scene where the powers of evil have just been overthrown, and from which Satan has just been banished, his people ' reign with Christ a thousand years.' When the white throne is seen, He is seen already present to occupy it ; and not a word is given to indicate a fresh arrival, of Him who sits to execute the judgment. All converges on the advent before this vision, all centres on a personal advent of the Word in the vision itself, all implies a previous advent in the visions which follow. And hence the internal evidence that the real advent is here described, is complete."* Now this vision which presents Christ and his saints coming forth to judge and to reign is *followed* by others which present the judgment and the reign ; *i.e.,* the destruction of the hosts of Antichrist, and the millennial reign of the risen saints with their Lord. We have there-

---

* " Outlines of Unfulfilled Prophecy,' Birks, p. 83.

fore in the *last* prophecy on the subject, the *clearest* proof that the second coming of the Lord is to be premillennial. Will any one assert that a millennium, *unnoticed and undescribed in the Apocalypse*, has *preceded* this advent vision? What! the glorious times of restitution of all things, passed over in silence, as unworthy of a place in the great chart of the future? Impossible! and even granting it possible, whereabouts could we insert a millennium, in the long list of evil event and sore judgments of which the book consists? and even if any one find room for it, and satisfy himself by conceiving it may come in here or there, what then will he do with the millennium that *is noticed and described after* this advent vision? Are there to be two millennia? Does the word of God sanction such a thought? Are we to have a spiritual millennium preceded by a spiritual coming, and then a literal millennium preceded by a literal coming? To ask the question is to answer it! The whole Bible forbids the notion of a third advent and second millennium!

The only other alternative, is to deny that this is a vision of a personal advent of Christ at all. But then *what is it?* It cannot, as we have seen, be a figurative coming. *What can it be?* Does it describe nothing at all? Is the most magnificent vision in the book destitute of signification? Is it conceivable, that the greatest event in the future history of our world is not made the subject of a vision in the Apocalypse at all? Where else can we find it? Nowhere! Christ acts on earth afterwards, He does not *come to earth*. This then is the ADVENT VISION, or—there is none! And why should we doubt that this is its character? Does it clash with any previously revealed truth? Nay, but it harmonizes most sweetly with all! He is to come after the resurrection, for He brings the risen saints with him. Here the marriage of the Lamb, that perfect union of Christ and his people, which cannot take place prior to resurrection, immediately precedes this advent vision. He is to come to destroy Antichrist and to take vengeance on those that know not God and obey not the gospel. Here this destruction of Antichrist and the kings of the earth and their armies, immediately follows this advent vision.

Suppose for a moment, that the place occupied by it were left a blank, that the prophecy passed at once, from the marriage of the Lamb, to the destruction of the antichristian host. *Other scriptures would force us to place the second coming of Christ between those two scenes.* The destruction of the beast and the false prophet, demand a previous epiphany, according to 2 Thessalonians ii. ; and the rapturous marriage of the Lamb in heaven, the meeting in the air of Christ and his saints, requires a subsequent manifestation, according to 2 Thessalonians i. 10.

When therefore we find a vision, symbolising in the most consistent and magnificent way, a personal advent of Christ, just where we might have expected to find it, just where all prophecy would conspire to fix its place, just where its absence would render it impossible to harmonize multitudes of other predictions ; when we find it written large in letters of light, and stamped with a sublimity of symbol and circumstance worthy of *such* an event, and too grand for any other, we bow to this final testimony of the prophetic word, and admit that Scripture leaves no room to doubt, that the Lord Jesus will come again in person, to this earth, before the millennium, in other words, that the second advent will be premillennial.

CHAPTER III.

WE turn now to consider the teachings of the Apocalypse as to the events to succeed the second advent of Christ, and it is here that the application of the principle of progressive revelation becomes of peculiar importance.

That principle requires, as we have seen, that we receive the teachings of this inspired prophecy on its authority alone, when they are unconfirmed by other Scripture ; and it requires also that we be prepared to modify impressions derived from earlier and more elementary predictions, whenever this latest revelation of the future demands it. No author expects to have the latest and fullest edition of his book corrected by an earlier and less explicit one; no author but would wish on the contrary that early editions should be read in the light of the last. The Apocalypse contains undoubtedly, the last and the fullest revelation of God on these subjects, the final expression of his purpose ; prior statements must be conformed to this, and not this to prior statements.

The advent vision is followed by a vision of the judgment on Antichrist and his associates, and immediately after this we have

THE VISION OF THE MILLENNIUM.

And I saw an angel come down from heaven,
Having the key of the bottomless pit, and a great chain in his
hand ;
And he laid hold on the dragon, that old serpent, which is the
Devil and Satan,

And bound him a thousand years, and cast him into the bot-
tomless pit,
And shut him up, and set a seal upon him,
That he should deceive the nations no more, till the thousand
years be fulfilled,
And after that he must be loosed for a little season.

And I saw thrones, and they sat on them ;
And judgment was given unto them ;
And I saw the souls of them that were beheaded,
For the witness of Jesus, and for the word of God :
Who had not worshipped the beast, nor his image ;
Neither had received his mark in their foreheads, or in their
hands ;
AND THEY LIVED AND REIGNED WITH CHRIST A THOUSAND
YEARS.

But the rest of the dead lived not again,
Until the thousand years were finished ;
THIS IS THE FIRST RESURRECTION.
Blessed and holy is he that hath part in the first resurrection ;
On such the second death hath no power,
But they shall be priests of God and of Christ
AND SHALL REIGN WITH HIM A THOUSAND YEARS.

The twentieth chapter of Revelation, as is evident to every
student of Scripture, contains several new predictions peculiar
to itself.

The broad fact that there is to be a reign of Christ and his
saints on earth is not new. Though little is said about it in
the gospels and the epistles, for the reason previously assigned
that they occupy themselves rather with the previous *advent,*
yet the law, the psalms, and the prophets, teem with predictions of this *reign* of Christ.

But that it should be introduced by a binding of Satan, that
it should last a thousand years, these facts, dimly intimated
elsewhere, are revealed here *for the first and only time.*

Are we therefore to stand in doubt about them, or try to explain the revelation in some non-natural sense? God forbid! The God who cannot lie, *inspired* this single prediction of them; is not that enough? We need not hesitate to believe what GOD says, even if He say it only once; and indeed we might reject most of the revelations of the Apocalypse, if we adopt the maxim, of doubting all that is only once predicted.

Not only does this prophecy require us to believe two *new* revelations, but it also necessitates a modification of previously entertained views, on two familiar and all important points of our creed, the RESURRECTION OF THE DEAD and the JUDGMENT TO COME. It reveals, what had never previously been clearly made known, that both are to be accomplished *in two successive stages*, with a thousand years between them, and *not* in one great act, as, but for this chapter, we might have supposed.

Are we then to distort the declarations of this chapter, in order to bring them into harmony, not with previous predictions, but with the impressions we have derived from previous predictions? No! but we must bring our impressions into harmony with the joint teaching of earlier and later revelations, which, seeing both are Divine, cannot be contradictory. No one would dream of doing otherwise, in the case of an earlier and later communication from some superior authority. Say, for instance, that the Admiralty issue a notice, that a certain squadron is to sail next month for the Mediterranean. After a few weeks a subsequent order provides, that three vessels are to leave on the 1st of the month, for Besika Bay; and three more on the 30th, for Malta. Shall the commanders hesitate about giving credence to the *later* sailing orders, because they had received from the *earlier* notice an impression that all the ships were to start simultaneously, and for one and the same destination? Clearly not! There is no discrepancy or inconsistency in the orders; the difference is simply, that the later directions are more ample and detailed than were the earlier. From the earlier, the commanders received the erroneous impression they entertained; an impression they would of course abandon immediately the second order arrived.

But as regards these later visions of the Apocalypse, too many act in an opposite way. "We thought," they say, " that Scripture foretold one simultaneous resurrection of all mankind, to take place at the end of the world, and to be immediately followed by the general judgment, the final separation of the righteous and the wicked, and the eternal state. What? *two* resurrections? *two* judgments? and a thousand years apart? What? Christ and his risen saints, reigning over mortal men on the earth, for an entire age, while the rest of the dead lie in their graves? Impossible! The Bible never says so anywhere else! And Satan to be imprisoned for a thousand years, *before* he is cast into the lake of fire? This cannot be, we never gathered *this* from any other part of Scripture! Either these visions do not teach such heterodox novelties, or they are not inspired! True, they *say* this, but they must *mean* something else, for such doctrines are quite contrary to our creed, altogether at variance with the impressions we have derived from previous revelations on the subject."

Such reasoning is not true wisdom, it is prejudice, and it is a denial of God's right to make *progressive revelations.* Wisdom, while perceiving clearly the discrepancy, would say : " Contrary as these new revelations are to the impressions derived from previous scriptures, let us see if any real variance exist, and if not, let us abandon our imperfect and consequently erroneous ideas, and receive with meekness, *all* the light on these subjects graciously granted by God."

We propose therefore first to examine what the *peculiar* teachings of these visions *are,* and secondly whether these teachings, taken in their most obvious and natural sense, are *inconsistent with* other scriptures, or merely *in advance* of them.

Let it be noted then, first, that this is not a vision of the resurrection of saints, but of their *enthronement* and *reign.* As far as they are concerned, the resurrection is past already before this scene opens.

Other scriptures definitely fix the moment of the resurrection of saints. " They that are Christ's " rise *at his coming;* his saints meet their Lord in the air, and come with Him to the earth (Col. iii. 3, 1 Thess. iv.). The resurrection must therefore have taken place *before* the advent described in the previous vision. What was the immediately preceding act in this Divine drama?

Multitudinous voices in heaven, are heard asserting, that Christ has assumed his kingly power, and that *the marriage of the Lamb is come.* Now this marriage, celebrated by the glad hallelujahs of heaven, can be nothing else than that full union of Christ and his church which is to take place at the resurrection. The angelic host describe the bride, as made "ready," as arrayed in fine linen clean and white which is the righteousness of saints, and John is instructed to write down " blessed' those who are called to the marriage supper. Now not till after resurrection, can Christ present his church to Himself "a glorious church, not having spot, or wrinkle, or any such thing, but holy and without blemish," according to this scene : *resurrection must therefore have preceded this vision of the marriage supper.* No vision of it is given in the Apocalypse ; how could there be ? It is the event of less than a moment, it occupies only the twinkling of an eye. It could not be represented as an occurrence *on earth,* for the risen saints are, in a second, caught up to meet their Lord in the air; nor as an occurrence *in heaven,* for it is connected with the earth and the air. The precise locality of the nuptial feast is not indicated, a veil of privacy is thrown around the meeting of bridegroom and bride; it *takes place,* and this is all that we know. Whether any interval elapse between the resurrection rapture and the glorious epiphany, is not revealed to us here. But the epiphany *has occurred;* and the church, under the symbol of the armies that were in heaven, has shared in the work of judging the antichristian hosts, before this millennial vision opens. In it, consequently, we have not the resurrection, but the enthronement, of the risen saints. The expression " this is the first resurrection" is not a note of *time*, but of *character:* it is tantamount to, this is the company who rise in the first resurrection, *not* this is the chronological *point* at which the first resurrection takes place; and the company here spoken of, like those called to the marriage supper, are declared *blessed and holy.*

There is similarly no vision of the second stage of the resurrection in verse 12; the dead are presented as already raised, and standing before God. But though these verses give no vision of either the first or the second stage of the resurrection, they give much new light about it; *they distinctly reveal, that there is never to take place, a simultaneous resurrection of all mankind,* but that on the contrary, the distinction so marked in this life, between the godly and the ungodly, is to be more marked still in the resurrection. It shows us that the righteous shall rise before the wicked; rise to live and reign for a thousand years with their risen royal Lord; and that the "rest of the dead" rise not again till the thousand years be fulfilled.

"And I saw thrones, and they sat on them, and judgment was given unto them." To whom? To Christ and his risen saints, to the King of kings, and to the armies which were in heaven; for we must go back to the 13th verse of chapter xix. for the occupants of these thrones. There intervenes no plural or collective noun, for which this pronoun *they* could stand. We may therefore paraphrase the words thus: "I saw Christ and his risen saints enthroned and governing the world." John noticed especially among the latter, the martyrs and confessors who had figured so prominently in previous stages of this long drama; their cries, and groans, and sufferings, and blood, had been main features of its different stages, and they are therefore singled out from among their brethren for a special mention, which marks the unity of this scene with the whole Apocalypse. In this final righting of the wrongs of ages, the sufferers are enthroned beside the great Sufferer, the overcomers sit with Him in his throne, the faithful witnesses of Christ, reign with their Lord, the oppressed and slaughtered saints, judge the world. But this mention of a special class is by the way : the main stream of the prophecy continues thus : " I saw thrones, and they sat on them, and judgment was given unto them, and they lived and reigned with Christ a thousand years; but the rest of the dead lived not again until the thousand years were finished. This is the first resurrection."

Subsequently, the "rest of the dead" are seen standing in the last assize, before the great white throne, to be judged. " I saw the dead small and great stand before God." The dead are thus divided into two portions ; there are the dead who rise and reign, and the dead who rise not and reign not with them. There are the dead who rise to judge the world with Christ, and there are the dead who rise to be judged according to their works by God. There are the dead who rise to sit on thrones, and the dead who rise to stand before the great white throne. There are the dead who rise with spiritual bodies; how else could they last a thousand years ? and the dead who rise as they died, to die a second death. There are the dead who rise emphatically "blessed and holy," and the dead who rise only to be tried, condemned, and cast into hell. There are the dead who rise immortal, for on them the second death hath no power, and the dead who rise only to become its victims. Throughout, these two classes are presented in marked and intentional contrast; the latter are beyond all question literal dead, SO THEREFORE ARE THE FORMER.

This passage then teaches that the resurrection of the dead will take place in two stages, with a thousand years between. Taken in its apparent, most natural, and consistent meaning, nothing else can be made of it. Why then has it been made the victim of more distortion than almost any passage in the Bible ? And why, after the ablest champions of the truth, have in unanswerable argument, defended its right to mean what it seems to mean, why to this day, do multitudes still read it with the coloured spectacles of preconceived opinion, so as to change its clear blue of heavenly doctrine, into the muddy grey of mystical unmeaningness? Why will multitudes still derange its majestic harmonies, so as to produce ungrateful discord? why make of this graciously given clue to the labyrinth of previous prophecy, a snare to entangle our feet the further, in a maze of doubt and difficulty?   Let an intelligent child, or any one who simply understands the terms used, read these verses attentively, and then answer the question, "will the dead all rise at the same time?" We will venture to assert they would unhesitatingly answer : " No ! this passage declares the contrary, the righteous will rise a thousand years before the wicked."

Such is the obvious meaning of the prophecy, and the more closely it is analysed, the more clearly is it perceived to teach this doctrine.   The difficulty arises from the mistaken attempt to put new wine into old bottles, to reduce the fulness of a last revelation to the dimensions of a more elementary one. Let us reverse the process, and applying the principle of progressive revelation, let us see whether every previous prophecy on the subject of resurrection, may not without any distortion at all of the text, be harmonized with this latest prophecy.

There is but little in the Old Testament on the subject of resurrection, for it was Christ who brought life and immortality to light ; but, though revealed only dimly in the olden time, they *were* revealed.   Isaiah wrote : " Thy dead men shall live, . . . my dead body, they shall arise ; awake and sing, ye that dwell in dust."   Can this allude to a resurrection of others than saints?   Shall " the dead, small and great," *sing* before the great white throne?   But, to pass by other less clear statements of the doctrine of resurrection in the Old Testament, we find in Daniel xii. a passage more quoted than almost any other, in support of the idea that the resurrection of the righteous and of the wicked will be at one and the same moment.   "Many of them that sleep in the dust of the earth shall awake, some to everlasting life, and some to shame and everlasting contempt."   The time of this resurrection is fixed in the previous verse to be the time of the deliverance of Daniel's people from their great tribulation, that is, the time of Israel's restoration, Antichrist's destruction, and the second advent.

It seems to require some ingenuity to make out a contradiction between this prophecy and that of John. It places resurrection at the same *point* in the great chart of the future ; it makes the same moral distinction, and in the same order, as our Lord in John v., and it omits in the same way all allusion to a chronological interval. It neither specifies nor excludes one, as was natural in a prediction so brief and elementary, of an event at that time so distant. The apparent discrepancy is clearly caused by *defect of detail* in this early prophecy; and we have only to *add* to its statement, the new particulars given in the later revelation, to produce perfect harmony.

Some expositors, however, render the original of this verse differently from our authorized version ; translating it " the many," or " the multitude of," which is equivalent to *all.* Others consider that it will not bear this version, but rather that the two classes contrasted in the latter part of the prophecy refer to the many who rise, and to the " rest of the dead," whose resurrection is not here mentioned, but who are destined to shame and everlasting contempt.* Whichever view may be the true one, neither, it is evident, presents any important variation from the Apocalypse ; the two predictions harmonize *as far as the first goes.* No contradiction can be alleged between them ; we must not wonder that we do not find in the pages of Daniel, that which we cannot discover even in the gospels, a doctrine that it was reserved for the final prophecy of Scripture, to reveal.

The passage of Scripture which more fully than any other

---

* " I do not doubt that the right translation of this verse is,—' and many from among the sleepers of the dust of the earth shall awake, these shall be unto everlasting life, but those (the rest of the sleepers who do not awake at this time) shall be unto shame and everlasting contempt.' "—Tregelles on Daniel, p. 102.

dwells on the subject of *the resurrection*, the passage which has illumined the darkness of death to successive generations of Christians, and like the bow in the cloud, thrown a gleam of glory over ten thousand graves, is the fifteenth chapter of the First Epistle to the Corinthians.

To the sound of its majestic and marvellous strains, we commit to the dust, those whom we bury in sure and certain hope of a glorious resurrection. But why does an intelligent and conscientious Christian, shrink from sounding over the grave of the ungodly those triumphant and heart cheering strains?

Because that chapter treats exclusively of *the resurrection of those that are Christ's at his coming!* There is no assertion here of a simultaneous rising of all mankind! In vain we search for any allusion at all to a *resurrection of the wicked.* " It is sown in corruption, it is raised in incorruption ; it is sown in dishonour, it is raised in glory ; it is sown in weakness, it is raised in power ! " Believers only can be included in the statement. " We shall not all sleep, but we shall all be changed ; in a moment, in the twinkling of an eye, at the last trump ; for the trumpet shall sound, and the dead shall be raised, *incorruptible*, and we shall be changed ; for this corruptible must put on incorruption, and this mortal must put on immortality " ; that death may be swallowed up in victory, and we obtain the victory, through our Lord Jesus Christ. There is nothing here at variance with the vision we have just considered ; on the contrary, there are two distinct harmonies with its teachings.

1. The resurrection of those that are Christ's is spoken of as a distinct event. " Christ the firstfruits, afterward *they that are Christ's* " (not " afterward all mankind ").

2. This resurrection is said to be, *not* at the end of the world, but " *at his coming,*" which, as we have seen, is 1000 years before the end of the world.

It is added " *then cometh the end,*" and as well nigh two thousand years have already intervened between *the first two*

events here predicted, it is doing no violence to the passage to assert, that one thousand years will intervene (according to the twentieth chapter of Revelation), between *the last
two.* The prediction marches with majestic step, measuring
millenaries, as it passes from one scene of resurrection to another.

1. Christ the firstfruits.
2. Afterward, they that are Christ's, at his coming.
3. Then cometh the end.

Three great epochs of resurrection : that of Christ, that of
Christians, that of the ungodly ; the latter not being named or
described here, though its chronological point is intimated, it
is at the end.*

It is the same with the other great statement of our hope in
1 Thessalonians iv. It speaks of a resurrection of the dead in
Christ, and of *such only* at his coming ; and thus *suggests*, what
the Apocalypse *states*, that "the rest of the dead live not again"
till after an interval of whose length it says nothing.

In Acts xxvi. 15, Paul, stating his own faith and that of the
Jewish nation on this point, says " there will be a resurrection
of the dead, both of the just and of the unjust." The vision
we are considering shows this double resurrection, and adds
the information, that its chronology is as twofold as its character, that the resurrection of the just, will take place a thousand
years before the resurrection of the unjust. There is no contradiction here.

In Philippians iii. 11, Paul,—expressing his own ardent desire
and aim,—says, " if by any means I might attain, to the resurrection of the dead." Had he put before himself as an object or
attainment, and of difficult attainment too, a resurrection com-

---

* In the typical "feasts of the Lord" (Lev. xxiii.) there were similarly
THREE INGATHERINGS. The *firstfruit sheaf*, on the morrow after the paschal
sabbath ; seven weeks later the *firstfruits of the harvest*, " two wave loaves";
and at the *end* of the Jewish sacred year, the ingathering of all the fruits of
the earth, including *the vintage.* These were the three feasts, in which all
Israel's males were to appear before God. "Thrice in the year shall all
thy males appear before God " (Exod. xxiii. 14-17).

mon to all mankind, and consequently inevitable for him? No!
but a *peculiar* resurrection! A resurrection which was to his
heart, as the pole to the magnet, a resurrection ἐκ τῶν νεκρῶν,
"*from among*" the dead, the first resurrection, in which only
the blessed and holy have part. In the same way our Lord
spoke of being "recompensed at the resurrection of the just;
could He have used such language if there were no distinction
between the resurrection of the just and that of the unjust?

In John v. 28, 29, our Lord says, "the hour is coming, in
which all that are in the graves, shall hear his voice, and shall
come forth; they that have done good, unto the resurrection of
life, and they that have done evil, unto the resurrection of
judgment."

It must be admitted that if we were obliged to take the word
"*hour*" here in its most limited sense, this passage would undoubtedly teach, a simultaneous resurrection of all the dead.
But we are not. The word ὥρα admits of wide extension, its
primary meaning is "season," and our Lord Himself, in a sentence immediately preceding this, employs it to cover the whole
of this gospel dispensation, in which the spiritually dead are
being quickened to life by his voice. If it admit of extension
to eighteen hundred years in the twenty-fifth verse, it may well
include a thousand in the twenty-eighth, and this is all that is
requisite, to make it agree perfectly, with the apocalyptic vision.
This grand and solemn prediction of our Lord announces that
morally there will be two resurrections, first of the just, and
secondly of the unjust; the twentieth chapter of Revelation
adds, that *chronologically also* there will be two, first of the
just, and secondly of the unjust. There is no discord here,
but there is on the contrary a marked harmony.

There is a parallelism also between the spiritual resurrections that are going on in this "hour," and the bodily
resurrections that shall occur in that "hour." Neither are
simultaneous; though the latter according to the Apocalypse, take place only at two epochs, at the beginning, and
at the close, of the millennium; while the former are, as

experience teaches, still less simultaneous, and take place day by day, throughout the whole course of the dispensation. Would our Lord have used the two striking, distinct, names He does use, had He foreseen one general resurrection? Would He have spoken of "the resurrection of life" and "the resurrection of damnation"?

These are the main passages in the Bible bearing on the doctrine of resurrection. We now inquire, where does Scripture teach a simultaneous resurrection of all mankind? And echo answers, where? Yet many have so strong an impression that it is a fundamental doctrine of the Christian faith, that they feel bound to evade in some way, the simple obvious conclusions to be drawn from the visions we are considering.

So far from being *at variance* with previous inspired teachings on the subject, the fresh revelations of the Apocalypse enable us to perceive the Divine accuracy of many delicate touches in earlier scriptures, which would have remained unperceived but for our knowledge of this truth. Such, for instance, is the discriminating use of the four Greek expressions, rendered indifferently in our version "the resurrection OF the dead." Moses Stuart says: "after investigating this subject, I have doubts whether the assertion is correct that such a doctrine as that of the first resurrection, is nowhere else to be found in Scripture. The laws of philology oblige me to suppose, that the Saviour and St. Paul have both alluded to such a doctrine." The Greek expressions used may be literally translated "resurrection of dead ones," "resurrection from among dead ones," "the resurrection : that one from among dead ones," and "the out resurrection of or from the dead." The Greek expressions are not used indiscriminately; and it is evident that, had they been uniformly translated by exactly corresponding phrases, the thought of a resurrection of some of the dead, and not of all the dead, would have been a familiar one to students of Scripture. The phraseology employed on the subject is, in other words, precisely what would naturally be selected by the

Holy Spirit, if resurrection were foreseen to consist of two
stages ; but unaccountable, if it were all to consist in one
act.*

It should be remembered also that a resurrection of some,
which leaves others behind, is the only kind of resurrection of
which we have any example. Such were the three resurrections miraculously wrought by our Lord ; such was his own
resurrection, and such was the rising which took place, when
" many bodies of the saints which slept arose, and came out of
the graves, after his resurrection, and appeared unto many."
Why should not that which *has* happened on a small scale
happen on a large ?

The Final Judgment.

The commonly received opinion on this subject, that the
whole race of man will appear simultaneously before the great
white throne of God, to be judged according to their works, at
the coming of the Lord, is based upon a great many passages
of Scripture, and is tenaciously held, with a conviction that any
departure from it is grave heresy. But this twentieth chapter
of Revelation, taken in its context and in its natural sense,
requires a modification of this theory. It does not deny that
the whole human family will appear before the judgment seat
and throne of God ; but it teaches that they will not do so
simultaneously, that the act of judgment, like that of resurrection, will take place in two stages, divided by an interval of a
thousand years.

---

* The expression " out of " or " from " the dead is never used in the
New Testament except of a resurrection in which others are left behind;
it is used thirty-five times of the resurrection of Christ (and save in two
passages where the ἐκ is omitted for the sake of euphony no other *is* used).
The natural inference is that when this expression or a stronger one is
applied to the resurrection of Christ's people, it implies a resurrection of
some in which others are left behind. One who has examined this subject
very fully says : " I am prepared to affirm that whenever ἐκ or ἐξ is used in
connection with ἀνάστασις, it is the resurrection of the just that is referred
to ; or at least, a resurrection in which some are left behind."—See Wood's
" Last Things," p. 59.

The Vision of the Final Judgment.

And I saw a great white throne, and Him that sat on it ;
From whose face the earth and the heaven fled away,
    And there was found no place for them.
And I saw *the dead* small and great, stand before God ;
    And the books were opened,
And another book was opened which was the book of life,
    And the dead were judged
Out of those things which were written in the books
    According to their works.

And the sea gave up the dead which were in it ;
    And death and hades
Delivered up the dead which were in them ;
    And they were judged,
    Every man according to his works.
And death and hades were cast into the lake of fire.
    This is the second death,
And whosoever was not found written in the book of life
    Was cast into the lake of fire.

This passage taken in its natural obvious sense, and with its context, is clearly a sequel to the previous vision, and can be interpreted only in connection with it.

The "rest of the dead," who lived not again then, *do* live again now ; those that had done good, rose in the bright morning of this day of the Lord, to the resurrection of life, those that have done evil, rise now at its lurid close, to the resurrection of judgment.

The expression "the dead small and great" includes all who were dead, at the inauguration of this great session of judgment : not only the "rest of the dead" left behind at the time of the first resurrection, but all cut off during the course of the millennium, as well as the immense company of rebels, destroyed by fire from heaven, at its close.

A little reflection will convince the thoughtful of the impossibility, that the church of the firstborn should be summoned to this bar of judgment. They have already been tried, condemned, and executed, viz., in the person of the Surety. Rom. vi. 7, (Gr.) "He that has died is justified from sin (guilt):" death exhausts the penalty. Ever since the marriage of the Lamb, a thousand years before, they have been publicly owned as the bride of Christ, *one* with the occupant of the great white throne, united to Him, not only secretly by faith, but publicly in the eyes of the universe. They are his body, a part of Himself; because He lives, they live also. And will He summon his dearly loved, blood-bought, long glorified bride, to be judged amid "the dead small and great"? Shall the saints stand and be tried, in company with their enemies and persecutors? Why, Christ Himself is their righteousness, they are pure as He is pure; shall they mingle again in the common herd of the fearful, and the unbelieving, and the abominable, and murderers, and whoremongers, and sorcerers, and idolaters and liars, from whom grace made them, ages ago, to differ? God covenanted with them to remember no more their sins and iniquities, and to blot out as a thick cloud their transgressions. Shall they now be called to account for the long cancelled score? Ages since, they received the gift of God, eternal life; shall *He* now call in question their right to his own gift? For a thousand years they have been, by the Divine Judge himself, vindicated from every shade and suspicion of guilt, before the holy angels and the entire universe; and shall they now descend from their priestly thrones, and with "blessed and holy" inscribed on their brilliant brows, and clad in their fine linen clean and white, as no fuller on earth can white it, stand amid the throng of the unholy and impure, to be *judged*, and judged according to their works? To what end should they mingle with the "lost," from whom conversion long since severed them, and with the dead, from whom resurrection long since divided them? To be afresh acquitted, say some, and to hear again the "Well done, good and faithful servant." Be it so! but then *why is neither their presence, nor their acquittal,*

nor their eternal portion, even so much as alluded to in the vision?
Why is there no mention of these? Why do we read only of
"the dead small and great," and of *their condemnation* alone?
The answer is clear. Because the dead only are there! They
seek in vain, who seek the living among the dead!

Such then is the apparent teaching of this vision, on the
subject of judgment. It remains to be examined, whether the
strong impression in the minds of many, that this doctrine is
not only additional to, but *contrary* to, the doctrine of other
parts of Scripture, is well grounded or not.

We must, then, inquire on what passages this strong conviction is based, and whether they *do* definitely teach a *simultaneous* judgment of the just and of the unjust. Let it be borne
in mind that *this* is the point; not the broad truth that both
classes are to be judged. "It is appointed unto men once to
die, but after this the judgment," is a rule without exception,
as far as we learn from Scripture. "Every one of us shall give
account of himself to God." "We shall all stand before the
judgment seat of Christ." There is no possibility of mistaking
the all-inclusive character of these and similar assertions; but
they leave untouched the question we have to consider. The
statements, "the commander in chief will review the army,"
"he will review every regiment," "every officer and every
private will pass in review before him," prove that all are to be
reviewed, but not that all are to be reviewed *at the same time.*
Those who are forced by its internal evidence to deny that the
judgment vision of Revelation xx. includes the righteous, are
not thereby forced to assert, that the righteous are to go
unjudged. The point to be decided is exactly similar to
that we have considered in connection with resurrection; do
earlier scriptures oblige us, by unequivocal assertion of *simultaneousness,* to give a non-natural interpretation to these final
prophecies? or do they, in the light reflected back from these
latest revelations, accommodate themselves naturally to a
different sense?

The close connection which exists between resurrection and

judgment, would lead us to expect that what has proved true in the one case, will do so in the other. The resurrection of the dead and eternal judgment, are never separated by any considerable or defined interval. If therefore the former is proved to be divided into two widely distant stages, the presumption is strong, that this will be the case also with the latter. The two resurrections indeed receive their distinctive appellations from the results of the judgments which accompany them; the " resurrection of life," and " the resurrection of damnation."

In reviewing the testimony of other scriptures on this subject, we are likely to find—in harmony with the principle of progressive revelation—many statements of the broad fundamental doctrine of future judgment, which fall in equally well with either view; some few which at first sight seem to teach simultaneousness, but which on closer examination will be seen to leave the point undecided; and some, which can only be fairly interpreted, or fully understood, by assuming two epochs and scenes of judgment.

Of the first class are such passages as, "we must all appear before the judgment seat of Christ, that every one may receive the things done in his body, according to that he hath done, whether it be good or bad." " God will render to every man according to his deeds" (Rom. ii. 5). "The Son of man shall come in the glory of his Father with his angels, and then shall He reward every man according to his works" (Matt. xvi. 27).

Many such passages exist; it is not needful to multiply quotations, no argument can be built on them, in favour of either view. Without further revelation we should doubtless have understood them to teach a simultaneous judgment; *with* further revelation, we can read them as broad comprehensive statements, made by One who *knew*, but did not at the time wish to *reveal*, modifying details. Such passages mention the universality of the judgment, the twofold result, the fact that it is to follow our Lord's return, and they show that in either case the issues will be eternal; but they do not touch the question of *simultaneousness.*

With the closing parable of Matthew xxv. it is otherwise. This is the leading passage, of the second class above alluded to; those which seem at first sight distinctly to teach a simultaneous judgment of the righteous and the wicked. On any theory this passage is one difficult of interpretation, owing to its peculiar semi-parabolic form; the difficulty of deciding whether it is a judgment of the dead or of the living; the principle of the judgment,—*works,*—taken in connection with the eternity of the issues in either case; the limited nature of the test, on which the great award is made to depend; its relation to the previous parables; its likeness to, yet dissimilarity from, other parallel scriptures; and other features. But the following considerations seem to make it clear, that the scene here described is not identical with that in Revelation xx. 12. *This* presents *an award* only, *that* an *investigation,* for "the books were opened and the dead were judged out of those things written in the books;" this presents the righteous and the wicked, and mentions the eternal portion of each, that, is silent altogether as regards the righteous; this parable in describing those gathered before the Son of man, makes use of an expression applicable to *the living,* πάντα τὰ ἔθνη, "all nations" or "the Gentiles;" while the vision in the Apocalypse shows only the dead, "the dead small and great"; in the former, the wicked are condemned *en masse,* on the negative ground of what they have *not* done; in the latter, as individuals, on the positive ground of what they *have* done, "the things written in the books."

If this parable does describe a judgment of the dead, (which is most unlikely,) then we are compelled by the later revelation to apply to it the same rule, as to the first class of passages, and to conceive that our Lord presented the judgment as a great whole, and was purposely silent, as to the interval between its two stages. Other great and important events had to intervene; the moral effect to be produced on the minds of his disciples by this truth of judgment to come, was the same, whether it were to take place at once, or at intervals; and the object He had in view did not require that He should enter into details, for which they were not prepared. The same Divine reticence, which had purposely hid from their view the interval between his own approaching departure and his return, hid also the interval between the stages of this judgment. In this view of the passage the first session of the judgment is at the advent, when the righteous are rewarded with the kingdom ; the whole millennium is included under the phrase, "then shall He sit on the throne of his glory" ; and the concluding session of the judgment is at its close, when the wicked are doomed to everlasting fire.

A considerable part of the impression of simultaneousness which it produces on the mind, is to be attributed to the parabolic form of this prophecy. Divested of this, and translated into a plain declaration of the future, it would seem as natural, to apply to it, as to any other passage on the subject, the principle of prophetic perspective.*

Our Lord's parables in Matthew xiii. are also adduced as teaching the simultaneousness of the judgment, but the same

---

* Professor Birks, of Cambridge, to whose writings on prophecy frequent reference is made in these pages, while holding that there will be *two resurrections* of the dead, the first at the beginning and the second at the end of the thousand years of Revelation xx., lays stress on the *simultaneousness* of the judgment of the saints and that of the ungodly, as involved in the discriminating character of the first resurrection. In a letter to the author, written after he had read the first four hundred pages of this work, Professor Birks says : "I agree fully with almost every sentence in the first four hundred pages, except one small section, pp. 68–78. I think the vision from Revelation xvii. I to xxi. 8 is one integral part of the prophecy. I fully agree with what you write on the first resurrection, but I think you overlook the fact that this resurrection is a public act of Divine acquittal to those included in it, and by the distinctness of the two resurrections is implied sentence of condemnation to those excluded from it. This account of final judgment then I thus hold to be parallel to Matthew xxv., and that the simultaneousness of the twofold judgment is more strongly affirmed here than even there ; but with regard to the judgment on degrees of glory or of punishment, this extends over the whole day of judgment of a thousand years, and the two parts belong to its evening and its morning.

"May God give an abundant blessing to your work, which I think to be one of great importance and interest to the Church, from the amount of precious and important truth which it unfolds. "

thing is true of them. Their object is to unfold the present *mixed* state of things in the kingdom of heaven, in contrast with the *pure* state of things that shall exist after the end of this age. The division between the wheat and the tares, between the good fish and the bad, which takes place as we are expressly told at the end of this age, is a division effected at the advent, among the *living* not the dead; it is a severing between real believers, and false professors; between the true, and the apostate church. The tares are still growing with the wheat in the harvest field; "the field is the world." The fish are still struggling together in the gospel net; there is no thought here of a resurrection of the dead, it is a severance among the living. Other scriptures teach us that a resurrection of dead saints will take place at the advent, but that is not alluded to here. The tares are gathered in bundles to be burned, and the wheat is gathered into the garner. "One shall be taken and another left." "We who are alive and remain shall be caught up in the clouds to meet the Lord in the air." The parables of Matthew xiii. present the thought of severance, and not that of judicial investigation and award.

We next look at the passages which teach more directly the truth, that judgment to come will take place in two stages. Foremost among them is our Lord's own memorable declaration, John v. 24: "Verily, verily, I say unto you, he that heareth my word and believeth on Him that sent Me, hath everlasting life, and shall not come into condemnation, but is passed from death unto life." It is well known that the word here translated condemnation, κρίσις, means *judgment*, and is so translated in the verse but one previous. The believer shall not come into judgment, when judgment is to be to condemnation. Not, he shall not be condemned in the judgment, but he shall not even *come into it*. The same word is used in verse 27 and again in verse 29, where it is translated "damnation." Now this resurrection of damnation, or resurrection to judgment, is clearly that spoken of in Revelation xx.; *and into that, our*

Lord Himself declares his people shall not come. There shall be a reckoning of Christ with his people, as many passages which shall be examined presently teach ; but this is not judgment. Alford says : " the reckoning which ends with ' Εὖ ἀγαθὲ δοῦλε,' is not 'κρίσις,' the reward is of free grace. In this sense the believers in Christ will not be judged according to their works. They are justified before God by faith, and *by God;* Θεὸς ὁ δικαιῶν—τίς ὁ κατακρίνων; Their passage over from death to life, *has already taken place,*—from the state of spiritual death, to that ζωὴ αἰώνιος which they ἔχουσι already. It is to be observed that our Lord speaks in very similar terms of the unbelieving being *condemned already,* in chapter iii. 18. The perfect sense of μεταβέβηκεν must not be weakened or explained away." Let those who hold that there will be a simultaneous judgment of the just and of the unjust explain this statement of our Lord. He does not say that believers shall not be *condemned* in the judgment, but that they shall not *come into it.* Can anything be clearer than this ?

Into what judgment then shall they come ? Into one, distinct alike in its objects, principles, results, and period, from the judgment of Revelation xx. 12.

In the judgment of sinners the object is to determine their eternal destiny ; in the judgment of saints *their* eternal destiny is already determined ; they are, from the moment they believe, indwelt by the Holy Ghost, one with the Lord Jesus, possessors of eternal life, and heirs of eternal glory. The resurrection which precedes their judgment has manifested this ; for when Christ their life appears, they appear with Him in glory, they see Him and are like Him, conformed to the image of God's Son. Now it is clear, that when these *already glorified saints* stand before the judgment seat of Christ, the point to be investigated and settled is *not* whether they deserve and are to have eternal life and glory ; grace has already given them these, though they deserved eternal condemnation : but the point to be investigated and decided is, how far they have been faithful servants and stewards of their absent Lord ; how far their works, as saved persons, can stand the test of Christ's judgment, and what measure of reward each is to enjoy. Their common possession of eternal life does not forbid degrees in glory, and the fact that they are saved by grace does not forbid that they shall be *rewarded* according to their works. That this is a very different thing, from the eternal destiny of each individual, being made to depend on his own works, is evident.

The judgment of sinners is on the ground of "rendering to every man according to his works,"—justice ; the judgment of saints is on the ground of grace, for it is grace alone that rewards any of our works.

The judgment of sinners ends in the blackness of darkness for ever ; the judgment of saints ends in "then shall every man have *praise* of God." The one is a judgment of *persons*, the other of *works only*. The one as we have seen is prefigured in symbolic vision in Revelation xx. ; the other is spoken of in various places, in the epistles addressed to the early church. "Every man's work shall be made manifest, for the day shall declare it, because it shall be revealed by fire ; and the fire shall try every man's work, of what sort it is" ; that is, the searching, penetrating, soul-discerning judgment of Christ, shall put the works of his people to the test, and only the perfectly pure shall abide the test. Some works, like wood, hay and stubble, will be destroyed by this "fire" ; but, even so, the man who did them shall be saved ; his works may perish but he shall "never perish" according to his Saviour's promise. In Romans xiv. Christians are urged in view of this judgment, not to judge each other, "for we shall all stand before the βῆμα or judgment seat of Christ," not the "throne," as in Revelation xx.

The period of the judgment of sinners before the great white throne, is a thousand years or more *after* the coming of the Lord. The period of the judgment of saints is fixed to be *at* the coming of the Lord. 1 Corinthians iv. 5 : "therefore judge nothing before the time, *until the Lord come*, who both will bring to light the hidden things of darkness, and will make manifest the counsels of the hearts, and then shall every man havé praise of God."

We conclude therefore that these two judgments cannot be the same, and that so far from being at variance with other inspired prophecies, the twentieth chapter of Revelation enables us to understand and combine previous statements, and sheds new light on many also. Judgment will no more be simultaneous than resurrection ; both will take place at two grand epochs, marking respectively, the morning and the evening, of the day of the Lord ; the former will be a resurrection and a judgment unto life, the latter a resurrection and a judgment unto condemnation.

Whence then has arisen the exceedingly prevalent opinion to the contrary ? From the littleness of the finite mind, that comprehends with difficulty the vast, far reaching, and complete designs of the Infinite ; from the lack in us of the patient continuance of searching the Scriptures ; from the irreverent neglect with which the last prophecy of the Bible is too often treated ; and from the not giving it, even when studied, its due authority—the non-recognition of the principle of PROGRESSIVE REVELATION.

From Dean Alford's Commentary on the New Testament we extract the following testimony to the doctrine of two distinct resurrections of the dead.

" I cannot consent to distort its words (Rev. xx.) from their *plain sense* and *chronological place* in the prophecy, on account of any considerations of difficulty, or any risk of abuses which the doctrine of the millennium may bring with it. Those who lived next to the apostles, and the whole Church for 300 years, understood them in the plain literal sense ; and it is a strange sight in these days to see expositors who are among the first in reverence of antiquity, complacently casting aside *the most cogent instance of consensus which primitive antiquity presents.* As regards the text itself, *no legitimate treatment of it will extort what is known as the spiritual interpretation now in fashion.* If, in a passage where *two resurrections* are mentioned, where certain ψυχαὶ ἔζησαν at the first, AND THE REST OF THE νεκροὶ ἔζησαν ONLY AT THE END OF A SPECIFIED PERIOD AFTER THAT FIRST,—if in such a passage the first resurrection may be understood to mean *spiritual* rising with Christ, while the second means *literal* rising from the grave ; then there is an end of all significance of language, and Scripture is wiped out as a definite testimony to anything. If the first resurrection is spiritual, then so is the second, which I suppose none will be hardy enough to maintain ; but IF THE SECOND IS LITERAL, THEN SO IS THE FIRST, *which in common with the whole primitive Church and many of the best modern expositors, I maintain and receive as an article of faith and hope.*"

END OF PART I.

PART II.

PROGRESSIVE INTERPRETATION.

CHAPTER I.

HUMAN COMPREHENSION OF DIVINE PROPHECY HAS BEEN AND WAS INTENDED TO BE, PROGRESSIVE.—THREE IMPORTANT INFERENCES FROM DANIEL XII. 9.—THERE IS A BLAMELESS AND A GUILTY IGNORANCE OF THE FULFILMENT OF PROPHECY.—INSTANCES OF EACH.—REASONS FOR A PARTIAL AND TEMPORARY OBSCURITY OF PROPHECY; AND MEANS BY WHICH PROGRESSIVE COMPREHENSION OF ITS SIGNIFICATION HAS BEEN GRANTED.

WE have seen that God has been pleased to reveal the future to men only by degrees; that both in the number of subjects on which the light of prophecy has been permitted to fall, and in the clearness and fulness of the light granted on each, there has been constant and steady increase, from the pale and solitary ray of Eden, to the clear widespread beams of Daniel, and to the rich glow of the Apocalypse.

We now proceed to show that human comprehension of Divine prophecy has also been by degrees; and that in certain cases it was evidently intended by God to be so. Light to understand the prophetic word, is as much a Divine gift as that word itself. The sovereignty of God was exercised in the selection of the matters to be revealed by prophecy, the time of the revelation, and the individuals to whom, and through whom, it should be communicated. And it is equally exercised in the determination of the degree *to* which, and the time *at* which, the true meaning of certain prophecies shall be un-veiled, as well as in the selection of the individuals to whom the interpretation shall be given. "The Lord hath not only spoken by dreams and visions of old, but He speaketh also every day, even as often as He enlighteneth the minds of his servants, that they may be able to search out the hidden truth of his word, and bring it forth unto the world." *

Prophecy, being essentially a *revelation* of the future, is of course designed to be understood ; but it does not follow that it is designed to be understood immediately on its being given, nor by all who become acquainted with its announcements. The Most High has various ends to answer in predicting the future ; and though we may not *always* be able to discern his reasons for making revelations before He intends them to be comprehended, yet in some cases they are sufficiently clear.

In foretelling, for instance, the first advent of his Son, God might have been pleased to predict its *results*, in as clear and unmistakable a manner as He predicted the event itself. But *plainly* to have foretold the rejection and crucifixion of the Lord Jesus by Israel, would have been to interfere with the free agency of man ; it must either have had the effect of pre-venting the crucifixion of Christ, or else have given the Jews a valid excuse for killing the Prince of life.

Not to have foretold the actual results *at all*, on the other hand, would have been to deprive Christianity of one of its main pillars of evidence, the fact that the events of the life and death of Jesus of Nazareth *were predicted* centuries before they took place ; it would have been to give some ground for pre-sent Jewish unbelief. The alternative was to *reveal* the suffer-ing and death of Christ, but to reveal them *in such a manner* that "both Herod and Pontius Pilate, with the Gentiles and the people of Israel," when banded together to carry out their own wicked wills, were quite unconscious that they were therein

---

* See preface to Brightman's "Revelation of the Revelation," 1615.

doing, what his hand and his counsel had "determined before to be done." This secured the good, and avoided the evil; the predictions were full and definite, and yet capable of being misunderstood: as a fact, they were not understood even by the disciples at first, nor are they understood to this day by the Jewish nation. They ought to have known Him, but "because they knew Him not, *nor yet the voices of the prophets which are read every sabbath day*, they fulfilled them in condemning Him."

Thus it is possible to possess prophecies of certain events, to read them diligently all our lives, and yet not to understand their fulfilment, even when it takes place before our own eyes. This is sinful unbelief; but there is a temporary inability to understand Divine predictions, which is entirely free from sin, which is inevitable, and indeed ordained of God.

The book of Daniel is one of the fullest revelations of the future contained in the Bible; it is unequalled for the variety and minuteness of its historical detail, and for its breadth of range, both chronological and geographical. It is closed by this remarkable injunction, (which applies, however, *mainly to the last prophecy in the book*): "But thou, O Daniel, shut up the words, and seal the book, *even to the time of the end;* many shall run to and fro, and knowledge shall be increased . . . none of the wicked shall understand, but the wise shall understand."

This passage seems to warrant three inferences of importance.

1. That though God for certain reasons saw fit to give this revelation of the future to Daniel at a certain date, *He did not intend it to be understood for centuries;* since, whatever may be the exact limits of the "*time of the end*," it could not include *more* than the course of this dispensation, and the *commencement* of this dispensation was several centuries distant, when Daniel wrote.

2. That even when in the lapse of ages the meaning of this prophecy should become apparent to some, even when "know-

ledge " should " be increased " and the wise understand, it was
the will of God that it should still remain a dark mystery to
others, that " none of the wicked should understand."

3. And thirdly that the comprehension or ignorance of this
prophecy, when the time for its being understood at all arrived,
would depend rather on the *moral* than on the intellectual state
of those who should study it. The *wise* alone should understand it ; the *wicked* should not.

The first of these inferences is confirmed by 1 Peter i. 10 :
" The prophets inquired and searched diligently . . . what
manner of time the Spirit of Christ which was in them did signify, when it testified beforehand the sufferings of Christ, and the
glory that should follow. Unto whom it was revealed that *not
unto themselves, but unto us they did minister* the things . . .
the angels desire to look into." Peter here alludes evidently
to this very passage of Daniel who " inquired and searched
diligently " about the *time* of the events revealed to him, (" O
my Lord, what shall be the end of these things ? ") but he lays
it down as a general principle, applicable to other prophets as
well, that when they " testified beforehand, of the sufferings of
Christ and the glories that should follow," they ministered NOT
unto themselves but unto *us.* That is, they revealed not a
proximate future, interesting themselves and their brethren of
the Jewish economy especially, but a more distant future, pertaining to another dispensation altogether, and *not designed to
be understood till that dispensation dawned.*

The second of these inferences, that even when light was
vouchsafed it would be partial, is confirmed by the words of
our Lord, " it is given unto you to know the mysteries of the
kingdom of heaven, but to them it is not given." " Thou hast
hid these things from the wise and prudent, and revealed them
unto babes."

The third inference, as to the moral character of those
who receive prophetic light, is also confirmed by his words,
" if any man will do his will, he shall know of the doctrine."
It is " scoffers walking after their own lusts " who are repre-

sented as saying "where is the promise of his coming?" and as being "willingly ignorant" of the purpose of God as expressed in type, and in prophecy about the future.

It is evident therefore that there may be such a thing as a blameless ignorance of the meaning of prophecy, as well as a blameworthy and guilty ignorance of it. The prophets were not to be blamed, for not understanding what God did not intend them to understand. Jews and infidels now, are to be blamed for a guilty unwillingness to perceive, the accomplishment of Old Testament prophecies, in New Testament events.

Take as an instance of blameless ignorance, that of the apostles, even after Pentecost, as to the calling of the Gentiles. This, though in one sense a hidden mystery (Eph. iii. 9), had as a matter of fact, long been a revealed purpose of God. It had been foretold in type, in prophecy, and in promise, so that in Romans xiv. the apostle makes no less than four quotations in succession, to prove that *it was written*, and in Acts xv. James admits that "to this agree the words of the prophets." It was revealed, but not designed to be understood till a certain time, and then a special vision was sent to Peter, and a special revelation on the subject granted to Paul (Eph. iii. 3), to prepare their minds for the fulfilment of these long extant predictions, and to induce them to preach among the Gentiles the unsearchable riches of Christ.

Take as an instance of guilty ignorance, in the face of actual fulfilment, Jewish misunderstanding respecting the prophecies of the rejection and death of Messiah the prince. These events were, as we have seen, distinctly revealed ; He was to be " despised and rejected of men," " led as a lamb to the slaughter," "cut off yet not for Himself" ; but the revelation was understood neither by " wise " nor " wicked" for a time. When the event had fulfilled and interpreted these predictions, the risen Saviour had still to address, to the two disciples going to Emmaus, that rebuke which assumes both the fact of the revelation and of their duty to understand it : " O fools and slow of heart to believe, all that the prophets have spoken ; ought not Christ

to have suffered these things, and to enter into his glory?"
To this day, those who have their minds still blinded
through Jewish unbelief, find " a vail untaken away in the reading of the Old Testament " and cannot perceive the accomplishment of the Messianic prophecies in the life and death
of Jesus of Nazareth.

Our Lord Himself revealed much that He knew his disciples did not and could not understand at the time ; though
He also withheld much that they were unprepared to receive. " Destroy this Temple, and in three days I will raise
it up." It was not till after He was risen from the dead,
that they caught the deep meaning of those pregnant words.
" I have yet many things to say unto you, but ye cannot
bear them now." " The Comforter which is the Holy Ghost,
shall teach you all things, and bring all things to your remembrance, whatsoever I have said unto you."

Even after the resurrection had taken place we read, "as yet
they knew not the scriptures that He should rise again from
the dead." They were familiar with the words " Thou wilt not
leave my soul in hades, neither wilt Thou suffer thine Holy One
to see corruption "; but, even standing beside the empty sepulchre, the true *meaning* of the words failed to penetrate the mists
of Jewish prejudice, which darkened their minds. After Pentecost however, when Peter had not only the inspired prophecy,
but the inspiring Spirit to interpret it, how lucid and authoritative his explanation of these words : " men and brethren, let me
freely speak unto you of the patriarch David, that he is both dead
and buried, and his sepulchre is with us unto this day.
He being a prophet, spake of the resurrection of Christ, that
his soul was not left in hades, neither *his* flesh did see corruption. This Jesus hath God raised up, whereof we all are
witnesses." On the same occasion he asserts that the pentecostal
effusion of the Spirit, at which his audience were ignorantly
marvelling, was the fulfilment of Joel's familiar but little understood prediction : "*this is that* which was spoken by the
prophet Joel." How did he know it ? The " untoward gene-

ration" whom he addressed thought not so, nor dreamed that they were witnessing the fulfilment of a Divine prophecy. Their account of the matter was very different; "these men are full of new wine." This proves that *spiritual enlightenment is required, for the perception of the fulfilment of prophecy, even in startling events which may be taking place before our eyes.*

It is not too much to assume that the Apocalypse of St. John was also designed to be progressively understood; that it forms no exception to the general rule, but was given *to reveal the future by degrees, and only in proportion as the understanding of it might conduce, to the accomplishment of God's purposes, and the good of his people.* Analogy forbids us to suppose, that such a prophecy could be clear all at once, to those to whom it was first given, and it equally forbids the supposition that it was never to be understood or interpreted at all. Can we not perceive reasons why God should in this case, act as He had so often acted before, and progressively reveal its meaning? and can we not also perceive means by which such a progressive revelation of the meaning of this prophecy, might, as time rolled on, be made?

These questions may be unhesitatingly answered in the affirmative. There are evident and weighty *reasons* why, in this prophecy above all others, the truth should not have been all at once apparent; and although this book was the last work of the last apostle, and closes the canon of Scripture, it is not difficult to see the *means* by which God Himself might unveil its signification, at an advanced period of the dispensation.

Let it be granted for a moment, (as it shall we hope be subsequently proved) that this prophecy contains an outline of all the great events of interest to the church of God, which were to happen prior to the second advent of Christ, as well as of that advent itself, and subsequent events; and that not only are the events themselves predicted, but that the actual chronology of some of them is predicted also, the duration for instance of the antichristian apostasy for a period of 1260 years. Supposing this to be the case, it is clear that God, though giving the prophecy in the apostolic age, cannot have *intended* it to be understood for many many subsequent generations. It was the express will of Christ that the church should be ever waiting and watching for her Lord, uncertain as to the time of his return. The Holy Spirit could therefore no more have *revealed clearly* to the early church 1260 years of apostasy prior to the return of Christ, than He could have revealed a thousand years of millennial blessedness; which as we have previously shown would have been inconsistent with his purpose.

Must we therefore conclude : "*this then cannot be the character of the Apocalypse; the same argument that proves that the millennium must succeed the advent, proves also that no long period of apostasy can be predicted as to precede it*"? No! but we conclude hence, that if such a period be revealed, it must be in a mysterious form, not intended or adapted for comprehension at the time. If an apostasy of such duration be predicted, it must be *so* predicted as that the true, full, meaning of the prediction, should not be obvious for centuries, and yet be evident, as soon as altered circumstances should render the understand-ing of the prediction, desirable for the glory of God and the good of the church.

A consideration of the problem shows, that the very same end that was to be attained by the church's ignorance of the true nature and duration of the apostasy in early ages, will in these last days be better attained by her acquaintance with both; and will lead us to admire the wisdom and the grace of Him, who in this prophecy secured for her that ignorance while it was best, and laid up in store for her that knowledge, against the time when it should, in its turn, be most beneficial.

"Known unto God are all his works from the beginning;" the real history and length of this dispensation were of course not only foreseen, but foreordained of God. For certain reasons Christ never mentioned them to his disciples, and the Holy Ghost revealed but little about them to Peter and Paul. What were those reasons? To keep alive loving expectation of the Lord's second coming, to encourage believers to constant watchfulness, to cheer them by a present hope, and to weaken the power of temptation to earthliness and worldliness, by stamping on all things here uncertainty and evanescence. Her ignorance of the time of the Master's return, is made a motive to "patient waiting for Christ." The first generation of believers took all the promises of his speedy return literally, and lived in the hope that they might remain to the blessed moment, and not sleep but be changed. The Holy Ghost did not undeceive them to any considerable extent; in one case, where the due balance of patience and hope had been in measure lost, express revelations of intervening events were given to restore that balance, but no *periods* were assigned to these events (2 Thess. ii.); the hope was left vivid as ever, if not quite so close at hand. But *this hope was born of inexperience;* blessed and beautiful as it was, it was destined to wither away and be disappointed. The cold logic of facts proved it ill founded and mistaken, but did not render it the less sanctifying and cheering : blessed be God, there is another kind of hope, born of patience and experience, and founded not on ignorance, but on knowledge. This hope dawned on the church, as the other sank beneath the horizon, and has gradually brightened ever since ; and it is a hope that shall " not make ashamed." Now it is clear, that had God revealed the duration of the long antichristian apostasy to the early church, they would at once have been deprived of *their* holy, happy, hope. What help or consolation could the sufferers and martyrs of early days have found, in gazing forward through well-nigh two thousand years of pagan and papal persecutions, of decay and death, and spiritual corruption ? The appalling prospect was in mercy hidden from their view, foreshortened almost to a point ; and the advent which was to close it all, was the grand object presented to their gaze. How could they have watched for an advent two thousand years off? what present practical influence could it have exerted over their lives ? Their ignorance was evidently best for them, and God in mercy did not remove it. They held in their hands the prophecy, big with the mournful secret; but they guessed not its burden, in their blissful and blameless ignorance they concluded that the " I come quickly" of their absent Lord, meant "quickly" according to human calculations. To leave them in their ignorance was the gracious purpose of God, and his motive was their comfort and sanctification.

But it is equally clear that for us, believers of the nineteenth century, the case is reversed. A knowledge of the limits of the great antichristian apostasy, would not now *deprive us of hope*, but the very contrary : in fact we need some such revelation to sustain our faith and hope to the end of the long delay; without the chronological data afforded us by the prophecies of Daniel and John, *we* should be in a position of fearful temptation to doubt and despair. *They were entirely ignorant of the length of the interval which we know to have occurred*, and this knowledge absolutely *prevents* the general promises of the nearness of the second advent, from having the same power over us that they had over them. Those statements cannot convey to us, after a lapse of well-nigh two thousand years, the impressions they conveyed to the primitive saints. They seemed to justify *them* in expecting the coming of Christ in their own day ; but each succeeding generation would have less and less ground for such an expectation ; and when the promise was already one thousand years old, who could avoid the reflection, " since it has included one thousand years it may include another "? We, after nearly two thousand years, could not, as we read the promise, escape the conviction, that having already included two thousand years, it was perfectly possible that two thousand more were yet to come. Each century of delay would thus increase the heart-sickness of hope deferred, and the church of these last days, might well hang down her head in the sorrowful but irresistible conviction, that her redemption might still be at an immeasurable distance ; she could have no well grounded hope that the Lord was in any strict sense " at hand."

Now one generation of his saints is as dear to God as another; we may be sure He did not secure the holiness and

happiness of the early church, at the expense of ours, nor conceal what might be a blessing to us, because the knowledge
might not have been a blessing to them. No! He provided
some better thing for us, than that we should float uncertainly on
the stream of time, not knowing whether we were any nearer to
the future than to the past advent of Christ. He *revealed*, but
revealed *in a mystery*, all the main events of this dispensation,
and nearly two-thirds of its duration ; He revealed them, in just
such a way, as best to secure a renewal of hope that should give
consolation, and revive in these last times a "patient waiting
for Christ." Since *continued* ignorance of the true nature and
length of this dispensation, as determined beforehand in the
counsels of God, would have produced the very opposite effects
designed by the permission of *temporary* ignorance, we have
every reason to conclude, that God would in due time replace
this latter by knowledge, and give a gradually increasing
understanding of the inspired predictions.

And if it be asked *how* this could be done, since inspiration has passed away and apostolic explanations can no longer
be enjoyed, we reply, by the same means by which the interpretation of earlier prophecies was given to Peter, *by their
fulfilment before our eyes*, and by the teaching of the Holy Ghost,
enabling us so to discern the true nature of events, as *to
recognise the correspondence between them and the long familiar
predictions.* When the heart is docile, and the mind free from
prejudice, a comparison of inspired prediction and historic
fulfilment, is sufficient to show the relation between them ; to
whatever extent prejudice exists, spiritual perception is blunted;
where it reigns supreme, as in the case of the Jewish nation,
"blindness in part has happened," and the ignorance being
wilful, is necessarily a guilty ignorance, like that of Israel in
apostolic days. Oh, how it behoves Christians to take heed,
that they be not *thus* ignorant of the real meaning of apocalyptic prophecy !

Another observation may confirm our conviction, that it was
the intention of God in the earlier parts of the Apocalypse, to

conceal for a time the real nature of the events, and the true length of the periods, therein revealed. The future, which for the sake of the early church required to be hidden under a veil of mystery, was of course only the future of *this* dispensation. No prolonged interval was to be interposed between the church and her hope,—the return of her Lord ; but the same concealment was not requisite as regards *subsequent* events and their duration. If then the principle for which we contend be true, there will be found an air of mystery about the times and seasons mentioned prior to the advent vision, and an absence of it subsequently. This is exactly what exists. There are eight passages in the earlier part of the book, where periods of time, are named by phrases which are obviously uncommon, *not* the ordinary or natural mode of designating the period they seem to suggest, but all having an air of mystery. In the vision which immediately follows that of the advent, on the contrary, a period is six times over mentioned in *the simplest possible form,* " a thousand years." Why this difference ? The real length of *this* age of sin and suffering was to be hidden for a time ; but there was no need to hide the real length of the blessed age of purity, peace, and joy which is to succeed it.

We conclude then, that since God has constantly acted on this principle, of gradually revealing the meaning of his own predictions, both in the Old and New Testaments, since we can see special reasons why He should do so, and a simple means by which He could do so, in this case, and since the construction of the book affords internal evidence of such an intention, that there is the strongest presumption that the *meaning* of the apocalyptic prophecies was designed to become clear to the church *only by degrees.*

We conclude, that though the Apocalypse was not, like the visions of Daniel, to be supplemented by later revelations, and understood only in the light reflected back from these, yet it was to receive explanation from other sources, so that while it was a mystery in the early ages of the church, it should unfold its own meaning gradually, during the course of the dispensation, and become increasingly clear and consequently increasingly precious, in the last days.

We conclude also, that like Daniel's predictions and all other prophecy, it is not intended *ever* to become *self-evidently clear,* that even when understood by "the wise," its meaning will still be hidden from the world, and that consequently the true interpretation, whenever it shall arise, will have many adversaries, and be rejected with contempt by "the wicked," even while it is being fulfilled before their eyes.

These legitimate conclusions will lead us to expect *the primitive interpretation of the premillennial visions of the Apocalypse, to be the least correct;* though it might be, probably would be, right as to events *subsequent* to this dispensation. They prepare us to weigh with candour, the interpretations of later times, and forbid us to reject, on the ground of novelty, any view that attaches to these mysterious predictions a meaning worthy of Divine inspiration, and calculated to accomplish good in the church, even though it may have been unknown to the fathers, and even though it may be rejected and ridiculed by multitudes. These conclusions will lead us to expect the true interpretation *to arise* only after many many centuries of the church's history had rolled away, when the bright hope of early days had quite died out ; and to *have the effect* of quickening the church afresh to the patient waiting for Christ. But we should expect also that the true clue to the mysteries of the Apocalypse, once discovered, would not be immediately applied correctly ; so that it would never practically have the effect of leading the church to think the Lord's return a very distant event, however much it might, theoretically considered, seem likely to do so. In other words, that God would not suddenly illuminate these predictions and so translate the church at a bound from perfect ignorance to perfect knowledge of the fore-appointed length and character of this dispensation ; but that He would *enlighten her darkness gradually*, by leaving a measure of obscurity till towards the close ; would allow her

still, as at the first, to expect the great consummation long
before its predestined date, and sustain her by revealing fresh
grounds of hope, based on more accurate apprehension of the
truth, as each erroneous anticipation was disappointed by the
event. We shall consequently expect to find every generation
of saints, after the true key to the book has once been found,
making advances on the last, and the *discrepancies existing between their views will not stumble us, or lead us to reject them all
as ungrounded.* We shall trace the vein of truth growing wider
and deeper ; we shall watch the ever brightening dawn of the
true light ; and far from deeming this gradual discovery of the
meaning of the apocalyptic prophecies, with its consequent
inevitable discrepancies, a proof that they have no meaning, or
none worth seeking, we shall accept it as a proof, of the purpose of God to act, still, as ever, on the principle of progressive
revelation.

Now on reviewing the history of apocalyptic interpretation
we find that the early church were right in their interpretation
of the visions which follow the second advent, they understood
correctly, that which it was not the purpose of God to *conceal*
from them. *All the primitive expositors and teachers were pre-
millennialists.* With the exception of Origen, who spiritualized
everything, and of a few who denied the inspiration and
apostolicity of the book, all the early fathers up to the time
of Constantine, including Justin Martyr, Irenæus, Tertullian,
Hippolytus, Victorinus, Methodius, Lactantius, held that the
first resurrection of Revelation xx. was a literal resurrection, prior to a personal reign of Christ on earth. The expectation of a spiritual millennium, to precede the coming of the
Lord, grew up only in the more corrupt ages of the church,
after her union with the world in the days of Constantine.*

As to the previous predictive visions of the book, the
numerous commentaries on the whole, and the almost innumerable explanations of parts of it, which have appeared,

---

* Elliott, " Horæ," vol. iv., p. 306.

may be arranged in three distinct classes, which for couve-
nience' sake have been denominated Preterist, Futurist, and
Presentist schemes of interpretation; each of these classes
embraces a great variety of expositions, but the interpretations
of each class have a *fundamental* resemblance to each other,
and differ *fundamentally* from those of the other two.

The first or PRETERIST scheme, considers these prophecies
to have been fulfilled in the downfall of the Jewish nation and
the old Roman empire, limiting their range thus to the first
six centuries of the Christian era, and making Nero Antichrist.

This scheme originated with the Jesuit Alcazar towards the
end of the sixteenth century; it has been held and taught
under various modifications by Grotius, Hammond, Bossuet,
Eichhorn and other German commentators, Moses Stuart, and
Dr. Davidson. It has few supporters now, and need not be
described more at length. Moses Stuart bases it on the denial
of the very principle for which we are contending; he takes it
for granted that the writer had an "*immediate* object in view
when he wrote the book," and that the *original readers of the
Apocalypse understood it;* and argues that it must therefore
treat of such matters as they could understand. But his only
reason for this assertion is that *he cannot conceive* how "a
sensible man" could write a book "which would be unin-
telligible to those to whom it was addressed;" and he proceeds
to admit that there is no *evidence* extant to show that the early
Christians understood it. Further on he says that "very soon
after this age, it was *so* interpreted that grave obstacles were
raised to the reception of the book as canonical." And looking
back from the end of the eighth century, after reviewing all the
previous expositors of Revelation, he says "we find that no
real and solid advances were yet made" towards a satisfactory
explanation of the book. Thus he *assumes* that its first readers
were intended to understand it, and assumes that they did do
so, while admitting that there is not the slightest *proof* to
support either assumption, and that the light if ever possessed,
was very quickly lost. His work evinces much learning but

little spirituality, and treats the Apocalypse too much as a merely human production; his views are happily not shared by many.

The second or PRESENTIST interpretation, is that historic Protestant view of these prophecies, which considers them to predict the great events to happen in the world and in the church, from St. John's time to the coming of the Lord ; which sees in the Church of Rome, and in the Papacy, the fulfilment of the prophecies of Babylon and of the Beast, and which interprets the times of the Apocalypse on the year-day system.

This view originated about the eleventh century, with those who even then began to protest, against the growing corruptions of the Church of Rome.   It grew among the Waldenses, Wickliffites, and Hussites, into a consistent scheme of interpretation, and was embraced with enthusiasm and held with intense conviction of its truth, by the Reformers of the sixteenth century. In their hands it became a powerful and formidable weapon, to attack and expose the mighty apostasy, with which they were called to do battle.   From this time it spread with a rapidity that was astonishing, so that ere long it was received as a self evident and fundamental truth, among Protestant churches everywhere.   It nerved the Reformers of England, France, Germany, Switzerland, Denmark, and Sweden, and animated the martyrs of Italy and Spain ; it decided the conscientious and timid adherents of the Papacy to cross the Rubicon, and separate from the so called Catholic Church ; and it has kept all the Reformed churches since, from attempting reunion with Rome.

It was held and taught by Joachim Abbas, Walter Brute, Luther, Zwingle, Melanchthon, Calvin, and all the rest of the Reformers ; by Bullinger, Bale, and Foxe ; by Brightman and Mede, Sir Isaac and Bishop Newton, Vitringa, Daubuz and Whiston, as well as by Faber, Cunningham, Frere, Birks and Elliott ; no two of these may agree on all questions of minor detail, but they agree on the grand outline, and each one has added more or less to the strength and solidity of the system, by his researches. During the last seven centuries this system has been deepening its hold on the convictions of the Christian church, and has been embraced by some of her wisest and best guides and teachers. It originated with martyrs and confessors, exerted a sanctifying and strengthening influence over those who received it ; it tended to revive the hope of the premillennial coming of the Lord, which had long lain in abeyance, leading naturally to many false anticipations of that event, which have been disproved by time, as well as to many very remarkable approximations to the truth, as to the time of other events. It met *of course* with intense and bitter opposition from the church it branded as Babylon, and the power it denounced as Antichrist, and to this day is rejected by all who in any way maintain or defend these, as well as by some who do neither.

The third or FUTURIST view, is that which teaches that the pro phetic visions of Revelation, from chapters iv. to xix., prefigure *events still wholly future* and not to take place, till just at the close of this dispensation. It supposes "an instant plunge of the apocalyptic prophecy, into the distant future of the con summation." * This view gives the literal Israel a large place in the Apocalypse, and expects a personal infidel Antichrist, who shall bitterly oppress the saints for three years and a half, near the date of the second advent, thus interpreting *time* as well as much else in the Apocalypse, *literally*.

This view is, in *a certain sense*, the most ancient of the three 'for the primitive fathers agree in several of these latter points. In its present form however it may be said to have originated at the end of the sixteenth century, with the Jesuit Ribera, who, moved like Alcazar, to relieve the Papacy from the terrible stigma cast upon it by the Protestant interpretation, tried to do so, by referring these prophecies to the distant *future*, instead of like Alcazar to the distant *past*. For a considerable period this view was confined to Romanists, and was refuted by several

---

* Elliott, iv., 561.

masterly Protestant works. But of late years, since the commencement of this century, it has sprung up afresh, and sprung up strange to say among Protestants. It was revived by such writers as the two Maitlands, Burgh, Tyso, Dr. Todd, the leaders of the "Brethren" generally, and by some Puseyite expositors also. It is held thus by *extreme* parties ; by those who though Protestants, are ashamed of the Reformation, speak of it as an unwarrantable schism, and verge as closely on Rome as is possible ; *and* by those, who though Protestants, deem the glorious Reformation to have stopped grievously short of the mark, and see so much of Babylon still, in the Reformed churches, that they refuse to regard them as having come out of Babylon, or as victors over Antichrist. It is held under a greater variety of modifications than the other two, no two writers agreeing as to what the symbols *do* prefigure, but all agreeing that they do *not* prefigure anything that has ever yet taken place.

Those who hold this view support it, among other arguments, by the authority of the primitive church. They say : "the fathers had apostolic tradition ; they had no controversial bias ; their opinion ought to have great weight ; the historical interpretation was unknown in the church for one thousand years or more ; our view is the original view of the early Christians *They* expected that Antichrist would be an individual man ; *so do we. They* expected him to be an infidel atheistic blasphemer, not a Christian bishop ; *so do we. They* believed his tyranny would last three years and a half immediately prior to the coming of Christ ; *so do we. They* took the days, weeks, and months of the Apocalypse literally ; *so do we.*"

Now we readily admit this agreement (though indeed it is by no means so perfect as is implied[*]), and reply that herein lies a *very strong presumption against the Futurist scheme. It is a return to that early interpretation of the prophecies, which was necessarily defective and erroneous, seeing it was not*

---

[*] See Elliott, " Horæ Apocalypticæ," vol. iv., p. 612.

the purpose of God, to permit a premature comprehension of the nature and length of this dispensation. It is a view which rejects the light as to the *purposes* of God, which experience of the *providence* of God has afforded. It exalts the impressions of ignorance, above the ripe results of mature knowledge, and claims prestige for primitive views, on points where posterior views are necessarily preferable. It treats inexperience as wisdom, and despises as folly the wisdom acquired by eighteen hundred years' experience, of the most wonderful providential dealings of God. It recommends those who are of full age to return to the opinions of childhood, forgetting that errors excusable in children are inexcusable in men. The early church knew nothing of the marvellous ecclesiastical phenomena with which we are acquainted; their ignorance of the true scope of the prophecy was unavoidable; we have seen the awful apostasy that has lorded it for more than twelve hundred years in the church of God; similar ignorance in us is without excuse, for experience ought to teach. *The Futurist view denies progressive revelation,* and asserts that the early church understood the Apocalypse better than the church of after-times, which is contrary to the analogy of Scripture, and to the apparent purpose of God.

Two main systems of interpretation of this final revelation of Scripture, are then before us: which is likely to be the true? The one characterized the infancy of the church, the other was the offspring of mature experience: the one sprang up amid utter ignorance of the actual purpose of God; the other in view of his accomplished providence: the one can never be brought to any *test;* the other at every point exposes itself to critical examination: the one was and is held by the apostate and persecuting church of Rome; the other by multitudes of confessors and a glorious army of martyrs: the one leaves us to form our own opinion of the greatest fact in the history of the church, the papal system of ecclesiastical corruption and tyranny; the other gives us God's infallible and awful judgment about it: the one was never more than a barren speculation; the other has

H

been and is, a *mighty power for good:* the one leaves us in dismal doubt as to our place in the prophetic calendar; the other makes us lift up our heads, to catch the glow of the coming sunrise.

The presumption is surely *against* the modern revival of the primitive view. A return to primitive *doctrine* is good; no progressive revelation of the dogma of justification by faith, for instance, was to be expected; innovation in questions of faith is condemned; we are "earnestly to contend for the faith *once delivered to the saints.*" But prophecy is not doctrine, and its very nature implies that it must be capable of receiving elucidation from the course of providence. *The Protestant historical system of apocalyptic interpretation is based on this fact, and has consequently a strong presumption in its favour.* But presumption is not proof; and the question is of such importance that a fuller examination must now be attempted.

Three main points require to be settled before we can hope to arrive at the meaning of the prophecies of the Revelation.

1. Is the Apocalypse to be understood literally? and if not, on what principle is it to be interpreted?

2. Is it a fulfilled or partially fulfilled prophecy? or does it refer to events still future?

3. Is it a Christian or a Jewish prophecy? That is, does it bear to the church, and to her fortunes in the world, the same relation that earlier prophecy bore to Israel, and to their fortunes in the world? These questions will be considered, in the chapters which follow.

CHAPTER II.

IT is clear that before a student can understand a given work, he must be acquainted with the language in which the book is written ; and he must read it *as* written in that language, not in another. If the work be in French, he will fail to decipher its meaning if he reads the words as Latin or as English.

In what language is the Apocalypse written ? Is it to be understood *literally* ? If not, on what principle is it to be interpreted ?

It is obvious to the most superficial reader, that in its actual texture and construction, the Apocalypse is *a record of visions that are past.* All allow that it is nevertheless, as to its meaning, *a prophecy of events that are future,* or *were* future at the time that the visions were granted to St. John. The angel calls the book a prophecy, "seal not the sayings of the prophecy of this book, for the time is at hand." Of its *prophetic* character there can therefore be no more question, than that its *form* is a record of past visions. In the strictest sense then no one understands the book *literally* ; for the statement, "I saw a beast rise up out of the sea," taken literally, is in no sense whatever a prophecy ; it is a narrative of a past event, not a prediction of a future one.

Such literalism as this is divinely excluded. John beheld things which were to take place "hereafter," but the future was signified to the apostle in a series of visions.

The book is "The Revelation of Jesus Christ, which God

gave to Him, to show unto his servants things which must shortly come to pass; and He sent and signified it by his angel, unto his servant John."

To "signify" (σημαίνω) is to show by signs, to intimate your meaning, not in plain words, but by signs and symbols.

Now it were clearly folly, *to confound the sign with the thing signified.* In a language of signs, each sign and each combina- tion of signs, has a definite meaning. The first verse of the book therefore answers our first question about it : is it to be understood literally? No! IT IS A BOOK OF SIGNS. Its true meaning is veiled under significant figures, and a process of translation must take place, ere that true meaning can be reached. Each symbol used, must be separately studied, and its force gathered, from its context, from comparison with other scriptures, from its own nature, and from such explana- tions as are given in the prophecy itself, before we can expect to discover the mind of the Spirit of God in this book.

If on opening a letter from a friend, the first sentence that met the eye was "I write in Latin in order that my letter may not be understood by all," we should at once be prepared to translate as we read; we should not pore over a certain com- bination of letters and syllables, trying in vain to make some intelligible English word out of them; we should say the *word* is so and so, but the *meaning* is so and so. In reading the symbolic portion of the Apocalypse, we are bound to do the same; on no other principle can anything like a consistent interpretation be attained. The nature of the case forbids it. And yet an opposite maxim of interpretation is often laid down; it is said, take everything literally unless you are forced by impossibility in the nature of things, to give a symbolic signifi- cation. This is like saying, if you can find any combination of letters or syllables in this Latin letter, that will form any English word, take it as English, but where you cannot pos- sibly make anything out of them as English, then no doubt they are Latin. What a singularly lucid communication would be the result of such a system of interpretation! And yet, alas! it is in connection with the Apocalypse too common, among some, whose spirituality and intelligence ought to be fruitful of more wisdom. Such interpreters argue in defence of the monstrosities evoked by their hybrid system, somewhat in this way : "The Nile was once literally turned to blood, we doubt not therefore that this prediction, Revelation viii. 8, 'the third part of the sea became blood,' means just what it says ; God, who wrought the one miracle, can accomplish the other." Undoubtedly : the question is not what God *can* do, but what He here says He *will* do. Now Exodus is a literal history ; when it says the river became blood *it means it ;* Revelation is a symbolic prophecy, when therefore it says "the third part of the sea became blood," *it does not mean it*, but it means something entirely different ; and it is needful not only to substitute a future for a past time, but to translate these symbols into plain language, in order to ascertain what the meaning really is.

It would be ludicrous, were it not painful, to contemplate the absurdities and inconsistencies, which have arisen from a neglect of this simple and almost self-evident maxim of interpretation, demanded by the opening verse of the book, as well as by its whole construction. To overlook it is to turn the most majestic and comprehensive prophecy in the Bible, into a chaos of vague monstrosities, unworthy of being attributed to inspiration ; it is "to degrade the highest and latest of God's holy revelations, into a grotesque patchwork of unmeaning prodigies."*

Prophecy like science has its own peculiar language ; *for understanding the prophecies, therefore,* as Sir Isaac Newton justly observes, *we are in the first place to acquaint ourselves with the figurative language of the prophets.* "In the infancy of society ideas were more copious than words ; hence . men were obliged to employ the few words which they possessed, not only in their natural and direct sense, but likewise in an artificial and tropical sense. . . . Half civilized nations abound in

---

* Birks.

metaphor and allegory. . . . Why is it that a Cherokee
warrior talks of burying the hatchet and of lighting the pipe?
. . His meagre language cannot supply him with the various
terms, which the precision of modern diplomacy has rendered
familiar to Europeans, and therefore he expresses the making
of peace by allusion to certain well known ceremonies attendant upon it. . . . If such then of necessity was the language
of defective civilization, such also would be the first rude attempt to express it *in writing.* The earliest manuscripts were
neither more nor less than *pictures*, but these pictures closely
followed the analogy of spoken language : . . . hence they
were partly proper, and partly tropical. A member of a half
civilized community, who wished to express to the eye the naked
idea of *a man*, would rudely delineate the picture of a man,
. . . a brave, and ferocious, and generous man, he was already
accustomed to *denominate a lion*, if therefore he wished to express such a man in writing, he would *delineate a lion.* . . .
Nation bears to nation, the same relation, that individual bears
to individual.   Hence, according to their attributed characteristics, this nation would be *the lion*; that would be the bear;
and that would be the tiger.   The general prevalence of
the science of heraldry in all ages, under one modification or
another, perpetuated and extended the form of speech to which
it owed its origin.   Thus the dove was the ancient banner of
the Assyrian empire.   Such is the principle on which
is built the figurative language of prophecy.   Like the ancient
hieroglyphics, and like those non-alphabetic characters which
are derived from them, *it is a language of ideas rather than of
words.* It speaks by pictures, quite as much as by sounds . . .
Nor is this derogatory to the all-wise spirit of prophecy . . .
when God deigns to converse with man, He must use the language of man.   The Scriptures were designed for the whole
world; hence it was meet, that their predictions should be couched
in what may be termed a universal language.   But the only
universal language in existence, is the language of hieroglyphics.
To understand this character, we have not the least occasion to

understand the spoken language of the nation who uses it, . . . not being alphabetic it is the representative, not of words but of things. . . . Let the conventional mark be extended to the whole world, and we have forthwith *a written universal language.* Our common numerical cyphers, so far as they extend, form a universal language; for the figures 1 2 or 3 convey the same ideas to each person that uses them, by whatever different *names* the numbers themselves may be called. In the use of this language there is by no means that obscurity and uncertainty which some pretend. They might just as reasonably throw aside a Chinese inscription as incapable of being deciphered. Without a key neither can be understood, but when the key is procured, the book will very readily be opened. *Now the key to the scriptural hieroglyphics, is furnished by Scripture itself,* and when the import of each hieroglyphic is thus ascertained, there is little difficulty in translating, as it were, a hieroglyphical prophecy, into the unfigured phraseology of modern language. When once it is known that a wild beast is the symbol of an idolatrous and persecuting empire, and when the empire intended, has been satisfactorily ascertained, it matters not whether this deed or that deed be verbally ascribed to the empire, or symbolically ascribed to the wild beast. Either mode of speech is equally intelligible. . . . In any case the elements of a language must be first learned, but when that has been accomplished, the rest will follow of course, whether the language in question be verbal or hieroglyphical."*

It is hardly needful to add that there are exceptions to this rule as to every other. Plain predictive sentences and literal explanatory clauses are interspersed here and there, amid the signs of this book. They stand out from the general text, as distinctly as a few words of English introduced here and there in a page of a Greek book would do; it needs no signpost to say "adopt a literal interpretation here." They speak for them-

---

* Faber's "Sacred Calendar of Prophecy," vol. i., chap. i.

selves, common sense dispenses with critical canons, and re-cognises them unaided.

Any system of interpretation that violates this fundamental law of the book is thereby stamped as erroneous. The system that says : " Babylon means Babylon ; and the literal ancient Babylon will, we are bound to believe, be revived," must be false. In the Apocalypse, Babylon does *not* mean Babylon, nor Jerusalem Jerusalem, nor a Jew a Jew, nor the temple the temple ; the system therefore that says " all this Jewish imagery proves that the book has reference to the future of the Jewish nation, and not to the future of the church," must be false. All this Jewish imagery is *symbolic;* these things are used as *signs.* Everything connected with Israel was typical of things connected with the church. The *things signified* must therefore be *Christian,* otherwise the sign and the thing signi-fied, would be one and the same. The system that says the New Jerusalem is a literal city, 1500 miles square and 1500 high (l), made of gems and gold, *must be false;* the New Jeru-salem is a sign ; the thing signified, is the glorified church of Christ, as comparison with other Scripture proves.*

The Divine explanation attached to some of the earliest symbols employed in the book, furnish the key by which much of its sign-language is to be interpreted. They are to the sym-bology of the Apocalypse, what the Rosetta stone was to the hieroglyphics of Egypt. " The seven stars are the angels of the seven churches, and the. seven candlesticks which thou sawest are the seven churches." The seven branched candle-stick, was one of the most important emblematic vessels in the tabernacle " which was a figure for the time then present " of spiritual realities. John saw seven separate candlesticks, and saw Christ the great High Priest, walking in their midst, like

---

* " The application of symbols literally seems to me to be very false in principle, and a very unsuitable mode of interpretation. It is the denial that they are symbols. I believe the language of symbols to be as definite as any other, and always used in the same sense as much as language is." --J. N. DARBY, " Notes on Revelation," p. 31.

Aaron, trimming his lamps. He tells John what the emblem represents; the seven candlesticks symbolised the seven churches of Asia. This explanation authorizes us whenever we meet the same symbol of a candlestick, to attach to it the same signification; and it does more. The candlestick was *one* feature of the tabernacle and temple economy, in which *every* feature was typical of heavenly things; many other symbols borrowed from the same system, appear in the Apocalypse: *this one key unlocks them all.* We have no right to say that the ark of the covenant, the altar, the sea of glass, the temple of the tabernacle of the testimony, the court, the holy city, the New Jerusalem, the priests and their garments, or the worshippers, are to be taken literally. We are bound on the contrary to interpret them *all* on one harmonious principle. The seven candlesticks mean seven Christian churches, that is, they are a perfect representation of the Christian church. *A Christian and not a Jewish sense, then, must attach to all the rest.* The seven stars are not a part of the tabernacle system, but they are equally symbols, standing for a reality of an entirely different nature. Whatever the angels of the churches were, they were not *stars ;* and whenever we meet with this symbol in the book, we may be sure from the Lord's translation of it here, *that it will not mean literal stars,* but rulers, governors, chief men, messengers, or something analogous. " The seven stars are the angels of the seven churches." What sort of consistency would there be in the book, if a star in one place meant a ruler, and in the next a literal star ? Language used in so indeterminate and inexplicable a way, would cease to answer the purpose of language, no definite meaning could attach to it. The study of the Apocalypse might well be abandoned, as more hopeless than that of the hieroglyphics, or the arrow-headed inscriptions of remotest antiquity ; for these we possess keys, for the Apocalypse none, *if our Lord's own explanations are rejected as such.* There is another indication of the same kind in the twice repeated expression, " which say they are Jews and are not, but do lie." The parties alluded to, clearly were literal Jews, but being unbelievers, our Lord here denies to them the name, thereby taking from "*Jew*" thenceforth, its old literal meaning and confining it to a higher sense. "He is not a Jew which is one outwardly, neither is that circumcision which is outward in the flesh : but he is a Jew which is one inwardly, and circumcision is that of the heart." These explanations and indications at the commencement of this prophecy, are like a Divine warning against the error of taking these Jewish emblems literally ; in the Apocalypse they must uniformly be interpreted as *signs of other things.*

In every part of Scripture it is the spirit, and not the letter, that is life and light giving ; how especially must this be the case in a part where the letter, that is the outward form and expression of the truth, is so mysterious, so enigmatical, so unspiritual, as in the Apocalypse ? Popery has surely read the church of Christ a lesson, as to the danger of a false literalism; and yet if there be an apparently simple sentence in the Bible it is surely "this is my body." How can they who object to a literal interpretation of these words, consistently claim one for the strange supernatural symbolisms of the Apocalypse? "That literalism is to be renounced which involves a contradiction to the purified reason, or narrows and contracts the messages of God below the instincts of a holy and spiritual mind."*

Another argument for the symbolic and Christian nature of this book may be drawn from the fact that it is written by *John.* A unity of character and style generally attaches to the different writings of the same author ; and, subordinate to the higher unity of inspiration, this may be detected in the writings of the New Testament. One who is familiar with the style of Paul, for instance, would find it hard to believe that any one else was the author of the epistle to the Hebrews; and one who has entered into the peculiar matter and manner and spirit of John's gospel would, even were they anonymous, assign his three epistles to him.

---

* Birks, " Elements," p. 252.

They are characterized by the same selection of high and deep truth; by the same spirituality and unearthliness; by the same profound simplicity of style; by the same massive divisions, which overlook all minor distinctions; by the same unguarded breadth ot statement, which leaves aside qualifying limitations; by the same marked, abrupt,. contrasts; by the same ignoring of the Jews, and disowning of everything Jewish, based on the great fact stated at the commencement of the gospel, "He came unto his own, and his own received Him not"; and by a recurrence of many of the very same ideas and forms of expression. It may safely be asserted that · John, is the least Jewish and the least earthly of all the apostles, and of all the writers of the New Testament.

The Apocalypse is written by this same John; not only it claims to be so, and is proved by external evidence to be so, but it bears internal evidence of the fact. Though in very different connections, we meet with too many ot the peculiar thoughts and expressions of John, to admit of any doubt as to the authorship of the book. "The Word of God," "the light," "a voice," "the Lamb of God," "the witnesses," the ascending and descending angels, the temple, the temple of his body, the living water, the shepherd leading the sheep; these and many such points of resemblance, recall continually, that the apostle favoured to receive the Revelation of Jesus Christ, was "that disciple whom Jesus loved," and of whom He said, "if I will that he tarry till I come, what is that to thee?"

Now, if we take the Revelation as a symbolic prophecy, predicting the fortunes of the Christian church throughout this dispensation, it is harmonious with all the rest. The strange outward material symbols are only signs; the things signified are mighty spiritual realities; the book is one grand contrast throughout; it traces the long and deadly conflict between the Lamb and the Beast, θηρίον and ἀρνίον, and their respective armies, between the whore associated with the Beast, and the bride of the Lamb, the false and faithless church, and the true and faithful church. In spite of all the Jewish symbolism, (which is natural from the typical character of the Jewish economy, and the antitypical character of the Christian) the Jews and their fortunes, are scarcely glanced at in the book; which, starting from a period subsequent to the final destruction of Jerusalem, and to the dispersion of the Jews, occupies itself entirely, with the history of that church in which is neither Jew nor Gentile. The whole drama as it is enacted before us, recalls such words of John's earlier writings as, "ye are from beneath, I am from above"; "ye seek to kill Me"; "ye are of your father the devil "; the time cometh that whosoever killeth you will think that he doeth God service "; " in the world ye shall have tribulation, but be of good cheer, I have overcome the world "; " O righteous Father, *the world* hath not known Thee, but *these* have known Thee "; "art Thou a king then? for this end was I born, and for this cause came I into the world"; "behold your king"; " he is antichrist that denieth the Father and the Son "; "the world passeth away"; " it is the last time "; " when He shall appear we shall be like Him ", " for this purpose was the Son of God manifested, that He might destroy the works of the devil "; " boldness in the day of judgment, because as He is so are we in this world "; "this is the victory that overcometh the world, even our faith "; "he that hath the Son hath life, and he that hath not the Son of God hath not life."

These and many other thoughts, familiar to us from the gospel and epistles of John, shine out with their old lustre in their new surroundings; reading Revelation as a symbolic prophecy, we feel that it is as characteristic of the soaring, eagle eyed, spiritual apostle, as any of his writings.

But if it be a record of mere material wonders to happen after the Christian church has been removed to heaven, in connection with a future Jewish remnant, how singularly unlike is it, to anything John was ever inspired to write! What a rude and incomprehensible contrast, would exist between this and all his other productions!

And finally the principle of progressive revelation, demands that these visions should not be taken as literal predictions of a coming crisis at the end of the age. Other previous prophecies, had already brought down the chain of events to the destruction and fall of Jerusalem, and our Lord Himself in treating of it, passed on to the final crisis, of which it was a precursor. The one and only period, unillumined by prophetic light was *the church's history on earth.* Our Lord had revealed little, save its general character as a time of tribulation ; the other apostles had foretold certain events which were to characterize its course ; it remained for the Revelation of Jesus Christ which God gave to Him, and which He now sends, as his last gift to the churches, to map it out in detail, and present in a mystic form, all its leading outlines. If the Apocalypse merely went over again, the events of the final crisis, it would not be an advance on all previous revelation, as its place in the canon of Scripture warrants our concluding that it is. To be this, it must be a symbolical history of the Christian dispensation.

CHAPTER III.

THE APOCALYPSE IS A CONTINUOUS PROPHECY EXTENDING FROM
ITS OWN TIME, TO THE CONSUMMATION OF ALL THINGS.—IM-
PORTANCE OF HISTORICAL KNOWLEDGE, IN ORDER TO ITS
CORRECT INTERPRETATION.—IT IS A PROPHECY CONCERNING
THE EXPERIENCES OF THE CHRISTIAN CHURCH, IN THE WORLD,
AND NOT CONCERNING THOSE OF THE JEWISH NATION.

VERY serious are the consequences of a refusal to admit
uniformly and consistently, this symbolic character of the
visions of the Apocalypse. Like most errors it brings further
error in its train, and renders almost impossible any advance
in the comprehension of the book. It answers beforehand,
independently of investigation, the question whether the prophecies of the Apocalypse are fulfilled or not. It stands to
reason, that if these emblematic visions are read under the impression that these things are to come to pass *literally*, the
conclusion that the book consists entirely of unfulfilled prophecies is inevitable, for most assuredly no such things ever have
come to pass.

Literalists must therefore be *futurists*, and the abandonment
of the first error, is almost certain to lead to the abandonment
of the second. The moment we begin to translate the symbolic into ordinary language, the prediction assumes such a
very different shape, that it is no longer a self-evident fact that
it must be unfulfilled. The inquiry is on the contrary awakened,
has this happened? and we turn to history for an answer. If
a fulfilment have taken place, we shall then be on the road
to discover it; one such fulfilment clearly established will be
a clue to others; and every fulfilment so discovered, will be
an argument for the truth of that system of interpretation which
led to the discovery.

Here we are met by an objection; some are found rash enough to condemn that system of interpretation which leads to the comparison of prophecy with history, on the ground that it does so. The sun, say they, requires no candle to show that it shines; the Bible requires no light from history; history is merely human; we are told to search the Scriptures, but we are nowhere told to search Eusebius, or Gibbon, or Hallam. God is his own intrepreter; He can explain his own word without human help; history was not written in heaven, it is the wisdom of this world, foolishness with God, and so on.

Now this reasoning, though often advanced in the most oracular way as if it settled the question, is shallow, and based on fallacies; and yet, alas! it misleads many, calculated as it is to flatter ignorance, to foster indolence, and to encourage dogmatism, by throwing the reins on the neck of imagination, which is by it left free, to invent future facts and fulfilments, as it lists. A little reflection will show the superficial nature of the objection.

A knowledge of history *is* needful to the intelligent comprehension of prophecy. The Bible itself contains a large amount of history, from which alone we learn the fulfilment of many of its earlier prophecies, and without which we might still be expecting a fulfilment, which took place hundreds of years ago. What are the four gospels, and the book of Acts, but histories, divinely inspired histories of course, but under the point of view we are now considering, their inspiration is mainly important as securing their accuracy and authenticity. They are *authentic records* of a series of facts, which took place eighteen hundred years ago, in a distant land; for a knowledge of which consequently we *must* be indebted to the testimony of others. By the help of such testimony we compare the facts that have occurred, with the predictions of prophecy, and perceive the marvellous and accurate fulfilment. Without such testimony we never could have done this; and to be ignorant of the existence and nature of such testimony, is to be practically without it. But Bible history, while it begins with the first Adam and the first paradise, does not, like Bible prophecy, reach on to the coming of the Second Adam in glory to re-establish paradise on earth. It ends about A.D. 60, and we have only uninspired though authentic records of all that has happened since. Now according to these objectors, we are not to make use of these ; not to compare New Testament prophecy with profane history. Either then there must be absolutely no prophetic light thrown by the Holy Ghost on the last eighteen hundred years, or else God does not intend us to have the benefit of it. Supposing a fulfilment clear as daylight to have taken place, we must remain in ignorance of it, unless God were pleased now to add an appendix to the Bible, to record facts which many trustworthy historians have already recorded. Revelation never teaches things which common sense is sufficient to discover. For instance, a tenfold division of the Roman empire was predicted by Daniel, prior to the establishment of the kingdom of Christ on earth. The Roman empire was still existing in its integrity when John closed the canon of Scripture by his prophecy, which repeats the prediction. Blot out now all historical records, deprive the church of the help of all uninspired testimony, and Christians must to this day remain in ignorance of the solemnly momentous fact, that this prediction has been fulfilled during the last twelve hundred years, and the strong presumption to be derived therefrom that the coming of the Lord is nigh, even at the doors. Nor will it do to say, ah, but that is a notorious fact, evident to our senses without historical testimony. No : our knowledge of it depends upon uninspired testimony, historical or otherwise ; and the question is not, to what *extent* may we make use of uninspired records to elucidate inspired predictions, but, may we make use of them *at all ?* The answer is clear, *we must,* or for ever remain ignorant, whether the holy prophecies of the word of God regarding post canonical events, are fulfilled or not.

A still more rash assertion is also made ; it is said that no events of this parenthetical church dispensation (save those of its closing crisis) are, or could be, subjects of prophecy.

That this statement is not true is proved by the above instance, and by many more that might be alleged. But it is evident that a knowledge of history is needful to warrant the statement! How without such knowledge, can it be ascertained that the visions of Revelation for instance, do *not* present a connected outline of the leading events between the past and future advents of Christ? A knowledge of what has actually taken place is as ·needful to justify a denial, as an assertion of the fact. We must know a person as well before we can pronounce that a certain portrait does *not* resemble him, as in order to assert that it *does.*

This prejudice against the use of history in the interpretation of prophecy, seems frequently to be based on a confusion which is made, between the facts recorded by historians and the opinions of the historians who record them. Grant that the latter being merely human are worthless, the former are none the less important. Trustworthy historians record events which *they* neither invented nor caused, but which occurred under God's providential government; it was He who caused or permitted these events; they are in one sense as Divine, as prophecy; that is, both proceed from Him. Prophecy is God telling us beforehand what shall happen; authentic history is men telling us what has, in the providence of God, taken place. In truth each is best understood in the light of the other; the moral features of events, occupy the main place in the prophecy, so that by its study we learn to weigh things in God's balances, to judge of men and systems by a Divine standard. But the history also elucidates the prophecy; when we see what has been allowed to occur in fulfilment of a prediction, we learn what was intended in the announcement, and understand the perhaps previously mysterious form, in which it was made. Apparent contradictions are reconciled, difficulties are removed, and we are filled with admiration and awe at the foreknowledge and wisdom evinced in predictions, over which the ignorant can only puzzle or speculate. Authentic history ought not to be deprecated as merely the wisdom of this

world; it is something more, it is a record of God's providential government of the world.   Besides it is vain and
foolish to deny, that mental cultivation in general, an acquaintance with ancient languages and literature, with history and
with science, *are* a help, in the understanding of Scripture
and especially of prophetic Scripture.   They are not needful
to a spiritual apprehension of saving truth, thanks be to God,
nor to growth in grace and in the experimental knowledge of
the Lord.   God can and does dispense with them, but He
can and does also sanctify and use them, for the elucidation
of his word.   By themselves they are worthless, for they deal
only with the letter; but, sanctified and used by the Holy
Ghost, they are invaluable, as helping to explain the letter, in
and through which we grasp the spirit.

It is a strange estimate to form of the dignity of the inspired book of the all-wise God, that those ignorant of his
works in nature and providence, are as capable of understanding it, as those familiar with them.   It is true that the un-
learned Christian has, equally with the learned, the indwelling
Spirit to guide him into all truth.   But it is also true that
he needs in addition *ministry*, human teaching; else why
has Christ given *teachers* to his church?   Books are but
written ministry.   Ignorance is an infirmity, an unavoidable
one with many it is true, and one for which help is provided; •
but it is as much an infirmity of the mind, as blindness or
lameness is of the body.   We blame not the blind and the
lame for not seeing and walking, but we should blame them
for refusing the help of those who possess the powers of which
they are deprived.   We blame not the ignorant for their
ignorance when it is unavoidable; but we should blame them
for refusing assistance, and for glorying in that ignorance as a
peculiar advantage.   The ignorant Christian must be indebted
to the learned in many ways; but for the labour of such, he
would indeed have no Bible; for what could *he* learn from the
original text? and if the translation put into his hands be
defective, how but from the criticisms of the learned, shall he

remedy the defect? This is surely designed of God, and is one of the ways in which "the whole body, compacted to. gether by that which every joint supplieth, according to the effectual working in the measure of every part, maketh in. crease of the body unto the edifying of itself in love." It is impossible to assign any reason, why the wisdom and knowledge derived from historical research, should not be made available, as well as every other kind of science, for the elucidation of Scripture.

We dare not for these reasons exclude the light afforded by history, in the endeavour to answer the questions sug gested above, *is the prophecy of the Apocalypse fulfilled or partly so, or is it still entirely unfulfilled?* and is it in its general scope Christian or Jewish? The two inquiries are so closely re lated, that it is impossible to pursue them apart; it is evident that if the Revelation be partially fulfilled, it is in the history of the Christian church we shall be able to trace the fulfilment, seeing the Jewish nation was already cast away,—"broken off" for a time,—before this prophecy was published; and it is equally evident that if it relate to the future history of restored Israel, no fulfilment can have yet commenced, seeing Israel is still scattered, and Jerusalem trodden down of the Gentiles.

We have therefore to ascertain from the internal evidence of the prophecy itself, and from the external evidence of analogy and history, the truth as to these two closely connected points.

And first what says the Apocalypse of itself? To whom is it addressed? This is a fair and fundamental question; it is thus that we judge of the object and scope of the epistles of the New Testament, and of the "burdens" of the ancient prophets. The epistles are addressed "to the saints and to the faithful in Christ Jesus," or "to the church" in such and such a place. Observing this, we argue, the Jews and the ungodly have no right to appropriate the contents of these letters; they are for believers in Christ alone; confusion will result if unbelievers take to themselves these Divine messages. The argument applies with equal force to the Apocalypse. It is addressed to Christ's "servants," "to the seven churches of Asia." This is reiterated; the expressions occur both at the opening and at the close, of the book. "The Lord God of the holy prophets sent his angel to show unto *his servants* things which must shortly be done." "I Jesus have sent mine angel to testify unto you these things, *in the churches.*" On reading these distinct declarations, simple unsophisticated minds would surely conclude, that the Jews and unbelievers in general, have no more to do with this prophecy than they have with the Epistle to the Ephesians. They may possibly be alluded to in the one, as in the other, but it is not for them, it is not mainly concerned with them; *it is for us;* Christians alone were Christ's servants in the days of Domitian, when John saw and heard these things; to Christians alone was it sent, the seven churches represented the *whole* church, the prophecy is for the Christian church, and they take the children's bread to give it to outsiders, who would rob the church of her Lord's last gift.

It is no use to say, yes! but though given to the church, it might still be a revelation of the counsels of God about others than herself. *It might;* the Epistle to the Ephesians *might* have been a treatise on the state and prospects of the lost ten tribes, but it was not; the vision of Nebuchadnezzar, might have been a vision of the restoration of Israel, but it *was* not; the visions of Daniel might have been visions of the seven churches in Asia, but they *were* not, nor was it likely that they would be, nor is it likely that the Lord Jesus in his last prophetic communication to his cherished church, from whom for eighteen hundred years He was to be hidden, would have nothing more pressing, personal, and important to reveal to her, than the destiny of a future Jewish remnant, with which she has nothing in common, and the final judgments on a world, from which she is already delivered, and from which, according to this theory, she will have been previously removed. Did she need no guidance, no comfort, no sustainment with the cordial of hope, for the years of earthly pilgrimage that lay before her? True, He had before, revealed in broad outline the sufferings that awaited her, and the glories that should follow ; but had He, who knows the end from the beginning, and who foresaw all that has since happened, no further words of warning and of cheer for his long-to-be-tempted, and sorely-to-be-persecuted church? Strange, that such an idea should find place in Christian hearts! What! shall our Lord be less kind and careful than an earthly friend or parent? A father sends forth his young son into a world which he must face alone, into circumstances in which he cannot further communicate with him for some years ; he foresees that the separation will be far longer than the lad conceives, that his son will be exposed to temptations and snares, into which he will be only too prone to fall, that he will meet a crafty, specious, dangerous, deadly foe, in the guise of a friend, and that he will have to undergo sufferings that will be hard for him to bear, before he regains the paternal roof. He puts a long prophetic letter into his hand as they part, with solemn, earnest, repeated, injunctions to him to read and mark its contents. In distant lands and dreadful difficulties, the son opens this letter, and finds—suited advice and encouragement? helpful warning and direction? Oh no ! but an elaborate description of what his father intends to do for his younger brother, after his own return home ! What should we say of the wisdom or tenderness of such a parent? Do these interpreters indeed believe that God inspired this prophecy, and that Christ loves his church?

Farther, what does the Apocalypse say about its own scope, and about the time to which it refers? Again the first verse of the book supplies a simple and direct answer. It was given to show to Christ's servants "*things that must shortly come to pass,*" and the next verse urges the study of the book, on the ground that "*the time is at hand.*" In the last chapter the angel speaks of these things as "things that must shortly be done," and commands John not to seal the sayings of the prophecy, for the same reason, "*the time is at hand.*" These words *may* measure time by the thousand-years-to-a-day scale, may not mean "at hand" according to human, but only according to Divine chronology.   But it is not likely that this is the case, because in another closely related prophecy, we have expressions *of an exactly opposite character*, which can be proved to measure time by the *ordinary standard.*   Daniel is twice or thrice told to shut up and seal certain parts of his prophecies, which related to events to take place in this dispensation, "even to the time of the end," because "the time appointed was *great*" and "the vision for *many days.*"   Now the most distant of those events was *near* if measured by the Divine scale, distant only according to the common computation.   *If these expressions in Daniel are used in their merely human sense, we have every reason to suppose that it is the same with the similar expressions in Revelation.*   To Daniel, Christ said, "shut up the words and seal the book even to the time of the end," and to John, when these things had already begun to come to pass, the angel says, "seal not the sayings, for the time is at hand."   It would not have been at hand in the ordinary sense, if the prophecy relates mainly to still. future events.   We have every reason therefore to believe, that it relates, on the contrary, to events that began soon after the apostle received the revelation, and that the fulfilment has been in progress ever since.

Another strong presumption that the visions of the Apocalypse form a continuous prophecy, stretching over the whole of this dispensation, exists in their analogy with the prophecies of Daniel.   The resemblance between these two is marked and close ; both are in the symbolic language, both were given to aged saints who were greatly beloved, who were confessors and all but martyrs ; the "Man clothed in linen and girded with the gold of Uphaz, whose face was as lightning, whose eyes were as fire, and whose voice was as the voice of a multitude," who addressed Daniel, on the banks of the Hiddekel, is unquestionably the same Divine Being who addressed John in Patmos.   The prophecies were in both cases communicated when the temple was in ruins, and the Jews dispersed ; and both Daniel and John, had been trained in a school of peculiar experiences, to fit them to become recipients of these sacred revelations. We take then the symbolic prophecies of Daniel, as those likely to afford the most direct analogy to the symbolic prophecies of the Apocalypse, and we ask, do *they* date from contemporary events, or from a far distant future? and do they present a *continuous* sketch of the interval they cover, or do they dwell exclusively on salient and distant crises ?

The question scarcely needs a reply. The fourfold image seen by Nebuchadnezzar begins with the Babylonian monarchy of which he was the first great head. " Thou art this head of gold." It pursues its even course down through all the times of the Gentiles, and ends with the millennial kingdom of Christ.

The second prophecy of Daniel, that of the four great beasts or empires, was given forty-nine years later, in the first year of Belshazzar, that is towards the end of Israel's captivity, when the days of Babylon's glory were fast drawing to a close, when the time was rapidly approaching for the kingdom to be numbered, finished, divided, and given to others. Accordingly, while the first beast is still the Babylonian empire, the first particular noticed in the prophecy, is the plucking of the eagle's wings, on the lion's back. The prophecy thus starts from the diminished glory of the latter end of Babylon, rather than from the golden splendour of its commencement, that is, *from contemporary events.* It presents a second and fuller sketch of the political history of the Gentile world, (for the spiritual power, the little horn, is glanced at principally in its political aspects,) and traces the main features of the times of the Gentiles, down to the same point as its predecessor, the everlasting kingdom of the Most High.

The third prophecy of Daniel, that of the ram and the he-goat, with its four horns and its little horn, was given, as its opening states, in the third year of Belshazzar, two years later than the preceding prophecy. It opens with the Medo-Per-

sian empire, and the conquests of Cyrus.   Now when this prophecy was given, Cyrus had already been reigning seven years
in Persia, and the rise of his universal empire was close at
hand.   It gives a continuous history of the Medo-Persian and
Grecian empires, and of the Mohammedan politico-religious
power, thus ranging from soon after its own date, to far on in
the Christian era.

The fourth prophecy of Daniel, that of the seventy weeks to
elapse between the end of the captivity, and the coming of
Messiah the Prince, began to be fulfilled about eighty years
after it was delivered, when Artaxerxes gave the commandment
to restore and to build Jerusalem.   But the decree of Cyrus,
to restore and build the temple, and to liberate the Jews from
captivity, was promulgated only two years after the date of this
prophecy, and would no doubt be taken by the Jews at first, as
marking the commencement of the seventy weeks.   This prophecy includes a period of about five hundred years, and reaches
from the restoration under Nehemiah to the final destruction
of Jerusalem by Titus.   Its object was less to indicate intervening events, than to measure *the period up to the great event
of human history;* the previous and the following prophecies,
delineate the main outlines of the history of the period.

And lastly the fifth and great closing prophecy of Daniel,
given by our Lord Himself, and recorded in the 11th and 12th
chapters, *begins with the date of the vision,* "the third year of
Cyrus king of Persia," and takes even a retrospective glance
to the first year of Darius the Mede (chap. xi. 1).   It predicts the succession of the Persian monarchs, condensing into
one sentence the reigns of Cambyses, Smerdis, and Darius
Hystaspes, down to the overthrow of the rich and mighty
Xerxes, who stirred up all against the realm of Grecia.   It traces
next the history of the Ptolemies and of the Seleucidæ, down
to the desolations and persecutions of Antiochus Epiphanes,
gives full detail of the career of the wilful king, and of the
closing events of this dispensation, ending with the deliverance
of Israel, and the resurrection of the just.   It embraces thus a

period of at least 2400 years, and extends from the fall of the *typical*, to the fall of the *antitypical* Babylon ; so that *all* the historical prophecies of Daniel start from events close at hand when they were given, and predict with varying degrees of fulness, a series of other events, to follow in regular sequence, to the point at which they close.

Now, judging by analogy, we should expect that when He who revealed to Daniel the things noted in the Scripture of truth, came six hundred years later, to reveal to John "things that must shortly come to pass," He would follow the same method. ·On opening the Apocalypse, this expectation is confirmed ; we find that it starts, like all Daniel's prophecies, from "the things that are," and that it ends like them, with the great consummation. In the nature of things, it could not go over *all* the ground of the older prophecies. Many of the events foretold by Daniel had already transpired. The three great empires had risen and fallen ; the fourth was then in its glory. Antiochus had desolated Judæa and defiled the temple ; Messiah had come, and had been cut off ; Titus had destroyed Jerusalem. So much of the journey lay behind John in Patmos ; these facts were no longer themes for prophecy, but materials for history. Israel's fortunes were no longer the object of main interest, either to Him who was about to give this last of all prophecies, or to him who was about to receive it, or to those for whose sakes he was to write it. Blindness in part had happened to Israel, until the fulness of the Gentiles should be come in. The Apocalypse was not given in the sacred tongue of the Hebrews consequently, but in gentile Greek, just as Daniel's two earlier prophecies, which refer to the times of the Gentiles, without much allusion to Israel, are in gentile Chaldee. Taking these altered circumstances into account, what should we expect the last revelation granted to John in Patmos to contain ? Should we, judging by analogy, expect that, passing over in silence eighteen hundred years, crowded with events of deep interest, of stupendous importance to seventy or eighty generations of his saints, the Lord Jesus would reveal through this Christian apostle, only the particulars of a brief closing crisis of earthly history, subsequent to the church's removal, and relating mainly to a future Jewish remnant? Assuredly not! We should expect this final prophecy, sent directly by Christ Himself to his church, through his most spiritually minded apostle, to contain *an outline of all that should befall that church, from the time then present, until the Lord's return, with perhaps brief indications of subsequent events.* A first perusal of the prophetic part of the book, gives the impression that our expectation is correct. We find a series of symbolic visions, and we observe a perceptible correspondence between some of them, and some of Daniel's, exactly as would be the case supposing these visions to traverse the same ground as his *later* ones. We find in the Apocalypse no beasts answering to Daniel's first three, but the fourth reappears very prominently with his ten horns ; we find no periods corresponding to the seventy weeks or the 2300 days, but the "time times and a half" is repeated in several forms, and in the same relative connection. We find in the closing visions, features that identify them with the final scenes of Daniel, and it is difficult to resist the conviction, that the intervening apocalyptic visions, must be *symbolic predictions of the moral and spiritual aspects, of all that has happened to the church of Christ, from John's day to the present time, and of all that shall happen, to the close.*

But analogy furnishes a stronger argument still. "The Old Testament, when rightly understood," says Augustine, "is one great prophecy of the New." The records of the past are pregnant with the germs of a corresponding but more exalted future. The history of the seed of Abraham after the flesh, is, throughout, typical of the history of his seed by faith. The Lord's dealings with them, were types of his dealings with us; for every fact in their history, some counterpart may be noted in our own; our experiences are but a new edition, on a different scale, of theirs. Now under the old covenant, prophecy threw its light beforehand, on almost every event of importance that happened to the nation of Israel, from the days of Abraham to the days of Christ, the fall of Jerusalem and its temple, the dispersion of the Jews, and the end of that age.

The light of prophecy is a privilege, a blessing, a gift; it is always so spoken of in Scripture ; " He *gave* them prophets," " He gave gifts unto men, . . . apostles, *prophets*, evangelists, pastors, teachers "; and though Christianity possesses many higher privileges, and nobler gifts than Judaism, it lacks none of the real blessings of that earlier economy. We have exchanged many a shadow for substance, but lost no substantial good. New Testament prophecy may therefore be expected to throw its light, on every event of importance to. happen to the church of Christ, from the fall of Jerusalem to the second advent, that is, from the end of the Jewish, to the end of the Christian age.

Among the events made subjects of prophecy in the Old Testament were the birth of Isaac, the rapid increase of Israel. the descent into Egypt, the sufferings of the Israelites under the Pharaohs, the duration of their bondage, the exodus, the forty years in the desert, the possession of Canaan, its very division among the tribes ; the characters of Saul, David, Solomon, and many other individuals ; the building of the temple, the division of the kingdom into two, the Assyrian invasion, and Israel's captivity ; the Babylonian invasion and the seventy years' captivity of Judah, the return from Babylon, the time to elapse, and many of the events to occur, between it and the coming of Messiah the Prince, his birth, character, true nature, ministry, sufferings, and death ; the ministry of John the Baptist, the rejection of Israel, the call of the Gentiles, and the destruction of Jerusalem under Titus.

Was *Israel* ever left during a long period, full of momentous changes, and events of solemn national importance, without the light and guidance of prophecy? Is there in *their* history any " mighty unrepresented vacuum," of the occurrences of which we can say, great as are these events in human estimation, they are deemed unworthy of Divine notice in prophecy? If such be the case there will be a distinct analogy, on which to base the theory, that the Apocalypse is still wholly unfulfilled. But such is not the case. The chain is almost unbroken, and though four hundred years elapsed between the last of the prophets and the coming of Messiah, Daniel's prophecy fills in the events of the interval, so that no gap of even a century occurs in the long series.

Is it likely that there should be no analogy, but a perfect contrast, in the history of the antitypical Israel? Has she no Egypt to leave and no wilderness to traverse, no land to inherit, no oppressors to tyrannize over her, no evil kings to mislead her, no reformers and deliverers to arise, no BABYLON to carry her captive, no temple to rebuild, no Messiah to look for, no judgments to apprehend, no rest to inherit? Are *hers* less important than theirs? Are her foes so much more obvious, her dangers so much more patent, that it should be superfluous to supply her with prophetic light to detect them? Because *they* were an earthly people, and *she* a heavenly church, is she therefore not on earth, and not amid the ungodly? Are her enemies heavenly because the church is so? Nay, but most earthly, for the wicked spirits against whom the church wrestles, wage their warfare incarnate in earthly, sensual, *devilish* systems, and in actual men, as did Satan in the serpent in Eden. Every conceivable reason would suggest her *greater* need of prophetic light. Now the Apocalypse is the book of the New Testament which answers to "the prophets" of the Old. If then it contain predictions of the first spread of Christianity, of the hosts of martyrs who sealed their testimony with their blood, during the ten pagan persecutions, of the reception of Christianity by Constantine and the Roman empire, of the gradual growth of corruption in the church, of the irruptions of the Goths and Vandals, and the break up of the old Roman empire into ten kingdoms, of the rise and development of popery, of the rise and rapid conquests of Mohammedanism, of the long continued and tremendous sufferings of the church under papal persecutions, of the fifty millions of martyrs slain by the Romish Church, of the enormous political power attained by the popes, of their Satanic craft and wickedness, of the Reformation, of the gradual decay of the papal system and the extinction of the temporal power of the popes : *if it contain predictions of these events, which we know to have taken place in the history of the antitypical Israel,* then we have a *perfect analogy* with the Old Testament. If on the other hand, the Apocalypse alludes to none of these events, but passing them all over in silence, gives only the history of an Antichrist who has not yet appeared, and of judgments not yet commenced, nor to be commenced until the church is in heaven, then instead of a striking scriptural analogy, we have a glaring and most unaccountable contrast.

We say advisedly *unaccountable,* for none of the reasons assigned for this supposed contrast between Israel's experience and our own in this matter, are satisfactory. Their calling was an earthly one, ours is a heavenly one, it is true ; nevertheless our calling from heaven, and to heaven, leaves us still on earth. We have earthly connections and relations ; we are not of the world, but we are in the world. The acts of earthly monarchs and the changes of kingdoms and dynasties, affect the church even as they affected her Lord, in the days of his flesh. How came the prophecies " I called my Son out of Egypt," and " He shall be called a Nazarene," to be accomplished ? What took the virgin mother to Bethlehem ? Why was Paul left bound two whole years ? Secular political events have their influence, their mighty influence, on the church, notwithstanding her heavenly calling, and may therefore well be revealed to her by the spirit of prophecy. It is evident there is nothing in the peculiarity of this dispensation, which precludes the church from receiving predictions, of specific events to take place during its course, because *the epistles contain such predictions.* The fact that the Holy Ghost has announced to the church, events reaching through the whole dispensation cannot be denied. " He who now letteth will let until he be taken out of the way ; and then shall that wicked be revealed, whom the Lord shall consume with the spirit of his mouth, and shall destroy with the brightness of his coming." The hindering obstacle, whatever it was, was in existence when the apostle wrote, and was to continue in existence until another event took place, the rise of the man of sin, and that wicked one was to continue till the Lord's coming. Here we have a prophecy the fulfilment of which, starting from its own date, reaches to the consummation, and covers the whole interval, leaving no room for a break.

There is therefore no ground for asserting,' that the fulfilment of the Apocalypse must be future, because the church cannot be the subject of prophecies whose sphere is earth. If she may be the subject of one or two, she may equally well be the subject of a hundred, and the question must be decided on other grounds. If the first generation of Christians were forewarned of the fall of Jerusalem, we may be forewarned of the fall of Babylon. If they knew beforehand that Jerusalem was to be compassed about with armies, we may know that the power of Turkey is to decay. In principle there is no difference ; a dispensation that admits of the one, admits also of the other.

The interpretation of this book which asserts a past historic fulfilment of the greater part of its mystic visions, is then in perfect harmony with strong scriptural analogies ; and the interpretation which asserts them all to be future and unfulfilled, is in violent and unnatural opposition to all analogy, and would require the strongest internal evidence to support it. But such internal evidence it can never receive, seeing it is a negative, and not a positive theory ; it denies the historic fulfilment, but substitutes no other that can be tested by its correspondence or otherwise with the terms of the prediction. Internal evidence in its favour is therefore impossible ; there is no analogy to support it ; and we are driven to the conclusion that it is untenable.

The principal test, however, by which to determine the

period covered by this prophecy is a comparison with history. Can any series of events be indicated, which have transpired since the Christian era, which bear a sufficiently clear resemblance to the symbolic visions of the Apocalypse, to justify the assertion, that the prophecy is for the most part a fulfilled one? If so, candour would admit, that it settles the question.

We firmly believe that such a fulfilment is clearly traceable. Yet as Jewish unbelief refuses to perceive that the character and mission, the life and death, of Jesus of Nazareth, fulfil the long series of Messianic predictions, so there may be a Christian unbelief, which refuses to perceive, that the events of the Christian era, answer to the predictions of this Christian prophecy.

Yet if such a series of events have taken place, it ought not to be difficult to observe the resemblance between the history and the prophecy. It is not a question of minor details, but of events of stupendous magnitude, affecting a vast extent of the earth, and reaching through centuries of time. It is not a question of remote antiquity, nor of half explored, dimly known regions; no such difficulties encumber the problem. The things that have transpired in the Roman earth, since the days of Domitian, when the Apocalypse was written, especially those concerning the Christian church, both true and false, and those transpiring in our own day, are not things done in a corner, concerning which there may exist a great variety of opinions and of questions that can never be decided. On the contrary, we have records abundant and varied enough of the whole period, to enable us to live it over again in imagination ; and we have remains, and monuments, and present facts, which are so linked with all that eventful past, that no ingenuity can distort or deny, any of its main features. The last eighteen hundred years, present no *terra incognita* to the historian ; explorers may not conjure up characters, or concoct transactions, to suit their taste ; dates cannot be adapted to fit theories ; every error is sure to be detected, and every assertion sifted. Very narrow are the limits within which invention may act ; almost boundless is the field for examination and research. This being the case, it must be not only possible, but easy, to recognise the fulfilment of the apocalyptic prophecies if it exist, provided only we are sufficiently acquainted with the facts of history, and rightly understand the predictions themselves.

If a photograph of an extensive and varied landscape, be presented to a person familiar with the scene, he will not fail to recognise its main features ; he might not be immediately able to detect the miniature of his own homestead, amid the many similar to it, nor to identify every spire of the neighbouring city, and every little detail of the picture. But the more he studies it, the more he will see in it, and the microscope will enable him to identify objects, which one without a microscope and with less knowledge of the neighbourhood, would never notice. It is thus with a student of the Apocalypse who is familiar with history. Or, to reverse the simile ; one who has long being acquainted with a series of photographs, say of the Holy Land, who has pored over them with loving interest and impressed them deep in his memory, is transported to Palestine, and wanders amid those very scenes. He stands on the shores of a blue lake which reflects a snowy cone that rises far away to the north ; the level tops of a range of barren mountains stretch along the opposite shore ; a ruined, earthquake-shaken town and castle lie behind him ; and away to the south a river makes its way out of the lake. He needs no guide to tell him where he is ; he stops not to observe the details of the scene ; this combination of broad features so often noted in the photograph is enough : " Hermon," he exclaims " that exceeding high mountain apart ! Tiberias, solitary survivor of sister cities ! mountains of Bashan, river Jordan, I know ye all " ; and he would smile incredulously at any one who should say, " Well, in spite of the general resemblance, I question after all whether this is the sea of Galilee ! "

It is thus with a student of history who is familiar with the Apocalypse. The remembered photograph serves to identify the real scene, as in the former case the well remembered scene interpreted the picture ; if there be a resemblance it would be impossible that either could be known, and the other not recognised, if contemplated with sufficient care and attention.

The reason that the resemblance is not more uniformly perceived, between the predictions of Revelation and the facts of history since the Christian era, must then lie, either in a want of thorough acquaintance with one or other, or else in a want of careful and unprejudiced attention to the correspondence between them. Those who have taken the Apocalypse literally, have of course little idea what it predicts when translated into unsymbolic language ; and history is too often contemplated, from the worldly political point of view in which it is generally written, for the resemblance between the Divine delineation of its facts, and the facts themselves, to be easily recognised.

Besides this, a foregone conclusion that the book of Revelation is unfulfilled, prevents many from perceiving the proofs to the contrary. But we feel no hesitation in asserting, that a candid student, who admits the Apocalypse to be symbolic, and patiently endeavours by the help of other Scripture to translate its symbols, and who then proceeds to compare its predictions, with the authentic historical records of the Christian era, will be driven to admit, that there is as clear a correspondence between the two, as between any other prophecy and its fulfilment.

We cannot enlarge on this argument here ; to do it justice would be to give an exposition of the greater part of the book. The correspondence will be traced somewhat fully as to one or two of the visions, in the third part of this work ; and any force of truth therein perceived, must be allowed to lend its aid in deciding our present point, the general principles on which the book ought to be interpreted. We entreat the Futurist reader to remember, that it is possible for the plainest and most satisfactory fulfilment of a prophecy, to be forced on the attention, and yet be unperceived : witness the Jews in the days of Christ; witness the disciples by the empty sepulchre. And yet if

a fulfilment of the Apocalypse has been accomplishing for
more than seventeen hundred years, and if there remains very
little now to be fulfilled, *it is of momentous interest to the
church of Christ that she should be aware of the fact.* If in
watching an exhibition of dissolving views we judge of the
nearness of the conclusion, merely by the time that has
elapsed since it began, we may have a vague impression that
the end cannot be far off; but if we have held a programme
of the proceedings in our hand all the time, and have observed that each scene appeared as announced, and that
only the final one remains, we have a certainty that *the end
must be close at hand,* which is a very different state of mind.

A Divine programme of the proceedings of this dispensation
has been placed in our hands; they who avail themselves of
it, they who study it, and watch the dissolving views presented
on the stage of history, know how many of the pre-appointed
configurations have appeared, melted away, and been replaced
by others; they know the position on the programme of the
one now on the stage, and they know what remains! They
lift up their heads, they know that their redemption draweth
nigh, yea very, very nigh!

Nor are the claims of this principle of historical interpretation in the least invalidated by the fact, that interpreters differ
among themselves as to the precise application of some of the
visions. Nearly all the writers of the first fifteen centuries of
the Christian era, entertained the view that the Apocalypse
was a comprehensive prophecy, reaching from the date of its
publication to the end of all things, and endeavoured consequently to find its historical solution. It can be no wonder
that, as the page of history has unrolled itself, greater accuracy
should have been attained, than it was possible for early
students to possess. At the time of the Reformation, and
subsequently, the great body of commentators still interpreted
the Apocalypse on the same principle, but naturally with a far
closer approximation to the truth, though they were by no means
unanimous in their expositions of detail; and many are the

points of controversy which still exist.   But the essential agreement, more than counterbalances the minor differences,* and it would be strange indeed if such differences did *not* exist.

Prophetic interpretation is not milk for babes, but rather strong meat for those that are of full age, and have their senses exercised by reason of use.   But which of the very simplest doctrines of Scripture excludes controversy ?   Is it an argument against the true view of the atonement, that numerous erroneous

---

* We extract the following note from an admirable little pamphlet by P. H. Gosse, F.R.S., entitled, " The Revelation : How is it to be Interpreted ? " (London : Morgan and Chase, 23, Warwick Lane, Paternoster Row) which we earnestly commend to the consideration of those who hold Futurist views.   "The following list of Presentist expositors of the Apocalypse includes, so far as I have been able to ascertain, all of any note from the era of the Reformation to the publication of the ' Horæ ' of Mr. Elliott : Luther, Bullinger, Bale, Chytræus, Marlorat, Foxe, Brightman, Pareus, Mede, Vitringa, Daubuz, Sir Isaac Newton, Whiston, Beugel, Bishop Newton, Bicheno, Faber, Frere, Irving, Cunningham, Habershon, Bickersteth, Birks, Woodhouse, Keith, Elliott, twenty-six in all.   Out of these there are agreed as follows :

1. That seals I. to IV. are the decline of the pagan empire . .   10
2. That seal VI. is the fall of paganism under Constantine   11
3. That trumpets I. to IV. are the Gothic invasions 15
4. That trumpet V. is the Saracens. 17
5. That trumpet VI. is the Turks 21
6. That the little opened book refers to the Reformation. .   12
7. That chapter xi. is the papal persecution of saints as heretics . 22
8. That chapter xii. is the depression and recession from view of
      the true church during the papal ages   18
9. That the beasts are aspects of the Papacy 25
10. That the vials are the great French revolution and its results   8
11. That chapter xvii. is Rome   26
12. That chapter xviii. is the Papacy.   26
13. That a day is the symbol of a year 19

It is right to observe that, the first four seals and first four trumpets referring each to several things, the agreement must be understood as admitting some diversity in details.   Also that the application to the French revolution of the vials, could not possibly be made by expositors who wrote before the close of the last century, that is more than half of the whole number.   Sir Isaac Newton and Whiston, however, shrewdly foresaw the great infidel revolution, as the earthquake of the seventh trumpet, " that infidelity was to break in pieces the antichristian party which had so long corrupted Christianity." (Whiston, p. 46.)

and defective views exist? Is there no revealed truth on
the subject of church government, because such widely differing creeds on the point prevail? If we cannot see eye to
eye on such subjects as these, shall we marvel that differences
appear in the application of the symbolic visions of Revelation
to history? The multitude of the events predicted, their range
and variety, the peculiar language in which they are foretold,
the fact that they bear a strong testimony against existing corruptions in the church, and consequently enlist the antagonism
of all who uphold these corruptions, these things are quite sufficient to account for the measure of disagreement, which is
found among interpreters, and which decreases in proportion
as acquaintance with the subject increases, and as every fresh
phase of contemporary history, adds its testimony to the previously existing mass.

But it is needful to notice one or two objections, com-
mouly advanced by a certain school of Futurist interpreters,
who hold very strongly the parenthetical character of the present dispensation; because they appear to have more weight
than on examination they prove to possess. They settle the
question as to the character of the Book of Revelation, in a
summary and apparently conclusive way, but in reality on
superficial and unsubstantial grounds. The first is a sort of
attempt to prove an *alibi* on behalf of the church : " the church
cannot be in any way the subject of the prophetic visions of
Revelation (chapter vi.—xix.) because she is already seen in
heaven in the two previous chapters. All that happens after
chapter v. is subsequent to the rapture of the church ; it must
therefore refer to the Jewish remnant." " The church is never
seen on earth, or anywhere but in heaven, from the end of
chapter iii. till in chapter xix. Christ comes forth from heaven,
and the armies which were in heaven follow in his train." *

Fully admitting that the four-and-twenty elders and the
cherubim of Revelation iv., v., include the church, we hold,

---

* " Eight Lectures on Prophecy." W. T.   3rd edition, p. 192.

that it would be a sufficient answer to this objection to say, part of the church are seen in heaven, while part are still represented as suffering on earth ; or to say " He hath raised us up together, and made us sit together, in heavenly places in Christ" even now, while we still groan, and fight, and toil, and die, on earth. But the chapters themselves supply a more conclusive answer. The church is not only seen in heaven, but she is seen taking part in the action of the beautiful introductory episode of this Divine drama. What is that action? It is the taking and opening by the Lamb, of the seven sealed book. *This action took place while John was an exile in Patmos ;* for ever since, the mysteries hidden under those seven seals have been discovered and published to the world.

Clearly the book is not now shut and sealed ; for we know its contents ; each seal covered or contained a vision, *not be it observed the fulfilment of a vision, but the vision itself.* The visions were not seen till the seals were broken, and the seals were not broken till the Lamb took the book. But the visions were seen eighteen hundred years ago ; therefore the Lamb took the book and broke the seals thereof, eighteen hundred years ago ; that is, *the scene in which the church is represented as taking part in heaven occurred eighteen hundred years ago.* But the church *was not actually* in heaven eighteen hundred years ago, and therefore there is no ground for the assertion that the church *will be actually* in heaven before the events symbolised in chapters vi. to xix. take place. The church was in heaven, *in the only sense in which she will be there till the marriage of the Lamb shall come,* when John was in Patmos. In other words the Apocalypse represents the church as mystically in heaven, while still actually on earth, even as Ephesians ii., Philippians iii., and other scriptures do.

So, while we gladly grant to our Futurist brethren, that a portion of the church is represented as in heaven, in chapters iv., v., we ask them to grant with equal candour that a portion is represented on earth in the subsequent chapters. The one is just as evident as the other ; and to deny it is both to destroy

the dramatic unity so markedly stamped on this prophecy, and
to obscure one of its grandest lessons.

The prophecy is addressed, as we have seen, to *Christ's
servants* and to the *churches ;* the ascription of praise in chap.
i. 5 is evidently *Christian* praise, it is the praise of those who
have been loved by Jesus, and washed from their sins in his
blood. John speaks of himself as the brother, and fellow
sufferer of those to whom he wrote, and John was a *Christian*
confessor, a prisoner of Jesus Christ in Patmos, as much as Paul
had been in Rome. He says he was in exile "for the word of
God, and for the testimony which he held," which expression
therefore means *Christianity.* Under the fifth seal we catch a
glimpse of a company of martyrs who were slain "for the word
of God and for the testimony which they held," that is, for con-
fessing their *Christian faith*, like John ; they were slain because
they were Christians. White robes are given to them, and
they are told to wait till another company of martyrs should
be killed *as they were,* that is *as Christians.* In chapter vii.
we have presented to us a company in heaven, unquestionably
Christians also, for they are gathered out of every nation,
kindred, and tongue, and they have washed their robes and
made them white in the blood of the Lamb. In chapter viii.
"the prayers of all saints" and "the prayers of the saints"
are mentioned ; now prayer ascends from suppliants on earth,
and "saints" in New Testament phraseology means *Christians.*
We have no right in the last book of the New Testament to
revert to an Old Testament signification of this word. Let
the general tone of John's gospel and epistles be recalled, and
his choice of *this* word to designate true Christians, in the
midst of an ungodly world and falsely professing church, will
be felt to be in beautiful harmony. What is the grand distinction made in John's epistles between true Christians and
those who are not ? It is *holiness, saintship.* "If we say we
have fellowship with Him, and walk in darkness, we lie and do
not the truth ; but if we walk in the light, we have fellowship one
with another, and the blood of Jesus Christ his Son cleanseth

us from all sin." "These things write I unto you, that ye sin not." "Every one that doeth righteousness is born of Him." "Every man that hath this hope in Him, purifieth himself even as He is pure." "Whosoever abideth in Him, sinneth not." "Whosoever is born of God doth not commit sin." "In this the children of God are manifest, and the children of the devil· whosoever doeth not righteousness, is not of God." "This is the love of God, that we keep his commandments." "Whatsoever is born of God sinneth not." "We know that we are of God, and the whole world lieth in wickedness." "He that doeth good is of God, but he that doeth evil hath not seen God."

Such language shows that in the eyes of John, practical purity and holiness, *saintliness*, is the grand characteristic ou Christians. When therefore we find *him*, consistently designating a certain body, by the distinctive appellation of "the saints," we conclude that those so called are *true Christians*, in opposition to the ungodly, or to false professors. Where does John, ever apply such a term to *Jews?* Where in the whole New Testament can the term be found so applied? Why then should we assert that it is applied to Jews here? Paul uses it forty-three times, and in every case as a synonym for Christians. Luke uses it four times, in the Acts, and Jude twice in his epistle, in the same sense; in fact only once is it used in any equivocal sense in the whole New Testament. ("Many bodies of the saints which slept arose." Matt. xxvii. 52.)

Besides, we observe these "saints," who are thirteen times mentioned in the Apocalypse, doing and bearing exactly what we know from other scriptures, the saints of the Christian church must do and bear in this dispensation. We find them watching, waiting, praying, enduring tribulation (chap. xiii. 10), resisting unto blood (chap. xvi. 6), resting in heaven (chap. xiv. 12, 13), and at last manifested as the bride of Christ, and as the "armies which were in heaven," clad under both emblems with the "fine linen clean and white, which is the righteousness of *saints*"; we find them associated with the martyrs of *Jesus*, (chap. xvii. 6), a clear proof that they cannot be Jewish saints.

In short, so far from the church being actually and exclusively in heaven, at the commencement of the prophetic drama of this book, *she is seen on earth during its entire course.* She is seen collectively under various symbols, such as the one hundred and forty-four thousand, the two witnesses, the sun-clad woman, the armies of heaven, the New Jerusalem; and her members are seen severally as " the saints." They are seen first in their sufferings, and then in their glory; first slain for Jesus' sake, then enthroned beside Him. Can it be questioned that the saints who pray, and wait, and suffer, and die as martyrs of Jesus, are the *same* saints, the " called, and chosen, and faithful," who are seen with the Lamb afterwards, as his bride, and as his white-robed followers? If they are *not,* the unity of the book is gone, it becomes an incomprehensible confusion. If the saints who form the bride of the Lamb in chap. xix., are not the saints who in the previous chapters witnessed for Him in life and in death, then the lesson written most legibly on the pages of the prophecy,—the lesson that, in spite of ignorance and obscurity, the church in all ages has learned from it,—the truth that sustained millions of martyrs in their protracted sufferings and cheered them in their dying agonies,—the truth with which this prophecy seems instinct, " IF WE SUFFER, WE SHALL ALSO REIGN WITH HIM," is utterly obliterated from its pages! The suffering "saints" get no reward ; and the happy, blessed bride, rises not from a surging sea of sorrow and suffering, to the joy of her Lord's embrace and the glory of his throne. One of the great *morals* of the book is gone, as well as its dramatic *unity.* The exigences of a false system alone could suggest such a wresting of Scripture as this.

This system of interpretation, involves besides, a logical inconsistency. The bride is the Christian church ; her raiment *identifies* her with the previously mentioned "saints," and the "saints" are—a Jewish remnant !* This is as if we should say :

---

* The future existence of a Jewish remnant is not denied, though their history and experiences are mapped out by a certain school of prophetic the army is composed of *soldiers*, they wear *uniforms;* whenever you meet men in uniform they are—*civilians !* Surely they who teach thus should be ashamed for not rightly dividing the word of truth. " Be not carried about with divers and strange doctrines," is an exhortation we have need to remember. Let simple minded saints be reassured, and fear not to claim and appropriate, their divinely bestowed name !

The only way of avoiding the force of this argument is, to deny that the bride of the Lamb is the church ; for it is evident that the bride is identical with the saints, and it is evident also that the saints are on earth, during the whole course of the book. Those who are resolved to prove that the church is *not* represented as on earth in these visions, must therefore not only deny that the saints *are* the church, but seeing the saints are identical with the bride, must also *deny that the bride is the church.*

It is a painful and humiliating illustration, of the length to which the desire to uphold a favourite theory, will carry Christian men, that many Futurists are to be found, who actually *do* deny this, and even glory in their shame in so doing, as if this departure from one of the first principles of Christ, were an attainment of advanced truth !

The bride of Christ a Jewish remnant ! ! It is then of the Jewish remnant that the apostle Paul speaks in Ephesians v. ; it is of the Jewish remnant that Eve, and Rebecca, and Rachel, and Asenath, and Zipporah, and Ruth, and Pharaoh's daughter are types ! It is of a Jewish remnant that Paul says, "I have espoused you as a chaste virgin to Christ ! "

Even so. " The bride is not the figure of nearest associa-

---

interpreters, far more definitely than by the word of God. That the remnant or remainder of the Jewish nation, will be restored to Palestine before the millennium, brought there into great trouble, and prepared by it to say, " Blessed is He that cometh in the name of the Lord," that Christ will appear for their deliverance, and that they will be converted at the sight of Him, this much seems clear from Scripture. The gifts and calling of God are without repentance, and He has not cast away his people whom He foreknew.

tion," say our accurate Futurist friends; "the *body* is still
nearer." "The church is his body, the fulness of Him that
filleth all in all." True! but have ye not read, "he that loveth
his *wife* loveth *himself*"? in a sense the bride is the body, and
the body is the bride. The figures are twain, the truth is one.
Such is the union, that Christ and his church are separate
existences, as are bridegroom and bride; such also is the union,
that Christ and his church are one, as is the body with the
head. "He that is joined to the Lord is one spirit"; "because
I live, ye shall live also." Let any one read Ephesians i. and
v., and say is it not making a distinction without a difference,
to assert that the bride and the body do not represent the
same reality.

Let it be granted then that, fulfilling all these types from
Eden downwards, and realizing all the figures of most intimate
association and union which language can convey,—the vine
and the branches, the head and the members, the bridegroom
and the bride,—the white robed saintly bride of Revelation
xix. is the church of the redeemed; and we claim that without all contradiction, THE CHURCH IS ON EARTH DURING THE
ACTION OF THE APOCALYPSE, AND THAT THEREFORE THE APOCA-
LYPSE IS A CHRISTIAN PROPHECY, FULFILLED IN THE EVENTS
OF THE CHRISTIAN ERA.

END OF PART II.

PART III.

FORETOLD AND FULFILLED.

CHAPTER I.

THE PROPHECIES OF "BABYLON," AND "THE BEAST."—REA-
SONS FOR THE EXAMINATION OF THESE TWO PROPHECIES.
—FUNDAMENTAL, DIVINELY INTERPRETED ; PRACTICALLY IM-
PORTANT.—BABYLON THE GREAT REPRESENTS THE APOS-
TATE CHURCH OF ROME.

THE scope of this work, prevents our attempting to enter
into a detailed examination, of the symbols of the Apocalypse.   The book itself, as we have seen, interprets some of
them, and other parts of Scripture interpret others.   It would
not be difficult to form a tolerably complete dictionary, of the
meaning of the Apocalyptic symbols, by placing over-against
each, passages of Scripture in which the same symbol is employed in contexts which indicate its meaning ; or in historical
narratives, ceremonial observances, or legal enactments, which
throw light upon it.   To search the Scriptures, is to find the
solution of many a difficulty in this book, for it is more closely
related to the rest of the Bible, than would by superficial
readers be supposed.

We proceed, however, briefly to examine, two of the leading
prophecies of the Revelation, a clear understanding of which,
is of itself, sufficient to determine its whole scope and character.   They are two of the most important symbolisations in
the entire series, they occupy several whole chapters, and are
alluded to in others ; they are closely related to each other,
and one of them is *divinely interpreted.*   This is the vision of

BABYLON THE GREAT, in the seventeenth chapter of the book, a prophecy which by its synchronical connection with almost all the other predictions of the Apocalypse, furnishes a most valuable clue to the meaning and application of the whole series of visions. This prophecy has besides a solemn practical importance, rendering it peculiarly needful that it should be rightly interpreted.

Immediately prior to the fall of Babylon, described in the 18th chapter of Revelation, a voice from heaven cries, " Come out of her, my people, that ye be not partakers of her sins, that ye receive not of her plagues ; for her sins have reached unto heaven, and God hath remembered her iniquities." Is it not all-important that Christian people, should be very clear, as to the system thus solemnly denounced by a voice from heaven ? And similarly, immediately after the fall of Babylon, "a great voice as of much people in heaven," is heard saying, with reference to it, "Alleluia; Salvation, and glory, and honour, and power, unto the Lord our God : for true and righteous are his judgments : for He hath judged the great whore, which did corrupt the earth with her fornication, and hath avenged the blood of his servants at her hand. And again they said, Alleluia. And her smoke rose up for ever and ever." If this symbol represents an evil so gigantic, that heaven itself is moved to psalms of praise, on the occasion of its overthrow, should not the church on earth be anxious to recognise it, and to avoid all connection with it?

The deep depravity attributed to "Babylon the Great," the peculiarly solemn adjuration to God's people to come out of her, and the utter and awful destruction denounced against her, all combine to attach great practical importance to the inquiry, *what system is intended by this symbol?*

A perusal of the 17th and 18th chapters of the Book of Revelation, shows that "Babylon the Great" represents a system which should last long, exert a subtle and extensive influence, and be guilty of exceeding iniquity and cruelty. This system must *still be in existence*, seeing its destruction takes place, simultaneously with "the marriage of the Lamb," an event which we know to be, still future ; and seeing also that up to the moment of its destruction, or very nearly so, children of God will be found, more or less closely connected with it, so that a need will exist, for the urgent call, " *Come out of her, my people.*"

This system is prefigured as a cruelly persecuting one, as one that would " shed the blood of saints, and martyrs of Jesus," one on whom the Lord God would ⁀ avenge the blood of his servants." The Lord Jesus Christ, who loves his church, foreseeing the existence and career of this terrible system, forewarned, and thus fore-armed her by this prophecy. He furnishes her with abundant marks whereby the foe may be recognised, and solemnly warns her against making any truce or compromise, while He stimulates and encourages her for the long and bitter conflict, by a view of the final result. He would have his people in no perplexity or doubt on so momentous a question, so He has made this prediction peculiarly clear ; has placed it in marked and intentional *contrast* with another prophecy, which makes its meaning still clearer ; and He has added besides, *an explanation* which leaves no room for the candid student to err.

Let the reader note the contrasted features of the two symbolic prefigurations.

"THE WHORE THAT SITTETH UPON MANY WATERS."	"THE BRIDE, THE LAMB'S WIFE."
" BABYLON THE GREAT."	" THE HOLY JERUSALEM."
"There came one of the seven angels which had the seven vials, and talked with me, saying, Come hither ; I will show unto thee the judgment of THE GREAT WHORE that sitteth upon many waters.	" There came unto me one of the seven angels which had the seven vials full of the seven last plagues, and talked with me, saying, Come hither, I will show thee THE BRIDE, the Lamb's wife.

"So he carried me away in the spirit into the wilderness: and I saw a woman sit upon a scarlet coloured beast, full of names of blasphemy, having seven heads and ten horns.

"And he carried me away in the spirit to a great and high mountain, and showed me," (the bride, the Lamb's wife, under another symbol). (Rev. xxi.)

"And the woman was arrayed in purple and scarlet colour, and decked with gold and precious stones and pearls, having a golden cup in her hand full of abominations and filthiness of her fornication. And upon her forehead was a name written, Mystery, BABYLON THE GREAT, the mother of harlots and abominations of the earth.

"To her was granted that she should be arrayed in fine linen, clean and white : for the fine linen is the righteousness of saints " (Rev. xix. 8).

This Bride is described as "THE HOLY JERUSALEM, descending out of heaven from God, having the glory of God · and her light like unto a stone most precious " (Rev. xxi.).

"And I saw the woman drunken with the blood of the saints, and with the blood of the martyrs of Jesus " (Rev. xvii. 1–6).

The dragon "persecuted the woman," and "the dragon was wrath with the woman, and went to make war with the remnant of her seed, which keep the commandments of God and have the testimony of Jesus Christ " (Rev. xii. 13–17).

As to Babylon, John adds, "when I saw her, I wondered with great admiration. And the angel said unto me, Wherefore didst thou marvel? *I will tell thee the mystery of the woman.* . . . The seven heads are seven mountains, on which the woman sitteth. The waters, are peoples, and multitudes, and nations, and tongues   And the woman which thou sawest is that great city, which reigneth over the kings of the earth " (Rev. xvii. 7).

These prophecies present, two broadly contrasted *women*, identified with two broadly contrasted *cities*, one reality being in each case, doubly represented, as *a woman*, and as *a city*, the harlot and Babylon are one ; the bride and the heavenly Jerusalem are one.

It is evident that the true interpretation of either of these double prefigurations, must afford a clue to the true interpretation of the other.

The two women are contrasted in every particular that is mentioned about them ; the one is pure as purity itself, "made ready" and fit for heaven's unsullied holiness : the other, foul as corruption could make her, fit only for the fires of destruction.

The one belongs to the Lamb, who loves her as the bridegroom loves the bride ; the other is associated with a wild beast, and with the kings of the earth, who ultimately hate and destroy her.

The one is clothed with fine linen, and in another place is said to be clothed with the sun, and crowned with a coronet of stars ; that is, robed in Divine righteousness, and resplendent with heavenly glory ; the other, is attired in scarlet and gold, in jewels and pearls, gorgeous indeed but with earthly splendour only.

The one is represented as a chaste virgin, espoused to Christ, the other is mother of harlots and abominations of the earth.

The one is persecuted, pressed hard by the dragon, driven into the wilderness, and well-nigh overwhelmed ; the other is drunken with martyr blood, and *seated on* a beast which has received its power from the persecuting dragon.

The one sojourns in solitude in the wilderness, the other reigns "in the wilderness" over peoples and nations and kindreds and tongues.

The one goes in with the Lamb˙ to the marriage supper, amid the glad hallelujahs of heaven ; the other is stripped, insulted, torn, and destroyed, by her guilty paramours.

We lose sight of the bride, amid the effulgence of heavenly glory and joy, and of the harlot amid the gloom and darkness, of the smoke that " rose up for ever and ever."

It is impossible to find in Scripture, a contrast more marked ; and the conclusion is irresistible, that whatever the one may represent, the other must prefigure *its opposite.* They are not two disconnected visions, but a pair—a pair associated, not by likeness, but by contrast.

Now Scripture leaves us in no doubt, as to the signification of the emblematic bride, the Lamb's wife, the heavenly Jerusalem. We read, " Husband, love your wives, even as Christ also loved the church, and gave Himself for it ; that He might sanctify and cleanse it with the washing of water by the word, that He might present it to Himself a glorious church, not having spot, or wrinkle, or any such thing ; but that it should be holy and without blemish." " For we are members of his body, of his flesh, and of his bones." The purpose of Christ's love, as regards his blood-bought church, is, that she should be with Him, and be one with Him for ever ; that she should behold and share his glory, being perfectly conformed to his image. Here in prophetic vision, we see this blessed design accomplished, and the complete and perfectly sanctified church, clad in spotless robes of righteousness, brought to the marriage supper of the Lamb. We see her persecuted like her Lord, and like her Lord and with her Lord, glorified. Beyond all question, the New Jerusalem bride represents *the true church of Christ.*

What then must the contrasted symbol, the Babylonian harlot represent ? *Surely some false and apostate church,* some church which, while professing to belong to Christ, is in reality given up to fellowship with the world, and linked in closest union, with the kings of the earth ; a worldly church, which has left her first love, forgotten her heavenly calling, sunk into

carnality and sin, and proved shamelessly and glaringly faithless to her Lord.

Be it observed, that these symbols, a woman and a city,
prefigure definite systems, corporate bodies, not merely a
multitude of similar, but disconnected individuals. The tares
of a wheat-field, the bad fish in the net, may represent such ;
but here we have neither true Christians nor worldly professors, as *individuals*, but two corporations, two definite
bodies. The true church of Christ is a body ; its members
are united in the closest union to their Head and to each
other ; one life animates them : " because I live, ye shall live
also ; " one spirit dwells in them, they are one habitation of
God. The link that unites them is however a *spiritual* one ;
the body, is consequently invisible *as such.* A false church can
have no such spiritual link. The bond that unites *it* must
therefore be carnal, outward, visible ; the church represented
by Babylon, must be *a visible church*, an earthly corporation,
and as such capable of being discerned and recognised. Nor
can the symbol comprise all false and faithless churches : to
the harlot is expressly assigned a local connection—the woman
and the city are one—if we can discover the name of the city,
we shall be able to identify the church intended.

The last words of the angel to John, seem to leave no
possibility of mistake as to the city. " The seven heads are
seven mountains on which the woman sitteth   and
the woman which thou sawest is *that great city which reigneth
over the kings of the earth.*" What city was that ? There was
but *one* great city, which in John's day *reigned over the kings
of the earth.* It was ROME ; and Rome is the *only* city which
was great then, *has been* great, in one way or other, ever since,
and *is* so still. And Rome was seated on seven hills, " the
seven mountains on which the woman sitteth." Her common
name with the classic writers of St. John's age, is " the seven
hilled city ;" an annual festival used to be held in honour of
the " seven hilled city ;" every Latin poet of note during a
period of five hundred years, alludes to Rome's seven hills ;

their names were the Palatine, the Quirinal, the Aventine, the Cælian, the Viminal, the Esquiline, and the Janiculum hills. The medals and coins of the day, *represent Rome* as a woman sitting on seven hills; and her titles show with sufficient clearness, how thoroughly she *reigned.* She was styled "the royal Rome;" "the mistress of the world;" "the queen of nations." Her sway was all but universal. She was the metropolis of that fourth great empire which Daniel had foretold would break in pieces and subdue all things, "dreadful and terrible and strong exceedingly;" and at the time of the Apocalyptic visions, her power was at its height. Rome, and no other city can be intended here; the woman is in some way identified with *Rome.* We previously saw that she must represent a church, now we know what church. The harlot is the *Church of Rome;* for simple minds there seems no escape from this conclusion. And it is a singular and notable fact, that no other city but Rome, has ever given its name to a church, which has embraced many kindreds and nations. Many *countries* have done so, and even individuals; but as far as we are aware, no other *city.* We have the Greek Church, the Armenian and the Coptic Churches, the Lutheran Church, the Protestant Churches of various countries, the English Church, the Scotch Church, etc.; but the papal system is styled, not so much the Latin Church, as the CHURCH OF ROME. "The woman which thou sawest is that great *city*" (not empire or country) "which reigneth over the kings of the earth."

The question, however, naturally suggests itself, If the woman be identified in some way with ROME, why is her brow emblazoned with the name of BABYLON? The answer is evident; the Apocalypse is a book of mysteries; things are represented by signs; realities are veiled; and it would have been altogether inconsistent with the whole style of this prophecy to have written ROME on the harlot's brow. The woman is a figure of a church, a corrupt idolatrous church; that is, the *symbol* seen by John was suggestive of something widely different from itself; so the name with which that symbol was stamped, was also suggestive of something widely different from itself, though mysteriously similar. The harlot is "Mystery, Babylon the Great." That the *literal* Babylon was not intended, is perfectly clear, since that city was neither built on seven hills, nor reigning over the kings of the earth, in John's day. But that the literal Babylon was a most appropriate symbol for Rome, is equally evident. Analogies of the most remarkable kind, geographical, historical, and moral, existed, which fully account for the selection. Both were situated in the midst of vast plains, both largely built of brick made out of their own soil, the one had been Queen of the East, the other was then Queen of the West, Babylon of old had called herself "the golden city," "the beauty of the Chaldees' excellency," and claimed eternity as well as universal supremacy. (Isa. xiv. 4–7.) Rome similarly styled herself "the eternal city," "the mistress of the world." But especially, both had been employed by God, as scourges for the guilty city of Jerusalem and people of Israel ; and to each in its turn, had the sacred vessels of the Temple been carried as spoil ; Belshazzar abused them at his banquet, and Titus engraved them on his arch.

Even had the plan of the Apocalypse not demanded it, circumstances would have rendered it needful, for St. John to use a mysterious designation, in speaking as he here does of Rome. It would not have been safe in the days of Nero and Domitian, to expose the corruption, and predict the downfall and utter overthrow, of their capital. Persecution was already bitter enough, as St. John was experiencing in Patmos ; and *reserve* on such a subject was evidently needful. But in spite of reserve and mystery, the true meaning of this symbolic name "Babylon," was early perceived by the Christians, and divined even by their enemies. Irenæus, who was a disciple of Polycarp, who was a disciple of John himself, says, that "Babylon" in the Apocalypse signifies Rome ; and Tertullian says, "names are employed by us as signs, Samaria is a sign of idolatry . Babylon is a figure of the Roman city, mighty, proud of its sway, and fiercely persecuting the saints." So Jerome and others, in unbroken sequence, to the present day. When accused by their heathen Roman adversaries of holding sacred, predictions of the downfall of Rome, the early Christians *never denied the charge*, but merely replied, that they were far from *desiring* that downfall, since, little as *Rome* favoured Christianity, the *Antichrist* whom they expected immediately to succeed, would do so still less.

BABYLON, then, in this prophecy means ROME; even Roman Catholic writers are constrained to admit this. Bellarmine and Bossuet do not attempt to deny that these predictions concern Rome. They admit it freely, but assert that they refer to Rome *as a heathen city merely*, and not as a Christian church; and they maintain that the prophecy of the fall of Babylon, was fulfilled in the destruction of Rome, by the Goths, in the fifth century. " Babylon," say they, is *Rome Pagan*, not *Rome Papal;* and they defend this position with considerable skill, and some show of reason. This interpretation originated with Bossuet in the 16th century; till that time it had never been supposed by any expositor, that the fall of Rome under Alaric, exhausted the prediction about the fall of Babylon. But as soon as the Protestant application of this prophecy to the *Church* of Rome, was felt to be a tremendous weapon against that church, its advocates were driven in self-defence, to find some interpretation which should turn its edge.

It must not be supposed, however, that the interpretation now called *Protestant*, originated out of the party feeling and antagonism produced by the Reformation. On the contrary, the view that Babylon meant the Church of Rome, was held long prior to the Reformation, and may be said, to some extent, to have produced it. As soon as the Church of Rome began to put forth her unscriptural claims, and to teach authoritatively her unscriptural doctrines, so soon did the faithful begin to recognise her, as the predicted Babylon of the Apocalypse. The earliest fathers of the church, who lived while Rome was Pagan, could not, of course, hold such a view.

Little did *they* dream that Rome, the persecuting pagan city, would ever become the seat and centre of a Christian church. Nor could this application of the prophecy arise, while Rome remained a faithful and pure Christian church; but at the close of the 6th century, Pope Gregory the First made a strong protest against the assumption of the title of "*universal bishop.*" He went so far as to assert that "the first bishop who should assume it, would thereby deserve the name of Antichrist." From that time to the present day, the testimony that the Church of Rome is Babylon, has *never been dropped*; and though, through all the middle ages, this view was held at great risk and peril, we can trace an unbroken succession of witnesses, each one bolder and more decided than the last, up to the time when Luther and the Reformers sounded aloud over Europe the trumpet-call, " Come out of her, my people, that ye be not partakers of her sins, and that ye receive not of her plagues."

The argument, therefore, that the Protestant interpretation is a modern innovation, unknown to the first fathers of the Christian church, is valueless. We must now briefly examine the considerations which prove it to be the true view.

And first, seeing the rise, pretensions, persecutions, domination, and decay, of the Papal Church, have been beyond all controversy *the greatest and most important facts in church history*, is it not incredible, that the prophecy intended to guide and sustain the church all through its course, should not allude to these facts, or even glance at the existence of this church? And yet, if Babylon be *not* the Papal Church, we must agree with Bossuet, that that church is *not so much as mentioned* in the whole Apocalypse.

And wherefore should so elaborate a prophecy, have been given about the character and doom of Rome Pagan, which was sacked by Alaric A.D. 410? Was it for a brief period of about 300 years only, that the Apocalypse was to afford guidance, support, and instruction to the church? Even admitting this improbability, what were the few, who in this

case were alone to benefit by the prophecy to learn from it?
To shun heathen idolatry? Not to bow down to the many
gods of the Pantheon? Not to burn incense to Jupiter? But
it did not need the Apocalypse to teach them that. Surely
the martyrs who died in multitudes before this last prophecy
was given to the church, had learned that lesson without its
aid! The early Christians were in no danger of relapsing into
heathen idolatry; but a *Christian idolatry* was to arise; Antichrist was to sit on the throne of Christ, in God's temple; a
fearful apostasy was to take place in the church itself; it was
an object well worthy of Divine inspiration, to indicate *this
new and specious form of evil*, which, rising slowly and imper-
ceptibly, was destined to attain such gigantic proportions, and
to endure for more than a thousand years.

But there are statements in the prophecy itself, which entirely
preclude its application to Pagan Rome, and its Gothic destruction. This harlot city, Babylon, rules and rides upon the Roman
beast in its *ten horned state.* Now the ten crowned horns, or
ten kingdoms, of the Roman empire, did not make their appearance until *after* the barbarian eruptions, and the sack of Rome
by Alaric. Rome Papal, on the other hand, rose into power
simultaneously with these ten kingdoms, who " gave their power
and strength" to her. Rome Papal ruled rulers, who *voluntarily*
submitted to her authority, as is here predicted. Rome Pagan
never did any such thing, she put down all kings, and ruled over
them *against their will.* When did ten kingdoms agree to *give*
their power to Imperial Rome? Never! To Papal Rome?
Throughout the dark ages ! By her alluring devices, she obtained
their *willing* subjection, and she still *claims* it as her due.
To every Pontiff who assumes the tiara she says, " Know thyself
to be the father of kings and princes, the ruler of the world."

The prophecy further represents, that the harlot shall ultimately be destroyed by the ten kingdoms which had previously
supported her. The destruction of Rome Pagan was not by
old friends, but by new enemies, who had never been in subjection to it, and cannot therefore be regarded as a fulfilment
of this prophecy.

A further proof is found, in the condition to which Babylon is, as represented here, reduced by her overthrow. She becomes "the habitation of devils, the hold of every foul spirit, and the cage of every unclean and hateful bird." Now if the fall of Babylon be the sack of Rome by Alaric, this *subsequent* condition must denote the state of *Rome Christian*, a portrait Roman Catholics will hardly care to appropriate. It is added, that Babylon is to be burnt with fire and become utterly desolate, and that she is to be plunged like a great millstone into the sea. But neither of these prophecies were fulfilled, in the Gothic destruction of Rome, and they must therefore be still unfulfilled; in other words, their fulfilment must occur, in connection with *Rome Papal*, and not with Rome Pagan.

St. John saw this Babylonian harlot in a state of intoxication, "drunken with the blood of saints, and of the martyrs of Jesus;" at which he says he "wondered with great admiration." This is a proof that *he* did not conceive the symbol to prefigure *heathen* Rome. It could have caused him no astonishment that the *heathen city* should persecute Christianity. He was painfully familiar with that characteristic of the Roman Empire, having seen thousands of his fellow-Christians martyred, and been all but a martyr himself. But that Rome should not only become a Christian church, but, *being such*, should be also a bitterer persecutor of Christians, than ever heathen Rome had been, *this* was indeed astonishing, and John might well wonder !

That the Church of Rome deserves pre-eminently to be stigmatized as "drunk with the blood of saints," cannot be disputed. What other church ever established an Inquisition, instigated a St. Bartholomew, and gloried in her shame in having done so? What other Christian church has slain *fifty millions* of Christians for *no crime but Christianity*, as she has done ?

The Babylonian harlot is represented as enthroned upon many waters, which are nations and peoples. She is not only a church, but *a church ruling nations;* that is, she claims a temporal as well as a spiritual sway. She governs the beast

and his ten horns; and so unites a civil and a religious supremacy.   Now this is one of the most striking characteristics of
the Church of Rome, and of that church only.   Other churches
may be so united to the State, that the State assumes the unlawful right to govern *them;* but no other church assumes the
right to govern the State, yea, and *all States,* and to make all
men her subjects.   Rome did this, and does so still, even in
her decrepitude and decay.   She claims two swords, she holds
two keys, she crowns her Pontiff with two crowns, the one a
mitre of universal bishopric; the other, a tiara of universal
dominion   " There is indeed a mystery on the forehead of the
Church of Rome, in the union of these *two supremacies ;* and it
has often proved *a mystery of iniquity.*   It has made the holiest
mysteries subservient to the worst passions; it has excited rebellion on the plea of religion ; it has interdicted the last spiritual
consolations to the dying, and Christian interment to the dead,
for the sake of revenge, or from the lust of power.   It has forbidden to marry, and yet has licensed the unholiest marriages.
It has professed friendship for kings, and has invoked blessings
on regicides and usurpers.   It has transformed the anniversary
of the institution of the Lord's Supper, into a season of male-
diction,   and fulminated curses according to its will.
Pius IX., in the year 1848, addressed the people of Rome thus,
" It is one of the many great blessings which God has lavished
on Italy, that *our three millions of subjects should have two
hundred millions of brother subjects of every language and nation.*"
So that to the present day, Rome, by her extravagant and
guilty claims, does all in her power to identify herself with the
harlot of the Apocalypse, who sits upon many waters, which
are peoples, and multitudes, and nations, and tongues."
    The title emblazoned on the brow of this mystic woman, is
not only " Babylon the great "; but " mother of harlots and
ABOMINATIONS of the earth."   This word *"abominations"*
designates, as is well known, *idols.* *   The literal ancient

---

* See Hyslop's " Two Babylons."

Babylon, was the mother of almost all the *literal* idolatries, that the earth has ever known. The spiritual Babylon is here charged with being a source and fountain of spiritual idolatry ; in other words, it is here predicted, that the Church of Rome would be an *idolatrous church.*

It needs but to recall a few of the world-wide and long-enduring customs of that church, to prove how strikingly this prediction has been fulfilled. Rome enjoins the worship of a bread-god—the wafer, or sacrament ; and anathematizes all who refuse to render it. The Council of Trent plainly declares the doctrine of transubstantiation, that the bread and wine in the sacrament are " changed into our Lord Jesus Christ, true God and true man," and adds, " there is therefore now no room to doubt, that all the faithful in Christ, are bound to venerate this holy sacrament, and to render thereto the worship of *latria*, which is due to the true God. . . . If any one shall say, that this holy sacrament should not be adored, nor carried about in processions, nor held up publicly to the people, to adore it, or that its worshippers are idolaters, *let him be accursed.*" This worship is rendered to " the Host " by Roman Catholics, not only when it is elevated at the time of the sacrament, but whenever it is carried in procession in the streets. All persons are by the sound of a bell, admonished to worship the passing God, and accursed if they refuse. On all the millions of her members in every land, Rome enjoins as a solemn and indispensable duty, the adoration of a bit of bread which a man may eat or a mouse may nibble.

Millions of martyrs have perished for protesting against this idolatry, and asserting that it is blasphemy to say, man can first make God, and then eat him ; a creed more degrading than any that the heathen hold. In the days when the " Corpus Christi" procession was a most imposing and dazzling ceremony, when friars, and monks, and priests, and prebends, and canons, and bishops, and archbishops, in varied and splendid costumes attended the bread-god through the streets of crowded cities, amid the clang of bells, bands of military music, choral hymns, and clouds of incense, it was no easy matter for a heretic to escape detection. From the moment the Host came in sight, until it had passed right out of the range of vision, the multitudes were commanded to bow in profound adoration and awe! And woe to the man who dared to do otherwise, the Inquisition speedily became his home, and the *auto da fé* his portion.

Nor is this the worst form of Rome's idolatry: her mariolatry—her worship of the Virgin, is worse. We hesitate to record the profane blasphemies found in the writings of the Popes, prelates, and divines of Rome on this subject. Entire litanies of supplication are addressed to the Virgin; attributes which are the glory of God alone, are ascribed to her; the most extravagant and fantastic devotions are offered at her shrines; the whole of the hundred and fifty Psalms of David, have been *altered*, so as to substitute for the Great Jehovah, the Virgin Mary, as an object of prayer and praise and holy trust: "Into thy hands I commend my spirit, O Lady, in thee have I reposed my hope! Blessed is the man that loveth thy name, O holy Virgin, thy grace shall strengthen his soul. In thee, O Lady, have I hoped, I shall never be put to shame." This "Psalter of Bonaventura, Cardinal Bishop of Albano," has never been disowned, or prohibited by the Church of Rome.

How completely the human mother has taken the place of her Divine Son, in the minds of Roman Catholics, may be gathered from a favourite story recorded by St. Francis. A monk had a vision; he saw two ladders: one red, at the summit of which was Jesus Christ; and the other white, at the top of which presided his blessed mother. He observed, that many who endeavoured to ascend the first ladder, after mounting a few steps, fell down; and on trying again, were equally unsuccessful, so that they never attained the summit; but a voice having told them to make trial of the white ladder, they soon gained the top, the blessed Virgin having held forth her hands to help them! False doctrines, such as the fabulous "assumption of the Virgin" and the unscriptural "immaculate conception," are freely invented by the Church of Rome, to justify this idolatrous adoration of the creature; the latter, promulgated so lately as 1854, by the Pope in St. Peter's, in the presence of two hundred bishops, filled the Catholic Church with joy. The following passage is from an encyclical letter of Pius IX. :

"But that our most merciful Lord may the more readily lend an ear to our prayers, and grant our petitions, let us ever call upon the most holy mother of God, the immaculate Virgin Mary, to intercede with Him ; for she is the fond mother of us all, our mediatrix, our advocate, our securest and greatest hope, than whose interposition with God, nothing can be stronger, nothing more influential !"

The "Te Deum" itself, has been parodied, in honour of Mary, "We praise thee, O Mother of God ! we acknowledge thee, O Virgin Mary ! All the earth doth worship thee, the spouse of the everlasting Father ! Holy, holy, holy, Mary, Mother and Virgin. The church throughout all the world joins in calling on thee, the Mother of the Divine Majesty !" And the creeds, have in like manner been parodied.

Nor is it the Virgin alone who is worshipped. Images of her—mere dolls, are also adored; witness the degrading ceremony of the annual "coronation of the Virgin," in which the Pope himself takes part; witness the worship of the "Madonna of the Augustinians" and other Madonnas. Mariolatry, among the ignorant masses, is pure image worship, idolatry in its most sensual and childish form, the adoration of a doll !

Space forbids more than a passing allusion to the other forms of idol worship, characterizing the Romish Church, the worship of the "wooden cross," the worship of the "bambino," the worship of the image of St. Peter, the worship of saints, the worship of relics, and similar profanities. When the subject is even superficially examined, the conviction that Rome Papal has exceeded Rome Pagan, in the degradation of her idolatries, becomes irresistible ; and the mind is overwhelmed with admiration of the wisdom and foreknowledge of the inspiring Spirit, who prefigured, ages before it existed, the Church of Rome, as the "mother of abominations" or "idols."

To conclude—in the true and eloquent words of another— "The Holy Spirit, foreseeing, no doubt, that the Church of Rome would adulterate the truth by many gross and grievous abominations ; that she would anathematize all who would not communicate with her, and denounce them as cut off from the body of Christ and the hope of everlasting salvation; foreseeing also that Rome would exercise a wide and dominant sway for many generations, by boldly iterated assertions of unity, antiquity, sanctity, and universality ; foreseeing also that these pretensions would be supported by the civil sword of many secular governments, among which the Roman empire would be divided at its dissolution, and that Rome would thus be enabled to display herself to the world in an august attitude of imperial power, and with the dazzling splendour of temporal felicity ; foreseeing also that the Church of Rome would captivate the imaginations of men, by the fascinations of art allied with religion, and would ravish their senses, and rivet their admiration, by gaudy colours, and stately pomp, and prodigal magnificence ; foreseeing also that she would beguile their credulity by miracles and mysteries, apparitions and dreams, trances and ecstasies, and would appeal to such evidence in support of her strange doctrines ; foreseeing likewise that she would enslave men, and (much more) women, by practising on their affections, and by accommodating herself with dangerous pliancy to their weakness, relieving them from the burden of thought, and from the perplexity of doubt, by proffering them the aid of infallibility ; soothing the sorrows of the mourner by dispensing pardon, and promising peace to the departed ; removing the load of guilt from the oppressed conscience, by the ministries of the confessional, and by nicely poised compensations for sin ; and that she would flourish for many centuries in proud and prosperous impunity, before her sins would reach to heaven, and come in remembrance before God ; foreseeing also that many generations of men would thus be tempted to fall from the faith, and to become victims of deadly error; and that they who clung to the truth would be exposed to cozening flatteries, and fierce assaults, and savage tortures, from her; the Holy Spirit, we say, foreseeing all these things, in his Divine knowledge, and being the ever blessed Teacher, Guide, and Comforter of the church, was graciously pleased to provide a heavenly antidote, for all these dangerous, wide-spread, and long-enduring evils, by dictating the Apocalypse. In this Divine book, the Spirit of God has portrayed the Church of Rome, such as none but He could have foreseen that she would become, and such as, wonderful and lamentable to say, she *has* become. He has thus broken her magic spells : He has taken the wand of enchantment from her hand; He has lifted the mask from her face, and with his Divine hand, He has written her true character in large letters, and has planted her title on her forehead, to be seen and read of all, " MYSTERY, BABYLON THE GREAT, the mother of harlots and abominations of the earth."

The Church of Rome holds in her hand the Apocalypse, the Revelation of Jesus Christ ; she acknowledges it to be Divine. Wonderful to say, she founds her claims on those very grounds which identify her with the faithless church, the Apocalyptic Babylon. As follows :—

1. The Church of Rome boasts of universality ·

And the harlot is seated on many waters, which are nations and peoples and tongues.

2. The Church of Rome arrogates indefectibility :

And the harlot says that she is a queen for ever.

3. The Church of Rome vaunts of temporal felicity, and claims supremacy over all :

And the harlot has kings at her feet.

4. The Church of Rome prides herself on working miracles :

And the minister of the harlot makes fire to descend from heaven.

5. The Church of Rome points to the unity of all her mem-

bers in one creed, and to their subjection under one supreme visible head ·

And the harlot requires all to receive her mark, and to drink of her cup.

Hence it appears that Rome's notes of the church, are marks of the harlot : Rome's trophies of triumph, are stigmas of her shame ; the very claims which she makes to be Zion, confirm the proof that she is Babylon.

We have been contemplating the two mysteries of the Apocalypse. The word "mystery" signifies something spiritual; it here describes a church. The first mystery is explained to us by Christ Himself : "The mystery of the seven stars which thou sawest ; the seven stars are the angels of the seven churches, and the seven candlesticks which thou sawest, are the seven churches." The second mystery is explained also : " I will tell thee the mystery of the woman. The woman is *that great city* which reigneth over the kings of the earth."

The first mystery is the mystery of the seven stars.

The second mystery is the mystery of the seven hills.

The first mystery represents the universal church in its sevenfold fulness, containing within it all particular churches.

The second mystery represents a particular church, the church on seven hills, the Church of Rome, claiming to be the church universal.

The first mystery represents *the universal church*, liable to defects, but not imposing errors as terms of communion ; and, therefore, by virtue of the word and the sacraments, held together in apostolic communion with St. John, and with Christ, who walketh in the midst of it, and governed by an apostolic ministry, shining like a glorious constellation, in the hand of Christ.

The second mystery represents *the particular Church of Rome*, holding the cup of her false doctrines in her hand, and making all nations to drink thereof.

The first is a mystery of godliness.

The second is a mystery of iniquity."

The foregoing is quoted from an admirable pamphlet, entitled, " Babylon ; or, the Question examined, Is the Church of Rome the Babylon of the Apocalypse? " by Chr. Wordsworth, D.D., Canon of Westminster (present Bishop of Lincoln). This book may fairly be called an unanswerable argument for an affirmative reply to the above inquiry. In 1850 the author challenged the Church of Rome to answer his argument in the following words : " If any minister or member of the Church of Rome, can disprove this conclusion, he is hereby invited to do so. If he *can*, doubtless he *will;* and if none attempt it, it may be presumed that they cannot ; and, if they cannot, then, as they love their salvation, they ought to embrace the truth which is preached to them, by the mouth of St. John, and by the voice of Christ." Sixteen years ago, when the above work was published, the author reiterated the challenge, and no reply has as yet been made to it by any member of the Church of Rome ! " *Speech-less !* " " Guilty before God."

CHAPTER II.

The Man of Sin, or Antichrist.

A Great Fourfold Prophecy of Fundamental Importance
(Dan. VII. 7–27 ; Rev. XIII. 1–9 ; Rev. XVII. ; 2 Thess. II.).—
The Roman Power.—Its Last Form as Predicted Here.—
Individual and Dynastic Use of the Word "King."—
An Apostate, Blasphemous, and Persecuting Power,—
Exactly Answering to the One Here Predicted, Has
Been in Existence for More Than Twelve Centuries,
in the Succession of the Popes of Rome.—Origin of
This Power.—Its Moral Character.—Its Self-Exalting
Utterances.—Its Self-Exalting Acts.—Its Subtleties,
False Doctrines, and Lying Wonders.—Its Idolatries.
—Its Dominion.—Its Persecution of the Saints.—Its
Duration.—Its Doom.

INTIMATELY associated with the Apocalyptic prophecy
of Babylon the Great, which foretold, as we have seen, the
existence, character, career, and doom, of the apostate church
of Rome, is another prophecy so closely related to it, that the
one cannot fairly be considered apart from the other.

The woman which symbolises the corrupt church, is seen
seated on a " scarlet-coloured beast, full of names of blasphemy,
having seven heads and ten horns." As the angelic interpretation connects the woman with Rome, by the words : " the
woman which thou sawest is that great city which ruleth over the
kings of the earth," so it also connects this "beast" with Rome;
for, interpreting its seven heads as seven successive forms of
government, the angel says of them, " five are fallen, and one
is." Under one of its seven forms, then, the power here intended *was the ruling power in the days when the Apocalypse
was granted.* That power was, as we know, the Roman Em-

pire; it was by the tyrant Domitian that the Apostle John was exiled to Patmos, and it was under the Pagan persecutions of the Roman Emperors, that the saints of that age were suffering martyrdom.

The past as well as the future history of this power, is sketched by the angel. Five of its forms of government had, at that time, already passed away. The sixth was then in existence, a seventh was to follow and last a short time, and then should come *the eighth and last;* and it was on the beast as governed by this eighth and last head, that the woman was seen seated. Speaking of the "heads," or forms of government, the angel says, "Five are fallen, and one is, and the other is not yet come, and when he cometh he must continue a short space; and the beast which thou sawest . . . *he is the eighth,* and is of the seven, and goeth into perdition."

This scarlet-coloured beast is then a symbol of *the final form of the Roman power,* the last phase of that power whose entire course is represented by the fourth great beast of Daniel. (Dan. vii.) A careful perusal of these prophecies, leaves no room to doubt, that the *same* power is symbolised a third time in the "beast from the abyss," described in the thirteenth chapter of Revelation. These scriptures present a threefold prophetic history, of one and the same power; and that power, beyond all question, is the great, the terrible, the exceeding strong, ROMAN Empire, the fourth universal monarchy from that of Babylon, the one which, both in Daniel's vision of the four beasts, and in Nebuchadnezzar's vision of the image, is represented as continuing, till the establishment of the everlasting kingdom of the God of heaven.

In common with the three preceding empires this power is represented as *a beast,* that is as degraded, ignorant, and ferocious. Daniel, in the days of Belshazzar, long before the first Advent, saw it as a *one*-headed beast, John in the days of Domitian, when it had already been more than eight centuries in existence, saw it as a *seven*-headed beast, fuller detail being naturally revealed to the later seer.

As a matter of fact, the great Roman power, did actually exist under seven distinct and constantly recognised forms of government, enumerated by Livy, Tacitus, and historians in general, as such. Rome was ruled successively by kings, consuls, dictators, decemvirs, military tribunes, military emperors, and despotic emperors ; the form of government being entirely dissimilar under these two last, though the name Emperor was common to both.

This empire is represented as existing first in an undivided state, and secondly in a divided *tenfold* state. As a matter of history, it is notorious that the Roman power has done this. From its rise to the fourth century it was one and undivided ; since its decline and fall as an empire, it has been broken up 'nto many independent sovereignties, held together by a common submission to the Popes of Rome. The number of distinct kingdoms into which the Roman Empire in Europe has been divided, has always been about ten, at times exactly ten, sinking at other times to eight or nine, and rising occasionally to twelve or thirteen, but averaging on the whole *ten.** This is generally admitted, and indeed cannot be denied ; the fact lies on the surface of the history of Europe since the break-up of the Roman Empire, and serves as an important clue to the true scope and fulfilment of these predictions.

The point of supreme importance, in connection with this thrice-symbolised Roman Empire, is (to judge from the great prominence given to it by the inspiring Spirit), *its connection in its second stage* with a *peculiar and diabolical power of evil*, the

---

* " It seems unnecessary," says Wordsworth, present Bishop of Lincoln, " to specify *ten* particular kingdoms into which the Roman Empire was divided ; or even to demonstrate that it was divided into precisely *ten* kingdoms. The most ancient passage of Scripture in which the prophecy of the future division of the Roman Empire is found, is the vision of the image (*Dan.* ii. 42), where these kingdoms are represented by *the toes* of the image. Being toes they must be ten. Hence, when this dismemberment is described in other successive prophecies this denary number is retained : and thus the number *ten* connects all these prophecies together, and serves to show that they all point to the same object." (Wordsworth on the Apocalypse, p. 524.)

rise, character, and actings of which, are delineated with greater fulness, than are those of the Empire itself. It is evident that the " little horn " of Dan. vii., and the " eighth head " of the beast in Rev. xiii. and xvii. represent *some important and mysterious power of evil*, distinct from, and yet connected with, the Roman Empire, in its second or divided stage. How important this power is in the Divine estimation, may be gathered from the fact, that more than ten times as much space devoted to a description of *it*, than is occupied by the whole course and continuance, of either of the first three universal monarchies. These are each dismissed in a single verse ; the little horn occupies ten or eleven, as if ten times more importance were attached to this strange power destined to arise in ʾhe second stage of the Roman dominion, than to any one of the vast and mighty empires of antiquity. Moreover, it is evidently the character and actings of this horn, or head, or power, that determine the doom of the beast.

Before we inquire *what this power is*, we must associate a fourth prophecy with these three, and consider very briefly St. Paul's prediction of the *man of sin*.

" Now we beseech you, brethren, by the coming of our Lord Jesus Christ, and by our gathering together unto Him, that ye be not soon shaken in mind, or be troubled, neither by spirit, nor by word, nor by letter as from us, as that the day of Christ is at hand. Let no man deceive you by any means : for that day shall not come, except there come A FALLING AWAY first, and that MAN OF SIN be revealed, the SON OF PERDITION ; who opposeth and exalteth himself above all that is called God, or that is worshipped ; so that he as God sitteth in the temple of God, showing himself that he is God. Remember ye not, that, when I was yet with you, I told you these things? And now YE KNOW what withholdeth that he might be revealed in his time. For the mystery of iniquity doth already work : only he who now letteth will let, until he be taken out of the way. And then shall THAT WICKED be revealed, whom the Lord shall consume with the spirit of his mouth, and shall destroy with the brightness of his coming even him, whose coming is after *the working of Satan* with all power and signs and lying wonders, and with all deceivableness of unrighteousness in them that perish ; because they received not the love of the truth, that they might be saved. And for this cause God shall send them strong delusion, that they should believe a lie " (2 *Thess.* ii. 1-11)

In this passage, Paul,—in his endeavour to remove from the minds of the Thessalonians, the erroneous expectation of the immediate advent of Christ, which they were entertaining, and which they had perhaps derived from the expression in his previous epistle, "we who are alive and remain,"—reminds them of something he had before *told* them, that certain events had to intervene, that an apostasy had to take place in the church, whose incipient workings might already be detected. It was to issue in the development of a terrible power of evil, which he proceeds to describe, but which he tells them, could not be fully manifested, till a certain hindrance, (and what that is, he adds, "*you know*") should be removed.

The very earliest traditions tell us, that the hindrance here alluded to was *the Roman Empire* as then existing, and that Paul having previously by word of mouth made known that fact to the church, avoided, from prudential reasons, more explicit reference to it in this written communication. He did not wish to expose the persecuted Christians to fresh dangers, by putting into the hand of their enemies, proof of what would by them have been considered, a seditious creed.

Tradition is often an unsafe guide; but in this case it seems peculiarly entitled to respect. The point was both an *important*, and a *simple* one; those who received the information from the apostle were not likely to forget it, and could scarcely err in repeating it; and from no other source than tradition, *could* the church of later ages learn, a fact, *communicated by word of mouth only*, and *purposely* omitted from the inspired letter of the apostle. We may therefore be thankful, that the tradition as to what this hindrance was, is of a very early date, is explicit, and agrees with what we learn from other scriptures; as well as that there is no counter-tradition on the point. From Irenæus, the disciple of Polycarp, the contemporary of St. John, we first hear, that the hindrance mentioned by Paul when he was with the Thessalonians, and alluded to in his second epistle, was THE ROMAN EMPIRE; and from him downwards the fathers are unanimous in this assertion. Paul says to the early church, "ye know;" the early church, (though not the identical generation,) tell us what they knew, and who are we, that we should say they are mistaken? How can *we* be in a position to correct *their* error?

Besides, there is the strongest presumption that they were right, for how should Irenæus and the fathers *invent* such an improbable notion? They were far more likely to imagine the Roman Emperor to be Antichrist, than to imagine him to be the great obstacle to Antichrist's development! Its truth alone can account for the existence of this tradition, at the date at which we first meet it.

The point is important, because his connection with THE ROMAN EMPIRE, is one of the links in the chain of evidence, which proves, that the "man of sin" and "son of perdition" here foretold, is identical with the power described in the three prophecies we have just considered. He was to reign at ROME, else why would the then regnant power be a hindrance to his development? He was to succeed soon after the fall of the Roman Emperors, "*then* shall that wicked be revealed;" he was to emanate from Satan, "whose coming is after the working of Satan;" he was to wield an ecclesiastical power, though succeeding purely secular rulers, "the temple of God," or Christian church, being the special *scene* of his ostentation and pride; he was to be an opposer of Christ and his laws; and he was to be consumed like the "little horn," by the brightness of Christ's coming. In all these respects, the power here foretold by Paul exactly resembles that predicted by Daniel and John, and as two such powers could not co-exist, it must be the same power. Its rise, actings, character, and doom, are here foretold in plain words, while in the other prophecies, they are veiled in symbolic language.

In seeking the fulfilment of this fourfold prediction, we must therefore combine the features given in each separate prophecy, and, recognising the principle of progressive revelation, we must modify the views derived from the earlier, by the later prophecies, and those derived from the later by the latest.

The particulars revealed about this great and peculiar power of evil, or "man of sin," are neither few nor vague; but, like those given by the spirit of prophecy respecting the Lord Jesus Christ before his advent,—they are numerous, full, and most definite. They comprise explicit information as to the time, place, and mode of his origin, and as to the attendant circumstances; they assign to him various and deeply significant names; they describe his character and his actings toward God and toward man; his official position; his pride; his idolatries; his blasphemies; his lying wonders and false miracles; the extent of his dominion; his coadjutors; his persecutions of the saints of God; his opposition to the Lamb of God; the duration of his prosperity and power; the causes of his decay and fall; his end, and his eternal portion. There is added, besides, a mysterious numerical mark, designed to secure his recognition by the wise   This is indeed the object for which this prophetic portrait is given to the church, that she might recognise her great enemy when he should appear, be sustained in her sufferings under him, and be encouraged to resist him even to blood. It is not a portrait easily to be mistaken : the features are too terrible and too peculiar, to belong to more than one incarnation of evil.

Interpreting, then, by the help of Scripture itself, the symbols under which realities are veiled, and blending in our minds the scattered intimations of this fourfold prophecy of the man of sin, and son of perdition, we will endeavour to point out the power, that in every respect answers to the portrait, sketched by the pen of inspiration. That power we are fully persuaded, and hope to be able to prove to the satisfaction of every unprejudiced reader, is, the succession of the Roman Pontiffs, the line of tiara-crowned monarchs, who for more than twelve centuries governed Papal Europe, who ranked as temporal sovereigns, and united under their sway the kingdoms of western Christendom.

As the Futurist school of interpreters hold a contrary view to this, and maintain that the fourfold prophecy in question refers to *a single individual*, and not to a succession of rulers, we must examine the symbols employed, and the statements made in these predictions, to see which view has most Scripture authority.

In Daniel's vision, the power in question is represented as a horn of the Roman beast—" a little horn." Now a horn in these symbolical prophecies signifies sometimes an individual king, and sometimes a dynasty or race of rulers. In the " notable horn " of the he-goat, or Grecian Empire, universally admitted to have prefigured Alexander the Great, we have an instance of the use of the symbol in the former sense ; and in the " four horns," which came up in the place of that notable horn, and represented the dynasties of the Ptolemies, the Seleucidæ, etc., we have an instance of its use in the latter sense.

It is an exceedingly important inquiry, in *which* sense is the symbol used in the prophecy we are considering. Are the ten horns and their cotemporary the " little horn " *individual rulers*, or are they *races of rulers?* We turn to the angelic interpretation of the vision for additional light. " The ten horns are the ten *kings* which shall arise, and another shall rise after them." If the word " king " here, *necessarily* signifies an individual monarch, the question is answered ; the ten horns must be ten individual kings, and their cotemporary, the " little horn," must in that case be an individual also. If this be so, the Futurists are right ; for since we know the " man of sin " is to be in existence at the coming of Christ, it follows, that his career is *future;* since an individual can live only the ordinary life of mortals. *If,* we say again, a " king " *must* signify one man, and not a race of men, then the whole Protestant system of interpretation is erroneous ; then the innumerable multitude of martyrs, confessors, and commentators, who have deemed that they recognised Antichrist, and heard his voice, and felt his oppressions, were deluded, and betrayed into gross perversion of the word of God ; then the Waldenses, and the Wickliffites, and John Huss, and Jerome of Prague, and all their fellow-sufferers were deceived on this most important subject; and then, moreover, the event, which the church of the 19th century has to expect, is not the speedy coming of Christ, but, as the Futurists assert, the very same that the Thessalonians of the first century were directed to look for, a prior advent and revelation of Antichrist.

It is therefore a momentous inquiry, which must not be lightly passed over, *Does the word " king," in common and in Scripture usage, necessarily mean an individual ?* On the answer to this question, depends in great measure our judgment, as to whether the long-predicted Antichrist is a past and present power, or whether we are still to look forward to his reign as a future event.

It is a maxim of the English Constitution that "the king cannot die." Does that maxim assert the immortality of an individual? or does it not rather assert the perpetuity of *the Royal Office?* "The king of England is a constitutional monarch," is a statement, which as much includes Queen Victoria as George III., though she is not a king at all, because it asserts what is characteristic of the whole line of English monarchs. If we read "the king of Prussia was at war with the emperor of France," we do not imagine that the two men were fighting a duel, but perceive that the word is used in a *representative* sense, the "king" including his kingdom, and the emperor representing his empire. In ordinary language, then, the word "king" may have a personal, an official, or a representative force; the context must in each case determine its signification. In treating of brief periods, and trivial events, the word is generally used in the *personal* sense; but in treating of long stretches of history, and great abstract principles, in the *official* or *representative* sense.

As far as ordinary usage can be a guide, the extended sense of the word, is therefore most likely to be the true one in the passage under consideration, which treats of the succession of empires, and gives an outline of the world's history to the end of time.

But we are not left to this presumption; the prophecy itself *uses* the expression in the extended official sense, immediately before the sentence in question. (Dan. vii. 17.) "These great beasts which are four, are four *kings* which shall arise out of the earth." Did this mean four individuals? Nay! but *four great universal empires*, each of which endured for centuries, under a succession of monarchs.

This proves that the ten horns and the little horn *may* be dynasties and not individuals; it does not prove that they *must*. It shows that Scripture uses the word in both senses, and many confirmatory instances of this official use of it, might be quoted. (Compare Jer. xxv. 9-12; xxvii. 6, 7.)

The great question is, How is it used in the symbolic prophecies of Daniel? A little investigation will show that *out of six instances in which it occurs, five require the extended official sense, and in the other, the two meanings of the word coincide.* The *probability*, therefore, is, that governments, and not individual men, are intended by the ten horns and the little horn.

A further argument for the same view is found in the fact that these prophecies are evidently *continuous.* There are no gaps, between the parts of the image seen by Nebuchadnezzar; the ten toes, (which are evidently identical with these ten horns,) are joined on to the legs of iron. The interpretation links the history in the same way. Every subsequent stage follows immediately on the preceding one. There was no interval between the fall of Belshazzar and the rise of Darius the Mede. "In that night he took the kingdom." So in each case. How contrary then to all analogy to suppose an interval of over 1200 years, between the close of the undivided state of the Roman Empire, and the commencement of the divided state, which is presented as immediately succeeding! And this, when it is an undeniable and notorious *fact*, that a tenfold division *did* take place immediately after the dissolution of the old Roman Empire, and has continued more or less definitely from that day to this!

Prophecy foretells that the Roman Empire, when it ceased

to exist as one kingdom, should begin to exist as ten ; history
tells us that it *did* so ; and as we adoringly admire this correspondence, between the prediction and the fact, Futurist interpreters try to persuade us, that the prophecy does not predict
this fact at all, that the ten horns do not symbolise the ten kingdoms into which the old Roman Empire was broken up ; but
that, leaping over the *twelve centuries marked by this fact*, to a
period still future, it predicts the rise, of ten individual men,
whose brief career of a few years, is to be terminated by the
Epiphany of Christ !

Is not this to make the prophecy of God of none effect
through their interpretation ?

And further, as we shall hereafter prove, the *chronology*
of these visions, is as symbolic as their other features, and is
expressed on the year-day scale. The duration assigned to
this great power of evil, is therefore 1260 years (time, times,
and half a time) ; and this alone decides the question. The
ten horns, and their cotemporary the little horn, represent
dynasties, like the four horns of the Grecian he-goat and the
two horns of the Medo-Persian ram.

The symbol employed in the Apocalyptic prophecy to prefigure this evil power, equally demands its dynastic character,
and forbids the thought that an individual man is intended.
It is represented as an *eighth head* of the Roman beast, an
eighth form of government, having its seat at Rome. Now
none of the previous "heads" of the Roman world, were
individual rulers ; but each consisted of a *series of rulers*. Seven
kings formed the first head, and lasted 220 years ; consuls,
tribunes, decemvirs, and dictators, were the next four heads,
and governed Rome in turn for nearly 500 years ; sixty-five
emperors followed, and ruled the Roman world for 500 years
more. Now the man of sin, Antichrist, is to be the last, *and
the most important " head " of this same Roman beast.* If he be
a race of rulers enthroned at Rome, and governing thence
the Roman world for more than twelve centuries, it is in harmony with all the rest. But if the eighth head represent one

individual man, who exercises authority for only three years and a half, there is an utter violation of all symmetry and proportion in the symbol. Analogy demands that the last head, be like all the previous ones, *a race or succession of rulers.*

The Thessalonian prophecy leads us to the same conclusion. The mystery of iniquity was already working in the apostle's day; that mystery which was to result in the development of the man of sin. Now, *if* he be not yet come, and *if* when he comes he is to reign only three and a half years, we have this extraordinary fact; that it has taken Satan eighteen or nineteen centuries to produce this single, short-lived enemy of the church. *Reductio ad absurdum!*

If, on the other hand, Antichrist rose on the fall of the Roman Empire, all is reasonable and natural. Satan worked secretly for three or four centuries, corrupting the church by false doctrine, worldliness, etc., and at last, having gradually prepared the world and the church to receive him, he enthroned the Antichrist at Rome, in a race of rulers, who, combining temporal and spiritual power, and using both to hinder the spread of the truth, were to be for more than twelve centuries, his principal agents upon earth.

It is not denied that the Thessalonian prophecy gives the impression, *on a cursory perusal*, that it predicts a single individual. This is exactly in harmony with the style of prophetic chronology, with that mysterious year-day system which was selected by God to keep alive the hope and expectation of the coming of Christ, throughout the whole course of the dispensation. Had the dynastic character and real period of the son of perdition been revealed clearly, the return of Christ would to the early Christians, have been postponed to a hopelessly distant future. But, though the early church knew (after the publication of second Thessalonians) that the advent of Antichrist was to precede the advent of Christ, they supposed he would be an individual, whose period would be brief; and the expectation formed no hindrance to their watching and waiting for the Lord's return.

Many other arguments in favour of the dynastic character of the power answering to the "little horn" and "eighth head," might be adduced; but these must suffice. *The fulfilment is the great proof.* Such a power as is here predicted, *has existed*, has done the things this power was to do, has borne the character and undergone the experiences here described; it rose at the crisis here indicated, lasted the period here assigned, answered in every point with the most marvellous exactitude to these prophetic prefigurations, and was recognised by those who suffered under it, as *the* power here intended. If a singularly complex lock is opened by a key equally complex in its structure, who doubts that the one was made to fit the other?

So copious is the evidence, of the fulfilment in the history of the Popedom of this remarkable fourfold prophecy, that it is almost impossible fairly to present it in a brief compass. Learned and able writers have filled volumes without number, with proofs, that the Papacy has accomplished every clause of these predictions. Every history of the middle ages, every description of the monastic orders, and of the Jesuits, every narrative of the Papacy and its proceedings, every bull, and every decretal, issued by the sovereign Pontiffs, many a monument, and many a medal, and many a mournful martyrology, lend their witness to the fact. Space oblige us to confine ourselves here, to the *merest* outline of the overwhelming mass of historic testimony, that might be adduced on the subject. We append a list of works from which fuller information may be obtained.*

I. ORIGIN.

The "little horn," in Daniel, is a horn of the ROMAN beast, that is a political power, which rules over part of the territory formerly governed by the Cæsars. The eighth head in Revelation is similarly a head of the ROMAN beast, the same beast that was in power when the Apocalypse was written, and had been for centuries previously. Two intimations exist that

---

* See Appendix A.

ROME ITSELF was to be the seat of this ruling power : it is an *eighth head,* and the seven previous ones had all ruled at ROME; and Paul says that the removal of the Imperial power?*from* Rome, was a needful preliminary to its rise.

As a *horn,* this power was to be little—"a little horn;" its dominions were never to be territorially large, nor its *mere* political influence great; and yet it was to be more influential and important than all the rest. It was to displace three horns, as it grew up among the ten, but these were apparently to be replaced, for the horns are always spoken of as "ten." Though only a *horn,* this power has some of the attributes of a *head,* for its "eyes and mouth" impart to it an incontestable superiority over the rest. In the later vision of John, the same power is represented *as a head,* an "eighth head," representing a former seventh head, which had received a deadly wound. By both emblems it is presented, as in some important sense *a prolongation of the power of the old Roman Empire.* The immediately preceding head, or form of government, was to receive a deadly wound, so that the beast should seem to be for a time destroyed ; but under this eighth head it should revive, and become as strong as ever. The one original Empire was to be broken up ; in its stead a number of smaller kingdoms were to arise ; and cotemporaneously with their rise, was to spring up also this mysterious, peculiar, "little horn," this unique and singularly evil power, territorially small, but yet so all-influential, that it would take the lead of the rest, become their head, and so *reunite, by a new bond, the recently dissevered and independent portions of the Western Empire of Rome.*

Now to any one familiar with the history of Europe from the division of the Roman Empire, into Eastern and Western under Valens and Valentinian, to the time of the Reformation, this prophecy *reads like history.* So exact, so singularly descriptive is the figuration, that if it were proposed as a problem, to present the phenomena attending the rise of the Papacy, in a single symbol, it would be impossible to discover one more appropriate.

What are the notorious facts of the case, facts attested by historians of unquestionable accuracy and impartiality, admitted by Roman Catholic writers, and confirmed by redundant evidence? Briefly these,—

After the reception of Christianity by Constantine, and its establishment as the religion of the Empire, corruption and worldliness, which had long been rife in the Church, increased with fearful rapidity. At the close of the fourth century, the bishopric of Rome was already deeply sunk in these and other vices, and full of earthly ambition; rival bishops contended for the episcopal authority with the carnal weapons and fierce passions of secular rulers, and indulged in luxury and pomp that imitated those of the Emperors themselves.

When the Empire expired under Augustulus, (the hindrance mentioned in Thessalonians, being at last removed,) the mystery of iniquity so long working, began to develop itself rapidly. The spiritual power and pretensions of the Papacy were great, though some time still elapsed ere it became *a temporal power.* When the dismemberment of the Roman world by the barbarian invasions began, Italy fell first to the share of Odoacer and the Heruli. But theirs was never a firm or strong kingdom. The bishops of Rome hated the authority to which they were obliged to submit, and desired its overthrow. In about twenty years from its establishment, this was accomplished, and the *first* "horn" that had sprung up in Italy and hindered (like the defunct Empire) the development of the little horn, was rooted up before it.

A new power, however, succeeded, and for two generations held dominion over Rome and her bishops. Theodoric, the Ostrogoth, became master of Italy, and the Popes for sixty years had to own him and his successors as superiors and rulers. But their own pretensions and claims were rapidly increasing, and keeping pace with the growing corruption of the Church. The Gothic yoke became unbearable to them, and, mainly through the influence of the Popes, Belisarius, the great general of the Eastern Emperor Justinian, expelled the Ostrogoths from

Italy. A *second* horn had now fallen before the rising power; the Exarchate of Ravenna was established, and very shortly a *third* barbarian power obtained the greater part of Italy. Alboin and his Lombard followers held sway over its fairest territories, though they avoided making Rome their capital. Degraded to the rank of a second city, Rome was left to the care of her bishops, whose authority began to assume a *mixed* temporal and spiritual character. They had as yet no temporal *dominions*, but they were striving to take their place among earthly sovereigns, and even already asserting a superiority to them in certain respects. The ancient metropolis of the world had at this time sunk very low in political influence and power.

" The lofty tree under whose shade the nations of the earth had reposed, was deprived of its leaves and branches, and the sapless trunk was left to wither on the ground. The ministers of command, and the messengers of victory, no longer met on the Appian Way, and the hostile approach of the Lombards was often felt, and continually feared. . . . The Campagna of Rome was speedily reduced to the state of a dreary wilderness, in which the land is barren, the waters impure, and the air infectious. Like Thebes, or Babylon, or Carthage, the name of Rome might have been erased from the earth, *if the city had not been animated by a vital principle, which again restored her to honour and dominion.* A vague tradition was embraced, that two Jewish teachers, a tent-maker and a fisherman, had formerly been executed in the circus of Nero; and at the end of 5oo years their genuine or fictitious relics, were adored as the Palladium of Christian Rome. . . . The temporal power of the Popes insensibly arose from the calamities of the times, and the Roman bishops who have (since) deluged Europe and Asia with blood, were compelled to reign as the ministers of charity and peace. . . . The misfortunes of Rome involved the apostolical pastor in the business of peace and war."*

The Lombard sway, in its turn, became intolerable to the

---

* Gibbon, " Decline and Fall," chap. xlv., p. 7o1.

ambitious Popes of Rome ; and at last, through their earnest entreaties, and awful threats, Pepin and Charlemagne came to their rescue, uprooted the Lombards from Italy, overthrew their power, *and presented their dominions as a free gift to the Pope.*

The *third horn* had fallen before the rising power of the Papacy, and it stood forth at last firmly settled in its place on the head of the Roman beast. "The ancient patrimony of the Roman Church, consisting of houses and farms, was transformed by the bounty of these kings, into *the temporal dominions of cities, and provinces;* and the donation of the Exarchate to the Pope was the first-fruits of the victories of Pepin. . . . The splendid donation was granted in supreme and absolute dominion, and the world beheld for the first time, *a Christian Bishop, invested with the prerogatives of a temporal prince:* the choice of magistrates, the exercise of justice, the imposition of taxes, the wealth of the Palace of Ravenna."*

Thus as to the time, place, and manner of its origin, the power of the Popes of Rome fulfilled the symbolic predictions · "I considered the horns ; and behold there came up among them another little horn, before whom there were three of the first horns plucked up by the roots." "The ten horns out of this (fourth) kingdom, are ten kings that shall arise ; and another shall rise after them, and he shall be diverse from the first, and he shall subdue three kings."

The following extract, is from a recent work by a Roman Catholic writer who has given a description of the rise of the Papacy, which could hardly have been differently worded, had he intended to point out its fulfilment of the prophecy of the "little horn."

"The rise of the temporal power of the Popes, presents to the mind one of the most extrordinary phenomena, which the annals of the human race, offer to our wonder and admiration. By a singular combination of concurring circumstances, *a new power and a new dominion, grew up, silently but steadily, on the ruins of that Roman empire,* which had extended its sway over,

---

* Gibbon, "Decline and Fall," chap. xlix., p. 885.

or made itself respected by, nearly all the nations, peoples, and races, that lived in the period of its strength and glory ; and that *new power, of lowly origin*, struck a deeper root, and soon *exercised a wider authority*, than the empire whose gigantic ruins, it saw shivered into fragments, and mouldering in dust. In Rome itself, the power of the successor of Peter, grew side by side with and under the protecting shadow of that of the Emperor ; and such was the increasing influence of the Popes, that the majesty of the supreme Pontiff was likely ere long, to dim the splendour of the purple. The removal by Constantine of the seat of empire from the West, to the East, from the historic banks of the Tiber to the beautiful shores of the Bosphorus, laid the first broad foundation, of a sovereignty, which in reality commences from that momentous change. Practically, almost from that day, Rome which had witnessed the birth, the youth, the splendour, and the decay, of the mighty race by whom her name had been carried with her eagles, to the remotest regions of the then known world, was gradually abandoned by the inheritors of her renown ; and its people, deserted by the Emperors, and an easy prey to the ravages of the barbarians, whom they had no longer the courage to resist, beheld in the bishop of Rome, their guardian, their protector, their father. Year by year the temporal authority of the Popes, grew into shape and hardened into strength ; without violence, without bloodshed, without fraud, by the force of overwhelming circumstances, fashioned, as if visibly, by the hand of God."

II. CHARACTER.

The circumstances connected with the *origin* of the Papacy fulfil then the indications of the prophecy. Has the *character* of this power, answered to that attributed to the predicted Antichrist ? Certain definite phases of evil, expressly noted in the prophetic word, will be considered further on ; but we ask now, What has been the *general* character of the Papal power ? If the question were proposed, Do the prophecies of the Messiah of Israel, find a fulfilment in Jesus of Nazareth ? it might be answered, not only by an appeal to definite predictions exactly fulfilled, but by a comprehensive glance at the general scope of the mass of Messianic prophecy. The coming Messiah was to be a wondrous supernatural being, endued with heavenly power and wisdom, marked by matchless meekness, pure and holy, just and merciful, great yet lowly, a sufferer and yet a king, a victim and yet a judge, a servant of God, and yet Lord of all. By these general features, Jesus Christ was demonstrated to be the hope of Israel, as well as by his being born at Bethlehem, and brought up at Nazareth.

Now the Antichrist has similarily his broad characteristics; his very names imply some of them. He is called "that wicked," or the lawless one, who sets God's revealed will at defiance; his coming is "after the working of Satan;" he "opposeth and exalteth himself," against God, and against his people. He is to be the "man of SIN," the outcome of the working of "a mystery of INIQUITY." He is the very opposite of all that is holy and good, the oppressor of all that love God, for Satan animates him. Further, he is called "the son of perdition," and this name, applied by our Lord to Judas Iscariot, the traitor, would prepare us to find the man of sin, the Antichrist,* *not* in some openly and avowedly infidel power, but in a *professedly Christian* one. The "son of perdition" was an

---

* "Antichrist" is a name used only in John, in four passages, as follows, "Children, it is the last time : and *as ye have heard that the Antichrist cometh*, even now are there many Antichrists" (1 John ii. 18). "Who is the liar (ὁ ψεύστης) but he that denieth that Jesus is the Christ? This is the Antichrist which denieth the Father and the Son ' (ii. 22). "This is the spirit of *the Antichrist, respecting which ye have heard that it cometh* " (1 John iv. 3). "Many deceivers are gone forth into the world, who confess not that Jesus Christ is come in the flesh ; this is the deceiver and the Antichrist." The repeated statements that Christians *had heard* of the coming of this Antichrist, prove that John alludes under this name to the "little horn " of Daniel, and the "man of sin " of Paul. The name itself means, not as is sometimes asserted, an avowed *antagonist* of Christ, but one professing to be a *Vice-Christ, a rival-Christ*, one who would assume the character, occupy the place, and fulfil the functions of Christ. The incipient Antichrists of John's own day, denied the Father and the Son, *by their false doctrines about them.* Etymologically the word does not mean a person opposed to Christ, but *an opposing Christ*, a vice-Christ, one assuming to be Christ.

apostate disciple, who betrayed his Lord with a kiss of seeming reverence and affection. This name would lead us to expect that *a Judas character* will attach to the great apostacy and its head, and lead us therefore to look for it *in the professing Christian Church*, the sphere in which Paul indeed distinctly states, that it will be revealed.

So dark is the moral aspect of the power predicted, whatever it be, that many conceive that *no* power that ever has had an existence, can approach its enormity of guilt and evil; and they look, in consequence, for some future monster of iniquity who shall better fulfil the predictions of Scripture.

When this impression is not the result of ignorance of history, it illustrates the mournful facility with which familiarity with evil, diminishes its enormity in our sight; for it may be safely asserted that all, not to say more than all, these prophecies foretell, has found its realization in the line of Roman Pontiffs.

It must be remembered that the Popes of Rome are guilty before God, not only for all the sins they have committed, but for all the sins they have connived at, for all the sins they have suggested, for all the sins they have encouraged and sanctioned, and, above all, for the sins they have *commanded*. When their personal character and the influence of their examples, are considered, when the tendency of the institutions they have invented and maintained are examined, when their bulls and laws are studied, and their effects observed; and when all these results are multiplied, by the extent of their dominion, the length of its duration, and the assumption of infallibility and *Divine* authority that accompanied it, the impression of unparalleled iniquity produced on the mind, defies all power of expression; language seems too weak to embody it, and the words of inspiration seem to fall short of, rather than to exceed, the reality.

Not only have an appalling number of the Roman Pontiffs been personally, *exceedingly* wicked men, as reference to any authentic history of the Popedom will show, (so wicked that it were a shame even to speak of the things that were done by them ;) not only have they thus abused their high position, by setting examples of sin of the most flagrant kind ; but by their laws, exempting their innumerable clergy in all lands from the jurisdiction of the civil power, they have protected others in sinning in the same way : and they have, by their countless sinful and sin-causing enactments and institutions, *led others into sin*, on a scale that it is positively appalling to contemplate.

Take for instance Papal doctrines and practices on the subject of forgiveness of sin—*indulgences*. The Pope made a bargain with sinners, and on certain conditions, such as the joining in a crusade, the helping to extirpate so-called heresy, the performance of certain pilgrimages, the repetition of prescribed formulas, or the payment of money, he agreed to give them *pardons for sin*. Finding this traffic singularly lucrative,—for what will not men do to indulge in sin with impunity,—it was developed into a system of fabulous wickedness. Indulgences for the dead, as well as for the living, were freely sold, and thus the affections as well as the selfishness of men, were turned to account for the replenishment of the papal treasury. Some of these indulgences expressly mentioned the very sins, which the Scriptures declare, exclude from the kingdom of heaven, and bade those who practised them not doubt of eternal salvation, if they bought a papal indulgence.

The number of years by which the torments of purgatory were to be abridged by some of these indulgences, was extravagant to the last degree. John XII. granted " ninety thousand years of pardon for deadly sins," for the devout repetition of three prayers, written in the chapel of the Holy Cross at Rome. Indeed, such has been the profligate extravagance with which these pardons have been dispensed, and the excessive facility with which they may be procured, that if they had been made available according to the intention of the Church, then must purgatory, again and again, have been swept out,—nay more, it must for ever be kept empty, and the sins of all the sinners that ever lived, must have been forgiven over and over again.

The *sale* of these indulgences for money, was the proximate cause of the glorious Reformation. The intense disgust, and the utter abhorrence, with which they came to be regarded, in consequence of the unblushing effrontery, and shameless trickery, connected with their sale, roused all Germany to resist their introduction, and stirred up Martin Luther to examine into the rotten foundation on which they rested. The deeply interesting story must not be told here—how Tetzel the indulgence-monger, bearing the bull of Leo X. on a velvet cushion, travelled in state from town to town in a gay equipage, took his station in the thronged church, and proclaimed to the credulous multitudes, "Indulgences are the most precious and sublime of God's gifts; this red cross has as much efficacy as the cross of Jesus Christ. Draw near, and I will give you letters duly sealed, by which even the sins *you shall hereafter desire to commit*, shall be all forgiven you. There is no sin so great that indulgence cannot remit. Pay, only pay largely, and you shall be forgiven. But more than all this, indulgences save not the living alone, they also save the dead. Ye priests, ye nobles, ye tradesmen, ye wives, ye maidens, ye young men, hearken to your departed parents and friends, who call to you from the bottomless abyss, 'We are enduring horrible torment, a small alms would deliver us, you *can* give it, *will* you not?' The moment the money clinks at the bottom of the chest, the soul escapes from purgatory, and flies to heaven. With ten groschen you can deliver your father from purgatory. Our Lord God no longer deals with us as God—he has given all power to the Pope." The indulgences sold were in the following form "Our Lord Jesus Christ have mercy on thee, M. N.; and absolve thee by the merits of his most holy sufferings. I, in virtue of the apostolic power committed to me, absolve thee from all . . . excesses, sins, and crimes, that thou mayest have committed, however great and enormous they may be, and of whatever kind. . . . I remit the pains thou wouldest have had to endure in purgatory, . . I restore thee to the innocence and purity of thy baptism, so that at the moment of death, the gates of the place of torment shall be shut against thee, and the gates of Paradise open to thee. And if thou shouldest live long, this grace continueth unchangeable, till the time of thy end. In the name of the Father and of the Son and of the Holy Ghost, Amen. The brother John Tetzel, commissary, hath signed this with his own hand."

For the wonderful and horrible account of the excesses of this abandoned agent of the Popes, we must refer the reader to D'Aubigné's History of the great Reformation, and similar works.

There was a published scale of the prices for which different sins could be pardoned ; and that the gain of money was the only object was clear, from the enormous price charged for indulgences for certain crimes, likely to be committed by the rich, —crimes only by the laws of the *church*,—while the grossest violations of the law of God were excused for a trifle. The royal, and merely conventional crime, of marriage with a first cousin, cost £1000, while the terrible sins of wife murder or parricide cost only £4 !

"The institution of indulgence," says Spanheim, " was the mint which coined money, for the Roman Church ; the gold mines for the profligate nephews and natural children of the Popes ; the nerves of the Papal wars ; the means of liquidating debt ; and the inexhaustible fountain of luxury to the Popes." The curse fell on Simon Magus for thinking that the gift of God might be *purchased* with money ; what shall we say of him, who pretends that he has Divine authority to *sell* the grace of God for money ? Of him, who *leads* millions of immortal souls to incur the guilt and curse of Simon Magus, under the delusion that they are securing salvation ? and who leads them to do this for his own wicked and selfish ends ? Is it possible to find guilt of a deeper die, perfidy of a more atrociously cruel and satanic character ? Even the Jews could say, " None can forgive sins save God only ; " what shall we say of him who professes to blot out guilt, and remove its penalty, from countless thousands who repose unlimited confidence in him, in order to secure his own evil ends ?

"Whoso confesseth and forsaketh his sin, shall find mercy;" what shall we say of him who offers boundless mercy, to those who so love and cleave to their sins, as to be willing to pay enormous prices for permission to commit them? of him who makes plenary pardon dependent on mere outward acts, prayers, pilgrimages, payments, or even on the commission of other gross sins, massacres, extirpation of heretics, etc.? The Psalmist prayed "Keep back thy servant from presumptuous sins, O Lord;" what shall we say of him, who encourages to presumptuous sin, by the prospect of plenary pardon at the moment of death, on condition of holding a candle, or kissing a bead?

That this practice is a mighty and effective inducement to sin, no one acquainted with human nature, and the operation of moral causes, can question : and, worse still, it misrepresents the atonement of Christ, asserting its insufficiency to put away sin ; it denies the boundlessness and freedom of the love of God, and of the Gospel of grace, which offers pardon without money and without price ; it gives false impressions of the true nature of sin, the guilt of which is so great that blood-shedding alone can remove it; it separates what God has indissolubly joined, justification and sanctification, providing pardon apart from a change of heart ; it conceals from view the tribunal of the righteous Judge, and draws men to a fellow-man, sinners to a fellow-sinner, for pardon. It is opposed to the doctrines of "repentance toward God, and faith in our Lord Jesus Christ," as well as to all practical godliness, and is a characteristic creation of "that wicked, whose coming is after the working of Satan."

Its institution and patronage of the *Order of the Jesuits* is another of the exceedingly sinful deeds of the Papacy. This Society, which has dared to appropriate to itself the Name which is above every name, by calling itself "The Order of Jesus," deserves rather, from the nature of its doctrines, and from the work it has done in the world, to be called "The Order of Satan." Founded by Ignatius Loyola, a Spanish officer, cotemporary with Luther, its great object was, to sub-jugate the whole human race, to the power of the Papacy. From the book of the "Constitutions" of the Jesuits, we obtain the evidence that condemns their Order as a master-piece of the father of lies.

Expediency, in its most licentious form, is the basis of their whole system of morality. Their doctrine of "probability;" their doctrine of "mental reservation," by which lying and perjury are justified; their doctrine of "intention," which renders the most solemn oath of no power to bind a man; the way in which, by their glosses, they make void the law of God in every one of its precepts, and give licence to every crime, not excepting murder, and even parricide, all these render their whole system of morals a bottomless abyss of iniquity.

This is no mere Protestant account of the Jesuits; their extraordinary viciousness, has led to their suppression, and expulsion, at various times, by different Catholic sovereigns in Europe. In stating their grounds for such action, these monarchs give descriptions of Jesuit morality, which could scarcely be worse. The Catholic king of Portugal says: "It cannot be, but that the licentiousness introduced by the Jesuits, of which the three leading features are falsehood, murder, and perjury, should give a new character to morals. Their doctrines render murder innocent, sanctify falsehood, authorize perjury, deprive the laws of their power, destroy the submission of subjects, allow individuals the liberty of killing, calumniating, lying and forswearing themselves, as their advan-tage may dictate; they remove the fear of Divine and human laws, so that *Christian and civil society could not exist*, where they are paramount."

In 1767 they were expelled from Spain on similar grounds. They were also expelled from Venice (1606); from Savoy (1729); from France (1764); from Sicily (1767), and from various other States. From 1555 to 1773 they suffered no less than *thirty-seven expulsions*, all on account of *their iniquitous doctrines and evil practices*.

The Catholic University of Paris, in 1643, said of them: " The laws of God have been so sophisticated by their unheard-of subtleties, that there is no longer any difference between vice and virtue ; they promise impunity to the most flagrant crimes ; their doctrines are inimical to all order ; and if such a pernicious theology were received, deserts and forests would be preferable to cities ; and society with wild beasts, who have only their natural arms, would be better than society with men, who, in addition to the violence of their passions, would be instructed *by this doctrine of devils*, to dissimulate and feign, in order to destroy others with greater impunity. *It is a device of the great enemy of souls.*" The Parliament of Paris, in 1762, used language quite as strong in a memorial to the king, accompanying a collection of extracts from 147 Jesuit authors, which they presented to him, "that he might be acquainted with the wickedness of the doctrine constantly held by the Jesuits, from the institution of their Society to the present moment—a doctrine *authorizing* robbery, lying, perjury, im purity ; all passions, and all crimes ; *inculcating* homicide, parricide, and regicide ; overturning religion and sanctioning magic, blasphemy, irreligion, and idolatry."

The book of "secret instructions," generally attributed to Lainez, the second Father-general of the Order, contains directions so unprincipled, that on the first page it is ordained that, if the book fell into the hands of strangers, it was to be positively denied that these were the rules of the Society ! This book gives directions for the attainment of power, in fluence, and wealth, by means of the vilest intrigues : the vices of the rich and great, were to be pandered to in every way ; spies were to be diligently sought and liberally rewarded ; animosities were to be fostered and stirred up among enemies, in order to weaken them ; the dying were to be watched as if by vultures, and promised *canonization* by the Pope, if they would bequeath their property to this Order. Women who were found in confession to have bad husbands, were to be instructed to withdraw a sum of money secretly, to be given to the Society, as a sacrifice for their husbands' sins. To all classes, but especially to the great and rich, any vicious indulgence they desired might be allowed, in order to soothe and win them, provided public scandal were avoided. These and multitudes of similar injunctions, are based on the doctrine, that we may do evil that good may come, that "the end sanctifies the means." Scripture says of those who hold and teach this doctrine, that their " damnation is just."

The same principle led Jesuit missionaries into the most sinful compromises with heathen superstitions and philosophies in different parts of the world. In India they swore that they were Brahmins of pure descent, sanctioned some of the most abominable habits of idolatry, and practised some of the worst Hindu austerities, to acquire fame. In China, they pretended that there was only a shade of difference between the doctrine of Christ and the teachings of Confucius ; and to make proselytes, they taught, instead of pure Christianity, a corrupt system of religion and morality, that was quite consistent with the indulgence of all the passions. Nay, so far did they go, that, finding the Crucifixion was a stumbling-block to the philosophic Chinese, as to the Jews of old, they actually *denied that Christ was ever crucified at all*, and said it was a base calumny invented by the Jews, to throw contempt on the Gospel ! They told the Red Indians that Jesus Christ was a mighty chief, who had scalped more men and women and children than any warrior that had ever lived ! Having no real principles, they were willing to make *any* compromise, no matter how foul, provided they could by it advance the interests of their Order, or swell the roll of recruits to the Roman army.

Now, when we remember that the teachings of these Jesuits are not only permitted, but received as standard authorities in the Roman Catholic Church, and directly sanctioned by the Popes, what shall we say of the so-called Vicar of Christ ? Is not this the deceivableness of unrighteousness ? Is not this the doctrine of devils ? And is not he who sanctions and patronizes such an "Order" of Satan, "the lawless one"? Is he not, and does he not richly deserve to be, "a son of perdition"? Is he not a "man of *sin*" who speaks lies in hypocrisy, having his conscience seared with a hot iron? Where, if not here, shall we ever detect the predicted mystery of iniquity?

That the line of Roman Pontiffs, have been for the most part personally wicked men, there can be no doubt ; that many of their institutions, besides the two just considered, have been fearfully fruitful sources of deep deluges of sin, is also unquestionable; but perhaps nothing more fully warrants the application to them of the distinctive title, "The Man of Sin," than the fact that they have *commanded* sin. If Aaron was doubly guilty because he *led the people* to worship the golden calf; if the wickedness of Jeroboam the son of Nebat, is intensified by the fact that he "*caused Israel to sin*," what must be the dark guilt, and the dreadful doom of those, who have *led* the professing Church of Christ into the foulest idolatry, and into sin of every conceivable kind, not only by example, not only by false doctrines and evil practice, but also by direct *commands*—commands delivered in the name of the Lord, and believed by the people to have Divine authority ; and this not to a few, not as an occasional thing, or during a brief period, but to all papal Christendom and throughout long ages!

This double dyed guilt, lies at the door of the power we are considering. Did not the Popes of Rome, for their own selfish ends, *command*, what Scripture forbids, *the celibacy of the clergy*, and thus lead the whole body, in all lands, into disobedience to God in this respect, a disobedience that was the *direct cause* of the wide-spread and unfathomable flood of moral corruption, that deluged Europe for ages? Have not the Popes, times without number, commanded idolatries, persecutions, treasons, rebellions, regicides? Any collection of papal bulls, presents a very harvest of commands to sin, commands which were, alas! only too faithfully obeyed by multitudes.

And how often have they prohibited, the very things enjoined by God! Is not this a negative command to sin? Christ bids all men, for instance, "Search the Scriptures," "prove all things, and hold fast that which is good." On no one point, are the Popes more resolved to enforce disobedience to the Divine will; in bull after bull they have forbidden the use of the Scriptures in their own tongue to the people, saying, "Let it be lawful for no man whatever to infringe this declaration of our will and command, or to go against it with bold rashness." When Wickliffe published his translation, Pope Gregory sent a bull to the University of Oxford (1378) condemning the translator as having "run into a detestable kind of wickedness." When Tyndale published his translation, it was condemned. In 1546, when Luther was preparing his German version, Leo X. published a bull, couched in the most vile and opprobrious language. The indignation of Pius VII. (and other Popes) against Bible Societies, knows no bounds. He speaks of the Bible Society as a "crafty device by which the very founda tions of religion are undermined," as "a pestilence dangerous to Christianity;" "a defilement of the faith, eminently dangerous to souls;" "a nefarious scheme," etc., and strictly commands, that every version of the Scriptures into a vulgar tongue, without the church's notes, should be placed in the Index among prohibited books. Curses are freely bestowed on those who assert the liberty of the laity to read the Scriptures, and every possible impediment is thrown in the way of their circulation. Bible burning is a favourite ceremony with Papists; and their ignorance of the real contents of the book, is almost incredible. The famous bull "Unigenitus," A.D. 1713, condemns the proposition that "the reading of the Scriptures is for everybody" as "false, shocking, scandalous, impious, and blasphemous."

What must be the guilt, in the eyes of God, of the men who thus withhold the word, by which alone they can be born again, from myriads of perishing sinners, over whose consciences they have perfect sway!

III. SELF-EXALTING UTTERANCES.

One of the leading characteristics of the power symbolised by the "little horn" is "a mouth speaking great things." The destruction of the beast is said to be, "because of the great words which the little horn spake." The same point is noted also in Rev. xiii. 5, where the beast is said to have "a mouth speaking great things, and blasphemies."* Paul similarly predicts of the man of sin, that he will oppose and *exalt himself* above all that is called God or that is worshipped." We must therefore inquire whether *self-exalting utterances of a peculiarly impious nature*, have been a characteristic of the Papacy? We turn to the public documents, issued by various Popes, and find, that they have fulfilled in a marvellous way this prediction; the pretensions they have made are blasphemies, the claims they have put forth, are, to be equal, if not superior to God Himself; no power on earth has ever advanced similar pretensions.

Fox, in his "Acts and Monuments," gives extracts from two hundred and twenty-three authentic documents, comprising decrees, decretals, extravagants, pontificals, and bulls, all of which are indisputable evidence. Twenty pages of small type in a large volume, are filled with the "great words" of the Popes, taken from these two hundred and twenty-three documents alone. What a crop would a complete collection of Papal publications afford! Space forbids many quotations;

---

* "Blasphemy in Scripture means not so much a speaking against God, as the assumption of Divine attributes or Divine power where no rightful claim to do so exists. Thus, in Matt. ix., the scribes said of Jesus, 'this man blasphemeth,' because He said to the sick of the palsy, 'thy sins be forgiven thee.' Jesus *could* rightly say so, therefore their charge was false. Rome, through her priesthood, can *not* rightly say so, therefore our charge against her is true; she blasphemeth. Again, in John x. 30–33, we read that, when Jesus said, 'I and my Father are one,' the Jews took up stones to stone Him, saying, 'for a good work we stone Thee not, *but for blasphemy*, and because that Thou, being a man, makest Thyself God.' Jesus and his Father were one, therefore the charge of blasphemy was vain; the Pope and God are not one, therefore our charge of blasphemy is true. He that says, 'I am the sole last supreme judge of what is right and wrong,' blasphemeth."—"Words of the Little Horn," by Rev. H. E. Brooke.

let the reader judge of the mass from the following samples, which we blend into one, in order to help the conception. If " he that exalteth himself shall be abased," what degradation can be commensurate with such self-exaltation as this ?

" Wherefore, seeing such power is given to Peter, and to me in Peter, being his successor, who is he then in all the world that ought not to be subject to my decrees, which have such power in heaven, in hell, in earth, with the quick, and also the dead. . . . By the jurisdiction of which key the fulness of my power is so great that, whereas all others are subjects —yea, and emperors themselves, ought to subdue their executions to me ; only I am a subject to no creature, no, not to myself ; so that my papal majesty ever remaineth undiminished ; superior to all men ; whom all persons ought to obey, and follow, whom no man must judge or accuse of any crime, no man depose but I myself. No man can excommunicate me, yea though I commune with the excommunicated, for no canon bindeth me : whom no man must lie to, for he that lieth to me is a church robber, and who obeyeth not me is a heretic, and an excommunicated person. . . . Thus, then, it appeareth, that the greatness of priesthood began in Melchisedec, was solemnized in Aaron, continued in the children of Aaron, perfection-ated in Christ, represented in Peter, exalted in the universal jurisdiction, and *manifested in the Pope*. So that through this pre-eminence of my priest-hood, having all things subject to me, it may seem well verified in me, that was spoken of Christ, ' Thou hast subdued all things under his feet, sheep and oxen, and all cattle of the field, the birds of heaven, and fish of the sea,' etc., where is it to be noted that by oxen, Jews and heretics ; by cattle of the field, Pagans be signified. .   By sheep and all cattle, are meant all Christian men, both great and less, whether they be emperors, princes, prelates, or others. By birds of the air you may understand angels and potentates of heaven, who be all subject to me, in that I am greater than the angels, and that in four things, as afore declared ; and have power to bind and loose in heaven, and to give heaven to them that fight in my wars. Lastly, by the fishes of the sea, are signified the souls departed, in pain or in purgatory. . . . For, as we read, ' The earth is the Lord's and the fulness thereof ; " and, as Christ saith, ' All power is given to Him, both in heaven and in earth : ' so it is to be affirmed, that the Vicar of Christ hath power on things celestial, terrestrial, and infernal, which he took immediately of Christ. . . . I owe to the emperors no due obe-dience that they can claim, but they owe to me, as to their superior ; and, therefore, for a diversity betwixt their degree and mine, in their consecra-tion they take the unction on their arm, I on the head. And as I am supe-rior to them, so am I superior to all laws, and free from all constitutions ; who am able of myself, and by my interpretation, to prefer equity not being written, before the law written ; having all laws, within the chest of my breast, as is aforesaid. . . . What country soever, kingdom, or province, choosing to themselves bishops and ministers, although they agree with all other Christ's faithful people in the name of Jesu, that is, in faith and charity, believing in the same God, and in Christ, his true Son, and in the Holy Ghost, having also the same creed, the same evangelists, and scriptures of the apostles ; yet, notwithstanding, unless their bishops and ministers take their origin and ordination from this apostolic seat, they are to be counted not of the church, so that succession of faith only is not sufficient to make a church, except the ministers take their ordination from them who have their succession from the apostles. . And likewise it is to be presumed that the bishop of that church is always good and holy. Yea, though he fall into homicide or adultery, he may sin, but yet he cannot be accused, but rather *excused* by the murders of Samson, the thefts of the Hebrews, etc. All the earth is my diocese, and I the ordinary of all men, having the authority of the King of all kings upon subjects. I am all in all and above all, so that God Himself, and I, the Vicar of God, have both one consistory, and I am able to do almost all that God can do. In all things that I list, my will is to stand for reason, for I am able by the law to dispense abave the law, and of wrong to make justice in correcting laws and changing them. . Wherefore, if those things that I do be said not to be done of man, but of God : WHAT CAN YOU MAKE ME BUT GOD ? Again, if prelates of the Church be called and counted of Constantine for gods, I then, being above all prelates, seem by this reason to be ABOVE ALL GODS. Wherefore, no marvel if it be in my power to change time and times, to alter and abrogate laws, to dispense with all things, *yea, with the precepts of Christ ;* for where Christ biddeth Peter put up his sword, and admonishes his disciples not to use any outward force in revenging themselves, do not I, Pope Nicholas, writing to the bishops of France, exhort them to draw out their material swords? And, whereas Christ was present Himself at the marriage in Cana of Galilee, do not I, Pope Martin, in my distinction, inhibit the spiritual clergy to be present at marriage-feasts, and also to marry ? Moreover, where Christ biddeth us lend without hope of gain, do not I, Pope Martin, give dispensation for the same ? What should I speak of murder, making it to be no murder or homicide to slay them that be excommunicated? Likewise, against the law of nature, item against the apostles, also against the canons of the apostles, I can and do dispense ; for where they, in their canon, command a priest for fornication to be deposed, I, through the authority of Silvester, do alter the rigour of that constitution, considering the minds and bodies also of men now to be weaker than they were then. . . . If ye list briefly to hear the whole number of all such cases as properly do appertain to my Papal dispensation, which come to the number of one-and-fifty points, that no man may meddle with but only *I myself alone*, I will recite them :—

"The Pope doth canonize saints, and none else but he.

"His sentence maketh a law.

"He is able to abolish laws, both civil and canon.

"To erect new religions, to approve or reprove rules or ordinances, and ceremonies in the Church.

"He is able to dispense with all the precepts and statutes of the Church.

"The same is also free from all laws, so that he cannot incur any sentence of excommunication, suspension, irregularity, etc., etc.

"After that I have now sufficiently declared my power in earth, in heaven, in purgatory, how great it is, and what is the fulness thereof in binding, loosing, commanding, permitting, electing, confirming, disposing, dispensing, doing and undoing, etc., I will speak now a little of my riches and of my great possessions, that every man may see by my wealth, and abundance of all things, rents, tithes, tributes, my silks, my purple mitres, crowns, gold, silver, pearls and gems, lands and lordships.   For to me pertaineth first the imperial city of Rome ; the palace of Lateran ; the kingdom of Sicily is proper to me, Apulia and Capua be mine.   Also the kingdom of England and Ireland, be they not, or ought they not to be, tributaries to me ?   To these I adjoin also, besides other provinces and countries, both in the Occident and Orient, from the north to the south, these dominions by name (here follows a long list).   What should I speak here of my daily revenues, of my first-fruits, annates, palls, indulgences, bulls, confessionals, indults and rescripts, testaments, dispensations, privileges, elections, prebends, religious houses, and such like, which come to no small mass of money ? . . . whereby what vantage cometh to my coffers it may partly be conjectured. . . .   But what should I speak of Germany, when the whole world is my diocese, as my canonists do say, and all men are bound to believe ; except they will imagine (as the Manichees do) two beginnings, which is false and heretical? For Moses saith, In the beginning God made heaven and earth ; and not, In the beginnings.   Wherefore, as I began, so I conclude, commanding, declaring, and pronouncing, to stand UPON NECESSITY OF SALVATION, FOR EVERY HUMAN CREATURE TO BE SUBJECT TO ME."

Add to these utterances, which might be multiplied by the thousand, the usual formula of investiture with the papal tiara : " Receive this triple crown, and know that thou art the father of princes, and *the king and ruler of the world.*"   And in proof that the claims here advanced are no obsolete mediæval assumptions, abandoned in modern times, but the unchangeable voice of the Papacy, take a few "great words" from a comparatively recent sermon of the principal representative of Rome in England, Cardinal Manning, who puts the following similar language into the mouth of the Pope.

"You say I have no authority over the Christian world, that I am not the Vicar of the Good Shepherd, that I am not the supreme interpreter of the Christian faith. I am all these. You ask me to abdicate, to renounce my supreme authority. You tell me I ought to submit to the civil power, that I am the subject of the King of Italy, and from him I am to receive instructions as to the way I should exercise the civil power. I say I am liberated from all civil subjection, that my Lord made me the subject of no one on earth, king or otherwise ; that in his right I am Sovereign. I acknowledge no civil superior. I am the subject of no prince, and I claim more than this. I claim to be the Supreme Judge and director of the consciences of men ; of the peasant that tills the field, and the prince that sits on the throne ; of the household that lives in the shade of privacy, and the Legislature that makes laws for kingdoms. I am the sole, last, Supreme Judge of what is right and wrong."

In full harmony with this assumption is the new definition of Papal infallibility : "The Roman Pontiff, when he speaks 'ex cathedra,' that is, when, in discharge of his office of pastor and doctor of all Christians, by virtue of his supreme apostolic authority, he defines a doctrine regarding faith and morals, to be held by the universal church, *he enjoys infallibility*, and that therefore such definitions of the Roman Pontiff are irreformable of themselves, and not from the consent of the church. And if any one presume to contradict this definition, let him be anathema."

But actions speak louder than words ! The Popes have not confined their self-exaltation to empty boastings. They have *practically* exalted themselves "above all that is called God, or that is worshipped." The following is extracted from the "Ceremoniale Romanum," and describes the first public

O

appearance of the Pope in St. Peter's, on his election to the Pontificate. After the investiture with the scarlet papal robes, the vest covered with pearls, and the mitre studded with precious stones, the new Pope is conducted to the altar, before which he prostrates himself in prayer, bowing as before the seat of God. An awful sequel then follows. We read : " The Pope rises, and, wearing his mitre, is lifted up by the cardinals, and is placed by them *upon the altar to sit there.* One of the bishops kneels, and begins the Te Deum. In the mean time the cardinals kiss the feet and hands and face of the Pope." This ceremony is commonly called by Roman Catholic writers " The adoration ; " it has been observed for many centuries, and was performed at the inauguration of Pius IX. A coin has been struck in the papal mint which represents it, and the legend is, " Quem creant adorant," " whom they create (Pope) they adore." The language in which this adoration is couched is blasphemous to a degree. At the coronation of Pope Innocent X. Cardinal Colonna on his knees, in his own name and that of the clergy of St. Peter's, addressed the following words to the Pope : " Most holy and blessed father, head of the church, ruler of the world, to whom the keys of the kingdom of heaven are committed, whom the angels in heaven revere, and the gates of hell fear, and all the world adores, we specially venerate, worship, and adore thee."

The very assumption the Pope makes, to be Christ's Vicar involves self-exaltation. How should one representing the Judge of all be judged by any ? He might *make* laws, but he held himself above all law. Was not Christ King of kings and Lord of lords ? How then could *he*, the representative of Christ, do other than regard all kings, and rulers, and potentates, as his subjects, to be crowned and uncrowned by him at his pleasure ? His dominion he likened to that of the sun, all other dominion being like that of the moon and satellites, immeasurably inferior. Pope Celestine III., when crowning Henry VI., expressed in action his sense of his own superiority to all monarchs : " The Lord Pope sat in the pontifical chair, holding the golden imperial crown between his *feet;* and the Emperor, bending his head, and the Empress, received the crown *from the feet* of the Lord Pope. But the Lord Pope instantly struck with his foot the Emperor's crown, and cast it upon the ground, signifying that he had the power of deposing him, from the empire, if he were undeserving of it. The cardinals lifted up the crown, and placed it upon the Emperor's head."

"Is not the king of England my bondslave?" said Innocent VI. "Hath not God set me as a prince over all nations, to root out and to pull down, to destroy and to build?" asks Boniface VIII. The glorious declarations of the world-wide homage yet to be paid to Messiah the Prince, have been applied by the Popes as descriptive of the respect due by earthly monarchs to them : "All kings shall fall down before Him, all nations shall serve Him ;" and since Christ was God, and he was Christ's representative and Vicar, was he not also to be regarded by men *as God?* Even to this height of blasphemy and folly did Antichrist push his pretensions. Witness the address of Marcellus to the Pope at the Lateran Council : "Thou art another God on earth ;" and the oft-accepted title, "Our Lord God the Pope." And since the Pope by his power of *transubstantiation* can even *make* God, and by his power of ordination can enable his countless priests to do the same, is he not in a sense the superior of God Himself? What adoration can be too profound for one exalted so high? Such worship is accepted by the Roman Pontiffs.

We read, "great is the mystery of godliness ; God was manifest in the flesh," the Most High stooped and made Himself of no reputation. May we not say, in considering the self-exaltation of the Popes of Rome, great is the "mystery of iniquity," man, sinful, mortal man, exalting himself to be as God! And strange to say, men allowed it : "All the world wondered after the beast." It was no empty boast of Gregory II. · "All the kings of the West reverence the Pope as a god on earth." Sismondi describes how Pepin and the

Franks received him "*as a divinity.*" The mighty Emperor
Charlemagne consented to receive his title and empire as a
donation from the Pope ; and ere long the coronation oath
of Western kings came to include a vow, to be "faithful and
submissive to the Pope." Kings and emperors consented,
like our own John, and like the Emperor Otho, and many
others, to hold their dominions as vassals of the Pope, and
to resign them at his bidding : to hold his stirrup, and lead
his palfrey, like servants, to kiss his feet and bow in his
presence like slaves. In his full fame, and flushed with victory,
the great Francis I., of France, in his interview with Leo X. at
Bologna, just before the Reformation, "knelt three times in
approaching him, and then kissed his feet." The Emperor
Henry of Germany, driven to the most abject humiliation by
the terror of a papal interdict, sought pardon, barefoot and
clothed in sack-cloth, and was kept waiting three wintry days
and nights at the doors of the supreme Pontiff, ere he could
secure an interview.

It is difficult in this nineteenth century to credit the records
which reveal, the unbounded power of the Pope during the
dark ages, and the nature and extent of the claims he
asserted, to the reverence and subjection of mankind. If kings
and emperors yielded him abject homage, the common people
regarded him as a deity. His dogmas were received as oracles,
his bulls and sentences were to them the voice of God. The
Sicilian ambassadors prostrated themselves before Pope Martin, with the thrice-repeated cry, " Lamb of God, that takest
away the sins of the world." " The people think of the Pope
as the one God that has power over all things, in earth and in
heaven," said Gerston. The fifth Lateran Council subscribed,
just before the Reformation, a decree which declared, that "as
there was but one body of the church, so there was but one
head, viz., Christ's Vicar, and that it was *essential to the salvation of every human being to be subject to the Roman Pontiff.*"

" Every spiritual as well as every ecclesiastical office of
Christ, was arrogated to himself by the 'man of sin.'" " If

Christ was the universal Shepherd of souls, was not he, the Pope, the same? If Christ was the door of the sheep, was not he the door? If Christ was the truth, was not he the depositary, source, and oracular expounder of the truth, authoritative, infallible, independent of Scripture, and even *against* it? If Christ was the Holy One, was not he the same, and did not the title, *his holiness*, distinctively and alone belong to him? If Christ was the husband of the Church, was not he the same? With the marriage ring in the ceremonial of his inauguration he signified it; and with his great voice in his canon law and papal bulls he proclaimed it to the world. The power of the keys of Christ's Church and kingdom, given him, extended into the invisible world. He opened with them, and who might shut? He shut, and who might open? . . . the souls in purgatory and the angels in heaven were subject to him; and it was even his prerogative to add to the celestial choir; by his canonizing edicts he elevated whom he pleased of the dead to form part of heaven's hierarchy, and become objects of adoration to men." *

IV. SUBTLETIES, FALSE DOCTRINES, AND LYING WONDERS.

The foregoing are not the only characteristics which lead the careful student of Scripture and of history, to recognise in the Papacy, the great predicted power of evil, that was to arise in the latter times of the fourth great empire, and fix its seat at Rome. The coming of the Antichrist was to be "with all power and signs and lying wonders, and with all deceivableness of unrighteousness." We must inquire whether this mark has been visibly impressed on the papal dynasty, whether subtleties, false doctrines, and lying wonders, have been an essential part of its policy. Again the abundance of evidence alone makes reply difficult!

Macaulay says: "It is impossible to deny, that the polity of the Church of Rome, is *the very masterpiece of human wisdom.* In truth nothing but such a polity could, against such assaults,

---

* Elliott, "Horæ," III., p. 161, condensed.

have borne up such doctrines. The experience of twelve hundred eventful years, the ingenuity and patient care of forty generations of statesmen, have improved that polity to such perfection, that *among the contrivances which have been devised for deceiving and oppressing mankind, it occupies the highest place.* The stronger our conviction that reason and Scripture were decidedly on the side of Protestantism, the greater is the reluctant admiration with which we regard *that system of tactics* against which reason and Scripture were employed in vain." This wonderful policy of the Papacy may be viewed as an expression of Satanic genius, if we may use the expression, or as a fruit of human genius. Regarded as " the working of Satan," it is in perfect harmony with all the other workings, of him, who has been a liar from the beginning. It has been by means of a *counterfeit Christianity* that Satan has, through the Papacy, resisted the spread of true Christianity. The Papacy has its counterfeit high priest, the Pope ; its counterfeit sacrifice, the mass ; its counterfeit Bible, tradition ; its counterfeit mediators, the Virgin, the saints, and angels ; the forms have been copied, the realities set aside. Satan inaugurated and developed a system, not antagonistic to Christianity, but a counterfeit of it ; and *as* Jannes and Jambres withstood Moses, *so* (*i.e., by imitation*) he has withstood Christ.

But viewed as a fabrication of human ambition and wickedness, the subtlety with which the Papacy has adapted itself to its end, is a marvel of genius. That end was, to exalt a man, and a class of men, the Pope and his priesthood, to the supreme and absolute control of the world and all its affairs ; to reign, not only over the bodies, but over the minds of men. To attain this object it employed a policy, unmatched in dissimulation and craft, a sagacity distinguished by largeness of conception combined with attention to detail, irresistible energy, indomitable perseverance, and, when art was unavailing, overwhelming physical force.

In the selection of ROME as its seat of empire, the Papacy

secured enormous prestige. "In no other spot, would its gigantic schemes of dominion have been formed, or, if formed, realized. Sitting in the seat which the masters of the world had so long occupied, the Papacy appeared the rightful heir of their power. Papal Rome, reaped the fruit of the wars and the conquests, the toils and the blood, of Imperial Rome. The one had laboured and gone to her grave, the other arose and entered into her labours. The Pontiffs were perpetually reminding the world, that they were the successors of the Cæsars, that the two Romes were linked by an indissoluble bond, and that to the latter had descended the heritage of glory and dominion acquired by the former. . . . The Pontiffs also claimed to be successors of the Apostles : a more masterly stroke of policy still. As the successor of Peter, the Pope was greater, than as the successor of Cæsar. The one made him a king, the other made him king of kings ; the one gave him the power of the sword, the other invested him with the still more sacred authority of the keys. The Papacy is the ghost of Peter crowned with the shadowy diadem of the old Cæsars." *

Every doctrine and dogma of the Papacy is framed with a similar design, *to exalt the priesthood*, at the expense of the intellect, the conscience, and the eternal well-being, of mankind. By the doctrine of *tradition*, the priest becomes the channel of Divine revelation, and by that of *inherent efficacy in the sacraments*, the channel of Divine grace : men are wholly dependent on the priesthood, for a knowledge of the will of God, and an enjoyment of the salvation of God.

Recognising that no religion enjoining a high morality could ever be a popular one, in a world of sinners, who love sin, the Papacy presented a religion of ritual observance, instead of one of spiritual power : heaven could be secured by outward acts ; obedience to the church, not a change of heart, was the great essential of salvation. Men naturally seek *to earn* heaven ;

* Wylie's " Papacy," p. 414.

Popery sets them to work to do so, teaching salvation by merit, and denying salvation by faith. " It provides convents for the ascetic and the mystic ; carnivals for the gay ; missions for the enthusiast ; penances for the man suffering from remorse ; sisterhoods of mercy for the benevolent; crusades for the chivalrous ; secret missions for the man whose genius lies in intrigue ; the Inquisition, with its racks and screws, for the cruel bigot ; indulgences for the man of wealth and pleasure ; purgatory to awe the refractory, and frighten the vulgar ; and a subtle theology for the casuist and the dialectitian." * Its marvellous flexibility, its adaptation of its doctrines to all classes and conditions of men, is one phase of the exceeding *subtlety* of the Papacy. Many others might be adduced, as for instance its encouragement of ignorance, in the people, in order to the production and maintenance of that superstition, which alone makes spiritual imposture easy or even practicable.

The absurd and childish doctrine of *purgatory*, unknown in the church till the end of the sixth century, could never have obtained currency, but for the aid of fictitious miracles,— visions of departed persons broiling on gridirons, roasting on spits shivering in water, or burning in fire, etc. Such "lying wonders" were therefore freely invented by the priests, and readily credited by the people ; and by their means the doctrine, which was one of the most *lucrative* ever invented, was soon firmly established. Time would fail us, to speak of the "lying wonders" connected with the relics, shrines of pilgrimage, and false miracles of the Papacy : their name is legion, and their folly is exceeded by their guilt.

V. PERSECUTIONS.

We must pass on to note *its persecutions of the saints*, for in the prophecies of Antichrist under consideration, this feature is prominently conspicuous. Daniel says of the "little horn " that "he shall *wear out* the saints of the Most High, and they shall be given into his hand." And John says, " It was given

---

* Wylie's " Papacy," p. 414.

him to make war with the saints, and to overcome them," and that he "opened his mouth to blaspheme," or speak evil of them.

Now it is a notorious fact that the Church of Rome considers heresy (*i.e.*, any dissent from her teachings,) the worst crime of which a man can be guilty; she asserts that no heretic can be saved. She teaches that no faith is to be kept with heretics, that they are to be cut off from all social intercourse, deprived of all natural, civil, and political rights; that they forfeit all claim and right to their property; that they are to be put to death, and that if they have died a natural death, their very bones and dust are to be taken up and burnt. And who are to be regarded as heretics? Let the bull In Coena Domini (or, "at the supper of the Lord") answer. Every Thursday of Passion Week, that is the day before Good Friday, this bull is read in the presence of the Pope, Cardinals, Bishops, and a crowd of people. His Holiness appears with a pair of peacock's feathers, one on each side of his head, and when the bull is finished, flings a lighted torch into the court of the palace, to make the effect of the anathema the more dreadful. The object of the bull, as defined by Pope Paul III., is "to preserve the purity of the Christian religion, and to maintain the unity of the faithful." The following is one of its clauses. "We excommunicate and anathematize in the name of God Almighty, Father, Son, and Holy Ghost, and by the authority of the blessed Apostles, Peter and Paul, and by our own, all *Hussites, Wickliffites, Lutherans, Zuinglians, Calvinists, Anabaptists, Huguenots, Trinitarians, and apostates from the faith, and all other heretics,* by whatsoever name they are called, and of whatsoever sect they be, as also their adherents, receivers, favourers, and generally all defenders of them; together with all who without our authority, or that of the Apostolic See, knowingly read, keep, print, or any way for any cause whatsoever, publicly or privately, on any pretext or colour, defend their books, containing heresy or treating of religion."

These are the *principles* of Popery, as stated by acknowledged authorities of her church, and pronounced applicable to all times.

As to the *practice* of this unchangeable church, there is *not a statement in the following quotation which history does not abundantly substantiate.* "As some luxurious emperors of Rome exhausted the whole art of pleasure, so that a reward was promised to any who should invent a new one ; so have Romish persecutors exhausted all the art of pain, so that it will now be difficult to discover or invent a new kind of it, which they have not already practised upon those marked out for heretics. They have been shot, stabbed, stoned, drowned, beheaded, hanged, drawn, quartered, impaled, burnt, or buried alive, roasted on spits, baked in ovens, thrown into furnaces, tumbled over precipices, cast from the tops of towers, sunk in mire and pits, starved with hunger and cold, hung on tenter hooks, suspended by the hair of the head, by the hands or feet, stuffed and blown up with gunpowder, ripped with swords and sickles, tied to the tails of horses, dragged over streets and sharp flints, broken on the wheel, beaten on anvils with hammers, blown with bellows, bored with hot irons, torn piecemeal by red-hot pincers, slashed with knives, hacked with axes, hewed with chisels, planed with planes, pricked with forks, stuck from head to foot with pins, choked with water, lime, rags, urine, excrements, or mangled pieces of their own bodies crammed down their throats, shut up in caves and dungeons, tied to stakes, nailed to trees, tormented with lighted matches, scalding oil, burning pitch, melted lead, etc. They have been flayed alive, had their flesh scalped and torn from their bones ; they have been trampled and danced upon, till their bowels have been forced out, their guts have been tied to trees and pulled forth by degrees ; their heads twisted with cords till the blood, or even their eyes started out ; strings have been drawn through their noses, and they led about like swine, and butchered like sheep. To dig out eyes, tear off nails, cut off ears, lips, tongues, arms, breasts, etc., has been but ordinary sport with

Rome's converters and holy butchers. Persons have been compelled to lay violent hands on their dearest friends, to kill or to cast into the fire their parents, husbands, wives, children, etc., or to look on whilst they have been most cruelly and shamefully abused. Women and young maids have also suffered such barbarities, accompanied with all the imaginable indignities, insults, shame, and pungent pangs, to which their sex could expose them. Tender babes have been whipped, starved, drowned, stabbed, and burnt to death, dashed against trees and stones, torn limb from limb, carried about on the point of spikes and spears, and thrown to the dogs and swine." If such treatment as this, inflicted on successive generations of disciples of Christ, for centuries together, be not " wearing out the saints of the Most High," what could be? History affords no parallel, for the Pagan persecutions were brief in comparison to the Papal.

The following is one of the authorized curses, published in the Romish Pontifical, to be pronounced on heretics by Romish priests, " May God Almighty and all his saints curse them, with the curse with which the devil and his angels are cursed. Let them be destroyed out of the land of the living. Let the vilest of deaths come upon them, and let them descend alive into the pit. Let their seed be destroyed from the earth ; by hunger, and thirst, and nakedness, and all distress, let them perish. May they have all misery, and pestilence, and torment. Let all they have be cursed. Always and everywhere let them be cursed. Speaking and silent let them be cursed. Within and without let them be cursed. By land and by sea let them be cursed. From the crown of the head to the sole of the foot, let them be cursed. Let their eyes become blind, let their ears become deaf, let their mouth become dumb, let their tongue cleave to their jaws, let not their hands handle, let not their feet walk. Let all the members of the body be cursed. Cursed let them be standing, lying, from this time forth for ever ; and thus let their candle be extinguished in the presence of God, at the day of judgment

Let their burial be with dogs and asses. Let hungry wolves devour their corpses. Let the devil and his angels be their companions for ever. Amen, amen; so be it, so let it be."

Entire volumes would be requisite to give an adequate idea of the way in which the Papacy has worn out and overcome the saints of the Most High, by her cruel persecutions. The Apocalypse presents us with two great companies of martyrs (Rev. vi. 9 ; xv. 2) one slain by Pagan Emperors, on account of their testimony against heathen idolatry ; the other slain by Christian Popes, on account of their testimony against Christian idolatry, against the corruptions and false doctrines of the Papacy. The latter company in number *enormously exceeds the former;* it cannot be numbered by hundreds, or by thousands, or by tens of thousands, or by hundreds of thousands, or even by millions ; we must rise to *tens of millions,* to express the multitude of the saints of Christ, whose blood has been shed, by the self-styled Vicar of Christ on earth !

The INQUISITION,—a name at which humanity has learned to shudder,—is a long and supremely cruel and wicked history compressed into one word! Instituted for the avowed purpose of suppressing heresy, it was established in every country which submitted to Papal authority. In Spain alone it has been proved by the careful statistical investigations of Llorente, that between the years 1481 and 1808 over *three hundred and forty-one thousand persons* were condemned by this " Holy Office," of whom 31,912 were burned alive, 17,000 burned in effigy, and nearly 300,000 tortured and condemned to severe penances. Every Catholic country in Europe, Asia, and America, had its INQUISITION, and its consequent unexplained arrests, indefinitely long imprisonments of innocent persons, its secret investigations, its horrible torture chambers, and dreadful dungeons, its *auto da fés,* or burnings of obstinate heretics, and its thousand nameless cruelties and injustices.

When the French took Toledo, and broke open the Inquisition prison there, we read, " Graves seemed to open, and pale figures like ghosts issued from dungeons which emitted a sepulchral odour. Bushy beards hanging down over the breast, and nails grown like birds' claws, disfigured the skeletons, who with labouring bosoms inhaled, for the first time for a long series of years, the fresh air. Many of them were reduced to cripples, the head inclined forward, and the arms and hands hanging down, rigid and helpless : they had been confined in dens so low they could not rise up in them : in spite of all the care of the surgeons, many of them expired the same day. The light of the sun made a particularly painful impression on the optic nerve. On the following day General Lasalle minutely inspected the place, attended by several officers of his staff. The number of machines for torture thrilled even men inured to the battle-field with horror ; only one of these, unique in its kind for refined cruelty, seems deserving of more particular notice.

" In a recess in a subterraneous vault, contiguous to the private hall for examinations, stood a wooden figure, made by the hands of monks, and representing the Virgin Mary. A gilded glory encompassed her head, and in her right hand she held a banner. It struck us all, at first sight, as suspicious, that, notwithstanding the silken robe, descending on each side in ample folds from her shoulders, she should wear a sort of cuirass. On closer scrutiny, it appeared that the fore part of the body was stuck full of extremely sharp nails and small narrow knife-blades, with the points of both turned towards the spectator. The arms and hands were jointed ; and machinery behind the partition set the figure in motion. One of the servants of the Inquisition was compelled, by command of the General, to work the *machine*, as he termed it. When the figure extended her arms, as though to press some one most lovingly to her heart, the well-filled knapsack of a Polish grenadier was made to supply the place of a living victim. The statue hugged it closer and closer ; and when the attendant, agreeably to orders, made the figure un-

clasp her arms and return to her former position, the knapsack was perforated to the depth of two or three inches, and
remained hanging on the points of the nails and knife-blades.
To such an infernal purpose, and in a building erected in
honour of the true faith, was the Madonna rendered subservient !"

Gigantic enterprises of EXTERMINATION of Christian confessors were from time to time undertaken by the Popes of Rome.
Witness the bloody " crusade," against the Albigenses, described by Sismondi, and the religious wars against the Waldenses, narrated by Monastier and others. Pope Alexander
III. began the persecution against these " saints," whose only
crime was, that they held the truth of the Gospel and read the
Scriptures ; he confined himself to excommunications, anathemas, and decrees, by which they were rendered incapable of
holding offices of trust, honour, or profit, and by which their
lands were seized, and their goods confiscated. Innocent III.,
finding that they grew and prospered in spite of this, instigated
sterner repressive measures ; and the fierce and bloodthirsty
cruelty with which his behests were obeyed, has added to
history one of its very darkest chapters.

The populous and beautiful Val Louise (Dauphiny) was
deserted on the approach of the Papal army, the Waldenses
fleeing to the caves of the mountains. They were followed,
caught, thrown headlong over the precipices, dashed to pieces ;
others who took refuge in caves where their persecutors could
not follow them, were suffocated with the smoke of huge fires,
lit in the cavern's mouth ; 3000 men, women, and children,
with 400 infants, were found so smothered in one cave, at one
time ! At the Lateran Council, A.D. 1179, a decree was issued
against all heretics of whatever name, anthematizing them, and
forbidding any to harbour them while alive, or give them
Christian burial when dead. Lucius III. gave them up to the
secular arm, and to the Inquisition, for detection and suppression. Innocent III. charged every bishop to gird himself for
the work of extermination, and to employ both princes and

populace in the cause. Then followed the proclamation of a Crusade, with all its horrors, against the faithful witnesses for the truth. At the siege and sack of Beziers alone, sixty thousand Protestants were slain, and this was a specimen of the whole crusade. Vassals, were by the Pope absolved from allegiance to their superiors, should these latter refuse to join in the work of extermination ; the lands and goods of heretics, were given to their murderers ; and plenary indulgence to the day of death, was granted to every one taking part in the persecution.

The dreadful sufferings inflicted on the peaceful and industrious Vaudois, in the fifteenth and sixteenth centuries, are too well known to need repetition. The wretched villagers, surprised in the night, and hunted from rock to rock, by the light of the flames which were consuming their homes, escaped one snare, to fall into another. Surrender did not save the men from slaughter, nor the women from brutal outrage at which nature revolts ! All were forbidden to afford succour to the fugitives. At Cabrières more than 700 men were butchered in cold blood, and the women were burned alive in their houses.

The "bloody ordinance of Gastaldo," issued in 1655, decreed, that all who would not embrace the Catholic faith, must quit the valleys within a few days. Upwards of 1000 families were driven by this edict from their homes, in the depth of winter, to the shelterless recesses of the Alpine heights. The general to whom the execution of the edict was entrusted, fearing the consequences, if the Vaudois should resist in the defiles of their mountain passes, resorted to treachery, persuaded the villages, by fair promises, to receive his 15,000 soldiers in small detachments ; and when the simple, unsuspicious people, complied with his desire, he ordered the massacre, which filled Protestant Europe with horror. Four thousand victims suffered death, under cruelties too horrible to relate, and the carnage was repeated in valley after valley.

In 1686, a fresh persecution was organised against the remaining Vaudois, by the Duke of Savoy; terrible devastation was carried again into their quiet vales; unheard-of barbarities committed, on every age and sex; life could be saved only by submission to overwhelming force, and a remnant did submit. The whole Protestant population were consigned to prison, and their lands, houses, and possessions, were divided among the Catholic soldiers of Victor Amadeus. The gaols were so crowded, and the treatment of the prisoners so cruel, that multitudes of the poor captives perished; they slept on bare bricks, in dungeons thronged to suffocation, in the intense heat of summer; and the disease and death engendered were horrible in the extreme, so that in six months only 3000 of the Vaudois survived. Urgent representations from the Protestant powers of Europe, procured the liberation of this remnant; but the wretched exiles were sent out destitute, after having been, in many cases, deprived of their children, and of their pastors. They turned their steps to Switzerland, and had to make their way over the Alps, in the depth of winter; hundreds perished of cold and hunger on the road. Three years later, a little band of eight hundred of these intrepid exiles, made their way back to their valleys, under the leadership of Arnaud, who himself recounts their triumph over apparently insuperable difficulties. *

Is further proof of the persecuting spirit of the Roman Pontiffs needed? Look at IRELAND in 1641, when the Romanist Bishops, proclaimed a "war of religion," and incited the people by every means in their power, to massacre the Protestants. North, south, east, and west, throughout the island, Protestant blood flowed in rivers; houses were reduced to ashes, villages and towns all but destroyed, in the deadly strife; the very cattle of the Protestants were inhumanly tortured; the only burial allowed to the martyrs was the burial of the living, and their persecutors took a fiendish delight, in hearing their cries and groans, issuing from the

---

* "Glorieuse Rentrée des Vaudois dans leurs Vallées" : Arnaud.

earth. Popish children were taught to pluck out the eyes of their Protestant playmates, to hack their little limbs, and hunt them to death. Some were forced to murder their own relatives, and then butchered themselves over the bleeding remains ; the last sounds that reached their dying ears, being the savage assurances of the priests, that these agonies were but the commencement of eternal torment. Dublin alone escaped, and became a refuge for the distressed, but all its Popish inhabitants were forbidden, under pain of the direst curse, to afford the slightest succour to the sufferers. Thousands died of cold and hunger ; thousands more emigrated, and perished in the wintry weather, from hunger and exposure.

In Armagh, four thousand Protestants were drowned; in Cavan, the road for twelve miles together was stained red with the gory track of the wounded fugitives ; sixty children were abandoned in the flight, by parents fiercely hunted by the blood-hounds of the Papacy, who declared that any who helped or even buried these little ones, should be buried by their sides ; seventeen adults were buried alive at Fermanagh, and in Kilkenny seventy-two. In the province of Ulster alone, upwards of one hundred and fifty-four thousand Protestants, were massacred or expelled from Ireland. O'Niel, the Romish Primate of all Ireland, declared this rebellion to be " a pious and lawful war;" and Pope Urban VIII., by a bull, dated May, 1643, granted "full and absolute remission of all their sins," to those who had taken part in " gallantly doing what in them lay, to extirpate and wholly root out, the pestiferous leaven of heretical contagion." *

But France was the scene of the greatest national crime which even the Papacy has ever instigated and approved, THE MASSACRE OF ST. BARTHOLOMEW'S DAY, planned by the infamous Catherine de Medicis, and ordered by her weak and wretched son, Charles IX. The horrible story of this unparalleled atrocity, is too well known to need recounting

---

* " History of the Attempts of the Irish Papists to Extirpate the Protestants in the kingdom of Ireland." By Sir John Temple, Master of the Rolls.

here. In Paris alone the blood of over ten thousand innocent Protestant citizens, deluged the streets, and for a whole week the shouts of "Kill, kill," resounded on every hand. In Rouen from one to two thousand were slaughtered; and a similar number at Lyons, at Orleans five hundred; every town and village became a scene of carnage. Some writers compute that at least one hundred thousand persons fell in this terrible massacre; others put the number lower. At the most moderate calculation, thirty to forty thousand Protestants, perished on account of their faith, in that fatal month of August, 1572. All the Princes of Europe expressed their indignation at the foul treachery, excepting the King of Spain and the Pope. The former wrote to congratulate Charles IX., on the "triumph of the Church militant," which his conduct had secured. The Pope, Gregory XIII., who was privy to the plot, celebrated a TE DEUM on hearing the news, ordered a jubilee, and a solemn procession, which he accompanied himself, to thank God for this glorious success; he sent a nuncio to Paris to congratulate the king, had a medal struck in memory of the happy event, and a picture of the massacre, painted and hung in the Vatican. A scroll at the top contained a Latin inscription to the effect, *The Pontiff approves the murder of Coligny*.

Tremendous as this blow had been, it did not crush Protestantism in France; a twelfth part of the entire population of the country were still attached to the Reformed religion. Henry IV., on ascending the throne, issued, in 1598, the Edict of Nantes, which placed Protestants on an equal footing with Catholics in regard to civil rights, and the free exercise of their religion. The Huguenots soon began to recover from the effects of past persecutions; but the gleam of prosperity was of short duration. With the murder of Henry IV. it passed away, and by the loss of La Rochelle the political power of the Protestants was extinguished. Oppression and injustice gradually increased, till, on the accession of Louis XIV., they were so galling, that eight hundred thousand of the best

Huguenot families of France, emigrated to England and other countries, to find the liberty to worship God denied them in their own. At last, in 1685, the Edict of Nantes, and all the other concessions made to the Reformed, were *revoked completely;* their churches were demolished; their meetings prohibited; their schools closed; their children, from five to sixteen, taken from them to be educated as Catholics; while at the same time they were forbidden to emigrate. A reward of five thousand five hundred livres was offered, for information leading to the capture of any one of the Huguenot preachers. Persecution waxed hotter and hotter; secret meetings, surprised by the dragoons, were at once turned into scenes of butchery and slaughter. Incredible tortures were invented, and cruelties, the recital of which is almost impossible, were perpetrated by the Romish party, on their unoffending fellow-subjects. The Protestants, driven to desperation, rose at last in the Cevennes, and in 1702, the war of the " Camisards " began. A Huguenot historian of this dreadful civil war, says, " Never did hell in the direst persecution, invent or employ means so diabolical and inhuman as the dragoons, and the monks who head them, have used to destroy us. These cruelties were general in France, but most violent in our Cevennes." The Pope, Clement XI., did all in his power to secure the utter extinction of the persecuted Camisards. He promised complete exemption from the pains of purgatory, to all who took up arms to exterminate " the accursed and execrable race." For three years this cruel crusade continued, till the fair and fruitful hills and valleys of the Cevennes, were turned into desolation, and the Protestants completely crushed.

Time and space fail to tell the sickening and similar stories of the papal persecutions in Spain and Portugal, in Savoy, in Poland, in Bohemia, and in the Thirty Years' War in Germany ; the horrible persecutions of the Emperor Charles V., and above all of the dark deeds of the Papacy, wrought through the infamous Duke of Alva, in the Low Countries. Let the thrillingly interesting story of the holy heroism of hundreds and thousands of Christian martyrs, as told in Motley's "Dutch Republic," add its testimony to the fact, that the Papal power has fulfilled the inspired prediction, "he shall wear out the saints of the Most High," and "make war with the saints and overcome them;" let Foxe's "Book of Martyrs" do the same; let the records of the Lollard persecution in our own land, and of the reign of "bloody" Mary, do the same; let Mexico, and Abyssinia, and India, tell their tales of the Holy Inquisition and its doings, and of the Jesuits and their proceedings; and let Italy itself unveil the scenes that Ferrara, and Venice, and Parma, and Calabria have witnessed, in confirmation of the fact. In the mouth of many many witnesses, the charge is proved, and one single statement makes all argument on the subject needless. *It has been calculated that the Popes of Rome have, directly or indirectly, slain on account of their faith, fifty millions of martyrs;* fifty millions of men and women who refused to be parties to Romish idolatries, who held to the Bible as the Word of God, and who loved not their lives unto death, but resisted unto blood, striving against sin.

VI. Dominion.

One of the most marked features of the great power of evil predicted in the four prophecies we are considering, is, ITS WIDE DOMINION.

Of this revived head of the Roman earth we read, (Rev. xiii. 7,) "*power* was given him, over all kindreds, and tongues, and nations"; and other clauses in the chapter show that so absolute was this power to be, that all, small and great, rich and poor, free and bond, were to be brought into subjection to it, and that it would become almost impossible, for those who refused such subjection, to exist; they would not even be permitted to buy or sell.

A peculiar mark of the nature of this power is also given. The subjection yielded to it would be a *voluntary* one. It is said of the ten horns, that they shall "have one mind, and shall *give* their power and strength unto the

Beast"; that is, it is predicted that the kingdoms into which the Roman earth would be divided, on the fall of the Empire, would *voluntarily* place themselves, in some sense, under the dominion of this final form of Roman power. Their subjection would not be effected by conquest, but by the arts of persua-sion and subtle influence. They would be deceived and cajoled into submission, by fair words, by false miracles, by lying wonders, by superstitious fears, and by the influence of others, acting on behalf of this power, rather than by its own direct efforts.

This feature is so peculiar, so unlike the analogous features of the three first Beasts or Empires of Daniel, whose dominion was acquired by devouring, pushing, running furiously, smit-ing, breaking, stamping in pieces, in a word, by exercising physical force, instead of subtle spiritual influence, that it serves at once to indicate the power intended. The Papacy is the only great political power, which has ever held sway over all kindreds, tongues, and nations, without having to fight for it, and with the consent of the subjected kingdoms. The pro-found ignorance of the dark ages, so zealously fostered by the Papacy, created a degree of superstition, which rendered kings and peoples alike, willingly obedient to this power, which boldly claimed to be supernatural, and to exercise dominion in heaven and in hell, as well as on earth, and over the souls, as well as over the bodies of men; and that both for time and for eternity.

The prophecy further distinctly intimates, that this power will not be universal or all-inclusive, even in the lands where it should prevail. It would be resisted by a certain class: "all that dwell upon the earth shall worship him, *whose names are not written in the book of life of the Lamb slain from the foundation of the world.*" This foretells that the godly—"the saints"—the chosen and called and faithful, and they *alone*, will refuse to bow to this power; and the vision shows also, that they will do it at the *risk*, and too often at the cost of the *loss of*, life itself. How literally and fearfully this prediction has been fulfilled in the history of the Papacy, the preceding outline of the persecutions inflicted on so-called "heretics," shows.

The extent and the character of Papal dominion, during the dark ages, is, in our days, little realized. It is not easy, gazing on the rotten stump of an old oak, to picture to one's self what the tree was in the days of its glorious youth, and of its mighty maturity; how its immense branches shot out on every side, overshadowing a thousand lower growths; how the tempests attacked it in vain, and the hurricanes only rooted it more firmly in the soil. How beautiful it looked in its light green robe in spring; how magnificent in its ruddy autumnal brown; how generation after generation of birds sheltered amid its branches, and of wild boars fed upon its acorns. The centuries that have rolled over the tree have left little trace of what it *was*, and yet the very size of the stump tells the tale of its bygone might and glory. It is just so with the power of the Roman Pontiffs. The world can smile now at the puerility of the proud and preposterous pretensions, of the poor old man who occupies the chair of St. Peter, in his Vatican prison in Rome. It listens to his loud claim to infallibility with a laugh of contempt, and to his fierce anathemas on science, and literature, and social and religious liberty, with the calm and compassionate scorn, with which the wanderings of a lunatic are regarded. But of yore it was quite another thing. Every utterance of the tiara-crowned monarch was heard with awe, every command was implicitly obeyed. Men trembled under his curse, and gloried in his benediction, as if they had been those of Deity. The thunders of his interdicts shook the nations, and the fires of his excommunications spread death and destruction abroad. The imperial edicts of the Emperors Justinian and Phocas gave the Popes of Rome a legal power in all religious matters; and very early the various Gothic princes of Western Christendom showed a disposition to yield submission to the Roman Pontiff, as children to a father, or inferiors to a superior. Already, in the eighth century, Gregory II. boasted to the Greek Emperor, " all the kings of the west reverence the Pope *as a God on earth,"* and facts fully justified the assertion. Pepin, for example, when aspiring to the crown of France, prayed the Pope to authorize his usurpation; and as soon as he had done so, the Franks, and indeed the whole Western World, recognised his title. Even the great Emperor Charlemagne, was willing to receive from the Roman Pontiff his crown and dominion. "The Lord John, apostolic and universal Pope," says the Council of Pavia, "hath at Rome *elected*, and anointed with the holy oil, Charlemagne, as Emperor." The western kings of Europe accepted the position of subserviency to the Sovereign Pontiff, by admitting into their coronation oaths a promise, "to be faithful and submissive to the Popes, and the Roman Church."

In its earlier days the Papacy, restrained by princes from exercising civil dominion, was equally restrained by the independence of bishops, and the authority of councils, from assuming despotic power, even in the church. "From the time of Leo IX.," says Mosheim, "the Popes employed every method which the most artful ambition could suggest, to remove these limits, and to render their dominion both despotic and universal." Hildebrand, one of the most ambitious, sagacious, crafty, and arrogant of men, when he became Pope under the title of Gregory VII., "looked up to the summit of universal empire, with a wistful eye, and laboured up the ascent with uninterrupted ardour and invincible perseverance." He laboured indefatigably to render the universal church, subject to the despotic government of the Pontiff *alone*, as well as to submit to his jurisdiction the emperors, kings, and princes of the earth, and to render their dominion tributary to the see of Rome. Even when the Pope reclaimed a crown he had conferred, he was often met with the most abject submission. The Emperors Rodolphus and Otho, of Germany, not only received the crown as a Papal grant, on the Pope's deposition of previous emperors, but they resigned, at his bidding, the crowns so received. Peter II. of Arragon, and John, king of England, and other monarchs also, gave up their independence, that they might receive back their realms as *vassals of the Pope.* "Under the sacerdotal monarchy of St. Peter," says Gibbon, "the nations began to resume the practice of seeking on the banks of the Tiber, their kings, their laws, and the oracles of their fate." And similarly, in speaking of the first Norman king of Sicily, he says, "The nine kings of the Latin world might disclaim their new associate, unless he were consecrated by the authority of the supreme Pontiff."

If kings and emperors bowed thus before the Pope, it will easily be believed that the reverence of the common people for his person and office, and their submission to his arrogant and blasphemous pretensions, was complete. "Not in respect of his power in secular things, but in things much higher, who knows not of the universal reverence and faith in his blasphemous pretensions exhibited throughout the long middle ages by Christendom? Look at the thronging multitudes on pilgrimage to Rome, in assurance of the salvation he promises them! Look at their reception of his dogmas in matters of faith, as very oracles from heaven! Look at their purchasing of his indulgences with their often hard earned money, in the belief of delivering thereby the captive souls of departed relatives, as well as their own souls, from the pains of purgatory and of hell!" * Look at the way in which thousands of all classes engaged in crusades and religious wars at the bidding of the Popes, and refused aid, even to their nearest and dearest friends, if they came under his ban! From the most private domestic relations of individuals, to the most public national acts of empires, all fell under the rule, direct or indirect, of the Papacy. It was the last solemn united act, before the Reformation, of the deputies of Christendom assembled in council, to subscribe the bull *Unam Sanctum,* which declares that AS THERE IS BUT ONE BODY OF THE CHURCH AND CHRISTENDOM, SO THERE IS BUT ONE HEAD, THE VICAR OF CHRIST—THE POPE; AND THAT IT IS ESSENTIAL TO THE SALVATION OF EVERY HUMAN

---

* Elliott, vol. iii., p. 171.

BEING, TO BE SUBJECT TO THE ROMAN PONTIFF ; and no subsequent Council ever revoked this decree.

It is clear, then, that a widespread and all-pervading power, of the most despotic, absolute, and blasphemous character, *was* wielded for a thousand years by the Popes of Rome, and is claimed by them still; that this power was submitted to by all the nations of Western Christendom for many centuries; and that it is still acknowledged by all Roman Catholics everywhere. The late Pope, in addressing the people of Rome on one occasion, congratulated them, that they had more than *two hundred millions of fellow subjects* elsewhere, speaking all languages, and dwelling in all nations.

In the Papacy, has therefore been fulfilled to the letter, and in the most marvellous way, the prediction, " Power was given unto him over all kindreds and tongues and nations." *

The growth of this power to these gigantic proportions, was a most singular phenomenon. Tyndale the Reformer speaking of it, says : " To see how the holy father came up, mark the ensample of the ivy ! First it springeth up out of the earth, and then awhile creepeth along by the ground, till it

---

* The application of this prophecy to the Popedom has sometimes been doubted, because of the wide universality of this expression. But comparison with other scriptures removes this difficulty. We read in Matthew iii. 5 : " Then went out unto him Jerusalem and all Judea, and all the region round about Jordan, and were baptized." And again, Acts ix. 35, " And all that dwelt in Lydda and Saron saw him, and turned to the Lord." " All " in these passages must be taken with *limitations,* which are not expressed. So in Daniel iii. 7, it is said that when Nebuchadnezzar set up his image, " all the people, the nations, and the languages fell down and worshipped." Now, the second verse of the chapter shows, that only the princes and governors of those nations were *present ;* they are regarded as *representatives* of their people. In the same way all Christendom submitted to the Popes of Rome, through the Councils which represented them. The exception in the text of those whose names are written in the Lamb's book of life shows that—just as all were not Israel that were of Israel—so all were not Papists that were subject to the Papacy. This must never be forgotten. At the last the cry goes forth, " Come out of her, *my people,*" a call which implies that—as Lot dwelt in Sodom—so some true believers will be found in the Roman Catholic system, even just prior to its final destruction.

find a great tree. Then it joineth itself beneath, unto the body of the tree, and creepeth up a little and a little, fair and softly. At the beginning, while it is yet thin and small, the burden is not perceived; it seemeth glorious to garnish the tree in winter. But it holdeth fast withal, and ceaseth not to climb up till it be *at the top*, and even *above all.* And then it sendeth its branches along by the branches of the tree, and overgroweth all, and waxeth great, heavy, and thick; and it sucketh the moisture so sore out of the tree and his branches, that it choaketh and stifleth them. And then the foul, stinking ivy waxeth mighty in the stump of the tree, and becometh a seat and a nest for all unclean birds and for blind owls which hawk in the dark, and dare not come to the light.

"Even so the Bishop of Rome, now called Pope, at the beginning crope along upon the earth, and every man trod on him. As soon as there came a Christian emperor, he joined himself to his feet and kissed them, and crope up a little, with begging now this privilege, now that. . . . And thus with flattering and feigning and vain superstition, under the name of St. Peter, he crept up, and fastened his roots in the heart of the emperor, and with *his* sword climbed up above all his fellow bishops, and brought them under his feet. And as he subdued *them* by the emperor's sword, even so after *they* were sworn faithful, he, by their means, climbed up *above the emperor*, and subdued him also, and made *him* stoop unto his feet and kiss them! . . . And thus the Pope, the father of all hypocrites, hath with falsehood and guile perverted the order of the world, and turned things upside down."

VII. Before closing this chapter, we must notice the *doom* of the great power of evil predicted in the fourfold prophecy we are considering.

It consists of two parts, gradual consumption, followed by sudden and final destruction. The latter, being still future, affords no opportunity of comparing the prophetic announcement with the historical fulfilment; but the former, being already partially fulfilled, and still in progress of fulfilment;

does, and the correspondence between prediction and event is nowhere more clear and unmistakable.

In Daniel, in Thessalonians, and *in the Apocalypse*, the final destruction of this last form of the Roman power, is connected with the personal appearing of Christ to establish his millennial kingdom. But in each prophecy it is also intimated that a consuming and destroying process, would go on for some time, *previously* to the end, so that the once mighty power would be weakened and impoverished, before it is finally destroyed.

"They shall take away his dominion, to *consume* and destroy it unto the end" (Dan. vii. 26). "Whom the Lord shall *consume* with the Spirit of his mouth, and *destroy* with the brightness of his coming" (2 Thess. ii. 8). "The ten horns shall hate the whore, and shall *make her desolate and naked*, and *shall eat her flesh*, and burn her with fire" (Rev. xvii. 16).

The final destruction of the power in question is described in Rev. xix. 20, "The beast was taken and cast alive into a lake of fire burning with brimstone." This is his *destruction* with the brightness of Christ's coming; and the *consumption* by the spirit of his mouth, must have preceded this final judgment.

Pharaoh and the hosts of Egypt were similarly wasted and consumed by the ten plagues, before they were whelmed in the waters of the Red Sea. The consuming process is figured in the Apocalypse as taking place under the outpouring of certain vials of wrath, on the kingdom of the Beast, and on his followers.

We inquire, then, whether there have been in the history of the Papacy any events answering to this emblem, whether any process of *consumption* is distinctly traceable, any wasting to decay of its resources, any conspicuous diminution of its dominion, and reduction of its influence and authority.

The facts of the case are so notorious, that it is needless to set them forth in detail. The political power of the Roman Pontiffs, once, as we have seen, a dread reality in Europe, is gone. It is a memory of the past, not an existing fact. The territorial possessions of the Pope are gone; the States of the

Church form part of the dominions of the king of Italy, and Rome itself has become his capital. Within the last twenty years all the Concordats made between the Pope and the various countries of Europe, have been brought to an end. The immense *landed property*, belonging to the various orders of monks and nuns on whom the Papacy relied as its universal agents, has all been confiscated and secularized in Italy, in France, in England, and in other lands. In 1513, when the great Lateran Council was held, there was not a "heretic" to be found. There are now nearly eighty millions of PRO-TESTANTS, who abjure Papal doctrines and practices. The dominion of the Popes, over the bodies and minds of men, is therefore marvellously diminished, though the latter is not yet destroyed.

And it is specially worthy of note that the means by which this conspicuous and undeniable "consumption" of Papal power has been accomplished, are precisely the means speci-fied by the Apostle Paul in Thessalonians. He says that the Lord shall consume this evil power *by the spirit of his mouth*, *i.e.*, by his word.

Holy Scripture is of course the form in which the word or spirit of the Lord's mouth, retains a sensible existence, and influences human society. "The words that I speak unto you, they are spirit, and they are life."

Does not the extreme jealousy with which the Papacy has always endeavoured to bury the Bible in an unknown tongue, or to undo its teachings by false interpretations, betray its inveterate antagonism to the power destined to "consume" it? "There is an instinct of apprehension, a consciousness, which, antecedent to experience, divines danger; it seems discernible in the alarm with which Romanism recoils from Holy Scrip-ture." *

The Creed of Pius IV.—that creed, a belief in which is, ac-cording to Papal declaration, essential to salvation—expressly

---

* "The Apostasy": O'Sullivan.

states that the Bible is not for the people : "Whosoever will be saved," must *renounce* it. It is a forbidden book. Bible Societies are "Satanic contrivances." Bible burnings are most Catholic demonstrations. All this dread of Scripture, all this violent opposition to its circulation, is a plain proof that *the Papacy recognises in the Word of God its worst antagonist.* Experience shows it is right.

Wherever the Word of God has free course, the power of the Papacy is at an end. The Reformation sprang from a recovered Bible ; and wherever, as in Scotland, the popular mind is imbued with Scripture, Romanism has no chance. It is the absence of Bible knowledge that enables the Papacy to retain its sway, in Spain and other European countries, in Mexico, in Brazil, and in parts of Ireland.

The fact was stated in evidence before the Commissioners of Education, that in 1846, among 400 students attending Maynooth College, only ten had Bibles or Testaments, while every student was required to provide himself with a copy of the works of the Jesuits, Bailly and Delahogue.

The failure of the Hibernian Schools, in which the Bible without note or comment was used, was attributed by Lord Stanley to that fact alone : the priests exerted "themselves, with energy and success, against a system to which they were in principle opposed." The parents were told that it was "mortal sin" to send their children to such schools ; and if they persisted, the sacrament was withheld from them, even when dying.

Pius IX., in his Encyclical Letter of 1850, speaks of Bible study as "poisonous reading," and urges all his venerable brethren with vigilance and solicitude to put a stop to it. A clergyman lost his wife in Rome, and wished to put a text on her tombstone. The Pope refused permission, not only on the ground that it was unlawful to express a hope of immortality as to a "heretic," but because it was "contrary to law, to publish in the sight of the Roman people any portion of the Word of God"!

" Rome is constrained to do homage to the majesty of the Bible ; she has done her best to exile that book from the world, with all the treasures it contains,—its thrilling narratives, its rich poetry, its profound philosophy, its sublime doctrines, its blessed promises, its magnificent prophecies, its glorious and immortal hopes.   Were any being so cruel as to extinguish the light of day, and condemn the successive generations of men to pass their lives amid the gloom ot an unbroken night, where would words be found strong enough to execrate the enormity ?   Far greater is the crime of Rome.   After the day of Christianity had dawned, she was able to cover Europe with darkness ; and by the exclusion of the Bible, to perpetuate that darkness from age to age.   The enormity of this wickedness cannot be known on earth.   But she cannot conceal from herself that, despite her anathemas, her *indices expurgatorii,* her tyrannical edicts, by which she still attempts to wall round her territory of darkness, *the Bible is destined to overcome in the conflict.*   Hence her implacable hostility— hostility founded to a large extent on fear   .   To Popery a single Bible is more dreadful than an army ten thousand strong. . . .   When she meets the Bible in her path, she is startled, and exclaims with terror, I know thee who thou art !   Art thou come to torment me before the time ? " *

For the last three hundred years, ever since the Reformation, the Papacy has been in process of consumption by the spirit of the Lord's mouth.   It will ere long be " destroyed by the brightness of his coming."

VIII. This leads us to the last point we must notice in our brief examination of this remarkable fourfold prophecy of the Papacy,—ITS DURATION.

The period of the dominion of the little horn, is fixed in Daniel vii. as "time, times, and the dividing of time ;" and that of the last head of the Roman beast (which is, as we

---

* Wylie's " Papacy."

have seen, only another symbol of the same power), as "forty and two months," the same period under a different designation. This period is identical, and synchronous with, the 1260 days of parallel prophecies. Interpreted according to the year-day system, it has had a most evident fulfilment in the duration of the power of the Papacy; and it is besides A KEY TO THE WHOLE SYSTEM OF TIMES AND SEASONS, NATURAL AND REVEALED.

The entire system thus opened up, is a confirmation of the interpretation which opens it : its universal range, its exquisite internal harmonies, and its deep underlying connection with the profoundest truths of our faith, make this system a grand witness to the true interpretation of the mystic phrases which furnish the clue for its discovery.

To enter more largely on this point here would be to anticipate subsequent chapters. For the present we must content ourselves with asserting simply that the *predicted period* of the great power of evil we have been considering, 1260 years, points out the Papacy as the proper fulfilment, as clearly as any of the other features. The Bishops of Rome assumed universal supremacy in the beginning of the seventh century, and have exercised it ever since. It is a solemn fact, that these inspired prophecies,—every other prediction in which has been so marvellously fulfilled,—foretell that it will not last much longer. Its days are numbered. Its end is near.

To conclude. The origin of the Papacy corresponded with every indication furnished by these four prophecies. Its character answers exactly to the singularly wicked and evil character assigned by the inspiring Spirit to the predicted power. Self-exalting utterances, great words, against God and man, have been one of its most distinguishing features ; idolatries and false doctrines have been inculcated and promulgated throughout Christendom by its instrumentality ; it has made war with the saints and overcome them, fifty millions of evangelical martyrs having been slain by its authority ; it has ruled over all the kindreds and nations of Catholic Christendom, and that for more than twelve centuries; and it has for the last three hundred years been wasting to decay, undermined and exposed by the Reformation movement, which itself was the direct result of the revival of scriptural teachings and the dissemination of Bible truth. The Papacy was never so low, in power, in resources, in prestige, as it is at this moment. According to the Divine programme afforded by these sacred, once mysterious but now clear predictions, the Papal drama is played out. The final scene alone remains,—the destruction of the Papacy by the brightness of Christ's coming.

In the face of such a fulfilment as this,—a fulfilment on so grand a scale, as to the area involved, the events comprised, and the time occupied,—a fulfilment affecting countless myriads of human beings during its course of more than twelve hundred years,—a fulfilment of immense spiritual importance, to thirty or forty generations of professing Christians, throughout the world,—a fulfilment so little to have been expected, and therefore so peculiarly worthy of being made the subject of prophetic forewarning,—in the face of *such* a fulfilment, surely candour would admit, this is that which was spoken by the prophet; *this* is that system of supernatural and soul-destroying error, that dire and dreadful apostasy, revealed by the inspiring Spirit, as the principal power of evil, to arise between the first and second advents of the Lord Jesus Christ.

When the four symbolic beasts were presented to Daniel, it was *the fourth* that arrested his gaze, and it was the " little horn " of that fourth empire, that mainly attracted his attention, and the angelic interpreter dwells with tenfold fulness on the power represented by this symbol. So when Paul predicted the future of the church on earth, it was the rise, domination and decay of this same evil power that he presented, as the main event to intervene before her rapture to meet the Lord in the air; and so when John received the revelation of Jesus Christ, which God gave to him, the central symbol of the entire group of hieroglyphs, the one which occupied the most prominent place in the prophecy, was one of this same power.

"the beast," the great antagonist of the Lamb and his followers.

How worthy of such conspicuous mention in the sacred oracles, of such solemn denunciation by the Holy Ghost,—how worthy of such pre-eminent fame (or rather infamy!) among the gigantic evils that have afflicted mankind,—how deserving of every dark designation bestowed, and of the dread doom denounced, has THE PAPACY proved itself to be. The self-styled vicar of Christ has been his worst enemy in the world, the crowned priest on the papal throne has been the undoing of the church on earth. The system which asserts salvation impossible beyond its borders, has destroyed the spiritual and temporal well-being of untold multitudes of men. Unutterably disastrous as have been its direct effects, its millions of slaughtered saints, its myriads of deluded disciples, its indirect effects have been hardly less terrible. By its priestly assumptions and pious frauds, by its notorious cupidity and mercenary practices, by its gross perversions of the truth, and unblushing corruptions of morality, by its reason-revolting dogmas, childish superstitions, and endless old wives' fables, by its uniform opposition to social progress, and its habitual alliance with political tyranny, it has brought all religion into contempt, and filled Catholic Christendom with scorners, infidels, and atheists.

As to every single particular noted in the sure word of prophecy, the plainest correspondence can be traced between the fourfold prediction and the Papal fulfilment; and we cannot refrain from deprecating most earnestly, the mischievous system of interpretation, which teaches that this clear, undeniable, and grandly terrible accomplishment, *is not the fulfilment intended.*

Standing face to face with Jesus Christ, the disciples of John inquired in their master's name, "Art Thou He that should come, or look we for another?" They were answered by deeds, not words. The Lord wrought Messianic miracles in their presence, and said, "Go and tell John what thing ye have seen and heard;" that is, *He did the deeds which it had*

Q

been predicted that the Messiah would do, and all were responsible to draw thence the inference *that He was the Messiah*. So, pointing to the church history of the last twelve centuries, we say, lo! the Papacy has done the deeds which were to be done by the oft-predicted power of evil, foretold in the word of God! And we believe that Christians are responsible to draw from the historical fact, the inference, *the Papacy is the power that was thus predicted*.

To neglect the evidence which proves this fact almost to demonstration, and to speculate about possible future literal fulfilments, as the intended and main accomplishment of these sacred symbolic prophecies, is to denude them of their sanctifying power, and to turn their keen edge of practical application. If the Papacy is the real fulfilment, if it is THE evil that was *foreseen* as of supreme importance (as it has certainly proved *to be*), it is surely no light matter for teachers of the word to mislead others on the point. To do so, is to relieve Popery of the fearful stigma cast on it by the spirit of prophecy, to deprive the church of the Divine estimate of this Antichristian system, and to substitute instead, wild and unauthorized speculations, about some coming man, who is, in three years and a half, to exhaust these divinely given predictions, which the church has for eighteen centuries been studying.

We entreat our Futurist friends to consider, whether it is more likely that the all-wise God indited these solemn predictions for the benefit of *many* generations of his saints, or exclusively for the guidance of *the last* generation of this age? Did He *pass by* unnoticed, the gigantic and universally influential power, which ruled the whole of Christendom with despotic sway and inconceivably evil results for more than a thousand years, in order to describe in detail, and many times over, the doings of *one man*, the brief career of a single individual, who has not yet appeared? Was it to warn the church of the nineteenth century against some short-lived Napoleon, that the Holy Ghost unveiled the future to the prophet Daniel, and that the Lord Jesus gave the Apocalypse to the saintly John?

The ample and repeated descriptions of this power of evil, the unparalleled denunciations against it, the solemn adjurations to the people of God, to avoid any connection with it, all forbid the idea. Not for one, but for fifty generations of saints, were these prophecies indited; not to be fulfilled on the petty scale of three years, but on the majestic one of twelve centuries; not to indicate gross material dangers, but subtle spiritual and ecclesiastical evils, of long duration, and world-wide prevalence. The coming of Antichrist is no brief future event, lying between us and our blessed hope, the glorious appearing of our Saviour; he was revealed more than a thousand years ago, he has run his course, and lasted his pre-appointed period; for three hundred years, he has been consuming by the spirit of Christ's mouth, and of all the momentous series of events connected with his long-predicted career, nothing remains to be fulfilled save his final conflict with the Lamb, and destruction with the brightness of Christ's coming.

To conclude. *The correct interpretation of the prophecy of Babylon the great,—that it is the Church of Rome—confirms the above view of this prophecy of " the beast," and is indeed the key to the whole Apocalypse.*

There is a vast difference between the Papacy, and the corrupt church, which it founded, governed, and used as its tool; a difference, less in degree, but similar in character, to that existing between the Head of the true church, and that church which He founded, governs, and employs as an instrument to accomplish his will in the world. Many things are true of the Lord Jesus, that are not true of the church which is his body, close and inseparable as is the connection between them. So, many things are true of the Popes of Rome which are not true of the Roman Catholic Church, close as is the connection between *them.* Widely dissimilar hieroglyphs are selected to prefigure the two, in the Apocalypse, and yet the connection between them is very clearly indicated; they are never confounded, yet never disjoined.

Now the duration of the corrupt church is not mentioned

in this prophecy, though long duration is implied ; but her *name* is given, and it demonstrates with all but mathematical certainty, as we have seen, that the church intended is the *Church of Rome.* That church has, we know, as a matter of history, already lasted in a condition of corruption and apostasy, for more than twelve centuries. Its *fall* is in the Apocalypse represented as taking place under the *seventh* vial (Rev. xvi.), and as synchronizing with the marriage of the Lamb (Rev. xix. 1–4).

The power of " the beast " (or Papal dynasty) is also represented as being consumed under the outpouring of the vials, while he himself and his armies are destroyed by the advent, which synchronizes with the marriage of the Lamb. That is, " Babylon " and " the beast " are represented as *coming to an end at one and the same time.*

Their careers are also cotemporaneous, for the woman is represented as *seated on* the Roman beast—" the beast that was and is not "—that is, not old Pagan Rome, but Rome *revived,* in a totally new form of domination. This beast " that was and is not " is expressly said to be *the eighth* (v. 11), that is *the last* terrible form of revived Roman power, so fully described in chapter xiii.—the power of which we have been treating.

It follows, that since the Church of Rome has already lasted more than twelve centuries, the last ruling head of the Roman world, the blasphemous, persecuting, self-exalting head or power here predicted, *must have been in existence for the very same period,* which is indeed the duration assigned to it, in symbolic language by the prophecy—1260 years.

Now *what power* has actually ruled the nations of Christendom *from Rome as its seat, during the last twelve centuries?* THERE CAN BE BUT ONE REPLY—THE PAPACY : IT MUST THEREFORE BE THE POWER PREFIGURED BY THE SYMBOL OF " THE BEAST."

Further, the vials, under which Babylon and " the beast " are represented as being brought to an end, synchronize with the close of the period of the trumpets. The events prefigured under the *earlier* trumpets must therefore be sought in the previous history of Christendom ; *i.e.*, in the time of the *undiminished* power of the Papacy, and in the events which preceded and accompanied its *rise*.

The martyrs represented in the fifteenth chapter of the book, standing as victors on the sea of glass, having "*gotten the victory over the beast*, and over his image, and over the number of his name," must be those slain by Papal Rome. A previous group of martyrs are represented in the sixth chapter, who must therefore be those slain by Pagan Rome in the ten great persecutions of the church by the Cæsars.

Now it is under the *fifth seal* that this earlier company is seen under the altar, and consequently the events figured as taking place under the four *previous* seals, must be sought in days *prior to the last great persecution under Diocletian*, that is, in the first three hundred years of church history.

Thus we are led by clear and simple synchronisms, afforded by the book itself, to a conclusion respecting the Apocalypse, similar to that which we reached by other lines of argument ; namely, that its fulfilment is to be sought in the events of the Christian era, and that so far from all its visions, from chap. vi. to chap. xix. being still wholly *future*, they are almost wholly *past*. Nor can the force of this argument be avoided, save by denying that the Babylon of the Apocalypse represents the Church of Rome.

In the remaining portion of this work we shall find all the conclusions we have reached in its three earlier parts, respecting the second advent and the millennium, the resurrection and the judgment to come, the true scope and nature of the Apocalypse, and the signification of these, its two leading prefigurations, —abundantly confirmed from independent sources, and by arguments drawn from the realms of natural science.

END OF PART III.

PART IV.

INQUIRY INTO THE DIVINE SYSTEM OF TIMES AND SEASONS NATURAL AND REVEALED.

SECTION I.

SOLAR AND LUNAR DOMINION CAUSAL AND CHRONOLOGICAL.

CHAPTER I.

CHRONOLOGY, BIBLICAL AND NATURAL. IS THERE HARMONY BETWEEN THE TWO?

SOLAR AND LUNAR DOMINION IN THE INORGANIC WORLD. SOLI-LUNAR CONTROL OF TERRESTRIAL REVOLUTIONS.—WINDS.—RAINS.—OCEAN CURRENTS.—TIDES.—ELECTRIC AND MAGNETIC VARIATIONS.

OUR subject in this volume so far, has been sacred pro-phecy. We have observed the manner in which the Omniscient God has been pleased to reveal the future to man—progressively ; we have investigated some of the main prin-ciples, on which the symbolic predictions of Scripture should be interpreted ; and we have traced the historic fulfilment of two of the most important of them. We must now turn to the distinct yet cognate subject of CHRONOLOGY, and examine *the times and seasons* of some of the events foretold in pro-phecy, and those of Scripture in general.

Every Bible student is aware, that prophecy has its chron-ology, that various *periods* are assigned to events forefold by holy men of old, who spake as they were moved by the Holy Ghost. Empires have their duration, dynasties and kingdoms, last for certain periods, and as predicting these, prophecy can no more be divested of the chronological element than history. Indeed prophecy being simply history anticipated, the times and seasons of the one, become in due course, those of the other ; they are two parts of one whole ; and now that history unrolls before our eyes a record extending over six thousand years, very few are the prophetic periods whose fulfilment cannot be traced in some part of the scroll.

But further ; there exists, not in sacred prophecy alone, but throughout the entire Bible, a *system* of times and seasons. Chronology is a prominent feature of the Holy Scriptures. In the account of the creation, in the narrative of the flood, in the biographies of the patriarchs, in the Mosaic economy with its legal and ceremonial enactments, in the history of the Jewish nation ; in the prophets ; in the gospels, and in the Apocalypse ; statements of *time* abound. Not only is the creation work recorded, but the time it occupied ; not only are the waters of the flood described, but we are told how many days they took to rise, and how many to fall ; how many years Noah had lived prior to the crisis, how many days he waited before he sent out the dove, and how many more before he went forth from the ark, himself. It is so throughout. In fact the science of true chronology is based upon the statements of Scripture : the first of chronologers, Clinton, accepts its data as correct, and draws from thence his conclusions as to the age of the world. Unlike the sacred books of all false religions, Bible stories are no vague myths, or fabled occurrences, referred to some remote intangible past. The time of the events recorded is accurately measured, and they are all fitted into a framework of true chronology. And while the times and seasons of Scripture are substantial historical periods, bearing the stamp of accuracy and veracity, they form part of a series, and belong to a system, the features of which it is not difficult to trace. Not only are there chronological statements in abundance in the Bible, but there is, underlying them all a system, a peculiar system, harmonious with all the other features of that marvellous volume.

A moment's reflection will satisfy every well informed person that *nature* has also its times and seasons; that the outward material universe in which we dwell, and the laws which govern it, are marked by a well defined *periodicity*. The entire solar system is one great chronometer, the animal and vegetable worlds, are regulated by unchangeable laws in respect of *time*, as well as in every other respect; and nature being, in all its grandeur, its beauty, its complexity, its variety, its mystery, a revelation of its great Creator's wisdom and power, the system of times and seasons which characterizes it, may be called *a Divine system of times and seasons.*

There is no chance in the length of celestial revolutions, or in the duration of cycles of organic change : all is regulated, fixed, appointed. "He appointed the moon for seasons, the sun knoweth his going down. Thou makest darkness and it is night, wherein all the beasts of the forest do creep forth. The sun ariseth, they gather themselves together, and lay them down in their dens." As to man, "his days are determined, the number of his months are with Thee, Thou hast appointed his bounds, that he cannot pass." As the apostle Paul proclaimed to the Athenians of old, "God hath determined *the times* before appointed" as well as the bounds of the habitation, of all men, and of all living things; and He has fixed the orbit of every rolling globe in space, and timed its various revolutions. The mighty machine of the universe, has been wound up and regulated by its great Creator; all its myriad parts keep march and measure, and move according to the Divine will and purpose.

Now if there be a system of times and seasons, in nature, which is *unquestionably* from God, and a system also in the Bible, which *claims* to be a Divine revelation, it is evidently an inquiry of the deepest interest, *are these two systems one?* Can any principles or peculiarities be observed, which indicate that the two are the offspring of one and the same mind? Is the system of nature, the system of the Bible? Can the Bible system be traced in nature? Two books are before us, one certainly, the other professedly, the work of a given author. A marked peculiarity pervades the latter, with which long study has made us familiar. If on examination we find the very same singular feature to be prominent in the former, who would hesitate to conclude that both were written by one hand?

We propose now, in the last part of this work, to investigate this interesting and momentous point; to examine into the question, whether the natural system of times and seasons, is identical with, or related to the Bible system, whether the periodicity of nature, and the periodicity of Scripture, are demonstrably two parts of one whole.

The inquiry, it will be granted is a most legitimate one, for both the material universe, and the volume of inspiration are open revelations. We are not prying into hidden mysteries, or seeking to be wise above what is written "The secret things belong to God, but the things that are revealed, to us and to our children:" we are at liberty to study such a subject, "whoso is wise and will observe these things" shall behold more and more of the glory of God, for the diverse revelations which He has made, throw light the one on the other.

Moreover a pleasing element of certainty, attaches to such a research : science astronomic, biologic, physical, botanical, chemical, optical,—science in all its branches, deals with *facts*, and there is no refusing the testimony of ascertained and well established facts. Nature can be watched and tested, and no baseless theories stand a chance against her silent testimony. Nor can the chronology of secular and sacred history, be made to fit a false system. It is too angular, too solid, to adapt itself to a scheme for which it was not designed. The most remote pre-historic periods are spaced out for us by Bible statements only, but by far the larger part of the annals of the human race, are bathed in the double light of sacred and profane history.

The importance of such an investigation will scarcely be questioned. In these days of supercilious scientific contempt for Scripture, we can ill afford to leave unemployed, any single line of evidence, which may strengthen the argument for the Divine origin of the Bible. To demonstrate *this*, is to enable Christianity to dispense with other evidence, for if Scripture be from God, Christianity is unquestionably true. Now if Bible times and seasons harmonize with the system by which the entire universe is regulated, he will be a most uncandid and unscientific sceptic, who refuses to believe that Scripture *is* from God. The harmony once proved, will demand a modification of many a theory of unbelief, and to account for it will tax the ingenuity of infidels.

In the following pages it will be our endeavour to show, that the natural and Biblical systems are one—two parts of one whole,—and may the proof redound to the glory of God, and confirm the faith of his servants, in the inspiration of his Holy Word.

We shall examine first the periodicity of nature, inorganic and organic, and subsequently that of Scripture history and prophecy, gathering from the latter strong confirmation of the views of prophetic interpretation already advocated, and convincing, unmistakable evidence of the nearness of the end of the age : and may the Holy Spirit, whose office it is to teach us all things, and show us things to come, Himself be our instructor and guide !

On the very threshold of this subject, however, we are met by a question evidently so fundamental to its clear conception, that we must pause to give it a reply :—

What is Time ?

Time is " duration set forth by measures " * ; the ticking of a clock, the beating of a pulse, the burning of a candle, the falling of sand through a certain aperture,—these, and a thousand similar regular movements, may serve as measures, more or less exact, of time.

But its uniform and accurate measurement, being a matter of

---

* Locke " On the Human Understanding."

vast and universal importance, and standards of a great variety of lengths, being needful to beings who take an interest in the past, the present, and the future, including periods the most remote ; measures of a far more stable, accurate, regular and comprehensive character than these, are evidently needful.

Such measures the great Creator has provided in the revolution of the heavenly bodies. The diurnal, annual, and secular movements of the globe on which we dwell, give rise to exceedingly various celestial phenomena, which as the principal hands of a complex dial plate, indicate the lapse of time.

The best measures of time must of course be those which are most obvious, regular and universal, and in these and other respects, there are no standards that can for a moment compare, with the apparent and real movements of the sun and moon. The motions of the planets are slow, inconspicuous, and variable ; now forward, now retrograde ; difficult to detect, and observed by very few. The motions of the comets are still more irregular, and are for the most part altogether lost to sight ; but those of the sun and moon are universally conspicuous, they combine regularity with variety, and revolutions of considerable rapidity, with others of a slow and stately character, including some whose periods are of enormous duration. Above all, the sun and moon exercise an unrivalled dominion in the control of terrestrial movements and changes. They combine, and that to a marvellous extent, the two distinct elements of POTENCY and PERIODICITY. While they originate and rule almost all the physical changes continually taking place upon the surface of the globe, they are eminently periodic, and from the combination of these two elements it results, that they alone of all the heavenly bodies, create and control *terrestrial times and seasons.* We name the primary periods which they measure, *days, months, years ;* and all our times and seasons are either *these,* or *multiples of these.*

In investigating the question of Times and Seasons, we will commence then by considering the almost boundless DOMINION exercised by the sun and moon, over the inorganic and organic

worlds, and we will then advance to the subject of the periodicity of their movements, and the relation of these and other
natural times and seasons, to those revealed in the Word of God.

SOLAR AND LUNAR DOMINION IN THE INORGANIC WORLD.

"And God made two great lights; the greater light to rule the day, and
the lesser light to rule the night. And God set them in the firmament of
the heaven to give light upon the earth, and to rule over the day and over
the night, and to divide the light from the darkness. And God said, let
them be for signs and for seasons, and for days and years."—Gen. i.

The inspired writings were never intended to reveal to men,
those truths of science, which their own God-given intelligence would ultimately enable them, by means of humble, diligent, and patient observation, to discover. Yet the Scriptures
never darken counsel by words without knowledge, involving
scientific blunders, and they often use, in a passing way,
expressions which harmonize with the teachings of the most
advanced modern science.

The statement above quoted, that God made the sun and
moon "to RULE," is one of these. To rise to a conception of the
vastness and universality of solar influence in the creation and
control of inorganic and organic terrestrial change, is difficult
for us even now, and must have been impossible for the ancients.

Yet that this great light of our globe, is also its great ruler,
is beyond all question, and is a point we must seek to
establish, for the sake of those who scarcely recognise its
full import, before we endeavour to unfold some of the chronological laws of this dominion.

So numerous and important are the effects which Almighty
Power accomplishes through solar and lunar agency, that *the
sun and moon may be said to drive the whole clockwork of terrestrial nature.* The swift and ceaseless translation of the earth
through space; the curving of its path and its retention in an
annual orbit; the slow secular alteration of the direction of its
axis; the periodic donation and withdrawal of various degrees
of light and heat, with resulting days, and nights, and changeful

seasons; the movement and circulation of all winds, from the
gentlest zephyr to the most terrible tornado; the circulation of
all water currents, including on the one hand, the innumerable
rills and rivers of the land, and on the other, the equally countless currents of the ocean; the whole phenomena of tides, with
their varied and vasts results; and that of rains, from the up-
raising of waters in the form of vapour, and their transportation as clouds, to their condensation and descent in fertilizing
showers; the formation and fall of dews, of snow, of hail; the
control of all-pervading electric, magnetic, and chemical
changes; these, together with the constant exercise of the most
potent of all physical influences, in the development and support of vegetable and animal life, constitute a sum of solar and
lunar operations, which seems to leave but little to be effected
by other agencies.

It is needful that we should recall some familiar scientific facts, to justify
this statement and give it its due weight.

First, then, as regards the relation of soli-lunar influence to *inorganic*
changes, and primarily to the continual change in the earth's own position;
i.e., to the earth's varied and complicated *movements,* be it remembered
that every atom in the universe attracts every other atom with a force inverse
to the square of the distance. Such is the great and universal law of
gravitation. What then must be the attractive power exercised on our globe
by its closely-attendant satellite, the moon, which is a world 7000 miles in
circumference, with a mass estimated at 78,000,000,000,000,000,000 of
tons? And how stupendous and overmastering must be the attractive force
brought to bear upon the earth by the supreme *central* orb of the system,
which is 700 times greater than all the planets put together, and a million
times larger than the earth itself! A ponderous luminous globe, equal to
a *million worlds* in magnitude, is ever exerting on our world, all its might
of irresistible attraction. The globe we inhabit, vast relatively to us though
it be, yields to its influence, as the wave to the wind!

The earth moves in its orbit 120 times more swiftly than a cannon ball.
This almost inconceivable velocity, imparts to it, of course, an inconceivably
strong impulse or tendency to fly off at a tangent, and move on in a straight
line, from every point of its orbit. It is for ever struggling with tremendous
energy to be free from its lord paramount, seeking, with all the force of
the well-nigh irresistible laws of motion, to break away into space and
escape beyond the influence of the sun's light and heat. But it may not

be ! The great ruler of the system asserts his absolute dominion ; no laws of motion can resist the superior law of his attraction ; the earth owns her complete subjection, and is compelled to travel continually in her elliptical orbit around the sun. Yet the struggle is maintained age after age, and age after age the victory rests with the sun. When, at one part of her orbit, the earth's speed is increased to its maximum, she has power for awhile to increase her distance from the central orb round which she so reluctantly circulates. Further and further she retires, as if approaching the independence and the straight line to which she inclines ; but as she retreats her speed diminishes, and when it has reached a minimum, the never relaxed attraction of the central sun is felt with increased power, and she is obliged slowly to approach again the distant but resistless ruler. Distance and velocity may change within certain limits, but the earth's orbit, and the period in which she journeys through it, are invariable, owing to the supreme overmastering dominion of the sun.

Other influences exerted on the earth, as that of the moon, and that of her sister planets, are not without their effect ; but they are no more able permanently to change the earth's orbit, or alter her period, than are the sticks or stones of the river bank, able to stay the rushing river.

Again : steady though the earth's axis seems to be, pointing faithfully to the pole star, yet, in obedience to solar and lunar influences, it changes slowly its direction in the course of ages, so that the pole star of to-day, is not the pole star of the creation, nor will it be the pole star of a thousand years hence. This change in the direction of the axis of the earth, causes the entire starry firmament, to seem to revolve around the ecliptic, and makes the sun appear to fall back, through all the signs of the zodiac, in a direction contrary to that of its annual movement. This revolution, which occupies the immense period of 25,850 years, is called the precession of the equinoxes, or the advance of the equinoctial points. This is a year on a grand scale to our earth, a revolution occupying hundreds of centuries, performed under the double influence of solar and lunar attraction, and illustrating strikingly the complete and perpetual subjection of our globe, to these greater and lesser lights.

There is a second motion of the axis called "nutation," (nodding or tilting), caused by the moon's attraction alone. It is owing to a change in the plane of the moon's orbit, which causes the place of its intersection with the ecliptic to vary month by month, and year by year, for 19 years, in which period the series of changes is completed. During half that time, the axis of the earth is slightly tilted in one direction, and during the other half in the other ; an instance of purely lunar dominion.

And on a grander scale than any of these, is the ruling power of the greater light displayed. It is an ascertained fact, that the sun, instead of being fixed and motionless in the heavens, as was at one time supposed, is leading his whole train of attendant planets, with their satellites, on an immense and immeasurable journey through space. At the rate of four or five hundred thousand miles every day, the sun is drawing his magnificent train after him, our globe included, in a direction which can be distinctly traced, but whose far-sweeping orbit and amazing period, no power of man has been able to calculate.

It is therefore evident, that in obedience to the sun's attraction, and, in a much smaller degree, to that of the moon, our globe is continually performing movements which are vast, varied, and complex.

They range from daily, monthly, and annual effects, to secular changes of enormous though calculable period, and to some whose periods are incalculable.

The slowness of some of these movements, the amazing velocity of others, the variety of their form, and the vastness of their sweep, fill the mind which contemplates them as affecting the globe on which we dwell, with awe and admiration, and with a profound sense of the reality of solar and lunar dominion. The *rule* of these worlds over our own, is not in word, but in power. It is a rule, unlike the most despotic rule with which men are familiar, that makes itself felt at all times, in all places, in spite of all counteracting influences, and it is a rule that nothing can in the long run resist; apt image of the power exercised by Him of whom Gerhardt wrote,—

> "He everywhere hath sway,
> And all things serve his might;
> His every act pure blessing is,
> His path unsullied light."

And not only does the earth itself perform these marvellously complex and mighty motions under soli-lunar influence, but the very same power is the cause of almost all the incessant changes and movements which take place on its surface, and in its constituent elements.

Nothing in all its vast extent, as a moment's reflection will show, no single atom in the material substances which form and clothe the crust of the earth, is long at rest. And this unending and infinitely varied movement, may be traced to the influence of the sun and moon. Their rule not only embraces the greatest things, but is felt also by the least. The huge world itself submits to it, and every drop of water, every leaf, every insect, is similarly subject.

It is principally by means of its attraction that the sun governs the motions of the globe; but it is more through its heat, its light and its actinic, magnetic, and electric influences, that it operates on the atmosphere of our earth, on its seas and continents, on its flora and fauna, and on mankind. These forces, acting separately or in combination, produce almost all the changes and movements of matter which we witness, from the hurricane that cools and clears the heated atmosphere, to the opening of the rose-bud, and the painting of the petal or the leaf.

Its *heat* is the first great means by which the sun originates terrestrial change and motion. Heat, as is well known, expands and so rarefies all matter. The amount of solar heat received by the earth is enormous. It has been calculated that on one square mile exposed at noon under the equator, 26,000 tons of ice would be melted in an hour; and fifty million times this amount of heat is actually received by the earth from the sun every hour. Were this amount of heat evenly distributed over the earth's surface, it would, in the course of a year, suffice to heat to the boiling point, an ocean of frozen water, sixty miles deep.

The amount of heat received by any one part of the earth's surface, depends mainly on the altitude in the heavens, attained by the sun in that particular locality. The higher the sun rises, the hotter are its beams, and the longer the period during which its light and heat are enjoyed.

When we remember that the three forms in which matter exists, solid, liquid, and gaseous, are due to different degrees of heat, we at once perceive the importance of solar heat, in relation to the state of inorganic matter. The results of its presence or absence, are seen at a glance, in the contrast presented by the tropic and frigid zones ; the flowing seas and rivers of the one, and the frozen floods and icebergs of the other, are due solely to the increase or diminution of solar heat.

The vast inorganic changes in the surface of the earth which geology reveals, were brought about mainly by the same cause. The slow degradation of its solid constituents was due, then as now, to the alternate action of heat and frost, aided by the continual beating of the waves of the ocean, driven by winds, themselves the result of varying degrees of heat. To the flow of rivers and ocean currents, (which spring ultimately from the same cause) was due the dissemination and diffusion of these abraded matters, and their re-arrangement in fresh deposits. The violent volcanic action which from time to time upheaved the aqueous strata, is itself partially traceable to the same cause, for the increase of pressure over large spaces in the beds of the oceans, occasioned by the immense transfer of matter just alluded to, naturally produced diminished pressure over corresponding portions of the land, and the elastic force of subterranean fires, repressed on the one hand, and released on the other, broke forth in the tremendous upheavals and eruptions of the geologic eras.

But it is in the case of the atmosphere surrounding our globe, that the effect of the sun's heat is most apparent. It is kept in a state of ceaseless and complicated motion by the variations of solar heat. The steady periodical trade winds and monsoons, are simply the currents of colder air which rush in to fill the spaces, in which, by the excessive heat of the rays of a vertical sun, the air has been rarefied to an extreme degree. They are an effect produced by the sun, in his apparent annual progress from one tropic to the other. So the familiar land and sea breezes, which may be recognised on every seaboard, though most distinctly in the tropics, arise from the unequal heating of the land and the water. From its low conducting power, the land during the hours of sunshine receives and retains more heat than the water. The superjacent atmosphere becomes more rarefied in consequence, and *ascends*, while the cooler air from the sea, flows in to fill the vacancy. In fact, fickle and uncertain as the winds appear, they are all the result of *law*, and all more or less directly produced by solar heat. In Europe the winds succeed each other in an order always the same, and so marked as to be called "the law of rotation of the winds." Where solar heat is *greatest*, as in the tropics, atmospheric changes are most violent ; where it is most constant, the general direction of winds is steadiest, as in the trade winds. In short the sun draws about the wind, as the loadstone the needle ; and its dominion over the atmosphere is as complete as it is over the solid globe.

Nor is the world of waters any exception to the rule of solar dominion. The whole system of water-circulation, for the cleansing, support and nourishment of the world, is worked by solar power ; the sun is the ever-acting pump or heart, by which the supply is raised from the great oceanic reservoir. Its heat lifts the water in vapours to the sky ; these vapours are transported by the heat-caused winds of which we have spoken, and condensed by the withdrawal of heat, into rain, snow, hail, or dew, as the case may be. Thus summer heat leads to mists and rains, and when excessive, to tropical deluges ; thus sunset is followed by the fall of dew, and the winter diminution of solar heat, by snow, and hailstorms.

The results accomplished by this water supply, are of the highest possible importance in the physical world. The circulation of water, is to the globe, what the circulation of the blood is to the animal frame ; it is the great means by which life is supported, and by which the elements of corruption and decay are removed. In each case the circulation is complete. "All the rivers run into the sea, yet the sea is not full ; unto the place from whence the rivers come, thither they return again." The sparkling springs and mountain rivulets, the murmuring brooks, the flowing rivers, and the broad estuaries, are the continual returning of this life-sustaining water supply, to the ocean from which the sun originally lifted it. This water-circulation, together with all its marvellous effects, in cleansing, nourishing, beautifying, moving, transporting, disintegrating, depositing, accumulating, channelling, changing, etc., is carried on from year to year, and age to age, simply by solar influence. The power required for the work, and actually exerted by the sun is enormous. It has been calculated that the production of one day's steady rain, over an area equal to that of the county of Middlesex, demands power, equivalent to the mechanical force which would be requisite to raise 1,000,000,000 tons, to a height of three miles. What then must be the solar force expended in the constant work of watering the whole world ?

Nor is this all ! The ocean reservoir is itself a maze of currents ; no portion of the mighty deep is ever perfectly quiescent. From its surface to its lowest soundings, and from pole to pole, its waters are in ceaseless circulation. A large number of its currents have been tabulated, and are laid down on our charts ; some of them are hundreds, and even thousands of miles in length. Their existence is clearly traceable to the effect of solar heat. The heated waters of the Gulf of Mexico, becoming lighter as they expand under the vertical rays of a tropical sun, flow off like oil. from the top of the heavier water which rushes in below to take their place, and guided by the conformation of the adjacent continent, and the direction of the prevailing winds, cross the Atlantic and form the well known " Gulf stream," whose waters are perceptibly warmer than the ocean through which they run. Similar warm currents are constantly flowing northward from the tropics, and cold counter-currents returning from the poles. Thus the cold of extreme northern latitudes is modified, while ice-floes and icebergs are transported southward, and melted in the solar ray ; marine life, both animal and vegetable, is preserved and propagated ; ships are carried to their destinations, and the equilibrium of nature maintained ; and it is the sun which is the source of all this motion in the depths of the sea, as in the heights of the atmosphere.

It is mainly to the *moon* that we are indebted for that marvellous, world-wide, daily-recurring, and most beneficent movement of the waters known as the *tides*. It is impossible to overrate the value of the ebb and flow of the tide to man. It is a mighty scavenger in the first place, and a most inexpensive and precious mechanical power in the second. By the attractive power of the moon, operating all over the world, the ocean is heaved up at opposite sides of the globe in two broad waves, which travel round the world, steadily following the advancing moon. Two similar but lesser waves follow the track of the sun, and the high bi-monthly wave known as spring tide, is caused by a combination of these two. The nearness of the moon, gives it over the waters of the ocean, a power greater than that of the larger but more distant sun.

There is no terrestrial phenomenon which manifests so marked and steady a periodicity as this ebb and flow of the waters of the sea ; and there are few whose general effect is more beneficial. But for it, our shores, where rivers run into the ocean, would become vast stagnant deltas of corruption ; sources of pestilence and death. Cities and towns naturally grow up on the banks of rivers, and have an inevitable tendency to pollute them. But twice a day, thanks to the tidal wave, their impurities, instead of being suffered to accumulate in their channels, or at their mouths, are carried out to sea, and lost or rendered harmless ; a most important advantage to mankind.

A transport service of enormous extent is also performed by the tide, on coasts and on rivers, and where wind and steam are not available.

The heavier traffic carried on by large ships and in barges, is often taken in tow by this quiet but powerful tug, which performs without expense, an amount of mechanical labour, the money value of which would be difficult to calculate, even for one large city.

The close connection between tidal phenomena and lunar movements, is demonstrated by the fact that the tides have their cycles, which have been reduced to tables, and found accurately to coincide with cycles of soli-lunar change. For many years tide-tables were constructed from the results of observation independently of science. But Mr. Lubbock, a mathematician, convinced that more accurate tables might be framed on a scientific basis, undertook the extensive labours needful for their preparation. Finding that regular tide observations had been made at the London Docks, from 1795, he took nineteen years of these, purposely selecting the length of a cycle of the motions of the lunar orbit ; constructed tables for the effect on the tide of the moon's declination, parallax, and hour of transit; and was able to produce tide-tables founded on the data thus obtained, which were more exact than those which were compiled from observation alone.

The sun exerts mighty and mysterious influences over the earth, independently of his attraction and of his heat. That there is a close connection between solar and lunar force, and *magnetism*, has been abundantly demonstrated, though the nature of that connection is still, to a great extent, a problem awaiting solution.

Distinct diurnal, monthly, and annual variations in the direction of the magnetic needle, have been discovered, indicating the existence of some hidden, but close, relation between the revolutions of the sun and moon, and this potent and all-pervading force. Universal magnetic variations, accurately and constantly correspond with the changes which take place in the position of the sun and moon with reference to the earth. "All the magnetic elements, are subject to periodical variations, dependent on the position of the sun with respect to the meridian, the period of which is accordingly, the solar day." "They are subject also to a small variation dependent on the position of the *moon* with respect to the meridian ;" * and to a third irregularity which is annual in character, attaining its maxima and minima in the spring and autumn in the northern hemisphere, and *vice versa* in the southern.

Besides this, the magnetic declination changes slowly at all parts of the earth, in the course of centuries. Thus in the year 1580, and onwards to the year 1657, the declination of the magnetic needle at London was in an easterly direction, but constantly *decreasing*. At the latter date it disappeared altogether, and for some years the magnetic meridian coincided with the astronomic. After the year 1660 the declination became westerly ; it

---

* "Treatise on Magnetism." H. Lloyd, D.D., Provost of Trinity College, Dublin.

attained its maximum in this direction in the year 1815, and has ever since been diminishing, and returning towards the true astronomic meridian as before.

In addition to these diurnal, monthly, annual, and secular variations in the direction of the magnetic needle, there is an eleven years' cycle of electric and magnetic change, corresponding constantly and accurately, both in its duration, and in its periods of maxima and minima, with the eleven years' cycle of solar change, or that of the increase and diminution of *sun spots*, whose very remarkable periodicity was discovered by Schwabe of Dessau.

The periods of scarcity and abundance of the spots on the sun, succeed each other every five and a half years, so that in eleven years, the sun passes through all its stages of purity and spottiness: that is, about nine times in the course of every century. Both the beautiful electric phenomena called the aurora borealis, and the magnetic currents which influence the compass, are closely connected with these spots on the sun, though in what manner cannot be explained. Magnetic storms, as they are called, or sudden and powerful currents which cause the needle to jump and jerk violently at the same moment, all over the earth, and singularly brilliant and widespread auroræ, have been observed to correspond with remarkable outbursts of light, in or near some of the solar spots. The years 1857 to 1861 were remarkable for spots: in September, 1859, a most singular appearance was noted by two separate observers, unknown to each other, and in different parts of the world. Great spots were on that day visible on the disc of the sun, and suddenly a brilliant luminous appearance, like a cloud of light more dazzling than the sun itself, appeared close to one of the spots; in about five minutes it swept across and beside it, travelling over a space which could not be less than 35,000 miles in that brief space of time. What was this? An explosion of gas? A conflagration? It is impossible to say; but observations made at the time prove, that the earth was in a perfect convulsion of electro-magnetism at the moment. The self-registering magnetic instruments at Kew, which are always at work, recording photographically every instant, the positions of three differently arranged magnetic needles, showed, when examined subsequently, that *each of the three made at that moment a strongly marked jerk from its former position.* Auroræ were seen at the same time, even in parts of the world where they are rarely visible; as near the equator, and in South Australia. In some places the electric telegraph refused to work, and at several towns in America the telegraph men received severe electric shocks. At Boston, a flame of fire followed the pen of Bain's electric telegraph, which writes down the message on chemically prepared paper. There can be no question whatever that the solar phenomena, whatever its nature, had *a direct and instantaneous terrestrial effect*, and the fact is a new proof of solar dominion in the inorganic world.

CHAPTER II.

SOLI-LUNAR DOMINION IN THE ORGANIC WORLD.

EFFECTS OF LIGHT AND HEAT ON THE DEVELOPMENT AND DISTRIBUTION OF PLANTS AND ANIMALS AND OF THE HUMAN RACE.—DIURNAL AND SEASONAL CHANGES IN RELATION TO HEALTH AND DISEASE.

WE have traced the supreme and all-pervading influence which the "two great lights" appointed to rule the day and night exert, in the production of inorganic terrestrial change. It remains to observe their effect on organized existences, on plants and animals, and on man himself. In this wide and interesting realm, as in the previous one, we shall find that solar influence is supreme.

Light and heat are the most powerful of all agents in the quickening and support of animal and vegetable life, and of these the sun is of course the great source and centre. By its presence or absence, are caused our day and night; and by its elevation or depression, our seasons. These, in their varied alternations, set in motion and control the entire world of organized existence.

What simplicity and sublimity in these solar revolutions and their results! The dawning of day is the signal for the world's awaking from that deathlike sleep which is the child of darkness; with the rising of the sun the flowers open, the birds burst forth into song, and everywhere is seen the stirring of life and activity. The duration of the day sustains and nourishes the infinitely numerous and complicated organic movements and revolutions it has awakened, and its termination reproduces universal silence and repose.

Were the days considerably to lengthen or shorten, were the seasons to change or cease, how immense and disastrous would be the results to all organized existences ! The permanence of seed-time and harvest, day and night, cold and heat, has been promised by the sure word of a gracious and bountiful Creator, and the accomplishment of that promise is effected by the permanence and stability of the earth's actual relations with the sun. These may slightly vary in the course of the prolonged secular changes, discovered by astronomic observation, but compensating powers exist which keep these changes within very narrow limits, and provide for the maintenance of equilibrium, thus securing that uniformity of solar influence, which is needful for the continuation of terrestrial life.

The inclination of the axis of the earth, to the plane of her orbit, for instance, is at present undergoing a steady, though very slow diminution. Were this to continue, unchecked, or to accelerate, a time must come sooner or later, when the equator and the ecliptic would coincide, and thus destroy the present succession of the seasons.

But this catastrophe will never happen ; the all-wise Creator has provided for a continuance of the works of his hands. Before the movement of the earth's axis in this direction can produce any perceptible results, in changing the climate of any part of the globe, it will cease. The axis will, under fresh influences, remain steady for a time, and then commence a retrograde movement, which will restore it to its original position. It will thus oscillate to and fro in the ages to come, without ever deranging to the slightest extent, the climate of the various parts of the earth.

The extent of solar influence in the organic world, is marvellous to contemplate. The sun is the glowing ever acting heart of organic nature ; the succession of day and night are the pulsation, the systole and diastole, the contraction and expansion of that heart. The sun is the all-important reservoir of life-supporting power, constantly sending its royal tide of vitalizing light and heat, through all the arteries of the mundane system, to its uttermost extremities, penetrating its utmost recesses and lowest depths, with its life-giving warmth.

Vegetable life, without exception, is generated under the sun's quickening influence; without it, not a seed would germinate, not a blade would spring, not a leaf would shoot, not a bud would burst, not a petal would unfold, not a flower would bloom, not a fruit would ripen. It alone raises and distils the dews and rains which feed and nourish the entire world of plants; it alone dyes the field and the forest with their verdure; it alone paints the blossom with its beauty, and tints with hues of loveliness both earth and heaven. It gives birth to the breezes, which stir the movements of every leaf and branch, scatter seeds and perfumes, and strip away all that has withered or yielded to decay. It is the joyful parent of spring, and the fruitful fount of summer wealth and autumnal glory.

Animals are equally indebted to the sun. Without it none of the innumerable forms of animal life could for a moment exist. Without its warmth all muscular power would be paralysed, the frozen blood would fail to circulate, respiration would cease, and life would inevitably become extinct. Its rising and its setting, its shining and withdrawing, its ascent in summer, its decline in autumn and winter, and return in spring, control the cycles and create the boundaries of all the phases of animated nature, the sleeping and the waking, the stillness and the activity, the silence and the song, the action, the passion, and the repose of innumerable tribes of living creatures, peopling air and earth and seas.

Man walks in its light, labours in its heat, basks in its smile, rejoices in its glory. It is the constant and irresistible ruler of days, and years, and seasons, and is enthroned as such, from generation to generation, and from age to age. In all these respects, it is the most glorious and sublime of all the material emblems of HIM, from whose creative fiat, it of old derived existence and dominion, and by whose unfailing power it is upheld; of Him who is the blessed and only Potentate, the King of kings and Lord of lords, the eternal and overflowing Source of light and love.

As the moon only reflects the sun's *light* in a very modified degree, and no perceptible portion of its *heat*, it exercises little direct influence on *organized* nature. Its indirect action upon the organized forms contained in, or affected by, the many seas, estuaries, and tidal rivers of the world, is very considerable. The existence of the immense variety of plants and animals which live on the shores or boundaries of sea and land, is to a large extent conditioned by the ebb and flow of tides. To man, the moon is a useful and beautiful night lamp, and an invaluable chronometer, while by its daily, world wide, tidal movement, it is as we have seen, next to the sun, his most powerful natural aid. It rules for him the night, and regulates his calendar, indicating by its movements, in conjunction with the sun, the measures of time which he universally adopts and follows.

A few familiar facts, illustrative of the above statements, may serve to give them the weight they deserve, and if any apology be needful for re-calling natural phenomena, with the existence of which many if not most are familiar, it must be found in the necessity which we are under, of firmly establishing the great truth of soli-lunar dominion over terrestrial move-ment and change, in order to the due appreciation of the subsequent portion of this treatise.

Be it then remembered that the sun not only produces day and night, and the succession of seasons in each particular locality, regulating by this means, the growth and activity of organized nature, but by its various degrees of elevation in different latitudes, it causes all the varieties of climates, and through these, the development and distribution of vegetable and animal life throughout the world. These various degrees of elevation, causing the sun to afford varying degrees of light and heat, produce the different zones into which our globe, as regards climate, is divided. The principal zones are the equatorial zone, the tropical zones, the subtropical, the warmer temperate, the colder temperate, the sub-arctic, the arctic, and the polar zones.

Now *life*, whatever may be its origin, clearly depends for its continuance, on the physical conditions by which it is surrounded. According to the degrees of moisture or drought, heat or cold, the plant or animal flourishes, or languishes and dies. It is only in the case of certain plants and animals, that "acclimatization" under non-natural circumstances is possible, and even with these, it is possible only within certain limits, and by the greatest care. The flora peculiar to a region of excessive drought, will not survive removal to a region of excessive humidity, nor will ferns and marsh plants thrive in the desert. It is obvious, therefore, that on a globe where the sun produces such diversity of climate, life must exist under widely diversified forms. No region, save the extreme polar perhaps, is utterly destitute, of it, but each has its own peculiar development. The intertropical regions of the earth, having in greatest perfection the conditions favourable to life, or in other words having a large share of solar heat and light, have an exuberant growth of vegetable life and a redundance of animal existence. This decreases in each zone as we proceed towards the poles, till we reach the boundary, where a minimum of solar light and heat forbid the exis-tence of any form of life.

Since temperature similarly decreases, as we ascend from the level of the sea into the higher regions of the atmosphere, vegetation varies, not only according to *latitude*, but according to *altitude*. The Alpine traveller may pass through the climates of the various zones in one day. He leaves the rich vineyards, and the flowering myrtle and pomegranate, the fruit-bearing orange and lemon-trees behind him, in the valley ; passes through woods of oaks, sweet-chestnuts and beeches, as he mounts the lower slopes ; and amid pines and birches, as he gains the higher parts of the mountain, till at last he finds only the short fine occasional pasture grass, and subsequently nothing but lichens and mosses, edging the beds of perpetual snow and ice. The vine disappears before he has climbed two thousand feet ; the chest-nuts have vanished at three ; the oak fails to put in an appearance at four, and the birch long before he has climbed five thousand feet. The spruce-fir greets him as high as 5,900 feet, but even it goes no further. For nearly two thousand feet above this last of the trees, the beautiful rhododendron and other shrubs, cover immense tracts of the mountain side ; the her-baceous willow, the saxifrages, the hardy dark-blue gentian and the grasses creep up to eight thousand feet, but only lichens and mosses go right up to meet the never melting snow which caps the mountain top.

It is the same in the world of waters. Marine plants are equally dis-tributed in zones, and have also a vertical arrangement. *Depth* regulates heat and light for aquatic vegetation, and each successively deepening zone has its own peculiar forms of life. The ocean is divided into littoral, circumlittoral, median, infra-median, and abyssal or deep-sea zones; in this last only the microscopic "diatoms" exist, at a depth of over six hundred feet. The ordinary algæ scarcely descend half that depth.

Animals have less precise geographical limits than plants, their powers of locomotion and self-dispersion modifying the influences which climate and external conditions have upon them. But there is a well marked horizontal and vertical arrangement of animals, from the equator to the poles, and from the sea level to the loftiest heights of land, and to the greatest depths of ocean. Thus the larger carnivora are pretty much confined to the tropics, as also the elephant, rhinoceros, and hippopotamus, the crocodile, boa, and larger reptiles, the ostrich, flamingo, parrots, humming birds, and the generality of birds of very brilliant plumage, together with a most varied and exuberant insect life, which for variety, size, activity, and brilliancy, attains its maximum in Brazil and the East Indies, decreasing towards the temperate zone.

The useful domestic animals—the horse, the ox, the sheep, the dog, are specially characteristic of the temperate zones, while the arctic regions have the polar bear and the reindeer, the musk ox, the wolf, the fox, and the sable : few species, but many individuals, and all sober and quiet in hue, and clad in warm furs. Reptile life does not exist in the arctic zone.

It is the same as regards the sea-animals, their range is by no means universal. In the torrid zone are found a vast variety of genera and of species, and in colder latitudes, fewer species, but enormous numbers of individuals. So the fishes and shell-fish of the sunny tropic are of beautiful tints and hues, while the seals and whales of the arctic regions, are sombre and uniform in colour. The seal and the walrus never visit the torrid zone, nor are sharks ever seen in polar seas. The great majority of the food fishes are only found in perfection in the cool waters of high latitudes ; and though the sea water contains everywhere the same constituents, the coral insect builds his reefs only in the subtropical expanses of the ocean.

When we pass on to notice the effect of solar dominion on human development, and on the distribution of men on the earth, we at once perceive that it must necessarily be of a far more indirect character, than that exercised over plants and animals, and more difficult to trace.

Man has not only power of locomotion, but he is imbued with curiosity, ambition, and many other motives, which impel him to wander, and therefore, though it is now confessed by all naturalists, that scientifically speaking, all the various races of mankind constitute a single species of a single genus, yet we find this species, domesticated under every variety of climate, and able to subsist almost equally well between the tropics and in the polar regions. At first sight this would seem to indicate, that as far as the development of the race is concerned, mankind is independent of climatic differences. But this is far from being the case, as a little consideration will show. Of the five great families into which the human race is divided, the Caucasian, Mongolian, Ethiopian, Malay, and American, the distinguishing characteristics have a marked relation to the climate, and consequent productions and physical peculiarities, of the lands inhabited by each. Man, it is true, can struggle against, or modify the physical conditions which surround him, but he is never independent of them. There can be no doubt that our own moderate climate, is more conducive to mental and bodily vigour, than is the relaxing heat of the great plains of Hindostan ; nor that the slight differences of the seasons to which we have to adapt all our habits and pursuits, have a stimulating effect on energy and activity, lacking to nations who are subjected to excessively hot summers and cold winters. But for our insular situation, Englishmen would probably never have been the traders and adventurers they are, and but for our natural supplies of coal and iron, we should never have acquired the mechanical and manufacturing character we now possess. Climate, food, and landscape, influence mental as well as bodily character. We speak of "depressing weather," of an " enervating " or of a " bracing " climate; of " inspiring " scenery, and so on, and the idea conveyed by these expressions, that the outer world affects the inner man, is true.

The White or Caucasian variety of the human family, is the one which exhibits in their highest degree, all the intellectual and moral powers of human nature. It belongs to the temperate zone in either hemisphere. " Man presents to our view his most perfect type at the very centre of the temperate continent, at the centre of Asia-Europe, in the regions of Iran, Armenia, and the Caucasus, and departing from this geographical centre, in the three grand directions of the lands, the types gradually lose the beauty of their forms, in proportion to their distance, even to the extreme points of the southern continents, where we find the most deformed and degenerate races, and the lowest in the scale of humanity." " The indigenous man of America," says M. Guyot, " bears in his whole character, the ineffaceable stamp of the peculiarly vegetative character of his country. Living continually in the shadow of those virgin forests, which overspread the country he inhabits, his whole nature has been modified thereby. The very copper hue of his complexion, indicates that he lives not like the Negro, beneath the scorching sunbeams. His lymphatic temperament betrays the preponderance in his nature of the vegetable element. . . . The Indian has continued the man of the forest ; he has seldom elevated himself above the condition of the hunter, the lowest grade in the scale of civilization ; he has never ascended to the rank of the pastoral man. With him no domestic animals are maintained to feed him with their milk, or clothe him with their fleeces, as they are by the nomadic races of the Old World. From one to the other extremity of America we find the same lamentable spectacle. The people of the elevated table-lands of Mexico and Peru are the only exceptions to this picture, and this exception goes far to establish *the influence of the vegetative and humid lower plains of America.*"

Thus it is evident that the advancement of man in civilization, depends in great measure on the physical conditions by which he is surrounded, and these in their turn depend, as we have seen, to a very large extent, on solar influence.

As the elevation or depression of the sun, with its resulting modifications of light and heat, in different latitudes, controls the distribution of plants and animals, and of the races of mankind ; so its elevation or depression at different hours of the day and at different seasons of the year, at any one given place, influences the development of human and other organic life, at those hours and seasons, and thus more or less affects the period of *birth*, the diurnal and annual process of *growth*, the increase or diminution of *nervous and muscular power and activity*, the changes and periods of *disease*, the stages of *decay*, and the season and moment of *death*. Statistics prove that the greatest number of births occur in December, February, and March, and the fewest in June, July, and August—a fact that can be accounted for only, by some annual or solar influence.

All paroxysmal diseases appear at some particular hour of the four and twenty. It is a well known fact, that gout and all arthritic diseases, as well as many purely nervous affections, attack their victims at two o'clock in the morning, and cholera usually just before daybreak. The paroxysm of a quotidian ague comes on at four or five o'clock a.m., a quartan at four or five p.m., and a tertian at noon or soon after. A quotidian comes on when the consumption of oxygen in respiration is at its lowest point, a tertian when it is at its highest. They also appear at one certain definite point in the deviation of the magnetic needle, and terminate at another. The baro·meter also is at its minimum variation when the paroxysms come on, and at its maximum when they end.

Hippocrates says: "Diseases of every kind may arise in any season of the year; others, however, increase, and are excited only in particular seasons." He then gives a list of the complaints peculiarly rife in each of the four seasons, which, though written two thousand years ago, is perfectly applicable to the case of Greece, in the present day.

"Spring and fall" have long been popularly known, as the seasons in which cutaneous eruptions are most apt to appear, and the habits of some of the exanthemata render it probable that there is a determination to the skin at these seasons. In pellagia, according to Dr. Holland's observations, the cutaneous affection remits in autumn, and recurs in the spring, with increased severity.

Diseases which arise from exoteric causes, at different periods of the year, may be arranged in two classes. Increase of heat produces decrease of density in the atmosphere; at each inspiration less oxygen is conveyed to the lungs in summer therefore, than in winter, less carbon is in consequence excreted by the lungs, and hence the necessity for increased action on the part of the liver, during the hot months. Thus liver complaints are more frequent in hot weather and in hot countries. The perspiratory organs of the skin are also more active in summer, and other secretions are proportionally diminished. Various diseases result from these and similar changes in the seasons. Another class arise from purely external causes, as hay fever, marsh and jungle fevers, sunstroke, etc. The action of remedies varies also under these circumstances. Diseases of the respiratory organs, being largely affected by temperature, are more frequently fatal in winter, than at any other season.*

Nor is it in the case of disease only, that this all-prevailing soli-lunar influence is perceptible. It has also a marked effect on certain perfectly

---

* *Deaths from Diseases of the Respiratory Organs.*

1840 { Summer		2981
{ Autumn		2999
1841 { Winter .		4732
{ Spring		3943

Deaths from Measles.

1840 { Summer		301
{ Autumn .		251
1841 { Winter .		346
{ Spring		102

Deaths from Scarlatina.

1840 { Summer		436
{ Autumn		534
1841 { Winter		294
{ Spring		125

Deaths from Small-pox.

1840 { Summer		213
{ Autumn		381
1841 { Winter . . .		850
{ Spring		354

Diseases.	Deaths in Summer and Autumn, 1840.	Deaths in Winter and Spring, 1841.
Respiratory Organs . .	5982	8675
Measles	552	448
Scarlatina	970	419
Small-pox	594	1204

Lancet, 1842–3. Vol. ii., p. 829.

Schweig inquired into the mortality at various hours of the day. The following table shows the result:—

	Morning.				
	4–5.	5–6.	6–7.	7–8.	8–9.
Winter . .	95	109	116	115	113
Summer .	120	119	99	100	107

natural and healthy phenomena, of which, in a subsequent chapter, we will speak more particularly.

How it affects these, it may be difficult to explain, but that it does so is an incontestable fact. These phenomena are based on healthy and natural

	Evening.					
	4–5.	5–6.	6–7.	7–8.	8–9.	9–10.
Winter . .	103	114	81	77	105	111
Summer. .	111	119	132	82	86	110

The following tables show the hour of the day most influential in determining death from consumption :—

Deaths in Berlin in 1836 *from Phthisis.*

Midnight to six o'clock a.m.	165.	Ratio per 1000	220.
Six o'clock a.m. to noon .	220.	,, ,, ,,	294.
Noon to six o'clock p.m. .	197.	,, ,, ,,	263.
Six o'clock p.m. to midnight .	167.	,, ,, ,,	223.
Total	749 cases.		1000.

Deaths from Phthisis in Carlsruhe in Eleven Years.

Midnight to six o'clock a.m.	187.	Ratio per 1000	239.
Six o'clock a.m. to noon .	218.	,, ,, ,,	280.
Noon to six o'clock p.m. .	195.	,, ,, ,,	250.
Six o'clock p.m. to midnight .	180.	,, ,, ,,	231.
Total	780 cases.		1000.

Med. Quarterly Review. No. 35, p. 175.

	Maximum.	*Minimum.*
Variations in the barometer :—		
(*a*) Near London, 1807 to 1816	December	July.
(*b*) In the Deccan . . .	December or January	July.
Variations in the hygrometer .	January	July.
,, ,, thermometer .	July or August	January.
Amount of evaporation . .	July	January.
Number of births (Belgium) .	February	July.
,, ,, deaths (Belgium) .	January	July.
Cases of Insanity . . .	June or July	December or January.
,, ,, Suicide	Summer	Winter.
Crimes against persons .	June	January.
,, ,, property . .	December	July.

Dr. LAYCOCK. *Lancet,* 1842-3, p. 828.

revolutions of the system, and may be dependent on cyclical processes inherent in the system itself, or on periodic agencies acting from without, or they may result from a combination of these two ; that is, the causes may be esoteric, exoteric or endexoteric.

The most important of these alternations, proper to the system is that of activity and repose. During sleep the nervous system undergoes a remarkable functional change, the brain and nerves being more or less physiologically paralysed, as the sleep is more or less profound.*

The foregoing facts prove that in appointing the sun as the

---

* " The period of repose or sleep may be defined generally as extending from ten or eleven o'clock, p.m., to four or five, a.m. ; and I would here remark, that there is a numerous class of affections of the nervous system, which I have elsewhere termed neuræmic, resembling sleep in this, that they are dependent on some temporary change in the functions of the brain itself, apparently connected with a disturbance of the capillary circulation of that organ, or, perhaps, with some passing change in the composition of the blood, but, like sleep, unconnected with any appreciable alteration in the structure of the brain. *Many, if not all affections of this class are periodic;* and it is obvious that these, as well as all other diseases primarily dependent upon morbid functional derangement of the nervous system, *are most likely to appear when the natural functional derangement is greatest:* that is to say, about two o'clock in the morning, when sleep is most profound. Probably connected with this periodic change in the nervous system, are *the equally periodic changes in the functions of the heart, lungs, etc., observed by physiologists to occur diurnally.* Dr. Prout found THE CONSUMPTION OF OXYGEN GAS IN RESPIRATION to vary during the day as follows :—The *maximum* consumption is from eleven o'clock, a.m., to one o'clock, p.m. ; it then gradually decreases to a *minimum* about half-past eight, p.m., at which point it is stationary until half-past three o'clock, a.m. The amount then suddenly increases ; at first slowly, to its maximum, about *noon; and from this point it almost immediately begins to sink,* at first quickly, to its minimum, at half-past eight, p.m. *Dr. Prout conceives that* THESE VARIATIONS ARE REGULATED BY THE PRESENCE OR ABSENCE OF THE SUN. THE CIRCULATION has also its regular periods of change. So long ago as 1815, Mr. Knox inferred, from a series of observations, that during the morning the mere change from the horizontal to the erect posture renders the pulse more frequent by about fifteen or twenty beats ; at mid-day the increase is about ten, and in the evening four or six. Mr. Knox, some years subsequently, confirmed these results, and showed that the diurnal revolution, both as to numbers and excitability, is altogether independent of food or exercise. More recently Dr. Guy has come to almost similar conclusions. According to his experiments, " the effect of change of posture is *greatest in the forenoon,* and *least in the afternoon,* the effect in the evening being the mean between the other two ; and the effect produced by change of posture on the same frequency of the pulse in the afternoon, forenoon, and evening, respectively, is as the numbers eight, nine, and ten."

great time-measurer, the Creator selected the physical ruler of the world, the lord paramount of all its movements, the source of its entire life and activity, of its rotation, revolution, heat, light, seasonal differences, magnetic impulses, and tidal changes; of its winds, waves, and currents; its rains, snows, and frosts; of the actual distribution of its plants and animals; and of many important phenomena connected with the course and development of the human race itself.

The sun and moon are all-powerful in their influence over the earth; no one, no thing, is unconscious of their presence or absence; they control this globe, in all its movements and changes, from the most obvious and sublime, to the most occult and complicated; not an atom of matter is uninfluenced by them, nothing can resist their might or alter their movements. Those movements, conspicuous, periodical, regular, and adapted as they are to the necessities of the animal and vegetable creation—produce our times and seasons. The periods measured by their simple primary revolutions, we call days, months, and years, and our ordinary computation of time is by fractions or multiples of these; while their vast and secular motions afford superior standards, for the measurement of longer and slower changes in the history of the earth, and of the human race.

The facts then of the all-controlling *potency* and of the accu-

---

Dr. Guy states that the observations of Nick. published at Tübingen in 1828, are equally corroborative of Dr. Knox's views.

DIURNAL CHANGES IN THE INSANE. A diurnally periodic state of excitement of the system generally has been observed in the insane, as *à priori* might be anticipated. Dr. Allen made observations regarding this point on the insane patients under his care. . . . The first period of *increased* excitement is from four to half-past nine in the morning, and the second period is from four to half-past nine in the evening. The periods of *diminished* excitement extend from half-past nine, a.m., to four, p.m., and from half-past nine, p.m., to four, a.m., the hours corresponding very closely with Dr. Prout's observation. IT IS OBVIOUS THAT THESE CHANGES IN THE NERVOUS, RESPIRATORY AND CIRCULATORY SYSTEM MUST NECESSARILY INFLUENCE IN SOME DEGREE THE TIMES OF ACCESSION OF ALL DISEASES, but particularly of the paroxysms of intermittents."—DR. LAYCOCK.

rate *periodicity*, of the two great rulers of our globe, the sun and the moon, impart to the greater and lesser SOLI-LUNAR MEASURES OF TIME a vast and supreme importance. Any system of chronology which neglects the periods resulting from their sole and joint movements, is an unnatural and unstable system. On the other hand the fact that the events and cycles of human life and progress, of history and of prophecy, from the most minute to the most extensive, measured by soli-lunar chronology, fall into order, and arrange themselves into a symmetrical system,—such a fact, if it can be demonstrated, will be in evident harmony with the established order in nature.

The periods resulting from combined solar and lunar movements, must therefore, in the investigation of the world's chronology, be allowed to have a place of paramount importance. To ignore *them*, is to ignore the golden clue to the complex labyrinth; while patiently and consistently to employ them, is to follow the guidance granted by the great Creator, through the phenomena of creation,—the only way of attaining scientific truth.

We turn therefore now to observe the remarkable fact, that many vital phenomena of world-wide and unceasing occurrence, and many historic and prophetic periods, of the first importance in the annals of humanity, have, when measured by these minor and major soli-lunar revolutions, a singular, septiform, chronology, which stamps them as parts of one and the same system.

SECTION II.

The Law of Completion in Weeks.

CHAPTER I.

THE WEEK IN RELATION TO THE PERIODICITY OF VITAL PHENOMENA. .

PERIODICITY IN THE DEVELOPMENT OF INSECTS, FISHES, BIRDS AND MAMMALIA.—PERIODICITY IN THE GROWTH AND FUNCTIONAL ACTIVITY OF MANKIND IN HEALTH AND IN DISEASE.

THE birth, growth, maturity, vital functions, healthy revolutions of change, diseases, decay and death, of insects, reptiles, fishes, birds, mammals, and even of man himself, are more or less controlled by a law of *completion in weeks*.

The hatching of the ova of insects occupies in a large number of cases, intervals varying from two to six *weeks*. Their continuance in the caterpillar or larva condition is seldom less than seven days, and varies from this period to four weeks, six weeks, or longer periods. The exuviation, or change of skin, which occurs during this larva state, frequently takes place at intervals of seven days.*

---

* From an interesting series of papers contributed by Dr. Laycock, to the *Lancet*, in the years 1842-3, on the subject of Periodicity in Vital Phenomena, we extract the following :—

"*I found the most remarkable illustration and confirmation of the law in insects.* The changes to be noticed in insects as being regulated, as regards the time they occupy, by this law, are as following :—

" 1. The hatching of the ova.

" 2. The caterpillar, or larva state, and the moults which take place at that stage of development.

" 3. The pupa, or chrysalis period.

" 4. The imago state, or puberty.

"THE OVA are hatched in periods varying considerably in length. The shortest is *half a week* or seven (half) days, as in the wasp, the common

The moults of insects, the exuviation of serpents, the renewal of the plumage of birds, and of the coats of other

---

bee, and ichneumon ; in some, as the cecidomia tritici, the period is *one week ;* in others it is a week and a half, as, for example, the black cater-pillar and the gooseberry grub (tenthredo capræa). *In the majority oj insects however it is from two weeks to six weeks.*

"The ova of the glow-worm occupy six weeks ; of the mole cricket only four weeks, in hatching.

"THE LARVA. The period passed by insects in the larva will vary in length as the insect varies ; but I think it is seldom less than seven days. In the common bee it is six days and a half, in the humble-bee seven days exactly. *In day papiliones it is four weeks, in moths six weeks.* In many insects it is a long period, continuing for months. The larva of a new British wasp, of the genus oplopus, occupies twelve weeks ; namely, from the period when its two first segments coalesced to the throwing off of its exuviæ was *three weeks*, and from the time of the latter change to its full development, *nine weeks*. It is worthy of notice that the time occupied between each exuviation of the larva is limited in the same manner as the period of the larva state itself is limited. Thus, the latter period of the common black caterpillar is twenty-one days, or *three weeks ;* during this period it exuviates, or *changes its skin three times, at intervals of seven days each.* The wood-piercer bee is in the larva state *four weeks ;* of these four weeks it fasts exactly one, just before it enters the pupa state

"THE PUPA. *The period spent in the pupa state is the most in accordance with the general law of limitation by weeks ;* in fact, the more exact the observations are as to the length of this period, the more confirmatory are they of the general rule. For example, Mr. Denny had three larvæ of the sphinx atropos, which went into the earth on August 22nd, 24th, and September 2nd, respectively. They appeared as perfect moths on October 16th, 18th, and 27th; or, in each case, *in exactly eight weeks.* If the pupa state is entered late in the summer, the perfect insect does not appear until the following spring. Larvæ and ova will also hybernate in the same way; *but in all cases the period occupied is a definite number of weeks,* some are forty, others forty-two, and forty-eight weeks.

"THE IMAGO. I have not been able to collate observations as to the duration of the imago state, very few having been made ; but the vital actions of the perfect insect appear subject to the same general law. Thus, twenty or twenty-one days after the queen bee has begun to lay the eggs of drones, the bees begin to construct royal cells. If the impregnation of the queen be retarded beyond the twenty-first day (Huber) or twenty-eighth (Kirby and Spence), of her whole existence, she lays only male eggs ; and Huber states that after the twenty-eighth day, under these circumstances, she loses all feelings of jealousy towards the young queens in the nymphine state, and never attempts to injure them. Some insects attain puberty almost immediately after leaving the puparium ; others are a considerable time before their organs acquire sufficient hardness, especially some of the beetle tribe. Thus the newly-disclosed imago of cetonia aurata remains *a fortnight* under the earth, and that of the lucanus cervus not less than *three weeks.*"

animals are similarly regulated by a law of weeks. So are the periods of the laying of eggs, and of incubation, in many birds. The common hen, as is well known, sits three weeks ; the pigeon two, after having laid eggs also for two weeks. The seal calves on the rocks, and suckles its young for two weeks, when the calf casts its coat and goes into the water.

The ova of salmon are hatched in 140 days, or twenty weeks ; and those of the aquatic salamander in two weeks or fifteen days. But the habits and physiology of fishes and reptiles are comparatively little known or observed, so that few confirmatory facts, can be drawn from this department of the animal kingdom.

The periods of utero-gestation in many of the mammalia, and of incubation in numbers of birds, have been accurately and carefully noted. Out of one hundred and twenty-nine species observed by Dr. Laycock, sixty-seven had periods which were an *exact* number of weeks or months, twenty-four were so within a day, and only four were exceptions to the rule, as far as could be ascertained.*

---

* " I turned my attention to the periods of utero-gestation in lower animals, as I felt anxious to learn *whether any such limitation of the period by weeks could be traced as affecting them.* I tabulated the periods of gestation in various mammals, and the period of incubation in birds, as they were stated in works on natural history, and as I could make them out from personal inquiries whenever opportunity offered. Of course rigid accuracy could not be looked for in observations of this kind, but, such as they were *they confirmed the general law of limitation by weeks observed in the sex.* I collected tolerably trustworthy observations of this kind referring to *one hundred and twenty-nine species of birds and mammals* (some being, indeed, rigidly exact), and in sixty-seven of these the periods of utero-gestation and incubation were a definite number of weeks or months; twenty-four exhibited periods being within a day of the definite number, and in the remaining thirty-nine the period was so loosely stated as not to be of much weight either for or against the general law, although by far the greater number were decidedly favourable. Altogether I judged that there were only four available exceptions. As examples of this law may be stated— in the grallidæ, tetraonidæ, and other birds of about the same size, the period is *three weeks ;* in the anatidæ, *four weeks ;* the cygnidæ, *six weeks ;* but in small birds, as the muscipáræ, only *two weeks.*

" The facts I have briefly glanced at are general facts, and *cannot happen day after day in so many millions of animals of every kind,* FROM LARVA OR OVUM OF A MINUTE INSECT UP TO MAN *at definite periods, from a mere*

And it is well known that when we mount still higher in the scale of animated existence, and study the entire system of vital periodicity impressed by its great Creator on the human family, this law of limitation by weeks becomes conspicuous and all-pervading. From the cradle to the grave, and from before the cradle, from the day of conception to the day of death, every man, woman and child of our race, is strangely amenable to it. Consciously to one sex, unconsciously, but none the less really to the other, there is an alternate loss and gain of physical substance, *every four weeks.**

In the human family, the period of utero-gestation, is accurately *forty weeks*, nor do differences of age, climate, or circumstances, cause any variation in this period. It is *the rule*, though it has of course exceptions.

Dr. Denman, in his work on midwifery, states, " The common time of utero-gestation is *forty weeks*   I do not mean that it is completed to a minute or an hour, as has been surmised, because the birth of the child may be delayed by a mul-

---

chance or coincidence ; and although temperature, food, domestication, and other modifying circumstances, may and do interrupt the regulaiity with which the various processes, I have alluded to, are conducted, yet upon the whole it is, I think, impossible to come to any less general conclusion than this, that, *in animals, changes occur every three and a half, seven, fourteen, twenty-one, or twenty-eight days, or at some definite number of weeks.*"—DR. LAYCOCK.

* " It is well known to physicians, that there is a large class of diseases, the symptoms of which recur at regular intervals of time. It so happened that I had appointed myself the task of investigating those nervous affections belonging to this class, and I directed my inquiries in particular to the rule or law by which the interval between the paroxysms is regulated. Of course *the phenomena of menstruation* first demanded my attention as a *normal periodic movement.* In the course of my inquiries I ascertained that the interval between each such period was not always *four* weeks ; but occasionally *two weeks, three weeks, five weeks,* and even *six weeks.* Facts being such, I determined on *counting the interval by weeks.* The circumstances connected with menstruation led necessarily to those connected with the period of utero-gestation. This, it is well known, is *usually forty weeks;* but here again I found exceptions to the general law, like those just now mentioned, that is to say, *the period was exceeded or shortened by weeks.*"—DR. LAYCOCK.

From some " statistical details respecting the menstrual periods," given in Schweig's researches, we learn that " the results of 200 menstruations in tiplicity of accidents. But parturition will be accomplished, or the parturient disposition will take place, before or at *the expiration of forty weeks from the time of conception.* Nor does it seem reasonable that A LAW OF NATURE, which is not altered by the differences of age, by the diet, by the extremes of climates, by the severities of slavery, or the indulgences of luxury, should be changed by circumstances of less importance." *

Thus throughout all ages, and in all countries, the initial stage of human existence, the intra-uterine life of every one born into the wide world, is measured by *weeks;* and not till forty weeks have run their course, does the human being attain independent existence. These are phenomena of universal occurrence, and of fundamental importance in the natural history of mankind; they are leading and unquestionable physiological facts. The periodicity of *life*, and the periodicity of *birth*, need no demonstration, for the experience of every individual bears witness to it, as well as to the fact that it is *regulated by a law of weeks.* And if this

thirty-four individuals, showed an average of 27-8 days, *the maximum number in the table being* 28 *days.*" (*Medical Review, July,* 1844.)

Even *exceptional* cases to the ordinary monthly period, are regulated by a *weekly* variation. "I sought the explanation of such cases, and found that, in one half of the *three-weekly cases*, the type was explained by ovario-uterine disease of an organic nature, or by chlorosis; and in more than one half of the *six-weekly* cases, the patient's health was habitually bad, owing in two instances to uterine disease, which was also the case with the one that assumed the *fortnightly* type."—(TILT, "On Uterine Inflammation.")

There is an analogous *monthly gain and loss of substance and weight in the case of men*, which was first discovered by Sanctorius. "Nature, animate or inanimate, is full of periodically recurring phenomena. The periodicity of our planetary system is felt by man, for he experiences, by insensible perspiration, a constant *periodical* loss, which was first discovered by Sanctorius, who established—that even those who are in a perfect state of health, and observe the utmost moderation in living, *once a month increase beyond their usual weight to the quantity of one or two pounds, and at the month's end return again to their usual standard*, and that this is accompanied by an important change in the secretions. A further analogy between menstruation and the monthly oscillation in the urinary discharge referred to, as observed by Sanctorius, is that, 'before the aforesaid crisis happens, there is felt a heaviness in the head, and a lassitude all over the body, which symptoms are afterwards removed.' "—(Tilt, p. 204.)

* Denman, vol. i. p. 306.

be the case in health, and with normal functions, so is it also with disease, and in abnormal derangements. From time immemorial, it has been observed that fevers, and intermittent attacks of ague, gout, and similar complaints, have a septiform periodicity; that the seventh, fourteenth, and twenty-first, are critical days.

In his investigation into the phenomena of fevers, Dr. Laycock states that,

" *Whatever type the fever may exhibit, there will be a paroxysm on the seventh day*, and consequently this day should be distinguished by an unusual fatality or number of crises. For analogous reasons *the fourteenth will be remarkable as a day of amendment*, the last paroxysm of a quotidian taking place on that day, and the last of a tertian on the day previous; for observation has established that if a tertian is to cease about the fourth paroxysm (the seventh critical day), the second paroxysm will be more severe than the first or third; but if the fourth be severe, and the fifth less so, the disease will end at the seventh paroxysm, and, of course, the change for the better, if this rule be applied to remittent or continued fevers, will be seen on *the fourteenth day*. Should, however, the exacerbation occurring on the thirteenth day end fatally, whether it be the seventh of a tertian or the fifth of a quartan, death will probably take place early on the fourteenth day, namely, about three or four o'clock, a.m., when the system is most languid."

That these theoretical inferences are borne out by facts, all medical writers agree, and indeed it may be proved numerically by tables of cases, compiled without the least reference to critical days.*

---

* Forestius relates forty-eight cases of acute fever, without any reference to critical days; five of these terminated on the fourth day, *twenty-two on the seventh*, two on the eleventh, and *seven on the fourteenth*. The cases detailed by Stoll in his ' Ratio Medendi,' exhibit the same general fact; the seventh and fourteenth days, and then the fourth and eleventh, are the most remarkable.

Nor is it in fevers alone that this law of septiform periodicity is traceable. Paroxysms of gout afford another illustration of its operation.

"A fit of the gout going regularly through its stages in a robust subject, observes *the following order :—*

" The patient retires to rest well, or perhaps in better spirits than usual, and is awoke at two o'clock in the morning by rigors, thirst, and other febrile symptoms, and with pain in the great toe, or heel, or other part. This pain and the febrile action go on increasing *for exactly twenty-four hours,* that is to say, until two o'clock, a.m., comes again, when a remission takes place, sometimes an intermission ; *the interval it occupies being another nyctemeron, or period of twenty-four hours,* at the end of which another febrile paroxysm comes on. And so paroxysm and remission or intermission alternate, until the fit terminates. A fit of the gout, under the circumstances stated, is a tertian intermittent (in the *measure of its intervals*), and, like a tertian, *it terminates in fourteen days, or after seven paroxysms.*

" If the patient go on luxuriating in his diet, the next fit, if left to flannel and patience, will be of a *double length,* or occupy *twenty-eight days,* and have *fourteen febrile paroxysms,* or exacerbations ; or it will be *tripled,* and be of six weeks' duration, and *so go on increasing in length by a definite ratio of weeks,* as the predisposing and exciting causes become more efficient, until the viscera and the general system become so deranged that no regular fit takes place."

It is important also to notice, that not only is *the week* an evident measure in such fevers, and intermittents, but *the half-week also.* His investigations of the subject of vital periodicity forced this fact on the notice of Dr. Laycock, and its agreement with the periods of prophecy, leads us to call attention to his statement.

" The complete day of twenty-four hours is the pathological period most generally noticed by physicians; but, as I have

---

* See *Lancet,* 1842-3, vol. i., p. 128.

shown, there are also *periods of three days and a half*, or *seven half-days*. *This is, in fact, the ancient division of the whole day, or* νυχθήμερον, *into two parts.* We must start with *this half-day, or day of twelve hours, as the unit* which will comprise the phenomena of the best-marked class of periodic disease, the intermittents. Dr. Graves is, I believe, the only physician who has made this observation, and applied it to pathology. He observed that, if this period were adopted, '*we should not count three days and a half, but seven half-days:* we would not say seven days, but fourteen half-days.' Reckoning thus, many of the anomalous critical effects, and critical terminations in continued fevers, would, I have no doubt, be found *strictly conformable to some regular law of periodicity.*" *

The operation of the law we are considering may be traced also in the growth of children and young people from infancy to maturity, in the duration of the human powers, in their fullest perfection, and in their gradual decay.

Dr. Laycock divides life into *three great periods*, the first and last, each stretching over 21 years, and the central period or prime of life lasting 28 years.

The *first*, which extends from conception to full maturity at 21 years of age, he subdivides into seven distinct stages, marked by well defined physical characteristics, as follows :—

" 1. Intra-uterine life ;

" 2. The period between birth and the first dentition ;

" 3. The time occupied by the first dentition ;

" 4. The period between the first and second dentition ;

" 5. The time of the second dentition ;

" 6. The period between the latter and commencing puberty ;

" 7. The time occupied in the evolution of the reproductive system.

"The *second* great period will comprise three minor periods :—

"1. The perfecting of adolescence, from 21 to 28 ;

"2. The climax of development, or status of life, from 28 to 42 ; and

"3. The septenary of decline in the reproductive powers, extending from 42 to 49 (after which latter age conception rarely takes place).

"The *third* great period comprises also three minor subdivisions :—

"1. The grand climacteric, from 49 to 63 ;

"2. Old age, from 63 to 70 ;

"3. The years of ætas ingravescence, or decrepitude, from 70 to death.

"In fixing these epochs," says Dr. Laycock, "I have followed the generally received septennial division, being reluctant to make any innovation thereon. It would I think, however, be more in accordance with modern science, *to date, not from birth, but from the conception of the individual.* If this be done, each great period, should be calculated as commencing forty weeks earlier."

The process of dentition affords also illustrations of the operation of the law of septiform periodicity in vital phenomena ; * and viability, or the probability of life, is highest at 14

---

* "The order of the development of the *teeth* in man is an interesting subject, as upon it we must principally rely for determining the periods of development in the system generally. Mr. Goodsir's researches are exceedingly interesting, as marking this gradual hebdomadal evolution in the embryo and fœtus, but are not sufficiently accurate for our purpose as to the *time* when the changes occur. Previous to the *eruptive* stage, or common dentition, there are three phases of development ; the *papillary*, commencing about *the seventh week* of fœtal life, the *pollicular* in the *tenth*, and the *saccular* in the *fourteenth week*, which continue until the eruptive stage, about *the seventh month after birth*, when the four central incisors present themselves. After this the other teeth appear at intervals not yet precisely fixed, the first dentition being terminated, however, by the end of the thirty-sixth month. All is then quiescent for three or four years, or until *the middle or end of the seventh year*, when the first true molar makes its appearance, which according to Mr. Goodsir, is analogous to the milk teeth in its mode of formation, the permanent central incisors appearing about the same time."—*Lancet*, 1843-4, vol. iii., p. 255.

years of age. Dr. Laycock puts the results of his careful re-searches, into the five following propositions :—

" 1. That there is a general law of periodicity which regulates *all* the vital movements in *all* animals.

" 2. That the periods within which these movements take place admit of calculations approximately exact.

" 3. That the fundamental unit,—the unit upon which these calculations should be based,—must for the present be con-sidered as one day of twelve hours.

" 4. That the lesser periods are simple and compound multi-ples of this unit, in a numerical ratio analogous to that observed in chemical compounds.

" 5. That the fundamental unit of the greater periods is *one week of seven days, each day being twelve hours ;* and that single and compound *multiples* of this unit, determine the length of these periods by the same ratio, as multiples of the unit of twelve hours determine the lesser periods. *This law binds all periodic vital phenomena together, and links the periods observed in the lowest annulose animals, with those of man himself, the highest of the vertebrata.* . . ."

He concludes his investigation with the following words :—
" The sure and steady course of proleptical science will be from particulars to generals, and if its foundation be firmly established on severe induction, we may hope at some future day to extend its principles to the cycles of the seasons, and to comprise within its sphere, not only individual men and women, but societies generally, and even the whole human race. The axiom that the whole is equal to the sum of all its parts, is universally true, whatever the whole may be; and there is really no reason for despairing that we shall attain to a knowledge of the whole alluded to, (a knowledge which must necessarily be derived from a knowledge of its parts,) because those parts are microscopically small to the intellect. The boundaries of astronomical science have been pushed from small and obscure beginnings, into the infinite in space, time, and number ; and who can tell but that *Providence may so assist*

the humble inquirer into nature, that science shall be extended to the infinite in littleness, and so man be able to look down, by the light of philosophy, upon the varied phenomena of terrestrial life,—their multifarious combinations and complexities, their cycles and epicycles,—as he looks into the planetary world; and see nothing but order and simplicity where now there appears inextricable confusion." *

" *There is a harmony of numbers in all nature ;* in the force of gravity, in the planetary movements, in the laws of heat, light, electricity, and chemical affinity, in the forms of animals and plants, in the perceptions of the mind. The direction indeed of modern natural and physical science, is towards a generalisation which shall express the fundamental laws of all, by one simple numerical ratio. We would refer to Professor Whewell's ' Philosophy of the Inductive Sciences,' and to Mr. Hay's researches into the laws of harmonious colouring and form. *From these it appears that the number seven is distinguished in the laws regulating the harmonious perception of forms, colours, and sounds,* and probably of taste also, if we could analyse our sensations of this kind with mathematical accuracy."†

There are probably few branches of natural science from which additional facts in confirmation might not be culled. But the above may suffice, for our object is less to trace the extent of the dominion of this law, than to prove its existence in nature. The realm of entomology recognises this law, ichthyology and ornithology do the same, and the mammalia equally bear witness to its prevalence. As to man, his birth, growth, dentition, development, maturity, vital functions, reproductive system, health, disease, life and death, all his times and all his seasons, are more or less distinctly controlled by the law of completion in weeks. His very pulse keeps time to the seven day period. Dr. Stratton states (as the result of several series of observations) that in health, the human pulse is more frequent in the morning than in the

---

* *Lancet,* 1842-3.   † *Med. Review,* July, 1844.

evening, for six days out of seven ; and that *on the seventh day it is slower.* *

And man's life as a whole is a week, a week of decades. "The days of our years are threescore years and ten " and that by Divine appointment. Combining the testimony of all these facts, we are bound to admit that *there prevails in organic nature a law of septiform periodicity, a law of completion in weeks.* We turn now to consider, the prevalence of the same law in Scripture.

---

* *Edinburgh Med. and Surgical Journal,* Jan., 1843.

CHAPTER II.

The Week in Scripture.

FROM the foregoing facts it is abundantly evident that the hand of the Creator has regulated a vast variety of world-wide vital phenomena, by a *law of weeks:* that a septiform periodicity has been, by God Himself, impressed upon nature.

The Holy Scriptures claim to be a revelation from the God of nature, and an orderly and consistent system of chronology is one marked feature of the sacred volume. *Now it is a most noteworthy and indisputable fact, that this system is, from first to last, a system of weeks: septiform periodicity is stamped upon the Bible, as conspicuously and even more so, than on nature.*

The whole of its chronology—beginning with the order of creation unfolded in its earliest chapters, including the entire order of Providence revealed in its succeeding portion, and the typical and actual chronology of redemption itself—is regulated by the law of weeks. The times prior to the existence of man; the times recorded by the histories of the Pentateuch; the times enacted by the Mosaic ritual; the times traceable in Jewish history; and the times unfolded by the prophets,—all are without exception characterized by this feature. The actual length of the days of creation, whether longer or shorter, does not affect this statement, for the septiformity of creation chronology is equally clear, whatever may have been the measures of the creation week; and the Bible system includes, as we shall see, weeks on a great variety of scales.

The Levitical law contained a ceremonial system which shadowed forth good things to come, and the chronology of its observances, which was one of its most marked features, was as typical as all the rest—typical of the chronology of redemption history. The Levitical chronology was a system of weeks on various scales of magnitude; one which employed the main natural divisions of time, the day, month, and year, as units for its weeks, and which also employed the largest of these weeks, as a unit for still larger septiform periods. And as the complete chronology of the typical *law* foreshadowed the wonderful history of redemption, so the chronology of Old and New Testament *prophecy*, has reference to the same; for prophecy is only history anticipated, as types are history foreshown in action. But the views of history given in divinely inspired prophecy, are wider, and more comprehensive than can be found elsewhere, and therefore in prophetic chronology, we find periods of vaster scope—plainly foretold, or obscurely intimated—and above all a key to the whole plan of history. In this grand prophetic chronology, we trace the same system; it is throughout septiform, it consists of *a series of weeks*.

Here, the legal week of seven years, the week whose unit is a solar year, is multiplied tenfold (70 years) and seventy-fold (490 years); and here on the same principle, only on a higher scale, as the year had been previously employed as the unit of a week, so it is now employed as the unit of a year; this is the year-day system of chronological symbolic prophecy.

Weeks of such years are appointed as the measures of vast periods of history, distinguished one from the other by moral features, and by varied degrees of Divine revelation, such as the Patriarchal, Jewish, and Christian dispensations.

In all these different departments of Scripture, we shall find a uniform consistent chronological plan—*the week* reigns supreme;

it measures alike the briefest and the longest periods, and can be traced in various forms, in the law, in the prophets, and in the gospel. It runs like a golden thread through the entire texture of the Bible ; and this fact alone, were there no other evidence on the point, proves *a unity of design*, pervading this collection of the writings of about forty different authors of various lands and ages, which argues it the product of one inspiring mind,—the mind of the great Creator. On the world his hands have fashioned, and on the Word his Spirit has inspired, He has stamped in equally indelible characters, *the week*, as the divinely selected measure of human time.

In connection with the first appearance of the week—on the opening page of Scripture in the narrative of the creation, we find an exposition of its profound meaning, the moral object and end of God in its selection. It is the period that leads up to, and terminates in, the *rest of God*. We read, " On the seventh day God ended his work which He had made, and He rested on the seventh day from all his work which He had made. And God blessed the seventh day and sanctified it, *because* that in it He had rested from all his work, which God created and made." The same reason is assigned for the enjoined observance of the Sabbath, in the law given at Sinai " Six days shalt thou labour and do all thy work ; but the seventh day is the sabbath of the Lord thy God, in it thou shalt not do any work. . . . for in six days the Lord made heaven and earth, the sea and all that in them is, and rested the seventh day, wherefore the Lord blessed the seventh day and hallowed it."

The rest of God, and of man his creature, with God, in the enjoyment of the results of the work of God,—results which God Himself sees to be very good,—this is the end attained, at the close of the week ; this is the sabbath. This was the creation sabbath, soon, alas ! marred by sin ; this shall be the redemption sabbath, when the second great work of God, the new creation in Christ Jesus, is complete. No sooner had sin destroyed the sabbath rest of creation, than the great

Creator, in his invincible goodness, began to work again. "My Father worketh hitherto, and I work," said Christ; and such is still the case, for redemption is not yet complete, and the rest of God, and of man with God, is still future.

The Hebrew word translated "week" means *seven*, and would designate any period composed of *seven shorter* periods, whether days, weeks, years, decades, centuries, millenaries, or any other unit. The following were the various weeks, appointed under the Jewish ritual, for perpetual observance in Israel :—

1. The week of days. Gen. ii. 2, 3; Exod. xx.
2. The week of weeks. Pentecost. Lev. xxiii.
3. The week of months. Jewish sacred year. Lev. xxiii.
4. The week of years. Sabbatic year law. Lev. xxv.
5. The week of weeks of years. The Jubilee. Lev. xxv.

(i.) THE WEEK OF DAYS.

Taking them in the above order, we glance first at the natural week, of seven days, established in Eden, and the perpetual observance of which was enjoined under the law. To this week the Divine hand has attached, as we have seen, the idea of labour issuing in rest, of the stages of creature development terminating in maturity, and thus of the attainment by the creature, of moral and spiritual perfection. The sabbath expressed the entire complacency of God, and the entire satisfaction of man, in all that God had created and made.

This was the period appointed under the Levitical law, for many of those consecrations, which were the impartation of ceremonial or typical perfection. The process of consecrating Aaron and his sons, to the work of the priesthood, that they might minister before the Lord, for Israel, lasted seven days. (Exod. xxix. 35.) That also of sanctifying the altar, that it might become an altar most holy, imparting sanctity to all that touched it, lasted similarly *seven days*. (Exod. xxix. 37.)

Thus also the period of the duration of ceremonial uncleanness, was in a number of cases, limited by *seven days*, at the close of which ceremonial purity was restored. On the birth of a male child for instance, a woman was considered unclean for *seven days* (Lev. xii. 2), nor could the child, during that week, be circumcised. Circumcision could not take place till the eighth day.

The firstborn of cattle devoted to God were not to be offered during the first seven days. "*Seven days* shall it be with its dam, and on the eighth day thou shalt give it to Me" (Exod. xxii. 30). "On the eighth day and thenceforth it shall be accepted for an offering made by fire unto the Lord" (Lev. xxii. 27).

Various other ceremonial observances, of a similar nature, were enacted in Israel. Defilement from a running issue, or from an issue of blood, lasted *seven days*. (Lev. xv. 13–19.) The suspected leper was to be shut up *seven days*, and even after he was pronounced clean, he was still to tarry abroad out of his tent *seven days*. (Lev. xiii. 14.) Miriam, on account of her leprosy, was shut out of the camp seven days. (Num. xii. 14.) The house, or the garment infected with the plague of leprosy, were similarly to be shut up *seven days*.

Defilement by contact with the dead, also endured *seven days*, that is the ceremonial purity forfeited by this contact, could not be restored in less than *seven days*. (Num. xix. 11.) Thus the purification of the men, after the slaughter of the Midianites, lasted *seven days*. (Num. xxxi. 19.)

It is much insisted on in the law that the feast of unleavened bread should last "*seven days*." Under pain of death, all leaven was, during this period, to be put away from Jewish dwellings. (Exod. xii.) The feast of tabernacles also lasted *seven days*: "Ye shall rejoice before the Lord your God *seven days*, and ye shall keep it a feast unto the Lord, seven days in the year; it shall be a statute for ever in your generations: ye shall celebrate it in the seventh month; ye shall dwell in booths *seven days*" (Lev. xxiii. 36, 39).

On the occasion of the siege of Jericho, seven priests bearing seven trumpets, compassed the city with the men of war, for *seven days*, and on the seventh day they went round it seven times, when the city fell.

The week, with its concluding sabbath, is therefore deeply engraven in a variety of ways, on the whole Jewish ritual and history. Nor on Jewish history alone. Although in the Christian dispensation, the eighth day, or first day of a new week, is substituted for the creation sabbath, indicating that rest is to be found only in a *new* creation, only in resurrection, —yet still the weekly division of time, and the weekly day of holy rest, continue, witnessing as ever to the rest that remaineth for the people of God. For,—like the Lord's supper, which shows forth his death till He come,—the sabbath, and the Lord's day which has taken its place, glance both backward and onward. The first day of the week recalls the glad morning of the resurrection, the completion of the redeeming work of Christ, just as the sabbath recalled the conclusion of the creation work of God ; and it foretells the remaining rest, when they that are Christ's shall rise at his coming. Thus we may say, that three hundred thousand earthly Sabbaths line the road that lies behind the people of God, pointing each with outstretched hand, like so many guide-posts, in the same direction, and agreeing with overwhelming unanimity in their testimony to the blessed fact, that there remaineth a sabbatism for the people of God.

(ii.) THE WEEK OF WEEKS.

Next in order to the week of days came the *week of weeks.* This was the period appointed to elapse between the first two of the great annual gatherings of the Jewish sacred year, Passover and Pentecost. Of the deep meaning of these ordinances, as unveiled by the sequence of events, connected with the true paschal sacrifice, we pause not here to speak, as we shall have to allude to it, in another connection, further on. We simply call attention to the ordinance, as one instance of the law of weeks, impressed on Jewish ritual "And ye shall count unto you, from the morrow after the sabbath from the day that ye brought the sheaf of the wave offering, *seven sabbaths* shall be complete. Even unto the morrow after the *seventh sabbath* shall ye number fifty days, and ye shall offer a new meat offering unto the Lord " (Lev. xxiii. 15).

Thus in every Jewish year there occurred not only fifty-two weeks of days, each with its concluding Sabbath, but a week of weeks, with its closing Pentecostal celebrations, full of hidden hopes of resurrection rest.

(iii.) THE WEEK OF MONTHS.

The entire circle of the feasts of the Lord, ordained in Leviticus, is comprised within the first *seven months* of the year. The *sacred* portion of the Jewish year therefore, its complete calendar of divinely ordained religious ceremonies, prefiguring the history of redemption, occupied *a week of months*. It commenced with the month Abib or Nisan, on the fourteenth day of which the Exodus took place, in memory of which the annual feast of Passover was instituted. There followed each in its appointed season, the feast of unleavened bread, and the first-fruit sheaf, the feast of weeks or Pentecost, the feast of trumpets, the great day of atonement, and the feast of tabernacles. This last was held in the seventh month, and with it closed, for the year, the special " feasts of the Lord." Thus the period marked off for holy convocations, from the Jewish year, was septiform in character; *a week whose days were months*, contained, by Divine direction, the observances of Israel's ecclesiastical year; while the feasts themselves, and the order in which they occurred, had undoubted reference to anti-typical events, on the scale of ages.

(iv.) THE WEEK OF YEARS.

It was the will of God that not only the *people*, but the *land* of Israel, should keep sabbath. " The Lord spake unto Moses in mount Sinai, saying, Speak unto the children of Israel, and say unto them, When ye be come into the land which I give unto you, then shall *the land* keep a sabbath unto the Lord. Six years thou shalt sow thy field, and six years thou shalt prune thy vineyard, and gather in the fruit thereof; but in the seventh year shall be a sabbath of rest unto the land. a sabbath for the Lord : thou shalt neither sow thy field, nor prune thy vineyard. That which groweth of its own accord of thy harvest thou shalt not reap, neither gather the grapes of thy vine undressed : for it is a year of rest unto the land" (Lev. xxv. 1-5). The Hebrew servant similarly was to serve six years, and go out free in the seventh. (Exod. xxi. 2.)

The period thus marked off had exactly the same character as the week with its six days of toil and seventh of rest ; it is simply the week on the scale of years. And it is worthy of notice that the observance of the ordinances respecting the land during the sabbatic years, was *possible* only by means of a stupendous miracle, to be repeated every seven years. "If ye shall say, What shall we eat the seventh year ? behold, we shall not sow, nor gather in our increase. Then I will command my blessing upon you in the sixth year, and it shall bring forth fruit for three years" (Lev. xxv. 20, 21). Here was a law perfectly harmonious as we have seen, and shall yet see more fully, with the order of sacred seasons observed by the Jews; a law in which there was nothing foreign to their whole system, but which was on the contrary an integral part of it, and yet it was made to depend, for the possibility of its fulfilment, upon a special periodical interposition of Divine power, as wide in its range, as the necessities of an entire nation. No merely human legislation would ever have originated such a law, on account of its incapacity to provide the conditions needful for its observance. This miracle in the land, was, on the scale of *years*, what the doubling of the manna, in the wilderness, was on the scale of *days ;* a miraculous arrangement, to render possible the keeping of the prescribed sabbath. There, the gift of manna was doubled every sixth day ; while in the land of promise, the produce was trebled every sixth year, the object in each case being to secure the sabbath rest.

(v.) THE WEEK OF WEEKS OF YEARS.

The largest week ordained in the Mosaic ritual was the week of weeks of years, the period including therefore seven sabbatic years, with their intervening years of toil, forty-nine years.

" Thou shalt number seven sabbaths of years unto thee, seven times seven years; and the space of the seven sabbaths of years shall be unto thee forty and nine years. Then shalt thou cause the trumpet of the jubilee to sound on the tenth day of the seventh month, in the day of atonement shall ye make the trumpet sound throughout all your land. And ye shall hallow the fiftieth year, and proclaim liberty throughout all the land unto all the inhabitants thereof; it shall be a jubilee unto you; and ye shall return every man unto his possession, and ye shall return every man unto his family. A JUBILEE shall that fiftieth year be unto you : ye shall not sow, neither reap that which groweth of itself in it, nor gather the grapes of thy vine undressed. For it is the jubilee ; it shall be holy unto you ; ye shall not eat the increase thereof out of the field. In the year of this jubilee ye shall return every man unto his possession " (Lev. xxv. 8–13). This larger week is perfectly harmonious in character with all the previous ones ; during its earlier portion, bondage, debt, and poverty lasted, at its close they passed away and disappeared. The jubilee was a year of rest and joy and liberty, that foreshadowed more than any preceding sabbath, the *full and varied* blessedness of the rest that remaineth for the people of God. Once at least in every ordinary lifetime, would this great prophetic ordinance arrive, laden with its wealth of joy and peace, and glowing with its beams of hope and promise.

In the light then of these five enduring ordinances,—ordinances some of which are observed by the Jews even to our own day,—ordinances embodied in the Bible, and presented to the study of every generation of the people of God—in the light of the weekly sabbath observed from Eden onwards ; of the Pentecostal sabbath ; of the sevenfold sabbath of the final feast of tabernacles ; of the sabbatic seventh year ; and of the yet more sabbatic year of jubilee; it is impossible to deny that a *septiform chronology was divinely appointed in the elaborate ritual of Judaism.* And further, since that ritual was unquestionably typical, this fact may prepare us to find *a similar law of weeks governing the chronology of the antitypical events.*

(vi.) THE WEEK OF DECADES.

But not in the Pentateuch only is this law of weeks to be traced; it pervades the Old Testament, and embraces not Jews only, but Gentiles. Of the whole human race the words are true, " The days of our years are *threescore years and ten,* and it by reason of strength they be fourscore years, yet is their strength labour and sorrow, for it is soon cut off, and we fly away" (Ps. xc. 10). Human life is a week, *a week of decades,* and the last decade, the evening of life, is the time of rest rather than of action. But there is no sabbath in man's life, in the fullest sense of the word; no rest, till it closes in the sad dark rest of the grave; sin has introduced the curse instead of the sabbath, and death with its dreary gloom, ends the lifetime week of sinners. But the exception only proves the rule, and bears its testimony to the true nature of the week. The failure of bodily and mental power which takes place generally about the age of seventy, attests the operation of this law of septiform periodicity, on the entire human race, while the recognition of the fact by the psalmist suggests the perfect harmony of this providential arrangement, with all the sabbatic legislation we have been considering.

This period of seventy years is besides a very notable one historically. It marked the duration of the captivity of Judah in Babylon. It was predicted by Jeremiah, that in consequence of their inveterate idolatry Israel should be carried captive by Nebuchadnezzar, "the whole land shall be a desolation, and an astonishment, and these nations shall serve the king of Babylon *seventy years*" (Jer. xxiv. 11). And subsequently a second time the same limit was assigned: "For thus saith the Lord, after *seventy years* be accomplished at Babylon, I will visit you, and perform my good word toward you, in causing you to return to this place" (Jer. xxix. 10). A dark and terrible week to Judah were those seven decades; the daughters of Israel hung their harps upon the willows by the rivers of Babylon, and wept as they remembered Zion. The desolate land enjoyed her sabbaths, while her sons languished in exile. But this week also closed with restoration and liberty, when the Lord turned again the captivity of Zion, and her children felt like those that dream. as they sang, "The Lord hath done great things for us, whereof we are glad."

(vii.) THE WEEK OF WEEKS OF DECADES.

It was towards the close of this long and dark week of the captivity, that there was revealed to Daniel a still larger week ; a week each of whose days was to equal the captivity week, a week of seven times "seventy years," or "seventy weeks" of years—a period of 490 years. This may be termed the restoration week ; it was the time that elapsed between Artaxerxes' decree to restore and to build Jerusalem, and the days of "Messiah the Prince," indeed it was revealed *as measuring the interval.* "Seventy weeks are determined upon thy people and upon thy holy city, to finish the transgression and to make an end of sins, and to make reconciliation for iniquity, and to bring in everlasting righteousness, and to seal up the vision and prophecy, and to anoint the Most Holy."

Had Israel known the day of her visitation, and received her Messiah when He appeared, what a glorious sabbath would have closed this week ! Its seventh day did actually include the incarnation and life of the Lord Jesus Christ, and,—since when He came unto his own his own received Him not,—it included also his atoning death, his triumphant resurrection, and the descent of the Holy Ghost ; the rejection of Israel, the destruction of their temple, and the first gathering-in of the Gentiles. So that even on this scale of centuries, God has adhered to the law we have noted above, and brought in the day of the greatest blessings the world has ever known, as the seventh stage of a previous history. The period is however designated as "seventy weeks" rather than as one week—and it is therefore even more conspicuously an instance of the prevalence, even in long stretches of history, of the law of weeks.

(viii.) THE WEEK OF YEARS OF YEARS.

Scripture presents us—in symbolic prophecy—with a week on a scale of greater magnitude than any of these, in the "SEVEN TIMES" of Daniel. As we shall have to treat more fully of this in the following chapter, we forbear to enlarge on it now. It is a week of years, whose days are years, in other words a week, each of whose days consists of 360 solar years. Its second half is frequently mentioned in symbolic prophecy, under various designations which all indicate one and the same period, 1260 natural years. This gigantic week includes the entire " Times of the Gentiles," the times during which supreme power on earth, is by God committed to Gentile instead of Jewish rulers. It dates from the captivities, and is still running its course, though rapidly nearing its close.

(ix.) THE WEEK OF MILLENARIES.

And all these various weeks, are included in a *sublime week of millenaries*, which is clearly intimated, if not distinctly revealed, in the Word of God. In the Apocalypse as we have seen, the glorious reign on earth of Christ and his saints, which is to be the world's real sabbath, and Israel's real jubilee, the antitype and fulfilment of the types and shadows of the all-embracing sabbatic law we have traced through Scripture—the great sabbatism—is six times over spoken of as a period of " a thousand years." This millennial age, being the true *sabbath* of the world, must be regarded as *a seventh day*—the seventh day of a week, whose six preceding unsabbatic days, were of *equal duration* with this its sabbath. So that the last page of the Bible shows, that the creation week whose occurrences are narrated on its first page, was the germ and type of the world's chronology, and foreshadowed the whole course of time; that the sabbath of Paradise, pointed to a great sabbath of a thousand years, with which God—to whom a thousand years are as one day—has from the beginning purposed to bless mankind ; the seventh day of the great week of time, which is to introduce the eternal state—the new creation.

The system of times and seasons thus unfolded, bears the

stamp of divinity : there is a consistency and a grandeur about
it, as well as an evident end and meaning, which are worthy of
the Bible, worthy of God! Its connection with creation, with
the moral law, with the chronology of redemption, both typical
and antitypical; its connection with the most solemn and
deeply interesting episodes in Jewish experience and history ;
with the advent of Messiah, and with the most important events
in his human life; its relation to various and distant lands, and
to so many important epochs, Jewish, Gentile, and Christian ;
its existence amid the eras of history, and its adoption in
the visions of prophecy, all these features unite *to stamp it as
Divine;* while the fact that it is identical with the system impressed by the hand of God on nature, leaves no room for
doubt on the subject.

We have been considering not theories, but facts; we have
adduced, not opinions or fanciful interpretations, but a mass
of unquestionable scientific and authentic historical evidence.
Is it by chance, that the law of septiform periodicity is engraven so widely and so deeply on the vital phenomena of the
animal creation, and of the human family? Is it by chance
that the existence, growth, and functional activity, of every
individual of our race, is, both in health and disease, regulated
by a law of *weeks*, of various magnitudes? Is it a mere
curious coincidence, that a *weekly* rest, has from creation
onwards been observed by men? and that the Jewish nation
for three thousand five hundred years, have acknowledged and
obeyed a ritual system. whose constantly recurring periods from
the briefest to the longest, were *weeks* of diverse dimensions?
Was it by accident that historical episodes like the Babylonish
captivity, and the restoration era, were *weeks* of still greater
magnitude, and that even the mighty dispensations of providence
are measured by the same septiform scale?

No ! these facts are too far-reaching, too all-comprehending,
too universal, to admit of any other explanation than the
existence of what men call a law of nature, that is a rule
ordained by the great Creator Himself. A law that regulates

ten thousand phenomena, physiological, and historical, from the transformation of an insect, to the majestic revolutions of redemption history—a law which no power on earth can alter, nor any lapse of ages obliterate; a law which, as we shall hereafter show, is inscribed in letters of light, by the glittering orbs of the solar system in their ceaseless revolutions, in the realms of space, such a law can have but *one* Source; to no other can its enactment be attributed, than to the blessed and only Potentate, the King of kings and Lord of lords, who only hath immortality, dwelling in the light which no man can approach unto, whom no man hath seen, nor can see, to whom be honour and power everlasting !

Our next chapter, unfolding the operation of the law of weeks in the general course of human history, will strengthen this conviction.

CHAPTER III.

The Week in History.

THE Bible is the only book in the world that gives us a view of human history as a whole, that carries us from the lost Paradise of Eden, to the restored Paradise of the Apocalypse, traces the course of the human race through every stage of its intermediate existence on earth, and on beyond the limits of time, into the boundless regions of eternity.

In it, and in it alone therefore, are we likely to find the key, if key there be, to the periodicity of history,—the underlying principle bringing the labyrinth of inharmonious periods and chronological irregularities which the annals of the human race at first sight present, into harmony with each other, and with the periods of nature and revealed religion.

The histories of Scripture reach back to the farthest past, and its prophecies extend to the most distant future ; taken together, as they are presented in the Bible, the two afford a panoramic view of the whole course of events, from the creation and fall of man, to the final judgment, and the inauguration of the new heavens and the new earth.

The Bible is therefore the chart of all history, and it gives us, not events only, but their moral character, tracing the motives that influenced the various actors in the drama, as well as the results of their action. Events are shown in connection with their causes and their effects, and the judgment of God as to their character is revealed. Without the Bible, history would be a spectacle of "rivers flowing from unknown sources, to unknown seas;" but under its guidance we can trace the complex currents to their springs, and see the end, from the beginning.

The entire story of mankind as presented in Scripture being composed of two parts, the historic and the prophetic, it is clear that the periods into which the history of man as a whole is divided, cannot be discerned, without taking both historic and prophetic *chronology* into account, and as *both* are subjects on which different views have been entertained, our examination of the periodicity of human history as a whole, must be preceded by a careful though necessarily brief investigation, of the questions connected with these controverted points.

1. What, according to Scripture, is the age of the human race? in other words,—how long is it since the creation?

2. What periods are intended by the expressions of time used in Daniel and the Apocalypse in defining the duration of events which were future when predicted by these prophets?

These questions we must now therefore consider, taking first that of

OLD TESTAMENT CHRONOLOGY.

The highest point of antiquity to which authentic profane history carries us, is the occupation of Babylon by an army of Medes in 2233 B.C., that is about 250 years after the flood. *

For our knowledge of the dates and durations of all previous

---

* "Fasti Hellenici": Clinton, p. 296.

events, we are indebted exclusively to the Hebrew Scriptures, and very full and explicit are the chronological data of this remote period, which the Bible supplies. " The history contained in the Hebrew Scriptures presents a remarkable and *pleasing* contrast to the early accounts of the Greeks. In the latter, we trace with difficulty a few obscure facts, preserved to us by the poets, who transmitted, with all the embellishments of poetry and fable, what they had received from oral tradition. In the annals of the Hebrew nation, we have authentic narratives, written by *cotemporaries*, under the guidance of inspiration. What they have delivered to us, comes accordingly under a double sanction. They were aided by *Divine inspiration* in recording facts, upon which *as mere human witnesses*, their evidence would be valid." *

The length of the lives of the early patriarchs, often bordering on a thousand years, made oral tradition a comparatively safe guide : but one link intervened between Adam and Noah, from whom the story of antediluvian events would be handed down in the line of Shem to Abraham and Moses. This latter, though not an eyewitness of many of the facts he narrated, is yet an authentic reporter; and in the subsequent history of Israel, from the Exodus to the rebuilding of the temple, the writers were, strictly speaking, witnesses.

The chronology of the Pentateuch is gathered, not from *dates*, as in ordinary history, but from accurate genealogical records; it is measured and marked out, not by centuries, but by generations. The brief chronology of the antediluvian world, is all contained in the fifth of Genesis; the age of the human race at the time of the flood, that is to say, the interval that had elapsed between the creation and the deluge, is ascertained by adding together the ages of the patriarchs at the birth of the sons, in whom the line from Adam to Noah is traced. These were not invariably the *eldest* sons; Seth, the second link in the chain, was we know the third son of Adam, and the

---

* " Fasti Hellenici " : Clinton, p. 283.

figures given make it very improbable that either Enos, Enoch, or Lamech, were eldest sons. Younger sons, are often throughout Scripture the heirs of promise, as witness Shem and Abram, Jacob, and Judah, David, and Solomon. "That was not first which is spiritual, but that which is natural." Barren wives caused to become joyful mothers, and younger sons chosen to be heirs of promise, often intimated in the older economy, that purpose of God unfolded in the New, to bring life out of death, and to substitute for the first and natural order of things, a second and spiritual order; to replace by a new creation, under the headship of a second Adam—the Lord from heaven—that creation which fell in the first Adam.

An examination of the fifth of Genesis will show that the flood, dating from the creation, took place in the year 1656 A.M., which was the 600th year of Noah's life.*

The correctness of this date however, as well as of that of the birth of Abram (which is derived in a similar way from the postdiluvian generations), has been called in question, because there exist important variations between the Hebrew Bible, and some of its most ancient versions, as regards these very genealogical statements. The Samaritan Pentateuch, the Septuagint version into Greek, some other ancient translations, and the writings of Josephus, make many of the generations, both before and after the flood, *longer* than they are represented in the Hebrew Scriptures, and in our authorized version which follows the Hebrew. Nor is the discrepancy a trivial one; the Septuagint places the birth of Abram, *thirteen hundred years later* than does the Hebrew Pentateuch, making the present age of the human family to be between seven and eight thousand years, instead of about six thousand years.

It is evident therefore that in our consideration, of the measures of the dispensations into which human history has been divided, it will not do to overlook this great chronological question and controversy. We must ascertain which of these

---

* 130 + 105 + 90 + 70 + 65 + 162 + 65 + 187 + 182 + 600 = 1656. Gen. v.

rival chronologies is the true one, since a difference bearing so large a proportion to the whole duration of history, must be material to our inquiry.

The writings of Josephus favour the longer system; but as they mainly follow the Septuagint, their evidence is not of independent importance. The Samaritan Pentateuch has been *proved* unreliable in other respects, and cannot therefore be accepted as an authority on this point. The real issue lies between the chronology of the *Hebrew* Pentateuch and the Greek translation of it, made B.C. 280, at Alexandria in Egypt, by order of Ptolemy Soter, for the great Alexandrian Library. This ancient version, commonly called the Septuagint, or translation of "the seventy," was in common use among the Jews in our Lord's time, and was universally employed by the fathers of the early church, who entertained for it, an almost superstitious reverence, and even considered it as inspired. Absurd fables about its origin (the true story of which is, as regards *its details*, lost in obscurity) were invented, to give colour to this notion, and the reverence which existed for it was so great, that its chronology seems to have been generally accepted, save by Jerome, Origen, and a few others, whose familiarity with the original Hebrew led them to reject it.

Now it is especially to be noted, that the difference between the two, is unquestionably, from its very nature, *an intentional alteration.* It is not the effect of accident, but the result of deliberate design. *An entire century is, twelve times over, added to the age of the patriarch, at the time of the birth of the son, in whom the genealogy continues; while the same period is deducted from the residue of the life, so as to leave the whole unchanged.* The Hebrew Bible for instance states, that Adam was 130 years old at the birth of Seth, that he lived 800 years after, and died at 930. The Septuagint on the contrary gives him as 230 at the time of Seth's birth, says he lived only 700 years after, but agrees that he died at 930. The following table presents the discrepancy both as to its nature, and as to

its amount; it will be observed that it affects the lives of six
antediluvian, and six postdiluvian patriarchs :—

	Hebrew.				Septuagint.
Adam	130	•	•	•	230
Seth	• • •	105			205
Enos	• • •	90	•	•	• 190
Cainan	• •	70	•	•	• 170
Mahalaleel	65	•	•	•	165
Enoch	65	•	•	•	165
Arphaxad	35	•	•	•	135
Salah	• • •	30	•	•	• 130
Eber	• • •	34	•	•	• 134
Peleg	• • •	30	•	•	• 130
Reu	• • •	32	•	•	• 132
Serug	• • •	30	•	•	• 130

Nothing but *design* can account for this uniform and repeated
alteration; it is too systematic to be the result of accident, and
is clearly an intentional and deliberate corruption in one docu-
ment or the other; an increase or decrease of these periods,
made with some ulterior object in view.

It has been a warmly disputed point among chronologers,
which of the two was most likely to be correct, whether the
Jews had falsified the Hebrew, or whether the seventy Egyptian
translators, are to be credited with having distorted in this
manner the chronology of the Septuagint.

Many arguments have been adduced on either side of the
controversy, which space forbids our reproducing here. Not
only Josephus, but most of the Fathers adopted the chronology
of the Septuagint, as was natural, seeing it was the version with
which they were familiar, while very few of them were acquainted
with the Hebrew. Jerome, who made the Vulgate translation
into Latin, however, and Origen, and some others, adhered to
the Hebrew. The revival of learning which preceded and
accompanied the Reformation, led to a more extensive use of
the Hebrew original, and more deference was thenceforth

U

shown to the Hebrew chronology. Archbishop Usher's great chronological work, published in the middle of the seventeenth century, recognised the Hebrew dates as the true; in 1834 the profoundly learned work of Mr. Fynes Clinton showed that the judgment of this most accurate and discriminating scholar was in favour of the Hebrew chronology: and in 1847, Browne's "Ordo Sæclorum" followed, and threw its weight into the same scale. Thus the upholders of the Septuagint version are found principally among those who were unfamiliar with the Hebrew, and a large proportion, if not the majority of those who have most fully examined and compared the two, believe the Hebrew to be the true text.

But common sense without learning seems almost sufficient to settle the question. The Hebrew is the original, and dates from the time of Moses; the Septuagint is a mere Egyptian translation, dating from B.C. 286. Which is most likely to be correct?

The Jews held their own sacred writings in profound and indeed superstitious veneration; they worshipped the letter, and would have been the last people in the world to tamper with it. The Egyptians had no such reverence for the Old Testament, and would not have hesitated to corrupt the text, supposing any sufficient motive made the doing so seem desirable.

It is hard to assign any motive which could have induced the Jews to alter the genealogies of their Pentateuch. It has been suggested indeed that they did so in the hope of invalidating the claims of Jesus of Nazareth to be their Messiah. But such a change in the chronology of their *early* history could in no wise have done this. Had it been possible for them to have lengthened or shortened the chronology of the period between their restoration from Babylon, and the first advent, such a step would indeed have had an important bearing on the question. But to prolong the days before the birth of Abraham, could apparently serve no such purpose.

On the other hand it is by no means difficult to conjecture why its Egyptian authors, whether Jewish or Gentile, may have falsified the original, which by the king's command they were to reproduce in Greek. "The Chaldeans and Egyptians, whose histories were about that time published by Berosus and Manetho, laid claim to a remote antiquity. Hence the translators of the Pentateuch might be led to augment the amount of the generations, by the centenary additions, and by the interpolation of a second Cainan, in order to carry back the epoch of the creation and the flood, to a period more conformable with the high pretensions of the Egyptians and the Chaldeans." *

The arguments alleged in favour of the longer chronology prove, when closely examined, to tell even more strongly in favour of the shorter; and it must be remembered that while differing from the Hebrew as to the age of the patriarchs, at the birth of their sons, the Septuagint *agrees* with it, as to the age ultimately attained by each; a strong confirmation of the authentic character of the chronology of the Pentateuch. There is no valid reason for assuming that the inspired original has been corrupted, and that the Greek translation deserves more confidence. On the contrary the former must be regarded as possessing on every ground the strongest claim to our belief, and the chronology given in our authorized version, may be relied on as correct.

There is no other disputed point in Biblical chronology that involves any material difference, or renders questionable any *considerable* interval. The whole period from Adam to Christ may be traced step by step from Scripture statements. We meet indeed two breaks in the chain, two brief chasms, which no ingenuity can bridge over. They have been allowed to occur in the wisdom of God, for some good and sufficient reason, and the result is that it is impossible for any one to accurately ascertain to within a few years, the age of the world, the exact period that has elapsed since the creation of Adam.

1. We are not informed what was the duration of the govern-

---

* "Fasti Hellenici" : Clinton, p. 297.

ment of Joshua and the elders, and of the interregnum or anarchy which followed. The interval between the death of Moses and servitude under the Midianites, can from Scripture statements be calculated with tolerable certainty, but not with actual precision. The years assigned to it must rest more or less on conjecture, not on testimony; it is the period spoken of in Josh. xxiv. 31. "Israel served the Lord all the days of Joshua, and all the days of the elders that overlived Joshua, which had known all the works of the Lord that He had done for Israel." Joshua was probably about the same age as Caleb, forty at the time of the spies; he wandered with Israel in the wilderness for thirty-eight years subsequently, before he took command of their armies on the death of Moses. He was therefore about seventy-eight when his government began, and he was 110 at his death (Josh. xxiv. 29), so that the above expression, "all the days of Joshua," must apparently include about thirty-two years; it is impossible to fix the period more closely, and it may well vary ten years in either direction. Clinton puts it at twenty-seven years.

2. The second chasm occurs between the death of Samson, and the election of Saul, and was occupied by the governments of Eli and Samuel. Josephus makes this interval fifty-two years. Clinton, for reasons which appear satisfactory, considers that the nearest approximation to the truth which scripture statements permit, is thirty-two years.*

We have not space to enlarge on the point, as our object in alluding here to these chronological chasms, is less to investigate their limits, than to show that *those limits are very narrow.* From forty to sixty years comprises, in all probability, the range of the uncertain, in the whole extent of Bible chronology. The various statements of Scripture given in the subjoined table leave little doubt that the creation took place about 4138 B.C. instead of 4004, as is commonly supposed.† But any attempt

---

* "Fasti Hellenici," pp. 304–320.
† The appended table is from Elliott's "Horæ Apocalypticæ," brought down to the present date, 1878.

THE SCRIPTURE CHRONOLOGY OF THE WORLD.

A.M.	Event	Period	Years	Reference	Quotation
1	Creation of Adam	to the birth of Seth	130 years.	Gen. v, 3.	"Adam lived 130 years, and begat a son, . . . and called his name Seth."
130	Seth born	" " Enos	105	" v. 6.	"Seth lived 105 years, and begat Enos."
235	Enos born	" " Cainan	90	" v. 9.	"Enos lived 90 years, and begat Cainan."
325	Cainan born	" " Mahalaleel	70	" v. 12.	"Cainan lived 70 years, and begat Mahalaleel."
395	Mahalaleel born	" " Jared	65	" v. 15.	"Mahalaleel lived 65 years, and begat Jared."
460	Jared born	" " Enoch	162	" v. 18.	"Jared lived 162 years, and begat Enoch."
622	Enoch born	" " Methuselah	65	" v. 21.	"Enoch lived 65 years, and begat Methuselah."
687	Methuselah born	" " Lamech	187	" v. 25.	"Methuselah lived 187 years, and begat Lamech."
874	Lamech born	" " Noah	182	" v. 28.29.	"Lamech lived 182 years, and begat a son, and he called his name Noah."
1056	Noah born	to the Flood	600	" vii. 6.	"Noah was 600 years old when he flood of waters was upon the earth."
1656	The Flood	to the birth of Arphaxad	2	" xi. 10.	"Shem begat Arphaxad 2 years after the Flood."
1658	Arphaxad born	" " Salah	35	" xi. 12.	"Arphaxad lived 35 years, and begat Salah."
1693	Salah born	" " Eber	30	" xi. 14.	"Salah lived 30 years, and begat Eber."
1723	Eber born	" " Peleg	34	" xi. 16.	"Eber lived 34 years, and begat Peleg."
1757	Peleg born	" " Reu	30	" xi. 18.	"Peleg lived 30 years, and begat Reu."
1787	Reu born	" " Serug	32	" xi. 20.	"Reu lived 32 years, and begat Serug."
1819	Serug born	" " Nahor	30	" xi. 22.	"Serug lived 30 years, and begat Nahor."
1849	Nahor born	" " Terah	29	" xi. 24.	"Nahor lived 29 years, and begat Terah."
1878	Terah born	to his death	205	" xi. 32.	"The days of Terah were 205 years; and Terah died." [xii. 1.] "Now the Lord," &c.
2083	The Covenant made with Abram to the giving of the Law		430	Gal. iii. 17.	"The Covenant . . . the Law, which was 430 years after, cannot disannul."
2513	The Giving of the Law	to the return of the Spies	1	Num. x. 11. (Compare Exod. xix, 1.)	
2514	The promise to Caleb on the return of the Spies to the division of the Land		45	Josh. xiv. 10.	"These 45 years, ever since the Lord spake this word unto Moses."
2559	The division of the Land	to Samuel the Prophet	450	Acts xiii. 20.	"After that, He gave unto them Judges, about the space of 450 years, until Samuel."
3009	Saul anointed	to the death of Saul	40	" xiii. 21.	"Afterward . . . God gave unto them Saul . . . by the space of 40 years."
3049	David began to reign	to his death	40	1 Kings ii. 11.	"The days that David reigned over all Israel were 40 years."
3089	Solomon ditto	ditto	40	2 Chr. ix. 30.	"Solomon reigned in Jerusalem over all Israel 40 years."
3129	Rehoboam ditto	ditto	17	" xii. 13.	"He reigned 17 years in Jerusalem."
3146	Abijah ditto	ditto	3	" xiii. 2.	"He reigned 3 years in Jerusalem."
3149	Asa ditto	ditto	41	" xvi. 13.	"Asa . . . died in the 41st year of his reign."
3190	Jehoshaphat ditto	ditto	25	" xx. 31.	"He reigned 25 years in Jerusalem."
3215	Jehoram ditto	ditto	8	" xxi. 20.	"He reigned in Jerusalem 8 years."
3223	Ahaziah ditto	ditto	1	" xxii. 2.	"He reigned 1 year in Jerusalem."
3224	Athaliah's usurpation	to her death	6	" xxii. 12.	"He (Joash) was with them hid in the house of God 6 years; and Athaliah reigned."
3230	Joash began to reign	to his death	40	" xxiv. 1.	"He reigned 40 years in Jerusalem."
3270	Amaziah ditto	ditto	29	" xxv. 1.	"He reigned 29 years in Jerusalem."
3299	Uzziah ditto	ditto	52	" xxvi. 3.	"He reigned 52 years in Jerusalem."
3351	Jotham ditto	ditto	16	" xxvii. 1.	"He reigned 16 years in Jerusalem."
3367	Ahaz ditto	ditto	16	" xxviii. 1.	"He reigned 16 years in Jerusalem."
3383	Hezekiah ditto	ditto	29	" xxix. 1.	"He reigned 29 years in Jerusalem."
3412	Manasseh ditto	ditto	55	" xxxiii. 1.	"He reigned 55 years in Jerusalem."
3467	Amon ditto	ditto	2	" xxxiii. 21.	"[Amon] reigned 2 years in Jerusalem."
3469	Josiah ditto	ditto	31	" xxxiv. 1.	"He reigned in Jerusalem 31 years."
3500	Jehoahaz ditto	to his deposition	0	" xxxvi. 2.	"He reigned 3 months in Jerusalem."
3500	Jehoiakim ditto	to his death	11	" xxxvi. 5.	"He reigned 11 years in Jerusalem."
3511	Jehoiachin ditto	to his deposition	0	" xxxvi. 9.	"He reigned 3 months and 10 days in Jerusalem."
3511	Zedekiah ditto	to the Captivity	11	" xxxvi. 11.	"[Zedekiah] reigned 11 years in Jerusalem."
3522	The Captivity	to the proclamation of Cyrus	70	Jer. xxv. 11.	"These nations shall serve the king of Babylon 70 years." (See 2 Chron. xxxvi. 22.)
3592	The Decree of Cyrus	to the birth of Christ	536		} According to the commonly received chronology.
4128*	The Christian æra	to the present year	1878		
6006	The present year A.D. 1878.		6006 years, since the Creation of man.		

to fix with greater accuracy than this, the actual age of the world, is futile, as no scriptural data exist by which the *precise* year of the creation *can* be ascertained.*

We accept then as about the nearest possible approach to truth, and as probably a very near approach indeed, the following dates given by Mr. Fynes Clinton :—

Deluge	1656 A.M.
Birth of Abram.	2008
Call of Abram	2083
Exodus	2513
Death of Moses	2553
First servitude . .	[2580]
Death of Eli	[3010]
Election of Saul	[3042]
Accession of David	[3082]
Solomon . .	[3122]
Rehoboam	[3162]
Nebuchadnezzar's capture of Jerusalem. } Temple burnt . . . . }	[3552]
The Nativity . . .	[4138]

PROPHETIC CHRONOLOGY.

We turn now from the past to the future, to gather from the inspired Word of God, its prophetic revelations of the chronology of the closing events of the history of the world.

From the earliest days, statements of time have been an important element in Divine predictions. The hundred and twenty years that should elapse before the flood, the four hundred years' affliction of Abraham's seed, the forty years

---

* It is interesting to note that Cuvier asserts that "one of the most certain, though least expected results, of sound geological pursuits, is the opinion that the last revolution which disturbed the surface of the globe is not very ancient ; and the date cannot go back much farther than five or six thousand years." " The Chinese date for the Deluge is A.M. 1713, and for the seven years' famine in the days of Joseph, B.C. 1729."—See Elliott, vol. iv. p. 236, 237.

in the wilderness, the seventy years of the Babylonish captivity, all these and many other periods were announced beforehand to Israel. And similarly in the New Testament, the
Lord Jesus Christ foretold the period during which He would
bow to the power of the grave, saying "the third day He
shall rise again." These and other predictions, given *simply*
to *reveal* the future, are accompanied by plain, literal, statements of time, such as those just quoted. But there is, as we
have seen, another series of predictions, in which a *double
object* may be distinctly traced, to reveal and yet to *conceal* the
future.

The glory of God is declared by every prophecy. His foreknowledge is one of his highest attributes. His people are
comforted, and their faith is strengthened, when they find, that
the experiences through which they are passing, the troubles
that are befalling them, or the difficulties that they encoun-
ter, have been foreseen and foretold by their God. But there
are some things which it is better for God's people not to
know beforehand; as for instance the true length of the
present period of the absence of Christ from his church.
Divine wisdom and love judged it best, as we have seen
to *conceal* from the early church the foreordained duration of
this Christian age, and to allow every generation of Christians
to live in the expectation of the speedy return of their Lord.
"Known unto God are all his works from the beginning of
the world." He of course knew that over eighteen centuries
would elapse before the second coming of Christ, and could
very easily have revealed this in plain words to the church.
He did not do so, as is proved by the fact that the early
generations of Christians expected the return of Christ in their
own day. If then God, for the guidance of his people especially during its later stages, wished to reveal *the events* of this
period, without revealing *its duration*, He must needs adopt
a style of prediction, which would reveal while concealing,
and conceal while revealing, the truth.

This is exactly what He has done. The revelations granted

to Daniel and John, relating to the events of this dispensation. are not couched in ordinary language, or made in plain terms, which admit of no second meaning. They are embodied in mysterious symbolic forms, which require to be translated before they can be understood. They are not incomprehensible ; very far from that ! Incomprehensible prophecy could answer no conceivable object. But prophecy which would be obscure for a time, and clear only after the lapse of ages, would answer the object supposed above, of concealing from one generation that which it would not be desirable for it to know, while revealing it to a succeeding one, to which the knowledge was indispensable. Now as statements of time occur, in connection with these symbolic prophecies, as well as in connection with plain predictions, the question arises, are these statements to be taken, in a literal, or in a figurative sense? Does a day mean a day, or does it in these prophecies, mean a year? Does a year mean a year, or does it mean 360 years. Does "a thousand two hundred and threescore days" mean a period of three and a half years, or does it mean a period of 1260 of our years?

It is evident that a consideration of the periodicity of history in its widest extent, including the revealed *future* of man, as well as his *past, requires a previous investigation of this question*, since it is necessarily vital to the subject. Before we can discern their mutual proportions and relations, we must understand what all the periods with which we have to deal, *really are.* We must no more omit future periods than past ones, and must know the true length of the former, as well as of the latter. We must take *all* the portions of the dissected map into account, before we can even form a hypothesis as to its true configuration and dimensions, or discern the plan on which it has been divided. We must bear in mind for instance not only that the patriarchal and Jewish ages have *preceded* our own, but that Scripture foretells a millennial age to *succeed* it. We must be aware not merely that the Babylonish captivity lasted seventy years, but that the dominion of a certain power symbolised by " the little horn " was fixed at "time times and half a time," and we must know what period is meant by this strange unusual description. In a word, we must not only take into account the prophecies of Daniel and John, but we must seek by patient investigation to ascertain the sense in which their chronological statements are to be understood.

A moment's reflection will show the great importance of this investigation, not only to our present subject, but to a right understanding of the prophecies themselves.

The *duration assigned* to the events and powers represented by these symbols, must evidently determine to a large extent, our opinion as to what the symbols *themselves* signify. The " little horn " is to exercise dominion for " time times and the dividing of time," three years and a half. Now if this be literal years, the power predicted may be an individual, a personal Antichrist, as the Futurists assert; but if on the other hand, it be symbolic language, signifying a period extending over twelve centuries, then the power predicted must needs be some *dynasty of rulers*, some succession of potentates, seeing no one man could live during so long a period. The chronology of these prophecies once made clear, research into their meaning becomes comparatively simple. On every account then the subject demands the earnest attention of those who desire to understand the oracles of God; and even if it be not so attractive as some others, it must not be lightly passed over. We may say of *it.* what Mr. Birks says of his exposition of the two later visions of Daniel, "from the nature of the details of which it is composed, it may perhaps fail to interest general readers. But those who study it will find themselves repaid by a more deep and lively sense than ever, of the actual Providence of the Almighty in this fallen world. Why have we, in the word of God itself. so many genealogies and lists of names, of offerings of princes, of journeys in the wilderness, and other passages, that seem dry and barren, but to teach us, that we *must stoop to details and individual names*, if we would rightly understand the condescension of our God, and the reality of his special oversight of the children of men? Those who are soon weary of these details, must pay the cost of their own impatient spirit, by a more loose, unreal and slippery faith. *The tree of faith must throw out ten thousand little roots, into the lowly soil of prophetic history, if it is to grow and expand into that noble confidence of hope, which no storms of temptation can uproot or destroy."* Here we have to deal with numbers and periods instead of with names, but these are perhaps even more unattractive to most people, as involving the mental effort of calculation; but we venture to assert that those who take the trouble to follow the investigation of this chapter, Bible in hand, will not fail to be at the close more profoundly convinced than ever before, of the inspiration of the sacred volume, of the all-embracing providence and foreknowledge of God, and of the near approach of the "end of the age."

On the judgment which we form as to the true meaning of the statements of time in symbolic chronological prophecy, depends also, we believe, to a great extent, the liveliness of our expectation of the Lord's speedy return. "That entire rejection of prophetic chronology which follows of course, on the denial of the year-day system of interpretation, is most of all to be deplored from its deadly and paralysing influence on the great hope of the church. No delusion can be greater than to expect, by excluding all reference to times and dates, to awaken Christians to a more lively expectation of their Lord's second coming. For in truth without reference to such dates, in an open or disguised form, not one solid reason can be given, why the church may not still have to wait two or three thousand years, before the promise is fulfilled. The declaration 'the time is at hand,' was true and pertinent when the event was eighteen centuries removed. It and similar general promises, form no barrier to the supposition, that eighteen centuries more may still have to intervene. Every sign of the times, is either too vague to direct us, or in proportion as it becomes distinct, assumes practically all the characters of a numerical date, and becomes exposed to the same objections.' The prophetic times indeed, when separated from the context, and viewed in themselves only, are a dry and worthless skeleton, but when taken in connection with the related events, clothed with historical facts, and joined with those spiritual affections, which should attend the study of God's providence, like the bones in the human frame, they give strength to what was feeble, and union to what was disjointed, and form and beauty and order, to the whole outline and substance of these sacred and Divine prophecies." *

The questions, then, which we have to investigate are these. How are we to understand the statements of times and periods, which occur in the visions of Daniel and John? Are we to take them as literal, or as symbolic? And if the latter, on what principle are we to translate them into plain language? Is there a key to the hieroglyphic numbers? and if so, what is it? It must be borne in mind we are not speaking of prophetic numbers and periods *in general*, but exclusively of those which occur in the above named books, and which relate mainly to the events of this dispensation.

The times and periods in question are the following :—

In Daniel.

1. That of the domination of the "little horn" Dan. vii. 24.
2. That of the desolation of the "sanctuary" „ viii. 8.
3. The interval between the restoration from
   Babylon, and "Messiah the Prince" ix. 24.
4. Time, times, and a half . . . . xii. 5, 9.
5. A period of 1290 days . . . . „ „ 11.
6. A period of 1335 days . . . „ „ 12.

In the Apocalypse

1. The ten days' tribulation of the church at Smyrna, Rev. ii. 10.
2. The duration of the scorpion torment . . „ ix. ͍

* " Elements of Sacred Prophecy " : Birks, p. 415.

3. The career of the Euphratean horsemen   Rev. ix. 15.
4. The time of the down-treading of the Holy City ,, xi. 2.
5. That of the prophesying of the two witnesses   ,, ,, 3.
6. The time they lay unburied .   . . .   ,, ,, 9.
7. The sojourn of the woman in the wilderness   ,, xii. 6, 14.
8. The period of the domination of the beast . ,, xiii. 6.

We believe that in all the above fourteen instances, the period of time mentioned is *a symbol of another and a larger period*, and we now proceed to give our reasons for this opinion.

If a geographer wish to represent the entire surface of our globe, on a sheet of paper, it is clear that he must do so on a *miniature scale*, and that the difference between the reality and the miniature must be enormous. He fixes his scale, 100 or 1000 miles to an inch, as the case may be, and if his delineation is to be correct, to that scale he must adhere throughout. He must not reduce the latitude a little and the longitude more, or diminish the seas in one proportion and the continents in another; such a proceeding would destroy all the resemblance and utility of a map. If the drawing were a *portrait*, it would produce still more incongruous results. What possible resemblance to the original could be traced in a portrait, which should reduce to miniature all the features but one, and leave that one life-size? All must be reduced, or enlarged, in proportion.

The ancients in their hieroglyphic delineations observed this law of proportionate reduction. These were in fact miniature representations of the events and characters of history, and a certain uniform scale was adhered to in every hieroglyphic record. Apparent violations of the law of proportion, are in reality, the contrary. When for instance we see a Pharaoh represented as ten times as big as the slaves or captives in his train, it is still a proportionate representation, because the idea to be conveyed by the hieroglyph is *not* the literal size of the individual, but his *relative social importance*. Pharaoh was ten times more important than his slaves, a ten times greater man, in that sense.

Now the symbolic prophecies of Daniel and John are of this character, they are *verbal descriptions of hieroglyphs seen by the prophet;* and these hieroglyphs were themselves, *divinely designed miniature representations of future events.* We *read,* the description of what Daniel and John *saw;* and they saw, not certain events (as the rise and fall of empires), but minia- ture symbols or hieroglyphs of certain events. These were exhibited to them, by Him who knows the end from the begin- ning, and who wished to reveal to them and to others through them, long series of great events, to happen in ages to come on a wide theatre, and to interest and affect the entire human race. For obvious reasons, this had to be done in a very narrow compass, and in a mysterious though comprehensible form; a form which "the wise" only should understand, and that only after the lapse of ages. To do it, while observing these conditions, Divine wisdom selected as the most suitable medium, the universal language of symbols, the language that needs no intervention of sounds to make it significant; the language that represents *ideas* not *words; things* not their *names,* which appeals to the eye rather than to the ear, and which is equally comprehensible by every nation, people and tongue. As these hieroglyphs are historic, chronology is necessarily one of their most important features, and as *dura- tion* cannot be expressed by symbolic *devices,* the time of the vision is given in *words.*

Now would it not be to impeach Divine wisdom, to suppose that God has, in these miniature symbols, violated the laws of proportionate reduction, in a way which the feeble intelligence of his creatures would forbid *them* to do? To suppose that He who endows the architect and the artist with wisdom to make *their* drawings to scale, has Himself adhered to no scale, and that without giving us any intimation of the fact, He has in these symbols, presented some features in miniature, and some as large as life? These prophetic hieroglyphs are from God, they are therefore perfect; they are miniatures; *every feature* is therefore on a reduced scale, and *among the rest, their chronology.*

The chronological emblem has to be conveyed to the mind through the ear, instead of like the rest, through the eye; a beast may image an empire; a horn may represent a dynasty, but on the duration of the empire or the dynasty, these symbols give no light.

It requires words to express a period of time, but the period so expressed, may be as much a symbol of some other period, as the beast or the horn are symbols of some other thing. The reality of Antichrist was for wise reasons, veiled for a time, under the symbol of the "little horn," the reality of the duration of his dominion, was for the same reasons veiled under the symbol of "time, times, and the dividing of time." We have to compare Scripture with Scripture, and Scripture with history, to learn the meaning of the "little horn," and we must do the same to learn the meaning of the "time, times, and a half," for the one is as symbolic as the other.

The next question is, on what scale are these hieroglyphs constructed? What for instance is the proportion between the θηρίον or wild beast of Dan. vii. 7, and the Roman Empire, of which it is the universally acknowledged symbol?

Evidently the reduction is on as enormous a scale as when our world is represented by a globe a foot in diameter. Reason then compels us to conclude that *in the chronology of the wild beast, an equally enormous reduction will be found.* Otherwise there would exist on the face of this prophecy, that incongruous mixture of some miniature and some life-sized features, that we dare not attribute to inspiration. The statement of time *must*, like the prophecy in which it occurs, be a symbolic miniature, intended to convey a reality immensely greater than itself. We do not assert that the *words* in which these statements of time are made, are symbolic: that a "day" means anything but a day, or a "year," anything but a year, but that the *ideas of time* conveyed to the mind, by these words, are symbols, intended to suggest *other ideas of time,* just as much as the ideas conveyed by the other parts of the hieroglyphs, are intended to suggest something different from themselves.

If this be granted, the next question is, does Scripture prescribe any scale by which these miniature numbers are to be enlarged? For in order to be of any use, chronological revelations must be *accurate.* If we desire to ascertain from a map the distance between any two given points, we take the apparent space in a pair of compasses, and measuring it against the scale at the side of the map, we perceive the actual distance. So with a chart of history, every inch may represent a century, and be divided into a hundred parts to represent years. A short line of definite length, then accurately expresses the duration of an empire, or the life of an individual, because we can compare the length of that line with the scale, and thus learn the real period. Without such a scale or key, map and chart would be equally useless, the one would give us no idea of actual dimension or distance, nor would the other inform us, as to actual duration.

The above named prophetic periods, are, it will be observed, described under the five main divisions of time, " hours," " days," " weeks," " months," and " years." There are mentioned 3½ days, 10 days, 1260 days, and 1335 days ; a half-week, a week, seven weeks, sixty-two weeks, and seventy weeks; five months and forty-two months; a " day, month, and year," and " time, times, and a half."

It is evident that in order to be intelligible, these measures of time must all be interpreted *on one scale.* What scale is it? Is it the grand Divine scale of " one day is with the Lord as a thousand years"? or is it an hour for a day? or a day for a month? or day for a year? or what is it?

The great answer to this important query is found in the fact, that one of these periods *has been fulfilled,* and therefore supplies *the key* to all the rest. The seventy weeks of Daniel ix. elapsed between the decree of Artaxerxes, and the advent of Messiah. That period was actually 490 years, the prophecy announced it as 490 days, or "seventy weeks," and we are therefore led to conclude, that in all the above analogous passages, where time is predicted in miniature and in mystery, in harmony with the miniature and mysterious nature of the symbols by which the prophecy is conveyed, *a year is represented by a day*, seven years by a week, thirty years by a month, 360 years by a "year," and so on.

This principle once *admitted*, the chronology of these prophecies becomes simple and accurate, and available for our present study of the periodicity of human history. The plan of times and seasons governing both past and future events is seen to be perfect, and marvellous in its comprehensiveness; in its harmony with other Scripture and with nature; and in its significance.

But if this system be *rejected*, the chronology of prophecy becomes a strangely unmeaning thing, and these magnificent harmonies entirely disappear. Chaos reigns where order reigned, and we look in vain for indications of Divine wisdom, in the plan of the ordering of the ages.

And yet, strange to say, this natural, simple, scriptural, "year-day system," of interpreting the mysterious dates connected with the symbolic prophecies, has been strongly opposed by Futurists, who maintain that statements of time should be taken *as literally* in Daniel and John as in Genesis and Exodus—be regarded as having precisely the same force, when connected with a mass of miniature symbols, as when associated with the plainest literal predictions.

This system of interpretation originated, as we before mentioned, with Riberæ and other Jesuit writers, who, anxious to turn off from the Papacy the tremendous arguments against it, furnished by the application to *it* of the predictions of God's word about Antichrist, and Babylon, were driven to propose some alternative. They could not admit that the dynasty of the Popes had fulfilled the prophecies respecting the "man of sin," or that the Roman Catholic Church was, as the Reformers boldly asserted, "BABYLON THE GREAT;" yet it was clear, no other power and system that had ever existed, so well answered the description. Lest this fact should strike the minds of men, they maintained that all these prophecies were still *unfulfilled*, and insisted upon the duty of *literal interpretation*, especially of the prophetic times. The fact that it has been held and taught by reformers and martyrs, who resisted unto blood the errors of Popery, and that it has been *opposed* by the champions of that corrupt and evil system, is itself a plea for the truth of the year-day interpretation. The solid and unanswerable arguments in its favour, adduced by the great Protestant expositors, gave currency to it, in spite of Jesuit opposition, and the system of prophetic interpretation with which it is connected, was soon so generally held in the Reformed Churches, as to be commonly known as the " Protestant " view.

During the last half century Futurist views have however gained ground even among Protestants ; and in a good deal of current prophetic exposition, they are quietly *assumed*, and dogmatically taught to many who have never studied the subject, or clearly understood what the Protestant view is. We believe the Futurist view to be an erroneous and mischievous one ; it precludes any adequate conception of the majestic range of the predictions of Scripture, it deprives the church of the guidance of Divine prophecy, as to the character and doom of the great Apostasy ; and of the stimulus to faith and hope, afforded by the true interpretation. We must therefore be excused for dwelling a little more at length on the subject, which is not only important in itself, but fundamental to our present inquiry into the periodicity of history.

An exhaustive and masterly treatise on the year-day system, from the pen of the Rev. T. R. Birks (Fellow of Trinity College, Cambridge, Professor of Moral Philosophy), appeared about thirty years ago, in his work entitled " First Elements of Sacred Prophecy," a work which it is now difficult to procure. To the arguments and reasoning adduced by this cautious and candid writer, little can be added. Every student of the prophetic word, who wishes to arrive at the truth on the subject, should carefully ponder this elaborate and thorough examination of it. Recast, so as to adapt it to the present day, the reproduction of this work would be of immense service to the church. We give some extracts, and a brief summary of the general scope of the argument.

"The year-day theory," says Professor Birks, "may be summed up in these maxims :—

1. That the church after the ascension of Christ was intended of God to be kept in the lively expectation of his speedy return in glory.

2. That in the Divine counsels a long period, of nearly two thousand years, was to intervene between the first and the second advent ; and to be marked by a dispensation of grace to the Gentiles.

3. That in order to strengthen the faith and hope of the church under the long delay, a large part of the whole interval was prophetically announced, but in such a manner that its true length might not be understood, until its own close seemed to be drawing near.

4. That in the symbolic prophecies of Daniel and St. John, other "times" were revealed along with this, and included under one common maxim of interpretation.

5. That the periods thus figuratively revealed are exclusively those of Daniel and St. John, which relate to the general history of the church, between the time of the prophet and the second advent.

6. That in these predictions each day represents a natural year, as in the vision of Ezekiel ; that a month denotes thirty, and a "time" or year, three hundred and sixty years.

The first of these maxims is plain from the statements of Scripture, and the second from the actual history of the world. The third is, on *à priori* grounds, a natural and reasonable inference from the two former, and is the true basis of the year-day theory viewed in its final cause. The three following present the theory itself under its true limits. Perhaps no simpler method could be suggested in which such a partial and half-veiled revelation could be made, than that which the Holy Spirit is thus supposed to adopt, resting as it does on a plain analogy of natural times.*

Now the mere statement of these axioms removes at once several main difficulties which have been used to perplex and embarrass the inquiry.

1. First it has been urged, that this larger interpretation of the prophetic times is inconsistent with the repeated commands of our Saviour, that the church should always be watching for his return. How could this be possible, it is asked, if it were revealed from the first, that 1260 years must elapse before that advent should arrive?

This objection disappears in a moment, when the *facts* and the *hypothesis* are simply compared together. The very reason for which the times are asserted to have been given in this unusual form is, that they might *not* be understood too early, when they would have interfered with the earnestness of continual expectation. . The only way to sustain this objection is to assume that the fact of such a revelation being given, made it the duty of the church to understand *at once* its true meaning. Two duties would then seem to contradict each other,—the obligation of continual watchfulness, and the duty of understanding the message, that more than twelve centuries would intervene before the advent. But the contradiction is not real . . . there could be no obligation to *understand* the times from the first.

2. Again it has often been argued, that the mystical interpretation would compel us to lengthen the millennium to 360,000 years. But the principle on which the theory has just now been founded, removes this objection also. The millennium is not included in that time of waiting, which made it desirable to conceal the times under a symbolic veil. . . . It has been

---

* The two great revolutions of the earth are apparently intended : the one on its axis occupies 24 hours, and gives rise to the "*day ;*" the other in its orbit occupies 365 days (or 360 soli-lunar reckoning), and gives rise to the "*year.*" The lesser is used as a symbol of the greater.

further objected that the year-day interpretation was totally un
known for twelve centuries. This was a natural and necessary
consequence of the principle on which it depends. Instead
therefore of being *a valid objection*, it forms a remarkable *presumption in favour of its truth*. In fact this exposition appeared first, at the very time when it must have appeared, if
the principles on which it is founded had a real existence."*

As a presumption in favour of the mystical meaning of these
dates, it must be observed, that they either occur in the midst
of the symbols, or else " bear plain marks of a singular, uncommon, and peculiar phraseology, or are prefaced by words
importing concealment." In the case of several of them, the
unit of time being left undefined, " days" is not more literal
than " years." The fact also that they occur exclusively in
two books of symbolical and mysterious character. suggests the
idea, that they have a covert and mystical meaning ; especially
when we recall the words of our Lord, " It is not for you to
know the times and the seasons " It should also be borne in
mind, that these dates (with the exception of the seventy weeks
of Daniel, which has been *fulfilled*, on the scale of a year to
a day) all pertain to the times of the Christian dispensation.
Peter tells us that it was not for the prophets themselves, but
for the Christian church that these " times " were revealed.
(Dan. xii.; 1 Pet. i. 10–12) Now the Christian dispensation
throughout is one of *antitypical realities*, instead of one of types
and shadows and symbols, and it is harmonious with its character to suppose, that there is a typical analogy between the
" day" of these predictions, and the " year" of their fulfilment.

Another strong presumption in favour of the same view
arises, from the singular impressiveness and solemnity which
accompanies the announcement of these periods, a special and
almost awful solemnity, which is hard to explain, if the periods
be the brief ones apparently suggested by the expressions used.

* " First Elements of Sacred Prophecy": Birks, p. 311.

"They are not given in passing, nor as matters of subordinate
importance ; . . . it is in connection with one of these
dates that our Lord receives the title of 'the Wonderful Numberer.' . . . The time, times and 'a half' are twice revealed to Daniel, in two visions at an interval of twenty years;
in the second of these the words are introduced with peculiar
solemnity. Two saints are exhibited as speakers ; one of them
inquires the duration of the predicted wonders, the reply is
given by our Lord Himself, with all the solemnity of a direct
appeal to God. 'I heard the man clothed in linen, which
was upon the waters of the river, when He lifted up his hand
to heaven and sware by Him that liveth for ever, that it shall
be for time and times and the dividing of a time.' No
words could well be more expressive of deep mystery, and
of the special importance to the church of the period thus revealed " That there was a mystery in these numbers was
recognised in the church long before its true nature could be
guessed. The strange and unusual adjuncts forbad expositors
to rest in the simple literal meaning of the language employed.
The Jews themselves supposed the time times and a half " to
have a century for its unit, and denote three hundred and
fifty years."

When we turn from *presumption,* to direct *evidence* in favour
of the year-day system, the prophecy of the seventy weeks
occupies the first place, and is indeed by itself an almost conclusive argument in its support. The only way in which its
force can be evaded, is by saying that the word employed in
the original (shabua) is ambiguous, meaning a hebdomad or
seven, not necessarily of *days ;* that the event has shown that
in this case it meant *years,* and that consequently the passage
affords no ground for the year-day view. The answer to this
is simple and conclusive. It is perfectly true that the original word does not define the unit, and *might* mean seven of
any measure of time ; but it is also a fact, that in Scripture,
where it occurs about ten times, it is invariably *used* to denote

seven *days;* we are therefore bound to suppose it is used in the same sense in Dan. ix., and thus the argument retains all its force. Seventy sevens of *days* was the symbol employed to denote seventy sevens of *years.*

And that this important passage affords the true key to the scale on which all these miniature symbols ought to be enlarged, appears the more likely when we consider two other passages in which God Himself declares that He adopts this scale. The first is the sentence on Israel in the desert: "after the number of the days in which ye searched the land, even *forty days,* each day for a year, shall ye bear your iniquities, even *forty years.*" The twelve men who searched the land were representatives of the twelve tribes of Israel; they were not *symbols* of them, but they were types—representatives—a few men representing a great many. So the forty days during which they searched the land, are made typical of the forty years, during which they should wander in the wilderness.

Now here, it is not as in Daniel, the fulfilment which proves the prediction to have been on this scale; but *the scale is fixed and adopted by God before the event.*

And it is the same in Ezek. iv. 4, where the prophet is commanded to enact a type, to become himself a living emblem of the house of Israel, by lying first on his left side for three hundred and ninety days, and then on his right side for forty days. Ezekiel here, like the spies before, was a type or representative of the nation; his recumbent position, a type of their degradation and debasement by national sin, and the period during which he was to maintain that position, divinely fixed beforehand, represented the period to be completed prior to the end of the judgment which was to fall on that nation. And as Ezekiel was *a small* emblem of *a large* nation, so the days were *a brief* emblem of *a long* period. " I have appointed thee a day for a year, a day for a year." In each of these periods *a day*, in the enacted prophetic type, represented *a year* in the subsequent history. When therefore in Daniel and the Apocalypse, we find a variety of enacted prophetic symbols of subsequent history, associated with the announce-ment of periods in days, why should we doubt, that the same scale is to be applied for their enlargement and adaptation to the reality? The word of God furnishes no single instance of the employment of any other.

Besides these three clear Old Testament instances of the employment of a year-day scale, there is one New Testament incident, in which it is almost impossible to avoid the con-clusion that our Lord Jesus Christ adopts the same symbolic phraseology, and that for the identical reason for which it is employed in prophecy,—to reveal while concealing, and to conceal while revealing, the future.

It is in his message to Herod, when informed by the Phari-sees of that monarch's intention to kill Him. "Go ye, and tell that fox, Behold, I cast out devils, and I do cures *to-day* and *to-morrow*, and the *third day* I shall be perfected. Neverthe-less I must walk *to-day*, and *to-morrow*, and the *day following*; for it cannot be that a prophet perish out of Jerusalem."

There is a peculiar precision in this twice-repeated statement of time, which forbids the thought that it was a mere *indefinite* substitute for "a little longer;" as if He had said, "I must continue a little longer my works of mercy." He twice over mentions a definite period of *three days*. But a much longer period than three *literal* days elapsed between the utterance of these words and the death and resurrection of Christ, so the expression cannot be taken literally. It is an admitted fact on the other hand, that *the ministry of Christ* lasted three com-plete years, the period which elapsed between that first pass-over at which He cleansed the temple at the commencement of his public ministry, and that fourth passover, which He eat with his disciples the night before He suffered. The sentence in question, would therefore exactly describe the *appointed dura-tion of his ministry, on the year-day principle*, and would point out his Divine foreknowledge of the time when He was to be delivered by the Jews into the hands of the Gentiles, crucified, and raised again, or "perfected." It was as though, hearing of

Herod's crafty intentions to kill Him, He had sent him word, "You have no power against me, till I reach the time and the place predetermined for my death and resurrection. My ministry must last for three years, and terminate as it began, at the passover at Jerusalem."

There are thus three plain cases in the Old Testament, and one scarcely less clear in the New, in which the year-day system is divinely employed, and we have consequently substantial scriptural grounds on which to base it. And in addition to these presumptions in its favour, and to these scriptural instances of its employment, it must be observed that each of the above-mentioned fourteen prophetic statements of time, which the Protestant system interprets on this year-day scale, affords *internal evidence* when carefully examined, that it is not intended to be interpreted literally.

1. The leading one—the "time, times, and dividing of a time," is, to begin with, a most *peculiar form* of expression by which to designate a brief period of three and a half years. "If the short reckoning were the true one, no reason can be given why the times should not be expressed in the most customary form. On the other hand, the year-day theory requires that a shorter term should be merely suggested, in such a way as to hinder us from resting in the typical phrase, as the true meaning. Now such exactly is the term before us. It doubtless suggests to the mind by comparison with other texts, three years and a half. But it is not the usual or literal expression for that period. Twice alone does that interval occur elsewhere (Luke iv. 25 ; Jas. v. 17), and in both it is expressed by the natural phrase, *three years and six months.* The same is true in every similar case. Paul abode at Corinth "one year and six months" (Acts xviii. 11), David reigned in Hebron "seven years and six months" (2 Sam. ii. 11). He was with the Philistines "a year and four months" (2 Sam. xxvii. 7). The form in which the periods of time are expressed, is thus invariably the same. And hence though three years and a half are suggested to the mind by this phrase, there is nothing in the words which fixes

it to this sense. This has not in truth any more claim to be the *literal* meaning than one thousand two hundred and sixty years.

2. But secondly, the fundamental term, *a time*, implies, rather than excludes, the wider sense. The natural series of words of time, consists of a day, a week, a month, and a year. The first three are retained in the prophetic calendar; but the last of them is replaced by this general expression—a time—which takes the lead of all the others. It occurs in the first of these dates, and in two or rather three others on which the rest chiefly depend. Now this substitution could not be without meaning. It leaves the analogy among the different periods unbroken; but at the same time, it sets loose this fundamental period, so as to be at liberty even by the common rules of language, to receive a larger signification.

This argument becomes much stronger, when we consider the actual use of the same term in other passages. It is of frequent recurrence in the Old Testament, and is employed to denote periods of various lengths, and even extending to many years. It meets us first in the narrative of the creation : " Let them (the sun and moon) be for signs and for *seasons*," where it is distinguished alike from days and years. It is frequently used to denote the appointed time of all the feasts of the law. (Lev. xxiii. 2, 4, 37, 44 ; Num. ix. 2, 3, 7, 13 ; x. 10 ; xv. 3.) It is employed with regard to the fall of Pharaoh Hophra, and the restoration of Israel. " Pharaoh hath passed *the time appointed*" (Jer. xlvi. 17) " The time to favour Zion, the *set time* is come " (Ps. cii. 13). "The vision (of the coming of Christ) is yet for an *appointed time*" (Hab. ii. 3). In these and several other passages an extensive interval is clearly implied : and the fundamental idea is one, which has no respect to the length or shortness of the period, but simply to its fixed and determinate character. It is plain how completely these two marks, that it is at once indefinite, and determinate, make it a suitable term to form the basis of a prophetic chronology, on the year-day system.

3. *The different terms used to denote the same period*, are a further proof that it cannot denote three natural years and a half. The same interval occurs seven times over. Twice it is mentioned as 'time, times, and a dividing of a time'; once as 'time, times, and a half'; twice as 'forty and two months'; and twice as 'twelve hundred and sixty days.' A comparison of these passages will show that they all relate to the same period. Yet the expression is varied in this remarkable manner, and in all these variations *is never once expressed by the natural and literal phrase.* How can we explain this remarkable feature, but by supposing it to indicate a mysterious and hidden sense? The Holy Spirit seems in a manner to exhaust all the phrases by which the interval could be expressed, excluding always that one form, which would be used of course in ordinary writing, and which *is* used invariably in Scripture on other occasions, to denote the literal period. The variation is most significant if we accept the year-day system, but quite inexplicable on the other view.*

Two arguments in favour of the extended view of these dates, may be drawn from the history of Nebuchadnezzar's dream and its fulfilment, one connected with the word "times," the other dependent on the typical character of the monarch.

Nebuchadnezzar beheld in vision a lofty tree, interpreted to denote the king himself, he heard a watcher, even a Holy one, proclaim a remarkable sentence on the tree, that it should be hewn down and stripped. " Let his heart be changed from a man's heart, and let a beast's heart be given unto him, and *let seven times pass over him.*" This sentence on the tree, was fulfilled in the period of the insanity of the king, which though nowhere stated to have lasted seven years, is by general consent allowed to have done so.

Now at first sight this seems to afford an argument against the year-day interpretation, for here "seven times" clearly denoted seven literal years; on closer examination, however, it

---

* Birks' " Elements of Prophecy," p. 350-352.

will be found to do the reverse. The expression "time" does not, as we have seen, imply any particular period; any definite season, a day, a week, a month, a year, or a century, would be equally well expressed by it. The conclusion that the king's insanity lasted seven *years*, is not based therefore on the force of the word, but on *the context and the nature of the case.* We cannot suppose that seven days, weeks, or even months, would have sufficed to teach the monarch the great lesson he had to learn and teach to others; the duration of his life excludes the thought that seven centuries, or seven of any longer measure of time, were meant, and all things considered, *seven real years*, seems the only period that can have been intended. But when the same expression "times" occurs in connection with an empire whose duration is 2000 years, every reason which has led us to conclude that in the case of the individual king it meant years of days, *now* leads us to conclude that in the case of the empire it means years of years. If an insanity of seven weeks would seem an event unworthy of such solemn prediction, or of such a prominent place in the life of an individual, how much more so, an apostasy of three and a half years, in the history of an empire which extends over twenty centuries!

But Nebuchadnezzar was a typical, representative man. Not only was he the golden head of the great fourfold image, but he stands as its representative, as the representative of the long succession of Gentile rulers, who were to succeed him, till the coming of the Son of man. The two characteristic marks of these Gentile rulers have been *idolatry* and *persecution* of God's saints; these two things are represented as characterzing Nebuchadnezzar. His image making, and image worshiping, typified the idolatry (Pagan and Papal), which has been so indelibly stamped on all the four great empires; his "burning fiery furnace" for the faithful witnesses, typified the persecution which has been inflicted on the people of God, by each of the four great ruling empires in turn, especially by the modern spiritual Babylon. These two characters of idolatrous debasement and fierce cruelty, are those which render the symbol of wild beasts, suitable to represent these empires; and thus Nebuchadnezzar too is presented as a beast; his degradation to a bestial condition, typified the moral degradation of the Gentile kingdoms, through idolatry, pride, and self-exaltation; his restoration to reason, prefigured the yet future day when the empires of earth shall own that "the heavens do rule." Now, over this typical man, passed a period of insanity, which was doubtless *equally typical*, and which is the only clue we have to the appointed duration of the "times of the Gentiles," for neither in connection with the fourfold image, or with the four wild beasts, have we any hint of the *length of this interval*.

But the image, the king himself, and the wild beasts, are three types of one and the same thing under different aspects; and thus the duration of Nebuchadnezzar's insanity becomes typical of the duration of the times of the Gentiles, the times during which supreme power in the earth, is *by God* committed to Gentile rulers, instead of to the seed of David. Now these "times" have already lasted more than 2400 years since the days of Nebuchadnezzar, and thus we see that the seven *years of days*, during which the king was insane, were intended to pre-figure *seven years of years* (2520 years) during which the moral and spiritual degradation and debasement of the kingdoms of this world, dating from himself, are destined to endure. *Now the oft-repeated interval of " time times and a half," " forty-two months," " 1260 days," all refer to the second half of this period, and must therefore be fulfilled on the same scale as the whole period. They are part, not of the type, but of the antitype, and they must be interpreted not on the scale of the type, but on the scale of the antitype, that is on the scale of a day for a year.*

This inference is strengthened by one further remark. If the whole interval from Nebuchadnezzar's reign be divided into two equal portions, the latter half falls exclusively within the times of the fourth or Roman empire, and soon after the time when its division into separate kingdoms was first completed. This is a pointed coincidence with the broader features of the prophecy, for in the vision also the "time times and a half" are all included in the period which follows after the ten horns have arisen. *

The vision of Daniel viii. gives the prophetic date of *two thousand three hundred days* as the duration of the restored daily sacrifice, and of the subsequent desolations.

Now if we take this literally, it makes a period of between six and seven years, analogous to nothing else in Scripture, and incomprehensible in connection with the question to which it is an answer. Besides, if this were the time intended it would have been far more natural to have described it in years than in days. No motive of concealment could exist, to require a veil of mystery; nor indeed is any veil of *mystery* used, for it is a simple question of arithmetical reduction to resolve these days into years. That it is not to be taken literally, however, is proved by the constant usage of Scripture. *Not a passage can be found in the Bible in which a period exceeding a year, is stated in days*—and only two, in which a period exceeding two months is so mentioned (except of course those in which these symbolic dates occur).

---

* "Elements of Prophecy": Birks, p. 356. Mr. Elliott says on this subject :—

"I do not except the 'seven times' specified in Nebuchadnezzar's vision as the appointed time of the royal tree continuing cut down, from the category of chronological prophecies to which the year-day principle is to be applied. The tree itself symbolised Nebuchadnezzar, and as there was nothing of a *miniature scale* in the symbol as compared with what it symbolised, the seven years might, without violation of propriety, symbolise an equal period of desolation to the monarch. But did he experience this extraordinary judgment and recovery simply in his individual character, *or as a symbolic man?* . . . For my own part, considering the extraordinary nature of the judgment, the fact of its being so fully recorded by Daniel, the circumstance of Nebuchadnezzar being addressed on occasion of another prophecy, as the representative of his nation ('Thou art this head of gold'), and that of the symbolic tree when cut down, being bound with a band of BRASS and IRON, the metals significant (in the fourfold image) of the Greek and Roman Empires, which did for ages hold sway over the prostrate region of Babylon; all these considerations . . . induce me to believe that the seven times 360 days that passed over Nebuchadnezzar in his madness, represent the 2520 years . . . of the 'times of the Gentiles.'" (Elliott, " Horæ," vol. iii., p. 247, foot note).

But the word *days* is not used; the real form of the expression indicates more mystery, and suggests on critical grounds, the idea that no unit of time is given at all, and that consequently "days" is no more literal than years. "Unto evenings and mornings, or unto evening morning, two thousand three hundred." That a *long* period is intended appears, from the angel's words, "shut up the vision, for it shall be for many days." Now six or seven years is but a brief period in *our* estimation, how much less in an angel's? Gabriel would not thus have spoken of so short an interval. But if the period intended were twenty-three centuries, his words have an appropriate dignity. If we interpret this date on the year-day principle, it reaches from the time of Daniel to the future restoration of Israel, and is a clear and satisfactory answer to the double question.* It marks the duration of the *restored daily sacrifice, and of the subsequent desolation ;* the five centuries between Cyrus and Titus during which Jewish sacrifices were daily offered in the restored temple being its first portion ; while the second and longer portion comprehends the final destruction of the city and temple, the treading down of Jerusalem by the Gentiles, and the dispersion of her people ; and stretches onward to the future advent when the sanctuary shall be finally cleansed. The period being so long, and the greater part of it being occupied by this gospel dispensation, its length is purposely veiled, under an enigmatical yet deeply significant form of expression, and was evidently not intended to be understood at first. "Shut thou up the vision, for it shall be for many days." It included a declaration of the long duration of that economy of grace to the Gentiles, whose occurrence at all, was for five hundred years afterwards, a hidden mystery. "The mystery which in other ages was not made known to the sons of men . . . that the Gentiles should be fellow-heirs, and of the same body, and partakers of his promise in Christ, by the gospel." Here is a *reason* for the enigmatical form of the

---

* Dan. viii. 13.

chronological announcement; they who take it literally and refer it to a distant future, make a *mystery without a meaning.*

"The strangeness of the expression being once proved, our choice lies between a mystery which means nothing, and a mystery which has a plain and definite cause in God's providence, and a key not less plain and definite, and three times repeated in God's holy word. Who would hesitate which alternative to choose?" *

It is the same with three dates given in Dan. xii.; they form one group, the last two being merely extensions of the great period "time, times, and a half," and they must of course be interpreted on the same principle. The interval covered by this last prophecy (which begins with chapter xi.), clearly extends from the time then present, to the resurrection; it commences with, "Behold, there shall stand up yet three kings in Persia," and reaches on in unbroken sequence, to that time when "many of them that sleep in the dust of the earth shall awake." A solemn importance is thrown around the announcement of the times, "I heard the man clothed in linen, which was upon the waters of the river, when he held up his right hand and his left hand unto heaven, and sware by Him that liveth for ever and ever, that it shall be for a time, times, and a half; and when he shall have accomplished to scatter the power of the holy people, all these things shall be finished." Now it seems incongruous to suppose that this singularly impressive oath applies to a brief period, not one six-hundredth part of the whole interval revealed.

We turn now to the book of Revelation, to discover whether its testimony confirms the evidence afforded by the prophecies of Daniel, that the principle on which these sacred dates are to be interpreted, is that of a year for a day.

As to the ten days' persecution of the church at Smyrna, a literal fulfilment is unknown to history, though this is of course no proof that it did not take place. But if Smyrna be only one

---

* "Elements of Prophecy": Birks, p. 363.

phase, moral and chronological, of the whole Christian Church, that of the closing days of Paganism, prior to the entrance of gross corruption, as seems probable, the ten years of Diocletian's last great persecution, would evidently be indicated by the expression. The passage does not however tell strongly either way, though it is almost absurd to suppose that a persecution of ten literal days would be made a subject of prophetic revelation at all.

In the case of the locust woe (Rev. ix. 5), the miniature symbol again demands a miniature period, and the one selected is that of the ordinary ravages of locusts, but it evidently requires the year-day system to make it commensurate with the events predicted to take place during its course. In the case of the Euphratean horsemen, the very peculiarity of the phrase (Rev. ix. 15) suggests as before a mystic meaning. Why, if the period intended were literal, should *an hour* be mentioned at all? and why should the ordinary way of mentioning the larger period first, be completely reversed? But an improved reading (given by Matthæi and found in seven or eight of the best manuscripts) would give the words thus, " the angels prepared for that hour and that day, were loosed both a month and a year," *i.e.*, 390 *days*. Now this was the exact period during which Ezekiel was commanded to lie on his side, to represent the 390 *years* of the judgment of Israel. Mr. Birks truly remarks, " this has not the air of a casual resemblance ; it is rather an express mark supplied to us by the Holy Spirit, and directing us to the true key by which to interpret these prophetic periods." The 390 years was in each case marked as one of stubborn unrepenting idolatry, closed by decisive overthrow and judgment, and the period occurs nowhere else in Scripture.

The forty-two months of the treading down of the holy city (Rev. xi. 2), if taken literally, seems strangely unmeaning. Jerusalem has already been trodden down of the Gentiles 1800 years, and it will, as we know from our Lord's own words, continue to be so till the close of the times of the Gentiles. In what sense can this period be defined, by "forty and two months"? And why if the period designed were really as brief a one, as that in which the heavens were shut up by Elias (alluded to in the passage), why was not the same expression used to designate it, "three years and six months"?

That the "three days *and a half*" during which the witnesses lie unburied (Rev. xi. 9) is symbolic, is proved by the fact that "we have about thirty passages in Scripture where three days are mentioned to define an interval, and four where four days occur; but nowhere else is the fraction of a day introduced into such a measurement of time   If the Holy Spirit had intended natural days only, would He have used a preciseness in the statement of time, which is nowhere else employed in nearly forty examples, not even in that most important of all facts, the resurrection of our Lord"? *

The previous remarks as to the congruity of miniature dates with miniature symbols, and as to the mystery indicated by the unusual phraseology, apply equally to the two chronological periods in Rev. xii. The sun-clad star-crowned woman is evidently a symbol of the true or spiritual Israel, and her flight into the wilderness, where she is nourished for 1260 days, of some period of the church's history. Now the natural Israel of old fled also from the persecution of a tyrant king, into the wilderness, where they were nourished with bread from heaven, and water from the rock ; and we know their wilderness history to have been typical to the highest degree. There is not a point in the type, for which we cannot perceive a corresponding antitype, and it is natural to expect some analogy in the periods of the two sojourns in the wilderness. Now the duration of Israel's wanderings in the desert, was unquestionably fixed and announced by God, *on the year-day principle;* "after the number of the days in which ye searched the land, even forty days, each day for a year, shall ye bear your iniquities. even forty years." Can we escape the conviction

---

* "Elements of Prophecy": Birks, p. 380.

that the same principle is to be applied to the 1260 days here specified, as marking the abode of the antitypical Israel in the wilderness?

The period of the domination of "the beast" is fixed (Rev. xiii. 5) as "forty and two months." This is the last of the mystic dates we have to consider. It must be compared with the explanation (ch. xvii. 9–11) :—" The seven heads are seven mountains, on which the woman sitteth. And there are seven kings ; five have fallen, and one is, and the other is not yet come ; and when he cometh he must continue a short space ; and *the beast* that was and is not, even he *is the eighth*, and is of the seven, and goeth into perdition." The argument in favour of the year-day interpretation yielded by this passage is of the following character :—Prior to the days of John, five forms of government had succeeded each other in Rome. These were the five fallen heads ; a sixth was then in being, a seventh was to follow, and occupy a *short* space, and the beast who was to continue forty and two months was to be the *eighth*. Thus the whole interval from A.D. 96, the date of the Apocalypse, to the still future destruction of the beast, is divided into three parts,—the *remainder* of the sixth head, the "short space " of the seventh, and the forty-two months of the eighth head, or "the beast."

Now since the first is only a *remainder*, and the second expressly predicted as *short*, we should naturally expect *the third to be the longest in duration*. The whole interval is already nearly 1800 years : how, then, is it possible to suppose this third to be only three years and a half? The second must, of course, in that case be still less, and the fractional first part would have to be extended over 1770 years! On the year-day principle all is harmonious : the forty-two months of the beast occupy 1260 years out of the whole period, leaving 516 years to be divided between the fraction of the sixth, and the "short space " of the seventh head.

Mr. Birks thus sums up his masterly argument, of which the foregoing is a mere outline :—" The year-day theory rests on a surprising combination of scriptural arguments, some of which, it is true, are indirect, and some doubtful; but the great majority are full, clear, and unambiguous. First of all there are four or five distinct presumptions of a general kind, that the dates have some secret meaning. There are, then, three plain and certain, and one more disputable passage, which supply an express *rule of interpretation*, and *a key* at once simple and comprehensive, the direct appointment of God Himself. When we further proceed to examine the passages in detail, we find that every one, without exception, yields some peculiar argument, in support of this same view; and several of them furnish us with two or three distinct proofs. And besides all these internal evidences for the system, it is found to have a basis in the heavenly revolutions themselves, and to be confirmed by its manifest harmony with the most exact elements of natural science." *

Thus we have shown,

1. THAT THE CHRONOLOGY OF THE HEBREW BIBLE IS OUR ONLY RELIABLE GUIDE, AS TO THE PERIODS OF REMOTE ANTIQUITY; and that the two gaps which occur in it, between the death of Moses, and the accession of Saul, have necessarily very brief limits, and cannot affect the question of the age of the world, to a greater extent than about fifty or sixty years.

2. And we have proved, as far as the point admits of proof, THAT THE PERIODS OF SYMBOLIC CHRONOLOGICAL PROPHECY, ARE TO BE INTERPRETED ON THE YEAR-DAY SYSTEM.

We are consequently in a position to consider the periodicity of history as a whole, taking into account the times foretold as in their day future, by Daniel and John, as well as those recorded as past, by other holy men of old.

We now proceed to *examine* these periods, to trace their mutual relations, and their relations to other series of periods,

---

* The meaning of this allusion will be explained in later chapters of this work.

and to show the Divine plan and system which underlies them, connecting them on the one hand with the periods of vital phenomena, and on the other with those of the whole magnificent solar system.

In pursuing this investigation, it must be borne in mind that the great end of all human history, like the great end of the existence of every human being, is *a moral one.* Existence to the entire race, like life to each individual, is a state of probation and education. The great objects of God, in his dealings with man from age to age, seem to have been, to reveal to him and to the universe, his true character and condition as a fallen being; while at the same time unveiling his own glorious, righteous, and gracious attributes, making known his purposes, and bringing forth his salvation.

Ignore this moral purpose of God, and human history becomes inexplicable, its chronology reducible to no system, and its study comparatively profitless and vain. Recognise it, and the whole outline and movement of the great drama, are at once intelligible, the plan underlying its periods is clear, and its study becomes fraught with lessons of the deepest and most solemn importance.

The true plan of history can therefore be found only in the Bible. The birth of humanity, its growth and maturity, its fall and its restoration, are all to be best traced in the Holy Word of God; and the key to its chronology and periodicity is also *there.* In vain do those who neglect the scriptures seek to understand aright, either man's past or his future.

The main divisions of history which we shall now proceed to present, will be found therefore to have a character more moral and dispensational, than political. Many of the greatest political events in the world's history will have to pass under our review, but we shall regard them as occupying a place of subordinate, and not of paramount importance. The central line, to which all political events have more or less reference, will be seen to be THE HISTORY OF THE TYPICAL AND OF THE ANTITYPICAL ISRAELS,—THE JEWISH NATION AND THE CHRIS-

TIAN CHURCH. Bible history and prophecy range themselves around these, just as Bible geography ranges itself around Jerusalem and the Holy Land; and the reason is obvious.

The natural and spiritual *seed of Abraham* are the line of promise, the peculiar people of God, in and through whom alone, mankind is to be saved and blessed. " In thee, and in thy seed, shall all nations of the earth be blessed."

As in each of the realms into which we have already glanced, so here in the realm of history, we shall find everything adapted to the great Divine septiform system. In a marvellous, hidden, and intricate manner, THE WEEK measures the periods of history, both great and small. Patient and accurate attention to the statements of Scripture is needful in order to trace out the arrangement of its periods, for it is purposely disguised and concealed, so as to elude the observation of the superficial reader. A comprehension of the biblical system of times and seasons, is calculated to fill the mind with awe and admiration, and to draw forth fresh worship of the omniscient God, who orders all things after the counsel of his own will, and knows the end, from the beginning.

There is, in the various particulars we shall have to pass in review, a cumulative force ; peculiarities observed in a few periods, or even in many, would be insufficient to prove the existence of plan and system, but when a vast multitude of events, and innumerable periods of the most various and apparently incongruous dimensions, ranging in duration from hours to millenaries, are found to fall into order and harmony, at the touch of a single wand, on the application of a single principle, then it will surely be clear to a candid mind, that history has been intentionally ordered on that principle ; and when, further, that principle is seen to be the same that regulates the phenomena of the organic and inorganic creations, and the same that is consistently adopted in Holy Scripture, the conclusion is as inevitable, as it is elevating and sanctifying, that it is the Almighty Maker of all worlds, the sole Lord and Giver of life, the Author of the sacred volume, who *so* orders it, who is the

Ruler of all events, the Disposer of all times and seasons. Our *times* are in his hands, and the times of all earthly empires, and kingdoms, and dynasties; and in *due time* his own kingdom shall overthrow all other dominion, and stand for ever. "The vision is yet for an appointed time, but at the end it shall speak, and not lie; though it tarry, wait for it, for it shall surely come, it shall not tarry."

> "God moves in a mysterious way,
>   His wonders to perform ;
> He plants his footsteps in the sea,
>   And rides upon the storm.
>
> Deep in unfathomable mines
>   Of never-failing skill,
> He treasures up his deep designs,
>   And works his sovereign will.
>
> His purposes will ripen fast,
>   Unfolding every hour ;
> The bud may have a bitter taste,
>   But sweet will be the flower."

The grand primary division of all human history, whether viewed from the moral, or from the chronological stand-point, is into three main, comprehensive, and long-enduring dispensations.

Scripture presents us with,—

    I. THE PATRIARCHAL AGE,

    II. THE JEWISH DISPENSATION, and

    III. THE "TIMES OF THE GENTILES,"

and with these great periods *only*, prior to the "Times of the Restitution of all things," or the Millennial Age.

The limits of the first or Patriarchal Age, are defined by the Apostle Paul in the 5th of Romans; "death reigned *from Adam to Moses.*"

The second, or Jewish Dispensation, dating from the Divine act of dividing the nations of the earth, and assigning a *pre-eminence* and a *sacred* character to the family of *Shem*, included *the entire history of the Jewish people and their fathers*, and

extended from the re-peopling of the earth after the Flood, to
the destruction of Jerusalem by Titus, A.D. 70–71, which was
the end of the Jewish temple, city, and polity.

The third is distinguished by our Lord Himself as a separate
period, under the title of "the times of the Gentiles" (Luke
xxi. 24); and is the period of the duration of the empires prefigured by *the great fourfold image of Nebuchadnezzar*, the
earliest, the simplest, and the most comprehensive of all the
symbolic prophecies. It is the great Gentile dispensation,
during which dominion in the earth, and *over Israel*, is by God
committed to GENTILE powers. Speaking generally, it dates
from the rise of the four great monarchies, and extends to the
Second Advent of Christ to establish the "kingdom of the God
of heaven, which shall never be destroyed." The inspired
statements of time connected with this last, give the clue to the
duration or chronological measurements of all three dispensations. As distinctly intimated in Daniel. it is *a great week*,
"seven times." Its latter half, is the oft-recurring "time, times,
and a half," or 1260 years. Its whole duration is *seven years of
years ;* that is, it is a week, each of whose *days* is a year of 360
years : in other words, it is a period of 2520 natural years.

Each of the two previous dispensations, has, as we shall
presently show, *a similar duration.* If therefore the three were
juxtaposed, if they had followed each other in chronological
sequence, their united period would be between seven and
eight thousand years.

But this is not the case. The second takes its rise two-thirds
down the course of the first, and the third takes *its* rise, in a
similar way, two-thirds down the course of the second, so that
the whole period comprised in the three dispensations, is nearly
6000 years, as will be seen by an examination of the accompanying diagram.

It will be observed that the dispensations are represented
not as *joined on to*, but as *growing out of*, each other. As we
proceed, it will become obvious, that there actually exists between them, not a mere lifeless sequence, but an intimate living

connection, which makes this theoretically proper, as well as chronologically true. The relation between them is not that of mere mechanical juxtaposition, but that of *vital ingrafting* and growth.

Before we enter into the *chronological* and *historical* details which justify these general statements, it will be well briefly to trace the *moral* features which characterize these three great dispensations.

They coincide with three distinct stages of revelation of the character and purposes of God : they have afforded three distinct probations to man, and they are represented in Scripture as closed by great judgments which display, each one with added clearness, God's righteous indignation against sin.

In the first, or patriarchal age, was made known, what the apostle calls, " eternal power and Godhead ; " the second, or Jewish dispensation, revealed the righteousness and justice of God ; its one ever-recurring refrain seeming to be, " Holy, holy, holy is the Lord of Hosts ;" and in the third, " the kindness and love of God our Saviour towards man appeared," " the *grace* of God, which bringeth salvation, appeared unto all men." Nature, the Law, the Gospel, such have been the three stages, by which God has been manifested to men, and by which fallen, humanity has been put to the test.

Of the PATRIARCHAL AGE, the leading characteristic was, that it had " no law " (Rom. v. 13, 14). Man during its course was left very much to himself, that he might show what was in him. *An immense week* of probation was granted to him ; for the Eternal God moves slowly and majestically in his dealings with his fallen creatures. For twenty-five long centuries no code of laws was laid on men, to restrain them from evil, or direct them to good.

Yet God left not Himself during this period without a witness, as Paul shows in the first and second chapters of Romans. He laid open before the eyes of men the volume of nature ; the starry heavens above, and the beautiful world around, teeming with infinitely varied forms of life, and filled with ten thousand evidences of benevolent design, spoke to man of the wisdom, power, and goodness of his Creator.

But man had no ears to hear its silent testimony, no eye to take in its expressive teachings, no heart to feel its sweet and melting influences. He saw indeed the sun, moon, and stars, he beheld them with admiration and awe, but instead of looking through nature up to nature's God, he worshipped and served the creature instead of the Creator, who is blessed for ever. He did not like to retain God in his knowledge ; he did not glorify Him as God ; he was not thankful ; he did not understand, as he should have done, the nature and character of the invisible Creator, from "the things which are made ;" he became vain, dark, foolish, utterly corrupt, and filled with a reprobate mind. In all this he was without excuse, for not only was nature a revelation of "eternal power and Godhead," which *should* have rendered impossible to intelligent beings, the degrading sin of idolatry, but God had added to this outward witness, an inward witness to Himself and his will, in the voice of conscience. Man had been made a law to himself, and left to follow or transgress the law thus written by the finger of God on the tables of his heart. The moral law within and the material universe without, were the double testimony to duty and to God, granted during the patriarchal age. In spite of both, men universally became idolaters ; worshippers, not only of the brightest and grandest natural objects, such as the heavenly bodies, but of the lowest and most degraded, such as birds and beasts and creeping things, stocks and stones and inanimate images. A reflex degradation was one punishment of this great sin ; the idolater was given up by God to the lowest and vilest immorality. The heathen of our own day, the savage cannibals of the South Sea Islands, the ferocious fetish worshippers of Ashantee, the degraded aborigines of Australia, are specimens of the depth of moral depravity to which man may sink, when left to his own reading of the revelation afforded by nature.

Corruption and violence were the characteristics of the central portion of the patriarchal age, which closed with the flood. Idolatry was the great sin of its final third, which extended from the Deluge to the Exodus.

Egypt, the first mighty kingdom of antiquity, was the home and hot-bed of idolatry. The land was full of idol temples and idol monuments; huge monsters in human form, men and beasts, and reptiles, and even insects and onions, were adored as deities, and God was utterly forgotten and ignored. When at last his Divine claims came into conflict with the will of man, human crime, as represented by that first kingdom, culminated in the cruel oppression of Israel, and haughty defiance of Jehovah. The proud monarch that bowed before loathsome reptiles, refused to bow before the King of kings. God-dishonouring idolatry, was mingled with God-defying audacity and rebellion; and judgment overtook the guilty: the ten plagues of Egypt were sent in sore and sad succession, ending with death—the death of the first-born, and the destruction of Pharaoh and all his hosts in the Red Sea

Then followed THE DISPENSATION OF LAW. Man was no longer left to conscience and the light of nature. God unfolded to him far more of his holy character and will, by means of the law promulgated from Sinai, while his purposes of mercy were darkly foreshadowed in the ceremonial worship which He thence enjoined on Israel. It was a new and advanced revelation. Amid thunders and darkness and thick clouds, God descended in the presence of the assembled thousands of his chosen people. The mountain smoked and burned with fire, while lightnings uplit the lurid spectacle with a terrific glare.

A double law—moral and ceremonial—was given. Ten commandments were the principal embodiment of the former, while the establishment of the Tabernacle, the priesthood, and the Jewish worship, were the leading elements of the latter. The first was to convince of sin, the second to foreshadow its remedy. "The law entered that the offence might abound," and its ceremonies were "a shadow of good things to come."

With wonderful clearness and fulness the law revealed the holiness of God, his mercy, and his justice. He passed by and proclaimed Himself "the LORD, the LORD GOD, merciful and gracious, longsuffering and abundant in goodness and truth; keeping mercy for thousands, forgiving iniquity, transgression and sin, and that will by no means clear the guilty; visiting the iniquity of the fathers upon the children, to the third and fourth generation." The whole Jewish dispensation was one long display of these Divine attributes, and afforded a revelation of God, deeper by far than that latent in nature. It had also the effect of testing man by a more searching probation, and revealing with additional clearness his true character. Sin became more evident in the light of the laws enacted against it: "sin by the commandment became exceeding sinful."

In the Jew, man stands forth, not merely as a sinner, but as a deliberate and persistent rebel against God, breaking every law imposed on him, abusing every privilege granted to him, and despising every blessing bestowed.

Before they had time to receive, in its written form, the law which had been orally delivered to them, Israel had violated its first great and fundamental command, "Thou shalt have no other Gods but me," and all their subsequent career was in harmony with this beginning.

They sinned, and committed iniquity, they understood not God's wonders nor remembered his mercies, they provoked Him and forgot his works, they waited not for his counsel but lusted exceedingly in the wilderness, and tempted God in the desert; they envied Moses and Aaron; they changed their glory into the similitude of an ox that eateth grass; they forgat God their Saviour and despised the pleasant land; they murmured in their tents and hearkened not to the voice of the Lord; they joined themselves to Baal Peor, and ate the sacrifices of the dead; they provoked God to anger with their inventions; they did not destroy, as commanded, the idolatrous nations of Canaan, but were mingled among the heathen and learned their works; they served their idols and sacrificed their sons and daughters unto devils; they shed innocent blood, even the blood of their sons and daughters whom they sacrificed to the idols of Canaan; they were defiled with their own works, and went a whoring with their own inventions, till the wrath of the Lord was kindled against his people, and He abhorred his own inheritance. Many times did He deliver them, but they provoked Him with their counsel and were brought low for their iniquity. They persecuted every prophet that was sent to them, and after every deliverance, fell lower than before, into all manner of sin and evil.

At last, long threatened judgment fell, and captivity after captivity came upon the tribes of Israel; Pul and Sennacherib invaded their land, Shalmanezer and Esarhaddon, kings of Assyria, conquered and enslaved the ten tribes, and Nebuchadnezzar took Jerusalem and carried Judah away captive to Babylon. The city that was full of people and esteemed " princess among the provinces," sat solitary and became tributary, the ways of Zion mourned, and her gates were desolate; her beauty departed from Jerusalem, and she came down wonderfully; God covered the daughter of Zion with a cloud in his anger, and cast down the beauty of Israel; He cast off his altar, and abhorred his sanctuary, gave his people into the hand of the enemy, and scattered their princes among the Gentiles. " The precious sons of Zion, comparable to fine gold," were " esteemed as earthen pitchers "—the adversary took possession of the gates of Jerusalem. The Lamentations of Jeremiah tell how deeply the chastisement was felt; the confessions of Daniel show what searchings of heart and what contrition it created.

But the restoration of Israel under Ezra and Nehemiah, and their prolonged probation, in their land, proved that the awful lesson had been all in vain. Prophet after prophet had announced to them the advent of Messiah the Prince. In due time HE came. God was manifest in the flesh. He came unto his own,—to this people whom for over two thousand years He had been preparing to receive Him; but " *his own received Him not."* They " despised and rejected Him ;" they hated Him because He testified of them that their deeds were evil; they blasphemed the Son of God, accusing Him of deriv-ing his power from the Prince of Devils ; they took counsel together to slay the Holy and the Just; they bore false witness against Him to put Him to death ; they became his betrayers and murderers ; they cried, " Crucify Him, crucify Him," and by their wicked hands, He *was* crucified and slain.

And when the still lingering longsuffering of God, sent them one more chance of repentance, and the risen Saviour told his apostles that remission of sins through his name, was to be preached among all nations, *beginning at Jerusalem*, when the Holy Ghost in Peter and in Stephen pleaded still with Israel to repent and be converted, they filled up the measure of their iniquities by rejecting this final offer of mercy. They slew Stephen, and persecuted the Church. " The Jews both killed the Lord Jesus, and their own prophets, and have persecuted us ; they please not God, and are contrary to all men, forbid-ding us to speak to the Gentiles that they might be saved, to fill up their sins alway, for wrath is come upon them to the uttermost " (1 Thess. ii. 15, 16).

A few years elapsed, after those words were written, and then that wrath was poured out. Jerusalem fell, and great was the fall thereof ! Signal, terrible and unparalleled was the Jewish war, ending with the siege and capture of Jerusalem by Titus. It needs a pen dipped in fire and in blood to write the story in its true colours ! The sufferings and miseries that overtook the Jewish nation in that age, are all but inde-scribable, the very record of them is appalling. One million one hundred thousand Jewish lives were sacrificed in the siege and capture of Jerusalem alone ; streams of human blood ex-tinguished the blazing fires that destroyed the houses of the city, and heaps of the unburied corpses of those who had died of starvation during the siege, hid from the Roman soldiers the immense treasures of the temple. From April 14th, when the siege began, to July 1st,—115,880 bodies were buried at the public expense, or thrown from the walls, not including those interred by their friends. Some said that 600,000 of the poorer people had perished of want; women cooked and ate their own children, " the maimed and defenceless people were slain in thousands "; when the temple at last fell, " they lay heaped like sacrifices round the altar, and the steps of the temple ran with streams of blood, which washed down the bodies that lay about." " The slaughter within was even more dreadful than the spectacle from without, . it was indiscriminate carnage. The number of the slain exceeded that of the slayers. The treasuries, with their wealth of money, jewels, and costly robes, were totally destroyed. . . . The value of the plunder obtained was so great, that gold fell in Syria to half its former value."

Milman, after describing the long and awful siege, and the multiplied suffering of the Jews, says, " Thus fell, and·for ever, the metropolis of the Jewish State. Other cities have risen on the ruins of Jerusalem, and succeeded as it were to the inalienable inheritance of perpetual siege, oppression, and ruin. Jerusalem might almost seem to be a place under a peculiar curse ; it has probably seen a far greater portion of human misery than any other spot upon the earth."

After its fall, " the markets of the Roman Empire were glutted with Jewish slaves ; the amphitheatres were crowded with these miserable people, who were forced to slay each other, not singly but in troops, or else fall in rapid succession, glad to escape the tyranny of their masters by the expeditious cruelty of the wild beasts. And in the unwholesome mines hundreds were doomed to toil for wealth not to be their own." " The political existence of the Jewish nation was annihilated ; it was never again recognised as one of the States or kingdoms of the world. Judea was sentenced to be portioned out to strangers, the capital was destroyed, the temple demolished, the high priesthood buried in its ruins, and the royal race extinct."

Titus had destroyed the temple and city of the Jews, and slaughtered and captured and sold into slavery millions of the people. About seventy years later, the Jews had sufficiently recovered from this crushing blow, to rise afresh in revolt against the Roman power, and then Adrian completed the work of their dispersion among all nations of the earth. He made the whole country of Palestine a desolation, expelled all its remaining Jewish inhabitants, forbade the Jews on pain of death even to *approach* Ælia Capitolina, the Roman city erected on the site of Jerusalem; he slaughtered 580,000 Jews in a murderous war which lasted three years and a half, and sold thousands of prisoners, at the lowest prices, into slavery. The rest took refuge in foreign lands, and Palestine has never since been inhabited by the children of Israel.

Eighteen centuries have elapsed, since that fearful judgment of fire and blood, attested the righteous " severity " of God against those who had despised his " goodness." It was but the beginning of the " indignation " against the Jewish people. Ever since they have been scattered among the Gentiles, in Europe, Asia, and Africa, denizens everywhere, citizens nowhere ; oppressed and persecuted in most countries, banished at times in turn from each; treated with indignity, injustice, and cruelty, they yet survive, a separate and peculiar people ; a nation without a land, while their land lies desolate, without a people ; and their city, as Christ foretold it would be, is trodden down of the Gentiles, till " the times of the Gentiles " shall be fulfilled.

THE THIRD DISPENSATION, "the times of the Gentiles," brought a revelation of God, fuller, truer, more glorious by far, than any that had preceded it. " *God was manifest in the flesh,*" men saw, and heard, and spoke with, incarnate Deity. " The law was given by Moses, but grace and truth came by Jesus Christ." " God, who at sundry times and in divers manners spake in time past unto the fathers by the propets, hath in these last days spoken unto us by his Son." " No man hath seen God at any time, the only begotten Son which is in the bosom of the Father, He hath declared Him." Not the power and wisdom only, not the righteousness and justice only, but the kindness and love of God our Saviour toward man, appeared, in the life and death of Jesus Christ our Lord. God was proved to be a gracious Redeemer, as well as a holy Lawgiver, and an Almighty Creator. The shadows of the Law were replaced by the realities of the Gospel, the New Testament was added to the Old, its key and its completion ; the great salvation so long foreshadowed, was accomplished and brought nigh to man. God had provided Himself a Lamb to take away the sins of the world, and that Lamb, his own glorious Son, the Lord of all ! " Herein is love ; not that we loved God, but that He loved us, and sent his Son to be the propitiation for our sins."

What a flood of light fell upon the world in the teachings of Christ and his apostles ! The gift of the Holy Ghost followed on the ascension of the risen Saviour ; the Christian Church was.founded, and gathered, from Jew and Gentile alike, a vast multitude into its bosom. In spite of persecution it grew and multiplied, for God was with his people ; they endured and conquered, winning the world to their creed. Paganism fell. The mighty Roman Empire shut up its idol temples, sheathed its persecuting sword, and sat down as a disciple at the feet of Christ and his apostles.

Grace had wrought a wondrous work, but nature was unchanged. The natural man was still at enmity with God, and the cloak of Christianity, could not long conceal his corruption.

An apostasy of a dark and dreadful nature arose, and in the progress of ages assumed enormous proportions, and a character so diabolic, as to exceed in guilt all the idolatries of the patriarchal and Jewish dispensations. The greater light granted was abused and perverted, until it became a darkness exceeding any previous darkness—and the central period of its duration is, by common consent, called " the dark ages."

The religion of Christ became gradually, as we have seen, the religion of Antichrist. Carnal observances replaced spiritual conversion, the ceremonial took the place of the moral, human tradition obscured the word of God, human authority asserted itself in opposition to Divine ; and idolatry, under the guise of Christianity, replaced true and spiritual worship.

When Pagan Rome fell, Papal Rome rose.   Corruptions, heresies, abominable practices abounded.   The teachings of Christ were forgotten, and the teachings of the church put in their place.   It became a sin to believe the truth and serve the living God, yea, it was soon esteemed the worst of crimes to follow the Lord wholly.   The saints were persecuted.   In streams, ay ! in rivers, their blood was ·shed, till the *professing* church of Christ became " drunk " with the blood of his true disciples.   Millions more martyrs fell under the sword of *Papal* Rome than were slain by the power of the *Pagan* Empire which ruled from the seven-hilled city.

The head of this great Apostasy put himself in the place of Christ as head of the church.   He wore a ring to snow himself bridegroom, husband of the church ; he proclaimed himself her prophet, priest, and king ; he assumed to be Prince of the kings of the earth : King of kings and Lord of lords.   He wore a triple crown, and claimed dominion in heaven, earth, and hell ; power to pardon sins on earth, to loose from pains in hell, and to canonise whom he would in heaven ; he carried two swords, to mark his temporal and spiritual government ; he sat in the temple of God ; received worship as God ; and arrogated to himself Divine attributes and authority.

Doctrines of devils were taught to the people instead of the precepts of the Gospel.   The mass was presented to the multitudes instead of the atoning Sacrifice of the Saviour, the wafer god, instead of Christ : indulgences for sin were sold for money, turning the grace of God into lasciviousness.   The true nature of holiness was completely obscured, as well as the true nature of sin, and the true nature of Christ's religion.   The priesthood, sunk in the profoundest ignorance and in the grossest corruption, kept the people in the dark, that they might the more readily prey upon them ; the Bible was buried in an unknown tongue, and might almost as well not have been in existence. Christianity retained no trace of its pure and holy original.

Human intelligence revolted from the gross and monstrous lie, and thus Christian corruption created a reaction, and called into existence indirectly, in early days, the Mohammedanism which protests against all creature worship, and in later days, the Infidelity which denies Christ altogether, and the Atheism which excludes all worship of God.

For a thousand years this Babylon reigned paramount in the Roman Earth, and then God began to consume and destroy it. He raised up holy men and wise, to protest against it; He gave back, by their means, his Word to the nations; He gave his people grace to love not their lives, but to sacrifice them freely, that the faith of Christ might be restored in the earth. A reformed church arose, and with its reformed doctrines, came reformation of manners, and something of a return to primitive Christian purity and practice. But even here darkness quickly entered again. The Reformation did not go far enough, it did not purge out all the old leaven, it retained some principles of corruption, which caused the reformed churches quickly to degenerate into worldly corporations, unable to protest, with the spiritual power of the first Reformers, against the corruptions of Popery, or to grapple with the more rapidly growing forces of the infidelity it had created.

As to the Apostasy itself, no protests availed to reform it, no teachings to enlighten it, no examples to shame it, no warnings to awaken it : and at length judgment fell. The godless infidelity which had sprung up in the earth, as the result of Papal deeds and doctrines, rose in arms against it, and plunged both Papacy and monarchy into a sea of blood. The French Revolution! Who can depict its horrors? Vials of wrath were poured out on the Papal kingdoms of Christendom. One country after another was visited with vengeance ; wars, and bloody revolutions, internal strifes and contentions, darkened the realms of the Papacy ; and the Popes lost gradually all their direct authority over the kingdoms of Europe ; all their political power ; and enormous wealth in the shape of landed property and buildings, monasteries and convents. And still the measure of their iniquity was not full; the sore judgments of God led them not to repentance. The crowning crime came at last, and the Papacy, which had decreed the "immaculate conception" of an idolatrously worshipped woman, proceeded to decree the "infallibility" of a sinful man.

By the consent and decree of the Œcumenical Council of 1870, the Divine title of *infallible teacher of faith and morals* was given to the Pope of Rome. After twelve centuries of heresy and hypocrisy, corruption and persecution, the "man of sin" seals all his awful errors, and all his flagrant and revolting crimes, with the seal of "infallibility," and claims for all his doctrines of devils the authority of Divine inspiration!

While the words were yet in his mouth, judgment fell. War burst forth; Sadowa and Sedan crushed the might of the two most powerful Catholic nations of Europe. France, overwhelmed by the victorious armies of Protestant Germany, was fain to recall from Rome the French bayonets, which had long been the sole support of the Papal throne, and Victor Emmanuel entered the city as King of Italy. The temporal power of the Papacy was swept clean away, the throne of a thousand years was overturned, the Pope became "a prisoner in the Vatican." The long drama of the Papal temporal power is ended; there remains that its spiritual power be also destroyed. The Lord has *consumed* it by the spirit of his mouth, He is to *destroy* it by the brightness of his coming.

Nor have those sections of Christendom, which escaped the influence of the *Romish* apostasy, continued in the goodness of God. Apostasy has been universal. If we trace the history, and note the condition, of the Eastern churches, the Coptic, Armenian, Nestorian, Syrian, or Greek professing Christian churches, we shall see the same thing. In all, sooner or later, the light of truth, so graciously granted, has been first obscured, and then lost, while a darkness, all the more dangerous in that it professes to be light, has taken its place. The worship offered in these churches, has for ages been little better than idolatry: the morality practised, and the doctrines in-

culcated, at fundamental variance with those of Christ. The
scourge of Islamism was the awful judgment sent as a woe on
the Eastern churches; but it did not lead them to repentance.
For twelve centuries they have groaned under its cruel op
pression, but they have not forsaken their idolatries and evil
deeds. They are now drinking the last dregs of the cup of
judgment; and the Porte like the Papacy, true to the last to its
character, is hurting, killing, and tormenting to the bitter end.
But its days are numbered: the full and final judgment of
God is soon to overtake both oppressor and oppressed: " when
the Lord Jesus shall be revealed from heaven, in flaming fire,
taking vengeance on those who,"—in spite of all his revelations
of Himself,—" know not God, and obey not the Gospel of our
Lord Jesus Christ."

Intensely mournful is the review of human history as regards
man's treatment of God, in his threefold revelation of Himself, as Creator, Lawgiver, and Redeemer.

Having the light of nature, fallen man sinned; blessed with
the additional light of law, including commandments, and
types and shadows, the ministry of inspired prophets, and the
incarnation of God Himself, he sinned *still worse;* and favoured
with the full blaze of grace and truth, in the teaching and
work of Jesus Christ, in the illuminations of the Spirit of God,
and the possession of the New Testament, as well as warned
by the awful judgments which closed the former dispensations,
man has sinned *worst of all*, and incurred the heavier judgments foretold in the Scriptures of truth, and soon to fall on
the earth !

How can the heirs of salvation ever be sufficiently grateful
for the sovereign, unmerited mercy that has delivered them
from the kingdom of darkness, and translated them into the
kingdom of God's dear Son? How can they ever be sufficiently earnest, in urging the ungodly to flee from the wrath
to come—the lost to seek, while there is time, the salvation
which is in Christ Jesus?

But unspeakably blessed, on the other hand, is this review

of human history, in the light of *God's treatment of man*, in his threefold and ever-increasing sinfulness. It is an illustration of his power, wisdom, and love in overcoming evil with good. For out of each dispensation, marred by the sin of man, God has delivered a ransomed people, and raised them to greater heights of blessing than before. In the patriarchal age, He brought through the waters of the flood, the family of Noah, and then from Shem He produced the Hebrew race, through which salvation to the ends of the earth was to come. From the destructive and overwhelming judgments of Egypt He delivered Israel, and their Exodus brought them into new and nearer relationships to Himself, than man had ever known before; "ye shall be unto Me a peculiar people;" and from the desolating captivities of Israel and Judah, a remnant returned, destined to see the Desire of all ages, to behold the rising of the Sun of righteousness, to welcome to his temple the Lord Himself.

From the still more awful and desolating judgments poured out on the Jewish nation in consequence of their rejection of Christ, God brought forth the Christian church. "Through their fall salvation is come to the Gentiles." The branches were broken off, but the wild olive was graffed in, the casting away of *them*, was the reconciling of the world.

And then,—God's ways progressing ever from evening to morning, from good to better,—out of the closing judgments of these "Times of the Gentiles" whose thunders are already breaking on our ears and whose lurid lightnings are already flashing in our skies, shall spring the restoration of Israel, the return of Israel's Messiah, the resurrection of the dead in Christ, the rapture of the entire Christian church, the times of the restitution of all things, the millennial reign of Christ.

That in its turn will, as the very brief notice in Scripture proves, be a fresh revelation of God, and a fresh probation of man, and will end, like all the rest, in judgment—the great dread, long-foretold Day of final Judgment, which will usher in the eternal day, the "new heaven and the new earth wherein dwelleth righteousness," into which sin shall never enter, and where consequently death and the curse shall be no more. (Rev. xx., xxi.)

This is the great climax which closes *the first week* of human history, introducing untold ages of unspeakable blessedness for the human race, those "ages to come," in which God will show the exceeding riches of his grace, in his kindness towards his people, through Christ Jesus.

Each of the three dispensations into which human history has been divided, has therefore its distinctive and peculiar character, though the three resemble each other in this, that each ends in apostasy on the part of man, and in judgment, and the introduction of a higher economy, on the part of God.

The patriarchal age is broadly distinguished by the fact of its having "no law," from the Jewish, and this again, by its limitation of nationality, from the Times of the Gentiles ; but the flood, and the exodus, and the captivities, and the fall of Jerusalem, and the yet future destruction of the beast and the false prophet, and Babylon the Great, at the Epiphany of Christ, mark out so many distinct closes and re-commencements, wherein God executes deserved and long-denounced doom on the guilty, while delivering and raising to a higher level an elect and ransomed people.

We proceed now to trace *the chronological measures* of these three dispensations, and their respective positions, in the great stream of time. We will take the Times of the Gentiles first, as it is the most important, the most closely connected with the prophecies of Daniel and the Apocalypse, and the one whose duration is most distinctly defined in Scripture.

CHRONOLOGICAL MEASURES OF THE TIMES OF THE GENTILES.

When the Egyptian captivity of his seed was announced to Abraham, chronological limits were assigned to it ; and when the Babylonish captivity was foretold by Isaiah, seventy years was fixed as its duration. It might therefore be expected that the *length* of the period of Jewish affliction and degradation, which is termed by our Lord "the Times of the Gentiles," would also be more or less distinctly foretold : yet as it includes the times of the Christian Church—those ages of waiting for Christ, over which in tender mercy God saw fit to throw, as we have seen, a veil of mystery,—it is improbable that its duration will anywhere be revealed in plain terms.

We have already shown that this period or dispensation is that, during which the Jews are either wholly cast out of their land, or allowed to occupy it as mere tributaries, and during which also, the throne is taken from the house of Judah, and from the seed of David, and given by God to Gentile monarchs. It is the period during which the *land of Canaan,* promised to the seed of Abraham, and the *throne of Israel,* secured by covenant to the seed of David, are both alienated, and occupied by Gentiles instead of Jews. During by far the greater part of this period, Israel has been scattered among all nations, Jerusalem "trodden down of the Gentiles," and the pleasant land laid desolate.

The whole period is occupied by the duration of the four great monarchies, and it is to be closed by a fifth great monarchy, "the God of heaven shall set up a kingdom which shall never be destroyed . . . it shall stand for ever"—a kingdom symbolised by the stone cut out without hands, which smites and destroys the image, becomes a great mountain, and fills the whole earth. (Dan. ii. 44.)

This kingdom is, as we learn from other Scriptures, the kingdom of Christ Himself, *and his accession to the throne of the earth marks the termination of the Times of the Gentiles.* "The Lord God shall give unto HIM the throne of his father David." David foresaw that of the fruit of his loins, God would raise up Christ, to sit upon his throne. God will overturn one monarchy after another, "until *He* come, whose right it is," and will give the throne to Him.

And prior to this restoration of the throne to the house of Judah in the person of Christ, will be the restoration of the land of Canaan to the seed of Abraham.

"And it shall come to pass in that day, that the Lord shall set his hand again *the second time* to recover the remnant of his people which shall be left, from Assyria, and from Egypt, and from Pathros, and from Cush, and from Elam, and from Shinar, and from Hamath, and from the islands of the sea. He shall assemble the outcasts of Israel, and gather together the dispersed of Judah, from the four corners of the earth " (Isa. ii. 11). God has not cast away his people whom He foreknew, they are still beloved for the fathers' sakes, and in due time, when the fulness of the Gentiles has been brought in, "all Israel shall be saved." The gifts and calling of God are without repentance; the land must revert to its rightful owners the seed of Abraham, and the throne must be filled by its predicted occupant, the Son of David, the Prince of peace, of the increase of whose government there shall be no end, who shall "order and establish the kingdom, with judgment and with justice, for ever."

However improbable it may appear that Palestine should ever again be the home of a mighty Jewish nation, Scripture leaves no room to doubt that such will be the case,—that the same Almighty arm, which to place Israel there of old, plagued Egypt, destroyed the host of Pharaoh, and extirpated almost entirely the seven nations of Canaan ; which subsequently overthrew the mighty Babylonian monarchy, in order to restore Israel to it for a comparatively brief period, by means of Cyrus and Artaxerxes, will in due time overthrow the Turkish power which has so long trodden down Jerusalem, defiled the sanctuary, and desolated the land of Israel, and will, *the second time*, restore his ancient people, to their inalienable inheritance. Every barrier must fall, every obstacle be overthrown, that the purpose of God may be accomplished, and the promises to Abraham and to his seed be fulfilled.

God has clearly revealed that all this shall be ; has He also revealed *when* it shall be ? He has revealed the *character* of the Times of the Gentiles ; has He also revealed their *duration ?* We believe He has, very distinctly, though not in plain statements. He has given many a clue and many a mystic intimation, which when combined, by those who compare Scripture *prophecy* with Scripture *history*, and with profane history, afford no indistinct reply to this inquiry. It is of course needful to take profane history into account in considering this question, as many of the events predicted extend beyond the point at which inspired records cease. Nor should we have the slightest hesitation in doing this, for we are evidently intended to make use of uninspired historical evidence. Scripture history *ceases* just at the point where by common consent profane history becomes reliable, and passes from the dim regions of fable into the broad daylight of well ascertained facts. God graciously presents us with inspired records of that far distant past of which no uninspired records exist; but where authentic histories *are* in existence, He leaves us to learn from them what the course of mundane events has been. He makes provision for our unavoidable ignorance, but none for our indolence. He puts into our hands the telescope of Scripture history, to enable us to see farther into the distant past, than would with the naked human eye be possible; but He does not embody in the sacred writings, matters, such as the fall of Jerusalem and the dispersion of the Jewish people in the days of Titus, which are sufficiently well attested by Josephus and other careful historians.

Looking then both at ancient prophecy and at sacred and profane history, what do we learn as to the duration of these " Times of the Gentiles "?

THAT THEY ARE APPOINTED TO EXTEND OVER A GREAT WEEK, OVER " SEVEN TIMES," SEVEN YEARS WHOSE DAYS ARE YEARS, 2520 NATURAL YEARS.

This is *inferred* from Scripture rather than distinctly *stated* in it; but the inference is so well grounded as to be of almost equal weight with a distinct declaration.

When this long period of Jewish desolation and chastisement was first threatened (Lev. xxvi.), the expression " seven times " was emphatically used in connection with it. That this had any chronological force, was not of course understood by those who received the warning, but it is almost impossible in the light of subsequent predictions, and in the light of history, to doubt that the Omniscient God used an expression in harmony with *his* foreknowledge of Israel's future, and expressive of his Divine purpose—a purpose which *we* have seen wrought out in history. By the lips of Moses, God forewarned his people, saying,—

"If ye will not yet for all this hearken unto Me, then I will punish you *seven times* more for your sins . . . and if ye will not be reformed by Me by these things, but will walk contrary unto Me, then will I also walk contrary unto you, and will punish you *yet seven times* for your sins .
And if ye will not for all this hearken unto Me . . . then I will walk contrary unto you also in fury, and I, even I, will chastise you *seven times* for your sins. . . . I will make your cities waste, and bring your sanctuaries unto desolation . . . and I will scatter you among the heathen, and will draw out a sword after you . . . and ye shall perish among the heathen, and the land of your enemies shall eat you up" (Lev. xxvi.).

Old Testament history shows that Israel's oft-recurring and inveterate idolatry brought upon them judgment after judgment; that again and again God " being full of compassion forgave their iniquity and destroyed them not; yea, many a time turned He his anger away, and did not stir up all his wrath ; for He remembered that they were but flesh, a wind that passeth away and cometh not again ; " but that at last the measure of their iniquity being filled up, He sent upon them a chastisement, the *perfect* character of which is marked out by the *perfection of its period,* " seven times."

Seventy years,—the first portion of this long season of rejection, dispersion, and affliction, were spent in absolute captivity in Babylon and Assyria. The second stage was longer —it was the " seventy weeks," or 490 years of the restoration of Judah, and was passed by the restored remnant of the two tribes in a subject, tributary, and troubled state, in their own land, while the ten tribes remained captives in Assyria. This extended to the coming of Messiah the Prince, and the destruction of Jerusalem consequent on his rejection; and then commenced the *third* and longest portion of the 2520 years, which the Jews have passed in miserable exile, scattered over all the countries of the earth.

Already their chastisement has extended over " seven times," dating from the *earliest* stage in their captivities : *it will soon have done so, dating from the latest.* Does not then, the solemn threat, fulfilled in such awful justice through a long succession of ages, gleam *now* with the light of hope, and assume the cheering tones of mercy ? " Seven times." *No more !* then the curse that has fallen so heavily, is all but exhausted, and everlasting blessedness is to succeed. The wrath has come upon Israel to the uttermost ; the fountain for sin and for un-cleanness, shall ere long be opened to the house of David, and to the inhabitants of Jerusalem.

And secondly, though the fourfold image which symbolised to Nebuchadnezzar, the succession of Gentile empires, which were to fill up this long interval of Jewish rejection, had no chronology attached to it, yet we know that those empires, the Assyrian, the Persian, the Grecian, and the Pagan and Papal Roman powers, have as a matter of history lasted for about 2520 years. Now history is the evolution of the determinate counsel and foreknowledge of God, which must therefore have before assigned to " the Times of the Gentiles " *at least* this duration.

The symbol of the fourfold image declared, that these Gentile empires were to be succeeded by the kingdom of the God of heaven, but it did not reveal or even intimate when, or after what lapse of time, this should be. A subsequent vision granted to Nebuchadnezzar, did. He saw a tree, which he was told symbolised himself, cut down, and its stump left to be wet with the dew of heaven, and its portion with the beasts in the grass of the earth, its heart changed from a man's heart, and a beast's heart given it, until " seven times " should pass over it.

This vision was, as Daniel told the monarch, a prophecy of *the seven years' insanity*, which, as a chastening for his pride, was to overtake *him*, and which was to teach him to know God, and to own that " the heavens do rule." "All this came upon King Nebuchadnezzar," and at the end of the days, that is, or the seven years of his insanity, he lifted up his eyes to heaven, his understanding returned to him, and he blessed and praised and honoured the Eternal God, whose dominion is everlasting, whose will is sovereign, whose power is infinite, and who is able to abase those who walk in pride.

Now the vision of the tree is not more clearly symbolic of this remarkable incident in Nebuchadnezzar's life, than that incident itself is typical of certain moral and chronological features, of the succession of Gentile monarchies, of which Nebuchadnezzar was both head and representative.

The leading moral characteristics of all the four great empires have been, ignorance of God, idolatry, and cruel persecution of the saints. Nebuchadnezzar, prior to this incident, knew not God ; he set up a great image, and commanded all men, on pain of death, to fall down and worship it. He cast into the burning fiery furnace the faithful witnesses who refused to obey the idolatrous mandate. How have all his successors with one consent followed this example ! *Idolatry*, literal or spiritual, and *persecution*, Pagan or Papal, have marked the whole succession of Gentile monarchies. These episodes in Nebuchadnezzar's life are clearly typical ; these features of his character have been stamped indelibly on all his successors. These incidents answer to events on the scale of nations and centuries with which history makes us familiar. So also does the *seven years' bestial degradation of the monarch during his insanity*, answer to the *period of Gentile rule* represented by the *four wild beasts* of a subsequent vision. " The king himself *represents* the succession of imperial sovereignty, till the kingdom of Christ shall come ; the ' seven times ' that passed over him must therefore *represent* the whole period of debasement in the Gentile kingdoms, from the times of Nebuchadnezzar till their full redemption." *

---

* Birks' " Elements," p. 353.

As we have alluded elsewhere to this subject we do not dwell further on it here; it affords strong confirmation of the view that the "seven times" of Lev. xxvi. has a chronological force. A further argument in support of the same view may be derived from the "time times and a half" of the "little horn." We have seen that prophecy assigns to the Apostasy of the latter days, a duration of 1260 years, and that this period is repeatedly spoken of as *half a week*. Where are we to find the other half of this great week? As the Apostasy is to be over-thrown finally by the advent of Christ, it is clear the other half cannot *follow* but must *precede* the half which measures the existence of the Apostasy, it must date back, that is, from its *rise*. Calculating backwards then from the rise of the Papal and Mohammedan powers in the beginning of the seventh century, 1260 years lead up to the days of Nebuchadnezzar. to the commencement of the Babylonish Captivity, the point at which we know the Times of the Gentiles began. Thus we see that the entire period occupied by the four great empires, re-presented by the golden image, and by the four beasts, is the *whole* week, whose *latter half* is the time of the dominion of the "little horn." During the whole of this period Israel has ceased to be an independent kingdom, and during two-thirds of it, Jerusalem has been trodden down by the Gentiles. Each of the four great monarchies in turn ruled over the seed of Abraham, until at length, the cup of Jewish iniquity being full, the Romans came, took away their place and nation, and almost destroyed them as a people. Seventy years before this final judgment, Messiah came and was cut off, and his rejection and crucifixion by the Jews, which sealed and brought on their doom, inaugurated the Gospel dispensation, and the ingathering of the Gentiles to the kingdom of God. Thus the Christian dispensation, so thoroughly *Gentile* in its aspect, fills two-thirds of the Times of the Gentiles, the first third having been occupied with the growth of Gentile dominion, to the extra-ordinary development it had attained in the days of Augustus Cæsar. We conclude therefore that the dispensation in whose

closing days we live, was fore-ordained and appointed by God
to run a course of 2520 years, or in symbolic language of
"seven times;" and that our Lord Jesus Christ had this
great week in his mind when He said, "Jerusalem shall be
trodden down of the Gentiles, until the Times of the Gentiles
be fulfilled," an expression which seems to imply that the
period so designated had definite chronological limits. We
proceed to inquire when it took its rise. From what great
event are we to date the commencement of these "Times of
the Gentiles"?

Happily the answer is not far to seek. We are not left to
select among the complex changes of history, one which seems
to us of paramount importance. Inspiration itself settles the
question. The entire course of Gentile supremacy is symbolised by *an image* whose *head* was its beginning, and whose
ten toes are chronologically its end.

Interpreting his dream by Divine revelation, to the proud
monarch of Babylon, the prophet says to him "THOU art this
head of gold." If by this be meant "thou" *personally*, then
the "terminus a quo" or starting point of the "Times of the
Gentiles" must be sought, as has generally been done. somewhere in the lifetime of Nebuchadnezzar.

But it seems clear that this was not the case, and that
Daniel addressed the Babylonian king not as an individual,
but as the representative of the empire, for immediately after
saying "thou art this head of gold," he adds, "and after *thee*
shall arise another kingdom, inferior to *thee*," alluding to the
Medo-Persian Empire which succeeded the Babylonian.

Now this empire did not rise after Nebuchadnezzar *himself*,
but after *his kingdom*. It rose on the fall of the Babylonian
Empire, but not till four successors of Nebuchadnezzar had
occupied the throne, of whom Belshazzar was the last.

Though undoubtedly its most illustrious ruler, Nebuchadnezzar was neither the first nor the last head of the Babylonian
Empire, which lasted 210 years. The "head of gold"
evidently represents the *whole* Babylonian power, just as the

"breast of silver" represents the whole Medo-Persian, and it seems natural therefore to suppose that one main starting point of those times of the Gentiles, which include the four great empires, will be found at the era of *the rise* of the first of the four, *i.e., of the Babylonian power.*

This great dispensational period, the times of the Gentiles, is characterized by two distinct features, the dominion of the four great empires, and the *loss* of dominion and independence on the part of the Jewish people ; their subjection to and sufferings under their enemies ; their dispersion among all nations, and the desolation of their land.

The commencing era of the " Times of the Gentiles " must be an era of *decay and fall of Jewish independence, coincident with a rise of Babylonian power.*

Now the seventy years' captivity of Judah in Babylon was not the beginning of the decay and fall of Jewish independence, nor was it the beginning of the rise of the Babylonian power.

The year of the accession of **Nabonassar**, the first king of Babylon, is an era of great historic importance. It ranks with the greatest eras of history : the Greek era of the Olympiads ; the Roman A.U.C. or era of the foundation of the city of Rome ; the Syrian era of the Seleucidæ ; the Christian era of the Nativity ; the Papal era of indictions (dating from the conversion of Constantine, the fall of Paganism, and the beginning of the Imperial Church); and the Mohammedan era of the Hegira.

Moreover, the exact chronological point of this " ERA OF NABONASSAR " (N.E.) is more certain than any other date of remote antiquity, because, with it are connected a series of ancient astronomic observations, which have been *verified* by the labours of astronomers, during the last three centuries. It is certain not only to a year, but to a day and hour. It is noon of the 26th of February, 747 B.C.

That this important era, marking the commencement of the Babylonian power, should be one starting point of the 2520 years of the " Times of the Gentiles," seems as natural and suitable as that the capture of Jerusalem by Nebuchadnezzar should be another.

Like other national changes, and like many great political revolutions, the subjugation of the twelve tribes of Israel to the Assyrian and Babylonian powers, was only *gradually* accomplished. Monarch after monarch came up against the land; and one deportation of captives succeeded another. Ephraim first fell, then Judah: and Judah fell first partially, into the rank of a tributary kingdom, then completely, into the bitterest bondage, captivity, and degradation. Pul and Tiglath-pileser, Shalmanezer and Sennacherib, Esarhaddon and Nebuchadnezzar, all played their parts in the great and mournful tragedy. The following brief summary of the facts may be verified by reference to Scripture.

The earliest invasion of the land, which resulted in a carrying captive of Israelites, was that recorded in 2 Kings xv. 19, in the reign of Menahem, king of Israel. "PUL, the king of Assyria came against the land, and Menahem gave him a thousand talents of silver." And in 1 Chron. v. 26 we read that this Pul, and also Tiglath-pileser, carried away the Reubenites and the Gadites, and the half tribe of Manasseh, and brought them "unto Halah and Habor, and to the river Gozan," *i.e.*, into Assyria.

Subsequently Ahaz king of Judah, when alarmed by the combined attack of Pekah king of Israel and Resin king of Syria, sent to Tiglath-pileser to come to his aid, instead of trusting in God as Isaiah counselled him, and being quiet. It was like the sheep calling the wolf to his aid! He invited an enemy who soon overran the land. After taking Damascus from the king of Syria, Tiglath-pileser took a number of places in the land of Naphtali, and "*carried their inhabitants captive to Assyria*" (2 Kings xv. 29).

His successor, Shalmanezer, invaded in force the kingdom of the ten tribes, and after a three years' siege took Samaria, the capital, and *carried all Israel away into Assyria* (2 Kings xvii. 3-6).

Sennacherib afterwards invaded Judah, and ravaged the country for four or five years, taking every place of any strength, and at last besieging Jerusalem. Brought to the very verge of ruin, the city was at that time saved by a stupendous miracle, in answer to the prayer of the good king Hezekiah, himself similarly saved from the jaws of death not long after. The day of *Jerusalem's* fall had not yet fully come (2 Kings xviii., xix.).

> For the Angel of Death spread his wings on the blast,
> And breathed in the face of the foe as he passed ;
> And the eyes of the sleepers waxed deadly and chill,
> And their hearts but once heaved, and for ever were still.
>
> And the widows of Asshur are loud in their wail ;
> And the idols are broke in the temple of Baal ?
> And the might of the Gentile, unsmote by the sword,
> Hath melted like snow in the glance of the Lord !

The impious and profane Sennacherib was murdered by his sons as he was worshipping in the house of Nisroch his god, and Esarhaddon his son reigned in his stead. This king carried captive another detachment of Israelites, thus finally destroying the national existence of the ten tribes, just sixty-five years after Isaiah's prediction to Ahaz, that before that interval had elapsed, "Ephraim should be broken and be no more a people." He also carried captive Manasseh king of Judah, who was however subsequently restored.

And then lastly, in the days of Jehoiakim, Nebuchadnezzar, king of Babylon, came against Judah, and made that king his tributary vassal, while his son afterwards became his captive. The story is given in full in 2 Kings xxiv. We read that,—

"Jehoiachin went out to the king of Babylon, he, and his mother, and his servants, and his princes, and his officers : and the king of Babylon took him in the eighth year of his reign. And he carried away all Jerusalem, and all the princes, and all the mighty men of valour, even ten thousand captives, and all the craftsmen and smiths : those carried he into captivity from Jerusalem to Babylon, none remained save the poorest sort of the people of the land."

Nebuchadnezzar left the uncle of Jehoiachin—Zedekiah—behind as his viceroy in Jerusalem; but this deputy proving faithless and rebelling, he returned, besieged and took the city, and carried Zedekiah, with his eyes put out, captive to Babylon. Nebuchadnezzar's captain, Nebuzaradan, finished the work of destruction, burned the Temple, and broke down the walls of Jerusalem, carrying captive the rest of the people. This was the final act in the long drama, and it is said of it, "so Judah was carried away out of their land" (2 Kings xxv. 21).

Now, as given in Scripture and verified by the most careful chronological investigations, the leading stages of this decline and fall of the Jewish monarchy were as follows :—

		B.C.
1.	The invasion of Pul, following Menahem's accession in	770
2.	The siege and fall of Samaria . . .	723
3.	The captivity of Manasseh and deportation by Esarhaddon	676
4.	Final fall of the throne of Judah . .	602–598

The invasion of Pul is probably to be assigned to the first half of Menahem's reign, the duration of which was ten years.

We have therefore first, in general, *the era* from B.C. 770 to B.C. 598, a period of one hundred and seventy-two years, as a "time of the end," a period conspicuously including all the main stages of the decline and fall of the Jewish monarchy, as well as those of the rise of Babylonian power. Wars and reverses had before been experienced by the Jewish nation; but it had never previously been subdued and carried captive as it was during this period. And the fall was final. A restoration was indeed enjoyed by two of the twelve tribes, but it was only partial and temporary; the temple was rebuilt, but not in its former glory; the city was restored, but never to *independent* sovereignty; and after "seventy weeks" of such restoration, a worse flood of desolation than ever, overtook both city, temple, and people, from which they have never yet rallied. The 168–172 years ending with Nebuchadnezzar's capture of Jerusalem,

was emphatically the era of departing glory, the time when
LO AMMI was inscribed on the brow of the daughter of Zion.
And *in this critical era* four epochs of *special crisis* stand prominently out, as we have seen, connected with the four conquerors, Pul, Shalmanezer, Esarhaddon, and Nebuchadnezzar,
the years B.C. 770-766, B.C. 723, B.C. 676, and B.C. 602-598.
The first three have relation mainly to the kingdom of
Ephraim or the ten tribes, the last to the kingdom of Judah
or the two tribes.

Now, if "seven times" be the appointed duration of the
"Times of the Gentiles" we may expect to find, after an
interval of 2520 years from this *Jewish captivity era* a corresponding "time of the end," a period of similar decline and fall,
overthrow and decadence, of the last form or forms of *Gentile
ruling power*, ushering in the close of the dispensation, the
restoration of Israel, and the kingdom of Messiah the Son of
David.

And this latter decline and fall, like the former, will take
place, in all probability, *under judgment from God*, on account
of long-continued and terrible sin. Just as the patriarchal
"seven times" died out amid the plagues of Egypt, and with
the overthrow of the Red sea; and as the Jewish "seven
times" expired amid the blood and the flames of Titus' siege
and sack of Jerusalem; so the Gentile "seven times" is
destined as the Apocalypse reveals, to come to an end under
the outpouring of the "seven golden vials full of the wrath
of God," against the sins of apostate Christendom.

A very simple arithmetical calculation shows that 2520
years from this Captivity era brings us to the epoch A.D.
1751-5—A.D. 1919-1923,* and we inquire, Has this period
of 168-172 years, as far as it has elapsed, had any such character? And further, Have there occurred in its course any
years marked by such events as to be unmistakable *crises* in the
process of decay and destruction? And if so, do such years

---

* One year has to be subtracted in adding A.D. to B.C. periods.

correspond as closing termini with the critical years of the Captivity Jewish period at an interval of 2520 years or "seven times"?

The answer to these questions is full of solemn interest and importance, nor is it hard to find. In seeking it we have *not* to take into account all the empires and kingdoms of the world. The range is limited by the prophecy itself.

Gentile supremacy over Israel has been confined to one line. The Chinese and the Americans never conquered Judea, nor held Jerusalem. They never defiled the sanctuary and persecuted the Israel of God, either literal or spiritual. The line of Gentile powers who *have* done both, is distinctly defined in the two fourfold visions in Daniel, the image, and the four beasts, in which were symbolised the succession of the Babylonian, the Medo-Persian, the Grecian, and the Roman Empires. The three former having passed entirely away, *our search is confined to the limits of the fourth of these.*

That fourth, or Roman monarchy, was foretold as existing in two states—an earlier undivided, and a later divided one. The former of these has passed away, equally with the Babylonian, Persian, and Grecian empires. *Our search is therefore confined to the time and sphere, occupied by the kingdoms which rose out of the ruins of the old Pagan Roman Empire.* Two politico-religious powers or dynasties, symbolised as "little horns," are represented as rising up and wielding supremacy among these kingdoms; these little horns,—the Papal and Mohammedan powers,—constitute therefore the last leading phase of Gentile power contemplated in the prophecy; both oppose God and his saints, defile his sanctuary, and tread down the holy city, spiritual or literal.

The question before us is therefore reduced to narrow limits. *Only in the history of these two powers need we look for the answer;* and in judging of the character and relative importance of events in their history, we must compare them, not with events in the history of other powers, or other parts of the world, but only with *other events in the history of these powers.*

Unless this is borne in mind, it is impossible rightly to estimate the historical incidents, which must past under review in connection with this question. Again we ask then, Has the 168 years between A.D. 1755 and A.D. 1923, or rather that portion of it which has elapsed, been, in any remarkable and undeniable sense, *a period of decadence and overthrow to the once mighty Papal and Mohammedan powers?*

Historians would with one voice reply, Beyond all question, it has! But as all are not familiar with the facts of modern history, and as many who are, have never considered them in this connection, it is needful to recall some leading events in the recent history of Popery and Mohammedanism.

France—ever since the conversion of Clovis, and the donations of Pepin and Charlemagne, had taken rank as *the first of Papal nations,* and her king as Eldest Son of the Church. France —long foremost in her persecutions of heretics,—had taken a leading place in her opposition to the glorious Reformation; by the iron heel of power, she had crushed down the new life and had extinguished the rekindled Gospel light of that glad era. In the massacre of St. Bartholomew she had all but extirpated Protestantism; and by the revocation of the Edict of Nantes, she had banished from her shores her surviving Huguenot subjects. Papist to the core, France was for more than a thousand years, *a main pillar of the Popedom in Europe.*

The middle of the eighteenth century saw the beginning of a marvellous change in France. In less than half a century from 1750, this first of Papal nations had become madly and violently *anti-papal;* and this most servilely superstitious people, had become openly and even fiercely infidel.*

---

* Voltaire's influence was at its height about the middle of the eighteenth century, *i.e.*, just at the beginning of the period in question.

Speaking of Voltaire, Vinet says. "À partir de *l'an* A.D. 1750, il fut encore le plus populaire et le plus puissant des écrivains. . . . La seconde partie du dix-huitième siècle leur dut un caractère, ou Voltaire ne reconnut pas toujours celui de ses opinions personnelles, ui l'impulsion de son esprit. . . . Lorsque nous comparons la première moitié du siècle que nous occupe, avec l'époque de Louis XIV, il nous semble déjà

The great apostle and arch-priest of French infidelity, VOL-
TAIRE, was in the height of his influence at this period. With
the aid of his associate Deistic and Atheistic philosophers,
he was deluging France with clever, anti-monarchical, anti-
ecclesiastical writings, of the most audacious and blasphemous
character. These men enlisted talent and science for the
attack, employed the keen shafts of ridicule, and appealed to
all the evil democratic and licentious passions. They held up
to hatred and contempt, the apostate and corrupt form of
religion with which alone the French were familiar, and with
fanatical zeal sought to overthrow all its power over the
popular mind. Unjustly, but naturally, they visited on Christianity all the falsehoods, absurdities, hypocrisies, immoralities,
cruelties, and manifold wickednesses of Popery. " Ecrasez
l'infame ! " (crush the wretch !) was their modern version of
" Crucify Him ! " and their avowed object was to bring about
the utter rejection of revealed religion.

They succeeded only too well ! France ceased to be
Catholic, and became—*infidel ;* and infidel France, having
thrown off all restraints of law and order, natural and Divine,
plunged, before the end of the century, into the maddest
excesses of revolution and crime.

In 1793 came to its crisis that tremendous, unparalleled,
irresistible movement, which put an end at once to absolute
monarchy, aristocracy, and to ecclesiastical power in France,
and which communicated to the neighbouring nations of

---

qu'on se trouve un plein dix-huitième siècle. Mais quand on passe à la
seconde moitié de cette grande période, on sent que la première n'était
que le prologue, l'exposition du drame. L'explosion n'a pas encore eu
lieu."—Vinet, "La Littérature Française au XVIII° Siècle," p. 63.

"Voltaire—c'est pour le coup le dix-huitième siècle personifié ; sa vie
même est partagée comme cette grande période."

"*L'an* 1750, ou plutôt 1746, *marque le point essentiel* dans la carrière
et dans la direction du siècle " (p. 64).

" *De l'an* 1750 *à l'an* 1780, époque où la publication complète de l'ou-
vrage de Raynal, est comme le dernier éclat d'une incendie, à qui rien ne
reste à dévorer " (p. 74).

The middle of the 18th century is thus regarded by historians as the era
of the rise of the French Revolution.

Europe the shocks of revolution, and the fierce fires of democracy, together with an anti-ecclesiastical mania that has never
since been allayed.

The French Revolution is by common consent regarded as
the commencement of a new era, for the nations of Europe;
but it is not always remembered that the proximate cause of
the French Revolution, *the infidelity of the nation*, dates from a
generation earlier. That Revolution could never have assumed
the character it did, had not the French people previously lost
all fear of God, and all respect for man ; had not the national
mind been blinded, and the national heart hardened, against
all claims human and Divine, by the pernicious teachings of
the infidel philosophers.

It is needless to give details of that Revolution here, our
readers will mostly be familiar with the tragic facts. How the
infidel democracy suddenly uprose in its might, destroyed the
Bastile, issued its declaration of the rights of man ; assaulted
the king and queen by night, at Versailles, and murdering
some of their body guard, forced them to proceed as prisoners
to Paris, the bloody heads carried on pikes before the royal
carriage. How the people confiscated all the vast revenues of
the Church, all the domains of the Crown, and all the estates of
refugee nobles, for the use of the State ; subjected to themselves
all ecclesiastical, civil, and judicial power throughout the
country ; murdered the royal guard, and some five thousand
leading Royalists; dethroned, imprisoned, tried, condemned,
and murdered the king, and then the queen ; declared war
against all kings, and sympathy with all revolutionists everywhere ; how the " reign of terror " witnessed the slaughter of
one million and twenty-two thousand persons, of all ranks and
ages, and of both sexes, till the streets of Paris ran with blood,
and the guillotines could not overtake their work. How
thousands were mowed down by grape-shot fusilades ; drowned
in " noyades," where, in loaded vessels, hundreds of victims
were purposely sunk in the rivers ; roasted alive in heated
ovens, or tortured to death by other infernal cruelties. How

Christianity was publicly renounced, and a prostitute en-throned as "goddess of reason" at Notre Dame, and wor-shipped by the National Convention and by the mob of Paris, with the wildest orgies of licentiousness (morality as well as mercy having perished with religion); how the most horrid mockery of the solemn rites of Christianity, was publicly enacted, an ass being made to drink the sacramental wine; how the Sabbath itself was abolished, and the decade substi-tuted for the week; and how hundreds and thousands of priests were massacred or driven into exile, and the churches and cathedrals turned into stables and barracks. Taken as a whole, the French Revolution was a convulsion, in which the angry passions of men, set free from all restraint, manifested themselves, with a force and fury unprecedented in the history of the world, against monarchical, aristocratic, ecclesiastical, and religious institutions.

Let these things be considered in the light of a mighty and successful revolt against, and overthrow of, absolute monarchical power, and Papal tyranny and usurpation, and it will at once be granted that *nothing similar had ever occurred previously*, in the history of the fourth great Empire.

Terribly iniquitous had been the career of the monarchical power thus rudely overthrown; and fearfully corrupt the priesthood and religion thus utterly and with abhorrence rejected. A solemn character of *retribution* attaches to even the worst excesses of the French Revolution. The Papacy, in the hour of its agony, was exultingly reminded of its own similar cruelties against Protestants; Papists were treated ac-cording to the example set by Papists of other days, and the worst barbarities of Revolutionary France could not out-Herod the previous barbarities of Papal France.

"The more deeply and earnestly the French Revolution is considered, the more manifest is its pre-eminence above all the strange and terrible things which have come to pass on this earth. . . . Never has the world witnessed so exact and sublime a piece of retribution. . . If it inflicted enormous evil, it pre-supposed and overthrew enormous evil. . . . In a country where every ancient institution and every time-honoured custom, disappeared in a moment, where the whole social and political system went down before the first stroke, where monarchy, nobility, and Church, were swept away almost without resistance, the whole framework of the State must have been rotten ; royalty, aristocracy, and priesthood must have grievously sinned. Where the good things of this world, birth, rank, wealth, fine clothes, and elegant manners, become worldly perils and worldly dis-advantages for a time, rank, birth, and riches must have been frightfully abused. The nation which abolished and proscribed Christianity, which dethroned religion in favour of reason, and enthroned the new goddess at Notre Dame in the person of a harlot, must needs have been afflicted by a very unreasonable and very corrupt form of Christianity. The people that waged a war of such utter extermination with everything established, as to abolish the common forms of address and salutation, and the common mode of reckoning time, that abhorred 'you' as a sin, and shrank from 'Monsieur' as an abomination, that turned the weeks into decades and would know the old months no more, must surely have had good reason to hate those old ways from which it pushed its departure into such minute and absurd extravagance. The demolished halls of the aristocracy, the rifled sepulchres of royalty, the decapitated King and Queen, the little Dauphin so sadly done to death, the beggared princes, the slaughtered priests and nobles, the sovereign guillotine, the republican marriages and the Meudon tannery, the couples tied together and thrown into the Loire, and the gloves made of men's and women's skins ; these things are most horrible ; but they are withal eloquent of retribution, they bespeak the solemn presence of Nemesis, the awful hand of an avenging power ; they bring to mind the horrible sins of that old France, the wretched peasants ground for ages beneath a weight of imposts, from which the rich and noble were free ; visited ever and anon with cruel famines by reason of crushing taxes, unjust wars, and monstrous misgovernment, and then hung up, or shot down, by twenties and fifties, for just complaining of starvation, and all this for centuries ! They call to remembrance the Protestants murdered by myriads in the streets of Paris, tormented for years by military dragoons in Poitou and Béarn, and hunted like wild beasts in the Cevennes ; slaughtered and done to death by thousands and tens of thousands in many painful ways and through many painful years.

" In no work of the French Revolution is this, its retributive character, more strikingly and solemnly apparent than in its dealings with the Roman Church and Papal power. It especially became France, which, after so fierce a struggle, had rejected the Reformation, and perpetrated such enormous crimes in the process of rejection, to turn its fury against that very Roman Church on whose behalf it had been so wrathful, ... to abolish Roman Catholic worship as she had abolished the Protestant wor-ship ; to massacre multitudes of priests in the streets of her great towns ;

to hunt them down through her length and breadth, and to cast them by thousands upon a foreign shore, just as she had slaughtered, hunted down, and driven into exile, hundreds of thousands of Protestants ; . . . . to carry the war into the Papal territories, and heap all sorts of woes and shames upon the defenceless Popedom. . . . The excesses of revolutionary France were not more the punishment than the direct result of the excesses of feudal, regal, and papal France. . . . In one of its aspects the Revolution may be described as a reaction against the excesses, spiritual and religious, of the Roman Catholic reaction from Protestantism. No sooner had the torrent burst forth than it dashed right against the Roman Church and Popedom. . . . The property of the Church was made over to the State ; the French clergy sank from a proprietary to a salaried body ; monks and nuns were restored to the world, the property of their orders being likewise gone ; Protestants were raised to full religious freedom and political equality ; . . . the Roman Catholic religion was soon afterwards formally abolished. . . . Bonaparte unsheathed the sword of France against the helpless Pius VI. . . . The Pontiff sank into a dependant. Berthier marched upon Rome, set up a Roman republic, and laid hands upon the Pope. The sovereign Pontiff was borne away to the camp of the infidels   from prison to prison, and finally *carried captive into France.* Here . . . . he breathed his last, at Valence, in the land where his priests had been slain, where his power was broken, and his name and office were a mockery and byword, and in the keeping of the rude soldiers of the unbelieving Commonwealth which had for ten years held to his lips a cup of such manifold and exceeding bitterness. . . . It was a sublime and perfect piece of retribution, which so amazed the world at the end of the 18th century ; this proscription of the Roman Church by that very French nation that had slaughtered myriads of Protestants at her bidding ; this mournful end of the Sovereign Pontiff, in that very Dauphiné, so consecrated by the struggles and sufferings of the Protestants, and near those Alpine valleys where the Waldenses had been so ruthlessly hunted down by French soldiers ; this transformation of the 'States of the Church' into the 'Roman Republic,' and this overthrow of the territorial Popedom by that very French nation, which just one thousand years ago, had, under Pepin and Charlemagne, conferred these territories. Multitudes imagined that the Papacy was at the point of death, and asked, Would Pius the Sixth be the last Pontiff? and if the close of the 18th century would be signalized by the fall of the Papal dynasty. But *the French Revolution was the beginning, and not the end of the judgment;* France had but *begun* to execute the doom, a doom sure and inevitable, but long and lingering; to be diversified by many strange incidents, and now and then by a semblance of escape, a doom to be protracted through much pain and much ignominy." * . .

---

* "The Papal Drama," Book x. By Thomas H. Gill.

The career of Napoleon,—the second phase of the French Revolution,—was a further, and even more illustrious, stage in the fall of the Papacy. He made open war against Pius VI., and compelled him to sign that most humiliating treaty of Tolentino, by which Ferrara, Bologna, and Romagna ("Peter's patrimony") were ceded to France, with an indemnity of a million and a half pounds, and a hundred of the finest pictures and statues in the Vatican. Berthier, a general of the French Republic, soon after took Pius VI. prisoner; the tricolor flag was displayed from the Capitol, and the Pope's temporal power declared to be at an end. He was carried captive to France, where, in 1799, he died in exile.

When Napoleon, for political reasons, restored the Roman Catholic religion in France, it was only to inflict on it, what its own dignitaries deem, additional insult and injury. It was put on a level with all other sects of religion, and merely tolerated.

No trace of an admission of Papal supremacy, or even of Papal influence, is to be found in the concordat between Napoleon and the Pope for France, in 1801, or in that for Italy, in 1803. At his coronation, in 1804, Napoleon required the Pope's attendance, and made Pius VII. cross the Alps in mid-winter, not to confer a crown, but merely to adorn a ceremony. Napoleon placed the crown on his own head himself; and the Pope stood by, "an important and imposing, but purposely slighted witness of the coronation." Napoleon did not at that time wish to annihilate the Popedom, as the revolutionary Directory had done, but to retain the Sovereign Pontiff as his vassal. But when, a few years later, the Pope resisted his will, he soon showed him who was master. In 1809, in the plenitude of his power, when he was supreme in Europe, he issued from the palace of the Schönbrunn in Vienna, a decree dividing and distributing the dominions yet remaining to the Pope in Italy, and constituting Rome itself the second city in the French Empire. At the same time he reduced the "Holy Father" to the rank of a French subject, and even in his sacerdotal character, a mere salaried official of the French Court, his income being fixed at £80,000 a year.

The bull of excommunication which the Pope fulminated against Napoleon in return, only made him ridiculous in the eyes of Europe ; like his predecessor, he was carried captive by the French army, first to Savona, then to Fontainebleau, where he was forced to sign another concordat, renouncing all claim to Rome for ever.

On the overthrow of Napoleon, the Pope was restored to Rome ; " but he sat not on his throne as once before ; his power was crippled, his seat unstable, the riches of his Church were rifled, and a mighty precedent and principle of action had been established against him, which could scarcely fail of bearing similarly bitter fruit afterwards." (Elliott, " Horæ," iii. p. 375.)

The restoration of Papal supremacy in France did not last long. The year 1830 brought about another thoroughly anti-sacerdotal revolution. Charles X., who had acceded to the throne in 1824, had to abdicate, and his ministry had to flee for their lives ; while the Duke of Orleans was proclaimed king under the title of Louis Philippe.

In 1848 another revolution again constituted France a republic ; tumults broke out in Paris in February, the Tuileries were ransacked, and frightful disorders committed. Louis Philippe was obliged to abdicate and take refuge in England ; and " the second republic " was proclaimed. A fortnight after the fall of Louis Philippe, the constitution was proclaimed in Rome, and the city and country were thrown into a state of revolution.

Before the end of the year Cardinal Rossi, the Pope's prime minister, was killed, and the Pope had to flee from Rome. He was deposed from his temporal authority, and an Italian re-public was proclaimed. It was only by the power of the French that the Pope was afterwards for a time restored, when Louis Napoleon had become President of the French Republic. With occasional parses, and with gleams of passing prosperity now and then, the course of the Papacy has ever since been one of downfall and decay. It is not needful here to recall the details of the consuming process that has during the last forty or fifty years been going on; but recent events must receive a brief notice. In 1866 the Romish Empire of Austria was worsted by Protestant Prussia at the memorable battle of Sadowa, a battle the results of which were as decisive as those of Waterloo. Austria received a shock from which it has never recovered, and was obliged to cede Venetia, which was annexed to the kingdom of Italy, while Prussia was raised to the rank of one of the great powers of Europe. In 1868, the Spanish Revolution took place, Queen Isabella fled, and Spain was plunged into years of cruel strife, in the course of which the Jesuits were banished, their monasteries and churches confiscated and sold or pulled down, and the bones of the martyrs brought to light at the Quemadero.

The same year Pius IX. sent out his famous encyclical letter *summoning* the Œcumenical Council for 1870. Six archbishop princes, 49 cardinals, 11 patriarchs, 680 archbishops and bishops, 28 abbots, 29 generals of orders, 803 spiritual rulers, representing the Church of Rome throughout the world, solemnly decreed the dogma that the occupant of the Papal Chair, is, in all his decisions regarding faith and morals, infallible! It is said that arrangements had been made to reflect a glory around the person of the Pope by means of mirrors at noon, when the decree was made (18 July, 1870). But the sun shone not that day. A violent storm broke over Rome, the sky was darkened by tempest, and the voices of the Council were lost in the rolling of thunder.

On the very day following this culmination of Papal arrogance and self-exaltation, was declared that terrible Franco-German war, in which the French Empire of Louis Napoleon,—by the soldiers of which the Pope was maintained on his tottering throne,—*fell. The temporal sovereignty of the Papacy fell with it.* No sooner had the French troops been withdrawn from Rome, and the French Empire collapsed, than the Italian

Government announced its intention of entering the Roman States, and did so. On the 20th of September, 1870, Rome was declared the capital of the kingdom of Italy, and became the residence and the seat of the government of Victor Emmanuel. The *Times'* summary for that year says, "The most remarkable circumstance in the annexation of Rome and its territory to the kingdom of Italy, is the languid indifference with which the transfer has been regarded by Catholic Christendom. A change which would once have *convulsed the world* has failed to distract attention from the more absorbing spectacle of the Franco-German war. *Within the same year, the Papacy has assumed the highest spiritual exaltation to which it could aspire, and lost the temporal sovereignty which it had held for a thousand years.*"

Taking these and similar facts into consideration, there can be no question that the years which have elapsed since 1755, have been years of conspicuous, unprecedented, fatal calamity to the papal power.

It has been the period of the outpouring of the vials of the wrath of God, to use the striking symbol of the Apocalypse, for the closing judgments of the dispensation. Those *vial-plagues* (Rev. xvi.), comprising "a noisome and grievous sore" or boil, darkness, frogs, and blood-changed rivers, cannot fail to recall the similar plagues sent upon Egypt prior to the Exodus and to the destruction of Pharaoh. Then they were literal, in harmony with a typical dispensation ; now they are the antitypical realities, of which boils, darkness, etc., are the symbols. But so appropriate and graphic are the symbols, so suggestive of the things, that under their guidance alone, we might have been led to discover the events we have been considering. The infidelity of the middle of the 18th century, and its fearful fruit in the enormities of the French Revolution, have long been recognised as the judgment symbolised by the eruption of the "noisome and grievous sore on the men that had the mark of the beast, and worshipped his image," that is on the inhabitants of papal Christendom. Such an outbreak in the natural body is a mark of deep-seated impurity and disease in the constitution. In the body politic the eruption of violent moral and social evil is the same, an indication of long-continued and all-pervading irreligion and corruption.

The second, third, fourth, and fifth vials predict, under various symbols, the judgments connected with the Napoleonic and anti-Papal wars which followed the French Revolution ; the outpouring of the sixth, brings us to the other event we are seeking, *the decline and fall of the Mohammedan power.*

The years which have elapsed since the middle of the 18th century have been almost as fatal to the Eastern, as to the Western little horn. We have not yet seen the *complete* extinction of the political power of the Sultan, as we have that of the Pope ; but it is already *almost* annihilated in Europe ; crippled and restricted where it still exists ; and events, as well as Scripture prophecy indicate, that its hold over Syria cannot last much longer.

The rise and fall of the Ottoman Empire are symbolised in the Apocalypse, by the overflow and drying up of the great river Euphrates. In other parts of Scripture the overflow of a river is, from its peculiar appropriateness, used as a symbol for the invasion of a land by a foreign conqueror. (See Jer. xlvi. 7 ; Isa. viii. 7, 8.) A modern " History of the Ottoman Turks"* opens with the following sentence. " Six centuries ago a pastoral band of four hundred Turkish families was journeying westward, *from the upper streams of the river Euphrates :* their armed force consisted of four hundred and forty-four horsemen, and their leader's name was Ertoghrul " This little band of Euphratean horsemen, were the ancestors of that terrible host or " army of horsemen two hundred thousand thousand" strong, whom the Seer of Patmos beheld, loosed *from the Euphrates,* and overflowing the Roman earth, carrying distress and death wherever they went—the " second woe " sent by God as a judgment on Christendom for its depravity and apostasy, the first having been the Saracenic.

---

* By Sir Edward S. Creasy, M.A. London : Bentley, 1877.

History tells us how this Euphratean flood covered land after land, with its irresistible advance. All over South-Eastern Europe, as far as Venice, the Turkish flood extended. Wherever it reached it carried misery and death, so that even the strong language of Rev. ix. 17 can barely convey an idea of the "woe" it was to Eastern Christendom.

The "drying up" of this flood, that is to say the liberation from Turkish oppressions, of the Christian nations and lands overwhelmed by it, began with the Greek rebellion in 1820. But fatal blows to the power and prestige of the Ottoman Empire, had previously been dealt by Russia. In the war of 1768 between the two kingdoms, the Turkish armies were beaten and destroyed, and ruin and disgrace attended each succeeding campaign. In 1770 the Russian admiral annihilated the Turkish fleet in the Ægean sea. In 1774 a large Turkish army was again most disgracefully beaten, and the humiliating peace of Kainargé, showed that the conqueror was in a position to dictate terms. Three years later, war again broke out between the two powers, and again the Russians had the mastery both by sea and by land, and obtained the cession of important towns and districts before concluding peace. In 1806 Russia occupied Moldavia and Wallachia, and the old hostility broke out afresh, the weakness of the Ottoman Empire becoming more apparent than ever. A new fleet, which had been created, was destroyed by the Russians at Lemnos. Mahmoud II. had to buy a peace, by the cession of all his territory north of the Pruth, of a number of fortresses on the Danube, and of a principal mouth of the Danube itself. In 1820 began a formidable insurrection in Greece, the finest province of the Turkish Empire, which quickly spread to Wallachia, Moldavia, and the Ægean Isles.

In 1826 the Porte surrendered to the Russians all the fortresses it retained in Asia ; in the same year civil commotions distracted Constantinople ; and the awful slaughter of the Janissaries took place, 4000 soldiers being shot or burned to death in their own barracks in the city, and many thousands more all over the empire, by the Sultan's own command.

The Greek rebellion continued till 1827, when, after a severe and prolonged struggle, Turkey was obliged to acknowledge the independence of Greece. The sympathies of Western Christendom had been aroused by the horrible cruelties perpetrated by the Turkish Admiral, in the conquest of Scio ; and England, France, and Russia intervened between the Porte and its Greek Christian subjects. At the great naval battle of Navarino, the fleet of Turkey was once more destroyed, and Greece became independent.

In 1829 the freedom of Servia was similarly secured by a treaty which forbade a single Turk to reside north of the Danube; and the same year the Turkish province of Algeria in Africa became a French colony.

Mehemet Ali, the powerful Pacha of Egypt, who had long been aiming at an hereditary kingdom for himself, rebelled against his master, and asserted his independence in 1832. He attacked and conquered Syria, and defeated the Turkish armies in three great battles. Nothing but the interference of the great powers of Christendom, at that time prevented his marching on Constantinople, and overthrowing the Sultan altogether. He was forced back into his own province, and made again nominally dependent on the Sultan by payment of an annual tribute, and the furnishing certain military aid when asked. But Egypt is virtually independent of the Porte, and her present ruler has assumed the title of Khedive, or king, in recognition of the fact.

In 1844 the Porte was compelled, under threat of European interference, to issue an edict of religious toleration, abolishing for ever its characteristic and sanguinary practice of execution for apostasy (*i.e.,* for the adoption of Christianity). This compulsory sheathing of its persecuting sword was a patent proof that its independence was gone, and a marked era in its overthrow.

Nor has it been under the judgment of the sword alone, that the Ottoman Empire has been sinking to decay. It is miserably perishing in its own corruption. Internal discord and insurrection, provoked by cruel tyranny and monstrous mis-government, have weakened the State. Polygamy and other vices have caused a depopulation so rapid as to be almost incredible. Pestilence, conflagration, earthquakes, civil commotions, massacres, slaughters, all have tended to reduce the population and weaken the empire. These attacks from without, rebellions from within, and this steady process of internal decay, have reduced Turkey, not only to financial bankruptcy, but to such a state of weakness, that, but for the policy of England and other European States, she must long since have perished. The notion that " the integrity of the Ottoman Empire" must be maintained in order to resist the encroachments of Russia, has for the last fifty years averted from this decaying power, long impending and richly deserved doom. But even this can avert it no longer. The atrocious cruelties and fiendish barbarities of the Turk, have alienated from him the sympathies and even the compassions of Christendom ; and in the recent war no hand has been upraised to avert the fate impending over the blood-guilty Ottoman Empire. Russia has this time all but accomplished the task, on which she has so long had her heart set—the liberation from Moslem tyranny of the Christians of South-Eastern Europe. If foreign interference *should* again avert the end (as it did in the case of the temporal power of the Pope), it can only be for a time. Forces are at work which must ere long destroy the foul tyranny which has so long ruined the fairest regions of the earth ; and must set, not Europe only, but Palestine, free from the Moslem rule.

The period that has elapsed since the middle of the 18th century, corresponding to the Jewish Captivity period, and closing the 2520 years, or " seven times " of Gentile supremacy, *has then been most conspicuously marked by the decline and fall of the two little horns, the final forms of Gentile rule over the Israel, and Sanctuary of God, spiritual and literal.*

And the years of special *crisis* in the former have been, as far as we have gone, answered by corresponding years of crisis in the latter, as will be seen by the following table. We have not yet reached the latest *terminus ad quem;* it is not yet 2520 years since the *final* fall of the throne of David, and the *full* establishment of Gentile supremacy by Nebuchad-nezzar's overthrow of Jehoiakin ; nor have the events pre-dicted as to *close* this time of the end all taken place as yet.

We do not wish to speculate as to the future ; of that, as the great Sir Isaac Newton said, " let time be the interpreter." We simply point to facts in the past. No one can question that the sudden and terrible outbreak of infidelity and atheism in the middle of the last century, marked by the publications of Rousseau and the Encyclopedists—the accession of the ill-fated king and queen who fell victims to the fury of the French revolution ; the culmination of that awful movement itself in the reign of terror, followed by the overthrow of the Papal power in Italy ; and, turning to the East, the compulsory signature by the Sultan of the first edict of religious toleration—no one can question we say, that these have been *marked and critical events,* in the downfall of the Papal and Mohammedan powers. Other indications will shortly lead us to other dates also ; but we are already in a position to see that between the critical years of the Captivity era, and the critical years of this time of the end, there lie exactly " seven times,"—2520 years.

For one such great " week," traced backwards from the middle of last century, takes us to the reign of Menahem, king of Israel and the invasion of Pul ; the same period traced back from the accession of Louis XVI. reaches exactly to the accession of Nabonassar, the first king of Babylon ; the same period traced back from the overthrow of the Papal power in the French revolution, leads up to the overthrow of Samaria by Shalmane-zer ; and the same period traced back from the Turkish edict of toleration reaches to the completion of the captivity of the ten tribes by Esarhaddon. A simple calculation will prove this, remembering that in adding A.D. to B.C. dates, one year has to be subtracted to obtain the *complete* interval elapsed.

TERMINI A QUO AND AD QUEM OF THE SEVEN TIMES.

I. From the first Assyrian invasion of Palestine (that by Pul, king of Assyria), and the carrying captive a portion of the Ten Tribes, to the outbreak of the grievous sore of infidelity, in the middle of the 18th century.*

B.C. 770_____2520 years._____A.D. 1750-1.

II. From the siege and fall of Samaria and more complete captivity of the Ten Tribes by Shalmanezer, to the judgments on the Papal Power in the French Revolution—

B.C. 723_____2520 years._____A.D. 1798.

III. From the captivity of Manasseh and coincident completion of the deportation of the remainder of the Ten Tribes by Esarhaddon, *to the first edict of religious toleration in the East,* issued by the Porte, the compulsory sheathing of its persecuting sword, a sign that its *independence* was gone—

B.C. 676-7_____2520 years._____A.D. 1844.

IV. From the full captivity of Judah, and final overthrow of the throne of David, accomplished by Nebuchadnezzar, to the still future *terminus ad quem* of the prophetic period of 2520 years.

B.C. 598_____2520 years._____A.D. 1923.

Historically, then, the Times of the Gentiles is a great dispensational week, of 2520 years, extending from the Captivity era, B.C. 770–598, to the era of the closing judgments on the kingdom of the beast, the vial era of the Apocalypse, A.D. 1750–1923. It is the "seven times" of Gentile dominion over Israel, included in the symbol of Nebuchadnezzar's image.

This great *week* has thus earlier and later commencements, incipient and then full starting points, and corresponding closes, just as in an eclipse, the penumbra first comes in contact, and after a brief interval the dark shadow. This is clearly the case with other chronological prophecies also. Jeremiah announced,

---

* Measured from the accession of Menahem, as the date of this invasion in his brief reign, is not given.

for example, that Judah should serve the king of Babylon "seventy years" (Jer. xxv. 11, 12). History shows that this period had a double commencement and a double termination,—*a twofold fulfilment.* First, from B.C. 606 to the decree of Cyrus, and again from B.C. 587 to the edict of Darius. This is easily explicable. The majestic movements of Providence and of history demand time ; empires do not rise and fall in a day ; and the omniscient God takes note of the comparatively insignificant *beginning* of a mighty movement as well as of its climax. We are witnesses that the decay of the Papal and Mohammedan powers demands *an era*, not an epoch merely ; and such has been the case with the decay of other great powers in other ages. Hence the propriety of indicating *various dates of rise and fall.* But it should be noted that the interval by which the earliest of these commencing and closing dates is separated from the latest is, *compared to the whole period*, so small as to be scarcely perceptible, so that it is even difficult to represent it to scale, on a diagram. Thus the statement that at the equinox the day is twelve hours long, is practically true of a day or two *before*, and of a day or two *after* the equinox, because the *variation is, compared to the length of the day*, hardly observable.

But while the measures of this great dispensational week are sufficiently clear, when we consider its main termini, they become increasingly so when we proceed to study its bisections and divisions. The measures of the whole week are evident ; but those of the half week, the "time, times, and a half" of prophecy, are still more so, and these we must now examine.

The *whole* week, or "seven times," dates from the era of the rise of the *literal* Babylon, and measures the entire course of the four great monarchies ; the *half* week, or "time, times, and a half," dates from the era of the rise of the *spiritual* Babylon, and measures the existence of the great apostasies which occupy the latter half of the "Times of the Gentiles." When did these arise ?

The Papal power rose in the interval between the fall of the

Western Roman Empire, under Romulus Augustulus, the last Emperor of Rome, and the Pope-exalting decrees of the Eastern Emperors Justinian and Phocas, which put the topstone on the slowly rising arch of Papal pretension and power, by constituting the Bishops of Rome Universal Bishops, and making them heads of all Christendom. And the Mohammedan power rose in the East during the very same interval; for, as Luther used to say, "the Pope and the Turk came up together." The fall of the Western Empire took place in A.D. 476, and the Hegira era of the Mohammedans is A.D. 622.

The century and a half intervening between these dates may be called *the era of the rise of the Western and Eastern Apostasies*. It embraces nearly all the main stages of the rise of the two little horns; it is analogous in character and in duration to the Captivity era, and it is central in position in the great "seven times."

1. It is analogous in *character*, for the Captivity era was one of decay and fall to the natural Israel, and one during which the power and dominion of the natural Babylon was rising steadily to its culmination in the reign of Nebuchadnezzar. This central era of the rise of the apostasies is one of decay and fall to the spiritual Israel, the true Church of Christ, and one during which the power and dominion of the spiritual Babylon was rising steadily to its culmination in the enthronement of the Papal dynasty—the great antichrist, the antitype of Nebuchadnezzar—at Rome.

2. It is analogous also in *duration*, for from the era of Nabonassar to the overthrow of Jehoiakim is 126 solar, or 130 lunar, years, and from the fall of the Western Empire of Rome (A.D. 476) to the date of the Hegira of Mohammed A.D. 622 is exactly the same period.

3. It is central in position in the great "seven times." The intervals which separate the commencement and completion of the Captivity era from the commencement and completion of this central era are respectively 1260 lunar years; and the intervals which separate these lunar dates from the corresponding

ing dates of the " time of the end " are also respectively 1260 years.

That this central era is the bisection of " seven times " has long been perceived in a general way by students of prophecy; but it is only by the application to the period of careful astronomical measures that the wonderful accuracy and exactness with which this is the case can be demonstrated.

Three sorts of years are, it must be premised, demonstrably employed by the Author of the prophetic periods : solar, calendar, and lunar years. Calendar years, or years of 360 days, are used in the predictions of Daniel and the Apocalypse ; for it is only three and a half *such* years that contain 1260 days.

Solar and lunar years are also taken into account, as is proved by the fact that in Dan. xii.—75 years are, as we have seen, added to 2520 ; and 75 is exactly the difference between 2520 *solar* years and 2520 *lunar* years.

We have a warrant therefore for measuring historic intervals by *any or all of these three standards;* and where, for any reason, it is the Divine purpose to conceal for a time, or partially, the actual measures of any interval, we may expect to find the *lunar* year employed in measuring it, inasmuch as this year gives rise to what may be termed a hidden chronology.

Before going further, it will be well to enquire what were the *critical years* in this era of the rise of the Papal and Mohammedan powers. We are in the broad sunlight of authentic profane history here ; there may be room for some difference of judgment as to the relative importance of certain events in the history, but there can be no question at all as to the dates of the events selected.

" He that letteth," or that which hindereth the development of the great apostasy, "will let, until he be taken out of the way," said the Apostle Paul, and *then* the antichrist will be revealed (2 Thess. ii.). There could be no chance for Popes while the Cæsars still ruled at Rome. The first step in the rise of the Papacy therefore was necessarily the complete *downfall* of the *Western Empire of Rome,* which, as we have seen, took place under Romulus Augustulus, in A.D. 476. From that time forth the claims of the Bishops of Rome in. creased continually, based at first on the metropolitan cha. racter of the see of Rome, and by degrees on more super. natural and spiritual grounds. But their claims to supremacy over other bishops received no *legal sanction* until A.D. 533, when, by his celebrated decretal letters, the Eastern Roman Emperor, JUSTINIAN, *recognised* the Bishop of Rome as *"head of all the holy Churches, and all the holy priests of God."* *

In the seventy-fifth subsequent year, A.D. 607, the Emperor PHOCAS promulgated another very notable decree, *confirming* the right of the Pope to the headship of all the Churches, *Eastern as well as Western,* and acknowledging him *primate of all other sees, that of Constantinople included.* In 608 Phocas bestowed upon the Pope the Pantheon of Rome, a temple formerly dedicated to Cybele and all the gods, and thenceforth to the Virgin Mary and all the martyrs; *i.e.,* formerly devoted to Pagan, and thenceforth to Papal, *idolatry.* Phocas died in A.D. 610. In 1813 the base of a pillar was excavated in Rome, bearing an inscription intimating that it was erected in honour of Phocas, A.D. 608, on the occasion of these his great concessions to the Pope.

The accession of the assassin Phocas was "joyfully" en- dorsed by Pope Gregory the Great,† *whose own accession* in A.D. 590, constitutes a very leading date in the rise of the Papacy. Gregory the Great was " the last of the Latin Fathers, and *the first in the modern sense of the word of the Popes,"* and he "did more than any other to set the Church forward upon the new lines on which henceforth it must travel to constitute a Latin Christianity, with distinctive features of its own, such as broadly separate it from Greek."‡

---

* See Appendix A., Justinian's decree.

† Gibbon, "Decline." Ch. xlvi.

‡ Archbishop Trench, "Mediæval Church History," p. 14.

One more remarkable step in the rise of the Papacy, and the extending over Europe of its peculiar evil influence, must be noticed. It is the decree of the Pope VITALIAN, ordering all the services of the Church throughout Christendom to be read in *Latin*,—a decree, as we know, still in fatal force, and obeyed by every Roman Catholic priest in the world. This was in the year A.D. 663. It gave a distinctly Roman, or Latin, character to the Church, secured perfect unity with Rome in all its ceremonial, and was surely one way in which the beast "caused all to receive his mark and the number of his name" (ΛΑΤΕΙΝΟΣ = 666). From the time of the division of the Roman Empire, the Western half, indeed, received the designation Latin, in opposition to "Greek," which, strangely enough, was soon applied by the Eastern Roman Emperors to themselves and their empire. In the West the word Roman was also dropped; it was the *Latin* world, the *Latin* kingdoms, the *Latin* Church, the *Latin* clergy, the *Latin* patriarch, the *Latin* councils. Gibbon, who is so accurate in his word-painting, always applies this epithet to the Western Papal kingdoms. "'They latinize everything,' to use Dr. More's words; 'mass, prayers, hymns, litanies, canons, decretals, bulls, are conceived in Latin. The Papal councils speak in Latin; the Scripture is read in no other language under Popery than Latin; in short, all things are Latin.'"* From the time of Vitalian's decree, public worship itself throughout the whole of Papal Christendom was in Latin only. Hence the truth and worship of God became mere unmeaning sounds to the mass of the people in all lands, and the power of the Papal priesthood proportionably increased.

We take then as the main epochs of the rise of the *Papal power*—

1. The decretal letter of Justinian ...   533.
2. The accession of Gregory the Great   590.
3. The edicts and donations of Phocas   ...   607–610.
4. The latinizing decree of Vitalian   ...   ...   663.

* Elliott, vol. iii., p. 232.

The main points or epochs in the rise of the Eastern little horn, the *Mohammedan power*, which sprang up during the same era, spread with extraordinary rapidity, attained enormous influence, and wielded it to the misery and destruction of the Christian nations subjugated by it,—are two.

1. The Hegira, or flight of Mohammed from Mecca to Medina, the turning point in the career of the false prophet, which transformed him from the despised leader of a sect of fanatics to the prince and prophet of his people.

2. The capture of Jerusalem and Syria by the Caliph Omar, when a mosque was erected on the site of Solomon's temple, from which, that Muezzin call to prayer which has never since ceased (save for a brief interval in the time of the Crusaders) was first heard in the city. It was on this occasion that Sophronius, the unhappy patriarch of Jerusalem, muttered as he followed the victorious caliph round the sacred sites, " The abomination of desolation stands in the holy place."

The ten years of the Caliphate of Omar from A.D. 634 to A.D. 644 were years of rapid extension of Mohammedan power. The Saracens during their course reduced to obedience 36,000 cities or strongholds, destroyed 4,000 Christian churches, and built 1,400 mosques.

" At the end of the first century from the Hegira, the Arabian Empire had been extended to 200 days' journey from east to west, and reached from the confines of Tartary and India to the shores of the Atlantic, " over all which ample space," says Gibbon, " the progress of the Mohammedan religion diffused a general resemblance of manners and of opinions,"—over all which ample space, we may add, the venom of the scorpion sting of their conquerors was made to rankle in the breast of the subject Christians. For, indeed, the bitter contempt and hatred flowing out from the Moslem faith towards them could not but be felt perpetually. It was marked in the terms " Christian dogs" and " infidels." The enactments of the capitulations granted them were their every-day remembrancers of it. Deprived of the use of arms, like the Helots of old, with a tribute enforced as their animal life redemption tax, with a different dress, enjoined on them from their masters, and a more humble mode of riding, an obligation to rise up deferentially in the presence of the meanest Moslem, and to receive and gratuitously entertain for a certain time any Mussulman who on a journey might require it, such were the marks of personal degradation ordained in the capitulations. And then, in token of the degradation of their religion,—to which, notwithstanding all their superstitions, they clung with fond attachment—there was a prohibition to build new churches, to chime the bells in those retained by them, or to refuse admission into them to the scoffing Moslem, though they regarded his presence as defilement. Add to which the inducements to apostacy, operating to an incalculable extent, on the young and thoughtless in families more especially, and then the penalty of death against their returning to the Christian faith, the insults, moreover, to the Christian females, and thousands of undefinable injuries of oppression, and how could it be but the bitterness of their loss should be felt, and the poison rankle within them, even as in other days with the Jewish captives in Babylon, so as to make life itself almost a burden?"*

The two principal *Mohammedan* dates of commencement then are—

1. The Hegira ... ... A.D. 622.
2. Omar's capture of Jerusalem A.D. 637.

Now let it be observed

1. That from the accession of Nabonassar, the first king of Babylon, to the deposition of Romulus Augustulus, the last Emperor of Rome, was *to a day* 1260 lunar years.†

2. That from the overthrow of Jehoiakim by Nebuchadnezzar (B.C. 602) to the Hegira of Mohammed is also 1260 lunar years.

3. That from Nebuchadnezzar's burning of the temple, in

---

* Elliott, vol. i., p. 424.
† See Calendar of the Times of the Gentiles, Appendix.

the 19th year of his reign (B.C. 587), to Omar's capture of Jeru salem (A.D. 637), followed by the erection of a mosque that bears his name on the site of the temple, is again 1260 lunar years.

4. That from the Mohammedan era of Hegira to the import- ant crisis in the *decay and fall* of Mohammedan power before alluded to, the end of its independence and *legalised* intoler- ance, A.D. 1844, is once more 1260 years lunar, and it should be remembered that the Mohammedan reckoning is lunar.

5. That from the celebrated Pope-exalting decree of Justi- nian, A.D. 533, which constituted the Bishop of Rome head of all the Churches, 1260 years reckoned as lunar, as calendar, and as solar, lead respectively to the important initial, and crisis dates of the French revolution ; thus :—

A.D. 533, Justinian's decretal letter

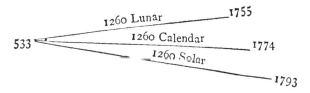

6. That from the decree of the Emperor Phocas, confirm- ing the primacy of the see of Rome over that of Constanti- nople and all the Eastern and Western Churches, 1260 years measured in the same three ways lead respectively to the three great modern overthrows of Papal power of which we have spoken : the revolutions of 1830, 1848-9, and 1866-70.

A.D. 607-10.   Phocas—

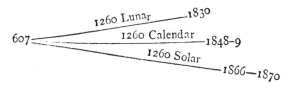

7. That measured from the important *central* date of the accession of Pope Gregory the Great, Sept. 3, A.D. 590, *the first properly speaking of the Popes,* the 1260th *solar* year

commences in Sept., 1849, which year is the terminus of 1260 *calendar* years from the decree of Phocas.

8. That from the captivity of Jehoiachin, and the final over-throw of Judah, B.C. 598, 1260 solar years lead to the promul-gation of the decree of Vitalian that the services of the Church throughout Christendom should be performed in Latin, A.D. 663. This latter date is, consequently, the *bisection* of "seven times" in solar years, as reckoned from the date of the final overthrow of the throne of Judah, and 1260 solar years from that point do not run out until the year A.D. 1923.

9. Further, from the capture of Jerusalem by Omar, A.D. 637, 1260 *calendar* years have brought us to the recent over-throw of Turkey by Russia, the Treaty of Berlin; the Anglo-Turkish Convention as to Cyprus, and the English protectorate of Asia Minor, unquestionably a fresh stage in the downfall of the Mohammedan power, whose present head is Constanti-nople. We have not yet reached 1260 solar years from the same date; they will run out in 1897 (and 1260 solar years from the Hegira date, the true commencement of Moham-medan reckoning, will expire in 1882).

It may be asked, How is it, if the fulfilment of these chro-nological prophecies be thus clearly traceable, that the fact has not been earlier perceived?

We reply, It is the revealed purpose of God that, for wise and gracious reasons, these chronological prophecies *should* become clear only in the "time of the end" (Dan. xii.).

In fulfilment of this design, not only is a symbolic system of predicting events and their duration adopted, but even when the chronological symbol employed is rightly translated on the year-day system, it is not necessarily clear *what kind of year* is the *reality*, for which a day is the *symbol;* hence the true length of the predicted period may still be to a certain extent hidden.

Some of the above periods are accurate even to a day when calculated by the true lunar year, though they present only distant approximations to accuracy when measured by the solar year.

But while comprehension of these Divine prophecies was impossible until partial fulfilment had given the true clue in the year-day system, and while the periods predicted still remained obscure even when the clue was obtained, their true scope has become clearer and clearer as each successive generation of students has searched into their meaning, till now, in the light of such fulfilments as the late loss of temporal power by the Papacy, and the present and imminent loss of power by the Ottoman Empire,—in the clear glow of light shed by fulfilments in this end of the age, and by the discovery of the astronomic measures of these mysterious times, *the whole series seem to range themselves into order and proportion,* and to present no longer a hopeless, puzzling, and intricate maze, but a complete, majestic, and clearly traceable plan.

CHRONOLOGICAL MEASURES OF THE PATRIARCHAL AGE AND THE JEWISH DISPENSATION.

It remains now to show that each of the two earlier dispensations lasted for a period similar to the Times of the Gentiles, and consisted of a great week of years of years—" seven times."

It should be noted, that Christianity, the religious system which has distinctively characterized the Times of the Gentiles, did not take its rise at their commencement, but on the contrary, when they had already run a third of their course. The rise of Christianity dates, not from the overthrow of Jewish independence in the Captivity era, but from the period of the abolition of Judaism, just before the fall of the city and temple of Jerusalem. Similarly Judaism, the distinctively characteristic religion of the previous or second great dispensation, dates, not from its commencement, but from SINAI, the giving of the law, the point where the Patriarchal dispensation closes. And just as the times of the Gentiles had an earlier commencement than Christianity, so the Jewish race and their special covenant privileges, had an earlier origin than the giving of the law. *In each case a people was first prepared to receive the new system of religious truth, and then the system was revealed.* Thus, as represented in the diagram, the dispensations overlapped; the second grew out of the first, and the third out of the second. The earliest date of the origin of the third, is, as we have seen, the beginning of the Jewish Captivities, the invasion of Pul, in the reign of Menahem, whose accession was in B.C. 770, 840 years before the destruction of Jerusalem, followed by the triumph of Titus, celebrated at Rome A.D. 70-71. Now 840 years is one-third of 2520 years; the times of the Gentiles took their rise one-third of " seven times," before the passing away of Judaism. We naturally inquire, Is any parallel fact observable in connection with the previous dispensation? Did the origin of the Abrahamic race precede the giving of the Law, by any such period?

The call of Abram preceded the Exodus by 430 years : " the covenant, that was confirmed before of God in Christ, the law, which was 430 *years after*, cannot disannul, that it should make the promise of none effect" (Gal. iii. 17). The birth of the Patriarch preceded his call by seventy-five years, and Abram the Hebrew was himself descended, through Eber, from SHEM, and with his race, inherited the blessing of that pre-eminently blessed son of Noah ; *his* was the specially privileged branch of the great Shemitic family. Now the blessing of Shem *immediately followed the flood ;* it dates from the recommencement of human history after the first great judgment of the world by water. Measuring, then, the Shemitic dispensation, or that of the Jewish people and their fathers, from this primary epoch, to the time of Messiah's advent and rejection, we find that another great "seven times" intervened ; that, as nearly as we can ascertain, such a week of years of years, divided these great termini from each other.

It must be borne in mind, that the two inevitable gaps in the world's chronology, occur in the course of this Shemitic or Jewish age, so that certainty, to within forty or fifty years, is unattainable. The date of the flood is A.M. 1656, which, according to Clinton's chronology is B.C. 2482. Adding twenty-nine years—to the date of the Crucifixion,—it will be seen that the latter event took place 2510 years after the flood, that is, only ten years less than the full "seven times," or 2520 years. Now it must be borne in mind that their rejection of Messiah the Prince, did not, as we have seen, cause at once, the full and final rejection of Israel by God. For some years subsequently the ministry of the Holy Ghost by the Apostles, appealed to them to repent and be converted, that the times of refreshing might come from the presence of the Lord. Ten or fifteen years later the sentence was pronounced by Paul and Barnabas, " It was necessary that the word of God should first have been spoken to you : but seeing ye put it from you, and judge yourselves unworthy of everlasting life, lo, we turn to the Gentiles. For so hath the Lord commandeth us " (Acts xiii. 46). Allowing therefore a few years for this final hovering of the Spirit of mercy and longsuffering over the guilty race, we may say that 2520 years, "seven times," elapsed between the bestowment of distinctive privilege on the race of Shem, and the utter rejection of the Jewish people, and transference of the kingdom of God to the Gentiles. It should be remembered that this is no question of brief periods ; it is a question of a period of over *twenty-five centuries ;* so that an inaccuracy of two or three years, even if it existed, would scarcely affect the conclusion.

But it cannot be proved that there *is* an inaccuracy, because of the acknowledged and inevitable uncertainty as to two of the minor intervals composing this long period, which may throw our accepted dates out, to the extent of forty or fifty years. Absolute accuracy is in this case unattainable ; the terminal event of the Shemitic or Jewish " seven times " may have been the Crucifixion itself, or it may have been the crisis indicated above, or it may have been the subsequent destruction of Jerusalem. There is no need to fix on any one of these, in order to recognise the broad fact, which is beyond dispute, that the Shemitic or Jewish age extended over a great week of prophetic times, exactly as does the succeeding dispensation, the times of the Gentiles. No trifling discrepancy of a few years,—a discrepancy which, as it is founded on ignorance, not on certain knowledge, may not exist, but be merely apparent,—can blind a candid observer to the fact, that here, in these major divisions of human history, there prevails the same law of completion in weeks, which we have traced in so many minor arrangements.

The first, or patriarchal dispensation, had a similar duration. "*From Adam to Moses*," when there was "*no law*," *i.e.*, from the Creation to Sinai, 2514 years elapsed, for the date of the Exodus (according to Clinton) is A.M. 2513, and the giving of the Law followed the Exodus, so that the "seven times" terminated within seven years of the Exodus. We may therefore boldly say that from Adam to Moses was "*seven times;*" from the incipient rise of the Hebrew nation and their peculiar privileges, to their utter rejection and fall, was "*seven times;*" and from the recognition by God of Gentile monarchy, down to its final overthrow, is also "*seven times.*" The three dispensations so clearly distinguished by their broad *moral* features, and marked off by their critical termini (the greatest events of all human history), are THREE GREAT WEEKS CHRONOLOGICALLY EQUAL TO EACH OTHER. Taking the prophetic "time" (360 years) as the unit, the first contained *seven* such; the second contained *seven* such; and the third contains *seven* such.

Symmetrical subdivisions of these great periods seem also clearly traceable. The second is divided into thirds, the last into halves. The Exodus marks the first third of the Shemitic or Jewish age, the Captivity era its second, and the fall of Jerusalem its close; the three periods representing respectively the rise, the prosperity, and the decay and fall, of the Jewish nation. The golden headship of the Babylonian power marks the rise of the times of the Gentiles, the *first* half of which is occupied by the four great Pagan Empires of antiquity, and the *last* by the domination of the "little horn," or Papal dynasty, for "time times and a half," 1260 years. The chronological harmony between these three great dispen-

THE THREE DISPENSATIONS.
Patriarchal;- Jewish;- Christian.

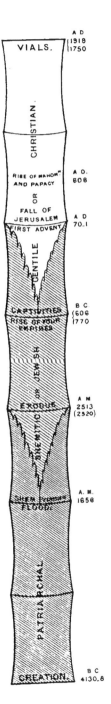

sations, or stages of progress, in the providential dealings of God with man, is of profound interest, especially when viewed in relation to the other scriptural uses of the week, and in relation to its prominence in natural and vital phenomena.

Owing to the *ingrafting* of these three dispensations, before mentioned, and represented in the diagram, their total duration is between 5880 and 6000 years. This commencement of a succeeding dispensation before the termination of a previous one, seems natural and appropriate, when the relation between them is remembered. Their connection is not one of mere succession or juxtaposition, but one of intimate relation, and of vital *growth*. The mature years of the parent coincide with the infancy and youth of the child ; indeed, there is always a period in which the lives of the mother and child are not twain, but one. So in the chronological arrangements of the law, one year began while another was still in progress, so that the two overlapped for several months. The year of jubilee, for instance, commenced in the midst of the ordinary current year, on the tenth day of the seventh month, the great day of atonement. (Lev. xxv.)

The deep reason for this arrangement is also obvious, it forms part of that hidden wisdom, of which Scripture is full. It is one feature of an underlying system of times and seasons, which, like all system in nature, is concealed from mere casual observers. Scientific classification has its basis in natural facts ; but the facts on which it is based are not conspicuously obvious to the superficial inquirer, so that the system is not self-evident. On the contrary, the facts must be carefully compared, before their mutual relations can be perceived, or the system which embraces them all, discerned. So it is with these biblical times and seasons. The moral distinctions between the three dispensations are clearly pointed out in Scripture ; the great crises in human history which form their respective termini, are fully narrated, the dates of the events and their duration are duly given, and the measures of the last are not indistinctly intimated in prophecy ; but it is nowhere *stated* that human history has been providentially divided into three great weeks of seven prophetic times each; we are left to discover from what *is* stated, what is *not* stated, *i.e.*, the plan that underlies the whole chronology of the Bible, and the harmony of that plan with the plan observable in nature, organic and inorganic. We are furnished with a clue, and then left to explore the labyrinth.

That there should be this analogy between *the mode* of God's revelation of his ways, in nature and in Scripture, is what might have been expected, even were no special reason assignable why, in the matter of the chronology of the ages, peculiar reserve should be employed. But, as we have previously seen, the purpose of God to conceal the fore-ordained duration of this Christian age, from all save the later generations of his people, is very distinctly intimated. "Shut up the vision and seal the book, even to the time of the end." "The words are closed up and sealed, even to the time of the end." The intimations which exist, of the uniform and septiform measures of the three dispensations, were therefore purposely slight and indirect, unlikely to attract attention in early days, or to be even surmised, till the fulfilment of the great prophetic "time times and a half" had so far progressed, as to illuminate with fresh light the entire book of chronologic prophecy.

And further, not only is the whole plan and system an underlying and half-hidden one, but even when perceived the providential gaps in Bible chronology necessarily prevent its being demonstrated, with that absolute evidence which would place it beyond dispute, or with that accuracy which would justify any prediction of "that day and that hour." "It is not for you to know the times and the seasons which the Father hath put in his own power," said our Master to his early disciples, when they inquired as to the time of the restoration of the kingdom to Israel. He did not abate their confident expectation that such a restoration was to take place; He implied, on the contrary, that the time and the season for it were appointed, but intimated that with that time and season *they* were not to become acquainted. A revelation of nineteen centuries of delay, would have been a test of faith and patience too severe to be imposed on the infant Church : a merciful veil of mystery was thrown over the subject, and the return of their Lord, after a longer or shorter delay, was the one hope and prospect left to the early disciples. But ages before, the promise had been given, that in the time of the end, the wise should understand the mysteries of chronologic prophecy (Dan. xii. 10, 11) ; and the promise has been fulfilled. Revelations that were dark to the fathers, are radiant with light to us ; and the perception of the true nature of the year-day system, and of the septiform measures of the Divine dispensations, so far from discouraging faith and hope, *now* only stimulate both. We humbly venture to regard the view unfolded in this chapter, of the uniform and harmonious ordering of the ages of human history, by the law of completion in weeks, as a fresh instance of progressive inter-pretation, another example of the way in which God, who is his own interpreter, makes plain in due time, the meaning of his own word.

SECTION III.

Soli-lunar Cycles, and their Relation to the Chronology of History.

CHAPTER I.

SOLAR AND LUNAR SUPREMACY
IN THE ORDERING OF TERRESTRIAL TIME.

WE have already called attention to the multiplied proofs afforded by every branch of science, of the universal dominion exercised by the sun and moon, both over the organic and inorganic creations.

We have shown that it is to its various relations, with these two vastly dissimilar, yet equally controlling bodies, that the earth owes its entire life and activity ; that its rotation, revolution, heat, light, seasonal changes, magnetic impulses, and tidal phenomena, its winds, waves, currents, rains, snows, and frosts, all proceed directly or indirectly from the influence of the sun and moon. We have also shown that the distribution of vegetable and animal life, on the surface of the globe, and many of the laws by which both—including the development of the human race itself—are governed, are distinctly traceable to the same cause. Solar influence is simply *supreme* in the production of all terrestrial change and movement, and in the sustenance and regulation of all vegetable and animal life.

We now turn to the second phase of solar and lunar dominion, and show the place of paramount importance occupied by these two great luminaries, in the regulation of times and seasons.

The three great tasks assigned to the sun and moon in the first of Genesis are to rule, to give light, and *to divide ;* to mark out the boundaries that separate day from night, month from month, year from year, "appointed time" from "appointed time." The sun and moon are thus constituted not merely beneficent fountains of light to a dark world, and all-influential rulers over our globe, but also principal hands of the divinely constructed and divinely appointed chronometer, by which, in all its course, terrestrial time is measured.

Nor does the record imply, that this chronometer is to be used by man alone! "Let them be for signs and for seasons," or appointed times, is an expression which may legitimately include a fact, which it is our object in the present chapter to demonstrate. God, who assigned to these worlds their paths and their periods, has regulated all his majestic providential and dispensational dealings with mankind, by *the greater revolutions of the same chronometer*, whose lesser revolutions mark our days and months and years. That chronometer is adjusted to measure not only the blossoming of the day-lily and the life-time of the ephemera, but also periods which are incalculable by human intelligence, and which border on infinity.

It must be noted that the inspired narrative says "let *them* be for signs and for seasons, and for days and years," *not* "let the sun" be so, or the moon, or the sun and moon separately, but let *them* in their conjoint revolutions be such. So obvious and influential are the *main* revolutions of these "great lights" that in all ages men have as a matter of fact, divided time by their means. But this is not all, they have in addition less obvious cycles, which have been, as we shall see, divinely employed as chronological measures.

Though time like distance, may theoretically be measured by comparison with standards of any length, yet practically, none are so convenient as those afforded by the conspicuous movements of the heavenly bodies. These provide not only obvious and universal standards, but what is equally needful, *varied* standards. For the subdivision of comparatively brief periods of time, a *short* standard is evidently desirable,— for longer periods a longer standard is required, while to measure periods which embrace hundreds of thousands of years, a standard of immense proportions is evidently needful. An inch is a good standard by which to divide into equal portions a yard, but it would be tedious to have to measure by inches the circumference of our globe. The distance of the earth from the sun may be measured by millions of miles, but for the almost infinitely greater distance of the fixed stars, we need a longer unit or standard of measurement, and find one in the velocity of light.

Thus the revolution of the earth on its axis, giving rise to the day, is a good unit of measurement for the month or moon's revolution in her orbit, and the month in its turn for the year, or earth's revolution in its orbit. This last is a good measure for centuries, but when we rise to millenaries and still longer periods we need larger units of measurement. These are afforded by the revolutions of the sun and moon, as we shall presently show, not by their obvious conspicuous axial and orbital movements merely, but by the cycles of discrepancy between them, and by their recurring epochs of harmony, as well as by their grand secular revolutions. The soli-lunar chronometer is adapted to measure any period, from an hour to an age of all but infinite extent. It has its second hand, its minute hand, its hour hand—its diurnal bell, its monthly chime, its annual peal, its secular thunder, its millennial choral-harmony. Man uses its minor measures, God requires its major standards; man counts by its days, and months, and years ; God's providence employs all its "appointed times."

"Let *them* be for times and for seasons." The movements of the sun and moon are such that naturally in most lands and ages, those of *both*, and not those of either alone, have been employed as measures of time.

The solar *day* is of course a division of time which both the physical constitution of man, and his occupations, have in every part of the world, and in every state of society, forced upon him, and compelled him to adopt as his fundamental unit of time.

The solar *year* as comprising the complete revolution of the seasons, and thus the entire round of the operations of husbandry, forces itself similarly into observance as a larger unit of measurement.

But the days of a whole year are far too numerous to admit of each one being distinguished by a name, and separately remembered and recognised. All nations have felt the necessity of grouping the days into smaller parcels which might be named, and the days in each distinguished by numbers.

The remarkably conspicuous revolution of the moon, being intermediate in its period between the solar day and year, has been adopted for this purpose, and *the month* has been the principal measure universally recognised, between the year and the day.

The marked phases of the moon, new, first quarter, full, and third quarter, might at first sight be supposed to have given rise to the fourth commonly received measure of time—the week. But while in a general way these phases harmonize with the week, they do not do so with sufficient accuracy to account for the use of this period, and *the week* evidently owes its origin *not* to any astronomical movement, but to the Divine institution of the Sabbath in Eden. (Gen. ii.)

CHAPTER II.

IT might have been supposed, that as solar and lunar revolutions were to be employed by man, as measures of time, God would have made them so harmonize, as that some definite number of the lesser, would be *exactly* commensurate with one of the greater, and a definite number of these again, with one of the greatest. We might have supposed for instance that thirty revolutions of the earth on its axis, would have occupied precisely the same time as one revolution of the moon in her orbit, and twelve such revolutions of the moon, precisely the same time, as one revolution of the earth in its orbit.

This arrangement would have made the month *exactly* thirty days, and the year *exactly* twelve months. Had it been selected by the Creator, the great natural chronometer in the heavens, would have acted, as do our little artificial time-pieces; its hands would, so to speak, have kept pace together, the second, minute, and hour hands, returning simultaneously to their common starting-point, at the close of every major revolution, and setting out again on a new round, in identically the same order as at first. New and full moon would have fallen invariably on the same day of the month, and of the year; and the endless variety we now experience in this respect would have been replaced by perfect uniformity.

Such a plan would have been, in some respects, convenient to mankind, and would have made the arrangement of the calendar an exceedingly simple matter, instead of as it is, a *most* complex and difficult one. But it would have been adapted to the measurements of short periods of time only, and would have afforded no standards for longer intervals.

The arrangement actually adopted on the other hand, while

it creates some difficulty in the exact and uniform adjustment of *days* and *months*, to *years*, gives rise to an infinite variety of cycles, or circles of change and harmony, which enable the soli-lunar clock to measure out the revolutions of ages, by standards, varying in length from three years to over a thousand years.

Of these cycles we shall have much to say presently ; and it must be distinctly borne in mind, that it is not in connection with them alone, that we employ soli-lunar reckoning, but that our ordinary computation of time is *soli-lunar*. Our calendar is neither purely solar—regulated by the sun alone ; nor is it wholly lunar—regulated by the moon alone ; but it is soli-lunar—regulated by both, adapted to the motions of both sun and moon.

As this soli-lunar reckoning of time is fundamental to our present investigation, it will not be out of place to dwell a little more fully on the subject of

THE CALENDAR AND ITS HISTORY.

It is evident that one of the first cares of every civilized or even partially civilized society, must always have been to establish some uniform method of reckoning time. Without such a standard of reference, the administration of public affairs would be impossible, and even the regulation of the common concerns of every-day life. For the adjustment of civil and religious ceremonies and institutions, for the fixing of the proper periods for seed-time and harvest, and for the transmission to later generations, of the dates of events worthy of remembrance, a well-regulated calendar is a matter of the utmost importance.

A moment's reflection will show the difficulty which must attend every attempt to construct a calendar, practically adapted to the wants of mankind, out of elements so inbarmonious as the natural day, month, and year.

The *day*, measured by the revolutions of the earth on her axis, and marked by the apparent diurnal revolution of the entire heavens,—contains twenty-four hours, and is the funda-mental measure of time.

The *month*, or interval between one new moon and another, occasioned by the moon's revolution in her orbit, contains 29 days 12 hours 44 minutes and 3 seconds.

The *year*, or apparent course of the sun round the earth, from any given point in his orbit, to the same point again, occupies 12 months 10 days 21 hours, or 365 days 5 hours 48 minutes and 49 seconds.

How many days make a month? How many months make a year? In either case the answer involves *a fraction*, and the fraction involves more practical difficulty, than can be easily conceived by the uninitiated.

Before observations were as accurate and information as full, or experience as great, as they now are, it is easy to under-stand that the ancients would grapple boldly with a difficulty which to them may have appeared slight. Twenty-nine or 30 days to the month, and 12 months to the year, was a fair approximation to actual facts, and would be supposed to be sufficiently near the mark. But the very purposes aimed at in the use of a calendar, would quickly be defeated by the employment of so inaccurate a one as this. It would for a time agree pretty well with the course of the moon; but each year it would get more and more out of harmony with the true course of the sun, by eleven days. Now as the seasons are regulated by the course of the sun, it is evident that practical confusions, and irregularities of a most embarrassing kind, would quickly arise. For supposing it to have been settled at any time, that the new year should begin in the spring, sixteen years afterwards, new year's day would fall in the autumn, and in thirty-three years it would have worked its way all through the seasons, back to spring again.

Intercalation, or the insertion of days at certain junctures, was the remedy employed to meet this difficulty; but it was an uncertain, awkward, and imperfect remedy. About the time of the Christian era, it was felt that a reformation of the calendar was urgently needed. Julius Cæsar, calling to his aid the most eminent mathematicians of his time, attempted the task. A careful consideration of the elements of the problem proved, that no satisfactory solution could be found which did not make *the sun's annual course* the *principal* measure and adapt to *it* the months and days. He therefore made the year to consist of 365 days for three years successively, and of 366 every fourth year, in order to take in the odd six hours.

This reformation was made B.C. 45, in the year of Rome 708. The beginning of the year was fixed to the 1st of January; and the months were made to consist of 30 and 31 days alternately, with the exception of February, which in ordinary years had only 28 days, but in the fourth year, when the new day arising from the odd six hours was added to it, 29 days.

This Julian calendar, though superior to any that had preceded it, was still far from perfect, for the odd six hours is not actually six full hours, but 5 hours 48 minutes and 49 seconds as we have said; so that the year of the Julian calendar exceeded the true solar year by 11 minutes and 11 seconds.

This difference amounts in 130 years to an entire day, and in process of time throws the whole seasons again out of course. In the 16th century the vernal equinox, which had by the Council of Nice in A.D. 325 been fixed to the 21st of March was found to happen instead on the 11th of that month, the error having, in the intervening period, accumulated to the extent of ten days.

The present and prospective inconvenience of this state of things was represented to the Councils of Constance and Lateran, by Cardinals Ailli and Cusa, and attempts to remedy it were proposed and discussed. Pope Sixtus IV., in the year 1474, called to Rome the celebrated mathematician Regiomontanus, and bestowed on him the Archbishopric of Ratisbon, that through his aid he might accomplish the required fresh reformation of the calendar. The premature death of the mathematical archbishop, disappointed however the project, and nothing was done for another century. Then Pope

Gregory XIII., after consulting mathematicians, and obtaining the consent of the various princes of Christendom, to a plan submitted to him by the astronomer Luilius, called a council of the most learned prelates to consider the question, and having with their concurrence decided it, he published a brief in March, 1582, abrogating the Julian reckoning, and substituting for it the Gregorian calendar which we now employ.

By this alteration, or " new style," the ten days which the civil year had gained on the true solar year, were deducted from the month of October of the year 1582, the equinox being thus brought back to the 21st of March, as it had been settled by the Nicene Council; and in order to prevent a recurrence of the irregularity, it was ordered, that instead of *every* 100th year being a leap year, as by the old style, only every 400th year should be such, and the rest be considered as common years. As a day had been gained by the former method every hundred and thirty years, or about three days in four hundred years, the omission of three leap years every four centuries, would evidently nearly rectify the defect. A much more difficult matter was to adjust the lunar to the solar year, and to settle the time for the observance of Easter and other moveable feasts.

It was ordered by the Council of Nice, that Easter should be celebrated on the first Sunday after the first full-moon, next following the vernal equinox. In order that this rule might be properly observed, it was needful to know the days when the full moon would happen, in any given year. This however it was extremely difficult to ascertain : for the nineteen-years' cycle discovered by the Greek philosopher Meton, which nearly harmonizes the movements of sun and moon, and brings the days of new and full moons back to the same days of the year, was found to be too long by an hour and thirty-two minutes (Julian year measure). After sixteen Metonic or lunar cycles the true phases of the moon would precede those shown in the calendar by a whole day.

At the time of the Gregorian reformation, the error occasioned by this means amounted to four days; had the old calendar still been followed, it would in time have announced full moon, at the time of change, and Easter would consequently have been celebrated at a period, exactly opposite to that commanded by the Church. By an ingenious device, Luilius, the astronomer employed by Gregory XIII. in this intricate business, succeeded in arranging a plan by which the period of the new moon may be ascertained for any month of any year.

He rejected the " Golden numbers " formerly employed for the purpose, and made use of Epacts in their stead.

The Epact is the moon's age at the end of the year. If for example the new moon occurs in a given year on new year's day, we should say there was no epact that year. But as twelve lunations (or lunar months) are completed in 354 days and the year is over 365 days, it is evident that on the second new year's day, the moon would already be eleven days old, while by the third, she would be twenty-two, or have twenty-two days' epact, and by the fourth *thirty-three.* But as the time of the entire lunation is never more than 29 days and a half, the epact cannot possibly exceed thirty. In the latter case, therefore, thirty must be subtracted, and at the beginning of the fourth year the epact would only be *three.* By observing this rule through a period of 19 years, the epacts would stand in the following order :—0, 11, 22, 3, 14, 25, 6, 17, 28, 9, 20, 1, 12, 23, 4, 15, 26, 7, 18.

As in sixteen lunar cycles, or 304 years, the slight error of that cycle amounts to an entire day, these numbers have then to be increased by unity, and for the second period of 304 years will stand in the order, 1, 12, 23, 4, 15, 26, 7, 18, 29, 10, etc.

Gregory XIII. ordered all ecclesiastics under his jurisdiction to conform to the new method of reckoning, and exhorted all Christian princes to adopt it in their dominions. The Catholic nations did so at once, the Protestant nations refused to for a time. But the difference between the "old" and new style, as the Julian and Gregorian accounts were called, occasioned so much confusion in the commercial affairs of the different states of Europe, that by degrees popular prejudice against the change was overcome even in Protestant countries, and in 1752, the new style was by Act of Parliament adopted even in England. A century having elapsed, instead of cancelling *ten* days as the Pope had done, *eleven* days were ordered to be left out of the month of September, and accordingly on the second of that month the old style ceased, and the next day instead of being called the third, was called the fourteenth. Russia still retains the old style.

This Gregorian calendar is practically correct for a very long period; it is not absolutely so, and it would probably be impossible to arrange a calendar that should be theoretically perfect for all time, but it is so accurately adjusted to actual solar and lunar movements, as to be free from the error of a day in some thousands of years. A better plan had been previously proposed which seems to have been unknown to Gregory XIII. Herschel says: "A rule proposed by Omar, a Persian astronomer of the court of Gelaleddin Melek Schah, in A.D. 1079 (or more than five centuries before the reformation of Gregory) deserves notice. It consists in interpolating a day, as in the Julian system, every fourth year, ónly postponing to the 33rd year the intercalation, which on that system would be made on the 32nd. This is equivalent to omitting the Julian intercalation altogether in each 128th year (retaining all the others). To produce an accumulated error of a day on this system, would require a lapse of 5000 years. So that the Persian astronomer's rule is *not only far more simple but materially more exact than the Gregorian.*

CHAPTER III.

CYCLICAL CHARACTER OF THE PROPHETIC PERIODS OF DANIEL
AND THE APOCALYPSE.

DISCOVERIES OF M. DE CHESEAUX.

THE perplexities and difficulties which encumber the attempt to adapt *brief* periods of time to both solar and lunar movements, as in the calendar, disappear, directly it is a question of *longer* intervals.

Short periods have to be artificially harmonized, longer ones harmonize themselves. There exist various times and seasons, which are *naturally* measurable both by solar years, and lunar months, without remainder, or with remainders so small as to be unimportant.

Such periods are therefore SOLI-LUNAR CYCLES, and we shall henceforth speak of them as such. They harmonize with more or less exactness solar and lunar revolutions, and they may be regarded as divinely appointed units for the measurement of long periods of time, units of precisely the same *character* as the day, month, and year, (that is created by solar, lunar, and terrestrial revolutions) but of larger *dimensions*. They are therefore periods distinctly marked off as such, on the same principles as those on which our calendar is based, that is they are natural measures of time, furnished by the Creator Himself for human use.

The lunar cycle of nineteen years employed by the Greeks is one of these periods, and the ancient cycle of Calippus is another. Their discovery has always been an object with astronomers, as their practical utility is considerable. But it was exceedingly difficult to find cycles of any tolerable accuracy, especially cycles combining and harmonizing the day, and the month, with the year.

About the middle of last century a remarkable fact was discovered by a Swiss astronomer M. de Cheseaux, a fact which
is full of the deepest interest to the Christian mind, and which
has never received either at the hands of the Church or of the
world, the attention that it merits.

The prophetic periods of 1260 years and 2300 years, assigned
in the Book of Daniel and in the Apocalypse, as the duration
of certain predicted events, *are such soli-lunar cycles*, cycles of
remarkable perfection and accuracy, but whose existence was
entirely unknown to astronomers, until, guided by sacred Scripture, M. de Cheseaux discovered and demonstrated them to be
such. And further, the difference between these two periods,
which is 1040 years, *is the largest accurate soli-lunar cycle known*

The importance of this discovery, and the fact that it is exceedingly little known, must be our apology for entering into
a somewhat full account of the matter here. It is besides vital
to our own more immediate subject, and was indeed the means
of leading us to the present investigation.

M. de Cheseaux's book is out of print, difficult to procure
and even to consult. A copy of it exists in the library of the
University of Lausanne, and another in the British Museum.
It is entitled "Mémoires posthumes de M. de Cheseaux" and
was edited and published by his sons, in 1754. It contains
" Remarques historiques, chronologiques, et astronomiques,
sur quelques endroits du livre de Daniel." The calculations of
the astronomical part, were submitted to Messrs. Mairan and
Cassini, celebrated astronomers of the Royal Academy of
Sciences at Paris, neither of whom called in question the accuracy of M. de Cheseaux's principles, or the correctness of his
results. M. Mairan, after having carefully read his essay, said
that "it was impossible to doubt the facts and discoveries it
contained ; but that he could not conceive *how* or *why* they
had come to be embodied so distinctly in the Holy Scrip
tures." M. Cassini wrote, after having read the treatise and
worked the problems, that the methods of calculating the solar
and lunar positions and movements, which M. de Cheseaux

had deduced from the cycles of the Book of Daniel, were most clear, and perfectly consistent with the most exact astronomy;" he wished the essay to be read before the Academy.

M. de Cheseaux was engaged in some chronological researches, and in order to fix with certainty the date of the Crucifixion, he was led to examine certain parts of Scripture, and especially the Book of Daniel. The first portion of his essay is purely chronological, and unimportant to our subject, we may say, however, that he clearly perceived that the "time times and a half" of Dan. vii. meant a period of 1260 years. "The importance of this conclusion and of some of the foregoing principles," he adds, "will be perceived, when we show how it led to a discovery of the singular relation which exists between this period of Daniel, and the facts of astronomy. However strange it may seem, I can positively deduce from the periods of Daniel, as accurately as by the best astronomical methods, and even *more* so, **the five** elements of the solar theory."

He goes on to explain what *a cycle* is : "a period which brings into harmony different celestial revolutions, containing a certain definite number of each, without remainder or fraction," and he shows that there are four different kinds of cycles connected with the sun, moon, and earth.

1. Those harmonizing the solar *day* and *year*.
2. Those harmonizing the solar *year* and lunar *month*.
3. Those harmonizing the solar *day* and lunar *month*.
4. Those harmonizing all three, day, month, and year.

M. de Cheseaux adds, "the discovery of such cycles has always been a great object with astronomers and chronologists. They have considered it so difficult a matter, that they have almost laid it down as a principle that it is impossible, at any rate as regards those of the fourth class. Till now, the discovery of a cycle of this kind has been to astronomers,—like perpetual motion to mechanicians,—a sort of philosopher's stone. Anxious to settle whether the thing were really impossible, I began some time ago to try for a cycle of the second kind."

D D

M. de Cheseaux then describes the process by which he was led to the discovery that 315 years is such a soli-lunar cycle, *ten times more exact* than the nineteen years Metonic cycle in use by the ancients; the sun and moon coming after a lapse of that period, to within three hours twenty-four seconds of absolute agreement: and he proceeds,—

"I had no sooner discovered this cycle, than I observed that it was *a quarter of the* 1260 *years of Daniel, and the Apocalypse,* and that consequently, *this period is itself a soli-lunar cycle,*" after which the sun and moon return, within less than half a degree, to the same point of the ecliptic precisely, and that within an hour of each other.*

"The relation of *this* period, assigned by the Holy Spirit as the limit of certain political events, to the most notable movements of the heavenly bodies, made me think it might be the same with the 2300 years. By the aid of the astronomic tables I examined this latter, and found that at the end of 2300 Gregorian years, minus six hours fourteen seconds, the sun and the moon return to within half a degree of the place from which they started, and that an hour later the sun has reached its exact starting point on the ecliptic: whence it follows that the prophetic period of 2300 years, is a cyclical period (also remarkable for the number of its aliquot parts, and for containing a complete number of cycles) and *one so perfect, that though it is thirty times longer than the celebrated cycle of Calippus, it has an error of only thirteen hours, a seventeenth part of the error of that ancient cycle.*

"The exact similarity of the error of these two cycles of 1260 and 2300 years, made me soon conclude that the difference between them, 1040 *years,* ought to be a perfect cycle, free from all error; and all the more remarkable as uniting the three kinds of cycles, and furnishing consequently a cycle of

---

That is, after 460,205 days 6 h. the sun and moon come into conjunction, and in 460,205 days 7 h. 23 m. the sun has returned to its exact starting point on the ecliptic—a period of 1260 solar years. (According to more accurate modern measures 1260 years are about three hours less.)

that *fourth kind*, so long sought in vain, and finally concluded to be chimerical, impossible to find.

" On examination of this period of 1040 years by the best modern astronomic tables *I found that it was even so.* Its error is absolutely imperceptible, in so long a period, and may indeed be accounted for by errors in the tables themselves, owing to the inaccuracy of some of the ancient observations on which they are founded.

" This period of 1040 years, indicated indirectly by the Holy Ghost, *is a cycle at once solar, lunar, and diurnal or terrestrial of the most perfect accuracy.* I subsequently discovered two singular confirmations of this fact, which I will explain presently, when I have adduced all my purely astronomic proofs ; may I in the meantime be permitted to give to this new cycle, the name of THE DANIEL CYCLE."

M. de Cheseaux then goes into full astronomic detail, of a kind that would fail to interest our readers, though proving the very remarkable nature of this cycle : and he subsequently continues, " As I before said, a cycle of this kind had long been sought in vain ; no astronomer or chronologist, had been able to light upon one for nineteen centuries ; and yet for two thousand three hundred years, there it has been, written in characters legible enough, in the Book of Daniel : legible, that is, to him who was willing to take the trouble of comparing the great prophetic periods, with the movements of the heavenly bodies ; in other words, to him, *who compared the book of nature with the book of revelation."*

" The slightest error, even of a few seconds, in the determination of the true length of the solar year, would remove altogether from these numbers, their cyclical character. Only the perfection of modern astronomical instruments in fact, can demonstrate it at all. So that we have the problem, How did Daniel, or the author of the Book of Daniel, whoever he was (if, as some assert, the prophecy is of a later date than Daniel), light upon these undiscoverable and undiscovered, yet excessively accurate celestial cycles, at a time when there were no instruments in existence capable of measuring solar revolutions with sufficient accuracy, to reveal the cyclical character of the periods?"

M. de Cheseaux adds, "I must close with one observation. For many ages the Book of Daniel, and especially these passages of it, have been quoted and commented on by numerous and varied authors, so that it is impossible for a moment to call in question their antiquity. Who can have taught their author the marvellous relation of the periods he selected with soli-lunar revolutions? Is it possible, considering all these points, to fail to recognise in the Author of the Book of Daniel, the Creator of the heavens and all their hosts, of the earth and the things that are therein?"

In a subsequent portion of his dissertation, M. de Cheseaux shows that not only can the five *solar* elements be deduced from the data in Daniel, but also the *lunar*. He compared his theoretic results with the observations recorded by the ancient astronomers Hipparchus and Ptolemy. Calculating forward first, he finds that the mean new moon of the vernal equinox of A.D. 1879 will, at Alexandria in Egypt, occur at 11.43½ p.m. on the 10th of March (O.S.). He then applies this cycle of 1040 years, and reckons backwards. Two such cycles, equal to 2080 years, from the above date, carry back to 11.43½ p.m. of March 26, B.C. 202 (*i.e.*, sixteen days later than March 10, reckoning by Julian calendar).

Now according to the tables of Hipparchus and Ptolemy the new moon of the vernal equinox that year, *did* at Alexandria fall on the 26th of March, at 11.39 p.m., not quite five minutes earlier than, by the cyclical calculation, it should have fallen! M. de Cheseaux adds, "I leave it to others to judge whether a slight difference such as this, may not well be attributed to the inevitable errors of the best ancient observations."

In his second dissertation this astronomer deduces the true size and figure of the earth, from these same cycles. and works by means of them some thirty or forty elaborate astronomical and geographical problems.

Such were M. de Cheseaux's discoveries; and they are of the deepest interest and importance, as manifesting, in a new light, the wisdom and glory of God in connection with his holy word. That the ancient prophet Daniel twenty-five centuries ago, and "the disciple whom Jesus loved" eighteen centuries ago, should both have incorporated in their mysterious books of symbolic prophecy, as the chronological limits of certain most important events, periods of time, which the accurate researches of modern science have proved to be cycles formed by vast, complex, long-enduring movements of the heavenly bodies, seems a marvellous fact, a fact to be accounted for *only* by the Divine inspiration under which these holy men of old wrote.

For it is certain, and none can dispute it, that these periods *are* accurate celestial cycles : it is equally certain, and few will be inclined to question it, that neither Daniel, nor John, the fisherman of the Sea of Galilee, were able to calculate these cycles, or were even aware of their existence. Had they been in intercourse with the first astronomers of their day, or even had they been themselves astronomers of the highest attainments, it would have been impossible for them in the then existing state of astronomic science, to have observed the cyclical character of these periods. There was no such exact knowledge of either the true length of the solar year, or lunar month, as would have made the discovery of these cycles *possible.* In Daniel's day even the Metonic or lunar cycle was unknown, and these larger but similar cycles, were as a matter of fact, discovered only last century.

It was therefore certainly not as moved by their own intelligence, that the sacred writers selected these periods; and if they were not moved by Divine inspiration, how is the fact of their use of them to be accounted for? Could it be by chance—by accident—that to certain supremely important series of events, were assigned as the period of their duration, these cyclical periods?

Such an explanation of the fact, would be improbable to the

last degree! Nothing but an unwillingness to admit the miracle of inspiration, could lead to its being suggested as an alternative. It would be an unsatisfactory account of the matter had there been one single cycle only, so employed, and the fact that there are *three*, makes it wholly inadmissible. But there are more, and even *many* such proofs, of the use in Scripture by writers ignorant of astronomy, of periods marked out distinctly as cycles, by the less obvious revolutions of the heavenly bodies. This fact, which has we believe never before been demonstrated, is of such importance as enhancing the evidence of the inspiration of Scripture, as to deserve the most careful consideration.

In the following chapters we shall endeavour to unfold the further multiplied, and most remarkable links of connection which we have ourselves discovered, between the chronology of Scripture, historic and prophetic, and the cycles of soli-lunar revolution.

CHAPTER IV.

PROPHECY, which occupies about a third of the Bible, threw its light beforehand, as we have seen, on all the events of importance which were to befall the typical and the antitypical Israels, and the empires, nations, and powers with which in the course of their long earthly histories they were to be brought more especially into contact. One large group of prophecies range themselves around the rise of the Jewish people, and a similar group clusters around its fall. The majority of these sacred predictions have in them, no chronological element, but in several, statements of time are embodied. The predictions we have now to pass in review, are the chronological prophecies, delivered about the time of the *fall* of the Jewish nation, by Isaiah, Jeremiah, and Daniel. Some of these prophecies are literal, and some symbolic. In the literal predictions, the chronological statements are made in plain terms, while in the symbolic, they are expressed on the year-day system, in harmony with the nature of the prophecy. The former generally relate to events near at hand, and were given for the benefit of the generation which received them, or of the immediately succeeding generations, while the latter foretell a remote future, and were given, less for the benefit of the men of that age, than for our admonition, on whom the ends of the world are come.

To the prophet who was privileged to receive these wonderful Divine revelations of the future, and to behold in vision mystic symbols of events to take place in the time of the end, it was said concerning them, "Thou, O Daniel, shut up the words, and seal the book, even to the time of the end;" and to others, as well as to this greatest of all chronological prophets, "it was revealed, that not unto themselves but unto us, they did minister" in their prophecies concerning the "sufferings of Christ, and the glories that should follow." These mystic revelations were not designed to be fully understood until after the lapse of ages, when the fulfilment of a portion should have thrown light on the meaning of the remainder, hence they were given in symbolic language, and their chronology expressed on the year-day system.

In this second class of prophecies are comprised Daniel's predictions as to the duration of the restored Jewish polity after the Babylonish captivity; the period to elapse before the advent and death of Messiah the prince, and the subsequent destruction of Jerusalem by the Romans, the rejection of the Jewish people, and desolation of their Sanctuary; the long course of the times of the Gentiles, with the events marking the close of that great dispensation; the resurrection of the dead; and the final blessedness of the righteous.

Thus, from the time of the prophet Daniel, right on over the first and second advents of Christ, and over all the intervening events, these far-reaching and majestic prophecies throw their Divine light, showing both the close of the Jewish economy, and the end of the Christian dispensation, and fixing beforehand, in mystic terms, the chronological limits of both.

They were not given for the wicked to understand, but for "the wise" to ponder in their hearts, and at the time of the end, when knowledge should be increased, to comprehend with ever growing clearness.

The predictions of the first, or literal class, which we shall have to consider are,—

1. That recorded in Isa. vii. 8; the "sixty and five years" foretold by the prophet, as to end in the cutting off of *Israel's* national existence by their Assyrian conquerors.

2. That given in Jer. xxv. 11; and xxix. 10; the "seventy years" twice predicted as the predetermined duration of that Babylonish captivity which was sent upon *Judah* as a punishment for sin.

3. The "thousand years" of the millennial reign of Christ. Rev. xx.

Those of the second, or symbolic class, which must pass under our review, are,

1. The "seventy weeks," or 490 years, foretold by Daniel as the interval destined to elapse between the *rebuilding* of *Jerusalem* and the advent and atoning work of the Messiah. Dan. ix.

2. The 2300 years, similarly predicted as the long extended period which would elapse before the final *cleansing* of *the Sanctuary*. Dan. viii.

3. The 1260 years predicted domination of the little horn, which is the assigned duration of other events also. This period is the base of several others. It is a half week ; "time times and a half," so we must consider the week of which it is half, the "seven times" or 2520 years of Gentile dominion : and it receives in Dan. xii. two additions, of 30 and 45 years, so it must be studied both alone, and *with its addenda, i.e.,* as 1290 and 1335 years. It is indeed the most important of these symbolic periods, and will repay the fullest investigation.

The periods we have to consider are therefore the following :—

65 years			.		Isa. vii. 8.
70 ,,	.	.			Jer. xxv. 11.
490 :		.	.	.	Dan. ix.
2300			.		Dan. viii.
1260 ,,	.	.		.	Dan. vii.
2520 ,,	.	.	.	.	Dan. iv.
1290 .	.	.	.	.	Dan. xii.
1335					,, ,,
30 :					
45 :		.	.	.	,, ,,
2595 .		.	.	.	,, ,,
1000 ,,	.	.	.	.	Rev. xx.

A little consideration will show a variety of beautiful and

harmonious relations between these apparently dissimilar and incongruous periods.

They are all proportionate parts of a great week of millenaries, and fit into each other, and into a framework of 7000 years, in a way that proves almost to demonstration, that they were designed so to do.

The 70 years of the Captivity may be regarded as *a day;* the 490 years of the restoration is then *a week* of such days; the 1260 years of the dominion of the little horn, is *eighteen* such days; the 2520 years of the times of the Gentiles is *thirty-six* such days (a tenth of 360 or *a year* of such days) and the 2300 years to the cleansing of the Sanctuary is a *third* of the whole period, the nearest third of seven millenaries, possible in centuries.

Of all these periods the *root* is evidently *the week of years,* the seven years which, under the Levitical economy, extended from one sabbatic year to another.

The 70 years during which the Babylonish Captivity was appointed to endure, were 10 such weeks, and the 490 years of the restored Judaism 70. The little horn was to reign 180 such weeks, and the " Times of the Gentiles " to extend over 360, or an entire *year* of such weeks, while the whole period of seven millenaries contains 1000 such weeks.

It must be remembered also that the Jubilee period established under the law of Moses, was *seven* such weeks, or 49 years ; so that the period of restored Judaism to the time of Messiah the Prince, was *a tenfold Jubilee,* or 490 years.

It should further be noted, that the *two principal* of these periods, the 2520 years, and the 2300 years, relate respectively the one to the THRONE, and the other to the SANCTUARY; the first embracing the whole period of Gentile *rule,* from the conquest of Judah by Nebuchadnezzar to the establishment of the *kingdom* of Christ, the true son of David ; and the other extending from the time of the Medo-Bersian kingdom, to the *final cleansing of the Sanctuary,* when Jerusalem ceases to be trodden down of the Gentiles, the Times of the Gentiles being fulfilled. The one is thus *civil*, and the other *sacred*, in character.

Harmonious and deeply significant mutual relations subsist therefore among these periods, and between them and the *legal and ceremonial times* established under the Mosaic economy. It remains to show that they are connected also with other periods of Jewish history, and that *though they are not all soli-lunar cycles, they form a series of septiform soli-lunar periods*, and that, of so marked and accurate character, as to preclude all thought of accidental coincidence, and to declare with unmistakable clearness the Creator's plan.

We proceed to consider them in detail.

THE SIXTY-FIVE YEARS OF ISAIAH VII. 8.

Chronological prophecy has always been given, not for seasons of prosperity, but for seasons of trouble and adversity : for nearly a thousand years,—ever since the prediction of Israel's forty years' wandering in the wilderness, it had been discontinued in Israel, when it was renewed shortly before the first captivity of the ten tribes, and continued at intervals during two centuries, up to the time of the last of Daniel's visions, and the restoration of Judah from Babylon.

In the year of the death of Uzziah,—the profane and presumptuous monarch who intruded into the Holiest, and was struck with leprosy in consequence,—there was granted to Isaiah the prophet a vision of the God of glory ; a vision of Christ the Lord, enthroned in heaven and adored, as the thrice Holy One, by the Seraphim.

The pollution and approaching rejection and desolation of Israel were also shown to him, and the future restoration of a remnant. This vision was immediately prior to the commencement of the " Times of the Gentiles," for it was given in the year of Uzziah's death ; and early in the reign of his grandson Ahaz, there was revealed to Isaiah the exact measures of the brief period that should elapse, before the commencement of the Captivity of Israel ; "*within sixty and five years shall Ephraim be broken, that it be not a people*" (Isa. vii. 8).

Called to his sacred office, and cleansed for it by a live coal from the altar applied to his lips, at this solemnly momentous crisis in the history of Israel, on the very verge of their incipient rejection by God, as his people, Isaiah was constituted *the evangelical prophet.*

He was commissioned to unfold the rejection and death of Messiah, the call of the Gentiles, and the final restoration of Israel. Through him, living as he did just before their incipient commencement, was revealed the general nature of the "Times of the Gentiles;" while to Daniel, living at their full commencement about a hundred and fifty years later, was revealed their duration, together with a multitude of important events, destined to take place during their course.

This *first* of the Captivity series of chronologic prophecies foretold the overthrow of the ten tribes only.

It dates from a well-marked epoch; a certain confederacy of the king of Syria, with Pekah king of Israel, and their joint invasion of Judah (B.C. 741).

This attack of the hostile allies, struck terror into the heart of Ahaz king of Judah, and into the hearts of his people; "their hearts were moved as the trees of the wood are moved with the wind" (Isa. vii. 2) ; and it was then that Isaiah the prophet was sent, to announce to the trembling king of Judah, as a message from Jehovah, the approaching downfall of one of his enemies. "*Within sixty and five years shall Ephraim be broken, that it be not a people.*"

This prediction received its fulfilment, in two stages. Shalmanezer, king of Assyria, came up against Samaria in the reign of Hoshea (B.C. 723) and after a siege of three years, took the city, carried Israel away into Assyria, placed them in Halah and Haber and other cities, and located colonies of Assyrians in the cities of Samaria, in their room. Subsequently, in 676 B.C., Esarhaddon the son of Sennacherib completed the work thus begun—carried away the remaining Israelites, replacing them by fresh parties of Assyrian colonists (from whom the Samaritans, with whom "the Jews have no dealings," sprung), and completing the destruction of Ephraim.

This period of sixty-five years stands chronologically thus,—

B.C. 741. SIXTY-FIVE YEARS TO EPHRAIM'S FALL. B.C. 676.

It comprised the period of the fall of the ten tribes, as distinguished from that of Judah; and its *close* synchronized with the *commencement* of Judah's captivities. It formed the gateway, so to speak, of the great seven times of Jewish desolation, for this completion of the judgment on the ten tribes, was quickly followed by the Babylonish captivity, and the total subjection of the entire Jewish nation to Gentile rule.

Now this period of sixty-five years, is not a soli-lunar cycle, but the solar gain on the lunar year during its course, is a septiform period, **seven hundred and seven days.**

SEVENTY YEARS.

By the mouth of Jeremiah, the weeping prophet, the Lord foretold a seventy years' captivity in Babylon, as the punishment shortly to overtake JUDAH for their long-continued sins of idolatry and obstinate rebellion against God. (Jer. xxv. 8–12.)

Unlike the judgment denounced against the ten tribes, to which no promise of speedy restoration was attached, a return to their own land was distinctly promised to Judah, at the expiration of this seventy years.

" Thus saith the Lord of hosts ; Because ye have not heard my words, behold, I will send and take all the families of the north, saith the Lord, and Nebuchadrezzar the king of Babylon, my servant, and will bring them against this land, and against the inhabitants thereof, and against all these nations round about, and will utterly destroy them, and make them an astonishment, and an hissing, and perpetual desolations. Moreover I will take from them the voice of mirth, and the voice of gladness, the voice of the bridegroom, and the voice of the bride, the sound of the millstones, and the light of the candle. And this whole land shall be a desolation, and an astonishment; and these nations shall serve the king of Babylon SEVENTY YEARS. And it shall come to pass, *when seventy years are accomplished*, that I will punish the king of Babylon, and that nation, saith the Lord, for their iniquity, and the land of the Chaldeans, and will make it perpetual desolations" (Jer. xxv. 8–12).

Towards the close of the captivity thus foretold, Daniel says, "In the first year of Darius . . . I Daniel understood by books the number of the years, whereof the word of the Lord came to Jeremiah the prophet, *that He would accomplish* SEVENTY YEARS *in the desolations of Jerusalem."*

Now this period of seventy years, is a remarkable one in many ways. It extends from the first destruction of Jerusalem by Nebuchadnezzar (2 Kings xxiv. 10; and Jer. xxv. 1), to the Edict of Cyrus for the return of the Jews, and the rebuilding of the temple (Ezra i. 2), that is to say, from B.C. 605 to the end of B.C. 536.

Its relation to the entire course of the history of the Babylonian Empire, and its chronological position *in* that history, must first be noted. The duration of that empire, dating from the era of Nabonassar (which is its own era), to the capture of Babylon by Cyrus, which preceded the restoration of the Jews, was 210 years; from B.C. 747 to B.C. 538.

Now 210 years, is *three times seventy years;* and the seventy years during which the captive Jews hung their harps upon the willows, and sat down and wept by the rivers of Babylon, almost exactly coincided with the closing third of the existence of the empire. In the year B.C. 538, Babylon fell, Darius the Median took the kingdom (Dan. v. 31), and the great Medo-Persian Empire succeeded the Babylonian.

This period of 210 years, is also *seven prophetic months* (30 × 7 = 210) so that the typical Babylon lasted seven such months, and the antitypical Babylon is twice over in the Apocalypse said to last six times seven—forty and two—such months. This is the period during which the symbolic holy city and temple court, are trodden under foot (Rev. xi. 2) and the period of the Beast (Rev. xiii. 5).

Seventy years was the life-time of the great king and sweet Psalmist of Israel, " David was thirty years old when he began to reign, and he reigned forty years " (1 Sam. v. 4). Moses the man of God, declares it to be the normal measure of human life, " The days of our years are threescore years and ten ; " and it is, as we have seen, the *day* of which other prophetic periods are multiples.

It is also ten times the sabbatic week of years, and indeed the Captivity may be regarded as a larger form of that week, during which the land, as God by Moses had threatened it should do, lay desolate and enjoyed its sabbaths.

Now this period, is astronomically, a soli-lunar cycle, in which the solar year gains on the calendar lunar year of 360 days, one entire year. *

The Seventy Weeks of Dan. ix.

When the seventy years of the Babylonish Captivity were nearly over, Daniel, " understanding by books " (the books of the prophet Jeremiah) that they must be well-nigh ended, gave himself to earnest supplication for his people, and about the city and Sanctuary, which, after a life-time of honourable exile, were still dear to his heart.

As David, when God had revealed to him his purposes of grace respecting his seed, cried, " O Lord God, the word that Thou hast spoken, establish it for ever, and do as Thou hast said ! " so Daniel, when he understood God's intention quickly

---

* Accurately, 367 days (a calendar lunar year, and a week) ; one day and a fraction in excess of the 365¼ days of the true solar year, but nearer to it, than would be the gain or epact of either 69 or 71 years, the nearest possible therefore.

to terminate the long captivity of the Jews, began to pray for the accomplishment of his purpose. What a lesson, that a knowledge of the purposes of God, so far from leading to a fatalistic carelessness about their accomplishment, should lead to earnest, believing, hopeful, supplication!

"Cause Thy face to shine upon Thy sanctuary! Behold the city that is called by Thy name! Defer not, O my God!" so pleaded this "man greatly beloved," this devout and intelligent student of prophecy, who became in his turn a prophet, and we may say, the prince of prophets.

While he was speaking in prayer, the answer was given. Gabriel was sent forth, commissioned to give him further understanding of the counsels of God, about the city and temple of Jerusalem, and the future fortunes of the Jewish nation.

Daniel's mind was full of the just expiring period of seventy years. Gabriel revealed to him, as determined by God, a new period of "seventy weeks." "Seventy weeks are determined upon thy people and upon thy holy city, to finish the transgression, and to make an end of sins, and to make reconciliation for iniquity, and to bring in everlasting righteousness, and to seal up the vision and prophecy, and to anoint the Most Holy. Know therefore and understand, that from the going forth of the commandment to restore and to build Jerusalem unto Messiah the Prince, shall be *seven weeks, and threescore and two weeks* : the street shall be built again, and the wall, even in troublous times. And *after threescore and two weeks shall Messiah be cut off,* but not for Himself : and the people of the prince that shall come *shall destroy the city and the sanctuary;* and the end thereof shall be with a flood, and unto the end of the war desolations are determined. And He shall confirm the covenant with many for *one week :* and *in the midst of the week* He shall cause the sacrifice and the oblation to cease, and for the overspreading of abominations He shall make it desolate [or, upon the battlements shall be the idols of the desolator], even until the consummation, and that determined shall be poured upon the desolate " [or, desolator].— Dan. ix. 24-27.

From the then approaching command to restore and to build again Jerusalem, to the coming of Messiah the Prince,—that grand goal of all Jewish expectations,—was to be "*seventy weeks.*" The event proved they were to be weeks of years, not of days ; the interval was to be a great week of Captivity periods, a week each of whose days should equal the seventy years of the Babylonish Captivity in duration. This had consisted of seventy *solar* years ; the new period was to include seventy *Sabbatic* years, 490 years. The reason why the chronology of this prediction is expressed in symbolic language, though all the rest is literal, is obvious.

It was needful so to word the prophecy, as to leave the Jews *free* to receive or reject Messiah when He should come, for He was not to be imposed on them against their will. His coming was to be a test : " It may be they will reverence my Son." Had the interval to the Advent been in the prophecy clearly defined as 490 years, Israel would not have been left free to say, as they alas ! did, " We will not have this man to reign over us." " He came unto his own, and his own received Him not." Messiah was, as predicted, cut off, which would hardly have been possible had the date of his appearance been beyond dispute. It was essential that the form of the prediction should not *compel* a recognition of Jesus of Nazareth : hence the adoption of language which time alone could interpret. A term of ambiguous meaning, though suggesting common weeks, was employed, and yet the larger reckoning was not by it excluded. On the contrary, it was the basis of the expectation of Messiah's immediate advent, so prevalent in Jerusalem when He did appear.

What then is this great period of four hundred and ninety years ?

In reply, let it first be noted that it was no new period in the history of Israel. It was their jubilee of forty-nine years on a larger scale, a tenfold jubilee measure ; and by it, previous

E E

chapters in their history had been regulated. It may be said indeed to be the peculiar period of the seed of Abram. The first stage of Jewish history from Abraham to the entrance into Canaan in the days of Joshua, is similarly a tenfold jubilee, a "seventy weeks," an interval of about 490 years. This was before actual jubilee reckoning began, for that was ordained to be from the time "when ye be come into your land." From Joshua's conquest of Canaan, B.C. 1585–6, to the commencement of the Jewish kingdom under Saul (B.C. 1096), was also, as far as can be ascertained, ten jubilees, or seventy weeks, that is 490 years, the period of the Judges, and of the prophet Samuel ;—the Theocracy of Israel.

From the accession of Saul, the *first* king (B.C. 1096), to the capture of Jerusalem by Nebuchadnezzar, in the days of the *last* king (B.C. 606), there elapsed ten jubilees more, another seventy weeks, or 490 years, the period of independent Jewish monarchy. So that *the* seventy weeks from the restoration to Messiah the Prince, was the fourth in a series of such periods, extending back to the days of Abraham, just as the seventy years of the Captivity was the third in a series of such periods, dating from the era of Babylon, the era of Nabonassar. God had *employed* both periods, before He *announced* either. This great period of 490 years is the connecting link between Old and New Testament times. Its closing portion was the period of the Advent, the atoning death, and the world redeem‧ing work of the Son of God.

The soli-lunar measures of four hundred and ninety years are as follows : they contain twenty-five lunar cycles ; and the solar gain on the lunar year in these twenty-five cycles, is twice seven lunar years and seven months.

There is a slight fractional remainder in years, the epact of which, added to that of the twenty-five lunar cycles, makes the epact of the whole 490 years, twice seven solar years and seven months, with a fractional remainder of about eight days, calculating by the *true* lunar and solar years. But calculating by the *Julian* solar, and *calendar* lunar years, the epact or difference is **seven calendar lunar years and seven weeks**, without remainder.

We may add, that in 490 years, *the equinoxes retrograde seven days.* Their annual retrogression is 20 m. 20 s., which amounts to seven days (within about two hours) in the " seventy weeks."*

THE " TIME TIMES AND A HALF," OR 1260 YEARS.
Dan. vii. 25.

This is the next link in the chain of chronological prophecy The period is mentioned, under different names, *seven times* in Scripture—in two chapters of Daniel, and three of Revelation. It is the duration assigned to,

1. The domination of the little horn over the saints	Dan. vii.
2. The closing period of Jewish dispersion .	Dan. viii.
3. The sojourn of the woman in the wilderness	Rev. xii.
4. The same, her flight from the serpent .	Rev. xii.
5. The treading under foot of the Holy City.	Rev. xi
6. The prophesying of the two witnesses .	Rev. xi.
7. The duration of "the Beast," or 8th head of the Roman Empire . . .	Rev. xiii.†

---

* We may also notice that the 49 years jubilee is a soli-lunar cycle, its error being one day and a fraction. In 490 years this error amounts to thirteen and a quarter days, or in whole numbers. *fourteen days, i.e., two weeks.*

† The following are the passages in which it occurs :—

1. Of the Little Horn of the fourth or Roman Empire it is said. "He shall speak great words against the Most High, and shall wear out the saints of the Most High, and think to change times and laws : and THEY SHALL BE GIVEN INTO HIS HAND UNTIL A TIME AND TIMES AND THE DIVIDING OF TIME. But the judgment shall sit, and they shall take away his dominion, to consume and to destroy it unto the end. And the kingdom and dominion. and the greatness of the kingdom under the whole heaven, shall be given to the people of the saints of the Most High. whose kingdom is an everlasting kingdom, and all dominions shall serve and obey Him " (Dan. vii. 25–27).

2. "And one said to the man clothed in linen, which was upon the waters of the river, How long shall it be to the end of these wonders? And I heard the man clothed in linen, which was upon the waters of the

It is of course evident that 1260 days are the same period as forty and two months ($30 \times 42 = 1260$), and that forty and two months are the same period as three years and a half

---

river, when HE HELD UP HIS RIGHT HAND AND HIS LEFT HAND UNTO HEAVEN, AND SWARE BY HIM THAT LIVETH FOR EVER, THAT IT SHALL BE FOR A TIME, TIMES, AND AN HALF; and when he shall have accomplished to scatter the power of the holy people, all these things shall be finished. And I heard, but I understood not : then said I, O my Lord, what shall be the end of these things? And He said, Go thy way, Daniel : for the words are closed up and sealed *till the time of the end.* Many shall be purified, and made white, and tried ; but the wicked shall do wickedly: and none of the wicked shall understand ; but *the wise shall understand.*" Connect verse 4, "But thou, O Daniel, shut up the words, and seal the book, even to the time of the end : *many shall run to and fro, and knowledge shall be increased*" (Dan. xii.).

3. It is the period of the sojourn of the woman in the wilderness. "And when the dragon saw that he was cast unto the earth, he persecuted the woman which brought forth the man child. And to the woman were given two wings of a great eagle, that she might fly into the wilderness, into her place, WHERE SHE IS NOURISHED FOR A TIME, AND TIMES, AND HALF A TIME, FROM THE FACE OF THE SERPENT" (Rev. xii. 13, 14).

4. "She brought forth a man child, who was to rule all nations with a rod of iron : and her child was caught up unto God, and to his throne. And THE WOMAN FLED INTO THE WILDERNESS, WHERE SHE HATH A PLACE PREPARED OF GOD, THAT THEY SHOULD FEED HER THERE A THOUSAND TWO HUNDRED AND THREESCORE DAYS" (Rev. xii. 5, 6).

5. It is the period of the treading under foot of the holy city. "And there was given me a reed like unto a rod : and the angel stood saying, Rise, and measure *the temple of God,* and the altar, and them that worship therein. But the court which is without the temple leave out, and measure it not ; for it is given unto the Gentiles : and THE HOLY CITY SHALL THEY TREAD UNDER FOOT FORTY AND TWO MONTHS" (Rev. xi. 1, 2).

6. It is the period during which the two witnesses prophesy. "And I will give power unto my two witnesses, and THEY SHALL PROPHESY A THOUSAND TWO HUNDRED AND THREESCORE DAYS, CLOTHED IN SACKCLOTH" (Rev. xi. 3).

7. It is the period of the Beast. "And I saw a beast rise up out of the sea, *having seven heads and ten horns,* and upon his horns ten crowns, and upon his heads the name of blasphemy. And the beast which I saw was like unto a leopard, and his feet were as the feet of a bear, and his mouth as the mouth of a lion : and the dragon gave him his power, and his seat, and great authority. And I saw one of his heads as it were wounded to death ; and his deadly wound was healed : and all the world wondered after the beast. And they worshipped the dragon which gave power unto the beast : and they worshipped the beast, saying, Who is like unto the beast? and who is able to make war with him? And there was given unto him a mouth speaking great things and blasphemies ; and POWER WAS GIVEN UNTO HIM TO CONTINUE FORTY AND TWO MONTHS" (Rev. xiii. 1-5).

$(42 \div 12 = 3\frac{1}{2})$, and that therefore, on the year-day principle, this seven times mentioned interval, is one of 1260 literal years ; *half* of the great week of " seven times," or 2520 years, which measures the Gentile dispensation.

It is primarily the period of the dominion of the little horn of the fourth beast of Daniel's vision. That beast as we know symbolised the Roman Empire ; and the little horn which had eyes and a mouth speaking great things, and which persecuted and wore out the saints of the Most High, represents a power which was to arise in the latter days of that empire, which would be *like* the other horns a *civil and political power*, and unlike them, at the same time, *a religious power*—unquestionably the Roman *Papal* dynasty.

The second symbol, to which the same period is attached is, as we have seen, the persecuting blasphemous eighth head of the Roman Beast, described in Revelation xiii. We have already shown that these represent one and the same power. They both rise in the latter stage of the Empire ; they both speak great words against the Most High ; they both wage war against the saints and overcome them ; and they both endure for this period. There cannot be *two* such powers, in the same days of the same Empire ; therefore these passages refer to the same power—the *Papacy*.

In Rev. xiii., a mysterious number is attached to this power, as " the number of his name," and special attention is called to it. " Here is wisdom, let him that hath understanding count the number of the Beast, for it is the number of a man, and his number is **six hundred, threescore, and six.**" **A trine of sixes,—666.**

Now in the Apocalypse especially, the number seven, is, as elsewhere throughout Scripture, prominent as the sacred number of perfection and completeness. The contents of the book which it represents as opened by the Lamb, is contained under seven seals, seven trumpets, and seven vials—*a trine of sevens*.

It is in *this* book that the number of the Beast is thus presented as a *trine of sixes*, and the contrast, as well as the intrinsic meaning of the numeral, intimates, that whatever else it may be, it is a perfect number of imperfection, or rather a number denoting *perfect imperfection.*

As this is the number of the Beast, we may expect to find it in various shapes in the chronology of the Beast, and in that of his most conspicuous Old Testament types. And *it is there;* a fact which has never before, we believe, been noted, but which is surely full of solemn importance. God has,—in secret cipher,—engraven this stigma, this mark of reprobation, on the very brow of the *period* of the self-exalting, blaspheming, saint-persecuting, power; and He has besides, in order that we may not fail to note the contrast, set it in the midst of a series of periods, whose septiform measures, bring out its peculiar and evil character.

There is nothing whatever sacred or septiform about this period, nothing sabbatic, nothing suggestive of rest, or worship, or liberty, as in the sevenfold sabbatic and jubilee series. Like some sounds in music, it is a discord, not a harmony; a symbol of what is imperfect and evil.

1. Twelve hundred and sixty years is, first, as we have seen, eighteen of the 70-years cycle. It is 6 + 6 + 6 such cycles.

2. And when we examine its lunar cycle measures we find that they similarly present a trine of sixes, for it is—

66 lunar cycles + 6 years.

(60 cycles + 6 cycles + 6 years).

Further; in the lunar cycles of this period, the sun's gain is 66 weeks of months, and in the 6 years remainder it is 66 days. Sixfold throughout! a clear link of connection between the number of the Beast and his period.

3. The dominion of the typical ancient Babylon over the typical Israel, lasted, as Clinton shows in his Chronology, accurately 66 *solar years,* for the remaining years of the Captivity were under the Medo-Persian power. The dominion of the antitypical modern Babylon, over the antitypical Israel—over captive Christendom—endures for 66 *lunar cycles, and 6 years.*

Another link between the *number* and the *period* of the Beast dependent on great, and apparent utterly disconnected facts, in the realms of history and astronomy.

4. It has been well said, that "history is prophecy," for all history has a tendency to repeat itself. But the saying is peculiarly true of Old Testament history. As Paul says of various incidents in the experience of Israel, " All these things happened unto them for ensamples (τύποι, types), and are written for our admonition, upon whom the ends of the world are come " (1 Cor. x. 11).

The literal Babylon was, as we have seen, a type of the spiritual Babylon—the Church of Rome ; and the great *king* of Babylon, the destroyer of the holy city and temple, the captor of the children of Judah, who set up a golden image of himself **60 cubits high and 6 broad** on the plains of Dura, and commanded all peoples nations and languages to fall down and worship it, and cast into a burning fiery furnace the faithful witnesses who refused—Nebuchadnezzar, who was a very incarnation of human pride, is a marvellous type of that Papal dynasty which is symbolised by the "little horn," and by "the beast." The Pope is the self-exalting monarch of the modern Babylon, who on a far wider scale commands all nations, and people, and languages, to bow down and adore him, and condemned to the flames the saints of the Most High, who refused compliance. The type-portrait is too like to be mistaken ; it has had but one antitype, the man who sits in the temple of God, showing himself as a God on earth, and claiming the infallibility of Deity. We ask then what was the *period* of this remarkably typical monarch, Nebuchadnezzar ?

Josephus tells us it was forty-three years, and the famous astronomical canon of Ptolemy confirms the statement ; as Clinton says, " The reign of Nebuchadnezzar is forty-three years, in all the copies of the canon of Ptolemy, and that number of years is also assigned to his reign by Berosus."

Applying the same standard as before, we look eagerly to see what are the soli-lunar measures of this singularly typical reign. and again the fatal trinity of sixes meets our view! The soli-lunar gain or epact in forty-three years is **sixty-six weeks, and six days. 66 weeks + 6 days.**

5. In considering the four hundred and ninety years' period, we observed, that whether regarded as consisting of true solar, or calendar lunar years, it equally afforded septiform results. when measured by soli-lunar epact. The elements of the calculation being different, the results are of course different, but *both are septiform.*

Similarly, with the period now under consideration, we have this true testimony of two witnesses. The twelve hundred and sixty years, may be taken either as true solar, or as calendar lunar years, the epact measurement affords in either case, *sixfold,* not sevenfold, results. Treating them as true solar and lunar years, they are, as we have seen, 66 lunar cycles and 6 years. Treating them as prophetic, or calendar years, on the other hand, we find **the gain of the true solar year in the whole period is 6606 days.***

There is a very noteworthy circumstance connected with this last measurement, to which we must direct attention. We have in a previous chapter spoken of the Reformation of the calendar effected by Pope Gregory XIII., A.D. 1582. But for the application to the period in question, of the more accurate measures of the solar year introduced by this Papal reformation of the calendar, the above results would have been hidden from view. The use of the *old style Julian year,* throws them out completely and make the solar gain in the 1260 years 6615 days. This is because the Julian year of $365\frac{1}{4}$ days is slightly in excess of the true solar year, and the error accumulates in this period to about ten days.

Now it will be remembered that Gregory XIII. cut off ten days from the year 1582, and commanded Christendom by a

---

* Accurately 6605 days and 7 hours, but in complete days, as above, 6606.

special Papal brief to count the 5th of October of that year as the 15th. *In this he legislated back for* 1260 *years*, thus changing times and laws for "a time, times, and the dividing of time," in remarkable agreement with the prophecy about the little horn.

This arose in the following way. The first general or Œcumenical Council, that of Nice, A.D. 325, had legislated with reference to the time of the observance of Easter. Gregory XIII. assumed this Council as a starting-point ; and as the error of the old Julian year, had, in the interval which had elapsed since the Council, thrown the vernal equinox out, by about *nine days and a half*, he arbitrarily ordained the removal of ten days from the calendar, at the same time that he introduced regulations to avoid irregularities in future.

Gregory XIII. died in A.D. 1585, *exactly* 1260 *years after the Council of Nice*, and his reformation of the calendar only came into use three years before his death, and that only in the Catholic countries which accepted it as a matter of course ; in Protestant Germany and Switzerland it did not take effect till A.D. 1700, and in England not till A.D. 1752.

It is a singular coincidence, to say the least of it, that this chronological legislation, emanating from the Pope who sanctioned and struck a triumphant medal, in memory of the bloody massacre of the Protestants of France, on St. Bartholomew's day, should have removed from a period of 1260 years (dating from the first General Council following the rise of *Imperial* Christianity) *the accumulated Julian error which concealed its true epact measures*, and that he should thus have unintentionally uncovered, as attached to it, one more form of the triple six, so solemnly linking *the period* with *the number* of the Beast.

The downfall of the temporal power of the Papacy is the event marking the close of this period of 1260 years, just as the rise of the Papacy marked its beginning ; and it is evident that neither of these events happened in a year, or indeed in a century. "Rome was not built in a day," it is commonly said ; and assuredly the Roman Catholic Church did not burst full-blown on the world. It rose into power gradually as the old Roman empire decayed and passed away; it had various marked *crises of rise*, and hence its great period of 1260 years, must have analogous successive termini, earlier and later, exactly as in the case of the Captivity era. The *earliest* possible conclusion of the period, is *the epoch of the Reformation.* Up to that time the saints had been delivered into the hand of this persecuting power without exception, and without appeal, or redress. Then, and thenceforward, a very considerable portion of Christendom was delivered from its spiritual and temporal oppression and tyranny. From the Council of Nice to the full end of the Reformation movement may therefore, perhaps, be regarded as an initiatory 1260 years.

The chronological legislation of Gregory XIII., took place at the close of this period, and corrected the error that had accumulated since its commencement. Sixtus V., who died five years after Gregory (A.D. 1590), was "the last pope who rendered himself formidable to European courts." From his time, to the present, Papal power has been passing through *its period of decline and fall,* just as from the fourth to the end of the sixth centuries, the system of the apostasy was gradually *rising and developing into the Papacy.*

A second and more evident and accurate measurement, is found by dating the 1260 years from the *Edict of Justinian,* which constituted the Bishop of Rome "*the head of all the Churches,*" A.D. 533. This date of the terminus *a quo,* gives as the terminus *ad quem* A.D. 1793, the time of the French Revolution, in the course of which, as we have seen, the Pope was carried captive from Rome, and the Papal power received a tremendous shock, from which it never fully rallied.

But the *main* reckoning of the period is unquestionably between the chronologic limits A.D. 606 *and* 1866-70, the former being the date at which the title of Pope, or universal bishop, was, by the Emperor Phocas, conferred upon Boniface III., and the latter, that of the overthrow of Austria and France, and the *consequent loss of the last vestige of temporal power, by*

Pius IX., when Victor Emmanuel moved his court to the Quirinal, and became sole king of united Italy. Then, and never quite *till* then, the Papacy, as a temporal power—a horn—ceased to exist. As a religion, it is destined to continue till the second advent of Christ, when the Lord will destroy it "with the brightness of his coming." The Beast is to be cast *alive* into the lake of fire, and therefore to be still in existence at the Epiphany.

To sum up : 1260 years, the foretold and fulfilled period of Papal domination in Christendom, and of the temporal political power of the Popes of Rome, has the following remarkable astronomic measures.

> 1260 years is **6 + 6 + 6 soli-lunar 70-year cycles;**
> 1260 years is **66 lunar cycles + 6 years.**
> 1260 years have **6606 days of epact.**

The 43-years type of the period of the Beast—the reign of Nebuchadnezzar,—whose image was 60 cubits high and 6 broad,—has

> **66 weeks + 6 days of epact.**

This period is then bound by multiplied links to the number of the Beast, **666.** And it is thus linked by *hidden* connections, not obvious ones; by great unobserved soli-lunar cycles, not by months and years of conspicuous recurrence ; linked therefore by the Hand that upholds the stars in their courses, by the Providence that orders all the events of history, and by the Mind that inspired the Apocalypse, and communicated to the man greatly beloved, the secrets of this "time of the end." "Known unto God are all his works from the beginning of the world."

The Two Thousand Three Hundred Years (Dan. viii.).

"And out of one of them [*i.e.*, one of the four kingdoms into which the empire of Alexander the Great was divided] came forth a little horn, which

waxed exceeding great, toward the south and toward the east, and toward the pleasant land. And it waxed great, even to the host of heaven : and it cast down some of the host and of the stars to the ground, and stamped upon them. Yea, he magnified himself even to the Prince of the host, and by him the daily sacrifice was taken away, and the place of his sanctuary was cast down. And an host was given him against the daily sacrifice by reason of transgression, and it cast down the truth to the ground ; and it practised, and prospered. Then I heard one saint speaking, and another saint said unto that certain saint which spake, [or to that wonderful numberer], How long shall be the vision concerning the daily sacrifice, and the making desolate [margin], to give both the sanctuary and the host to be trodden under foot ? And he said unto me, Unto two thousand and three hundred days [or evening-morning] ; then shall the sanctuary be cleansed.
I will make thee know what shall be in the last end of the indignation : for at the time appointed the end shall be. . . . In the latter time of their kingdom, when the transgressors are come to the full, a king of fierce countenance, and understanding dark sentences shall stand up. And his power shall be mighty, but not by his own power : and he shall destroy wonderfully, and shall prosper, and practise, and shall destroy the mighty and the holy people. And through his policy also he shall cause craft to prosper in his hand ; and he shall magnify himself in his heart, and by peace shall destroy many : he shall also stand up against the Prince of princes ; but he shall be broken without hand. . . . Shut thou up the vision; for it shall be for many days."

In the year 553 B.C., the third year of the reign of Belshazzar, and about fifteen years before his subjugation by Darius the Mede, there was granted to Daniel a third great symbolic vision, that of the ram and the he-goat, affording a fuller glance than the previous one, at the history of the *second* and *third* of the four great monarchies.

Given as it was at a time when the Babylonian Empire and Captivity were both rapidly drawing to a close, this vision naturally unfolds God's providence with regard to Israel and Palestine, under the MEDO-PERSIAN and GRECIAN empires. The symbols shown to Daniel prefigured their history with graphic accuracy : the successive rise of the two horns of the ram, foreshowing the sway of the two dynasties, which were afterwards merged in the great MEDO-PERSIAN monarchy ; the he-goat from the west,—with his rapid course, great strength,

wide dominion, and notable horn, abruptly broken, in the
plenitude of the goat's power, and replaced by four notable
horns,—prefiguring to the life the locality of origin, the character, the course of conquest, and subsequent history of the
Macedonian or Greek empire of Alexander the Great, as well
as its fourfold division consequent on his permature death. In
twelve brief years that European monarch overran and subdued all the fairest provinces of Asia ; and no sooner had he
reached the zenith of power than he died, and his empire, after
a period of confusion, was divided (subsequently to the battle
of Ipsus), among the four kings, Ptolemy, Seleucus, Lysimachus, and Cassander.

From one of these kingdoms, the prophecy foretells that
there would arise in the latter time a *little horn* which would
ultimately wax " exceeding great," greater apparently than the
" notable horn " itself, which is said to wax only " very great."

This " little horn " is evidently *a fellow* to the " little horn "
of the previous vision, only it rises, not amid the ten kingdoms
of the Roman earth, but from one of the four branches of
Alexander's Greek Empire. These four were, the SYRIAN kingdom of the Seleucidæ, the MACEDONIAN kingdom of Cassander, the EGYPTIAN kingdom of Ptolemy, and the kingdom of
Lysimachus, which included THRACE, BITHYNIA, and other
parts of Asia. It was from the kingdom of Ptolemy, as we
shall see presently, that this little horn arose. The direction of
the early conquests of this singular power, are distinctly given,
"toward the south, toward the east, and toward the pleasant
land." The main features of his conduct, as described in the
vision, are his self-exaltation against the Prince of princes,
his persecution of the saints, his taking away the daily sacrifice,
and defiling the sanctuary, and his casting down the truth to
the ground.

While beholding the vision, Daniel heard the question asked
of the " Wonderful Numberer" who made the revelation (apparently the Lord Himself), " *How long* shall be the vision
concerning the daily sacrifice, and the making desolate, to give

both the sanctuary and the host to be trodden under foot?" And it is in answer to *this* question, that the period we are considering is named.

"UNTO TWO THOUSAND AND THREE HUNDRED DAYS, *then* shall the sanctuary be cleansed."

Now, as this question was asked and answered before the close of the Captivity in Babylon, and when therefore the daily sacrifice and the sanctuary were not in existence, it is clear that this *prediction* of a *second destruction*, supposes *a prior restoration.*

This predicted period of 2300 years, commences, therefore, at some point in *the time of the restored national existence, and ritual worship of the Jews, and includes the entire period of their subsequent dispersion, and of the desolation of the sanctuary:* Its earliest possible starting point is the decree of Artaxerxes to restore and build Jerusalem; and, reckoned thus, its opening portion is the "seventy weeks," and its second portion the 1810 years which follow, and end in A.D. 1844, the terminus of so many prophetic times. (We previously mentioned that in this desolation period of 1810 years, the gain of the solar year on the lunar is 666 months.)

An important later starting point is *the era of the Seleucidæ,* or the era of the founder of the great *Syrian* dynasty which included *Antiochus Epiphanes*, the first of the three powers referred to in the prophecy, as defiling the sanctuary and causing the daily sacrifice to cease. Reckoned in *lunar* years from the era of the Seleucidæ (and it should be remembered that the long Mohammedan period of desolation which it *includes* is measured by *lunar* years) it terminates in A.D. 1919–20, or just 75 years later on, than when reckoned in *solar* years from the decree of Artaxerxes. Thus reckoned in *solar* and in *lunar* years from these two most important starting points, it terminates first *at the commencement* and then *at the close* of the last 75 years of the great "seven times" of prophecy.

The question may occur, *if* this prophecy embrace the whole period from the decree of Artaxerxes to the yet future restoration of Israel, why did the greatest event to take place in the course of those ages,—the first advent and death of Christ,— find no place in the revelation? The answer seems to be that the all-important coming and death of Messiah the Prince, and the events immediately subsequent, were to be fully treated in a revelation devoted entirely to themselves. They are similarly passed by in total silence, both in the vision of the four beasts, Chapter vii., and in that of the fourfold image, Chapter ii., though all three prophecies end with the *second* advent, or its connected events, the restoration of the throne to the seed of David, and the final cleansing of the sanctuary of Israel.

The place of paramount importance in this prediction, is given to the career and actings of an *Eastern* "little horn;" and our knowledge that the Papacy was the power predicted under the symbol of the Roman or *Western* "little horn" affords a clue to the meaning of this sister symbol.

The whole range of prophecy presents two, and only two, "little horns;" and the whole range of history presents two, and only two, powers, which exactly answer to the symbols; powers which, small and insignificant at first, gradually acquire empire on the ground of religion, and wax exceeding great by so doing; proudly oppose Christ, and fiercely persecute his people; repress and exterminate his truth; enjoy dominion for many long centuries (during which they tread down Jerusalem, either spiritual or literal), and perish at last under the judgment of God.

The Papacy does not stand out more distinctly as *the* great Apostasy of the West, than does Mohammedanism as *the* great parallel Apostasy of the East. The one originated from within the Church, the other from *without;* but *they rose together* in the beginning of the seventh century; they have run chrono· logically similar courses; they have both based their empire on religious pretensions; the one defiled and trampled down the Church, and the other defiled and trod down Jerusalem. In their life, they have been companion evils, and in their death they are not divided; for the one has just expired, politicallv, and the power of the other is fast expiring.

The Mohammedan power is, we think, unquestionably the main fulfilment of this symbol; but it is almost equally clear that it had a precursive fulfilment, on a smaller scale, in the person and history of ANTIOCHUS EPIPHANES. His career accords so closely with almost every feature of the prediction, as to leave little room for doubt that it was intended by the Holy Spirit, as one subject of the prophecy. For seventeen centuries all expositors, Jewish and Christian, held that the prophecy referred to Antiochus. The Books of Maccabees record his career with great detail, and trace in it, as does Josephus, the fulfilment of the predictions of this little horn. But Antiochus never waxed "exceeding great," he never "threw down the place of the sanctuary," though he took away the daily sacrifice; and he lived too near the time when the prophecy was given, to be the full and proper fulfilment of it, seeing it is said of the vision, "it shall be for many days," "at the last end of the indignation." Besides this, the time of the desolation effected by Antiochus,—just three years,—does not in any way, or on any system, correspond with 2300 days; so that we are driven to regard this, as one of those prophecies, which has undoubtedly had a double fulfilment, like Hosea xi. 1; or Psalm lxxii. Antiochus was a precursive little horn, Mohammedanism is the full and proper reality intended by the symbol.

A certain freedom in the construction of terms must be allowed in the case of all such double predictions, because the Holy Spirit, having more than one event in view, and selecting for description mainly those features which are common to both, may also introduce *some*, peculiar to the one or to the other.

Antiochus Epiphanes, the Romans, and the Mohammedans, have all taken part in accomplishing these predicted desolations of Jerusalem. The first two took away the daily sacrifice, the second cast down the sanctuary, all three have defiled the place of the sanctuary, and trodden it under foot, and by the last two especially have the "mighty and holy people" been "cast down," and "stamped upon," and "destroyed." But as the Roman power cannot be represented as "a little horn" arising out of one of the four kingdoms into which Alexander's empire was divided (Dan. viii. 9), whereas both Antiochus and Mohammed can, we conclude that they mainly are referred to in the prediction, and *especially the latter.*

It must be borne in mind that no sooner did the Roman Empire cease to tread down Jerusalem, than the Moslem power began to do so, and has continued to do so to this day. The utmost efforts of Christendom, expended in eight different crusades, failed to drive the Moslem out of the Holy Land ; for twelve centuries he has defiled the sanctuary, and stood up against the Prince of princes, casting down the truth to the ground, practising and prospering ; but it is written that when this period of 2300 years comes to an end, " he shall be broken without hand," and " then shall the sanctuary be cleansed."

First, then, with reference to the earlier of the two terminations of the 2300 years already named :—

B.C. 457 <u>*2300 years to the cleansing of the Sanctuary,*</u> A.D. 1844,—

Let it be remembered that all great movements have almost imperceptible commencements, just as great rivers spring from little brooks. Israel's restoration and the destruction of Mohammedan rule, *i.e.* "the cleansing of the sanctuary," are not events to be accomplished in a day or in a year, any more than the overthrow of the city and temple and national existence of the Jewish people, *was* accomplished in a day or in a year. From Ephraim's *earliest* down to Judah's *latest* captivity, a hundred and sixty-eight years elapsed ; and similarly at the restoration, from the first edict of Cyrus to the second of Artaxerxes, ninety-two years elapsed.

We need not marvel then to find that this *greater* restoration, from *this more than thirty times longer dispersion,* should apparently be destined to occupy a period of seventy-five years. In the year 1844, for the first time since the days of Mohammed,

F F

when the sanguinary laws of religious intolerance were enacted, the Turkish Sultan was obliged by the European powers, *to relinquish the practice of executions for apostasy and to make a decree granting religious toleration.**

---

* An abstract of the Parliamentary papers on this subject is given, as follows, by Rev. Edward Bickersteth :—

"The papers entitled 'Correspondence Relating to Executions in Turkey for Apostasy from Islamism,' were presented to Parliament, May 3, 1844, and having come before me through the kindness of Lord Ashley, I give the following abstract of them. The correspondence occupied a considerable part of a year—from Aug. 27, 1843, to April 19, 1844.

"The difficulties in the way were thus stated by the Grand Vizier, Aug. 24, 1843 : 'The laws of the Koran compel no man to become a Mussulman ; but they are inexorable, both as respects a Mussulman who embraces another religion, and as respects a person, not a Mussulman, who, after having of his own accord publicly embraced Islamism, is convicted of having renounced that faith. NO CONSIDERATION CAN PRODUCE A COMMUTATION OF THE CAPITAL PUNISHMENT, TO WHICH THE LAW CONDEMNS HIM WITHOUT MERCY. The only mode of escaping death is for the accused to declare that he has again become a Mussulman.' The same difficulties were pressed Dec. 1, 1843, when our Ambassador was assured, that although the Porte wished to avoid any recurrence of the atrocity, yet as *such executions were obligatory under the law, considered by Mohammedans Divine,* it would be embarrassing to give an official declaration. And again, Feb. 10, 1844, the Ottoman Minister for Foreign Affairs drew a strong line of distinction between custom and Divine law, intimating that a law prescribed by God Himself was not to be set aside by any human power ; and that the Sultan in attempting it might be exposed to a heavy, perhaps even a dangerous, responsibility.

"The causes of this intervention of the European Powers are remarkable. In August, 1843, an Armenian youth, who after, under fear of punishment, becoming a Turk, had returned to his Christian faith, was put to death. This called for the interposition of our Government and its serious remonstrances, and produced in November, 1843, some promises of terminating such affairs without capital punishment. In December, however, a young Greek, who had become a Mussulman, having returned to his own creed as a Greek Christian, at Biligik, adjoining to Brussa, was executed. This taking place in the midst of the correspondence, called forth Lord Aberdeen's decisive letter of Jan. 16. Thus we are indebted to the faithfulness of Greek and Armenian martyrs for this remarkable change. The energy put forth to accomplish this change required the concurrent exertions of the five European Powers—Austria, Prussia, France, Russia, and England.

"The able despatch of Lord Aberdeen of Jan. 16, 1844, is peculiar, and very honourable to our country. It is as follows,—

"'Despatch to Sir Stratford Canning, our Ambassador at the Porte, from the Earl of Aberdeen.

From that date to the present time, a process of elevation
and incipient restoration of Israel has been going on. It has
been so quiet, so gradual, so unobtrusive, that few have noticed
it; the turn of the tide has taken place, but the current has

---

" ' *Foreign Office, January* 16, 1844.

" ' SIR,—I have received your Excellency's despatch of the 17th of
December, reporting that a Greek had been executed near Brussa as an
apostate from Islamism, and enclosing a copy of the communication which
you had directed Mr. Dragoman Frederick Pisani to make to the Porte in
consequence of that transaction.

" ' I have to state to your Excellency that her Majesty's Government entirely approve the promptitude with which you acted on this occasion. But
the repetition of the scene of this revolting kind so soon after that which
had, in the course of last summer, excited the horror and indignation of
Europe, evinces such total disregard, on the part of the Porte, for the feelings and remonstrances of the Christian Powers, that it is incumbent upon
Her Majesty's Government, without loss of time, to convey their sentiments
on the matter still more explicitly to the knowledge of the Porte. They
take this course singly, and without waiting for the co-operation of the
other Christian Powers, because they desire to announce to the Porte a
determination which, though it doubtless will be concurred in by all, Great
Britain is prepared to act upon alone. Her Majesty's Government feel,
too, that they have an especial right to require to be listened to by the
Porte on a matter of this nature ; for they can appeal to the justice and to
the favour with which the vast number of Mohammedans subject to British
rule are treated in India, in support of their demand that all persons,
subjects of the Porte, and professing Christianity, shall be exempt from
cruel and arbitrary persecution on account of their religion, and shall not be
made the victims of a barbarous law, which it may be sought to enforce for
their destruction. Whatever may have been tolerated in former times, by
the weakness or indifference of Christian Powers, those Powers will now
require from the Porte due consideration for their feelings as members of a
religious community, and interested as such in the fate of all who, notwithstanding shades of difference, unite in a common belief in the essential
doctrines of Christianity ; and they will not endure that the Porte should
insult and trample on their faith by treating as a criminal any person who
embraces it. *Her Majesty's Government require the Porte to abandon, once
for all, so revolting a principle.* They have no wish to humble the
Porte by imposing upon it an unreasonable obligation ; but as a Christian
government, the protection of those who profess a common belief with
themselves, from persecution or oppression, on that account alone, by their
Mohammedan rulers, is a paramount duty with them, and one from which
they cannot recede. Your Excellency will therefore press upon the Turkish
Government, that if the Porte has any regard for the friendship of England
—if it has any hope that, in the hour of peril or of adversity, that protection,
which has more than once saved it from destruction, will be extended to it
again, it must renounce absolutely, and without equivocation, the barbarous
practice which has called forth the remonstrance now addressed to it. Your

not yet set sufficiently strongly in the other direction, to attract attention, yet the careful observer cannot fail to note the evident and rapid fall of Turkey and the incipient revival of Palestine. Jerusalem has not yet ceased to be trodden under

---

Excellency will require an early answer; and you will let the Turkish Ministers understand that if that answer does not fully correspond with the expectations which Her Majesty's Government entertain, your Excellency is instructed to seek an audience of the Sultan, and to explain to his Highness, in the most forcible terms, the feelings of the British Government, and the consequences, so injurious to Turkey, which a disregard for those feelings will involve. Her Majesty's Government are so anxious for the continuance of a good understanding with Turkey, and that the Porte should entitle itself to their good offices in the hour of need, that they wish to leave no expedient untried before they shall be compelled to admit the conviction that all their interest and friendship is misplaced, and that nothing remains for them but to look forward to, if not promote the arrival of, the day when the force of circumstances shall bring about a change which they will have vainly hoped to procure from the prudence and humanity of the Porte itself.

" ' Your Excellency will seek an interview with the Reis Effendi, and having read to him this despatch, leave a copy of it, with an accurate translation, in his hands.

" ' I am, etc., (Signed) ABERDEEN.' "

Count Nesselrode's despatch of February 27, 1844, on the part of the Russian Government, is instructive as opening out the weakness of the Ottoman Government. "It is the Emperor's intention that you should declare to the Ottoman Porte, in the form of friendly counsel, that we positively expect no longer to witness executions which array against it the indignation of all Christendom. It is with a view to its own interest, that we address to it this demand. The Porte must not delude itself with regard to the elements now in a state of fermentation in Turkey. Instead of alienating from itself the feelings of the Christian population, the Ottoman Government ought more than ever to labour to conciliate them to itself."

The magnitude of the question is thus forcibly stated, February 22, 1844, by the Turkish minister. "No fresh step was requisite to make us sensible of the importance of this question, with which we are deeply impressed. We are dealing with it with all the seriousness and all the care which its gravity requires. Yes, what your respective chiefs say is true; this question has its political as also its religious side. It is requisite, in fact, that we should separate ourselves from the nation, or otherwise from the Christian Powers; those are two great evils to be equally avoided. The Sultan has commanded that this question shall be discussed in the council of Oulemas, which will be opened on next Saturday, at the Sheik-ul-Islam's, to which the Gazi-Ashes, and the other principal persons among the men of the law will be summoned; after which the council of ministers will again apply themselves to it. Do not suppose, however, that we have confined ourselves to directing their attention, purely and simply, to the

foot ; but what of the two great Powers which for eighteen hundred years (with a few brief intervals) have successively trodden her down—Rome, and the various forms of that Mohammedan power, whose present head is Turkey?

question as it regards religion: we have likewise submitted to them the protocols of the conferences, the despatches of the two Governments, and even the extracts of the newspapers which have discussed this question ; and we shall likewise communicate to them the instructions which you have just delivered to me, and which, although superfluous as far as the Porte is concerned, may still add to the impression produced by the other documents in their hands."

In communicating the Queen's approbation, April 19, 1844, to Sir Stratford Canning, Lord Aberdeen ends the correspondence with these words, "You have brought to a successful close a question of which the importance cannot be too highly rated." Events will show the truth of these words.

The Porte, even on the 14th of March, 1844, would have put off the European Powers with a statement that the law did not admit of any change ; but such measures as were possible should be taken. The Ambassadors of the European Powers refused to receive this.

At length, on the 21st March, 1844, the question of religious execution was, as our Ambassador observes, "happily and, to all appearance, conclusively settled. The concession has been obtained with great difficulty; and even to the last moment it required the firmness of resolution, inspired by your Lordship's instructions, to overcome the obstacles which were raised against us."

He inclosed in this letter the following "Official Declaration of the Sublime Porte, relinquishing the practice of Executions for Apostasy."

(Translation.)

" It is the special and constant intention of His Highness the Sultan that his cordial relations with the High Powers be preserved, and that a perfect reciprocal friendship be maintained, and increased.

"THE SUBLIME PORTE ENGAGES TO TAKE EFFECTUAL MEASURES TO PREVENT HENCEFORWARD THE EXECUTION AND PUTTING TO DEATH OF THE CHRISTIAN WHO IS AN APOSTATE.

" March 21, 1844."

To this must be added the following " Declaration of His Highness the Sultan to Sir Stratford Canning, at his audience on the 22nd of March, 1844.

" Henceforward neither shall Christianity be insulted in my dominions, nor shall Christians be in any way persecuted for their religion."

" The date of the official declaration, March 21, is very remarkable as being in fact THE FIRST DAY OF NISAN, the first sacred month of the Jews. And this is the more remarkable, as IT IS CONNECTED WITH THE TERMINATION OF THE REMARKABLE DATE OF 2300 YEARS."

" It will be observed that Ezra is very specific in stating the dates

Rome trod down Jerusalem in the days of Titus, and Turkey holds her down now. "Rome cast her to the ground, and when she was down, Turkey set its foot on her neck. Rome hurled her to the dust, Turkey trampled her in the mire ; Rome

---

B.C. 457. On the first day of the first month began he to go up from Babylon (Ezra vii. 9) B.C. 457. And they made an end with all the men that had taken strange wives by the first day of the first month (Ezra x. 17). The whole time of the return and restoration taking exactly a year."

The prophecy of this period is in these words (Dan. viii. 13, 14): "How long shall be the vision of the daily sacrifice, and of the transgression of desolation, to give both the sanctuary and the host to be trodden under foot ? And he said unto me, unto two thousand and three hundred days (or evening-morning) ; then shall the sanctuary be cleansed." (For the proof of this being the period of 2300 years, the reader is referred to Birks' "Elements of Prophecy," pp. 356-363.) Ezra's commission for the restoration of the sacrifice (Ezra vii. 15 ; viii. 35) was 457 years B.C. The period of a year was occupied in his return, and the cleansing of the sanctuary, that is to B.C. 456 (Ezra vii. 9 ; x. 17.) The restoration of sacrifice continued with slight exceptions, to the destruction of Jerusalem by the Romans, since which Jerusalem has been trodden down of the Gentiles, to the period of March 21, 1844 ; this period, according to the Jewish year, ending March 20, 1844, makes 2300 years ; and on the 1st of Nisan, 1844, the power of the Mohammedans to persecute Christianity passed away, and liberty is given for Christian worship, the true cleansing of the sanctuary. THIS IS THE MORE REMARKABLE ALSO AS THIS IS THE 1260th YEAR OF THE HEGIRA (the date fixed by the Mohammedan Antichrist as the rise of this branch of the Apostasy) and so the closing year in Mohammedanism of that remarkable prophetical period, 1260 years. In a letter from Tangiers, dated June 20th, 1844, given in the public journals, speaking of the difficulties besetting the kingdom of Morocco, it is stated, "It seems that the Moors have always had forebodings of this year. For a long time they have been exhorting each other to beware of 1260 (that is, of the Hegira), which according to our reckoning is the present year."

"It was a common remark in Egypt in 1839, 'The spirit of the Arab is gone.' Events in Sidon, Acre, Persia, India, Affghanistan, Bokhara, Algiers, illustrate the same view."

"Another material point connected with this event is the passing away of the Turkish Woe. It is the general voice of Christian interpreters, that the sixth angel sounding the second Woe Trumpet, describes the Turkish Woe. We have in this event a most remarkable feature of the ending of that woe. The importance of this fact will be seen by the prophecy (Rev. ii. 14-18), 'The second woe is past ; and behold, the third woe cometh quickly. And the seventh angel sounded ; and there were great voices in heaven, saying, The kingdoms of this world are become the kingdoms of our Lord, and his Christ, and He shall reign for ever ;' and immediately associated with this is the coming of God's wrath, and the time of the dead that they shall be judged. We are therefore clearly on the verge of these great events."—*Bickersteth*, "*Guide to the Prophecies*," *Ninth Edition*, p. 341.

destroyed God's temple and ploughed up the sacred site on which it stood, Turkey maintains the Mosque of Omar on that sacred site ; and on the holy hill where Abraham offered Isaac, where David offered the oxen of Araunah, where Solomon built his temple, and where the Lord Jesus, the Son of David, cast out all that was unholy, there, by Turkish authority now stands a Mohammedan mosque, and there no Jew is permitted even to set his foot." *

But Pagan Rome passed away long since, and Papal Rome is no longer a political power in the earth ; the first oppressor is gone, and Turkey, the second, is fast going. " The foot of the sick man is the only one now remaining on the neck of Jerusalem, and the sick man is dying ; when he dies, why should not Jerusalem arise and be free ? " Every step in the downfall of Turkey, is a step in the direction of the cleansing of the sanctuary, and these steps are in our day succeeding each other rapidly. Since 1821, Turkey has lost Greece and Servia, Moldavia and Wallachia, Morocco, Algeria, and Egypt; and now in the recent war, Bosnia, Herzegovina, and Bulgaria. The once mighty Ottoman Empire is in Europe practically extinct. Its power in Asia is also seriously diminished, and notably so in Syria. Aliens, or non-Mussulmans, are now allowed to hold landed property in Palestine, and the number of Jews resident in their own land is every year on the increase. Thousands of intelligent Christians visit its shores annually, and the Palestine Exploration has completed a survey of its every square mile " Thy servants take pleasure in her stones, and favour the dust thereof." There is every sign, when the present is contrasted with the past, that the time for the complete liberation of Palestine from Moslem tyranny is at hand.

The second starting-point from which these 2300 years may be dated is the era of the Seleucidæ, B.C 312. The Seleucidæ were the race of monarchs (descended from Seleucus Nicator, one of the four notable horns of the he-goat,) from which ANTIOCHUS EPIPHANES sprung.

---

* " ROME, TURKEY, AND JERUSALEM," by Canon Hoare.

As this era of the Seleucidæ, long used by the Jews themselves, and still employed by the Nestorians and other Eastern nations, is dated from the great foun· der of the dynasty of the precursory "little horn," it is not an unsuitable point of departure. The period of 2300 years measured from *it*, and reckoned in lunar years, runs out in A.D. 1919-20, *seventy-five years* later than its first termin- ation in 1844, and the same year as the *main* measurement of the Times of the Gentiles, dated from Nebuchadnezzar's over- throw of Jehoiakim, B.C. 602.

B.C. 3 1 2, 2300 LUNAR YEARS FROM THE ERA OF THE SELEUCIDÆ, A.D. 1919-20.

It remains to show that the soli-lunar measures of 2300 years assign to it a place in the great septiform series of prophetic times.

The sun gains on the moon in this vast period of twenty- three centuries **seventy lunar years and seven months.***

2520 Years, or "Seven Times" (Dan. iv.).

As we have already considered this period pretty fully (p. 341) as to its distinctive moral characteristics, and as to its historical chronological features (p. 369), we need in this place dwell only on its arithmetical peculiarities and astronomic measures. It is the great dispensational week, the arc of time which spans alike each of the three moral divisions of human history ; it is the period of the fourfold image of Gentile rule, which is to introduce the everlasting kingdom of the Son of God. It is the most important of all the prophetic periods, and the oft· repeated 1260 years of the Apostasy, is its second half.

---

* The accuracy of these measures is very striking. In 2300 years there is a remainder of one year over and above 121 lunar cycles ; and the solar gain of this one year, just makes up for the loss occasioned by the 121 repetitions of the small error of the lunar cycle, so that the solar gain is as stated above, within *less than a quarter of a day ;* 2300 years is, in fact, as we have before said, the most perfect secular soli-lunar cycle known.

With regard to it we note in the first place, that 2520 is arithmetically a most remarkable number; a number as distinct from all other numbers as the circle is from all other forms. It is not a number that could possibly have been selected by chance, or put inadvertently into the important position it occupies in the prophetic word. Its selection in preference to all other numbers, is an indication of intelligent design which candour cannot fail to recognise. The omniscient God has deliberately passed by all other conceivable numbers, any one of which might have been made the basis of chronologic prophecy, that He might select, to occupy this position, a number which is *sui generis*, altogether unique, one which stands forth by its very nature as a king among other numbers, conspicuous and paramount. 2520 *is the least common multiple of the first ten numbers;* in other words, it is the first in the entire series of numbers, that is exactly divisible by all the first ten numerals.

1	is contained in it	2520	times without remainder.
2	,,	1260	,,
3		840	
4		630	
5		504	
6		420	
7		360	
8		315	
9		280	
10	,,	252	,,

Now *ten*, be it remembered, is a natural numerical radix, employed in Scripture and in world-wide use, so that the first *ten* numbers form a complete and fundamental series, and their least common multiple is a great fundamental number in arithmetic.

It is like a complex crystal, capable, from its very nature, of numerous regular divisions, and it is adapted to harmonize in one several series of periods of different orders and magnitudes, in a way that no other conceivable number could do. Is it by chance that *this* is the number of years of the great " seven times," which is the vertebral column of prophetic chronology ?

Further : perfect arithmetically, 2520 years is also perfect astronomically. It contains 132 lunar or Metonic cycles, in which the epact amounts to—

seventy-seven lunar years.

Over and above these cycles there is a remainder of twelve years, which raises the epact of the entire period to—

seventy-five solar years.

Now, here we are confronted with another startling fact, a fact which it will puzzle the ingenuity of sceptics to account for, a fact which must have been unknown to Daniel, for the state of astronomic science in his day (nearly six centuries B.C.), was such that he could not have been acquainted with it ; yet a fact which is absolutely indisputable, and which a very short calculation will demonstrate. In the last chapter of Daniel the angel intimates to the prophet in answer to his chronological inquiries, that while the scattering of the power of the holy people, should terminate at the end of the second half of the 2520 years, yet that there should be additions of thirty and forty-five years, before the era of full blessedness would arrive. (Dan. xii. 11–13.) In other words, to the long period of 2520 years Scripture adds a brief period of seventy-five years, and as we have just seen, astronomy does the same. **The difference between 2520 true lunar and the same number of true solar years is seventy-five years. In other words, the seventy-five years added in the prophecy is exactly equal to the epact of the whole " seven times."** If 2520 lunar, and the same number of solar years begin together, the former will run out seventy-five years before the latter. The seventy-five years added to the " Times of the Gentiles " are equal to the epact of that great dispensational period.

Was it by chance that Daniel lit upon these two periods, so widely dissimilar, and which yet bear to each other *this remarkable astronomic relation ?* Impossible ! as impossible as that he could either have known that 2300 years (Chap. viii.) was a soli-lunar cycle, or that he could have selected by *chance* the exact number of years in that cycle, as the period of the restored temple and subsequent desolation of the sanctuary. Such coincidences are not the work of chance. Such Bible statements must be accepted with reverential awe, as evidences that the Divine mind which planned the universe, inspired also the sacred Book.

In these added seventy-five years, having this peculiar astronomic character, we see also one of those evidently intentional elements of uncertainty which meet us so frequently in chronofogic prophecy. Just as it would be impossible, prior to fulfilment, to say which of several probable eras was the real commencing era of the seventy years captivity, and hence of the " Times of the Gentiles," so it is impossible in this case to decide, whether these *added* seventy-five years are to have an inclusive fulfilment in 2520 solar years, or an added fulfilment, or both. Regarding the 2520 years as lunar, and dating them from 598 B.C., which, as we have seen, is the *latest* commencement of the " Times of the Gentiles," they terminated A.D. 1848, and we are now living in the interval created by the inequality of solar and lunar movements during the lapse of the whole " seven times."

But if the 2520 years be regarded as *solar* years, and dated from the same commencing era, they do not terminate, as we have seen, until A.D. 1923, and the concluding seventy-five years may possibly be added to that date. But the prophecy implies an *end* at the *beginning* of this supplementary seventy-five years; a fuller and more blessed end at the close of their first section—30 years (a month) of years; and the fullest and most blessed terminal point at the close of the supplementary forty-five years; that is, at the close of the whole seventy-five. What mysteries are here indicated who shall say? The full establishment of Messiah's kingdom on earth may, even after his glorious epiphany, be a work of time. The downfall of the "little horn" seems to be the event presented in the prophecy as marking the first close. No *events* at all are assigned to the other two chronological points. They are simply indicated, and a character of final blessedness is stamped on the last; but this is all. It is vain to speculate where Scripture affords no clue. "The secret things belong unto God, but the things that are revealed to us and our children."

"Twelve Hundred and Ninety Days" (Dan. xii. 11).

We must briefly glance at the two periods of thirty years and forty-five years, by which the main period of 1260 years, the latter half of the "Times of the Gentiles," is lengthened.

The glorious One, who makes this final revelation to Daniel, swears by Him that liveth for ever and ever, that "time, times, and half a time," 1260 years, should bring to an end the scattering of the holy people, and the "wonders" of judgment which had been foretold to the prophet. Daniel, longing to know more, inquires, "O my Lord, what shall be the end of these things?" The answer is a refusal *at that time* to reveal more, or make plainer what had been revealed, coupled with an intimation that in the time of the end the prophecy should be better understood. "Go thy way, Daniel, for the words are closed up and sealed till the time of the end." In the meantime he is assured that the blessed sanctifying work of God in individual souls would go on, in spite of national apostasies and the machinations of the Evil One. "Many shall be purified, and made white, and tried, but the wicked shall do wickedly; none of the wicked shall understand" (these prophecies apparently), "but the wise shall understand." And then the great Revealer adds one or two further mysterious chronological hints, evidently designed for the guidance of the saints at the time of the end, which show plainly, what the analogy of the Captivity period not indistinctly intimates, that the time of the end, brief as it is when compared with the "time, times, and a half," and very brief when compared with the whole "seven times," is yet a *period*, and not a *point*—a course of years, not a crisis; that the full end is to come *gradually*, not suddenly

Thus the rising and falling of the waters of the flood were gradual; the enslaving and the redeeming of Abraham's seed from Egyptian bondage were gradual; the downfall of Jewish monarchy was by stages, and the final expulsion of the Jews from their land was equally gradual and by stages. These closing verses of Daniel prove beyond a doubt that the elevation of Israel, and the introduction of millennial blessedness, will also be gradual, and that marked stages will occur in its course.

" From the time that the daily sacrifice shall be taken away, and the abomination that maketh desolate set up, there shall be a thousand two hundred and ninety days. Blessed is he that waiteth and cometh to the thousand three hundred and five and thirty days."

The remarkable feature about these two closing chronological statements is, that *they name no terminal event;* the former does not even suggest any; the latter only implies that its close will introduce the era of blessedness. The emphatic " blessed is he that waiteth and cometh " to it, recalls the " Blessed and holy is he that hath part in the first resurrection," of Rev. xx.; and we may probably assume that the 1335 days is, in the fullest sense, "*the end,*" to which the Angel alludes in his closing words ; " Go thou thy way till the end be, for thou shalt rest (in death), and stand (in resurrection) in thy lot at the end of the days " (*i.e.,* of these 1335 days, or years).

In considering the 1290 years, we note that it passes beyond the limits of the primary period by thirty years, or ONE PRO- PHETIC MONTH.

As no event marking its close is given, in the prophecy, it is impossible to decide whether it is to be added to the *earlier* or to the *later* close of the " seven times," and its second half, the 1260 years of the domination of the Desolator.

Astronomically, *thirty years is a soli-lunar cycle in which the* solar year and the lunar month agree within a day.

In the whole 1290 years the epact amounts to the septiform period of 2004 weeks, or 14,028 days.

THIRTEEN HUNDRED AND THIRTY-FIVE DAYS (Dan. xii. 12).

Forty-five years more are in ver. 12 added to 1290, making 1335 years, carrying us seventy-five years beyond the termination of the Times of the Gentiles, and introducing the era of full blessedness.

An analogous forty-five years terminated in the inheritance of the typical rest of Canaan. It will be remembered that Caleb, when appealing to Joshua to give him the promised possession, said, "The Lord hath kept me alive these forty and five years, ever since the Lord spake this word unto Moses, while the children of Israel wandered in the wilderness, and now I am this day fourscore and five years old . . . Now therefore give me this mountain whereof the Lord spake in that day. And Joshua blessed him, and gave unto Caleb the son of Jephunneh, Hebron for an inheritance, and the land had rest from war" (Josh. xiv. 10–13).

Forty-five years was also a terminal period in the history of the Jewish dispensation. Our Lord's crucifixion took place in the year A.D. 29, and his ministry began 3½ years previously, or in the year A.D. 25 ; the destruction of Jerusalem by Titus was in the year A.D. 70, forty-five years from the commencement of our Lord's ministry.

The soli-lunar measures of this brief terminal period are strikingly septiform. During its course the sun gains on the moon **seventy weeks, or 490 days.**

In the whole period of "1335 days," or years, there are seventy lunar cycles, and five years over. The epact of these five years is 54 to 55 days, from which the slight error of the lunar cycle has to be deducted. In 1335 years this error amounts to nearly a week ; the result is, that the solar gain during the whole 1335 years is **seventy weeks of months, and seven weeks of days.**

Measured by the prophetic, or calendar year, the solar gain on the calendar year of 360 days in the 1335 years is **a thousand weeks.**

Two Thousand Five Hundred and Ninety-five Years.

These two brief periods of thirty and forty-five years make together 75 years, and are added to the second half of the great "seven times" of prophecy; if we consider them as *added* to the *whole* "seven times," or 2520 years, they raise that period to 2595 years.

We may therefore, in closing, glance at the astronomic measures of this period. It contains 136 lunar cycles, and the solar gain over the lunar year in this period, is

seventy-seven solar years.

In other words, this comprehensive period consists of

seventy-seven soli-lunar cycles.

There is a remainder of eleven years, which—minus the accumulations of the small error of the lunar cycle—gives an additional septiform solar gain of fourteen weeks, making the epact of the whole accurately

seventy-seven solar years, and twice seven weeks.

Grouping together the epacts of the prophetic times, we observe among them a striking similarity, and indications of the existence of some underlying law inviting research.*

I. Epacts of the Prophetic Times, as measured by True Solar and Lunar Years.

Prophetic Times.	Epacts.
45 years	Seventy weeks of days.
65 ,,	Seven hundred and seven days.
490 ,	Twice seven solar years, and seven months.
1290 ,,	Twice seven thousand and four times seven days (two thousand and four weeks).
1335 ,,	Seventy weeks of months, and seven weeks of days.
2300 .	Seventy lunar years, and seven months.

* See Appendix A.

2520 years	.	Seventy-five solar years.
2595 „	.	Seventy-seven solar years, and twice seven weeks.
1000 „	.	A month of solar years.
1260 ;		Sixty-six weeks of months, and sixty days.
1810 „	.	Six hundred and sixty-six months.

II. Epacts of the Prophetic Times, as measured by the Prophetic, or Calendar Year of 360 Days.

Prophetic Times.	Epacts.
70 years	One calendar year and one week.
490 „	Seven calendar years and seven weeks.
1335 „ .	A thousand weeks.
2300 ;	Thirty-three solar years.
1000 „ .	Twice seven calendar years and seven months.
1260 „ .	Thrice six calendar years, and thrice six weeks; or six thousand six hundred and six days.

CHAPTER V.

W E have shown in the foregoing chapters, that the leading prophetic times are accurate astronomic cycles,
cycles not remote from terrestrial affairs, but connected with
our ordinary calendar measurements of time—cycles harmonizing, more or less perfectly, the unequal yet intimately related
solar and lunar revolutions.

We have also shown that the epacts of these prophetic times
form, with one peculiar exception, a remarkable series of septiform periods or weeks, of years, months, weeks, and days;
and that, in the one instance where it is not septiform, the
epact assumes a strikingly *sixfold* character, in harmony with
the sixfold number, attached by Divine inspiration to the power
of which that period is the duration.

These prophetic times become in due course *historic times;*
and the question naturally arises, Will this principle of
epact measurement yield analogous results, when extended to
other historic times, and to the whole chronology of human
history ?

In what follows we must endeavour to show that it does,
and that a marvellous law of harmonious proportion is clearly
observable between the chronology of certain *types* of the
course of redemption history and that of the actual *events*
typified—the reality being to the chronological type, not as a
year to a day, but as a *soli-lunar cycle* to a day. And what is
still more remarkable is that this cycle—a cycle whose epact
is exactly one solar year, *measures the most important period*

G G

in all human history—the earthly lifetime of our Lord Jesus Christ.*

We ask special attention to this statement. The evidence which justifies it amounts—not to demonstration, for the nature of the case forbids this—but to so high a degree of probability, as to be almost moral certainty, and the fact, if it be such, is a deeply interesting and important one, indicating another underlying link of connection between the assertions of Scripture history, and the phenomena of astronomic science.

A brief consideration of the statements of the New Testament on the period in question is needful here.

We learn from St. Luke that at the time of his baptism, when the Holy Ghost, in bodily shape like a dove, descended on Him to anoint Him for his ministry, and when the voice from heaven proclaimed Him the beloved Son of God, " Jesus Himself began to be about thirty years of age."

His entrance on his career of public service to God at this age, was in accordance with the principles of the Levitical Law, and with the practice of the Levites. Thirty years of age is the time of mental, moral and physical maturity—a man's prime. " From *thirty years old* and upward, until fifty years old, shalt thou number them," was the law respecting the Levites, " all that enter in to perform the service, to do the work in the tabernacle of the congregation." This is seven times reiterated in the fourth of Numbers (vv. 3, 23, 30, 35, 39, 43, 47).

David a type of the Messiah, began to reign at this same age. " David was *thirty years old* when he began to reign, and

---

* In every solar year there is an excess of ten days and twenty-one hours, or nearly eleven days, over the lunar year, *i.e.*, over the year as measured by twelve revolutions of the moon, so that when the sun commences his second round, the moon is between ten and eleven days behind hand. In three solar years, the moon has fallen back rather more than a month, in nineteen years it has retrograded seven months, and in 33 years, 7 months and 7 days, it has fallen back *one solar year*. This period is therefore A SOLI-LUNAR CYCLE of a certain order, and seven such periods, or 235 solar years, is a cycle of the same kind, and at the same time a number of complete solar years.

he reigned forty years." So the Son of David was thirty years old when He began his public life.

The gospels nowhere expressly state the exact duration of our Lord's *ministry*, yet that it lasted three years and a half, is clearly deducible from what they do state. The gospel of John distinctly mentions three "feasts" of Passover in the course of our Lord's ministry, and implies a fourth. The first, at which He cleansed the temple (chap. ii.); the second, when He healed the impotent man at the pool of Bethesda (chap. v.); the third, about the time of his feeding the multitude (chap. vi. 3); and the fourth, which He ate with his disciples before He suffered, the same night in which He was betrayed (chap. xviii. 28). Four Passovers of course include *three years.* There was also evidently an interval of some months between our Lord's baptism by John in Bethabara beyond Jordan, and the first of these Passovers. The events which had intervened were his forty days' fast, and subsequent temptation in the desert of Judea; his return journey to Galilee; his visit to Cana at the time of the marriage, when He turned the water into wine; his subsequent brief visit to Capernaum; and his return to Judea. All this can scarcely have occupied less than six months; so that it is with good ground that, from the early Fathers onwards, our Lord's ministry is assumed to have lasted three years and a half.[*]

---

[*] "On the phrase *feast of the Jews* (ἑορτὴ τῶν 'Ιουδαίων), John v. 1, turns mainly the question as to the duration of our Lord's public ministry. *John notes distinctly three Passovers;* John ii. 13; vi. 4; xii. 1. If now this feast be another Passover, then our Lord's public labours continued during *three and a half years;* if not, then the time of his ministry must in all probability be reckoned one year less.

The only reasonable ground of doubt in this case, is the absence of the definite article before *feast.* But even as the text now stands, it *may* assuredly in itself just as well denote the great Jewish festival as any other. The following considerations seem to show that it does most probably thus stand for a Passover, viz. the *second* in our Lord's public ministry.

1. The word *feast* (ἑορτή), without the article, is put definitely for the Passover, in the phrase κατὰ ἑορτήν, Matt. xxvii. 15; Mark xv. 6; Luke xxiii. 17. Comp. John xviii. 39.

2. In Hebrew a noun before a genitive is made definite by prefixing the

We assume then, that at the time of his death, our blessed Lord was thirty-three and a half years of age. Now, the soli-lunar cycle of which we speak is thirty-three years, seven

---

article, not to the noun itself but to the genitive ; see Davies's translation of Gesenius's Heb. Gr. § 109 ; 1 Nordheim Heb. Gr. ii. p. 14, γ. This idiom is transferred by the LXX. into Greek ; *e.g.* Deut. xvi. 13, ἑορτὴν τῶν σκηνῶν ποιήσεις σεαυτῷ, Heb. הַסֻּכֹּת חַג *i.e. the* festival of tabernacles. So too in the New Testament; Matt. xii. 24, ἐν τῷ Βεελζεβοὺλ ἄρχοντι τῶν δαιμονίων, *i.e. the* prince of demons. Hence, in the passage before us, according to the analogous English idiom, we may render the phrase by *the Jews' festival;* which marks it definitely as the Passover.

3. It is not probable, that John means here to imply that the festival was indefinite or uncertain. Such is not his usual manner. The Jewish festivals were to him the measures of time ; and in every other instance they are definitely specified. So the Passover, John ii. 23 ; xii. 1 ; even when Jesus does not visit it, vi. 4 ; and also when it is expressed only by *the feast,* iv. 45 ; xi. 56 ; xii. 12, 20, al. So too the festival of Tabernacles, vii. 2 ; and of the Dedication, x. 22. This is all natural in him ; for an indefinite festival could afford no note of time.

4. The plucking of the ears of grain by the disciples shows that a passover had just been kept; which tallies accurately with this visit of our Lord to Jerusalem.

5. This *feast* could not have been the festival either of Pentecost or of Tabernacles next following our Lord's first Passover. He returned from Judea to Galilee not until eight months after that Passover, when both these festivals were already past. That it might by possibility have been the Pentecost after a second Passover not mentioned, and before that in John vi. 4, cannot perhaps be fully disproved ; but such a view has in itself no probability, and is apparently entertained by no one. At any rate, it would also give the same duration of three and a half years to our Lord's ministry.

6. Nor can we well understand here the festival of Purim, which oc-curred on the fourteenth and fifteenth of the month Adar, or March, one month before the Passover; see Esth. ix. 21, 22, 26–28. Against this the following considerations present themselves : (*a*) The Jews did not go up to Jerusalem to celebrate the festival of Purim. The observance of it among that people throughout the world consisted solely in reading the Book of Esther in their synagogues on those days, and making them "days of feasting and joy and of sending portions (dishes) one to another and gifts to the poor;" Esth. ix. 22; Jos. Ant. xi. 6, 13, Reland, Antiq. ; Heb. iv. 9. But the "multitude," John v. 13, seems to imply a concourse of strangers at one of the great festivals. (*b*) It is very improbable that Jesus would have gone up to Jerusalem at the Purim, to which the Jews did not go up, rather than at the Passover which occurred only a month later. His being once present at the festival of Dedication (John x. 22) is not a parallel case ; since He appears not to have gone up for that purpose, but this festival occurred while He remained in or near Jerusalem after the festival of Tabernacles, John vii. 2, sq. (*c*) The infirm man was healed on

months and seven days, so at first sight it seems more than
a month longer than the life of Christ, but it must be remembered that our Lord's connection with this earth did not

---

the sabbath, John v. 9 : which sabbath belonged to the festival, as the
whole context shows, John v. 1, 2, 10-13. But the Purim was never
celebrated on a sabbath ; and, when it happened to fall on that day, was
regularly deferred ; see Reland l. c.

7. The main objection urged against taking this *feast* as a Passover, is
the circumstance, that in such case, as our Lord did not go up to the
Passover spoken of in John vi. 4, but only at the subsequent festival of
Tabernacles in John vii. 2, sq., He would thus have absented Himself from
Jerusalem for a year and six months ; a neglect, it is alleged, inconsistent
with his character and with a due observance of the Jewish law. But a
sufficient reason is assigned for this omission, namely, "because the Jews
sought to kill Him " (John vii. 1 ; comp. v. 18). It obviously had been our
Lord's custom to visit the holy city every year at the Passover; and because, for the reason assigned, He once let this occasion pass by, He therefore went up six months afterwards, at the feast of Tabernacles. All this
presents a view perfectly natural ; and covers the whole ground. Nor
have we any right to assume, as many do, that our Lord regularly went up to
Jerusalem on other occasions besides those specified in the New Testament.

In this instance, the most ancient view is that which takes *feast* for a
Passover. So Irenæus in the third century : " Et posthac iterum secunda
vice adscendit [Jesus] in diem paschæ in Hierusalem, quando paralyticum,
qui juxta natatoriam jacebat xxxviii annos curavit ; " Adv. Hær. ii. 39.
The same view was adopted by Eusebius, Theodoret, and others ; and in
later times has been followed by Luther, Scaliger, Grotius, Lightfoot,
Le Clerc, Lampe, Hengstenberg, Greswell, etc. Cyril and Chrysostom
held to a Pentecost, as also the Harmony ascribed to Tatian ; and so, in
modern times, Erasmus, Calvin, Beza, Bengel, etc. The festival of Purim
was first suggested by Kepler ("Eclogæ Chronicæ," pp. 72, 129, sq. Fran-
cof. 1615) ; and at the present day this is the only view, aside from the Passover, that finds advocates. Those who hold it, as Hug, Neander, Olshausen,
Tholuck, Meyer, Wieseler (Lücke and De Wette leave the question undecided), regard John vi. 4 as having reference to the second Passover
during our Lord's ministry ; which thus becomes limited to two and a half
years. See generally, Greswell's Dissert. viii. vol. ii., Neander's *Leben
Jesu*, 3te Ausg. p. 434. Wieseler's *Chronol. Synopse der Vier Evangelien*,
pp. 211-222.

From "Harmony of the Gospels," following that in Greek, by Ed.
Robinson, D.D., LL.D., published by the Religious Tract Society (pp.
199-200). " *That this feast was a passover, was certainly the most ancient
opinion, and it is the opinion of the great majority of critics*, being that of
Irenæus, as early as the second century, Eusebius and Theodoret among the
fathers ; and of Luther, Beza, Maldonat, Grotius, Lightfoot, La Clerk,
Lampe, Hengstenberg, Greswell, Robinson, Tholuck in his 6th edition, and
apparently in his 7th and last, Middleton, Trench, Webster and Wilkin-
son," etc. Commentary on N. Test., Rev. D. Brown, on John v. 1.

terminate with his death and resurrection. He walked and talked with his disciples, He ate and drank before them ; and manifested Himself to them during forty days after his resurrection before He left the world altogether, and "a cloud received Him out of their sight." These forty days must therefore be included in any estimate of his earthly life, for not until the final parting on the mount of Olives did it cease to be true that God in human form was tabernacling among men.

Our Lord's life, then, was composed of the 30 years prior to his baptism, the three years and a half of his ministry, and 40 days after his resurrection, and as it terminated between the feasts of Passover and Pentecost, it must have commenced about the time of the feast of Tabernacles. Now from the day of ascension in A.D. 29, to the first day of the feast of Tabernacles in the 34th preceding year, the interval (as we show in the Appendix) was 33 solar years 7 lunar months and 7 days, which is the exact measure of the soli-lunar cycle in question.

If it be objected that while the first and last periods of our Lord's life were clearly 30 years and 40 days, yet that the central period of his ministry cannot be proved to have been just three years and a half, we reply that it cannot be proved to have been more or less than that period, and there are the following good grounds for believing that the general view as to its duration is correct.

(1) The Divine system of times and seasons is, as we have seen, one of *weeks.* Messiah's coming and death had been announced in the prophecy of " 70 weeks," and that prophecy speaks of a division in the midst of a week. A week of years and a half week of years, are periods recognised and often employed in Scripture, and the latter is notably used in connection with the testimony of God's faithful witnesses. " Elias was a man subject to like passions as we are, and he prayed earnestly that it might not rain ; and it rained not on the earth by the space of *three years and six months*" (James v. 17). Similarly the two sackcloth-clothed witnesses in Rev. xi. pro-

phesy during three symbolic years and a half (1260 days), and then during three literal years and a half (symbolised by "three days and a half") they lie unburied.

The great "seven times" of the "Times of the Gentiles" is divided as we have seen, into two equal portions, each consisting of "time, times, and a half," or three years and a half (symbolic).

Now since the first period of Christ's life (30 years) was in harmony with Old Testament chronological usage, and also the forty days closing period, it seems reasonable to suppose that the central, and most important section of it, occupied by his public ministry, should not have been an irregular interval, unlike any other in Scripture. In assuming it to have been the important definite period *to which we know it closely approximated*, we only assume that it was in full harmony with sacred analogy, and not at variance with the law of weeks, which pervades the Bible.

(2) The events which took place before the first passover of Christ's life, when compared with subsequent similar journeyings and tarriances, seem likely to have occupied about six months; and as there are no counter indications, but the reverse, we may safely assume that the Lord's ministry was three years and a half, so nearly as to justify our regarding his earthly life, including its 40 days post resurrection period as in close, if not exact agreement with the 33 years 7 months and 7 days cycle, and to warrant our naming this soli-lunar cycle, "THE MESSIANIC CYCLE."

Now the fact that this central and all important period—the lifetime of our Lord—was comprised in such a cycle, naturally suggests the use of that cycle, as *a unit* for the measurement of larger periods. Before we point out the results of regarding it as *one day* of a great *year* of similar cycles, it is needful briefly to recall two points already discussed.

In our study of the law of completion in weeks (p. 270), we showed that a Divine chronologic system exists in Scripture; that it is a system of weeks; that it pervades the law and the prophets, and is traceable in the Gospels and Epistles; that it is especially conspicuous in the Jewish ritual, and in the symbolic prophecies of Daniel and the Apocalypse; and that it comprises weeks, or septiform periods, on a variety of scales, according to the day, or unit of computation, employed.

We considered the week of days, of months, of years, of decades, of weeks of years, of months of years, of years of years, and of millenaries; and we saw good reason to endorse, on new grounds, the ancient view, that in the course of the six first days of the week on this *last* scale, the mystery of God is destined to be finished, and that the seventh millenary of the world's history is to be its sabbath—the millennial reign of Christ on earth.

In considering the week of months (p. 276) we showed further that seven lunar months comprised all the feasts of the Lord, and constituted the sacred portion of the Jewish year, and that these feasts of the Lord, the observances and chronology of which are set forth at length, and with great exactness in Leviticus xxiii., form A COMPLETE CALENDAR OF DIVINELY ORDAINED TYPICAL CEREMONIES, PREFIGURING THE GLORIOUS HISTORY OF REDEMPTION. The series of feasts thus prophetic of the future,—for the law had "a shadow of good things to come,"—is introduced by the great law of the sabbatic, or weekly *rest*, a law involving a main principle of all these religious festivals; redemption terminating in the rest of God, and the rest of man in and with his Divine Redeemer "There remaineth a rest—a sabbatism—to the people of God." Then follows the setting apart of the paschal lamb, and, after a definite period, its redeeming death, pointing to "Christ our Passover sacrificed for us."

The closely connected feast of unleavened bread, with its rigid exclusion of leaven in every form, the type of sin, succeeded. It is explained by the Apostolic commentary, "Therefore let us keep the feast, not with the old leaven, neither with the leaven of malice and wickedness, but with the unleavened bread of sincerity and truth."

Then on the day after the sabbath following the passover, a first-fruit sheaf of the early harvest was waved before God, emblematic of the resurrection of "Christ the first fruits of them that slept," and pointing with no obscurity to the occurrence of his resurrection on the first day of a new week.

Fifty days (*i.e.* seven weeks and a day) reckoned from this wave-sheaf day, brought Pentecost, or the feast of weeks, with another wave offering, emblematic of the church. It consisted not of a single first-fruit sheaf, but of *two loaves baked with leaven* (typical of evil), and consequently accompanied by a *sin offering.* These loaves prefigured the Church of redeemed sinners in their present imperfect state, accepted by God, but only in and through the Beloved.

The next feasts prescribed were the terminal group in the seventh month, the feast of trumpets, the great day of atonement, and the feast of tabernacles. The first seems to point to a universal gospel testimony and to the future awakening of Israel, and to be chronologically connected with the final trumpets of the Apocalypse; the second foreshadows the national repentance of Israel, when "they shall look upon Him whom they have pierced, and mourn because of Him"; and the third, the glad concluding harvest home feast of tabernacles, typifies "the times of the restitution of all things," " of which God hath spoken by the mouth of all his holy prophets since the world began."

The antitypical realities which these feasts prefigure centre in the incarnation. The rejection of "God manifest in the flesh," and dwelling among men, led to Christ, our Passover, being sacrificed for us. *At that historical point the type and the antitype met,* for the crucifixion, the great act of redemption, was accomplished on an anniversary of the Exodus Passover, and the resurrection itself fell on the very day of the annual wave sheaf, which had for ages prefigured it; while the descent of the Holy Ghost, which baptized the separate disciples into one Church and Body of Christ, took place on the "day of Pentecost fully come," so that the birth of the Christian

Church, in its corporate character, synchronized with the observance of the ceremonies which had so long foreshadowed it.

Thus three of the most momentous and sacred events in the whole course of history (events than which none of greater importance have ever taken place), the atoning death of the Son of God, his glorious resurrection, and the descent of the Holy Ghost, coincided chronologically with their *prefigurative* ceremonial observances enjoined in Leviticus xxiii.

Thus far the prophecy of the Jewish ritual is, therefore, fulfilled. The remaining three feasts have yet to receive their antitypical accomplishment, but we know from other scriptures that the restoration, repentance, salvation, and blessing of Israel which they foreshadowed, are to take place at the close of the "Times of the Gentiles." This is implied in our Lord's own expression, "Jerusalem shall be trodden down of the Gentiles, *until* the times of the Gentiles be fulfilled;" and in the statement of St. Paul, "blindness in part is happened to Israel, until the fulness of the Gentiles be come in" (Rom. xi. 25).

Now, the event which terminates the "Times of the Gentiles" is the coming of Christ and the establishment of his millennial kingdom on earth. But this event does not terminate redemption history. It is only at the close of his millennial reign, when the Son shall have put down all rule and all authority and power, subdued all things to Himself, and destroyed the last enemy, death; and delivered up the kingdom to God, even the Father, it is only *then*, that his peculiar work as Redeemer and Mediator is accomplished.

Redeeming work, therefore, extends, according to Scripture, from the days of Eden to the end of the millennium. Thenceforward the perfect results of the great work remain, but the work itself is accomplished and over. Satan and death and Hades are cast into the lake of fire. There is no more death, neither sorrow, nor crying. The former things are passed away, and the tabernacle of God is for ever with men.

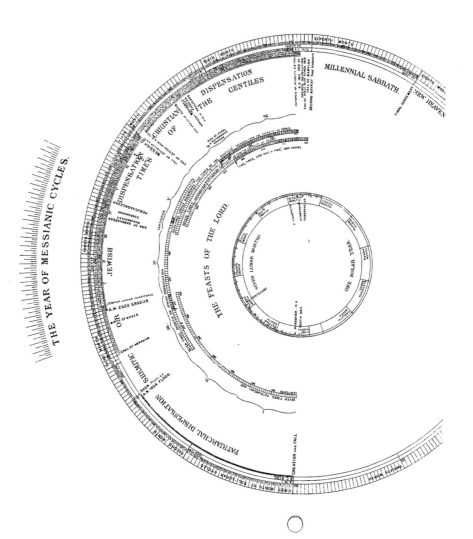

THE YEAR OF MESSIANIC CYCLES.

We have then two leading facts; first, that the *type* of redemption embodied in the Jewish ritual extended over seven
months of the ordinary year; and secondly, that as far as can
be ascertained from Scripture the actual *history* or course of
redemption extends over seven millenaries. Now the remarkable result of the application of the soli-lunar cycle
of 33 years 7 months and 7 days to these periods is, that
it brings the week of millenaries into close and special harmony with the week of months. A thousand years contains
as many of these soli-lunar cycles as there are days in a month,
and consequently *seven millenaries are seven months of such
cycles.* The agreement between the chronological type and the
great antitype is not, therefore, merely that between a week
of months and a week of millenaries, it is far more close and
remarkable. THE TYPE BEARS TO THE ANTITYPE THE PER-
FECT PROPORTION OF A WEEK OF MONTHS ON ONE SCALE TO
A WEEK OF MONTHS ON ANOTHER. Either may be regarded
as a week of months contained in a year; the former a year
of 360 to 365 *days*, the latter a year of 360 to 365 soli-lunar
cycles.

In the adjoined plate the millenaries measuring the course
of human history are divided into Messianic cycles, and may
be compared with the months and days of the Levitical
calendar sketched in the centre.

A thousand years equal 29¾ Messianic cycles (analogous with
the 29¾d. lunar month); *thirty* Messianic cycles (analogous with
the 30d. calendar month of the Prophetic Times) equal exactly
1007 solar years and 7 lunations; and 180 Messianic cycles
(half 360) equal 6045 solar years, 5 months.

According to the Hebrew chronology, as shown by Mr.
Clinton, we have now about reached the termination of the
first six thousand years of human history; and history as well as
prophecy abundantly confirm the view this fact suggests, that
we are now living in the last or closing days of the third great
dispensation, and on the verge of another and a better age.
Half a vast year of Messianic cycles, measured from the creation

of man, is now expiring; and as it expires, there dawns upon the world the light which immediately precedes the sun-rising; there arise around us the solemn yet joyful evidences of the nearness of the glorious kingdom of our God.*

---

* For further particulars with reference to the Messianic cycle see Ap·pendix.

CHAPTER VI.

CONCLUDING REMARKS.

WE have in the foregoing pages, traversed a considerable range of subjects; we have endeavoured to elucidate the fundamental principles of progressive revelation and progressive interpretation, and we have under their guidance traced the historic fulfilment of two of the main symbolic prophecies of Scripture. In this fourth part of the work we have directed attention to a variety of facts, in the realms of physiology and astronomy, and shown their connection with another series of facts, the facts of Biblical chronology. We have traced, very imperfectly, but still sufficiently to demonstrate its existence, *a system* of times and seasons running through nature—organic and inorganic,—and through Scripture —historic and prophetic :—a system which consequently we have ventured to call, *a Divine system* of times and seasons. We have shown that this system is characterized by soli-lunar dominion causal and chronological, and by a marked and peculiar septiformity; that a law of completion in weeks can be traced alike in Scripture, in physiology (normal and abnormal), in history, and in astronomy.

We have endeavoured to avoid mere hypothesis, and to build on the basis of solid unquestionable facts. It remains in conclusion to show the bearing of the facts of this Divine system of times and seasons,—

I. On some of the main controverted points of prophetic interpretation dealt with in the earlier part of this volume;

II. On the evidence of the inspiration of Scripture; and,

III. On the profoundly interesting question of the chronological point now reached in human history, and the nearness of "the end of the age."

I. The Divine system of times and seasons, which we have traced, strongly discredits the *futurist* system of interpreting the symbolic prophecies of Daniel and St. John, and in the fullest and most remarkable manner confirms *the Protestant historic system.* We have shown that if the true meaning of the *chronologic* statements connected with these prophecies can be *determined,* it would of itself and without the aid of further argument, settle the question at issue between these two schools of interpreters; inasmuch as the nature of the predicted Antichrist is decided by the duration of his existence. If the 1260 days of his dominion be (unlike all the other features of the prediction) *literal,* then the futurists are right in looking for a future division of the Roman earth into ten kingdoms with a coincident future rise of an individual Antichrist, whose advent shall precede by three and a half years that of Christ; and in denying that these prophecies have already received their fulfilment. But if the 1260 days be (like the predictions in which the period occurs), symbolic, then the little horn and the ten horns, *having a duration of* 1260 *years attached to them,* and their rise immediately succeeding the break-up of the undivided Roman Empire, the fulfilment must be looked for *in the past;* and can only be found in the history of the Papacy, and its relations to the kingdoms of Christendom, and to the true Church of Christ, during the last twelve centuries. In consequence of this, its great importance, we dwelt at some length on the evidence in favour of the year-day system of interpretation, and we must now direct special attention to the *confirmation of its truth* afforded by the Divine plan of times and seasons, which we have been investigating.

The period which,—as marking the duration, and therefore the nature of the great Antichristian Apostasy,—*is the disputed period,* is seven times designated by expressions synonymous with *half a week of years:* "forty and two months," 1260 days, etc. Now this alone would prove nothing, because weeks on an almost infinite variety of scale, are found, as we have shown, in the word and works of God. But *this half week leads up to a certain terminal point,* the establishment of the kingdom of the God of heaven, the overthrow of Antichrist and his armies, the cessation of the treading down of the holy city. These same events mark the termination of one of the *weeks* we have con-sidered, the last of the three great dispensational weeks, the times of the Gentiles ; this also ends in the establishment of the kingdom of God, the overthrow of Babylon and the beast, and the Second Advent of Christ. That is, we find a *whole* week of "seven times," or 2520 years, leading up to THAT ; and we find also a half-week of "time, times and a half," leading up to THAT. How can we question that the latter is half of the former ? that the half-week of years, is symbolic of a half-week of prophetic times, or years of years ? that the predicted 1260 "*days*" represent the 1260 years which are the last half of the Gentile dispensation ?

If this be so, if this period be the solemnly momentous and important last half of the last great dispensation, the twelve centuries which have rolled over Christendom since the rise of the Papacy, including the dark ages, the Reformation, and the modern revival of primitive Christian doctrine, and spread of missionary enterprise, with the coincident rise and spread of infidelity, then it is easy to understand the prominence assigned to it in the prophetic word. But if it be literally half a week of years, it is a brief half *without a corresponding half,* and no reason consistent with the wisdom and goodness of God can be assigned for the great importance which is attached to it in Scripture.

And when, further, TURNING TO THE SCROLL OF HISTORY, WE SEE THAT THE GREAT WEEK OF THE TIMES OF THE GEN TILES WAS, AS A MATTER OF FACT, BISECTED BY THE RISE OF AN ANTICHRISTIAN POWER, accurately fulfilling the conditions of the prophecy, and whose political existence demonstrably did endure 1260 years, or half a week on the year-day scale, it seems almost impossible to resist the conviction *that this is the scale employed, and this the Power foretold.*

It is a further argument in favour of the year-day system, that the periods of symbolic prophecy, interpreted in accordance with it, form parts of a great septenary system; the previous links in the chain being found in other portions of Scripture, and the subsequent ones in the movements of the universe. In the law, in the prophets, and in the Psalms, we found the week of days, the week of weeks, the week of months, the week of years, the week of weeks of years, the week of decades, and the week of weeks of decades. Now the dispensational "seven times," and its half, the 1260 years, are a week and a half-week of prophetic times, or *years of years*, the next step in advance ; and they are followed by the week of millenaries, and by the higher and vaster weeks marked out by the revolutions of the solar system. But for the clue afforded by the prophetic times interpreted according to the year-day system, the true measures of the dispensational divisions of history, would probably never have been surmised. Is it likely that a key which has unlocked so much, should be a wrong key, that the period which has proved a clue to the entire labyrinth, should itself have been misapprehended ?

But further, THE FACT THAT THESE PERIODS OF DANIEL, INTERPRETED ON THE YEAR-DAY SCALE, ARE FOUND TO BE NATURAL ASTRONOMIC CYCLES OF SINGULAR ACCURACY AND BEAUTY, UNKNOWN TO MANKIND UNTIL DISCOVERED BY MEANS OF THESE VERY PROPHECIES, SEEMS ALONE TO SETTLE THE QUESTION THAT THIS IS THE TRUE SCALE. Is it not most natural and suitable, that great events, deemed worthy of prediction by the Spirit of God ages before they occurred, *should* have had their fore-ordained duration marked off by the occult movements and coincidences of those orbs, which together constitute God's glorious chronometer ? Taken literally, the periods of symbolic prophecy, are astronomically *nothing*. Interpreted on the year-day principle, they are natural cycles, as distinctly marked out as such, as our ordinary months or years. Would this be so, were the brief symbolic period, everything, and the antitypical, the year-day period, nothing ? Taken literally, 2300 days are astronomically nothing; while 2300 *years* form precisely the largest secular soli-lunar cycle known.

When these dispensational, chronologic, and astronomic harmonies, are allowed their due weight in determining the true scale of prophetic chronology, only one conclusion seems possible. The system employed is that of denoting a year by a day ; not brief, but long periods, are therefore predicted, not passing events occupying only a few years, but stupendous ones, enduring through centuries, and affecting many generations of men. And these events are not to be looked for in the future, they are already for the most part fulfilled. This conclusion overthrows the entire futurist system, and fixes the application of the main symbolic prophecies of Daniel and the Apocalypse to the past and present, rather than exclusively to the future.

We invite futurist expositors of the prophetic word, to consider all the arguments on this subject which we have adduced, and either to refute them, or to acknowledge their force. Prophetic discussion and controversy are often feared and deprecated, because they have in other days degenerated into strife, and occasioned separation among brethren. These, however, are happily, not necessary results of searching the Scripture on this or any other topic, and they are evils from which humility and a real desire to discover the truth of God, will effectually preserve sincere inquirers and students.

We are strongly of opinion that the questions at issue between presentist and futurist interpreters of prophecy, *should* be both patiently studied, and fully discussed, both from the platform and by the press, with a view to their removal.

One system or other must be erroneous ; surely it is not hopeless to discover which ! No generation of Christians could ever have attempted the task with such a prospect of success as our own ; not only is there a special promise to the wise in the time of the end, that they *shall* understand these things, but the very nature of the case makes it clear, that if the historic system be the true one, *we* are in a better position to prove it, than our predecessors could be, for every fresh fulfilment that can be indicated, strengthens the proof. That most notable event the downfall of the Temporal Power of the Papacy exactly 1260 years after the edict of Phocas, *ought* to provoke a calm and thorough re-examination of the subject, on the part of our futurist friends.

"The days are at hand," and the effect of every vision, and the testimony of the Church on this great subject *should be as clear and as unanimous as possible*, for if the trumpet give an uncertain sound, who shall prepare for the battle? The world will never give heed to the warnings of the prophetic word, while the ministers of that word differ diametrically among themselves as to its true meaning; nor will Christians be roused to any such deep and real conviction of the nearness of the end as will produce practical results, by the exposition of varying and inconsistent views. At this eleventh hour, if ever, the predictions of the word of God ought to be clear to wise and humble students, nor should such rest content without an honest endeavour to compare and resolve their differences. We humbly hope that our own discoveries as to the epact measures of the prophetic times, may be helpful in the consideration of the question; and that, *the year-day system of interpreting the chronologic statements of symbolic prophecy,*— that main pillar of the Protestant historic view, may, in the light of the confirmatory evidence of its truth afforded by this investigation of the Divine system of times and seasons, be generally received among students of prophecy, as a truth which has been demonstrated.

II. The facts we have adduced have also an important bearing on the fundamental question of the inspiration of Scripture, and thus indirectly on the subject of Christian evidences. We have shown that nature is characterized by a septiform periodicity, and that many of its revolutions are regulated by a law of weeks; also that Scripture, in a great variety of ways, embodies the same septiform system. Now it must be borne in mind that the existence of this system in nature, has only been recognised of *late years*. Modern science,—with its careful and all-embracing scrutiny of investigation into natural phe-

nomena, with its reverential attention to even the minutest
details of physical function, with its rich accumulations of
tabulated records of observed facts, and its unprejudiced
candour in submitting all its theories to the test of experiment,
—has come to perceive, and for the first time, a law of septiform periodicity in nature. Mankind in all ages must of
course have been practically familiar with certain obvious
and universal instances of its prevalence; but the wide extent
of its operation, its exactness, and the variety of the spheres
in which it may be traced, is matter of very recent discovery.
The papers contributed by Dr. Laycock to the *Lancet*, which
we have quoted, were written less than forty years ago ; and
even now the subject is imperfectly understood.

It is thus abundantly evident that the writers of Scripture,
in attributing to their Mosaic legislation, embodying in their
historical narratives, and in concealing in their symbolic prophecies, *this same septiform system*, or law of completion in
weeks, were *not* adopting a principle already acknowledged in
the world at large, or even known to the men of science of
their day. They were entirely ignorant of the recently discovered septiformity of nature, and the exact harmony of their
writings with this widely operative, but to them utterly unknown
principle, must, on their part, have been perfectly undesigned.

On the other hand, it is equally impossible that this harmony
should be the result of chance : the use of the system in
Scripture is too thorough and all-pervading to admit of such
an explanation. It does not consist in a few minor arrangements enacted by a single legislator; it is the consistent and
complex system underlying the law and ritual, which, for
three thousand five hundred years have been obeyed by an
entire nation; a system running unperceived through the
historical records of the Old Testament, and lying hidden
under mystic expressions, in its symbolic prophecies—prophecies understood at the time neither by those who gave, nor
by those who received them, and whose true scale has only
become apparent in these latter days, in the light of their own

fulfilment. Creation, history, and Mosaic law, agree with the predictions of the prophets and apostles, and with the words of our Lord Himself, in recognising this system. It pervades Old and New Testaments, and harmonizes Jewish and Christian predictions. The actual events of redemption history, are found to be in chronological harmony with the octave or New Creation and Jubilee reckoning of the Law ; the chronology of the types of Leviticus is the chronology of Christianity anticipated. Intentionally then, and of set purpose, and in the most consistent way, the septiform law so prevalent and controlling in nature, is employed by the writers of Scripture, though they cannot have derived it from nature. *Whence then did they derive it ? How came they thus to employ it ?* There is only one reply ! Holy men of old spake as they were moved by the Holy Ghost.

Further ; we have seen that the septiform divisions of time in the Old Testament, run on constantly to an octave, and give a glad and glorious prominence to the eighth day and the fiftieth day, in connection with observances intimating that a new and better economy was destined to succeed the Jewish ; that in a New Creation, to follow the old, and in that alone, would full purity and peace, perfect joy and liberty be found. Would Jewish legislators and prophets have invented or conceived such an idea as this? Would *they,* of their own accord, have embodied in their law, in their history, in their prophecies, a silent testimony that Judaism was destined to be succeeded and set aside by a better order of things? Would they who held themselves to be the sole and peculiar people of God, have incorporated in their sacred books, a chronologic system, which points with no obscurity to the passing away of Judaism? No! Such a system cannot have originated in the *Jewish* mind, and yet the books are, as regards their human source, unquestionably Jewish. The fact can be explained only by admitting, that these Jewish minds were inspired, and these Jewish pens guided, by Him who from the beginning foresaw and planned the end, who intended Christianity to succeed

Judaism, the heavenly to follow the earthly, the substance to replace the shadow.

It may be urged, that though the law of septiform periodicity in vital function was unperceived by the ancients, that yet conspicuous celestial phenomena, such as the lunar quarters, may account for the Bible use of the week, without supposing inspiration. But the plea has no force, for the lunar quarter is not so near seven days as to make the observance of the week compulsory or inevitable, and as a matter of fact, it is *not* observed by two-thirds of mankind. China and, till quite recently, Japan, and all heathen nations, do not recognise the septiform division of time. Unlike the day, the month, and the year in this respect, the week is not marked out by an obvious and complete celestial revolution. Its observance evidently springs from a higher source, even the direct primitive mandate of the Most High: it has been imposed on man from Eden onwards (as well as indelibly impressed on his physical constitution), by the Creator Himself directly, and not indirectly, as the day, month, and year.

Again, what but inspiration of God can account for the fact that the prophetic periods of Daniel and St. John are found to be accurate soli-lunar cycles? and that their very epacts form a septiform series of periods as we have shown? Was Daniel acquainted with these facts? Could John have adapted his writings to the discoveries of modern science? Impossible! Candour must acknowledge that in the existence of such a system of times and seasons as we have traced, in the Bible, there is a proof of the Divine inspiration of the authors of that volume. Man never originated its holy and harmonious laws, with their wonderful septenary system of typical times and seasons, fulfilled, and still fulfilling, in the sacred events of Redemption Story. Man could not have invented its equally wonderful prophecies, unfolding as they do the whole plan and course of history, alike in its grand outline, and in its minor detail, and including even, in many cases, the accurate chronology of the things foretold. Man can never have been the

author of a system of times and seasons which involves the
co-ordination of things celestial and terrestrial; the mutual
adaptation of the periodicity of vital phenomena, the sacred
seasons of legal type, the periods of prophecy and the chronology of history, with the periods of the revolutions and cycles
of sun and moon and planet, or those of the movements of the
whole solar system.   Man can neither foretell the future nor
control it; man cannot order on a definite plan, the course of
ages, or so direct the revolutions of the moral world, as that
they shall harmonize with those of the material universe.   Such
operations can be accomplished only by Omnipotence, such
acts can be attributed to God alone.   The sacred volume,—
that unfolds the Divine world-system, including the course and
chronology of the ages of history, of ages future at the time
when it was written, as well as of ages past; foretelling periods
since fulfilled, and found, 2000 years after their prediction, to
be celestial cycles,—must be from God, and he who refuses to
acknowledge this, is bound to find some other satisfactory explanation of facts which true science cannot deny, nor common
honesty ignore.   And this evidence may be adduced in favour
of each portion of the sacred volume; the Pentateuch and the
prophets, the historical books of the Old Testament and the
gospels of the New, the Psalms and the Epistles and the
Apocalypse, all are more or less pervaded by the same system
of times and seasons.   A Divine unity pervades the volume in
this as in other respects, and the chronology of the Bible, independently of any other line of evidence, proves it to be the
word of God.

   III. And finally, the Divine system of times and seasons,
which we have been investigating, has an evident bearing on
the deeply important and profoundly interesting subject of the
nearness of the end of the age,—of the close of these Times of
the Gentiles, and the simultaneous inauguration of the "Times
of restitution of all things, of which God hath spoken by the
mouth of all his holy prophets since the world began."

   It bears on this question mainly by the evidence it affords

of the existence of a definite and predetermined chronological system, in the providential dealings of God with man; in the proof it gives that this system is a system of *weeks*, and that the great week of this third or Gentile dispensation, has almost run its course. Further, by confirming as we have seen that it does, in the fullest way, the year-day system of interpreting the chronology of symbolic prophecy, it brings the celebrated half-week of the great Antichristian apostasy into perfect harmony with all the other weeks of Scripture and of nature, determining its *character* thus by its *duration*, and leaving no doubt as to the power intended. The fulfilments which this system enables us to trace in the past, are so many guides as to the future, so that by its help chronologic prophecy, instead of being a puzzling mystery, is felt to become emphatically a light shining in a dark place,—a light which throws its beams back over the complex mazes of history, and forwards over the transcendently interesting events of the rapidly approaching crisis, which is to usher in the sabbath of humanity.

We must therefore briefly review *the evidence of the nearness of the end of the age* which is afforded by chronologic prophecy, and confirmed by non-chronologic predictions, and we must show, that while there is irresistible evidence to prove that the end is *near*, there are positively no data to enable us to fix on any exact year, as the probably predestined time of the consummation. According to the testimony of the sure word of prophecy, the end is *near*, but none can say *how* near, or determine its actual epoch.

First, then, in proof that it is *near*, let the measures of the three dispensations be remembered, and the wide and almost universal range of the law of completion in weeks. "Seven times" and seven times *only* are appointed as the period of Jewish degradation and dispersion. He who predicted the four hundred years affliction of the seed of Abraham at the beginning of their history, and who when those four hundred years were fulfilled, delivered Israel from Egypt, and judged the nation which had held them in bondage, predicted later on, that for a great week of 2520 years, Gentiles should rule over and afflict the Jewish people, and that at the end of that time Gentile monarchy should be destroyed, and the kingdom restored again to Israel, in the person of their Messiah. Independent Jewish monarchy fell as we know in the Babylonish captivity, since which event the tribes of Israel have existed only in bondage or dispersion. In about forty-five years from the present time (1879 A.D.) the great week of the Times of the Gentiles will have run out, even measured from its latest possible commencing date, the final conquest of Jehoiachin by Nebuchadnezzar, B.C. 598. The great image of Gentile monarchy has but a few years longer to exist; the period of Gentile supremacy is all but ended; the great but hidden dispensational prophecy of the "seven times" clearly teaches that we are *near* the end of the age.

And secondly, let the measures of the Antichristian apostasy, which is predicted under seven different aspects, be remembered. Half a week is assigned as its duration, half this great dispensational week of seven times—1260 years. Like all the other periods we have considered, this half-week may be dated, as we have seen, from a variety of starting-points ;* either from the decree of the Emperor Justinian constituting the bishop of Rome head of all the Churches, and so delivering the saints into his hands, (A.D. 533),—when it ends in the French Revolution, A.D. 1793 ; or from the decree of the Emperor Phocas, conceding to Boniface the Third, not only the primacy of the Church of Rome and all the Western Churches, but that of Constantinople and all the Eastern Churches (A.D. 606), which makes it run out at the recent complete destruction of the Papal temporal power and dominion (1866–70) ; or the period may be dated from the year A.D. 663, when Vitalian, the bishop of Rome, enjoined the services of the

---

* This is the case even with the comparatively brief period of the Babylonish captivity, whose seventy years may be dated either from Nebuchadnezzar's first invasion, B.C. 606, to the edict of Cyrus, B.C. 536, or from the destruction of the temple, B.C. 587, to the temple restoration, B.C. 517.

Church to be read in Latin throughout all Christendom,—
when the half-week would (like the whole week) expire, in A.D.
1923. We have seen the two first measures of this period
expire, and we have seen the events predicted take place.
The prophecy *implies* a brief succeeding period before the
close, " they shall take away his kingdom, to consume and to
destroy it to the end : and the kingdom and dominion, and
the greatness of the kingdom under the whole heaven, shall be
given to the people of the saints of the Most High, whose
kingdom is an everlasting kingdom, and all dominions shall
serve and obey Him." We have seen the kingdom taken
away; we wait to see the full consumption and destruction,
and the establishment of the kingdom of the Most High. The
prophecy of the " time, times and a half," *by its fulfilment*,
proves, that we are close upon the end of the age.

And thirdly, the prediction relative to the cleansing of the
sanctuary does the same. The Holy Land, the Holy City,
and the site of the Temple or Sanctuary of God at Jerusalem,
are to be finally " cleansed " 2300 years from some starting
point which is not exactly defined, but which appears from the
prophecy to be closely connected with the restoration of Judah
from Babylon ; that is, Jerusalem is, after that period, to cease
to be trodden down of the Gentiles, the times of the Gentiles
having been fulfilled. Dated from the earliest possible starting
point, the commission given by Artaxerxes to Ezra, B.C. 457,
this period expired as we have seen in 1844, which was a
marked epoch in the fall of that Mohammedan power which
has long defiled the sanctuary and trodden down Jerusalem.
But dated 145 years later, from the era of the Seleucidæ, this
period measured in *lunar* years expires, *seventy-five years later*, in
A.D. 1919. We have noted various indications in the condition
of Palestine and of Israel, and in the political events of our
own day which seem to indicate that the cleansing of the sanctuary and the restoration of Israel are not distant. When these
shall take place, when the Moslems, now driven out of Bulgaria,
shall be driven also out of Syria, when the nations of Europe,

actuated it may be merely by mutual distrust and political jealousy, or it may be by higher motives, shall conspire to re-instate the Jews in the land of their forefathers, *then* the last warning bell will have rung ; then the last of the unfulfilled predictions of Scripture as to events prior to the great crisis, will have received its accomplishment, then the second advent of Israel's rejected Messiah to reign in conjunction with his risen and glorified saints as King over all the earth, will be *close* at hand, then the mystery of God will be all but finished, and the manifestation of Christ immediate.* How long a time may be required to bring about this restoration of Israel—who shall say? Never within the last 1800 years has it seemed so likely as now, for never, since it first arose, has Moslem power lain so low as it does at the present moment. THE DESTRUC-TION OF THE POWER AND INDEPENDENCE OF THE OTTOMAN EMPIRE, LIKE THE ANNIHILATION OF THE TEMPORAL DOMINION OF THE PAPACY, SHOULD BE AS A TRUMPET-BLAST TO CHRIS-TENDOM, PROCLAIMING THAT THE DAY OF CHRIST IS AT HAND.

The sanctuary cycle of 2300 years, equally with the two pre-vions prophecies, indicates that the end is *near*.

Though differing as to many minor details, students of chro-nological prophecy with one consent *agree in this conclusion*, which is in itself a strong argument that it rests on a solid basis of revealed truth. The fact that many premature antici-pations of the end, have by the event been proved mis-taken, is sometimes adduced as a proof that all expectations based on chronologic prophecy, are of the nature of vain and foolish speculations, deserving only of ridicule and contempt from sober-minded practical Christian people. But when viewed in the light of the revealed purpose of God, to make known the future *only by degrees*, and only as the Church was able to bear it, the fact alluded to, is merely a proof that the symbolic language in which these chronological predictions

---

* We say emphatically "manifestation," because Scripture does not seem absolutely to exclude the possibility that the rapture of the Church (1 Thess. iv.) may have taken place before.

were expressed, has answered its divinely intended purpose, and disguised, till nearly the time of its accomplishment, the true meaning of the prophecy. To the early generations of the Church it was not given to understand these chronologic prophecies *at all;* later generations made a good guess at their general drift and scale ; the Reformers obtained approximately true ideas of their scope and application ; to many of the prophetic expositors and commentators of the last two centuries very clear light was granted, and (in spite of the obscurity which rash futurist speculations have cast over the subject) it may safely be said that in our own day the light has become so strong, clear, and bright, that the historic and doctrinal portions of Scripture are scarcely more simple and comprehensible than are its main prophetic outlines, to those who carefully study them.

And further, though foolish speculators have brought ridicule on the study of prophecy, by carnal, presumptuous, and baseless attempts to fix the day and the hour of the Second Advent, and though even cautious and learned students have often erred in their anticipations, yet it must in all fairness be granted on the other hand, that no sooner was the historic system of interpreting the Apocalypse received, and the true scale of enlarging the miniature periods of symbolic prophecy adopted, than some remarkably correct anticipations of future events were made and published. Since then, expositors of chronologic prophecy have proved over and over again, that they are on the right track, even though they may have erred in the application of certain principles, or in selection of certain data, on which to base their calculations. And it is evident that even when they had rightly accepted the year-day system, and when they had correctly apprehended the meaning of the symbols employed, and duly applied them to the events intended, they were by no means secure from minor errors. The very fact that all the prophetic periods have double, and some of them triple and even fourfold eras of commencement and conclusion,—coincident with definite stages of development and decay in the

Powers symbolised, leaves room for such errors, and accounts for them, without detracting from the value of the system employed. And if such false anticipations are noted, correct ones should in all fairness be remembered also. One of the earliest and most remarkable of these is that of ROBERT FLEMING, who in his work on the "Rise and Fall of Rome Papal," *published in the year* 1701 (a hundred and seventy-eight years ago), anticipated the years 1794 and 1848, as critical years in the downfall of the papacy; he added "yet we are not to imagine that these events will totally destroy the papacy, although they will exceedingly weaken it, for we find that it is still in being and alive, when the next vial is poured out." · Is it not a proof that this expositor was working on right lines, and had seized the true clue, that he should thus have fixed *nearly a century beforehand*, on the close of the 18th century, as the commencement of the era of Divine vengeance on the Papal power, and have pointed out within a single year, the very central period of that signal judgment? The year 1793 was that of the Reign of Terror, and of the temporary suspension of the public profession of Christianity in France, the first of Papal kingdoms; and five years later the Papal government in Italy was overthrown, and the Pope carried captive to Sienna. There was not a sign in the political heavens when Fleming wrote, that such events were impending; he foresaw them solely in the light of chronologic prophecy, and had he weighed a little more maturely the relative importance of the various Pope-exalting decrees and acts, which form the starting-points of the prophetic 1260 years, he would have fixed on that of Phocas, as the *most* important, and have added to the above two accurate and correct anticipations, a *third*, that the years 1866–70, would be years of even more decided crisis in the history of the Papal apostasy, and would probably witness the entire and final overthrow of the temporal sovereignty of the Popes. A very considerable number of expositors agreed, in indicating long before their arrival, the remarkable years A.D. 1848, and A.D. 1866–70, as years of crisis in the downfall of despotic power in Europe, and of Papal usurpation; while this half-century as the appointed period in which should be finished the long-continued exhaustion and decay of the Ottoman Empire, symbolised by the drying up of the Euphrates, has been indicated by an equally large number. Mr. Habershon, in his "Dissertation on the Prophetic Scriptures," published in 1834, pointed out that the year A.D. 1844 ought to be a year of crisis in this process, which, as we have seen it proved to be, the year in which the persecuting sword of Islam was by the power of the Christian nations of Europe, forced back finally into its sheath, since which Ottoman independence has never been a reality.

Let those who have justified themselves in turning from any deep or thorough study of the prophetic word, on the plea that interpreters differ among themselves, and that their prognostications have often proved false, remember that this must have been the case with regard to each one of the chronological prophecies that have now passed into the realms of history. Though each one has, as *we* can see, been fulfilled with marvellous exactitude, error would have been not only possible, but almost inevitable, in any attempt to fix beforehand the *exact* date of the predicted event. Had Israel in Egypt, or Moses in Midian, endeavoured to discover beforehand *the precise year* in which the 400 years of affliction and bondage predicted by God to Abram as to befall his seed, would terminate, they would have been sorely puzzled to select a commencing epoch. Was it to be dated from the call of Abram, or from the day the promise was given? or from the birth of Isaac, the promised seed? or from the descent into Egypt? or from the commencement of the cruel treatment of the children of Israel by the Egyptians, when there arose a king who knew not Joseph? There was a wide choice of possible commencing epochs, and it was easy to select a wrong one! The event proved that *none of these* was the real starting-point; that while the call of Abram was the *terminus a quo* of the main period, *modified by an addition of thirty years* (Exod. xii. 40–42; Gal. iii. 17), yet that the main period itself started from neither of the above-mentioned probable epochs, but *from the time when Isaac was five years old*; and to this day it is a matter of conjecture *what* the event was which marked that year, though there is little doubt that it was the casting out of the bond-woman and her son, on the occasion of the mocking of the heir of promise by the natural seed. This mocking, or "*persecuting*" (Gal. iv. 29) is the first *affliction* of Abraham's seed of which we have any record, and its result demonstrated that it was in Isaac the seed was to be called. The 430 years would thus start from the grant of the land to Abram's seed, and the 400 from the act showing *which* of the two seeds of Abram was to possess it. The important allegorical meaning attributed to this casting-out of Ishmael, confirms the impression that *it* was the starting-point; but the fact cannot be proved, and all we know is that the Exodus (which took place *on the self-same day* that the 430 years ran out—Exod. xii. 40) was 405 years after the birth of Isaac, *so that the 400 years dated from Isaac's fifth year.* How could Israel in Egypt possibly have guessed that? Their prophetic students (if they had any) would most likely base their calculations on the supposition, that the period started from the year the prediction was given,—twenty or twenty-two years before the true point. And when the 400 years from that epoch expired, sceptics and objectors may have derided them, and they themselves may have had their faith in the Divine prediction and their long-cherished hope of deliverance sorely tried, by the fact that their expectation had failed! But God is not a man, that He should lie; neither the son of man, that He should repent; hath He said, and shall He not do it? When the appointed period ended, the promised deliverance came. Little as Pharaoh and all Egypt feared their degraded bondslaves, or the God they professed to serve; little as either tyrant or captives foresaw any impending crisis of judgment and deliverance, suddenly and unexpectedly it came. In the short space of a few weeks, or months, Egypt was covered with confusion and horror and death. The fruits of the earth were blasted and devoured by locusts, the waters of the Nile were turned to blood, the cattle were destroyed throughout the land, filthy insects and noisome diseases afflicted the Egyptians, vermin filled their houses and their fields, thunder and lightning and fire and hail devastated the land of Ham, a horror of great darkness prevailed for three days, death raised a great cry in Egypt, and at last its proud monarch and all his hosts perished in the Red Sea, while Israel sang unto the Lord, who had triumphed gloriously, and who, according to his faithful word, had brought forth the people whom He had redeemed.

A longer bondage is now drawing to a close, and a greater Exodus awaits both the natural and the spiritual seeds of Abraham ; its date is similarly fixed in the purpose of God and similarly defined by chronologic prophecy, and though some students may mistake its exact era, and be discouraged by an apparent failure of their hope, and though the world may exult, and the mockers say, Where is the promise of his coming? yet the vision is for an appointed time, at the end it shall speak and not lie, or be found false ; therefore we will wait for it, "*for it will surely come, it will not tarry.*"

It was the same, both with the chronological prophecy of the seventy years' captivity in Babylon, and with that of the four hundred and ninety years, from the restoration to Messiah the Prince ; both were clear in their main tenor, but both obscure as regards their exact termini. As to the "seventy weeks," even when its true year-day scale was understood, it was impossible to fix its commencing date with any certainty, because there were several edicts of restoration issued by the Persian kings, any one of which might well have been *supposed* to mark the starting-point of the 490 years ; and there was no deciding whether the terminal event was to be the birth, or the maturity and presentation to Israel, or the death, of Messiah. Even now, in the light of the historic fulfilment, it is not altogether easy to affix the *exact* limits of these 490 years, though it is plain that such was the interval, because several important termini seem to possess claims to be the intended ones.

IN SHORT IT IS CLEAR THAT A KNOWLEDGE OF THE EXACT YEAR OF ITS TERMINATION, IS NOT NEEDFUL TO AN INTELLIGENT AND CORRECT APPREHENSION OF THE FACT, THAT A GREAT CHRONOLOGIC PROPHECY IS NEAR ITS CLOSE. Daniel understood by the writings of Jeremiah that the seventy years' captivity had nearly expired, and set himself to pray for the promised restoration. Those who looked for redemption in Israel were right in conceiving that the time for Messiah's appearance had come, though neither they, nor Daniel, could in all probability have assigned the correct chronological termini of the predictions on which their hopes were based.

This is exactly the position of the students of the prophetic word in our day; they *know* that they are living in the time of the end, but guided by the experience of these earlier saints, they see also, that the two great partially *fulfilled* chronological prophecies, that of the seven times, or 2520 years of Gentile dominion, and that of the 2300 years to the cleansing of the sanctuary, have several possible dates of rise and close. (The 1260 years of the duration of the Papal dynasty as a political power, must, since the events of 1870, be placed in the category of *fulfilled*, rather than unfulfilled predictions.) On this account, alone, as well as other grounds, the wise among them refrain from any attempt to assign the precise date of the consummation. These " times " appear to run out first in A.D. 1844-48 and fully in A.D. 1919-23, but whether these are the final dates, and what the *exact* nature of the terminal event may be, it is impossible to ascertain and foolish to surmise.* We are in the

---

* It should be noticed in this connection, that from the year 606 B.C., the year in which " the Lord gave Jehoiakim, king of Judah," into the hand of NEBUCHADNEZZAR, " with part of the vessels of the house of God, which he carried into the land of Shinar" (Dan. i.), to the year A.D. 637, in which Jerusalem was providentially given into the hands of the CALIPHS, there is a period of 1260 CALENDAR YEARS (1260 360-day years are 1242 solar years; and in adding B.C. to A.D. periods, *one* year has to be subtracted); and that from A.D. 637 to A.D. 1879 there is a similar period of 1260 calendar years, or together 2520 CALENDAR YEARS.

As to the first of these dates, B.C. 606, Clinton states that the fourth year

position of travellers, approaching a large and to them unknown
city, at the end of a long railway journey. They are aware of
the distance to be traversed, of the stations to be passed on the
way, and of the time required for the transit. The milestones
have long shown them that they are rapidly nearing their goal;
the time the journey was to occupy has elapsed, and they have
observed that the station just passed was the last but one.
Yet the terminus in the strange city may have several distinct
platforms, separated from each other by short distances; the
train may draw up at one or two before it comes to a final stand
at the last: they are ignorant of the exact localities in the great
metropolis, and hardly know at which station they will be met
by their expectant friends. Still they have no hesitation in
making their preparations for leaving the carriage, and in con-
gratulating each other with a glad " here we are at last!" They
would smile at the man who should dispute their conviction,
though they may be unable to decide whether it will be five
minutes or ten, or only two or three, before they actually reach
their destination. It is a mere question of minutes and miles;
if one platform is not the right one, the next may be; at any
rate, the long journey lies behind, the desired goal is all but

---

of Jehoiakim is to be reckoned from Aug., B. C. 606. The deportation
of Daniel was in the third year of Jehoiakim (Dan. i. 1) whence we may
place the expedition of Nebuchadnezzar towards the end of the third, and
beginning of the fourth year, in the summer of B.C. 606. In the fourth
year of Jehoiakim, Baruch writes the book : Jer. xxxvi. 1, 2. (Fasti
Hellenici, p. 328.) As to the second of these dates, A.D. 637, Clinton states
in his Fasti Romani, that "Abu Obeidah having received orders at the
close of 636 to besiege Jerusalem, sent Yezid hither first with 5000 men.
At last the patriarch Sophronius consented that the city should be surrendered upon condition that the inhabitants should receive the articles
from the Caliph himself. OMAR ENTERED THE CITY IN 637. Omar
while at Jerusalem divided Syria into two parts, and committed all between
the Hauran and Aleppo to Abu Obeidah. Yezid took charge of all Palestine
and the seashore" (Ockley). How grave the crisis just reached in
1878, in the overthrow of the once mighty Ottoman empire in the east !
THE MOSQUE OF OMAR still stands on the site of the ancient temple of
Jehovah, the temple which God of old filled with his glory. The Mohammedan is still the ruler of Palestine, but how soon we may see the
mosque of Omar taken down, and Palestine delivered from its last oppressor !

reached. It is easy to be patient, and not difficult to bear a momentary disappointment, because the main result is certain, and the end in any case close at hand.

Let it also be noted that the conviction of the nearness of the end derived from chronologic prophecy, and from a study of the Divine system of times and seasons, is abundantly confirmed by a multitude of predictions, wholly destitute of the chronologic element, as is proved by the fact, that the futurist school of interpreters, who are deprived by their system of all the guidance afforded by chronologic prophecy, are convinced equally with their opponents, that these are the last days.

Space obliges us to select only one or two "signs of the times" of this nature. The angel mentions to the prophet Daniel two very peculiar and definite characteristics of the last days. "Many shall run to and fro, and knowledge shall be increased." Now if any well informed and intelligent person were asked, What have been the leading and distinctive characteristic marks of the last half-century, as distinguished from any previous period in the world's history? he would at once reply, "steam locomotion, and the universality of education and spread of scientific knowledge." Where one person travelled formerly, ten thousand travel now; universally, incessantly, and in every corner of the earth, the wheels of locomotion are annihilating distance, and facilitating the running to and fro of millions, making the inhabitants of the most distant quarters of the globe almost like next-door neighbours. And never before in the history of mankind has this or anything like it been the case. Similarly, where one person could read and write in the olden time, ten thousand are fairly educated now; and where one secret of nature was known to the ancients, a thousand are known and turned to practical account by the men of our day. Knowledge is increased as it never was before; indeed, *the school and the locomotive* might be adopted as the devices of the nineteenth century.

Our Lord Himself gave another sign of the closing days of this age. He said, "This gospel of the kingdom must first be preached among all nations, and *then* shall the end come."

It may safely be asserted that never since the words were spoken, has the gospel been so widely preached among the nations as it has during the present century. Since the year 1801, when the Church Missionary Society was founded, almost all the Missionary Societies in existence have sprung up, as well as all the Bible Societies. Within the last fifty years, the gospel story has been translated into between two and three hundred additional languages, spoken by six or eight hundred millions of mankind. Colporteurs are distributing it, and preachers expounding it in all lands ; and though there are still alas ! countless tribes and peoples in the heart of Africa, in the continent of South America, and in the isles of the sea who have never yet heard the gospel message, yet we may say there is no kingdom, no regularly organized civilized " nation " or community, in which it has not been proclaimed, and in which it has not won some trophies. When it has been preached in *all* nations, then shall the end come.

But perhaps there is no sign of the times more solemnly indicative to the humble student of Scripture, of the approach of the end, than the confident conviction that seems universally to prevail in the professing church, and in the world, that all things continue as they were, *and will so continue*. Not only is there no expectation of impending judgment, there is a bold assumption that no change in the existing order of things is probable, or even possible.

The very idea of a Divine interference in the affairs of this world is scouted as foolish and fanatical ; the testimony of history to past interferences of the kind is superciliously explained away, or plainly pronounced to be myth, not real history, and any faith in the testimony of prophecy is regarded as antiquated folly. The reign of eternal law is proclaimed, while a Law-giver is ignored, the theory of progressive development is advocated, and the evidences of supernatural interruptions in the past, neglected. The state of popular opinion in

Christendom at this hour on this point is foretold with marvellous exactness by the Apostle Peter, and the true antidote to it prescribed. "There shall come in the last days scoffers, walking after their own lusts, and saying Where is the promise of his coming? for since the fathers fell asleep, all things continue as they were, since the beginning of the creation. For this they willingly are ignorant of, that by the word of God the heavens were of old, and the earth standing in the water, and out of the water; whereby the world that then was, being overflowed with water perished. But the heavens and earth which are now, by the same word are kept in store, reserved unto fire, against the day of judgment and perdition of ungodly men. But beloved be not ignorant of this one thing, that one day is with the Lord as a thousand years, and a thousand years as one day. The Lord is not slack concerning his promise as some men count slackness, but is long-suffering to usward, not willing that any should perish, but that all should come to repentance. But the day of the Lord will come, as a thief in the night."

This peculiar form of scoffing unbelief foretold as to characterize the last days, and most conspicuously characterizing these days, has never before prevailed widely in Christendom. It is an offspring of advanced scientific knowledge, a result and accompaniment of nineteenth-century attainments. The ignorance of other ages made men superstitious. Far from denying the existence of an invisible and immaterial world, far from questioning the possibility of the supernatural, they were slaves to credulity, and groundless apprehensions, and fell easy victims to the false miracles and lying wonders of a cunning and covetous priesthood. Apprehensions of an approaching end of the world, were from time to time widely prevalent in the dark ages. Bold infidelity, general scepticism as to all that is supernatural, gross materialism and positive philosophy, the foolhardy presumption that dares to assert "all things continue as they were since the beginning of the creation" and to argue "and will so continue for ever"—these features are peculiar to the last 150 years, and were never before so marked as they are *now*.

Were it otherwise, were men willing to heed the testimony of the word of God, were they observant of the fast thickening signs of the end, were they generally expecting the final crisis, we might be perfectly certain, *the end would not be near.* Such is not to be the tone and temper of the last generation. " In such an hour *as ye think not* the Son of Man cometh." Never was there a day when men were so firmly convinced, that no supernatural event is to be expected, as they are now. But "when they shall say, Peace and safety; then sudden destruction cometh upon them, as travail upon a woman with child ; and they shall not escape."

That the end of this Christian age, that end so bright with the glow of coming glory to the true Church, so lurid with the fires of approaching judgment to apostate Christendom, so big with blessing to Israel, and so full of hope for the nations of the earth,—is close at hand, seems for those who accept the testimony of Scripture, beyond all reasonable question.

It is true Israel must first be restored to Palestine ; it is true the gospel must probably first be preached more widely even than it now is ; it is true that " Babylon " must first fall more completely, as far as we can judge ; and it is true that these things take time. But when we consider the progress that has been made *in all these directions* during the *last* thirty or forty years—the elevation in the condition of the land and people of Israel, the removal of Jewish disabilities, the formation of the Universal Israelite Alliance, the exploration and survey of Palestine, the decay of the Turkish power ; the increase of missions, the opening up of China, Japan, and interior Africa, the revival of evangelical truth and effort in the Protestant Church, and the consequent increase of missionary effort; the separations of Church and State, and the disendowments of national Churches which have taken place ; the spread of infidelity in Christendom, and the increase of open ungodliness ; the overthrow of despotisms, and the establishment of democratic forms of government in their place,—we feel that supposing we are still thirty or forty years distant from the end of the age, all that is predicted may easily come to pass in the interval. Events in our day move rapidly, as if they too were impelled by steam, so that THE APPARENT RATE OF PROGRESS, AND THE APPARENT DISTANCE COINCIDE WELL.

Unless the entire biblical system of sabbatic chronology, have no application at all to the measures of human history as a whole, unless the moral and chronological harmonies which we have traced between the three dispensations be utterly illusive and unreal, unless the divinely instituted typical ritual of Leviticus, have no chronologic agreement with the long course of redemption history, unless there be no meaning in soli-lunar chronology, unless the employment of great astronomic cycles to bound the duration of historic and prophetic periods be a matter of pure accident, unless the singular septiform epacts of these periods be the result of chance, unless in short the whole system which we have traced out in the word and works of God, be utterly groundless and erroneous—then there can be no question that we are living in the very last days of this dispensation.

And what is the great event which is to close it? Speaking broadly and generally, it is the return in glory of the Son of God to this earth, to establish therein the kingdom of the Most High. Christ when on earth often alluded to the end of the age (or world, as αἰῶνος is often wrongly rendered in the A. V.), and He did so most definitely in his parting command to his apostles. "Go ye therefore and teach all nations, baptizing them in the name of the Father, and of the Son, and of the Holy Ghost: teaching them to observe all things whatsoever I have commanded you : and, lo, I am with you always even unto the end of age" (Matt. xxviii. 19, 20).

This commission and this promise taken together, clearly imply that evangelistic, missionary, and pastoral labours were to continue under the patronage and in the power of an absent and ascended Saviour, *until* the end of the age ; *till then* He promises to be with his people; *after that*, according to a pre-viously given promise, He would come again and receive them to Himself, that where He is they may be also. *He with them* till the end of the age by his Spirit, while still absent in per-son; *they with Him* after the end of age, "for ever with the Lord." The return of Christ, and the rapture of his Church to meet Him in the air, is then the great event which closes this age, and marks the transition to another age—even the millen-nial; that personal Epiphany which is the event symbolised by the fall of the stone cut out without hands, which destroys the image of Gentile monarchy, and becomes a mountain and fills the whole earth. We are living within half a century of what appears to be the latest close of the Times of the Gentiles, which introduces this millennial reign of Christ.

That the transition from this age to the next, will occupy a *period*, and not be a *point* of time, seems likely from analogy, and seems to be indicated in the two brief supplementary periods added to the main one, by the closing words of the angel to Daniel. That there will be marked stages in the accomplish-ment of the stupendous change from the world that is, to the world that shall be, and that it is impossible to fix their dates, or to determine beforehand the precise order of the various events, revealed as destined to occur in the course of the great crisis and consummation, may be freely admitted, without detracting in the least from the momentous weight and solemn importance of this most blessed conclusion. That the rapture will precede the glorious manifestation of Christ with his saints, and the marriage of the Lamb antedate the destruction of Antichrist and his host, is clear from New Testament pro-phecy, but what the interval between the two events may be, whether the twinkling of an eye or a longer space of time, there are no data to enable us to determine.

That a period of awful and destructive judgments on apostate Christendom, is to prepare the way for the full establishment of the millennial throne of Christ, and the world-wide recogni-tion of his peaceful righteous sway, is also abundantly clear

(2 Thess. i. ii. ; Rev. xix.) ; but the precise nature, duration, and effect of these judgments, it is impossible to define.

And while the chronological revelations of Scripture seem to prove that we are living within a few years of the latest close of all the prophetic periods, there is nothing whatever to forbid the thought that the end may come before that latest close. The main measures of the periods *may* be from the earlier *termini a quo.* We may be already far advanced in the supplemental seventy-five years. If the glorious Epiphany were to take place at any time, chronologic prophecy would still have been fulfilled, and as the Rapture of the Church precedes that Epiphany, who shall say how near that blessed hope may be? There is no ground for concluding it will *not* take place this year or next, any more than for asserting that it will. An intentional and impenetrable obscurity and uncertainty is even now, with all our perception of the Divine system of times and seasons, left around this point, and must be till the event itself shall occur. Each passing year diminishes the number of the few remaining years of this "time of the end," *somewhere in the course of which,* the advent apparently must take place, and should therefore quicken our hope, and increase our watchfulness : but to the last we shall not know the day or the hour.

This wholesome and divinely appointed ignorance of the exact period, is perfectly consistent with an intelligent apprehension of the true chronological character of the days in which we live, and a profound conviction that they are emphatically and literally, the last days. An approximate knowledge of the truth on this great subject is all we can gain, and it is *all that we require,* anything further would be injurious. SUCH A KNOWLEDGE WAS ALL THAT WAS EVER GRANTED TO THE SAINTS OF GOD IN CONNECTION WITH THE FULFILMENT OF OTHER CHRONOLOGICAL PROPHECIES IN OTHER DAYS ; FOR PROPHECY IS NOT GIVEN TO GRATIFY CURIOSITY, OR TO MINISTER TO MERE EXCITEMENT, BUT TO SERVE HIGH AND HOLY MORAL ENDS.

And our ignorance and uncertainty on the subject, are of a

very different nature from those which were appointed for the
early Christian church. Just as the patriarchs had the promise
and hope of Christ's first coming, but no clue whatever as
to the time of that greatly desired event ; while the expectations of the faithful in Israel *subsequent to the restoration from
Babylon* were definitely guided by the chronologic prophecy
of the seventy weeks, to the century and decade, though
not to the very year of Messiah the Prince, so the earlier
generations of Christians, had the blessed hope of Christ's
second coming, but no clue whatever as to its period. The
widest possible range was purposely left, for uncertainty on
the subject ; they were told that the Master might return in
the evening, or at midnight, or at the cockcrowing, or in the
morning, and they had no idea which period was the most
probable. For though they held in their hands chronological
prophecies containing mystic intimations of the appointed
duration of this dispensation, they knew not the language in
which the revelation was written, and to them it remained, as
the Lord had ordained that it should remain, a hidden mystery.

We are in a widely different position ; not a fresh revelation,
but new light on old revelations, has by the course of events,
and by the enlightenings of the Spirit of God been granted to
us. The facts of history have explained the predictions of
Scripture ; experience has demonstrated the true scale of the
chronology of symbolic prophecy, our expectations are consequently confined to a much narrower range. The evening
light of the early ages of church history faded away, long long
ago, into the " midnight " of the dark ages of the great
Apostasy ; the " cockcrowing " of the Reformation has already
brightened into the dawn of morning light, and *our* uncertainty
is limited to ignorance of the precise moment, at which the
Sun of Righteousness will rise in visible glory above our horizon.
The scheme of Divine providence has been by degrees unfolded, and the signs of the times assure us, that we are not
out in our reckoning. We are far advanced in the last days of
the Christian dispensation ; and though still ignorant of the

day and the hour of our Lord's return, we know that that great event must be close at hand.

If the uncertainty of the early Christians, was intended to have and calculated to have a sobering, sanctifying and stimulating effect on their minds, what should be the effect of this comparative certainty on ours? If there is immense practical power in the thought, *the Lord may come at any time;* how much more in the conviction *He is sure to come before many years are past.* This certainty is one which no previous generation of Christians could have had, because the great prophetic period of 1260 years was never demonstrably fulfilled before the complete fall of the temporal power of the Papacy in 1870, and the true nature of the Divine system of times and seasons, never before demonstrated, as now. The present generation ought therefore to exhibit fruits of holy living, and earnest service, never seen before, and if this truth were mixed with faith in the heart, *it would.* . Hence our deep regret that futurist expositions should take off the edge of this mightily practical truth; and just as at the Reformation they blinded the eyes of Papists to the true character of the Papacy, and to their consequent personal duty with regard to it,—so they should now blind Protestants to the real nature of the days in which we live ; depriving them of the certainty afforded by the sure word of prophecy in this time of the end, and throwing them back on the uncertainty of earlier ages.

A moment's reflection will show that in the past, while the beginnings of the ages and dispensations had general promises and predictions only, CHRONOLOGICAL PROPHECY WAS ALWAYS PERMITTED TO THROW ITS SOLEMNLY HELPFUL GUIDING LIGHT ON THE CLOSE. The first prediction of this character ever given was that of the 120 years to elapse prior to the flood, that great *close* of the antediluvian age. The second—the 400 years to the Exodus, marked the *close* of the entire patriarchal dispensation ; the third—the 65 years to elapse before Ephraim's overthrow, led up to the *close* of the kingdom of the ten tribes; and the fourth—the 70 years captivity of Judah, marked out by its commencement the *close* of Jewish monarchy, and by its own termination, the *close* of the Babylonian Empire; the fifth —the 490 years to Messiah the Prince, led up the *close* of the Jewish dispensation; and the remaining three great chronologic prophecies of the Bible, the 2520, the 2300 and the seven times repeated 1260 years, all indicate the *close* of the Times of the Gentiles, the oft-mentioned "end of the age." The reason seems to be, that each fresh age has been inaugurated and introduced by *miracle* on so grand a scale that faith needed for a time no further aid than that afforded by history and promise. But as the era of miracle receded, the temptation to doubt and unbelief strengthened, and God graciously provided the help of chronologic prophecy to sustain to the end, the faith and hope of his people. They who in this day despise that aid, or make it void by fanciful, unhistoric futurist interpretations, cast aside an invaluable weapon for the special conflict of these closing days. An age which rejects the argument from miracle, is confronted by that from the fulfilment of prophecy. As the evidence of the *first* becomes more questionable on account of its remote antiquity, that of the *second* becomes more irresistible year by year. Fulfilled prophecy is miracle in the highest sphere,—that of mind. It is the ever growing proof of Divine prescience in the authors of sacred Scripture.

To one who notes the peculiar characteristics of the condition of Christendom in our day, it seems evident, that the testimony which specially needs to be borne throughout its length and breadth at this solemn juncture, is a testimony not only to the goodness but the severity of God. "Behold therefore the goodness and severity of God," says the apostle Paul to the Gentile church, speaking of God's dealings with Israel; "on them which fell severity, but toward thee goodness if thou continue in his goodness, otherwise *thou also shalt be cut off.*" Christendom has no more continued in the goodness of God, than did Israel, and as surely as Israel fell and was cut off in judgment, so surely does a still more terrible doom await the apostate professing Christian church.

It needs faith in Divine revelation to believe this, and perhaps few of the clear teachings of Scripture are more generally disbelieved in our day; but unbelief will not make the promise or the threatening of God of none effect, and though myriads may ignore the solemn fact, and though myriads more may—as predicted—laugh to scorn the Divine denunciations of impending doom, *it is at hand.* If the Bible be true there can be nothing more certain than this, that Divine judgment must close this dispensation, and that in all probability within a brief period of time. Introductory and premonitory vials of wrath, have already been poured out on the Papal kingdoms of Western Europe, and on the Ottoman Empire of Eastern Europe; the sixth vial has been pouring out for the last fifty years, and seems to have all but accomplished its appointed task, of drying up the Euphrates, or wasting away the power of Turkey; *the seventh vial brings the fall of Babylon, the marriage of the Lamb, and the final destruction of Antichrist and all his hosts.* It is the vial of the consummation, and when it is poured forth the great voice out of heaven proclaims " IT IS DONE."

The political events of the last century have been the swift and sure precursors of the long-foretold destruction with the brightness of Christ's coming, which awaits the apostate church of this dispensation. But men's eyes are blinded and they see it not ! Let the watchmen who *do* see it, sound the alarm, if perchance they may awake some to the danger. Let the servants of the Most High preach to an unrepentant world, the preaching that He bids them, for "*yet forty days and Nineveh shall be destroyed !*" As foretold in the Apocalypse, all the sore judgments that have been sent on apostate Christendom have failed to lead it to repentance (Rev. ix. 21 ; xvi. 11), and a contemplation of its actual state affords the strongest of all arguments for a belief in its impending doom. There is such a thing as the measure of iniquity being full ; there is such a thing as the long-suffering of God being exhausted !

Let the universality and intensity of the apostasy of the professing Christian church be considered, and the length of time during which it has existed, as well as the way in which it has rejected every call to repentance. It is not the Papal church alone that has become apostate ; look at the lands where Christianity took its rise, and established itself in the earliest centuries. What is the state of the Syrian, the Nestorian, the Armenian, the Maronite, the Coptic churches, with their millions of so-called Christian adherents ? They are systems in which the grossest ignorance, idolatry, priest-craft, and corruption prevail, and in which the true gospel is almost as much ignored as among the heathen themselves. They who have traversed these lands, witnessed the unmeaning and degrading bodily exercises, and heard the endless vain repetitions which pass in their churches for Christian worship, have marvelled how anything so unlike the religion of Christ and his apostles, can retain even the name of Christianity. It should be remembered also that the majority of the population of these once Christian lands, long ago abandoned even the name of Christ, and under the pressure of Mohammedan conquest and persecution, became avowedly followers of the false prophet.

When from these smaller and more ancient Eastern churches we turn to the great Greek church with its ninety millions of members, and all its minor subdivisions of Syrian, orthodox and schismatic, Bulgarian and Russian, matters are little better · idolatry is universal, and the prevalent ignorance of the true gospel almost as great as in China or Japan. Do not the very missionary efforts we, as Protestants, are making in all these lands, prove, that we are driven by the appalling facts of the case to regard them as little more enlightened than heathen countries, as possessed merely of the names and forms of Christianity, but as destitute of its spirit and power ?

And what pen can paint in its true tints, the dark depths of apostasy in which *Papal* Europe has long been plunged ! Familiarity with its enormity may blunt *our* sense of its awful guilt, but this continuance in sin only serves to enhance the long slumbering wrath of God. Reformations have separated fragments from an idolatrous and Christless church, but the church as a whole has remained unreformed. Two hundred millions of souls are still bound in its hopeless bondage of soul-destroying error ; its blasphemous head still lords it, with ever increasing claims to Divine prerogatives, over all these multitudes. Religion is there, but it is a hollow mocking form : worship is there, but it consists in lip service and genuflexions, it is not worship in spirit and in truth ; the word of God is there, but it is locked in an unknown tongue, and studiously withheld from the people; adoration is there, but it is the adoration of saints and angels, of Pope and Virgin Mary, of picture and crucifix, of statues and dressed-up dolls, of shrines and relics, and of a breaden God. Before all these they bow l How *low* they bow ! How low the blind leaders of the blind bend, before the idol-God they create ! Dressed in fine linen and gorgeous silk, in lace and scarlet, and robes of glittering gold, they lead the people from the pure spiritual religion of Jesus Christ, to holy sacraments without regenerating power, to holy places of stone and marble, to holy fumes of burnt-wood, to holy days of their own appointment, to holy water which can never wash away sin, to holy candles which enlighten no dark mind, to the mass, to confession, to penance, to indulgences, to extreme unction, to anything, everything, *except* to God the Judge of all, to Jesus Christ the only Saviour, and to the Scriptures which testify of Him.

How much longer shall the poison-bearing vine of this Papal apostasy cumber the earth with its rank branches, and destroy men with its fatal clusters of falsehood? How much longer shall this man of sin and son of perdition show himself as God on earth, and blasphemously claim to be infallible? How much longer shall the nations of Europe be by it deceived and deluded into foul superstitions, or driven to revolt against God in open infidelity? Are these things to be suffered to continue under the name of the religion of Christ ? Zion has become Babylon, and the professing church a harlot; and Babylon has grown old in sin, and become ripe for retribution. All the judgments that have been sent on her, have failed to lead her to repentance, all protests against her corruption have proved powerless to abate one iota of her idolatries and false assumptions. Rome has proved herself irreformable and deserving of the dreadful doom so long decreed against her.

At the door of the apostate church of Rome lies the guilt of having given rise to modern continental infidelity, that plague which is ruining in its turn untold millions. Who shall number the so-called Christians in Europe and elsewhere, who scorn all religion as hypocrisy, and sneer at all sacred truth as legends and lies; who worship only self and mammon and pleasure, and live in the unceasing pursuit of vanity? What thousands of such, openly deride and deny Jesus Christ, and even make a mock at God; they refuse to the Creator a place in his own creation, and question his very existence.

And when we turn our eyes to the reformed Protestant churches of Germany, Denmark, Sweden, and England, what do we behold? The power of godliness to a greater extent, a purer creed, an open Bible, an educated people, a general respect for the things of God, and some vital godliness, some faith. But even here how much of covert or open infidelity, what rationalism, what scepticism, what "broad church" views, what oppositions of science falsely so called! What worldliness, what national sins, what confusion and strife in the church, what loathsome vice and ungodliness in the world! National churches honeycombed with infidelity, even when not relapsing back to Popery under another name, and Nonconformist churches fast admitting the same deadly leaven. Where can we find a Christianity worthy of Christ? Where a church, like a chaste virgin, fit to be his bride?

The Christian church as a witness for God in the world has failed, like the Jewish nation, and become apostate. There is a little flock, there is a true Church, but its members are scattered abroad and almost invisible in the great Babylon;

they are the seven thousand who have not bowed the knee to Baal, they are the called and chosen and faithful who follow the Lamb, they are those who have turned to God from idols, to serve the living and true God, and to wait for his Son from heaven; they are those who have not the form only, but the *power* of godliness, those who keep themselves unspotted from the world, and overcome through faith. They are found in every section of the professing church, and the Lord knoweth those that are his—"They shall be mine saith the Lord of Hosts, in the day when I make up my jewels."

But for the rest,—for the vast professing body which bears the name of Christ, it has not continued in the goodness of God, it has turned his grace into licentiousness, its sentence is gone forth, it must be "cut off." The long-suffering of God has been abundantly manifested, it is right that his holy severity should be again revealed. The professing church has long been unworthy of the sacred name it bears, and of the high and holy responsibility of being God's witness on earth, which belongs to it; it is time it should cease to hold the position it has so fearfully forfeited. Instead of being the instrument of spreading the truth of the gospel among men, it is the worst hindrance to their attaining that knowledge of God, and of Jesus Christ whom He has sent, in which life eternal lies; like the Pharisees of old it stands as the great obstruction, neither entering itself into the kingdom, nor suffering those who would, to enter in. The name of God is blasphemed among the nations, by reason of the corruption of the professing church; the light that should have been in it, is become darkness, and great is that darkness! The church is confounded with the world, and the true saints are strangers in its society; it is no longer the pillar and ground of the truth, it is the hotbed of heresy, false doctrine, and corruption of every kind. What contrast can be more complete, than that between the church as Christ intended it to be, and the church as it now exists in the world! An end must come to all this! Not only does the word of God predict it, not only does our own sense of righteousness demand it, but the solemn analogies of history distinctly intimate it. Let the undeniable fact that past apostasies brought down the judgment they deserved, forewarn men what must be the end of the existing apostasy of the professing people of God. Babylon must fall! Great Babylon must come in remembrance before God, who will give unto her the cup of the wine of the fierceness of his wrath, for her sins have reached unto heaven, and God hath remembered her iniquities! The testimony of the Apocalypse is full and fearful as to the doom that is now impending over Christendom. He who destroyed Pagan Rome, is about to destroy Papal Rome and all kindred apostasies; He who punished Jerusalem is about to punish Babylon; heaven waits to rejoice over her fall. The harpers on the crystal sea, the myriad martyrs who overcame her specious seductions, and endured her cruel torments, resisting unto blood her soul-destroying errors and superstitions,—wait to make heaven reverberate with the melodious voice of their triumph, over her utter downfall, and fiery destruction. The same severity of God, illustrated of old in the flood, in the plagues of Egypt, and in the fall of Jerusalem, is to be exhibited afresh in the cutting off of the apostate Christian Church; and the analogies of chronology teach us, that the great change and termination of the present state of things is near at hand. When the "seven times" of the patriarchal age of human history were finished, Egypt fell, and the Exodus of Israel took place. When the "seven times" of the Shemitic or Jewish age expired, Messiah appeared; and Israel, having filled up the measure of its iniquity by rejecting Him, was rejected in its turn, and given up by God to judgment. And now the "seven times" of this Gentile age are all but run out; the dispensation of the Christian Church has produced an apostasy worse than any preceding dispensation,—and shall the end be different? Only in this respect, that the judgment predicted is more terrible, as the sin has been more fearful and prolonged! Babylon must fall, and her fall will be great, for "strong is the Lord God who judgeth her."

K K

The prospect of the judgments which are to bring to a close this dispensation, and which are described in terms of appalling strength by inspired apostles (2 Thessalonians ii.; 2 Peter iii.; Revelation xviii., xix.), cannot *in itself* be an attractive one to the Christian heart. It must, when they realize it, excite in his people, the compassions of Christ; and incline them, as they see the ungodly turning from the only way of escape, to weep, as their Master wept over Jerusalem, in the prospect of *its* coming doom, and to exclaim with Him, "If thou hadst known, at least in this thy day, the things that belong to thy peace! But now they are hid from thine eyes!"

Yet, while sorrowing in Christlike compassion, we can also acquiesce in Christlike righteousness with the just judgments of God. It needs but a glance over the wide extent and awful character of the evils which those judgments are *to remove*, and the unspeakable, multiplied, and universal blessings which they are *to introduce*, to make a true Christian even from motives of humanity desire the hastening of the day of God. If use had not familiarized us with the miseries born of sin, if our standard of human duty and human privilege, had not been debased by ages of acquaintance with things as they are, if our ideal of the destiny of mankind was the true one,—that it is, "to glorify God, and to enjoy Him for ever,"—the present state of the wide world would fill us with grief and amazement, and with impatient longings for a change.

Two-thirds of the human race are buried still in heathen darkness, sensual and ignorant as animals, selfish and cruel as wild beasts, bowing down to the creature, and knowing nothing of the Creator; of the other third, a hundred millions, cursed with the degrading creed of the false prophet, are almost equally sensual and equally ferocious and cruel, while they dishonour God still more by blaspheming and rejecting His only Son; two hundred millions are nominally involved in the Papal apostasy, and about ninety millions in the Greek; how little is God either glorified or enjoyed among these! How little is his character understood, or his will done, or his communion sought! And in the small remainder, in the Protestant world, oh, what national sins bring national miseries even here, and how little is God either enjoyed or glorified! Take England, with her opium trade, her drink traffic, and her legalized immorality. Heathen China conceives us and our religion to be diabolic rather than Divine, since we deliberately persist in ruining her million-peopled empire for the sake of gold. At home the drink fiend is destroying our people and our national prosperity; sixty thousand drunkards die a miserable and disgraceful death annually in our land; murdered wives and starving children, and an immense and ever-increasing pauper, criminal, and lunatic population, cry aloud for some restraint to be put on the fell destroyer; but they cry in vain; our Government suffer and even encourage the traffic. It is acknowledged on all hands that in the metropolis of the greatest Protestant country in the world, where, if anywhere on earth, pure Christianity is acknowledged, *there*, instead of God being glorified and enjoyed, his laws are by the masses, trampled under foot, and sin and misery in one form or other abound.

Where in the wide world can we then find purity and peace? Where holiness and happiness? Oh, the foul lives, the defiled consciences, the troubled minds, the broken hearts, the crying oppressions, the multiplied miseries of our race! What a world of sin and woe is contained in that one word, WAR, and in that other word, SLAVERY! What famines and pestilences, and revolutions and massacres arise from MISGOVERNMENT! How truly the whole creation groans, and travails in pain together, waiting for the manifestation of the sons of God! The deepest and truest compassion for the sufferings of humanity must prompt the cry, How long, O Lord? And apart altogether from the joy that is to be brought to *her* by the revelation of Jesus Christ, the church must long for his coming, that the creation itself may be delivered from the bondage of corruption, and brought into the glorious liberty of the sons of God. Israel's conversion, and the world's jubilee of liberty and gladness, date alike from the coming of the Lord with all his saints, to execute judgment on the ungodly. Of the blessed condition of things which shall succeed, during the world's millennial sabbath, Scripture gives many a glorious sketch ! and though we may be, and must be, unable to image it to ourselves in its detail, we know its broad essential features, and they imply almost all we can desire. Satan, the source of all sin, the great deceiver and seducer of men, is to be bound, imprisoned, rendered perfectly powerless and inoperative; Christ, the source of all blessing, spiritual and temporal, is to *reign*, to govern the nations of the earth Himself, suffering no sin or oppression, and protecting the poor and needy. The seventy-second Psalm, the thirty-second chapter of Isaiah, and similar scriptures, describe his glorious, peaceful, righteous reign, and its blessed results to mankind.

And while compassion for our fellow-creatures would make us long for the dawn of the day of Christ, how much more, *desire for his glory !* Can we, who own Him Lord, be content to have Him despised and rejected still by his ancient people Israel, denied, mocked, and insulted by the vast infidel host, displaced from his rightful throne, by this self-styled Vicar on earth, robbed of all his peculiar glories by an apostate priesthood, unknown to the great majority of the sinners He died to save, poorly obeyed and honoured by his best friends and followers, and practically forgotten and disowned by the mass of those who bear his name ? Can we be content with a continuance of this treatment of the only begotten Son in whom God is well-pleased ? Can we endure to see this treatment still accorded to Him who for our sakes humbled Himself and became of no reputation, and took upon Him the form of a servant, and became obedient unto death, even the death of the cross ? Is He to have nothing but what He had before, the adoration and love of the heavenly hosts ? Or, rather, is not every knee to bow to Him, and every tongue to confess Him Lord, to the glory of God the Father ? Are not

our hearts impatient for the day when earth shall own her
King, and Israel its Messiah, and our blessed Lord alone be
exalted? Do we not cry,—

> Our longing eyes would fain behold
> That bright and blessed brow,
> Once wrung with bitterest anguish, wear
> Its crown of glory now?

And does not the cry gush from the depth of our souls?
The near approach of the day of Christ, must rejoice the heart
that adores Him ; for never till then will He have his rightful
place, or receive from the sons of men, the love and the sub
mission which He so richly deserves.

And without being selfish, we rejoice and must rejoice for
our own sakes in the prospect of the near approach of the end
of the age, notwithstanding its accompanying judgments.

For whatever the exact portion it may bring to others, whatever its immediate and precise effect on Israel, on Christendom,
and on the heathen nations of the earth,—and there may be room
for some doubts and differences of opinion as to these,—there
can be no question whatever, as to the portion it brings to the
true church and to each individual Christian. "In a moment,
in the twinkling of an eye," the dead in Christ shall rise, and
the living "in Christ" be changed, the corruptible put on incorruption, and the mortal immortality, when the Lord Himself
descends from heaven with a shout, with the voice of the arch-
angel and the trump of God ; we shall be caught up together
in the clouds to meet the Lord in the air, and so shall we be
for ever with the Lord. We shall see Him, and be like Him,
for we shall see Him as He is ; we shall go in, clad in pure
linen, clean and white, to the marriage supper of the Lamb;
we shall, as his blood-bought bride, sit with Him on his
throne, and share his glory, according to his word, "the
glory which Thou hast given Me, I have given them." Simple,
clear, abundant, and unmistakable are the predictions with
reference to our portion at the coming of the Lord. "It is a
righteous thing with God to recompense tribulation to those

that trouble you; and to you who are troubled REST WITH
US when the Lord Jesus shall be revealed from heaven with
his mighty angels, in flaming fire taking vengeance on those
that know not God, and obey not the Gospel of our Lord
Jesus Christ: who shall be punished with everlasting destruction from the presence of the Lord, and from the glory
of his power; when He shall come to be GLORIFIED IN HIS
SAINTS, AND ADMIRED IN ALL THEM THAT BELIEVE in that
day" (2 Thess. i. 6–10). Rest! that is to be one feature of
our portion, rest with Christ, rest with the saints and martyrs
that are gone before. Rest from conflict with the world,
the flesh, and the devil; rest from the life and walk of faith,
in the more glorious life and walk of sight, for we shall behold his face, and *see* Him, whom not having seen we love;
rest of heart in love's full fruition, in complete and eternal
union with our Lord,—the marriage of the Lamb; rest of
mind, in perfect knowledge, for then shall we know, even as
also we are known; rest from the burden of this body of
humiliation, rest from labouring in vain, and spending our
strength for nought, rest from all care and fear, from all strife,
and all pain and sorrow; and from the heart-ache produced by
the daily sights and sounds of ungodliness. The day of Christ
shall bring *rest* to the weary! Nor rest only, but fulness of
joy, and pleasures for evermore! The joy of seeing HIM
glorified and acknowledged by all, and the joy of being glorified and acknowledged ourselves by Him; the joy of perfect
holiness, the joy of possessing a new and incorruptible spiritual
body in which to serve Him as we cannot do here, and to
enjoy his glory, as would now be impossible. "Beloved! now
are we the sons of God; but it doth not yet appear *what we
shall be;* but we know that when He shall appear, *we shall be
like Him* for we shall see Him as He is." Ours shall be the
joy, not only of being like Him ourselves, but of beholding all
those we love like Him also—the joy of seeing eye to eye, and
of having every feeling in perfect unison, with all the children
of God, the joy of meeting the saints of other days, the

patriarchs and prophets and apostles, and the noble army of martyrs; of seeing, crowned with crowns of life, those who loved not their lives to the death—the joy of unhindered communion and worship, the joy of perpetual and perfect service. And all these joys sweetened by the assurance that they are ours for ever, that we shall go no more out from the temple of the immediate presence of God, that we are to be for ever with the Lord! Earth's millennium is to end, like all previous dispensations, in apostasy and judgment; but to the risen saints no change, no apostasy can ever come. Christ is their life; because He lives, they live also, in Him and with Him indissolubly and eternally one. Their eternal state begins at his Epiphany, at the Second Advent for which we wait.

Men and brethren, are these things so? *Have* we a hope thus full of glory, and *does* our hope draw nigh, yea very nigh? "What manner of persons then ought we to be in all holy conversation and godliness?" Ought we not to be persons filled with faith, even as the world is filled with scepticism? Ought we not to be moved with fear for the ungodly around us, and burning with earnest zeal for their salvation? If the day of Christ be so near, how should we employ the brief remaining interval? Many a task which it might have been wise and well to undertake in the earlier days of the dispensation, would be sadly out of place now! This is no time for controversies about ecclesiastical organizations and abstruse questions of doctrine. To proclaim far and wide throughout the earth the everlasting Gospel before it is too late; to lay hold of men and women and pull them out of Sodom ere the fire from heaven fall; to cry aloud as regards Babylon, "Come out of her, my people, that ye be not partakers of her sins, and that ye receive not of her plagues;" to spend and be spent in seeking to rescue the perishing, this is the work that becomes us. To warn the world that the sword of destruction is coming, to explain to men that the long-suffering of God is for salvation, and that it is nearly over, and to live as though we believed these things—this is our plain duty.

When the destruction of Jerusalem, and the ruin of Palestine were approaching, when fearful judgments were on the eve of being poured forth on the Jewish nation, our Lord forewarned his disciples against laying up treasures for themselves upon earth. He counselled and commanded them to lodge whatever treasures they had beyond the spoiler's reach. What the position of these early Christians in Palestine was, such is our position now. The judgment of God is at hand : destruction is about to break forth upon Christendom. In the coming conflagration, the church and her earthly possessions shall be parted. What a burning up of hoarded wealth shall take place then ! Let us be warned in time. Let us make haste to lay out all our buried talents in Christ's service, instead of laying them up for condemnation and confusion of face. Let none of us imitate an unbelieving selfish world. Oh the obstinate folly of those who spend all their strength in gathering worthless fuel for the flames of that great day ! Let every Christian bring forth his hidden treasures, if he has any, and use them as they are most needed, without delay, lest that day should come upon us as a thief, and our wealth become a witness against us. There is a deadly famine in the world. Men are perishing in every land for lack of that which we possess. We have, and they have not, the gospel. We have, and they have not, eternal life. Let us expend our means and lives in taking to them, or sending to them, that which has saved our souls, that we may be clear from the blood of all men, and may by all means save some. Love to men and love to God alike demand it, and the example of an impoverished and crucified Redeemer points us to this path. Behold the footprints of Jesus ! Let us trace and tread them till He comes ! How much there is to be done for a dying world ! How little time in which to do it ! Let us be up and doing. It is the evening of this dispensation. The harvest—alas, how little reaped—is red with the glow of the setting sun. Who will bring in these waiting sheaves? China's millions are there ; India's countless idolators, and Africa's innumerable degraded sons are there. The

children of error and superstition, the mass, the multitude are
there. Not a few whom we personally know and love are
there. Let us reap while the light lasts. Bring in these golden
sheaves! Now, or never, *bring them in!*

Brethren, let us lift up our heads, for our redemption draweth
nigh. We see on every hand the signs, the predicted signs of
the nearness of the Advent. Let us not wait till it comes to
rejoice in it. Let us rejoice now, because the joy of Christ
and of his church is near. Superstition's fall and error's flight,
the casting out of Satan, and the coming of the King are nigh!
Ye graves, how soon shall ye give up your prey! Resurrection
life and glory, how soon shall ye burst upon us! Children of
the coming kingdom, this is no time for gloom, for mourning,
or for tears,—let us *rejoice,* for our redemption, long waited-for
—our longed-for redemption is at hand.

And you who neither desire nor dread that day—you who
love not our Lord Jesus Christ—you whose busy thoughts,
and whose warm affections are still in the world, whose
motives and objects and treasures are of the earth, you whose
minds are in darkness ; whose consciences, when they speak
at all, accuse ; whose hearts and souls are *indifferent* to eternal
truth, *destitute* of real holiness, *dead* to Him in whom you live
—dead to God—through the darkness and the death of your
souls, let the light of the gospel you have heard but never
understood, now shine at length !

Hear ye the word of the Lord. God who is light and love,
"GOD WAS IN CHRIST, RECONCILING the world unto Himself,
not imputing their trespasses unto them ; and hath committed
unto us the word of reconciliation. Now then we are ambassadors for Christ, as though GOD did beseech you by us ; we
pray you in Christ's stead, BE YE RECONCILED TO GOD. For
He hath made HIM to be SIN for us who knew no sin ; that
we might be made THE RIGHTEOUSNESS OF GOD IN HIM." Oh
glorious gospel of the blessed God ! Shine, shine in some
dark heart through these most joyful words of saving truth !
Jesus made sin for sinners ! The Son of God suffering in the

sinner's place! The sinner who BELIEVES,—who TRUSTS in Him justified and saved! The darkness is past, the true light now shineth. O thou who hast hated HIM without a cause, He takes thy place, He gives thee his!

O THOU who hast taken on Thyself humanity, that Thou mightest bear our griefs, and carry our sorrows, and atone for all our sins,—Thou whose loud expiring cry upon the cross rung through the universe the triumphant truth that our redemption is accomplished, that its battle has been fought, its victory won; the foe vanquished; sin cancelled, made an end of, and known no more,—Thou whose tender sympathies and whose immortal love surpassing knowledge are with us still, whose sacred presence unseen, but ever felt, guards and guides thy redeemed in all their pilgrim way,—Thou who art COMING in the brightness of thy majesty, in the sweetness of thy grace, in the fulness of thy strength, to finish our redemption, and complete thy triumph over all our fears, and all our foes,—Thou whose unchangeable purpose it is to surround thyself with the spotless beauty of a new creation, whose voice shall yet proclaim the renovation of a ruined world, the completion of the conquest of our evil by thy good, the consummation of the moral movement of all these ages carried forward by thine unwearied Spirit in the souls of men, the perfecting of thy redeemed in the holy image of their Redeemer; whose faithful hand shall yet finish the true temple of Jehovah, the living temple of his fulness, and habitation of his glory for ever and for ever,—Thou whose latest promise and last recorded utterance is, "SURELY I COME QUICKLY," and whose coming is now near at hand—Life of our life—Light of our light—God manifested—God with us—our everlasting ALL—we long, we watch, we wait to welcome Thee, —come as Thou hast said—come soon—"EVEN SO, COME, LORD JESUS!"

APPENDICES.

APPENDIX A.

I. LEVITICAL CHRONOLOGY SOLI-LUNAR.

THE divinely ordained Levitical chronology was soli-lunar ; *i.e.*, it was regulated by the revolutions of both sun and moon. Its years were *solar*, for they followed the seasons, as in the various ordinances connected with the ingathering of the fruits of the earth ; while its months were strictly *lunar*— not artificial months, but lunations—certain ordinances being connected with the recurrence of every new moon. The adjustment of solar to lunar years was effected by the intercalation of months, as the epact grew by repetition to complete lunations.

II. TYPICAL FEASTS REGULATED BY LUNATIONS.

The feasts of the Lord, representing the history of redemption, were *connected with certain days of lunations and phases of lunar fulness ;* as the passover with the tenth and fourteenth day of the first month ; the feast of unleavened bread with the fifteenth ; the feast of trumpets, the day of atonement, and the feast of tabernacles, with the first, tenth, and fifteenth day of the seventh month, etc. Lunar revolutions were the chronometric wheels measuring the intervals of the Levitical calendar.

III. CLOSENESS OF THE ADJUSTMENT.

There is a close adaptation in lunar phases to the septiform arrangements of the calendar. The earliest *phasis* or appearance of the new moon occurs when the moon is eighteen hours old. Sir Isaac Newton mentions in his work on the Prophecies of Daniel that this number of hours was indicated by the *rule* which the Jews observed in regulating the commencement of their months, and to which they gave a name whose numerical value is *eighteen.* Now, from the eighteenth hour of *earliest* phasis to full moon is *exactly fourteen days*, which was the interval appointed to extend in the first month to the passover, which thus coincided with full moon ; and thus the fifteenth day, which was the first of unleavened bread in the first month, and the fifteenth day, which was the first of the feast of tabernacles in the seventh month, immediately followed the time of lunar fulness, in harmony with the *octave,* or new creation, character of these feasts.

IV. REMARKABLE ADJUSTMENT IN THE JUBILEE—THE 600 LUNATIONS.

The nature and closeness of this adjustment was very remarkable in the case of the jubilee. The jubilee reckoning, regulating important civil arrangements in the land of Canaan, began with the day on which Israel crossed Jordan and entered Palestine. Like the sabbatic law, of which it was an expansion, its point of commencement is thus defined, "when ye be come into the land " etc. (Lev. xxv.) Now, as the jubilee was regulated by *years,* for it recurred every forty-ninth year at the time of the autumnal harvest, and was also regulated by *months,* for it was reckoned from the tenth day of the first month when Israel crossed Jordan, and the jubilee day was the tenth day of the seventh month (that of atonement), it was important that the year and months should closely agree. It is most interesting to observe that such is their *natural* adjustment that, in the first place, forty-nine years form a soli-lunar cycle ; and in the second place the interval from the tenth day of the first month of the first year, to the tenth of the seventh month of the forty-ninth, is exactly 600 lunations.

(1) Forty-nine complete years are a soli-lunar cycle containing

606 lunations. The 606 lunations are less than forty-nine solar years by 1d. 7h. 58m.; an agreement of the month and year in the jubilee sufficiently close to render the intercalation of an extra month unnecessary in any period under one thousand years.

(2) The interval from the tenth day of the first month of the first year, to the tenth of the seventh month in the forty-ninth year, was exactly 600 lunations; (forty-eight solar years, six lunar months, nine days, and fourteen hours of a tenth day, or 17,718d. 8h., are the measures of 600 lunations.) It should be observed that the day of atonement was reckoned from the evening of the ninth day to the evening of the tenth, "in the ninth day of the month at even, from even unto even shall ye rest" (marginal reading).

It will be seen from this, that the jubilee redemption rest followed immediately on the expiration of the complete period of 600 months. As 600 months are exactly *fifty lunar years*, the fiftieth lunar year terminated on the day of atonement, on which day the jubilee year commenced. The jubilee year, which is called the fiftieth, extended from the day of atonement in the forty-ninth year to the same date in the fiftieth year, and was thus an overlapping year, the course of jubilees being 49 + 49 + 49 years, etc.

V. IMPORTANT ANALOGOUS ADJUSTMENT IN THE "SEVENTY WEEKS"—THE 6000 LUNATIONS; or, the correspondence between the *time* of our Lord's death, in the "seventy weeks," and that of the day of atonement and liberation in the jubilee.

There was a coincidence between the time of our Lord's death and the day of passover, a fact of very deep interest and importance in connection with the fulfilment in Christ of the Divine prophecies and foreshadowings of redemption. As our Lord's death coincided with the passover day in the first month, it could not coincide with the day of atonement in the seventh; yet the high priest entering within the veil on the day of atonement, set forth our Lord's entrance into heaven itself after He had obtained for us eternal redemption. It was impossible that the one event should fall on two distinct days; but was it not possible that our Lord's death, while coinciding with a passover day, should also have been accomplished at a time in some way analogous, and strikingly analogous, to that occupied by the great atoning day when the high priest entered within the veil? An attentive study of the subject will show that such a coincidence existed.

The day of atonement was annual, and its forty-ninth occur- rence *was the day of jubilee.*

The " seventy weeks " appointed to extend from the going forth of the commandment to restore and to build Jerusalem unto Messiah the Prince, was *an enlarged jubilee*—the former being forty-nine and the latter 490 years.

Now, the death, resurrection, and ascension of Christ, by which He atoned for sin, brought in everlasting righteousness, and entered within the veil, even into heaven itself, were ac- complished at the very time in the 490 years which perfectly answers to that of the atoning day in the forty-nine years jubilee. In order to demonstrate this it will be necessary to show the exact date from which the 490 years are reckoned, and also the date of the crucifixion.

The terminal point from which the 490 years are reckoned is " the going forth of the command to restore and to build Jerusalem," or the beginning of the passover month in the year 457 B.C. Of this we subjoin satisfactory evidence, drawn principally from the careful calculations of Sir Isaac Newton, with reference to the exact date of the seventh year of Arta- xerxes in which, according to the testimony of Ezra (chap. vii.), this edict went forth, and this restoration commenced. The record of several eclipses which occurred in the reigns of Darius and Cambyses enabled Sir Isaac Newton to fix the required date with great accuracy.

Our Lord's passion is assigned by Lactantius, Augustine, Origen, Tertullian, and other ancient authors to the year A.D. 29, and the correctness of this conclusion has been confirmed by Brown ("Ordo Sæclorum," sec. 2), and at a later date by Clinton ("Fasti Romani," p. 326). The interval between B.C. 457 and A.D. 29 is 485 years, and that period contains 6000 lunations, less 41–42 days. Now, the interval from our Lord's death to His ascension was 41–42 days; therefore 485 *solar years, terminating with our Lord's death, together with the 41–42 days which followed, to His ascension, are* 6000 *lunations.* We have previously shown that 600 lunations measured the interval in the jubilee which terminated with the day of atonement,—the tenth day of the seventh month or the forty-ninth year; it therefore follows that the time of the occurrence of the *true* atonement, and entrance "into heaven itself" in the 490 years, was in marked and perfect correspondence with the time of the *typical* atonement on the day of jubilee in the forty-nine years.

Proofs of the correctness of these conclusions will be found further on. In the first edition of this book, we assigned, in accordance with the most trustworthy authorities, the years B.C. 457 and A.D. 29 as those of the beginning of the " seventy -weeks," and of our Lord's crucifixion ; it has only been *in correcting for a second edition* that we have discovered the deeply interesting and important proportion which the interval connecting these termini bears to that which extended in the marvellous Levitical type to the great day of atonement and jubilee.

VI. THE GROUNDS OF THE CHRONOLOGY HERE FOLLOWED.

(1) As to THE TERMINAL POINT FROM WHICH THE "SEVENTY WEEKS" ARE TO BE RECKONED, we quote the following from the work of Sir Isaac Newton on the Prophecies of Daniel, part 1, ch. 10.

" 'Seventy weeks are determined (or " cut out ") upon thy people and upon thy holy city, to finish the transgi ession.'

" Here, by putting a week for seven years, are reckoned 490 years from the time that the dispersed Jews should be re-incorporated into a people

and a holy city until the death and resurrection of *Christ.* . , . Now
the dispersed Jews became a people and city when they first returned into
a polity, or body politic, and *this was in the seventh year of Artaxerxes
Longimanus*, when *Ezra* returned with a body of Jews from captivity and
revived the Jewish worship, and, by the king's commission, to judge and
govern the people according to the laws of God and the king. (Ezra vii.
7, 25.) There were but two returns from captivity—Zerubbabel's and
Ezra's ; in Zerubbabel's they had only commission to build the temple ; in
Ezra's they first became a polity, or city, by a government of their own.
Now, the years of this Artaxerxes began about two or three months after
the summer solstice, and his seventh fell in with the third year of the
eighteenth Olympiad ; and *the latter part thereof, wherein Ezra went up to
Jerusalem, was in the year of the Julian period,* 4257 (*i.e.* B.C. 457).
. . .

" The grounds of the chronology here followed I will now set down as
briefly as I can.

" The Peloponnesian war began in spring, An. 1, Olymp. 87 (B.C. 432),
Diodorus, Eusebius, and all other authors agree.   It began two months
before Pythodorus ceased to be Archon (Thucyd. l. 2), that is, in April, two
months before the end of the Olympic year.   Now, the years of this war
are most certainly determined by the fifty years distance of its first year
from the transit of Xerxes inclusively (Thucyd. l. 2), or forty-eight years
exclusively (Eratosth, apud Clem. Alex.); by the sixty-nine years distance of
its end, or twenty-seventh year, from the beginning of Alexander's reign in
Greece ; by the acting of the Olympic games in its fourth and twelfth years
(Thucyd. l. 5); and by three eclipses of the sun and one of the moon, mentioned by Thucydides and Xenophon.   Now, Thucydides, an unquestionable witness, tells us that the news of the death of Artaxerxes Longimanus
was brought to Ephesus, and from thence by some Athenians to Athens,
in the seventh year of the Peloponnesian war, when the winter half-year
was running, and therefore he died An. 4, Olymp. 88, in the end of An.
J.P. 4289 (B.C. 425), suppose a month, or two, before mid-winter ; for so
long the news would be in coming.   Now, Artaxerxes Longimanus reigned
forty years, by the consent of Diodorus, Eusebius, Jerome, Sulpitius, or
forty-one, according to Ptol. in Can., Clem. Alexand. (l. 1), Strom., Chron.
Alexandr., Abulpharagius, Nicephorus, including therein the reign of his
successors, Xerxes and Sogdian, as Abulpharagius informs us.   After Artaxerxes, reigned his son, Xerxes, two months, and Sogdian seven months ;
but their reign is not reckoned apart in summing up the years of the kings,
but is included in the forty, or forty-one, years reign of Artaxerxes ; omit
these nine months, and the precise reign of Artaxerxes will be thirty-nine
years and three months.   And, therefore, since his reign ended in the
beginning of winter, An. J.P. 4289 (B.C. 425) it began between midsummer
and autumn An. J.P. 4250 (B.C. 464).

"The same thing I gather also thus. Cambyses began his reign in spring, An. J.P. 4185 (B.C. 529), and reigned eight years, including the five months of Smerdes ; and then Darius Hystaspis began in spring, An. J.P. 4193 (B.C. 521), and reigned thirty-six years, by the unanimous consent of all chronologers. *The reigns of these two kings are determined by three eclipses of the moon, observed at Babylon, and recorded by Ptolemy ; so that it cannot be disputed.* One was in the seventh year of Cambyses, An. J.P. 4191 (B.C. 523), July 16th, at eleven at night ; another in the twentieth year of Darius, An. J.P. 4212 (B.C. 502), Nov. 19th, at 11.45 at night; a third in the thirty-first year of Darius, An. J.P. 4223 (B.C. 491), April 25th, at 11.30 at night. By these eclipses, and the prophecies of Haggai and Zechary compared together, it is manifest that his years began after the twenty-fourth day of the eleventh Jewish month, and before the 25th day of April, and by consequence about March. Xerxes, therefore, began in spring, An. J.P. 4229 (B.C. 485), for Darius died in the fifth year after the battle of Marathon, as Herodotus (lib. 7) and Plutarch mention ; and that battle was in October, An. J.P. 4224 (B.C. 490), ten years before the battle at Salamis. Xerxes, therefore, began within less than a year after October, An. J.P. 4228 (B.C. 486), suppose in the spring following, for he spent his first five years, and something more, in preparations for his expedition against the Greeks ; and this expedition was in the time of the Olympic games, An. 1, Olymp. 75, Calliade Athenic Archonte, twenty-eight years after the regifuge and consulship of the first Consul, Junius Brutus, Anno Urbis Conditæ 273 (B.C. 481), Fabio and Furio Coss. The passage of Xerxes' army over the Hellespont began in the end of the fourth year of the seventy-fourth Olympiad, that is, in June, An. J.P. 4234 (B.C. 480), and took up one month ; and in autumn, three months after, on the full moon, the 16th day of the month Munychion, was the battle of Salamis, and a little after that an eclipse of the sun, which, by the calculation, fell on October 2nd. His sixth year, therefore, began a little before June, suppose in spring, An. J.P. 4234 (B.C. 480), and his first year consequently in spring, An. J.P. 4229 (B.C. 485), as above. Now, he reigned almost twenty-one years, by the consent of all writers. Add the seven months of Artabanus, and the sum will be twenty-one years and about four or five months, which end between midsummer and autumn, An. J.P. 4250 (B.C. 464). At this time, therefore, began the reign of his successor, Artaxerxes, as was to be proved.

"The same thing is also confirmed by Julius Africanus, who informs us out of former writers that the twentieth year of this Artaxerxes was the 115th year from the beginning of the reign of Cyrus in Persia, and fell in with An. 4, Olymp. 83. It began, therefore, with the Olympic year soon after the summer solstice, An. J.P. 4269 (B.C. 445). Subduct nineteen years, and his first year will begin at the same time of the year, An. J.P. 4250 (B.C. 464), as above.

" His SEVENTH YEAR, THEREFORE, BEGAN AFTER MIDSUMMER, An. J.P. 4256 (B.C. 458), AND THE JOURNEY OF EZRA TO JERUSALEM, IN THE SPRING FOLLOWING, FELL ON THE BEGINNING OF AN. J.P. 4257 (B.C. 457) AS ABOVE."

(2) On THE THREE ECLIPSES in the reigns of Cambyses and Darius, by means of which Sir Isaac Newton determines the date of the seventh year of Artaxerxes (the starting point of the "seventy weeks,") we cite the testimony of *Ptolemy, by whom " a foundation has been laid for chronology sure as the stars."* Ptolemy's account of ancient eclipses, and of their connection with historic facts, is more precious than gold, and warrants a translation of the *Almagest* into every language. The astronomer Laplace says of this work, " *L'Almagest,* considéré comme le dépôt des anciennes observations, est un des plus précieux monuments de l'antiquité."

i. Of the eclipse in the seventh year of Cambyses (B.C. 523), Ptolemy mentions :

" In the seventh year of Cambyses, which is the 225th year of Nabonassar, between the 17th and 18th of Phamenoth, at one hour before midnight, the moon was eclipsed at Babylon by half the diameter on the north. At Alexandria the eclipse must thus have been nearly 1h. 50m. before midnight."

The era of Nabonassar (in whose 225th year this eclipse took place) is one fixed with certainty by recorded eclipses to Feb. 26th, 747 B.C. The month of Phamenoth is the seventh in the Egyptian year, and the time of this eclipse was July 16th, at 11 at night, B.C. 523.

ii. The eclipse in the twentieth year of Darius is thus described by Ptolemy :

"The second eclipse, which also Hipparchus employed, was in the twentieth year of the Darius who was after Cambyses, in the Egyptian month Epiphi 28 to 29, at 6¼ equinoxial hours of the night, at which time the moon was likewise eclipsed on the south by one-fourth of her diameter, and the middle time at Babylon was two-fifths of an equinoxial hour before midnight, since half the night was then 6¾ equinoxial hours nearly, but in Alexandria it was 1¼ equinoxial hours before midnight."

Epiphi was the eleventh Egyptian month. The time of the eclipse was Nov. 19th, 11h. 45m. at night, B.C. 502.

iii. With reference to the eclipse in the thirty-first year of Darius, Ptolemy writes as follows :—

"For the purpose of determining the node, we have taken the first eclipse observed at Babylon in the thirty-first year of Darius I. in the Egyptian month Tybi, third to fourth day, in the middle of the sixth hour, in which it is declared that the moon was eclipsed two digits on the south. With this we have compared another observed at Alexandria in the eighth year of Adrian," etc.

The month Tybi was the fifth in the Egyptian year, and the date of the eclipse, as given by Sir Isaac Newton, is April 25th, 11h. 30m. at night, An. J.P. 4223, which is B.C. 491. (The An. J.P., or year of the Julian period, is not reckoned from the creation, or from any historic date, but is a valuable artificial combination of several cycles in astronomical and chronological use.)

For commentary on these eclipses see the *Chrono-Astrolabe* by James Bowman Lindsay, pp. 75, 80–82 ; from which we have taken Ptolemy's statements as above given.

Having thus shown that the point from which the "seventy weeks" are reckoned—the going forth of the edict of Artaxerxes to restore the Jewish polity, in the seventh year of his reign—is the spring (passover month) of B.C. 457, we have now to establish, both by historical and astronomical means, as approximately as possible, the dates of the nativity, and of the death and resurrection of our Lord.

(3) AS TO THE PARTICULAR HISTORIC INTERVAL OCCUPIED BY OUR LORD'S LIFE, the following passage from Mr. Lindsay's valuable work, the *Chrono-Astrolabe,* presents the facts with great force and clearness :—

"Christianity exists now, and we know from Greek, Roman, and Jewish history that there was a time when it was not. The Jews were strictly forbidden to hold intercourse with foreigners ; but, notwithstanding their exclusiveness, the Gentile writers often mention them. The founder of Christianity, at what time soever He lived, gave His followers a law the very reverse of exclusiveness, by going to all nations to make known His doctrines. Not a word about Christianity is mentioned by Cæsar, Cicero, Livy, Virgil, or Ovid, and to believe that it existed without being mentioned by them is preposterous credulity. A century after these writers, Christians are mentioned by Josephus, Tacitus, Pliny, and Suetonius, and the *advent* of their Master must have been in the interval. Four different accounts of the life and death of Christ are given; the difference of authorship is proved by apparent discrepancies, and the truthfulness is confirmed by the general harmony. Luke relates several dates with great minuteness, and this affords a strong argument of veracity. He says that John commenced his preaching in the fifteenth year of Tiberius, and that soon after Jesus also commenced, when He was about thirty years of age. He also says that Christ was born in the reign of Augustus, and both he and Matthew place this event a little before the death of Herod. Now, from Ptolemy's canon we know exactly the times of Augustus and Tiberius, and the time of the death of Herod is determined from Josephus. The time thus obtained for the origin of Christianity *is just the interval of those Roman writers who do not mention it and those who do,* and there is no other time possible that can be fixed upon for its origin. False religions may arise from small beginnings as well as true; the utmost care and caution are necessary to discriminate, and credulity is as culpable as scepticism. A remarkable dissimilarity is observed in the teaching of the founder of Islamism and of the Founder of Christianity. The former affirmed that he had interviews with heaven, and, without giving any proof of the truth of his assertion, condemned all who disbelieved him to future punishment. The latter never found fault with the Jews for disbelieving His word, but for denying the evidence of their senses, or attributing His gracious miracles to demons. The Jews were trained from infancy to entertain the highest respect for the laws of Moses, and the most thorough contempt for all other religions. That a handful of persons thus trained should spontaneously arise and denounce those laws that they were taught to venerate is contrary to experience. No such example in the annals of history is anywhere found, and its occurrence would be as great a miracle as any in the Bible. No cause conceivable could effect such a change, except miracles addressed to the senses, or a direct voice from heaven; and those who deny those miracles as being contrary to experience, are compelled to admit a still greater miracle. Christianity certainly had an origin, and no other than that assigned to it would consist with experience. The books of the New Testament, also, can be proved to have been written in the first century, and not long after the events recorded in them. They could not have been written in the century before, *for the events recorded did not then exist,* neither could they have been written in the century after, *for they are quoted*

and commented upon by a host of writers that then lived. The writers of
the second century are quoted by those of the third ; and thus a regular
chain of writers, that has never been broken, never will, never can be
broken, has been formed from the apostles to the present day."—*Chrono-
Astrolabe,* Lindsay, p. 142.

(4) The Date of the Nativity.

Our present era for the nativity, or that in popular use, is
not of apostolic, or even of early, origin. It is that which was
fixed upon by Dionysius Exiguus, in the *sixth* century, and is
proved to be erroneous by the fact that it places the birth of
Christ no less than four years *after* the death of Herod—of
the Herod who, when our Lord was born, sought "the young
child to destroy him."

Our Lord was certainly born *before* the death of Herod,
and the time of Herod's death is ascertained by means of an
eclipse of the moon recorded by Josephus (Antiq. xvii. 4).
Just before his death Herod burnt alive, along with his companions, one Matthias, who had been made high priest,—
"*And that very night,*" says Josephus, "*there was an eclipse of
the moon.*" The passover occurred immediately after the
death of Herod, and before this came the funeral feast of
some days duration, which Archelaus appointed in honour of
his father. " Such an eclipse of the moon, visible at Jerusalem, as Ideler and Wurm have proved, actually occurred at
that time, in the night between the 12th and 13th of March,
and according to Ideler beginning at 1h. 48m., and ending
at 4h. 12m. The full moon of Nisan, *i.e.,* the 15th day of
Nisan, occurred in 750 A.U.C. (B.C. 4) on the 12th of April.
If, therefore, as we have seen above, Herod died some days
before this, and consequently at the beginning of April, this
note of time would harmonize most excellently with the date
of the eclipse of the moon."

" Wurm, considering that an astronomical datum furnished
a basis superior to all doubt, undertook the praiseworthy
labour of *calculating all the lunar eclipses from 6 B.C. to 1 B.C.,*

and has tabulated the results.   He shows that in the year
U.C. 750 (B.C. 4) the only lunar eclipse visible at Jerusalem was
that already mentioned, and that in the only other year which
can enter into consideration for the year of Herod's death,
there was not one."—Wieseler's "Chronological Synopsis of
the Four Gospels," p. 51.

(5) Kepler's Calculations as to the Star of the Nativity.

"The credit of having been the first to employ the data derived from
astronomical and chronological calculations respecting this star, as the basis
of his investigations concerning the year of our Lord's birth, is due to the
celebrated astronomer *Kepler*.   At the close of 1603, the very time that a
violent controversy was raging among theologians as to the year of our
Lord's birth, a phenomenon appeared in the starry heavens, which drew this
celebrated astronomer into the ranks of the combatants.   *On the 17th of
December of that year, there occurred a conjunction of the planets Jupiter and
Saturn.*   In the spring of 1604, *Mars also came to the same place,* and in
the autumn an entirely new body, resembling a fixed star, appeared in the
neighbourhood of those two planets at the east part of Serpentarius,
shining at first like a star of the first magnitude and very bright, but becoming gradually dimmer, until in October, 1605, it was scarcely visible,
and at last, in March, 1606, had totally disappeared.   Kepler, well aware
that the astrologers of all times, and therefore certainly also the Magi mentioned by Matthew, attached great importance to the conjunction of Jupiter
and Saturn, *which recurs about every twenty years,* and knowing that for
that very reason they had divided the zodiac, *which it traverses in about* 800
years, into four trigons, he calculated whether such a conjunction had taken
place shortly before the commencement of the era at which, according to
historical data, the birth of our Lord must be placed.   He arrived at the
remarkable result *that this conjunction had happened three times in* 747 U.C.,
B.C. 7, and that in the last half of Pisces, near the first point of Aries,
while *in the spring of the following year the planet Mars also came to the
same spot.   He therefore argued, that the star seen by the Magi from the east,
at the birth of Christ, was identical with the conjunction of those three
superior planets, and that probably an extraordinary star, like that which
had blazed forth in the foot of Serpentarius in his own time, was added to the
group.*   Accordingly he placed the birth of Jesus in the year
748 A.U.C., B.C. 6.

"Ideler, pursuing Kepler's view still further, has given us two calculations of the conjunction of the two planets.   The later, and, in Encke's

opinion, the most accurate, furnishes us with the following data to determine the three planetary conjunctions. The first took place on the 29th of May, in 21° of Pisces, when the planets were visible in the East before sunrise, and Jupiter and Saturn were only one degree apart; the second, on the 1st of October, in 18° of Pisces; and the third, on the 5th of December, in 16° of Pisces. Ideler, therefore, as had been previously done by Sanclemonti on other grounds, which Ideler accepts as valid, places the birth of Christ in 747 A.U.C."—Wieseler's "Synopsis of the Four Gospels," pp. 56-8.

The following passage on this remarkable conjunction at the time of the nativity is from Dean Alford's Commentary on the New Testament :—

" The expression of the Magi, 'we have seen his star,' does not seem to point to any miraculous appearance, but to something observed in the course of their watching in the heavens. We know the Magi to have been devoted to astrology, and, on comparing the language of our text with this undoubted fact, *I confess that it appears to me the most ingenuous way fairly to take account of that fact in our exegesis*, and not to shelter ourselves from an apparent difficulty by the convenient, but forced, hypothesis of a miracle. . . . Now, we learn from astronomical calculations that a remarkable conjunction of the planets of our system took place a short time before the birth of our Lord ; . these statements have been remarkably confirmed, except in the detail now corrected, 'that an ordinary eye would regard them (the planets) as one star of surpassing brightness,' by the Rev. C. Pritchard, in a paper read by him before the Royal Astronomical Society, containing his calculations of the times and nearnesses of the conjunctions, *as verified by the Astronomer Royal at Greenwich.* In the year of Rome 747, on the 20th May (29th, Pritchard) there was a conjunction of Jupiter and Saturn in the twentieth degree of constellation Pisces, close to the first point of Aries, which was the part of the heavens noted in astrological science as that in which the signs denoted the greatest and most noble events. On the 27th October (29th Sept., Pritchard), in the same year, another conjunction of the same planets took place in the sixteenth degree of Pisces ; and on the 12th November (5th Dec., Pritchard) a third, in the fifteenth degree of the same sign (Ideler, 'Haudbuch der Chronologie,' ii. 399). . . . It is fair to notice the influence on the position maintained in this note of the fact, which Mr. Pritchard seems to have substantiated, that the planets did not, during the year B.C. 7, approach each other so as to be mistaken by any eye for one star : indeed not 'within double the apparent diameter of the moon.' I submit, that even if this were so, the inference of the note remains as it was. The conjunction of the two planets, complete or incomplete, would be that

which would bear astrological significance, not their looking like one star."
—Alford, Comm. on Matt. ii.

With all due deference to Dean Alford as an able and
candid critic, we do not think that any of these conjunctions
can be referred to in the words, "*Lo, the star which they saw
in the east went before them, till it came and stood over where the
young child was.*" We think it not improbable that there was
a coincidence of the appearance of some bright particular
star with the earliest of these conjunctions *on the year which
preceded that of the nativity*, judging from the fact that
after Herod had "privily called the wise men and inquired
of them diligently *what time* the star appeared," he "sent
forth, and slew all the children that were in Bethlehem, and in
all the coasts thereof, *from two years old and under, according
to the time which he had diligently inquired of the wise men*,"—
a fact which implies that the first appearance of the star was
within two years of the slaughter in Bethlehem, which followed
the nativity. It seems to us that the star which, reappearing to
the wise men, " went before them and *stood over where the young
child was*," must have been something very different from the
mere proximity of two distinct planets revolving in common
with the rest of the stellar heavens in a westerly direction.

(6) Luke's Date for the Ministry of John.

The evangelist Luke connects the ministry and baptism of
John with the fifteenth year of the reign of Tiberius Cæsar
(Luke iii. 1).

" The fifteenth year of the *sole principate* of Tiberius, began August 19th,
U.C. 781 (A.D. 28) and reckoning backwards thirty years from that time
(see ver. 23), we should have the birth of our Lord in U.C. 751, or about
then ; for ὡσεὶ τριάκ. will admit of some latitude. But Herod the Great
died in the beginning of the year 750 (B.C. 4), and our Lord's birth *must*
be fixed some months, at least, *before* the death of Herod. If, then, it be
placed in 749 He would have been, at least, thirty-two at the time of his
baptism, seeing that it took place some time after the beginning of John's
ministry. This difficulty has led to the supposition that this fifteenth year
is not to be dated from the *sole* but from the *associated* principate of

Tiberius, which commenced most probably at the end of U.C. 764 (A.D. 11). According to this the fifteenth of Tiberius will begin at the end of U.C. 779." —Alford, on Luke iii.

(7) THE DATE OF OUR LORD'S PASSION.

We have already cited testimony (p. 451) to show that the ministry of our Lord included four passovers, and lasted for three and a half years.

His passion is placed in the year A.D. 29,—

" By many authors, by Lactantius, Augustine, Sulpicius, Idatius, Fast. apud Noris, the Catalogue Pont. Rom. apud Bucherium, by Origen, Hieronymus, and Tertullian. It is most probable that the nativity was in B.C. 5, that the ministry extended to a fourth passover, and that the crucifixion and ascension were in A.D. 29 " (*Clinton, Epitomy of Chron. of Rome*, p. 7). Among modern chronologists this date is accepted by Benson, Brown, Mann, Ideler, Bianchini, Sanclemonti, etc. "If the first passover after the baptism was in the spring of A.D. 26, the crucifixion and the fourth passover are determined to the year 29 ; and it remains to inquire whether the passover of that year was in March or April. The full moon of March is fixed by Mr. Cuninghame's calculation to Friday, March 18th, at 9h. 16m. p.m. If that was the paschal moon, we obtain these dates :—the 14th of Nisan began at 6 p.m. of March 17th, and the 15th of Nisan at 6 p.m. March 18th, 3h. 16m. before the full moon ; and the paschal lamb was slain at 3 p.m. of *Friday, March 18th*, 6h. 16m. before the full moon. It is no insurmountable objection that this was *three days before the equinox* ; for we have seen from the preceding testimonies that a Jewish passover was sometimes celebrated before the equinox ; and, as Mr. Benson properly remarks, in the Mosaic law there is no injunction which refers to the equinox at all. It has been objected, however, that March 18th is inadmissible, because if the 16th of Nisan is at March 20th, the corn would not be ripe for an offering. But the law seems only to require that when the sheaf was offered on the 16th of Nisan the barley should be in the ear. That it could be ripe enough to be reaped, and used for food, at that early season is scarcely credible. If the passover had been delayed until ripeness in the latter sense had been attained, not only a full moon at the equinox would have been excluded, but many vernal full moons after the equinox, and it could rarely happen that the passover could be celebrated at a full moon at all " (*Clinton, Epitomy Chron. Rome*, p. 326). The full moon of April, A.D. 29, fell on Sunday, the 17th, and if this was the month, the paschal lamb was slain at 3 p.m. of Friday, April 15th, *one day nineteen hours before the full moon ;* an irregularity and want of adaptation to the lunar revolutions measuring the feasts, which nothing short of absolute demonstration should compel us to admit in such a case. The conclusion is that the day of that supreme passover was according to the normal Levitical arrangement that of *full moon*, March 18th, A.D. 29, and that the resurrection *immediately preceded the vernal equinox*.

(8) Conclusions as to the Dates in the "seventy weeks" of our Lord's Death, Resurrection, and Ascension.

(*a*) We showed that the 490 years are to be reckoned from the beginning of Ezra's journey to Jerusalem, or "the first day of the first month," that of passover, in the year 457 B.C.

(*b*) We concluded that our Lord's death took place on the day of passover, Friday, March 18, A.D. 29. His resurrection followed two days later (Sunday), and his ascension forty days subsequently (the forty days apparently included the day on which He rose).

(*c*) The interval *in solar years* between these dates is 485 years, and 485 solar years equal 6000 lunations, less 41–42 days. Therefore reckoning from the spring of B.C. 457, when Ezra set out on his journey, 485 solar years, terminating with our Lord's death, together with the 41–2 days to his ascension, equalled 6000 lunations.

(*d*) The interval measured by *months*. Ezra began his journey on the first day of the passover month. Our Lord's death was on the 14th day of a passover month, and *his ascension near the end of the following month*.

Now, *by the most exact calculation* (given in the Tables in the fourth edition of the "Encyclopædia Britannica") the new moon of the passover month, B.C. 458, fell on March 31 (or April 6, O.S.).

From April 6, B.C. 458, to April 1, A.D. 29, are 486 equinoxial years. Now 486 years are one day less than 6011 lunations; therefore from April 6, B.C. 458, to April 2, A.D. 29, were 6011 lunations. To this add the lunation which followed, *near whose end* the ascension took place, and the sum is 6012 lunations. But B.C. 458 was, as Sir Isaac Newton has shown, the year which *preceded* Ezra's journey; therefore subtract for the Jewish lunar year 458-7 *twelve lunations*, and there remain, from the passover month B.C. 457 to the month which terminated with the ascension, 6000 lunations.

It follows from this that there exists *a perfect chronological analogy* between the date in the 49 years jubilee of *typical* atonement and liberty, and the date in the 490 years of the accomplishment of *true* atonement, ending with the glorious ascension of the great High Priest into heaven itself, there to appear in the presence of God for us, having obtained eternal redemption.

In the 49 years, exactly 600 lunations to a day terminated with the one ; in the 490 years, 6000 lunations terminated with the other.

How wonderfully does Jesus of Nazareth' fulfil the Divine Old Testament prophecies of redemption ! His death was on the very day of passover; his resurrection on the day of the presentation of the wave sheaf firstfruits of the early harvest ; the coming of his Spirit was on the day of Pentecost ; and his glorious ascension was accomplished at the close of *that month* whose end *in the "seventy weeks"* exactly answers to the position of the day of jubilee, and of the High Priest's entering within the veil, in the glad and beautiful Levitical symbol.

VII. THE DURATION OF OUR LORD'S TERRESTRIAL LIFE, AND
    ITS AGREEMENT WITH THE 33 YEARS, 7 MONTHS, AND 7
    DAYS SOLI-LUNAR CYCLE, THE CYCLE IN WHICH THE SUN
    GAINS ON THE MOON ONE SOLAR YEAR.

We have now cleared the way for a more accurate study of the duration of our Lord's life on earth. We have shown that his birth took place *before* B.C. 4, according to calculations of the eclipse which preceded Herod's death, and also that our Lord's death was accomplished in the year A.D. 29, on the day of passover, and that his ascension followed 41-42 days later.

We must now briefly consider the grounds of the popular

view that the *nativity* took place in the month of December, and endeavour to ascertain as nearly as possible the true date of the nativity.

"The vulgar DAY OF OUR LORD'S NATIVITY, Dec. 25, though an early tradition, as appears from the Apostolical Constitutions, lib. 5, cap. 13, was not established till the time of the Emperor Constantine, who died A.D. 337, when it was enacted, probably about the Council of Nice, A.D. 325, by the *Roman* Church, and adopted by the *Greek* Church ten years after at Constantinople, according to Chrysostom in his homily on the day of the nativity." "The true cause of their fixing on the 25th of December is thus perhaps best explained by Sir Isaac Newton."

"The times of the birth and passion of Christ being not material to religion, were little regarded by the Christians of the first age. They who began first to celebrate them placed them *in the cardinal periods of the year;* as the Annunciation of the Virgin Mary on the *25th of March*, which when Julius Cæsar corrected the calender was *the vernal equinox;* the feast of John Baptist on the 24*th June*, which was *the summer solstice;* the feast of St. Michael on *Sep.* 29, which was *the autumn equinox; AND THE BIRTH OF CHRIST ON THE WINTER SOLSTICE, DEC.* 25, with the feasts of St. Stephen, St. John, and the Innocents, as near as they could place them. And because the solstice in time removed from the 25th Dec. to the 24th, the 23rd, the 22nd, and so on backwards, hence some in the following centuries placed the birth of Christ on Dec. 23, and at length on Dec. 20, and for the same reason they seem to have set the feast of St. Thomas on December 21, and that of St. Matthew on Sept. 21. So also at the entrance of the sun into all the signs in the Julian Calendar, they placed the days of other saints; as the Conversion of Paul on Jan. 25, when the sun entered ♒; St. Matthias on Feb. 25, when he entered ♓; St. Mark on April 25, when he entered ♉; Corpus Christi on May 26, when he entered ♊; St. James on July 25, when he entered ♋; St. Bartholomew on Aug. 24, when he entered ♍; SS. Simon and Jude on Oct. 28, when he entered ♏; and if there were any other remarkable days in the Julian Calendar, they placed the saints upon them, as St. Barnabas on June 11, where Ovid seems to place the feast of Vesta and Fortuna, and the goddess Matuta; and SS. Philip and James on the first of May, a day dedicated both to the Bona Dea, or Magna Mater, and to the goddess Flora, and still celebrated with her rites. All which shows that these dates were fixed in the first Christian calendars by mathematicians at pleasure, without any ground in tradition; and that *the Christians afterwards took up with what they found in the calendars.*"—Sir I. Newton on Daniel, p. 145.

"Hospinian, a learned German antiquary, is of opinion that the Christians at *Rome* did not celebrate the 25th of December as thinking Christ was then born, but to make amends for the heathen *Saturnalia;* which was a season of great festivity, beginning on Dec. 16, and lasting three days, but usually prolonged to the end of the week on account of the succeeding feast of the Sigillarii (Macrob. Saturnal., lib. 1, cap. 10), and indeed the crowding together so many holidays near the end of December, as we find in the calendar, strongly confirms this opinion.

 " To determine the true day of Christ's birth, as Scaliger says, belongs to God alone, not man.   Of all the various conjectures that have been pro-posed, the most probable are, either (1) that 'Christ our Passover' was born about the time of the *vernal equinox,* when the *passover* was cele-brated ; or (2) ABOUT THE AUTUMNAL EQUINOX AT THE CELEBRATION OF THE FEAST OF TABERNACLES, when 'the WORD became flesh and (ἐσκήνωσεν) TABERNACLED among us '(John i. 14); or (3) on the great day of *Atonement,* the tenth day of the seventh month, as ' a faithful high priest in things pertaining to God, to make atonement for the sins of the people ' (Heb. ii. 17), to be Himself 'a propitiation for our sins, and not for ours only, but also for those of the whole world' (1 John ii. 2).   And if this last (adopted by Primate Usher) be preferred, it gives a peculiar emphasis to the declaration of the angel to the shepherds on the night of the nativity : 'Fear not: for, lo ! I bring you glad tidings of great joy, which shall be unto all people ; for unto you is born this day a Saviour, who is Christ the Lord.   Glory to God in the highest, and on earth peace, good will towards men ' (Luke ii. 10–14).   And indeed *either of the last two epochs agrees better than the first with the prevailing traditions of the duration of the ministry of Christ.*"—Hales' Chron. v. 1, p. 199.

The coincidence of our Lord's death with the passover, and of His resurrection with the wave sheaf offering, suggests the probability of the coincidence of his birth with some one of the feasts of the law.

That his birth should have coincided with the *passover* is not only most unlikely, if not inadmissible, from a chronolo-gical point of view, but also on the grounds (1) that it makes two so different events coincide with anniversaries of the same typical feast, and (2) that our Lord's birth *had not the sacrifi-cial character* which belonged to his death, and which justified the coincidence of the latter with the slaying of the paschal lamb.

On the same ground *the day of Atonement* is also excluded ; *the birth of Christ was not an atonement for sin*, neither did He enter on the day of his birth "within the veil," as the high priest did on the atoning day.

There remains then the probability, on typical and moral grounds, that the nativity coincided with *the feast of tabernacles,* that most joyous feast which celebrated the *dwelling of Israel in booths,* when God brought them out of the land of Egypt, a coincidence in perfect harmony with *Jehovah's tabernacling amongst us* when He became incarnate ("the word became flesh and TABERNACLED AMONG us") to bring us out of the antitypical Egypt in order that we may *dwell with Him* in the place He is preparing for us. This strong probability is confirmed by the age of our Lord at his baptism, and the three and a half years duration of his ministry, for as his death was on the day of Passover in spring, his birth, if thirty-three and a half years previously, took place *at the opposite season of the year,* near the *autumnal* equinox, and about the time of the *feast of taber-nacles.*

It becomes then a matter of much interest to ascertain what the exact interval was which extended from the day of our Lord's ascension back to the commencement of the feast of tabernacles in the thirty-fourth preceding year.

To render the calculation as simple as possible, we will show, first, the interval from the feast of tabernacles B.C. 6, to that of tabernacles in A.D. 29, and then subtract the difference be-tween the date of the ascension and that of this latter feast of tabernacles.

(1) From tabernacles to tabernacles *equals a number of com-plete lunations,* for the feast was regulated by lunations.

(2) From the feast of tabernacles, B.C. 6, to that of taber-nacles A.D. 29, extends 34 years, and in 34 years there are *twelve complete months of epact;* the months to be intercalated, therefore, are *twelve.*

(3) Thirty-four lunar years are 408 months, which with twelve months intercalation are 420 months.

(4) The feast of passover was on the 14th day of the first month, and the feast of tabernacles commenced on the 15th

day of the seventh, and therefore six months and one day later; we must, therefore, subtract six months from 420, leaving 414, and also *subtract* one day. We have then to *add* 41–42 days to the result to obtain the distance to the day of ascension.

414 months contain	12,225d. 15h.
Subtract one day	1d.
	12,224d. 15h.
Add 2d. and 40d. . . .	42d.
	12,266d. 15h.

We now compare this period of 12,266–7 days with the soli-lunar cycle in which the sun gains on the moon one solar year.

That cycle occupies exactly 33·585y.; or 33 *solar years, seven months, and seven days.*

We inquire what this period is in days.

Thirty-three solar years are a cycle of the day and year, and contain 12,053 days within ten minutes.

33 solar years contain . . .	12,053d.
7 lunations	206d. 17h.
7 days	7d.
Measure of the cycle . .	12,266d. 17h.

We previously concluded that as our Lord was thirty years old at his baptism, and as his ministry lasted for three and a half years, and terminated with a passover, He must have been born about the time of the feast of tabernacles, and now we find that *the interval from the commencement of the feast of tabernacles* B.C. 6, *to the day of our Lord's ascension, or* 12,266–7d., *was a soli-lunar cycle, in which the sun gained on the moon* EXACTLY ONE SOLAR YEAR.

This is the cycle which we consider to be the *unit*, or day, in the measurement of redemption history, and which we have named THE MESSIANIC CYCLE.

VIII. CONFIRMATION OF THE CHRONOLOGY THUS UNFOLDED.

1. As to the date of the first of Nisan, B.C. 457. 2300 years is a soli-lunar cycle; therefore the sun and moon occupy the same position at its beginning and end. From B.C. 457 to A.D. 1844 is 2300 years; and the new moon in March, 1844, occurred on the 19-20th (March 19d. 2h. 39m. astron. time of new moon at Jerusalem). The *phasis* occurred, of course, later, and stands in *the modern Jewish calendar* for that date *on March 21st.* This confirms the date March 19-20th for new moon of first Nisan, B.C. 457.

2. Reckoning the "seventy weeks" from B.C. 457, "the seventy weeks of years are Jewish weeks *ending with sabbatical* years, which is very remarkable." (Sir I. Newton.)

	TABLE OF SABBATIC YEARS IN THE "SEVENTY WEEKS."												
Wks.	1st 70 yrs.	W.	2nd 70 yrs.	W.	3rd 70 yrs	W.	4th 70 yrs.	W.	5th 70 yrs.	W.	6th 70 yrs.	W.	7th 70 yrs.
	B.C.		B C.		B.C.		B.C.		B.C.		B.C.		B.C.
1	457	11	387	21	317	31	247	41	177	51	107	61	37
2	450	12	380	22	310	32	240	42	170	52	100	62	30
3	443	13	373	23	303	33	233	43	163	53	93	63	23
4	436	14	366	24	296	34	226	44	156	54	86	64	16
5	429	15	359	25	289	35	219	45	149	55	79	65	9
6	422	16	352	26	282	36	212	46	142	56	72	66	2
7	415	17	345	27	275	37	205	47	135	57	65	67	A.D. 6
8	408	18	338	28	268	38	198	48	128	58	58	68	13
9	401	19	331	29	261	39	191	49	121	59	51	69	20
10	394	20	324	30	254	40	184	50	114	60	44	70	{ 27 34

It is needful to guard against the mistake that the sabbatic year exactly coincided with the interval, January to December, in any of the years in the above table. In each case it included parts of two years. The years on which it fell seem to have been 458-7 B.C., and so on to A.D. 33-34. The series is confirmed by the repeated statements of Josephus, that the capture of Jerusalem by Herod and Sosius, which took place at the end of B.C. 38, and the beginning of 37 (see Clinton, " F. Hellenici"), occurred *in a sabbatical year.*

There is some difficulty in adjusting its exact position, for in Ant. xiv. 16. 2 it is spoken of as current at the time of the siege : the Jews " erected new works when the former were ruined," etc., "and this they did while a mighty army lay round about them, and while they were distressed by famine and the want of necessaries, for this happened to be a sabbatic year "; and in Ant. xv. 1. 2 it is current after the capture, for then the distress was aggravated " by the sabbatic year, which was still going on, and forced the country to lie still uncultivated, since we are forbidden to sow our land that year."

It should be noticed that while the law commanded that the year of jubilee should commence on the day of atonement in the seventh month, it gave no such command with respect to the commencement of the sabbatic year. The *traditions* of the Talmud (Rosh Hashana) assign its beginning to the month Tisri. A tradition preserved by Maimonides informs us that "only Sh'mittahs were kept, and no Jobel, after the return from Babylon."

The Roman historian Tacitus testifies to the observance of the sabbatical year by the Jews in his time : "they give the seventh day to ease, because it put an end to labour ; moreover, through the allurements of idleness, *the seventh year also is given to inactivity* " (Tac. Hist. v. 4).

Compare also the very important testimony of Cæsar's decrees, recorded by Josephus, Ant. xiv. 10. 6 :

"Caius Cæsar, imperator the second time, hath ordained that all the country of the Jews, excepting Joppa, do pay a tribute yearly for the city of Jerusalem, *excepting the seventh, which they call the sabbatical year, because thereon they neither receive the fruits of their trees, nor do they sow their land;* and that they pay their tribute in Sidon on the second year (of that sabbatical period) the fourth part of what was sown ; and, besides this, they are to pay the same tythes to Hyrcanus and his sons, which they paid to their forefathers. And that no one, neither president, nor lieutenant, nor ambassador, raise auxiliaries within the bounds of Judæa, nor any soldiers exact money of them for winter quarters, or under any other pretence, but that they be free from all sorts of injuries; and that what-soever they shall hereafter have, and are in possession of, or have bought, they shall retain them all. It is also our pleasure, that the city Joppa, which the Jews had originally when they made a league of friendship with the Romans, shall belong to them, as it formerly did; and that Hyrcanus, the son of Alexander, and his sons, have a tribute of that city from those that occupy the land for the country, and for what they export every year to Sidon, twenty thousand six hundred and seventy-five modii every year; *the seventh year, which they call the sabbatic year, excepted, whereon they neither plough, nor receive the product of their trees."*

3. According to this chronology, *the seventh week of decades, or period of seventy years, in the* 490, *commences* with the taking of Jerusalem by Herod, and *the termination of the government of the Asmoneans.* "And thus did the government of the As-moneans cease, an hundred, twenty, and six years after it was set up. This family was a splendid and an illustrious one, both on account of the nobility of their stock, and of the dignity of *the high priesthood,* as also for the *glorious actions* their ancestors had performed for our nation" (Ant. xiv. 16). The sceptre did thus depart from Judah, and before the end of the government of the base and cruel monarch who seized it, *Shiloh* came.

4. Let the 490 years and the 2300 years of Dan. viii., which are clearly connected with the long Mohammedan down-tread-ing of the sanctuary, begin together, in the year B.C. 457; *then will the* 2300 *years end in the* 1260*th of the Mohammedan era.*

The Mohammedan year is strictly lunar—twelve lunations. The starting-point of the Mohammedan calendar is *the new moon of July* 15–16*th,* A.D. 622. This was the first of the Mulharram (or first month) preceding the so-called "flight of Mohammed." 1260 Mohammedan, or lunar years, are 1222 solar years and six months, so that the 1260th Mohammedan year coincides with A.D. 1844.

We have given (p. 437) the Mohammedan Edict of Tolera-tion, granted in 1844.

" It is an interesting fact connected with the duration of the Mohammedan power, that the firman, granted to the Society for Promoting
Christianity among the Jews, to build the Church of Christ in Jerusalem, in
the year 1845, was dated the first day of Ramazan, 1261, answering to our
September 10th, 1845 " (Letter of Rev. R. M. Chatfield in the *Record*,
dated December 13th, 1878).

An inspection of the subjoined Mohammedan calendar for
the present year (1879) will show its strictly *lunar* character,
i.e., that the first day of each month coincides with the first
appearance of the new moon. Ramadân is the ninth month;
and the first month (Mulharram) begins this time in December,
1878.

The *astronomic* new moons this year (1879) occur on the
following days : Jan. 22, 11h., m. ; Feb. 21, 4h., m. ; Mar. 22,
9h., aft. ; Apr. 21, 2h., aft. ; May 21, 5h., m. ; June 19, 8h.,
aft. ; July 19, 9h., m. ; Aug. 17, 8h., aft. ; Sept. 16, 6h., m. ;
Oct. 15, 3h., aft. ; Nov. 14, 0h. 38m., m. ; Dec. 13, 11h., m.
It will be observed that in the Mohammedan Calendar, the
commencement of each month takes place *about two days* after
astronomic new moon, soon after the lunar *phasis* (or appearance).

MOHAMMEDAN CALENDAR (Years 1296-97).			
Year.	Month.	Name of Months.	Month begins.
			A.D. 1879
1296	2	Saphar	Jan. 25
,,	3	Rabia	Feb. 23
,,	4	Latter Rabia	Mar. 25
,,	5	Gomada	April 23
,,	6	Latter Gomada	May 23
,,	7	Rajab	June 21
,,	8	Scbabân	July 21
,,	9	Ramadân	Aug. 19
,,	10	Schawal	Sep. 18
,,	11	Dulkaadah	Oct. 17
,,	12	Dulhagee	Nov. 16
1297	1	Mulharram	Dec. 15

5. This chronology is confirmed by the interval of *twelve* jubilees, which it shows, between the termination of the "seventy weeks," in A.D. 34, and the beginning of Mohammedan reckoning, A.D. 622—the Hegira.

The "seventy weeks," which, reckoned from B.C. 457, terminate in A.D. 34, are TEN JUBILEES, 490 years. The period which follows from that date to the setting up of the Mohammedan desolation, in A.D. 622, is TWELVE JUBILEES, 588 years.

The two periods together form twenty-two jubilees—1078 years; which is, as we have yet to show, a *perfect jubilee cycle*.

6. It is a further confirmation of Sir Isaac Newton's view that the "seventy weeks" are to be reckoned from B.C. 457, and not from B.C. 458, that the first of Nisan of the latter fell upon the Jewish *Sabbath*.

As the date of the new moon of March, B.C. 458, was on Thursday, March 30th, 14h. 48m. (according to Greenwich time), the *phasis*, or appearance of the new moon, did not take place till Friday evening, and the first of Nisan, therefore, fell on Saturday, the Jewish Sabbath. We are distinctly informed that Ezra commenced his journey on "the first day of the first month," which he would hardly have done had that day happened to be the Jewish Sabbath, seeing he attached so much importance to its strict observance as a day of rest.

7. It has been objected by some that if the passover in A.D. 29 coincided with the full moon of March 18th, it *preceded the equinox by about three days*. "This objection will be seen to be of no moment when it is considered that this very day, the 18th March, was regarded by the Western Church, prior to the Council of Nice, as the anterior paschal limit" (Browne's Chron. p. 55, who refers to the paschal cycle of St. Hippolytus).

Clinton, as previously quoted, says :—

"It is no insurmountable objection that this was three days before the equinox, for we have seen from the preceding testimonies that a Jewish passover was sometimes celebrated before the equinox, and, as Mr. Benson properly remarks, in the Mosaic law there is no injunction which refers to the equinox at all. It has been objected, however, that March 18th is inadmissible, because if the 16th Nisan is at March 20th, the corn would not be ripe for an offering. But the law seems only to require that when the sheaf was offered on the 16th of Nisan the barley should be in the ear, That it could be ripe enough to be reaped, and used as food, at that early season, is scarcely credible. If the passover had been delayed until ripeness in this latter sense had been attained, not only a full moon at the equinox would have been excluded, but many vernal full moons after the equinox ; and it could rarely happen that the passover could be celebrated at a vernal full moon at all " ("Epitome of Chron. of Rome," p. 326).

The fact that the full moon of March 18th, A.D. 29, *preceded the vernal equinox by about three days*, to our view only renders it *the more suitable* as the paschal date, *since it brings the resurrection and the vernal equinox into close proximity.* What more probable than that the new year, dating from the vernal equinox, and the new era, dating from the glorious resurrection, should commence together? The resurrection took place in the early morning *before* sunrise, and if in this month, but some hours before the sun entered the equinox of spring.

8. This chronology is further confirmed by the coincidence between the beginning of the " seventy weeks," and the date of *the vernal equinox* (or beginning of the equinoxial year). The "seventy weeks" began on the 1st of Nisan, which in B.C. 457 fell on the day of the vernal equinox, March 20–21 (March 26, O.S.), just as both new moon and vernal equinox fell on March 20–21, 2300 years afterwards, in A.D. 1844. The exact time of the passover new moon in 1844 was as follows :— Astronomical time of true new moon at *Jerusalem*, Tuesday, March 19th, 2h. 39m. Phasis *by the modern Jewish calendar*, Thursday, March 21st, first of Nisan. *New moon* thus fell on March 19–20, in 1844, and by the 2300 years cycle, it fell on the same date in the year B.C. 457. To this let it be added, that if the supreme passover was on March 18, A.D. 29, the resurrection day was March 20 (O.S.). With this month of Nisan and resurrection day, what a grand series of dates begins. This was the month of Israel's exodus from Egypt ; this was the date, 430 years before that exodus, of the call of Abraham and of his exodus. This was the month on whose first day the tabernacle was reared up ; and this the

mouth in which all Israel crossed Jordan, and entered the promised land. This was, from the exodus onwards, and still is, the *first* month of the sacred seasons of the Jewish people; and this has been for eighteen centuries the joyfully commemorated resurrection season in the Christian Church.

How eminently suitable that the " seventy weeks," extending to the time of Messiah the Prince, should commence with such a date! that its beginning should be in harmony with the subsequent starting-point in the wondrous history of the new creation!

9. The chronology we have reached is still further strengthened by *the solar date which it gives for the day of Ezra's reaching Jerusalem* on his divinely ordained mission of restoration, and the harmony of that date with a most important series of dates connected with the national calamities and deliverances of his people and of the city of Jerusalem.

" Upon the first day of the first month began he to go up from Babylon, and *on the first day of the fifth month* came he to Jerusalem, according to the good hand of his God upon him " (Ezra vii. 9).

As the 1st of Nisan, B.C. 457, fell on March 20–21, the first day of the fifth month, just four lunations later, fell on *July* 16*th.* Reckon from that date, July 16, 457 B.C., twenty-two jubilees (10 + 12), or 1078 years, a cycle of great importance in connection with the intercalation of months in the Jewish solilunar year,—reckon, we say, from the new moon of July 16, 457 B.C., 1078 years, and to what date does it exactly reach? It reaches just to the new moon of July 16, A.D. 622—the Hegira date, the first of Mulharram, or *the new moon from which the whole Mohammedan calendar has dated for now more than twelve hundred years.*

We may say, in passing, that the cycle of 1078 years is a combination of the most perfect soli-lunar cycle known, 1040 years (that which Mr. De Cheseaux named the Daniel cycle), and two lunar cycles of 19 years (the most perfect of short soli-lunar cycles), so that its accuracy is indisputable, the sun and moon returning at its close to within a very few hours of their position at its commencement. (We have yet to show that this cycle of 1111 *lunar years* 1 *month*, or 13,333 months, which just equal 1078 solar years, is *the astronomic foundation for a perfect jubilee reckoning.*)

From this era (July 16, A.D. 622,) dates the Mohammedan conquest of half the world, the chronology of the scourge of Eastern Christendom, and the period of the long *last* downtreading of Jerusalem.

From this era, July 15-16, A.D. 622, sweep forward 477 complete solar years to its anniversary on July 15, A.D. 1099. What date have we here? That of *the day of the recapture and rescue of Jerusalem in the first Crusade.*

In 1094, Peter the Hermit received his commission from the Pope to preach the Crusade. In 1096, Godfrey of Bouillon, Hugh of Vermandois, Robert of Normandy, Robert of Flanders, Stephen of Chartres, Raymond of Toulouse, Bohemond, and Tancred, set out with 600,000 crusaders, besides priests and monks, for the rescue of Jerusalem.

In 1099, on *July* 15, Jerusalem was taken by the Crusaders, and 70,000 Saracens put to the sword. Then was founded *the kingdom of Jerusalem* by Godfrey of Bouillon.

What an association of names : Ezra, Mohammed, Godfrey of Bouillon! What events linked with that date, July 15-16, and with that month of Ab!

This was the month of *the death of Aaron :* "Aaron the priest went up into mount Hor, at the commandment of the Lord, and died there, in the fortieth year after the children of Israel were come out of the land of Egypt, *in the first day of the fifth month*" (Num. xxxiii. 38).

Could the dying eyes of that first of Israel's high priests have but looked from the awful summit of mount Hor, down the long line of disasters and deliverances, which the recurrence of that memorable day and month should bring to his people, what scenes would he have beheld!

Far down the future he would have seen the burning of the

first glorious Temple, "the house of the Lord," and *beyond* it, the more awful burning of the second Temple! Both these burnings, the first by Nebuchadnezzar, the second by Titus, took place in the month of Ab, *and on the recurrence of the same day, the tenth of the fifth month.* The historian Josephus was much impressed by this solemn coincidence.

"As for that house," he says of the Temple, "God had for certain long ago doomed it to the fire, and now that fatal day was come according to the revolution of ages.

"It was the tenth day of the month Louis (Ab), upon which it was formerly burnt by the king of Babylon; although these flames took their rise from the Jews themselves, and were occasioned by them; for upon Titus' retiring, the seditious lay still for a while, and then attacked the Romans again, when those that guarded the holy house fought with those that quenched the fire that was burning in the inner (court of the) Temple; but these Romans put the Jews to flight, and proceeded as far as the holy house itself, at which time one of the soldiers, without staying for any orders, and without any concern or dread upon him at so great an undertaking, and being hurried on by a certain Divine fury, snatched somewhat out of the materials that were on fire, and being lifted up by another soldier, he set fire to a golden window, through which there was a passage to the rooms that were round about the holy house, on the north side of it. As the flames went upward the Jews made a great clamour, such as so mighty an affliction required, and ran together to prevent it; and now they spared not their lives any longer, nor suffered anything to restrain their force, since that holy house was perishing, for whose sake it was that they kept such a guard about it. . Now though any one would greatly lament the destruction of such a work as this was, since it was the most admirable of all the works that we have seen or heard, both for its curious structure and its magnitude, and also for the vast wealth bestowed upon it, as well as for the glorious reputation it had for its holiness; yet might such a one comfort himself with this thought, that it was fate that decreed it so to be, which is inevitable, both as to living creatures, and as to works and places also. *However, one cannot but wonder at the accuracy of this period thereto relating; for the same month and day were now observed, as I said before, wherein the holy house was burnt formerly by the Babylonians*" (Ant. vi. 4).

Eighteen hundred years have rolled away since that event, but to this day the Jewish nation scattered throughout the world *fasts on the ninth of Ab.* They regard this day as the most fatal in Jewish history, and consequently keep this fast " with greater rigour than any other in the Jewish calendar, the day of atonement alone excepted." In the synagogue service of the evening, the scriptures read are from the book of Lamentations. This year, 1879, the new moon of Ab (the phasis) falls on the 21st of July, and the feast of the ninth of Ab, on July 29.

"When the stars appear the feast is over; after which the month is generally called Menachem Av, *i.e.* Av the Comforter. All letters are particularly thus dated. And the Sabbath following the fast is called the Sabbath of Comfort" (Mills on the Religious Ceremonies of the Jews, p. 212).

(We should note in connection with this date Ezek. xx. : "It came to pass in the seventh year, *in the fifth month, the tenth day of the month*, that certain of the elders came to inquire of the Lord, and sat before me. Then came the word of the Lord unto me, saying, Cause them to know the abominations of their fathers." Also Zech. vii. 3 : " Should I weep in the *fifth* month, separating myself, as I have done these so many years?" Also Zech. viii. 19 : " Thus saith the Lord of hosts ; the fast of the fourth month, and the fast of the *fifth*, and the fast of the seventh, and the fast of the tenth, shall be to the house of Judah joy and gladness, and cheerful feasts ; therefore love the truth and peace.")

We have endeavoured to show that the seven months of the Levitical calendar correspond with the seven months of solilunar cycles, measuring the seven millenaries of redemption history. In this connection " the first day of the fifth month " corresponds with the end of the first four, and the beginning of the last three millenaries of the world's history, or in other words with the era which witnessed the advent and rejection of the world's Redeemer, and the simultaneous abolition of Judaism, a fact which casts fresh light on the suitability of the occurrence of Aaron's death, and of Ezra's arrival at Jerusalem on his mission of restoration on the typical date in question.

10. This chronology is confirmed by the coincidence in their termination of the following three great periods :—

Let the "seventy weeks," and with them the prophetic period and astronomic cycle of two thousand three hundred years, be reckoned from B.C. 457, then will the end of the 2300 years coincide, not only with *the 1260th year of the Mohammedan era*, but also with the end of the prophetic "*day, month, and year" period of the Ottoman Empire.*

The rise of the Ottoman Empire coincides with the capture of Constantinople in 1453, which was *the end of the Eastern Roman Empire.* In his magnificent history of the Decline and Fall of the Roman Empire, Gibbon traces the course of events from the days of Augustus Cæsar to this date and this event, and there terminates. The Constantine who fell before Mahomet II. was the last of the Romans. On the 29th of May, 1453, after a prodigious struggle and enormous loss of life, Constantinople was captured by the Ottomans, and *a Turkish empire founded on the ruins of the nominally Christian empire of the East.*

From that date the Cross, so called, throughout the entire East has been subject to *the Crescent.*

The predicted duration of the Turkoman power (the Euphratean woe) is "a day, a month, and a year " (Rev. ix. 15). This on the year-day scale is one year, plus 30, plus 360, or 391 years. The *terminus a quo* of the Turkoman power being the subversion of the Eastern Christian Empire in 1453, the 391 years must be reckoned from that date, and so reckoned they end in 1844, in the 1260th year of the Mohammedan era, and the 2300th year from B.C. 457.

11. A further confirmation is found in the fact that the year 1844, the terminus of the periods already named, is also the terminus of twice 1260 lunar years, or 2520 lunar years (" seven times ") as reckoned from the overthrow of the throne of David, B.C. 602.

CONVERGENCE OF 2300 SOLAR AND 2520 LUNAR YEARS IN A.D. 1844. Let the prophetic period of 2300 years be reckoned from B.C. 457, *then will its termination coincide with the close of 2520 lunar years, reckoned from* B.C. 602—the date of the subversion of the *throne* of David, and the transference of sovereignty to the Gentiles—*and the 2520 lunar years will be bisected by the Hegira date*, A.D. 622, that is, by the notable era of the rise of the Mohammedan power.

The commencement of the Babylonian captivity was B.C. 605–6.

"The *fourth* year of Jehoiakim, the son of Josiah king of Judah, that was the *first* year of Nebuchadrezzar king of Babylon" (Jer. xxv. 1). "Jehoiakim became his servant *three* years, *then* he turned and rebelled against him, and the Lord sent against him bands of the Chaldees . . . against Judah to destroy it according to the word of the Lord, which He spake by his servants the prophets. Surely by the commandment of the Lord came this upon Judah to remove them out of his sight, for the sins of Manasseh according to all that he did." The three years of Jehoiakim's servitude are, therefore, the fifth, sixth, and seventh of his reign, and in the eighth year occurred his rebellion and complete subjugation (B.C. 602), "Against him came up Nebuchadnezzar king of Babylon, and *bound him in fetters* to carry him to Babylon. Nebuchadnezzar *also carried off the vessels of the house of the Lord to Babylon, and put them in his temple at Babylon*" (2 Chron. xxxvi. 6, 7).

At this date "Jehoiakim is reconquered, removed from the throne, and, dying soon after, is succeeded by his son Jehoiachin, who is carried to Babylon, and remains in captivity many years, till his death. *The crown was then finally removed from Judah, and the sovereignty given into the hands of the Gentiles*" (Habershon on the Prophetic Scriptures, p. 444).

(1) 2520 lunar years are 2445 solar (for the difference between 2520 lunar years, and 2520 solar, is, as we have before shown, 75 *years*). The interval from B.C. 602 to A.D. 1844 is exactly 2445 solar years, and is, therefore, 2520 lunar years.

(2) 1260 years are consequently $1222\frac{1}{2}$ solar years (1222 solar years, 6 months), and from B.C. 602 to A.D. 622, there are 1222–3 solar years, and, therefore, 1260 lunar years.

(3) From A.D. 622 to A.D. 1844–5 are 1222 solar years, and

therefore 1260 lunar years. (The 1260th year of the Hegira began in the middle of January, 1844, and ended early in January, 1845.)

Thus, from the overthrow of the throne of David, B.C. 602, to the Mohammedan Edict of Toleration in 1844, there is an interval of "seven times" in lunar years, and this period is *bisected* by the rise of the Mohammedan power—"time, times, and half a time," extending to the Hegira date, A.D. 622; and "time, times, and half a time," from that date to the Edict of Toleration in 1844; which latter date is that of the termination of 2300 years from the commencement of the "seventy weeks," B.C. 457; and also of "a day, a month, and a year" (or 391 years) from the rise of the Ottoman Empire in 1453.

12. These dates are further confirmed by the following important harmony.

The complete overthrow of the THRONE of David was followed, *fifteen years afterwards,* by the destruction of the TEMPLE; and the setting up of MOHAMMEDANISM at the Hegira date was followed, *fifteen years afterwards,* by the CAPTURE OF JERUSALEM, and the erection of a Mohammedan mosque on the foundations of the Temple.

From this it follows that as from the overthrow of David's throne, in 602 B.C., to the setting up of Mohammedanism, A.D. 622, there are 1260 lunar years, so FROM THE DESTRUCTION OF THE TEMPLE BY NEBUCHADNEZZAR, B.C. 587, TO THE CAPTURE OF JERUSALEM BY OMAR, IN A.D. 637 (followed by the erection of *the mosque of Omar*), there are also 1260 lunar years (that is, "time, times, and half a time" in lunar years).

Through this memorable conquest by the Saracens—

"*Jerusalem*, once the glory of the East, was forced to submit to a heavier yoke than ever it had borne before. For though the number of the slain, and the calamities of the besieged, were greater when it was taken by the Romans; yet the servitude of those who survived was nothing comparable to this, either in respect of the circumstances or the duration. For however it might seem to be utterly ruined and destroyed by Titus, yet by Hadrian's time it had greatly recovered itself. *Now it fell, as it were, once for all, into the hands of the most mortal enemies of the Christian religion, and has continued so ever since; with the exception of a brief interval of about ninety years, during which it was held by the Christians in the holy war"* (Ockley's "History of the Saracens," p. 212).

The great battle of Yermouk, which decided the fate of Syria, was fought in November A.D. 636 (year of the Hegira 15). In that battle the Saracens were victorious. The siege of Jerusalem followed, and lasted for *four months*, the Saracen besiegers suffering much from the severity of *winter* (the winter of 636-7). On the Christian defenders yielding to the Saracens, "the Patriarch Sophronius appeared on the walls, and, by the voice of an interpreter, demanded a conference. After a vain attempt to dissuade the lieutenant of the Caliph from his impious enterprise, he proposed in the name of the people a fair capitulation, with this extraordinary clause, that the articles of security should be *ratified by the authority and presence of Omar himself*" (the successor of Abubecker, who was successor of Mohammed). "The question was debated in the council of *Medina ;* the sanctity of the place and the advice of Ali, persuaded the Caliph to gratify the wishes of his soldiers and enemies." Omar came, signed the capitulation, and entered the city. "Sophronius bowed before his new master, and secretly muttered, in the words of Daniel, "THE ABOMINATION OF DESOLATION IS IN THE HOLY PLACE." *"By his command the ground of the temple of Solomon was prepared for the foundation of a mosch."*

"According to the accurate survey of D'Anville ("Dissertation sur l'ancienne Jerusalem," pp. 42-54) the mosch of Omar, enlarged and embellished by succeeding Caliphs, *covered the ground of the ancient temple* (παλαιον του μεγαλου ναου δαπεδον, says Phocas), a length of 215, a breadth of 172, toises" (Gibbon, "Decline and Fall," p. 949). (The words of Sophronius were Το βδελυγμα της ερημωσεως το ρηθεν δια Δανιηλ του προφητου εστως εν τοπω αγιω (Theophan. "Chronograph," p. 281 ; footnote, Gibbon).

"Omar, while at Jerusalem, divided Syria into two parts, and committed all between Hauran and Aleppo to Abu Obeidah. Yezid took charge of all Palestine and the seashore. Amrou was sent to invade

£gypt" (Ockley). (Compare invasion of Egypt by Nebuchadnezzar after his conquest of Jerusalem, Jer. xliii. 10; xlvi. 13). "Aleppo and its castle was taken in four or five months"; Clinton says, "probably before the close of 637." Meanwhile Yezid attempted Cæsarea in vain, and Amrou "did not march directly to Egypt, but continued awhile in Palestine." "As he was marching towards Cæsarea the Saracens found the weather extremely cold." "Constantine guarded that part of the country." "We discern here the winter of 637-8" (Clinton, "Epit. Chron. Rome," p. 262).

Thus the capture of Jerusalem by the Saracens took place in the summer of A.D. 637, fifteen solar years after the Hegira commencement (*i.e.*, from July 15-16, A.D. 622), and this chronology harmonized with that of the destruction of the Temple and City of Jerusalem by Nebuchadnezzar "in the fifth month" of the year 587 B.C., 1260 lunar years before (1223 solar). (A.D. 637, the fifteenth solar year from the Hegira era, was the sixteenth year of the Mohammedan reckoning, the Mohammedan calendar being *lunar.*)

13. The foregoing chronology is confirmed by the interval which extended from the full commencement of the Times of the Gentiles, B.C. 602, to the supreme passover of A.D. 29 :—

That interval is 630 years, or just half of 1260 solar years; or, *one quarter of the great " seven times."*

Now, 630 solar years consists of two very perfect soli-lunar cycles of 315 years; and at its close the sun and moon agree within less than *seven hours.*

In other words, 630 solar years, and 7792 lunations, measure the same within six to seven hours.

It follows that the position of the passover month in the year A.D. 29 corresponded with that of the passover month in B.C. 602; and as the passover day in A.D. 29 seems conclusively fixed to March 18, it fell on the corresponding day in the year 602 B.C.*

---

* Lunations in 630 solar years $= 7777 + 7 + 7$, a perfect septenary, plus 1, which in this case coincides with passover month A.D. 29.

$7777 + 7 + 7$ lunations $= 159$ *lunu-diurnal cycles;* or cycles of forty-nine

14. Lastly, this chronology is confirmed by its remarkable agreement with that of the four empires and "Times of the Gentiles" as reckoned from the era of Nabonassar, B.C. 747. *From the rise of the Babylonian kingdom at that era, to the fall of the Western Roman Empire, the interval is exactly* 1260 *lunar years* (see appended calendar of the "Times of the Gentiles"); and the commencement of the "seventy weeks," B.C. 457, is in the 300*th lunar year* from the same starting-point, while the supreme passover year, A.D. 29, coincides with *the* 800*th of the same.*

Further, A.D. 29, the 800th lunar year from the beginning of Babylonian chronology, is the 777th Nabonassar year, for the Babylonian and Egyptian year was one of 365 days, and between Feb. 26, B.C. 747, and the corresponding date in A.D. 29, it fell back 187d. 17h. from the true solar year, which placed its commencement in A.D. 28, about seven months before the passover day, March 18, A.D. 29, making the latter year the 777th of the era. A.D. 29 was also the 70th year of the life of the Roman Emperor, Tiberius Cæsar; and March 18 (the passover day) was the 77th day of the year.

A.D. 29 was thus the 800th lunar year from the Babylonian starting point; the 777th year of the Nabonassar era; the 70th year of Tiberius Cæsar; and March 18, the 77th day of the year. The importance of these dates is confirmed by the consistency and perfection of the entire calendar of the "Times of the Gentiles" as reckoned from the Nabonassar era—a calendar which embraces not only the first four empires from the rise of the Babylonian to the fall of the Western Roman Empire, but also the whole duration of the

months, in which day and month agree within a minute and a half. The forty-nine months luni-diurnal cycle = 1447 days; and when it begins on the first day of week, succeeding cycle begins on Friday. If cycle of 630 years begin on first day of week, it *ends on Friday.* March 18, A.D. 29, *was Friday;* therefore March 18, B.C. 602, was Sunday: if the former was passover day, so was the latter.

empire of Eastern Rome, together with the rise and fall of the Papal and Mohammedan powers.

IX. GREAT JUBILEE CYCLE HARMONIZING THE MONTH AND YEAR.

The divinely instituted Jewish calendar was sabbatic, and consisted of a series of weeks of years, in which every seventh year was one of rest, and every forty-ninth a year of jubilee. The jubilee year began in the seventh month of the forty-ninth year, and extended to the same date in the fiftieth, and thus overlapped, and linked together, the forty-nine year periods.

Thus the great jubilee restoration period was not ten times fifty, but ten times forty-nine, or 490 years (the "seventy weeks" of Dan. ix.).

The Levitical calendar was both solar and lunar. Unlike the purely lunar Mohammedan calendar, it was adapted to the equinoctial, or solar year, for its feasts were linked with harvest ingatherings, while, at the same time, its months were strictly lunar. From this there necessarily resulted the *intercalation* of months of epact. As the annual difference between the lunar and solar year grew to months, such months were intercalated.

The Jewish calendar was thus a *natural*, and not an *artificial* one. Its months and years were those of nature, which is in harmony with the fact that the Author of that system was none other than the Author of nature.

Now, if this calendar was from the Author of nature, *it seems reasonable to believe that it was adapted to some natural system harmonizing the unequal measures of the month and year.* We inquire, then, to what system of intercalation was the Levitical calendar adapted—with what cycles of solar and lunar harmony does its chain of jubilees agree?

First, then, the forty-nine years jubilee period is a soli-lunar cycle, in which the epact amounts to eighteen months, or one and a half lunar years, so that in two jubilee cycles the epact is three lunar years; ninety-eight solar years equal 101 lunar (100 + 1, a measure analogous with octave numbers).

This ninety-eight years double jubilee cycle, or *first, plus a second, or new week cycle* (the octave principle), advances in its repetitions as follows:—2 jubilees; 4; 6; 8; 10; 12; 14; 16; 18; 20; 22 jubilees, or *thrice seven, plus one, jubilees* (an octave number) and then reaches a very perfect cycle of soli-lunar harmony. The lunar years in these periods are striking, and form the following series :—

101 lunar years; 202; 303; 404; 505; 606; 707; 808; 909; 1010; 1111 lunar years.

In 22 jubilees, or 1111 lunar years, the error of the jubilee cycle, which is 1d. 7h. 55m., amounts to just a complete month, which is then added by intercalation to the calendar, so that 1111 LUNAR YEARS, 1 MONTH, EQUAL EXACTLY 22 JUBILEES, OR 1078 SOLAR YEARS.

And in this period of 1078 solar years, or 1111 lunar years 1 month, the sun recedes in the zodiac (by precession) just half a sign; so that *in two such jubilee cycles, the equinoxes shift back one complete sign in the stellar heavens, and in twenty-four such jubilee cycles* (a new creation period 12 + 12) *the direction of the pole of the earth's axis completes the circuit of its revolution.*

The measure of the epact in this cycle of 1078 years is very remarkable, as being EQUAL IN AMOUNT TO THE FIRST CYCLE HARMONIZING THE LUNAR AND SOLAR YEAR. This fact connects the jubilee cycle with the *primary* cycle of the soli-lunar calendar. The LAW OF INTERCALATION may be stated as follows :—

1. The first cycle harmonizing the lunar *month* with the solar year is 19 solar years; but the first cycle of the lunar *year* and solar year is 32 solar years, which nearly equal 33 lunar.

2. The second and more perfect cycle of the lunar and solar year is 33 solar years, in which the epact amounts to one complete lunar year. This period is also the first most correct cycle of the solar year and day.

3. The calendar error introduced by this natural cycle *is corrected by the natural jubilee cycle of* 49 *years*, according to

which, instead of intercalating 3 lunar years in 3 times 33 solar, or 99 years, 3 lunar years are intercalated in *two jubilees*, or 98 solar years.

4. The jubilee cycle has itself an error of nearly $1\frac{1}{3}$ days, which is naturally corrected as follows : when the intercalated months in the jubilee accumulate to 33 lunar years, THAT IS, WHEN THEY EQUAL IN AMOUNT THE FIRST CYCLE OF THE SOLAR AND LUNAR YEAR, that error accumulates to just *one month*, and the period reached is a very perfect cycle, harmonizing year, month, and jubilee,—1078 solar years.

An examination of the appended "Calendar of the Times of the Gentiles," will show the coincidence of leading divisions of this cycle, as reckoned from the Nabonassar era, with certain great historic termini.

(1.) Measured from the Nabonassar era, the Babylonian *terminus a quo*, the duration of the first three empires was 707 lunar years, or 14 jubilees.

(2.) The death of Tiberius, under whom our Lord suffered, took place in the 808th lunar year from the same starting-point —or the completion of 16 jubilees.

(3.) The end of the Jewish war, A.D. 135, the full commencement of Jewish desolation, was in the 909th lunar year, —the close of 18 jubilees.

(4.) The dedication of Constantinople by Constantine the Great (called New Rome), and the rise of Arianism, in A.D. 330, 331, events which prepared the way for the division of the Roman world into the Eastern and Western empires, and the Eastern and Western Churches, occurred in the 1110th and 1111th lunar years from the Nabonassar era, or at the expiration of 22 jubilees,—the complete 1078 years cycle.

(5.) The final division of the Roman Empire by Valentinian took place in the 1111th *solar* year from the same terminus, A.D. 364. (Thus to the analogous events of the last two dates, there extend the analogous periods, 1111 *lunar* and 1111 *solar* years.)

(6.) From the death of Valentinian, A.D. 375, to the end of

the Eastern Roman Empire, at the fall of Constantinople, A.D. 1453, is one such cycle of 1111 lunar or 1078 solar years.

(7.) We may add that from the commencement of the great "seventy weeks" jubilee period, connected with Jerusalem, B.C. 457, to the year of the Hegira, A.D. 622, there elapsed *one such cycle* of 22 jubilees—*ten* jubilees to the close of the seventy weeks, and *twelve* jubilees from their termination to the beginning of Mohammedan reckoning; and from the new moon, or "the first day of the fifth month," July 16, B.C. 457, the date of Ezra's reaching Jerusalem, to the new moon of July 15-16, A.D. 622, the starting-point in the Mohammedan calendar, elapsed *exactly* one such cycle, or 1111 lunar years 1 month (1078 solar years).

The perfection of this cycle will be seen when it is added that *it is formed by the combination of two of the most perfect soli-lunar cycles known ;* viz. 1040 years, which is the most perfect soli-lunar cycle of large dimensions (named by Mr. De Cheseaux "the Daniel cycle"), and the nineteen years cycle, which is the most perfect among smaller lunar cycles.

(1040 + 19 + 19 years = 1078 years = 22 jubilees.)

The number of months to be intercalated in this 1078 years cycle is striking.

In one jubilee, or 49 years, 18 months; in ten jubilees, or 490 years ("seventy weeks"), 180 months—half a year of months; in twenty jubilees, 360 months—a year of months; in twenty-two jubilees, 36 months more, or 30 + 6 months, which, *with the one extra month then to be added to correct the error of the jubilee cycle,* amounts to 30 + 7 months, making the whole intercalation in the 1078 years cycle

360, plus 30, plus 7 months; or
A YEAR, A MONTH, AND A WEEK OF MONTHS.

Surely, the discovery of this 1078 years jubilee cycle is one of deep interest, as unveiling hidden features in the perfection of that sacred calendar whose observance was appointed by the all-wise Author of the perpetual revolutions of the solar system.

X. THE CYCLE OF THE PRECESSION OF THE EQUINOXES.

The year of Messianic cycles (12,091 years), which we have already considered, is not an actual year, marked off as such by a revolution of one of the heavenly bodies. It is a period whose epact is a year of years, or a prophetic "time," a period into which, regarded as a vast year, a variety of important biblical and historic periods fit, as proportionate parts.

We have now to deal with a period of still larger dimensions, which *is* definitely marked out as an immense year, by a slow but majestic motion of the axis of our earth; a motion imperceptible even by its results to the ordinary observer, but one with which astronomers are exceedingly familiar, and the results of which they have constantly to take into account; one which in the slow course of ages produces very palpable effects.

It is the revolution called the "precession of the equinoxes." Its precise scientific nature, and the mode and history of its discovery need not, however interesting, be here explained. It consists in a real but very slow change in the direction of the earth's axis, and may be detected by the change in the position of that point in the heavens, to which the earth's axis is directed. The star popularly supposed to mark that point, and called in consequence the "pole-star," is not really over the vanishing point of the earth's axis, conceived as indefinitely prolonged; it is nearer to it than any other conspicuous star, and it is every year getting nearer; in the year A.D. 2095 it will reach its nearest approximation as the earth's pole-star; but after the lapse of ages, it will cease to afford any indication of the true position of the pole; one star after another will become "pole-stars," and twelve thousand years hence, the peculiarly brilliant star VEGA in Lyra, will be in close proximity with the point in the heavens to which the earth's axis will then be directed.

This result is produced by a slow movement of the axis of

the earth, of which the motion of a well balanced top or tee-totum, when it is spinning not quite upright, may give a good idea. The handle or prolonged axis of the little toy will be observed to describe *a small circle* in the air ; just so, the pole of the earth's axis is directed in succession to every point in a circle in the northern heavens.

The direction of the earth's equator varies of course with this variation in the direction of its axis ; and the equinoctial points (or points at which the equator cuts the ecliptic, or sun's path in the heavens) must needs vary also. The equinoctial points slowly retrograde through all the signs of the zodiac, at the rate of *twenty minutes and twenty seconds of time every year.*

This is the movement called by astronomers the precession of the equinoxes. It is a distinctly *terrestrial* movement, and therefore as much adapted as the daily axial revolution of the earth, to measure terrestrial time. The mechanism of the solar system is like an elaborate and complex chronometer, with a variety of golden hands of different lengths, all in ceaseless and harmonious motion ; one marking seconds, another minutes, a third hours, a fourth days, a fifth weeks, a sixth months, a seventh years, an eighth cycles of years, a ninth cycles of cycles, and so on.

The advance of the moon in the ecliptic a distance equal to its own diameter, marks an *hour ;* the revolution of the earth on its axis, a *day ;* the lunar quarter, a *week ;* the complete lunation, a *month ;* the circuit of the earth in her orbit, a *year ;* the revolution of the lunar node, the nutation of the earth's axis, the falling back of the lunar year from the solar, the periods of the planets and their conjunctions, etc., measure various longer *cycles,* and this " annus magnus," or revolution of the equinoxes, measures the course of *ages,* for it requires *twenty-five thousand eight hundred* ordinary years to complete *one* revolution.

Can this vast period have any connection with mundane chronology and human history? Creation itself was less than three months ago on the scale of this great year ; is it likely that any harmonies exist, between its measures and those of human chronology? If the universe and its laws were the result of chance, nothing could well be less likely; but if they are the work of a God who governs all the events of history, and who inspired every record and every prophecy in the Bible—nothing would be more natural. Let then the following facts speak for themselves, and bear *their* witness along with a thousand others, to the wisdom and power of the eternal God!

We have seen in a previous chapter, that *the full normal period* of human existence (including its initial, intra-uterine stage), is *seventy years and from nine to ten months*.

In each of these years the equinoxes advance as we have said, *twenty minutes and twenty seconds*. Multiply this brief period by seventy and ten-twelfths, and the product is exactly four and twenty hours. In other words, **the rate of the precession of the equinoxes has been so adjusted that the full normal period of human life, is its day.***

So then, it is no mere figure of rhetoric that "our life is but a day;" no mere poetic simile! It is a hard astronomic fact, an accurate scientific statement! As really as the life of an ephemera, which is born at sunrise and dies at sunset, is a day measured by *one* axial movement of our globe, so really is our life a day, measured by *another!*

Nor should the duration of human life in this connection be regarded merely as an arbitrary appointment. Let its strange septiform stages of growth, maturity, and decay, its all-pervading septiform periodicity be borne in mind; and let it be realized that human life itself is a mysterious cycle of cycles of changes, adapted in a marvellous way to the changes of inorganic nature. And yet this complex, crowded, changeful, and

---

* Herschel assigns 25,870 years, and Chambers 25,817 years, as the period of precession. 70 years + 40 weeks = 70·7666 years, which multiplied by $365\frac{1}{4} = 25,847$ years, is a mean between the periods named. Seventy years and nine to ten months is as nearly as we can estimate the *day* of the vast equinox year. The average amount of precession in each such day is 59' 8", or one degree all but fifty-two seconds.

to the individual, all-important "threescore years and ten," is thus but a day, marked off as such by the ordinances of the sun and moon, and a slow majestic movement of our mighty globe! The morning of a day of the precession of the equinoxes, sees our conception and birth, its noon beholds our maturity, marriage, and multiplication, its night closes over our decay and death.

Is this accident? Consider! If the rate of precession differed from what it is, only by a single minute in a whole year, this harmony would be utterly destroyed! Or if normal human existence were only seventy years, as it is popularly considered, instead of as it is accurately, between nine and ten months more (dated from conception, its true commencement), this accurate coincidence would entirely disappear.* But the two widely severed and dissimilar phenomena, being *exactly what they are*, it is astronomically as well as figuratively true, that our life is a day, and we—ephemera!

The term appointed by God for Judah's captivity in Babylon, was "seventy years." As the mournful years of this week of decades of exile, drew to a close, it was revealed that a larger and a brighter week, each day of which should equal the entire captivity, was about to dawn upon the two tribes— and that its seventh or sabbath day, was to witness the advent of Messiah. The prediction was accomplished; the closing 70 of that 490 years, contained the life-time of our Lord Jesus Christ. This memorable period, the period of Judah's restored national existence, of the rebuilt city and second temple, with its deeply moving Maccabean exploits and episodes, and its eventful and all-tragic close; that period of final probation, between the Babylonish captivity and the present prolonged dispersion among the Gentiles—the "seventy weeks" of Daniel, was one week of the year of the precession of the equinoxes.

If now we examine *seven weeks* of the year of the precession

---

* See Dr. Laycock's statement, quoted p. 266.

of the equinoxes, plus a fiftieth day—a pentecostal period—
we find it is 3539 years. The period extending from the
Exodus (B.C. 1625) to the final close of the "Times of the
Gentiles" (A.D. 1919) is about this interval. Fifty days of
the ordinary year were appointed to elapse between Israel's
passover and the day of Pentecost; fifty such days *did* elapse
between the death and resurrection of Christ our Passover
and the outpouring of the Holy Ghost ; and fifty days of the
immense year of the precession of the equinoxes,—3539
years, seem to be similarly appointed to elapse, between the
exodus redemption of Israel from Egypt, and that yet future
Pentecost, when on the house of Judah and the inhabitants of
Jerusalem, shall be poured the spirit of grace and of supplication, leading them to national repentance ; when they shall
look upon Him whom they pierced and mourn because of Him,
and say "blessed be He that cometh in the name of the Lord."
Is not this the finger of God?   Who appointed the magnificent cycle of the precession of the equinoxes and measured
out its days and weeks?   He who enacted the ordinances of
Lev. xxiii., He who arranged in his providence, the historic
intervals of redemption history !

The adaptation of the precession of the equinoxes to the
measurement of long intervals of time, is one of its most important features.*   Just as in the course of one year the sun

---

* "Although this motion, slow as it is, is easily detected from year to
year by modern instruments, it was not until the sixteenth century that its
precise rate was ascertained.   Small as is its annual amount, its accumula-
tion, continued from year to year for a long period of time, causes a great
displacement of all the objects in the heavens, in relation to the equinoctial points from which longitudes and right ascensions are measured.
In 71·6 years, the equinoxes retrograde 1°, and therefore in that time, the
longitudes of all celestial objects of fixed position, such as the stars, have
their longitudes augmented 1°.   Since the formation of the earliest catalogues in which the positions of the fixed stars were registered, the retrogression of the equinoctial points has amounted to 30°, so that the present
longitudes of all the objects consigned to these catalogues is 30° greater
than those which are assigned to them."

"Since the equinoctial points thus *move backward on the ecliptic*, it follows
that the sun, after it has in its *annual* course passed round the ecliptic, will

advances through all the signs of the zodiac, so in the course of a number of ages it recedes through them all by another movement. Its rapid progressive motion, and its slow retrograde motion, through the same signs, measure the months and the ages, just as its apparent diurnal motion measures the day.

The precession of the equinoxes affords in consequence of this fact, an exceedingly interesting testimony to the truth of Scripture statements about the antiquity of the human race. The stars of the zodiac were at an early period in the world's history, divided into twelve groups or constellations corresponding with the twelve months of the year, and these were naturally known by names descriptive of the phenomena of the seasons in the northern hemisphere, in which, of course, the science of astronomy originated. Thus the constellations occupied by the sun, in spring and early summer, were called by names indicative of the fertilizing influence of the sun at that season ; that occupied by the sun at the summer solstice, when it reaches its highest elevation and begins to go back, was called "Cancer" from the supposed resemblance to the movement of the crab ; the powerful heat of the sun during the next month (the hottest in the year) suggested the name of the most powerful of beasts, "Leo," the lion ; the next constel-

---

arrive at either equinoctial point *before* it has made a complete revolution. The equinoctial point being 50·1″ behind the position it had when the sun started from it, the sun will return to it after having moved through 50·1″ less than a complete revolution. But since the mean hourly apparent motion of the sun is 147·8″, it follows that the centre of the sun will return to the equinoctial point $\frac{50 \cdot 1}{147 \cdot 8''} = 0\cdot33898$ hrs. $= 20$ min. 20·3 sec., before completing its revolution. Hence is explained the fact that while the *sidereal* year, or actual revolution of the earth around the sun, is 365 days 6 h. 9 m. 10·38 sec., the *equinoctial* revolution or *the time between two successive equinoxes of the same name*, is 365 days 5 h. 48 m. 50·4 sec., the latter being less than the former by 20 m. 20 s.

"The successive return of the sun to the same *equinoctial* point, must, therefore, always *precede* its return to the same point of the *ecliptic*, by 20 m. 20 s. of time, and by 50·1″ of space."—*Lardner's Astronomy* (pp. 710-11).

lation, the one in which the sun is in harvest-time, was taken to resemble a virgin bearing a sheaf of corn; the next, that of the autumnal equinox, when day and night are equal, was named "Libra," the balance; the remaining five traversed by the sun after the turn of the year—the winter months, of severe winds, rains and storms,—were called the scorpion, the archer, the goat, the pourer forth of water, and the fishes, or dwellers in water—Scorpio, Sagittarius, Capricornus, Aquarius, Pisces.

The characteristic *names* thus early attached to the twelve constellations of the zodiac, indicating the *season*, which, when the names were given, was connected with the sun's presence in any one constellation, have remained unchanged ; but the sun has been slowly passing out of its proper relation to them, in consequence of this precession of the equinoxes which we are considering. The sun of the vernal equinox is no longer in the constellation Aries, nor that of the autumnal in Libra. At the autumnal equinox *now*, the sun is in Virgo, and its distance from its old position indicates the length of time which has elapsed, since the autumnal equinox did take place on the sun's entering the constellation Libra.

Now astronomy is naturally one of the oldest of the sciences, and the naming of the signs of the zodiac would, of course, be one of its first achievements. We can judge from the *degree by which the signs now differ from the seasons* how long ago astronomy became a science, and approximately, therefore, the age or antiquity of man.

If that antiquity be as great as some surmise, men must have lived without becoming astronomers—or, at any rate, without naming the signs of the zodiac ; for, apart from all historical testimony, their very names tell us, that *they* were given only about the time to which Scripture assigns the rise of the earliest post-diluvian civilization—between two and three thousand years ago.

The position of the vernal equinox at the epoch of *the creation of man* was nearly one quarter of the heavens distant from its present place. Its close proximity to that grand starry circle, THE MILKY WAY, which cuts the sun's path at two opposite regions, and its nearness to the most splendid constellation in the heavens, ORION, gives the position of the vernal equinox at the creation of man a very marked place on the map of the heavens, and one suitable to be a starting-point in its measurement of the ages of history.

Seventeen centuries later, or at the time of the repeopling of the earth after the *flood*, the sun at the vernal equinox was near one of the most remarkable constellations in the zodiac, the PLEIADES, and at the summer solstice near the bright star REGULUS in Leo. The question addressed to the patriarch Job, " Canst thou bind the sweet influences of the Pleiades ?" may have alluded to the place of the sun at the *spring* equinox in that early age, and thus indicate the high antiquity of the period in which the patriarch lived, if not of the book which contains his story.

Our Lord's *nativity* took place probably about the time of the autumn equinox, which eighteen centuries ago occupied a place in the constellation VIRGO, near the star of the first magnitude in SPICA VIRGINIS.

> " The star which crowns the golden sheaf,
> And wants a name, O glory of the skies."

The constellation Virgo is remarkable for the number of its nebulæ, there being more in that region than in any other of equal space in the heavens (above three hundred).

At the present time the positions of the sun at the summer and winter SOLSTICES, coincide with opposite points of the sublime starry circle, or MILKY WAY, with which the equinoxes coincided at the time of man's creation.

The change in the direction of the earth's axis, which gives rise to the precession of the equinoxes, has caused the earth to have many a different pole-star during the last 6000 years ; but most of these have been too minute to attract attention. The pole-star of Abraham's day was, however, as conspicuous as our present one. It was the star "α Draconis." The pyramids of Egypt were so constructed, that the narrow passages by which alone they can be entered, opening on their northern sides, *pointed to its lower culmination.* There is evidence to show that it was a much brighter star formerly than it is now. The two well-known stars which we call the Pointers, indicate by the direction of a line passing through them, our present pole-star. A line through the other two bright stars of Ursa Major, which are nearly parallel to the Pointers, will indicate the pole-star of Abraham's day. It is interesting to look from one to the other of these two pole-stars, and to trace the arc in the heavens, through which the pole of the earth's axis has swept, since God led Abram forth at night, and bade him count the stars, saying to the childless patriarch, " So shall thy seed be ! " remembering, how while that arc has been slowly traversed, the promise has been fulfilled ; till Abraham's seed now embraces, not only the myriads of the natural, but the tenfold myriads of the spiritual Israel ! And yet the promise was only made two months ago, reckoning by the " annus magnus " of the equinoxes ! What will the seed of Abraham number, when it shall have completed its revolution, when the starry sphere shall have *returned* to the position it occupied when " God made promise to Abraham " ? *

---

* " Though the rate at which the equinoctial points move backward on the ecliptic is so slow, yet the accumulated effects in the lapse of ages become very sensible ; and even in a moderate number of years, astronomers are obliged by those effects to reconstruct their catalogues of the stars. About 2000 years ago, the 360° of the ecliptic were divided in twelve equal portions, each of 30°, and were named after the most remarkable constellations of the zodiac, which they respectively crossed ; thus, the first 30° of the ecliptic, running across the constellation Aries, was called the sign of Aries, and the equinox was called the first point of Aries ; at that time the constellations, and the divisions of the ecliptic were equally called signs of the zodiac, without causing confusion. Since that epoch, by reason of the annual increase of longitude of 50″2, common to all the stars, the constellations have all changed their places relatively to the divisions of the ecliptic. Though the vernal equinox is still called the first point of Aries, the circumstance which gave rise to that name exists no longer ; that point of the constellation is now removed 30° east of the equinox, and the beginning of Pisces has taken its place. Hence it is

XI. CYCLE OF THE REVOLUTION OF THE SOLAR PERIGEE.

Not only has the earth's *axis* the slow secular movement just described, but the earth's *orbit* has a similar one, which occupies even a longer period. The path in which the earth travels round the sun is not a circle, but an ellipse, the sun occupying one of the foci. The earth's distance from the sun consequently varies continually. The sun is three millions of miles nearer to the earth when in perigee, or at its nearest point, than it is when in apogee, or at its farthest point. When we speak of the sun's distance from the earth as ninety-two millions of miles, we allude to its *mean*, or medium distance. The line which joins the perigee and apogee points, is called the line of apsides. This line revolves from west to east,—in other words, the longer axis of the ellipse, turns gradually round in that direction. The motion is slower, even than that of the precession of the equinoxes, and is in the opposite direction. It has a perceptible effect on our seasons, as will be easily believed. When the sun is in perigee in summer, and apogee in winter, the former season will be hotter, and the latter colder, than when the reverse is the case. The sun is now in perigee in January, so that the winters in the northern hemisphere are milder, and the summers cooler. As the seasons are reversed at the antipodes, the opposite effect is produced there.

The period of the revolution of the perigee, according to its present rate, is about 109,800 years, or more than four times that of the precession of the equinoxes; but it varies enor-

---

necessary to make a distinction between the *signs* of the ecliptic, and those *groups of stars* which bear the same name; the former are spaces of 30° reckoned from the actual position of the vernal equinox; the latter also occupy 30°, but are in continual motion along the ecliptic, and are at present about 30° in advance of the signs of the same name. The beginning of the *sign* Aries will always be in the intersection of the ecliptic and equator, the beginning of the *constellation* Aries, only after intervals of twenty-six thousand years; when the sun enters the *sign* Cancer, it will always be midsummer; but he will, in the course of ages, enter the *constellation* Cancer at every season of the year."—*Hymers' Astron.*, p. 43.

mously at distant intervals. All the changes of human history are, of course, dwarfed into insignificance by such a stupendous year as this, and can have little relation to it as a *whole*, or to its *major* divisions. If the revolution of the line of the apsides is intended, as doubtless it is, to be a useful hand on the face of the great chronometer, it must be to future generations of men, and in the ages to come. Yet we may inquire whether there is any observable harmony between *its least* and *our greatest* measures, and we find that, as far as the thing is possible, relations similar to those we have noted elsewhere, exist here also.

The day of this great revolution is 300 years, and its week is 2100 years—nearly the same period as the month of the precession of the equinoxes, and measuring the Jewish age from Abraham to the fall of Jerusalem, and the patriarchal age from Abraham, back to Adam. This period was, by the Hebrew chronology, as nearly as can be calculated, 4200 years,—*two weeks* of the slowly accomplished year of the solar perigee, bisected by the life of the Father of the faithful.

Seven months of this great year comprise about three revolutions of the equinoxes with reference to the solar perigee,—another cycle which we must now consider.

XII. CYCLE OF THE VARIATION IN THE LENGTH OF THE SEASONS.

We have already considered two vast revolutions connected with the solar system : that of the equinoxes, and that of the solar perigee. We now glance at a third, which is created by the combined effects of these two, and which causes a cyclical variation in the length and character of our seasons.

Astronomically, spring, summer, autumn, and winter, are measured by the sun's passing the four quarterly points of his annual path, the vernal and autumnal equinoxes, and the winter and summer solstices. These four seasons are neither *equal* nor *uniform* in length ; they differ among themselves every year, and they all vary from year to year.

Were the earth's orbit a true cirole they would be of uniform length, and invariable. The existing irregularities are
occasioned by the *form*, and by the *movement*, of the earth's
orbit. Being elliptical, its quarters are of course unequal ; and
changing as it does continually, the direction of its longer axis,
the *relation* of the different quarters to the equinoxes changes
also.

The length of the seasons would therefore vary, even if the
equinoxes were stationary.* But we have seen that while the
solar perigee *advances*, they *retrograde*, in consequence of the
slow change in the position of the earth's axis ; and the cycle
of the variation in the length of the seasons, results from both
these movements. It is shorter consequently either than the
perigee or equinox cycle, and runs its course in 20,900 years.

The same causes affect the *comparative* length of the forenoon and afternoon of the day. These two are not equal as
might be supposed. Only four times a year, is the interval
from sunrise to noon (mean) equal to that from noon to sunset
The variation, as a glance at the almanac will show, sometimes
amounts to half an hour. This variation is not the same from
year to year, but changes throughout this same cycle of 20,900
years.

The equinoxes retrograde at the rate of one day in 70–71
years ; the perigee advances at the rate of one day in 300
years. The compound result in this cycle of the length of the
seasons, is an advance of the perigee, with reference to the
true equinoctial year, of **one** day in 57¼ years, or **one week in
400 years.**

On the scale of this great season year of 20,900 years, the

---

* In the year 1850, or the middle of the present century, the time elapsing
between the equinoxes and solstices was as follows :—

	d.	h.	m.
Spring equinox to summer solstice .	92	20	57
Summer solstice to autumnal equinox	. 93	14	0
Autumnal equinox to winter solstice	. 89	17	38
Winter solstice to spring equinox .	. 89	1	17

interval between the creation and the flood was about *one month.* According to the Bible chronology the creation took place 1656 years before the deluge. The flood lasted one year, so that the interval between the creation of Adam, and Noah's entrance on a new world, was 1657 years. This is 29 days or about one month, of the season cycle (four weeks and a day).*

The period revealed in vision to Abram, during which his seed should be a stranger in a land not their own, was a week of this cycle, "four hundred years." This was the period which terminated at the exodus passover. (Gen. xv. 13 ; Exod. xii. 41.)

In this vast cycle of 20,900 years the solar perigee coincides in turn with each of the four quarterly points, the equinoxes and solstices.†

---

* $400 \times 4 = 1600 + 57 = 1657.$

† "In the year 3958 B.C., or, singularly enough, near the epoch of the creation of Adam, the longitude of the sun's perigee coincided with the *autumnal* equinox ; so that the summer and autumn quarters were of equal length, but shorter than the winter and spring quarters, which were also equal. In the year 1267 A.D., the perigee coincided with the *winter* solstice ; the spring quarter was therefore equal to the summer one, and the autumn quarter to the winter one, the former being the longest. In the year 6493 A.D., the perigee will have completed half a revolution, and will then coincide with the *vernal* equinox ; summer will then be equal to autumn, and winter to spring ; the former seasons, however, being the longest. In the year 11,719 A.D., the perigee will have completed three-fourths of a revolution, and will then coincide with the *summer* solstice ; autumn will then be equal to winter, but longer than spring and summer, which will also be equal, and finally, in the year 16,945 A.D., the cycle will be completed by the coincidence of the solar perigee with the *autumnal* equinox. This motion of the apsides of the earth's orbit, in connection with the inclination of its axis to the plane of it, must quite obviously have been the cause of very remarkable vicissitudes of climate in pre-Adamic times. One result of this position of things we may readily grasp at this moment. As a matter of fact, in consequence of our seasons being now of unequal length, the spring and summer quarters jointly extend to 186^d. ; while the autumn and winter quarters only comprise 178^d. The sun is therefore a longer time in the northern hemisphere than in the southern hemisphere : hence the northern is the warmer of the two hemispheres. Probably it may be taken as an incidental proof of this fact, that the north polar regions of the earth are easier of access than the south polar regions. In the northern hemisphere navigators have reached 81° of latitude, whereas 71° is the highest attained in the southern hemisphere."—*Chambers' Astron.*, p. 75. 3rd edit. 1877.

These coincidences are the leading epochs in its long duration. Human history goes back far enough to take in two of
them only. The first—the coincidence of the solar perigee with
the autumnal equinox, took place near the era of the creation, B.C.
3958, or, according to the vulgar chronology, within fifty years
of that event. But the date of the creation as given by CLINTON,
probably the nearest possible approach to the truth (absolute
certainty being unattainable from lack of Scripture data, to within
forty or fifty years) is B.C. 4138. From B.C. 3958, to A.D. 29,
the date of the death and resurrection of the Lord Jesus Christ,
there elapsed ten weeks or *seventy days* of this year.*

The predicted interval (Gen. xv.) preceding the typical redemption of the Passover, was 400 years; the interval from
this great astronomic epoch to the antitypical redemption—
Christ our passover sacrificed for us—was ten times as long,
4000 years.

The second era of coincidence between the perigee and the
equinox revolutions, was in the middle of the 13th century.

" In the year A.D. 1250, the major axis was perpendicular to
the line of the equinoxes, the solar perigee coincided with *the
solstice of winter,* and the apogee with that of summer. On
that account Laplace proposed the year A.D. 1250, as a universal epoch, and that the vernal equinox of that year, should be
the first day of the first year."

The more accurate measures of modern astronomy, place
this coincidence in A.D. 1267, a few years later. It occurred
in the middle of the dark ages, and without laying much stress
on the fact, it is surely worthy to be noted. The solar perigee
influences had to struggle with the winter position of the sun;
and were reduced to a lower ebb than either before or since.
Two winters coincided, the lowest wintry depression of the
sun, and the shortest day of his influences, at the moment of
his nearest approach to the earth, or perigee, and winter, cold,

---

* B.C. 3958 to A.D. 29 = 3986 years, which wants only 14 years (a fraction of a day on this scale) of 4000 years.

dark, icebound, and fatal, in the moral world of Christendom. The 13th century was the darkest in all Papal history, persecution was at its height, the crusade against the faithful Albigenses raged for twenty years from A.D. 1208 ; the Inquisition arose about the same time. Riddle, the ecclesiastical chronologist, fixes on this period, and especially the year A.D. 1268, as that in which "the Papal dominion was at its utmost height." Astronomy assigns A.D. 1267, as the year of this coincidence of the solar perigee with the *winter solstice*. But whether any such harmony be admitted or not, the fact remains, this great turning point in the revolution of the perigee took place at a turning point of history—the culmination of the power of the Papacy, since which it has steadily declined to its fall.

And lastly, as *seven months* of the ordinary year comprehended the typical history of redemption, embodied in the ordinances of the feasts of the Lord, and as *seven months* of the year of Messianic cycles comprehend the entire range of the historic and prophetic times of human history as revealed in Scripture, so the entire year of Messianic cycles is about *seven months of this great cycle of the variation of the seasons*. We have reached here almost the top step of the ladder, the last "week" in the wonderful ascending scale of periods which we find in Scripture, in physical nature, and in the solar system. We have passed in review, the week of days, the week of weeks, the week of months, the week of years, the week of weeks of years, the week of decades, and the week of weeks of decades (490 years) ; the week of years of years, or the "seven times" of prophecy (2520 years) ; and the week of millenaries. Here where Scripture leaves us, astronomy takes us by the hand, and shows us that this vast and comprehensive week of millenaries, is only a week of months, seven months of a larger solar year, a year whose days are soli-lunar cycles, and that this year itself is again a week of months—seven months of a solar year, more gigantic still.

Nor have we any reason to suppose the series of septiform periods ends here ! As the telescope reveals worlds on worlds, system behind system, and nebula behind nebula, as far as human eyesight, aided by the finest optical instruments, can penetrate into the profundities of space, so this septiform system of measurement of times and seasons, may have pervaded all the past eras of geologic change, and may be destined to pervade all the ages to come, and the revolution of our own sun and all its attendant planets, in its incalculable orbit around *its* centre of gravity, wherever and whatever that be, a revolution whose period is so vast that inconceivable ages may roll away, ere it can even be calculated, that revolution itself, may prove to be only " a week " of some other, bordering even more nearly on eternity.

XIII. CYCLE OF THE EXCENTRICITY OF THE EARTH'S ORBIT.

Reference has already been made to the fact that the earth's orbit is not a perfect circle, but slightly oval in form, the excentricity of the ellipse being about one sixtieth part of its semi-diameter.

This excentricity is not uniform, but gradually decreasing. It will continue to decrease for many thousands of years, and then, having reached the nearest approach to a circular form which it will ever make, the orbit will, during succeeding ages, elongate once more, and slowly resume its more elliptical form.

A change in the excentricity of the earth's orbit means a diminution or increase in the length of its longer axis, and consequently of the mean amount of heat actually received from the sun ; and as animal and vegetable life are dependent on a certain uniformity in the supply of heat, the question as to the limits of change of excentricity in the orbit of the earth, becomes one of vital importance.

These limits have been ascertained. The amount of excentricity for many ages, past and future, has been calculated. It has been proved that the change has narrow limits, and a tendency to correct itself. M. Leverrier, with the aid of perfectly reliable data, as Herschel tells us, has assigned both the superior and inferior limits of the excentricity of the earth's orbit, and has shown that the inferior limit, or nearest approach to a circle, will be reached in about 23,903 years from the present time, A.D. 1879.

The revolution of the equinoxes occupies, as we have seen, 25,800 years. It follows, therefore, that the greatest event in all human history, the incarnation and death of the Son of God, took place about one revolution of the precession of the equinoxes from this great epoch of the inferior limit of the earth's excentricity: for 23,903 + 1879 = 25,782; and the equinox year is 25,800.

In other words, the immense interval between the accomplished advent of Immanuel, and that great astronomic era, the still far-distant "inferior limit," is measured by one revolution in the direction of the earth's axis.

Now, the precession of the equinoxes is a primary element in all astronomical calculations; it affects the place of every object in the heavens with reference to the earth. If we admit the principle that the revolutions of the heavenly bodies, have any connection with the cycles of history, as marking the chronological positions of their great crises, the question has a deep interest,—What was the position of the heavens when the Son of God was on earth, and when will that position be restored? The reply is: When the earth's orbit attains the inferior limit of its excentricity, and not till then, will the precession year have run its round, and the position of the pole, of the sun in the zodiac, and of the starry heavens above us, be restored to what they were when the star stood over the manger of the Babe of Bethlehem. The return of the universe to the position it occupied 1879 years ago, will be a milestone in the journey through endless ages.

XIV. THE PROPORTION WHICH SOLAR REVOLUTIONS BEAR TO LUNAR, AND DIURNAL TO ANNUAL, IS OCTAVE, OR JUBILAIC.

In order to understand and appreciate this remarkable fact, we must look at it in the light of the Divine system of times and seasons revealed in Scripture.

Scripture sets before us two creations, and two chronologies. Nothing can be more evident than that while SEPTENARY NUMBERS ARE LINKED IN SCRIPTURE WITH THE OLD CREATION, OCTAVE NUMBERS ARE AS CONSISTENTLY ASSOCIATED WITH THE NEW.

The day which commemorated the completion of the old creation was the seventh; whereas the day on which the glorious resurrection of our Lord took place, and which still commemorates it, the day which completed the work of redemption, is the eighth, or first of a new week. The same distinction pervades the whole Bible. The ancient ordinance of circumcision, which typified, as we learn from the Apostle Paul, the putting off of the old nature, in order to a renovation of the being, was appointed to take place on the eighth day after birth. The leper could not be cleansed till the eighth day. The first sheaf of harvest was presented on an eighth day, and the day of Pentecost, with its fuller first-fruit offering, was an eighth day, which was also a fiftieth. The feast of tabernacles both began and terminated on an eighth day, "the last day, that great day of the feast." The year of jubilee, with its restorations and rejoicings, was a fiftieth year.

Not only did our Lord's resurrection take place on an eighth day, a first day of the week, but by his subsequent appearances in the midst of his disciples on that day, He sanctioned the recognition of the first day of the week, instead of the seventh, as the day of Christian worship and rest. The early disciples met together to break bread on that day, the Apostle Paul enjoined collections to be made on that day for the poor, and the Christian Church in all lands and ages, has, ever since apostolic times, recognised the eighth, or first day, as the Lord's day.

The advent of the quickening Spirit, accompanied by the sudden coming of a sound from heaven as of a mighty rushing wind, and the appearing of cloven tongues like as of fire on the disciples, their baptism with the Holy Ghost, and endowment with power from on high, took place on an eighth

day, which was also a fiftieth; for it was "when the day of
Pentecost was fully come," that by one Spirit they were all
baptized into one body. (1 Cor. xii. 13.)

And as seven is a Scripture number of old creation completeness, so also is twelve.　There is an analogy between
'hese two numbers; the first is three added to four and
the second is three multiplied by four.　In the Jewish
tabernacle the seven-branched candlestick, and the table with
its twelve loaves of shew-bread, emblematized one and the same
Israel.　Of both, the tribes of Israel and the Apostles of Christ,
the primary number is twelve; but just as seven, and its square
forty-nine, are in the new creation numbers changed into
eight and fifty, so twelve in the same way is changed or merges
into thirteen.　The multiplication of Joseph, who was typically
raised from the dead, into two tribes, and the addition to the
number of the Apostles of the one born out of due time, the
Apostle of the Gentiles, Paul, raised the number of the tribes
of Israel, and the Apostles of Christ, respectively, from twelve
to thirteen.　In the new Jerusalem, where the two are united,
in the names on the gates and foundations of the city, the
thirteen are again resolved into twelve plus twelve, twenty-four
in all; and twenty-four symbolic elders are seen in vision, seated
around the throne.　To the twelve of the natural Israel, God
has added a new twelve; the final number is twice twelve,—
twenty-four.

From all this it is obvious that a transition from the sevenfold and the forty-nine fold, to the eightfold and the fifty-
fold, and from the twelvefold to the thirteen-fold, and the
final twenty-four fold, takes place in the formation of Bible
new creation numbers.

The principle of all this is simple.　It is a question of two
orders of things, a first and a second, an old and a new;
Creation and Redemption; the heaven and the earth that are
now, and the new heavens and the new earth, the earthly and
the heavenly; the first man a living soul, the second man the
Lord from heaven; man in Adam, and man in Christ; and as

the numbers seven and twelve are connected with the old, so eight and thirteen are linked with the new; the eighth is the first of a new seven, the thirteenth, of a new twelve.

Thus in music, the scale consists of seven tones (diatonic), or twelve semitones (chromatic). The eighth tone, or octave, and the thirteenth semitone are identical, and are the first of a new or second scale.

We shall now show that these are the numbers stamped on the proportion which solar revolutions bear to lunar, and diurnal to annual.

First: This is the case in the proportion which the solar day bears to the lunar quarter. Let it be noted that the lunar quarter is a distinct interval marked out by obvious phases, and by definite world-wide tidal phenomena. The lunar quarter contains always seven days, and nine hours of an eighth—its measures, as estimated by solar days, have an *octave* character.

Secondly: The same measure on a larger scale marks the proportion of the lunar quarter to the solar year. The solar year contains seven times seven, or forty-nine lunar quarters, plus half a *fiftieth*.

Thirdly: Octave measures mark the proportion which cycles of the day and month bear to cycles of the day and year. The first accurate day and month cycle is seven times seven months (in forty-nine months the day and month agree within a minute and a half). The first cycle of the day and year is four years (leap year). The four years cycle is the forty-nine months cycle, plus half a *fiftieth*.

Fourthly: Octave measures mark the still more perfect day and year cycle of thirty-three years—a cycle so perfect that its slight error does not grow by repetition to a day in less than 5000 years. The fraction of a 366th day in the solar year grows in 33 years to *eight days;* in other words, when the solar year fraction accumulates to a week, plus the first day of a new week, the solar day and year agree.

Fifthly: Analogous measures mark the proportion of the lunar month to the solar year. The eightfold and the thirteen-fold harmonize. Eight is the first of a new seven; thirteen the first of a new twelve. We have already observed that the eighth tone in music, and the thirteenth semitone, are identical. The solar year contains twelve months, and about the third of A THIRTEENTH. Further, this fraction of a thirteenth month grows to *a complete week of months* in the cycle of nineteen solar years; in other words, when the soli-lunar difference has accumulated to seven months, or when it has produced *a new week of months*, then solar year and lunar month agree.

Sixthly: The same thing marks the proportion of the calendar year of 360 days to the solar. The calendar year is a natural one. There are nearer 30 days in a lunar month than 29, and nearer 12 months in the year than 13; hence 12 months of 30 days each, form a natural calendar year. The difference between this year and the solar is $5\frac{1}{4}$ days, and this fraction grows first to a complete year in the septiform period of seventy years. Seventy solar years contain seventy soli-lunar, *plus a seventy-first*. A septenary measure of the one and an *octave* measure of the other, unite in a cycle of harmony.

Seventhly: There is a slow revolution of the equinoxes, in which the place of the sun at the equinox recedes 20m. 20s. every year, and recedes *one whole year* in 25,850 years. The *day* of this vast year measures seventy solar years plus nine to ten months of *a seventy-first:* and the sun gains on the moon every such day, *seven hundred and seventy days.* From the first to the last, all these proportions have an *octave* character. These are the mutual proportions which have been given by the Almighty Power which controls the revolutions of worlds, to days and months and years. These, too, are the measures which the Author of Holy Scripture has impressed on the entire system of *new creation numbers*, running through the whole complex economy of law and gospel. How profound the agreement between these two portions of the one glorious plan! How full of resurrection new creation hopes and harmonies, this wondrous structure of the works and word of God!

XV. GROWTH OF THE EPACT TRACED, FROM ITS PRIMARY CYCLES, TO ITS DEVELOPMENT IN THE PROPHETIC TIMES.

There are nearer twelve months than thirteen in the solar year, twelve months, therefore, constitute a lunar year.

The surplus fraction of a thirteenth month may be considered *a new lunar year element* in the solar year. It is commonly called " the epact."

We have already pointed out the association in Scripture of *eight* and *thirteen* as new creation numbers ; and we noticed the analogous fact that in the natural arrangement of sounds the eighth tone and thirteenth semitone are the same, and form the first note of a new scale.

We have now to trace the growth of this new lunar year element in the solar year, to complete periods of months and years. In doing so we shall follow its development in its elementary natural cycles, and in the Levitical and prophetic times.

1. THE FIRST PERIOD IN WHICH THE EPACT BECOMES A COMPLETE MONTH, IS THREE SOLAR YEARS.

Under the Divine law the time appointed for the presentation of tithe offerings was the end of every three years, an interval analogous with the oft-recurring three days resurrection period. Our Lord's ministry also extended over three full years.

(Three solar years exceed three lunar by one lunar month. and 3d. 2h. 17m.)

2. THE SECOND EPACT CYCLE, EIGHT YEARS.

As the seventh year was made Sabbatic in the Levitical law, the eighth was the first of a new series. In eight years the epact grows to *three months*. Both eight and three are used in Scripture as new creation numbers.

(Eight lunar years + three months, exceed eight solar years by 1d. 14h. 11m.)

3. The Third Epact Cycle, Eleven Years.

This cycle is a combination of the two previous ones; it is one-third of the thirty-three years cycle. Its epact is *four months*, or *the third of a lunar year.*

(Eleven solar years exceed eleven lunar + four months by 1 d. 12 h. 7 m.)

4. The Nineteen Years, or Lunar Cycle.

A celebrated soli-lunar cycle, discovered by the Greek Meton, and hence often called the Metonic cycle. As the eight years cycle errs by *excess,* and the eleven years by *defect,* the combination of the two makes this very perfect cycle.

Here we have the combination of two cycles whose epacts are *three* months and *four* months, producing a perfect cycle whose epact is *seven* months.

Thus, when the epact, or new month element, has so accumulated as to produce A NEW WEEK OF MONTHS, *the sun and moon almost perfectly agree,* and this cycle of their harmony becomes the *unit* of higher cycles.

(The 235 months of this cycle exceed nineteen solar years by only 2h. 4m. 4s.)

5. The Thirty Years, or Prophetic Month Cycle.

The combination of the nineteen years and eleven years cycles produces this cycle, which measured the life of our Lord up to his baptism, and is also the prophetic month.

(Thirty solar years exceed 371 months by 1d. 10h. 2m.)

6. The Messianic, or Thirty-three Years Cycle.

In this period the fraction of a thirteenth month in the solar year *grows to twelve complete months.*

In the same period the fraction of a day in the solar year *grows to eight complete days.*

This cycle measured the number of *complete* years in our Lord's earthly life.

He is the head of *the new creation,* the founder of *a second Israel,* building his church on *a new twelvefold foundation,* and his earthly days were measured by *the period in which the new month element in the solar year becomes twelvefold, and as such a new year.*

7. The full Messianic Cycle, Thirty-three Years, Seven Months, and Seven Days.

In the period of the previous cycle, *plus* seven *months*, and seven days, the epact becomes *a complete solar year—a complete new year.*

This soli-lunar cycle which we shall henceforth call the The Messianic Cycle, contained, as we have shown, the entire period of our Lord's life on earth.

This cycle is the day, or unit in the chronology of Redemption history.

8. The Thirty-eight Years Cycle.

This is two lunar cycles, and its epact *two weeks of months.* In the history of Israel it was the period which followed the solemn oath, that that generation should not enter into God's rest—the period of the wandering in the wilderness of the rejected race.*

9. Forty-five Years, the Terminal Period of the Prophetic Times.

This is an historic period, linked with full entrance into Canaan rest, and also, as we have seen, the terminal one in the *series of prophetic times.*

Its number of years is *the sum of the first nine numbers.*

It is not a cycle of the month and year, but its epact is *seventy weeks of days* (490d.).

The *week*, the *square* of the week, *ten times* the square of the week, are associated in Scripture with completeness. We have

---

* *Forty years*, the full term of the wilderness journey, contains ten cycles of the solar year and day, and consequently ten of the lunar month and day, or *seventy weeks of months*. The difference between these two sets of cycles amounts in forty years to a septiform measure, *twice seventy days*.

seen this in days, and in years; here it is in *epact.* Forty-five years is *a period producing a new seventy weeks of days in the inter-relation of solar and lunar years.*

10. The Jubilee, Forty-nine Years.

The seven weeks and a day of the pentecostal period in the Levitical calendar, and the seven weeks of years and a year, or fifty years, of the Jewish jubilee, were analogous, and proportioned to each other on the scale of a year for a day. Both terminated in seasons of sacred joy.

They were *simply octave periods on a higher scale.* The proportion of seven days to seven weeks is that of a week to its square. The eighth day follows the termination of the first, the fiftieth of the second.

The jubilee, or 49 years, is an epact cycle.

(49 years exceed 606 months by 1d. 7h. 55m.)

"The fiftieth year," or year of jubilee (Lev. xxv. 9, 10), *began on the 10th day of the seventh month of the forty-ninth year, the day of* ATONEMENT. All our deliverance, all our liberty, all our restoration, all our springs of joy, date from the atoning work of Him who has entered for us within the veil, having obtained eternal redemption. From his atoning work dates a new beginning, and nobler order of things, in the experience of his people.

11. The Millennial Cycle, 1000 Years.

The epact in 1000 years is A MONTH OF YEARS.

We stated that the chronology of Redemption history is measured by periods in which the epact (or new year element) grows to months and years, and to weeks of years, months of years, and weeks of months of years.

"A thousand years are with the Lord as one day," a millenary therefore may be considered *a unit in the Divine reckoning.* In this period the epact becomes also *a unit*—a month of years.

From this it follows that seven thousand years are as a week, and that *the epact of seven thousand years is a week—seven months of years.*

The week of millenaries is in obvious harmony with the Scripture series of weeks on various scales, *and its epact with the week of months of the sacred Levitical calendar.*

There are two kinds of months, the lunar and the soli-lunar ; the former is $29\frac{1}{2}$ to $29\frac{3}{4}$ days ; the latter is 30 days.

The epact in 1000 *years amounts to months analogous to these* In 1000 true solar years the epact is $29\frac{3}{4}$ solar years :

In 1000 solar years of 365 days measure (the Babylonian and Egyptian year), the epact is just 30 lunar years. (1000 365-days years are 365000 days ; and 1000 and 30 lunar years are 365000 days, less 2 days.)

The 365-days year has a 25-years cycle of remarkable exactness, in which the epact is just nine months. This cycle is more accurate than the lunar, and was known to the Egyptians. There are four times 25 years in 100, forty in 1000, and 280 in 7000 years ; consequently the epact is 3 lunar years in 100, 30 *lunar years in* 1000, and 210 *lunar years, or seven months of years, in* 7000 *years.*

In the period which exceeds 1000 *true* solar years, by 7 solar years, and 7 months, the epact is 30 *complete solar years* : 1007y. 7m. are a month of Messianic cycles.

12. EPACT IN THE "SEVENTY WEEKS" OF MESSIANIC PROPHECY.

The "seventy weeks," or 490 years, are a great jubilee. They bear the same tenfold proportion to the 49 years jubilee period, that the 70 years of Captivity bore to the Levitical week of years.

The epact of 490 years,—*twice seven solar years, plus seven months,* and by calendar measure *seven calendar years plus seven weeks,*—has the octave form of a larger week plus a lesser.

In the chronology of Redemption history the Messianic cycle is a *day,* and the millenary, a *month.* In 490 years there are fourteen and a fraction such days (half a month), so that

490 years bears the same proportion to the week of millenaries (7000 years) that half a lunar month does to seven lunar months in the Levitical calendar.

A half-month period in the Levitical calendar terminated with the feast of passover; as here, half a month of larger measure terminated in the accomplishment of Redemption.

13. The Sanctuary Cycle, 2300 Years.

This is the third in centuries of 7000 years. One-third of the seven months Levitical calendar terminated in the feast of Pentecost. One-third is a characteristic Scripture portion, whether of the week of months, or of that of millenaries.

One-third of seven lunar months is 68–69 days.

The epact in 2300 solar years is 68–69 solar years.

In 2300 365-days years, the epact is exactly 69 lunar years.

In 2300 solar years the epact (68–69 solar years) is *exactly seventy lunar years and seven months.* The accuracy of this measure is such as to make 2300 years a secular soli-lunar cycle.

14. The 1260 Years Papal Cycle contrasted with the 1335 Years Prophetic Period terminating in Resurrection Blessedness.

The first of these is the period of the dominion of the persecuting Papal power—" They shall be given into his hand until a time, times, and the dividing of time "—" It shall be for a time, times, and a half, and when he shall have accomplished to scatter the power of the holy people, all these things shall be finished." (Dan. vii. 25 and xii. 7.)

The second of these terminates in resurrection blessedness.

" Blessed is he that waiteth and cometh unto the thousand, three hundred, and five and thirty days."

The epact of the first is *eminently sixfold*, just as is the *mark or number* attached to the power of which it is the period.

The epact of the second is *eminently sevenfold*.

To exhibit the contrast, let us place them side by side.

1260 years contains 66 lunar cycles.

1335 years contains 70 lunar cycles.

(The lunar cycle is the first closely harmonizing solar and lunar movements. Its epact is seven months, as we previously stated.)

The epact in 66 lunar cycles is 66 weeks of months.

The epact in 70 lunar cycles is 70 weeks of months, or 490 months.

1260 years contain 66 lunar cycles, plus 6 years.
> Epact, 66 weeks of months, plus 60 days.

1335 years contain 70 lunar cycles, plus 5 years.
> Epact, 70 weeks of months, plus 7 weeks of days.

By Prophetic or Calendar year measure.

The epact in 1260 years is thrice six calendar years, plus thrice six weeks, or—

SIX THOUSAND, SIX HUNDRED AND SIX DAYS:

The epact in 1335 years is A THOUSAND WEEKS, (within a day.)

The contrast is complete.

15. THE "SEVEN TIMES," WITH ITS ADDED SEVENTY-FIVE YEARS.

The "time, times, and a half," is half a week of "times"— 1260 years.

To this period prophecy *adds* 75 *years*, making 1335 years. (Dan. xii.)

The week of which 1260 years is the half, is 2520 years.

The epact of 2520 years *is* 75 *solar years.*

THUS TO THE HALF WEEK OF "TIMES" PROPHECY ADDS A PERIOD EQUAL TO THE EPACT OF THE ENTIRE WEEK OF "TIMES."

The addition to 2520 years of a period equal to its epact is a remarkable fact, and cannot be accidental. Let it be noted that 2520 *lunar* years, *plus* 75 *solar years,* equal 2520 solar years. How came the prophet to add to the half week of times a period equal to the epact of the whole? He could not have known the epact of this period, for the true measures of solar and lunar years had not then been ascertained; nor indeed could he have known the true interpretation of the prophetic times which he announced,—that the 1260 and 1335 days would be fulfilled on the year-day scale ; and that the 1260 years would prove the second half of a great historic week of double the length. The correspondence of these astronomic measures of the "seven times" with the period which prophecy adds to its close, is a confirmation of the year-day interpretation, an astronomic seal on its correct-ness, and opens the way for a double fulfilment of the final 75 years, an inclusive and also a subsequent one.

The addition of 75 years to 1260 years, extending the prophetic interval to 1335 years, *raises the epact from sixfold imperfection to sevenfold completeness :* it raises it—

> From 66 weeks of months, plus 60 days,
> To 70 weeks of months, plus 7 weeks of days ;

And by a second measure (that of the prophetic or calendar 360-days year), the addition changes the epact—

> From SIX THOUSAND, SIX HUNDRED AND SIX DAYS—
> To A THOUSAND WEEKS.

In the same way this addition of 75 years, by extending the full period from 2520 to 2595 years, raises the epact of the whole

> From *seventy-five solar years,*
> To *seventy-seven solar years, plus twice seven weeks of days.*

It may also be noted that the epacts in 1335 and 2595 years are harmonious ; for—

> In 1335 years the epact is *seventy weeks of months and seven weeks of days,*

And in 2595 years it is *seventy-seven solar years, and twice seven weeks of days,*

16. THE EPACT IN THE REMAINING PROPHETIC TIMES.

The epact in the 65 years and the 1290 years are *equally septiform* with the preceding; in the one, *seven hundred and seven days* (101 weeks); in the other, *twice seven thousand and four times seven days* (2004 weeks).

The epact of 2300 years by *calendar* year measure (360-day years) is 33 SOLAR YEARS, and this 33 years is itself a cycle of the true solar and lunar years,—a cycle whose epact is twelve lunar months, or a lunar year. Thus, according to the calendar year measure, the epact of the Sanctuary cycle equals the soli-lunar cycle which comprehends the complete years of the earthly life-time of Immanuel.

17. THE EPACT IN THE FULL NORMAL PERIOD OF HUMAN LIFE AND IN THE ANNUS MAGNUS OF THE PRECESSION OF THE EQUINOXES.

In our chapter on periodicity in vital phenomena we showed that the full normal period of human life is forty weeks plus seventy years. The epact in this period is the septiform number of *seven hundred and seventy days.*

This period of human life bears the same proportion to the magnificent cycle of the precession of the equinoxes that a solar day does to a solar year, and as the epact of the former is 770 days, that of the latter is 770 solar years.

In conclusion: the simplest and most fundamental natural units of time are *the solar day, the lunar month, and the solar year.*

None of these is an exact multiple of any other. The lesser are contained in the greater with fractional remainders.

THESE FRACTIONAL REMAINDERS GROW TO COMPLETE DAYS, MONTHS, AND YEARS, AND TO WEEKS OF THESE IN THE PROPHETIC PERIODS, and in certain natural cycles fundamentally connected with the measurement of terrestrial time on a large scale.

We previously showed that the prophetic times are soli-lunar cycles ; we now see that they form a septenary series, as measured by the conjoint movements of the two glorious worlds which rule the orderly succession of terrestrial times and seasons. In conclusion we refer the reader to Sec. iii. ch. v., where we endeavour to show *what that whole is of which the prophetic periods and their epact measures are parts.*

Calendar

OF

"The Times of the Gentiles."

THIS CALENDAR

1. Presents in their order the leading events of the " Times of the Gentiles," with their dates B.C. and A.D., together with the names and periods of the reigns of an unbroken succession of Gentile monarchs, from the beginning of the kingdom of Babylon to the present day.

2. It gives the chronological distance of each reign and event from the accession of the first king of Babylon, both in solar and lunar years.

3. It also gives (Part II.) the chronological distances of reigns and events from the edicts of Justinian and Phocas, and from the era of the Hegira, the papal and Mohammedan starting-points ; the former being stated in solar, and the latter, in accordance with Moham-medan chronology, in lunar years.

4. It exhibits the fulfilment of the various chronological and other prophecies referring to these Gentile " Times."

The date of the commencement of the first of the four great monarchies, and thus of the whole "Times of the Gentiles," that of *the accession of the first king of Babylon,*—after the overthrow of the Assyrian empire,—is the well-known ERA OF NABONASSAR, from which all the reigns of the Babylonian kings and other events of history are computed by Babylonian, Egyptian, and other ancient chronologers and historians.

This date, the noon of Thoth I., Nabonassar I., is astronomically determined as February 26th, B.C. 747, by the records of a series of eclipses and planetary positions extending through nine centuries, all measured from that point by the astronomers who recorded them (notably Ptolemy).

These eclipses and planetary positions have, during the last three centuries, been verified by the labours of modern astronomers, and thus the exact point of the era of Nabonassar precisely ascertained.

The chronological starting-point of the Babylonian kingdom stands out therefore, in the providence of God, amid the mists of ancient chronology, as a clear, salient, accurately ascertained date, known to a year, to a month, and to a day—the noon of February 26th, B.C. 747.

From this date to the date of THE DEPOSITION OF ROMULUS AUGUSTULUS, THE LAST RULER OF THE WESTERN ROMAN EMPIRE, August 22nd, A.D. 476, the interval is

TWELVE HUNDRED AND SIXTY LUNAR YEARS.

"TIME, TIMES, AND AN HALF TIME."

Calendar

OF

"The Times of the Gentiles."

PART I. From the ERA of the RISE of the BABY-
LONIAN,
To that of the FALL of the WESTERN
ROMAN EMPIRE.

"TIME, TIMES, AND AN HALF TIME."

PART II. From the RISE to the FALL of the
PAPAL and MOHAMMEDAN
POWERS.

"TIME, TIMES, AND AN HALF TIME."

PART I.

CALENDAR OF THE FOUR GREAT EMPIRES,

BABYLONIAN, PERSIAN, GRECIAN, ROMAN.

From the ERA of the accession of NABONASSAR, the commencement of Babylonian Chronology,

Feb. 26th, B.C. 747

[DATE, Astronomically Determined],

To the END of the Government of

ROMULUS AUGUSTULUS,

August 22nd, A.D. 476,

a period of exactly

Twelve Hundred and Sixty Lunar Years

["a thousand two hundred and threescore days"]

First Empire—THE BABYLONIAN.

FIRST BEAST—Lion with eagle's wings. Kingdom of gold.

DURATION—210 years—seven prophetic months;
analogous with seven Babylonian months, or 210 days, and
also one-twelfth of SEVEN TIMES.

ANTECEDENT VISION OF

THE GLORY OF JEHOVAH SABAOTH,

AND OF THE DESOLATIONS OF ISRAEL
granted to the prophet ISAIAH
in the year that King Uzziah died, B.C. 757.

" HOLY, HOLY, HOLY, IS THE LORD OF HOSTS ·
THE WHOLE EARTH IS FULL OF HIS GLORY."

"Go, and TELL THIS PEOPLE, Hear ye indeed, but understand not ; and see ye indeed, but perceive not. Make the

heart of this people fat, and make their ears heavy, and shut
their eyes; lest they see with their eyes, and hear with their
ears, and understand with their heart, and convert, and be
healed. Then said I, LORD, HOW LONG? And He answered,
Until the cities be wasted without inhabitant, and the houses
without man, and the land be utterly DESOLATE, and the LORD
have REMOVED MEN FAR AWAY, and there be A GREAT FOR-
SAKING IN THE MIDST OF THE LAND. And still there shall
be A TENTH therein THAT SHALL RETURN, and there shall be
wasting; but as a teil tree and as an oak, whose life is in
them when they are cut down: the holy seed shall be the life
thereof" (Isa. vi.)

> B.C. 770. Accession of Menahem, king of Israel, who reigned
> 10 y. In his days Pul, the *first* king of Assyria
> named in Scripture, "came against the land," and
> in the reign of Pekah, Menahem's successor, Tiglath-
> pileser, king of Assyria, invaded it. By these were
> carried captive the Reubenites, Gadites, and half
> tribe of Manasseh (2 Kings xv. 17, 20; 1 Chron.
> v. 3, 25, 26).

LUNAR	SOLAR.	B.C.	KINGS OF BABYLON.
1	1	747	Accession of NABONASSAR, Thoth. 1, Feb. 26th. From the noon of which day Babylonian chrono-logy is reckoned—date accurately determined by the verification of a series of astronomical obser-vations, including eclipses, recorded by Ptolemy, the time of whose occurrence was measured by ancient astronomers *from this point.*
7	7	741	*FIRST CHRONOLOGICAL PROPHECY OF ISRAEL'S DESOLATION* [SIXTY-FIVE YEARS], *AND PROMISE OF* IMMANUEL (given on the very spot where Sennacherib's invading army afterwards stood: Isa. vii. 2, compare with xxxvi. 2), "within THREESCORE AND FIVE YEARS shall

LUNAR	SOLAR.	B.C.	
			EPHRAIM be broken that it be not a people" (Isa. vii.).
16	15	733	NADIUS. AHAZ. MICAH.
18	17	731	CHINZIRUS and PORUS. HOSEA.
23	22	726	JUGÆUS. HEZEKIAH. NAHUM.
26	25	723	SAMARIA BESIEGED, 4th year of Hezekiah; 7th of Hosea.
			SHALMANEZER (2 Kings xvii.).
28	27	721	MARDOCEMPADUS. FALL OF SAMARIA.
			(*First historical eclipse* is mentioned in Annals of Sargon, king of Assyria, and by Ptolemy. Total eclipse of moon, March 19th, four and a half hours before midnight, Babylon, B.C. 721.)
			## CAPTIVITY OF TEN TRIBES.
			(*Second historical eclipse.* Lunar eclipse, March 8th, 11h. 56m., B.C. 720, Babylon.—Ptolemy.)
			(*Third historical eclipse.* Lunar eclipse, September 1st, 10h. 18m., B.C. 720, Babylon.—Ptolemy.)
36	35	713	SENNACHERIB'S Invasion of Judea in 14th year of Hezekiah, 713 B.C. (2 Kings xviii., xix.; Isa. xxxvi. 39.)
41	39	709	ARCHIANUS. "I occupied the town of Samaria,
46	44	704	Interregnum. and brought into captivity 27,280 persons. . . . I took them to As-
			HAGISA, 30d. syria, and instead of them I placed
			MARUDACH men to live there whom my hand had conquered."—Annals of Sargon,
			BALDANES, 6mo. king of Assyria (Shalmanezer).
			"Records of Past," vol. vii., Assyrian texts.—Bagster.
			FROM THE SIEGE OF SAMARIA BY SHAL- MANEZER, B.C. 723, TO THE PAPAL OVER- THROW IN THE FRENCH REVOL., 1798 A.D. 2520 Y. OR "SEVEN TIMES." BISECTED BY PERIOD OF JUSTINIAN.
48	46	702	BELIBUS.
51	49	699	APRONADIUS or ASORDANES.
			MANASSEH, B.C. 697. JOEL.
57	55	693	REGIBALUS.
58	56	692	MESESIMORDACHUS.
62	60	688	Interregnum.

LUNAR.	SOLAR.	B.C.	
70	68	680	ASARIDINUS.
75	72–3	676-5	COMPLETION OF EXILE (OF ISRAEL) BY ESARHADDON (son of Sennacherib, 2 Kings xix. 37), and their replacement by heathen colonists. MANASSEH'S captivity in his 22nd year, B.C. 676–5 (2 Chron. xxxiii. 11, Ezra iv. 2), THENCE SEVEN TIMES, or 2520 SOLAR YEARS to the 1260th year of the Hegira.
84	81	667	SAOSDUCHINUS.
104	101	647	CHINALADINUS.
	.		JEREMIAH begins to prophesy in the 13th year of JOSIAH, B.C. 628.
127	123	625	NABOPOLASSAR.
			(*Fourth historical eclipse.* Lunar eclipse, April 21st, 18h. 22m., B.C. 621.)
			Birth of Anaximander, B.C. 610: discovered obliquity of ecliptic : disciple of Thales.
147	142	606	FULL DEVELOPMENT OF BABYLONIAN EMPIRE.
149	144	604	NEBUCHADNEZZAR. NINEVEH DESTROYED, 606. Prophecies of JONAH and NAHUM. *SEVENTY YEARS CAPTIVITY OF JUDAH BEGINS* (Jer. xxv. 1), B.C. 605 (in the year before the sole reign of Nebuchadnezzar. Clinton). NEBUCHADNEZZAR'S VISION OF THE GREAT IMAGE (Dan. ii.).
150-1	146	602	Complete subjugation of Jehoiakim (2 Kings xxiv. 1). THENCE 1260 LUNAR YEARS to the ERA of HEGIRA, A.D. 622.
155	150	598	FULL COMMENCEMENT OF THE "TIMES OF THE GENTILES" (2 Kings xxiv. 14). "ALL JERUSALEM carried away" captive. Thence 1260 solar to A.D. 663, commencing date of LATIN CHURCH, and "seven times" lunar to A.D. 1848 (2445 solar years = 2520 lunar) and seven times solar to A.D. 1923 (differ-

LUNAR.	SOLAR.	B.C.	
166	161	587	ence between the last two is the epact of the whole, or 75 years). 19th year of Nebuchadnezzar. THE TEMPLE BURNED, 10th day of the 5th month (2 Kings xxv. compared with Jeremiah lii. 12). THENCE an interval of 1260 LUNAR YEARS to the MOHAMMEDAN CAPTURE and DESOLATION of JERUSALEM, A.D. 637 (Mosque of Omar).
193	187	561	ABILMARODACHUS (Evil Merodach), 37th year of Jehoiachim's captivity, B.C. 562, falls within the 1st of Evil Merodach (2 Kings xxv. 27).
195	189	559	NIGLISSARUS (Neriglissar).
198	192	556	LABOSOARCHODUS.
199	193	555	BALTASARUS (Belshazzar). DANIEL'S VISION of the FOUR GREAT BEASTS in the 1st year of Belshazzar (Dan. vii.). DANIEL'S VISION of the RAM and HE GOAT in the 3rd year of Belshazzar (Dan. viii.).
217	210	538	BELSHAZZAR'S FEAST. "MENE, MENE, TEKEL, UPHARSIN" (Dan. v.). DARIUS. FALL OF BABYLON { BELSHAZZAR SLAIN. DARIUS THE MEDIAN takes the kingdom (Dan. v.).

Second Empire.—THE PERSIAN.

SECOND BEAST—The bear. Kingdom of silver (Dan. ii. 7).

DURATION—210 lunar years, B.C. 538 to B.C. 334—seven months of years.

In the first year of Darius,
DANIEL'S PRAYER.

The angel GABRIEL sent to reveal to him the
SEVENTY WEEKS RESTORATION PERIOD,
extending to the
ADVENT OF MESSIAH THE PRINCE (Dan. ix.).

LUNAR.	SOLAR.	B.C.	
219	212	536	CYRUS. First year of *sole* government of Cyrus, from death of Darius, called in Daniel 3rd of Cyrus.
			EDICT OF CYRUS. *END OF SEVENTY YEARS CAPTIVITY* (Ezra i., Dan. x.).
226	219	529	CAMBYSES (Dan. xi. 2).
			(*Fifth historical eclipse.* "In the seventh year of Cambyses, which is the 225th year of Nabonassar, between the 17th and 18th of Phamenoth, at one hour before midnight, the moon was eclipsed at Babylon by half the diameter on the north."—Ptolemy, July 16th, 11 p.m., B.C. 523.)
233	226	522	SMERDIS (Dan. xi. 2).
234	227	521	DARIUS HYSTASPIS. Second decree for rebuilding of THE TEMPLE (Dan. xi. 2 ; Ezra iv. 5, v. 6).
			HAGGAI, ZECHARIAH, ZERUBBABEL.
			(*Sixth historical eclipse,* 20th of Darius. Lunar eclipse, Nov. 19th, 11.45 at night, B.C. 502.)
			(*Seventh historical eclipse,* 31st of Darius. Lunar eclipse, April 25th, 11.30 at night, B.C. 491.)
271	263	485	XERXES. The fourth king of Daniel xi. 2, Ezra iv. 6. Passage of Hellespont. Battle of Salamis, followed solar eclipse verified as Oct. 2nd, B.C. 480.—Herodotus ix. 10.
			Birth of Socrates, April or May, 468 B.C.
292	283	465	ARTABANUS.
293	284	464	ARTAXERXES LONGIMANUS (Ezra vii.). Seventh monarch from Cyrus.
300	291	457	Issue of command "to restore and to build JERUSALEM." Latter part of 7th year of Artaxerxes. Thence 500 lunar years, or 6000 lunations, to the Ascension, A.D. 29; Phasis 1 NISAN, March 21st, B.C. 457.
			COMMENCEMENT OF THE SEVENTY WEEKS. Thence 2300 solar years to the 1260th year of the Hegira.

LUNAR.	SOLAR.	B.C.	
314	304	444	NEHEMIAH'S commission in 20th year of Artaxerxes (Neh. ii.).

METON commences his cycle with the new moon nearest the summer solstice, B.C. 432.

(Solar eclipse, August 3rd, 6h. 35m., B.C. 431, Athens.)

HERODOTUS, THUCYDIDES, HIPPOCRATES.

END OF O. T. CANON. CLOSE OF SACRED HISTORY.

BIRTH OF PLATO, May, B.C. 429.

333	323	425	XERXES II.

(Lunar eclipse, Oct. 9th, 6h. 45m., total, B.C. 425, Athens.)

333	323	425	SOGDIANUS.
334	324	424	DARIUS NOTHUS.

(Solar eclipse, March 20th, 20h. 17m., B.C. 424, Athens.)

Grecian defeat. Surrender of Nicias (Thucyd vii. 50, 75), eight or nine days after lunar eclipse, Aug. 27th, 10h. 15m., total, B.C. 413.

Temple erected on Mount Gerizim by Manasseh, B.C. 408.

354	343	405	ARTAXERXES MNEMON.

(Lunar eclipse, April 15th, 8h. 50m., B.C. 406, total, Athens.)

(Solar eclipse, September 2nd, 21h. 12m., B.C. 404, Athens.)

DEATH OF SOCRATES, at end of Thargelion, B.C. 399, when he had just entered his 70th year.

Johanan, the high priest, kills his brother Jeshua in the Temple, for which the Persian governor lays a mulct upon the Jews for seven years, B.C. 366.

401	389	359	OCHUS.

(Lunar eclipse, December 22nd, 19h. 6m., B.C. 383, Athens.)

(Lunar eclipse, June 18th, 8h. 54m., B.C. 382, Athens.)

(Lunar eclipse, December 12th, 10h. 21m., total B.C. 382, Athens.)

423	410	338	ARSES. Birth of Demosthenes, in July, B.C. 382.
425	412	336	DARIUS CODOMANNUS.

𝕿𝖍𝖎𝖗𝖉 𝕰𝖒𝖕𝖎𝖗𝖊.—THE GRECIAN.

THIRD BEAST—Leopard with four heads. Kingdom of brass
(Dan. ii., vii., viii. 5, xi. 3).

DURATION—from Conquest of Persian Empire, B.C. 334,
to end of Seleucidæ,
and capture of Jerusalem by Pompey the Roman, B.C. 63,
280 LUNAR YEARS, OR FORTY WEEKS OF YEARS.

LUNAR.	SOLAR.	B C.	
425	412	336	ALEXANDER THE GREAT. Accession about July. FIRST HORN OF HE GOAT (Dan. viii.). B.C. 334,—Crosses Hellespont, marches into Asia; conquers Caria, Syria, Tyre, Egypt, Babylon, Susa, Persepolis, and Persian Empire; Parthia, Media, Scythia, and invades India. Dies at Babylon, in June, B.C. 323, age 33. (Aristotle opens the Lyceum.) FOUR HORNS OF HE GOAT (Dan. vii. 6, viii. 8, xi. 4).
438	425	323	PHILIP ARIDÆUS. CASSANDER. Macedon and Greece. SELEUCUS. Babylon, Syria (Dan. xi. 5, 6). LYSIMACHUS. Thrace and Bithynia. PTOLEMY. Egypt ("The king of the south," Ptolemy, son of Lagus, Dan. xi. 5).
			MACEDON.
446	432	316	CASSANDER. (Solar eclipse, August 14th, 20h. 5m., B.C. 310, Sicily.) PTOLEMY SOTER (Satrap. Egypt, B.C. 323, Dan. xi. 5),

LUNAR.	SOLAR.	B.C.	KINGS OF SYRIA.
450	436	312	† SELEUCUS NICATOR (Dan. xi. 5, 6).
466	452	296	ANTIPATER. Era of Seleucidæ, Oct. 1, B.C. 312.
466	452	296	ALEXANDER.
468	454	294	DEMETRIUS.
477	462	286	PYRRHUS. Birth of Archimedes, about 287 B.C., at Syracuse.
483	468	280	† ANTIOCHUS I., Soter. PTOLEMY PHILADELPHUS, B.C. 285 (Dan. xi. 9).
485	470	278	FOR 16 YEARS 12 KINGS.
486	471	277	ANTIGONUS I., Gonatus.
502	487	261	† ANTIOCHUS II., Theos (Dan. xi. 1).
518	502	246	† SELEUCUS II., Callinicus (Dan. xi. 7, 8). PTOLEMY EUERGETES, B.C. 247 (Dan. xi. 7, 8).
525	509	239	DEMETRIUS II.
535	519	229	ANTIGONUS II., Doson.
538	522	226	† SELEUCUS III., Ceraunus (Dan. xi. 10).
541	525	223	† ANTIOCHUS III., THE GREAT (Dan. xi. 10). PTOLEMY PHILOPATER, B C. 222 (Dan. xi. 11, 12). ERATOSTHENES : Astronomer.
545	528	220	PHILIP. (Lunar eclipse, March 19th, 14h. 5m., total, B.C. 219, Mysia.) PTOLEMY EPIPHANES, B.C. 205 (Dan. xi. 14, 17).
579	561	187	† SELEUCUS IV., Philopater (Dan. xi. 20). (Solar eclipse, July 6th, 20h. 38m., B.C. 188. Rome.)
587	569	179	PERSEUS. PTOLEMY PHILOMETER, B.C. 181 (Dan. xi. 25).
591	573	175	† ANTIOCHUS EPIPHANES (Dan. xi. 21, II. Book of Maccabees). (Eighth from Seleucus Nicator, first of second seven.) Plunders the Temple, and dedicates it

LUNAR.	SOLAR.	B.C.	
			to Jupiter Olympius. Captures and miserably destroys Jerusalem. Jewish martyrs.
598	580	168	*Daily sacrifice ceases.*
			JUDAS MACCABÆUS.
			Asmonean deliverers and princes.
			(Eclipse of moon, June 21st, 8h. 2m., total, B.C. 168, Macedonia.)
601	583	165	Cleanses the sanctuary, 25th of ninth month, Cisleu, near time of winter solstice. Hence the feast of Dedication, John x. 22, "and it was winter."
			(Feast of Dedication, A.D. 1879, on Dec. 10th.)
			From the *Maccabean cleansing of the sanctuary,* B.C. 165, to the *First Crusade* for the deliverance of Jerusalem and the holy places from Saracenic desolation (A.D. 1096), 1260 solar years, or "time, times, and an half time."
602	584	164	† ANTIOCHUS V.
604	586	162	† DEMETRIUS I., Soter.
617	598	150	† ALEXANDER BALAS
			(Jonathan, Asmonean Prince).
621	602	146	† DEMETRIUS II., Nicator.
623	604	144	† ANTIOCHUS VI.
			(Simon, Asmonean Prince).
624	605	143	† DIODOTUS (Trypho).
628	609	139	† ANTIOCHUS VII. (First of third seven of Seleucidæ. Marries Cleopatra).
631	612	136	HYRCANUS I., High Priest.
			(Gen. xlix. 10.)
637	618	130	† DEMETRIUS II. (restored).
638	619	129	Hyrcanus conquers the Edomites, and compels them all to embrace the Jewish religion. From these sprang the Herodian family.

LUNAR.	SOLAR.	B.C.	
639	620	128	Hipparchus observes the vernal equinox March 22nd, B.C. 128. The star Spica (first magnitude) 6° behind the autumnal equinox.
640	621	127	† ALEXANDER ZEBINA (impostor).
645	625	123	† ANTIOCHUS VIII (Grypus).
			KINGS OF JUDEA.
661	641	107	ARISTOBULUS I., Son of Hyrcanus; first of Asmoneans who wore the diadem, and took the name of King. Slays his brother Antigonus, and is succeeded by his brother Jannæus.
663	643	105	ALEXANDER JANNÆUS. (Solar eclipse, July 18th, 22h., B.C. 104, Rome.) (The signs and constellations coincide about 100 B.C.)
668	648	100	BIRTH OF JULIUS CÆSAR, July 12th. (The Iron Subjugator.) Jannæus conquers Gilead and Moab B.C. 94; crucifies 800 of his rebel subjects, B.C. 86.
675	655	93	† PHILIP AND DEMETRIUS.
686	665	83	† TIGRANES (King of Armenia).
691	670	78	ALEXANDRA, Widow of Jannæus, conciliates the Pharisees. Dies, B.C. 70.
700	679	69	† ANTIOCHUS IX., Asiaticus. (21st and last of Seleucidæ.) HYRCANUS II., son of Alexandra. Seizes crown; forced to resign it after 3 months to his younger brother Aristobulus. ARISTOBULUS II.
704	683	65	(POMPEY CONQUERS SYRIA. END OF SELEUCIDÆ, B.C. 65.) CÆSAR ædile, B.C. 65.
706	685	63	HYRCANUS II.
707	686	62	POMPEY (ROMAN) having conquered Syria TAKES JERUSALEM, after a siege of three months, on day of a fast in

Q Q

LUNAR.	SOLAR.	B.C.	
			December, B.C. 63. Deposes Aristobulus and makes Hyrcanus king.
			Duration of First Three Empires—707 lunar years.
			BIRTH OF AUGUSTUS (CÆSAR) September 23rd, B.C. 63. Julius Cæsar elected Pontifex Maximus.
			(Lunar eclipse, Oct. 27th, 6h. 22m., total, B.C. 63, Rome.)
715	693	55	Julius Cæsar subdues the western tribes of Gaul, B.C. 56. Passes the Rhine, lands in Britain, B.C. 55. Second expedition of Cæsar into Britain, B.C. 54; returns and winters in Syria, crosses Rubicon, follows Pompey to Brundusium, conquers Afranius in Spain, B.C. 49.
724	702	46	Cæsar as Pontifex Maximus reforms the Calendar (inserts 67+23=90d. in year 46 B.C. Introduces *Julian year*). (The month Quintilis named Julius, B.C. 44.) Julius Cæsar slain March 15th, B.C. 44.
726	704	44	Age 56.
730	708	40	ANTIGONUS. Last of Asmonean princes. (Seventh from Hyrcanus I.)
732	710	38	HEROD and SOSIUS besiege Jerusalem, and after half a year's siege take it in December, B.C. 38.
733	711	37	(LAST SEVENTY YEARS of the 490 YEARS TO. MESSIAH begin, B.C. 37).
			HEROD THE GREAT (Idumean). 37.
			Murders Hyrcanus; by his instigation Antigonus is put to death at Rome.
			The sceptre thus departs from Judah (Gen. xlix. 10) in preparation for the immediate ADVENT OF SHILOH.
			Herod rebuilds the TEMPLE.
741	719	29	THE TEMPLE OF JANUS SHUT (cessation of war); shut a second time, B.C. 25.

fourth Empire—THE ROMAN.

FOURTH BEAST—"dreadful and terrible and strong exceedingly."
Kingdom of iron.

LUNAR.	SOLAR.	B.C.	EMPERORS.
743	$\frac{720}{721}$	27	AUGUSTUS CÆSAR.
			(Cæsar named Augustus, B.C. 27. The *Anni Augustani* computed at Rome from Jan. 1, B.C. 27. From E. Nab. to this point, two prophetic "times"—360 + 360 = 720 years of " seven times.")
			COMMENCEMENT OF THIRD PROPHETIC "TIME."
			(Three conjunctions of Jupiter and Saturn in the constellation Pisces, near the first point of Aries, B.C. 7. In spring of B.C. 6, the planet Mars came to same spot.)
			(B.C. 6 is first year of 40th lunar cycle from Nab. era. Epact in 40 cycles 280 months, or forty weeks of months.)
765	742	6	THE NATIVITY (Luke ii.).
		A.D.	MESSIAH THE PRINCE.
			Death of Herod a little before the Pass-over of B.C. 4 (Matt. ii. 19).
			(Date fixed by lunar eclipse in the night between March 12th and 13th, beginning at 1h. 48m., and ending at 4h. 12m. Ideler. Recorded by Josephus.)
777	754	7	Jesus goes up to Jerusalem at the feast of Passover when He is twelve years of age. Found "in the temple sitting in the midst of the doctors, both hearing them and asking them questions" (Luke ii. 46).
785	761	14	TIBERIUS (Luke xx. 22-25).
			Death of Augustus, Aug. 19th
			(Tacitus, Annals, Book I., mentions an eclipse of the moon soon after the death of Augustus. Verified as lunar eclipse Sept. 26th, 17h. 15m., total, A.D. 14.)

LUNAR	SOLAR.	A.D.	
			Tiberius Pontifex Maximus, March 10th, A.D. 15.
			MINISTRY OF JOHN THE BAPTIST (Luke iii.).
796	772	25	BAPTISM AND MINISTRY OF MESSIAH from Autumn of A.D. 25 (Luke iii. 23).
800	776	29	N. ERA, 777 (70th year of Tiberius).
			DEATH OF MESSIAH. DAY OF PASSOVER, March 18th. "About the ninth hour," or at 3 p.m. FULL MOON, 9 h. 16 m. p.m. (John xix. 28), (77th day of year), FRIDAY.
			BURIAL, Friday evening.
			Sabbath, March 19th, in the grave. "That sabbath was an high day" (John xix. 31).
			RESURRECTION AND ASCENSION OF MESSIAH (Matt. xxviii.).
			RESURRECTION, March 20th. FIRST DAY OF WEEK, Day of Wave Sheaf. Vernal Equinox. Sun in Aries.
			ASCENSION, 40 days subsequently, April 28–29 (Acts i. 3, 9).
			FOUNDATION OF THE CHURCH.
			Commencement of THE DISPENSATION OF THE SPIRIT (Acts ii.).
			The Gospel published in Judea, Samaria, and Antioch.
805	781	34	*END OF SEVENTY WEEKS.*
			The Gospel preached to the Gentiles.
			Labours of the Apostle Paul (Acts ix. to xxviii.).
808	784	37	CALIGULA. Assassination of Caligula, Jan. 24th, 41; age 29. Nero born.
			Herod Agrippa, king of Galilee.
813	788	41	CLAUDIUS (Acts xi. 28; xxviii. 2).
			Birth of Titus, Dec. 30th, 41. Herod Agrippa, king of all Palestine.

LUNAR.	SOLAR.	A.D.	
			Death of Herod Agrippa. All Palestine A ROMAN PROVINCE, A.D. 44.
			Cuspius Fadus, Procurator, 44. Claudius Felix, sole Procurator of Judea, A.D. 53.
826	801	54	NERO (Acts xxv. 8, 12; xxvii. 24). Claudius poisoned by Agrippina that her son Nero may succeed, Oct. 13th, 54.
			Festus, Procurator of Judea, A.D. 55.
			Albinus, Procurator of Judea, A.D. 62.
			Great fire at Rome; Christians falsely accused of having caused it, and suffer cruel persecutions. This first persecution lasted four years.
838	813	66	JEWISH WAR begins, May, 66. Christians flee from Jerusalem to Pella (Matt. xxiv.).
839	814	67	VESPASIAN conducts the Jewish war. Entering Galilee with his army takes Jotapata, after 47 d. siege, on 1st of Panemus or Thamuz, 67. Joppa and Tiberias then surrender. Josephus taken prisoner at Jotapata.
840	815	68	GALBA. Nero kills himself, June 9th, 68; age 30 y. 5 m. 26 d. (840 lunar years = ⅓ of 2520 y., or " seven times " lunar).
			Vespasian proceeds with the Jewish war; about Feb. 68 enters Gadara, and Jericho about May.
841	816	69	OTHO. Galba slain, Jan. 15; age 73.
			VITELLIUS. Proclaimed emperor by German legions. Disgraced by the grossest sensuality.
			VESPASIAN. Assumes empire, July 1, 69. Conquers Vitellius, who is beheaded, Dec. 21; age 55.
			Vespasian commits conduct of Jewish war to his son TITUS. Jerusalem a prey to fierce intestine factions.

LUNAR.	SOLAR.	A D.	
842	817	70	Titus marches from Alexandria to Jerusalem, arriving there a little before the Passover. Besieges the city nearly five months. Appalling sufferings of Jews. Encloses Jerusalem on every side (Luke xix. 41–44; xxi. 20, 24). Daily sacrifice ceased, 17th Panemus, Friday, 13th July. TEMPLE BURNED on the 10th day of the 5th month (Louis or Ab), August 4–5. Jewish war lasted 4 y. 4 m.; 1,100,000 Jews perish in the siege of Jerusalem; 97,000 captives.
843	818	71	TRIUMPH of Vespasian and Titus at Rome (commemorated by Arch of Titus at Rome). (Lunar eclipse, Rome, March 4th, 8h. 32m., A.D. 71, eclipsed at setting ; and 15 days after this the sun eclipsed at 9 in the morning.)
852	826	79	TITUS. Death of Vespasian, June 23rd, age 69. Pompeii and Heculaneum destroyed by an eruption of Mount Vesuvius, Aug. 23rd. Rome afflicted by a calamitous fire, followed by a pestilence, 80.
854	828	81	DOMITIAN. Death of Titus (attributed to poison), September 13th; age 40. Second persecution of the Christian Church. Gnosticism.
869	843	96	NERVA. Domitian slain on account of his barbarities, Sept. 18th, 96; age 45. Death of Nerva, Jan. 25th, 98; age 72. (Lunar eclipse March 21st, at 3 in afternoon, A.D. 98.—"Chrono. Astrolabe," Lindsay.)
871	845	98	TRAJAN. Bithynian persecutions under Pliny. Trajan, first emperor who enacts penal laws against the Christians. Death of the Apostle John. Martyrdom of Ignatius by Trajan, 115. CLOSE OF N. T. CANON.

LUNAR.	SOLAR.	A.D.	
891	864	117	HADRIAN. Proclaimed Aug. 11th, 117. Personally surveys all the provinces of the empire. Visits Syria, and on the ruins of Jerusalem builds ÆLIA CAPITOLINA, in which he dedicates a temple to Jupiter.

The aphelion of Mercury observed by Theon, July 5th, 131.

JEWISH rebellion under BARCHOCHEDAS, the false Messiah, 132. Persecutes Christians. Jewish war with Romans lasts from the spring of 132 to August, 135 (3 years and a half); 985 towns and villages and 580,000 Jews destroyed. Jews forbidden to approach Jerusalem; a new city built on its foundations and colonized by foreigners.

909	882	135	888 A.U.C. JEWISH DESOLATION COMPLETE.

Ptolemy (Claudius), astronomer, geographer, and chronologer, author of the Almagest. The eclipses he records extend through nine centuries. *Foundation of chronology.*

912	885	138	ANTONINUS PIUS. Death of Hadrian, July 10th, 138; reigned 20 y. 10 m. 30 d. Antoninus enacts that no Christian should be persecuted as such, 157. Died Mar. 7th, 161.
936	908	161	MARCUS AURELIUS (the philosopher), author of a systematic persecution. Justin Martyr's Apology. Martyrdom of Polycarp, 167. Pestilence rages several years.
956	927	180	COMMODUS. Death of Marcus, Mar. 17th, 180. Reigned, 19 y.; age 58 y. 10 m. 21 d. Commodus given to dissolute pleasures.

Increasing ascendency of Hierarchical Aristocracy in the Church. Montanism, 188.

LUNAR.	SOLAR.	A.D.	
969	940	193	PERTINAX. Murdered by Prætorians, March 28th, 193.
969	940	193	DIDIUS JULIANUS. Buys the empire. Slain, June 1st, 193.
969	940	193	SEPTIMUS SEVERUS. Early aggression of Church of Rome. Victor excommunicates the churches of Asia Minor. Irenæus. Tertullian. Edict prohibiting Christianity. Sixth persecution, 201.
988	958	211	CARACALLA. Oppressive taxation. Massacre at Alexandria by Caracalla, 215. Caracalla assassinated near Edesa, April 8th, 217; age 29.
994	964	217	MACRINUS. Succeeds, April 11th, 217. Beheaded, 218; age 54.
995	965	218	ELAGABALUS. A youth of 17, high priest of Temple at Emesa. Superstitious and profligate. Slain by Prætorians, Jan., 222; age 21. Origen at Alexandria.
999	969	222	ALEXANDER SEVERUS. In his 14th year, prudently guided by his mother, who is created Augusta, wages war with the Persians. Murdered, Feb., 235; age 28. The Canon Paschalis of Hippolytus begins, 222.
1012	982	235	MAXIMIN. Defeats the Germans. His ferocious tyranny in Sirmium excites universal horror. Partial persecution of Christians. Seventh persecution.
1016	985	238	THE GORDIANS. The Gordians proclaimed in Africa; defeated and slain. Toleration of the Church general.
1016	985	238	MAXIMUS and BALBINUS. Elected by the Senate, and murdered by the Prætorians.
1016	985	238	GORDIAN III. Age 13, proclaimed emperor. Murdered; age 19, 244.

LUNAR.	SOLAR.	A.D.	
1022	991	244	PHILIP THE ARABIAN. Openly shows favour to Christians. Makes peace with Sapor, 246.
			Origen, aged 60, writes cont. Celsum. Bishops now possess great and increasing influence.
1027	996	249	DECIUS. Eighth persecution; many apostatize. Persian and Gothic invasions.
			Origen suffers imprisonment and torture, 250.
1029	998	251	GALLUS. Appointed in association with Hostilianus, son of Decius. Ninth persecution. A pestilence begins which lasts fifteen years.
			Rise of monachism. Death of Origen, in his 69th year.
1032	1001	254	ÆMILANUS. Slain by his soldiers at Spoletum.
1032	1001	254	VALERIAN. Cyprian teaches that the Bishop of Rome is the successor of St. Peter, and that the Church of Rome is entitled to precedence from importance of the city, but not in point of jurisdiction.
			Persecution. Stephen, bishop of Rome, put to death. Many Christians sent to the mines.
1038	1007	260	GALLIENUS. Famine and PESTILENCE; diminution of the human species. Edict of Toleration. Christianity becomes for the first time a "religio licita"—a lawful method of worship.
1047	1015	268	CLAUDIUS. Gallienus slain, March, 268, age 50. Claudius overthrows the Goths, who, to the number of 320,000, had occupied Illyricum and Macedonia.
			Hierarchical pretensions on the increase. Celibacy in high esteem.
1049	1017	270	QUINTILLUS. Brother of Claudius, assumes empire, and in 17 days puts an end to his life.

LUNAR.	SOLAR.	A.D.	
1049	1017	270	AURELIAN. Makes peace with Goths and Vandals, unfriendly to Christianity; about to commence a persecution of Christians when he died, slain by the treachery of his notary; age 61.
			Interregnum of six months, ending Sept. 25th, 275.
1054	1022	275	TACITUS. Elected by senate, Sept. 25th. Dies while conducting an expedition against the Goths.
1055	1023	276	FLORIANUS. Brother of Tacitus. Killed by soldiers at Tarsus.
1055	1023	276	PROBUS. Proclaimed emperor by the army, and confirmed by Senate in spring of 276. Killed in a mutiny of army, October, 282; age 50.
1061	1029	282	CARUS. Subdued Sarmatians, slew 16,000 and captured 20,000; gives title of Cæsar to each of his sons, Carinus and Numerianus. Dies in November, 283; age 61.
1061	1029	282	CARINUS. Encounters Diocletian, who is advancing into Europe.
1061	1029	282	NUMERIANUS. Assassinated by his father-in-law, Aper.
			FIFTH SEAL. MARTYRS SLAIN UNDER PAGAN ROME.
1063	1031	284	DIOCLETIAN. Proclaimed emperor, Sept. 17th, 284. ERA OF DIOCLETIAN, or of MARTYRS, dates from 284.
1065	1033	286	MAXIMINIAN. Is associated by Diocletian with himself as joint emperor. Origenist controversy. Beginning of divisions in
1075	1043	296	the Christian Church. 1260 lunar years from laying Foundations of Samaria, B.C. 926.
1083	1005	303	Diocletian's systematic persecution of Christians commences with the publi-

LUNAR.	SOLAR.	A.D.	
			cation of his EDICT, at Nicomedia, on the 24th Feb., 303. This was the fiercest persecution the Church had endured, the "ten days" tribulation. It lasted ten years, and was the tenth persecution.
1085	1052	305	CONSTANTIUS CHLORUS. Diocletian abdicates at Nicomedia, May 1st, 305; and on same day Maximinian abdicates at Milan, and is succeeded by Constantius as Augustus.
1086	1053	306	CONSTANTINE THE GREAT. Constantius, after a victory over the Picts, died at York. His son, Constantine the Great, proclaimed Augustus by the army, 25th July, 306.
1092	1059	312	Conversion of Constantine. Indictions begin Sept. 1st, 312. Battle of Milvian Bridge, Oct. 28, 312.
1093	1060	313	Licinius's EDICT OF TOLERATION, 13th Jan., 313. Death of Diocletian, aged 68.

FALL OF PAGAN ROMAN EMPIRE.

Constantinople Founded, 324.

Rise of Arianism, A.D. 317, occasions council of Nice. Second stage in division of Christendom. 1260 calendar years after Foundation of Samaria, B.C. 926.

(Analogous with twofold division of Tribes,—Samaria and Jerusalem.)

Council of Nice, 325. Attended by 318 bishops. (First of the 21 Œcumenical or General Councils.) Dedication of Constantinople, 330. ARIANISM, 331.

LUNAR.	SOLAR.	A.D.	
1118	1084	337	CONSTANTINE II. Council of Tyre, Jerusalem, Arian, A.D. 335. 1260 solar years after Foundation of Samaria, B.C. 926. Arian council of Constantinople, 336. DIVISION OF CHRISTENDOM. The first controversial war. (The Church henceforth divided against itself.)
1118	1084	337	CONSTANS. Eusebius writes the life of Constantine.
1118	1084	337	CONSTANTIUS. Three sons of Constantine, divide the empire between them. The Cathedral of St. Sophia is dedicated at Constantinople, 360. One-half the inhabitants of the Roman Empire profess Christianity, which is now THE RELIGION OF THE STATE.
1142	1108	361	JULIAN. Openly renounces Christianity, and endeavours to re-establish Paganism. Restores heathen sacrifices.
1144	1110	363	Julian attempts to re-build the Temple at Jerusalem. The Jews assist. Undertaking abandoned on account of fire bursting forth from foundations. Julian wounded in battle, June 26th; expires at midnight, in his 32nd year, A.D. 363.
1144	1110	363	JOVIAN. Proclaimed emperor, June 27th. Restores privileges of the Church; recalls banished bishops. Dies Feb. 17th, 364.
1145	1111	364	VALENTINIAN. Makes his brother Valens emperor of the EAST, and takes the WEST himself. FINAL DIVISION OF EASTERN AND WESTERN EMPIRES. (Lunar eclipse Nov. 25th, 15h. 24m., total, A.D. 364, Alexandria.—Theon, in Commentary on the Almagest of Ptolemy.)

LUNAR.	SOLAR.	A.D.	
1157	1122	375	GRATIAN. Valentinian dies, Nov. 17th, 357; age 55. Succeeded by his son Gratian, who is the first emperor to renounce the heathen title PONTIFEX MAXIMUS (a title afterwards assumed by the Popes). Socrates, historian.
1157	1122	375	VALENTINIAN II. Younger brother of Gratian, associated with him. Ambrose, bishop of Milan. EARLIER TRUMPETS (Rev. viii.). OVER-THROW OF ROMAN EMPIRE.
1177	1142	395	HONORIUS. Removal of seat of government from Rome to Ravenna. Revolt of GOTHS. ALARIC commenced his ravages in Greece, 395 ; and in ITALY, 402.
1193	1157	410	SACK OF ROME BY ALARIC, Aug. 24th, 410. AUGUSTINE. Innocent I., bishop of Rome requires all the Western Churches to conform to the customs of the Church of Rome, 416.
1208	1172	425	VALENTINIAN III. Enacts that all bishops of the Western Empire obey the Bishop of Rome. Killed by Maximus for his adultery. Death of ATTILA, 453.
1239	1202	455	MAXIMUS. VANDALS under GENSERIC plunder ROME. Patricius, or Succoth (St. Patrick), 454. Genseric carries away the *sacred vessels* which Titus had brought from Jerusalem, about June 13-26, 455.
1240	1203	456	AVITUS. The VISIGOTHS establish their dominion in Spain.
1241	1204	457	MAJORIANUS. Assassinated, Aug. 7th, 461, by Ricimer, who places Severus on throne, but exercises imperial power himself.
1245	1208	461	SEVERUS. Proclaimed at Ravenna, 19th Nov., 461.
1252	1214	467	ANTHEMIUS. Inaugurated at Rome, 12th April, 467.

LUNAR.	SOLAR.	A.D.	
1257	1219	472	OLYBRIUS. Advance of Patriarchate. Olybrius reigned 7 months. Died Oct. 23rd, 472.
1259	1221	474	JULIUS NEPOS. Elevation, June 24th, 474.
1259½	1222	475	ROMULUS AUGUSTULUS. Orestes, the patrician, enters Ravenna with an army and drives out Nepos, who flies to Dalmatia, 28th Aug., 475. Orestes proclaimed his son ROMULUS emperor at RAVENNA, Oct. 31st, 475. ODOACER at the head of the HERULI invades ITALY; overthrows Orestes, who is slain at Placentia. ROMULUS AUGUSTULUS IS BANISHED. ODOACER makes himself KING OF ITALY, fixing his seat at RAVENNA. THE LAST AUGUSTUS reigned 10 mths.; from Oct. 31st, 475, to 22nd Aug.,
1260	1222½	476	*to Aug. 22.* 476. ("Fasti Romani," Clinton.)

END OF WESTERN ROMAN EMPIRE.

Period from Beginning of Kingdom of Babylon,
to Fall of Western Rome,—

From the Era of NABONASSAR, February 26th, 747 B.C.,
To the Fall of AUGUSTULUS, August 22nd, 476 A.D.,
there elapsed 1222 solar years and six months,

or

TWELVE HUNDRED AND SIXTY LUNAR YEARS.

"TIME, TIMES, AND AN HALF TIME."

1222 solar years 6 months = 446,503 days.
1260 lunar years, or 15,120 lunations = 446,502½ days.

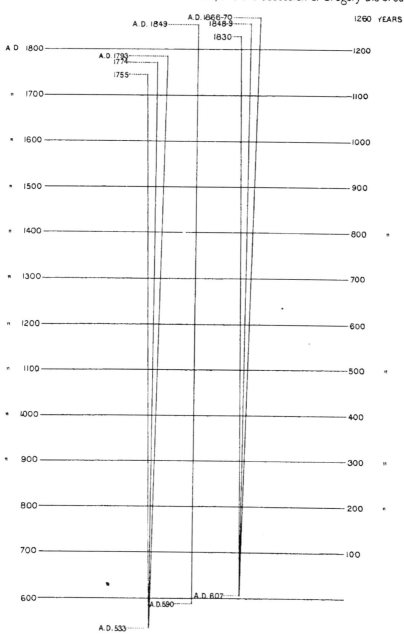

FROM THE RISE TO THE FALL OF THE PAPAL POWER;
1260 YEARS, IN SOLAR, CALENDAR AND LUNAR FORMS.
Reckoned from the Edicts of Justinian and Phocas; and the accession of Gregory the Great.

1260 YEARS

A.D. 1849
A.D. 1866-70
1848-9
1830

A D 1800 — 1200

A.D. 1793
1774
1755

" 1700 — 1100

" 1600 — 1000

" 1500 — 900

" 1400 — 800 "

" 1300 — 700

" 1200 — 600

" 1100 — 500 "

" 1000 — 400

" 900 — 300 "

800 — 200 "

700 — 100

600

A.D. 607
A.D. 590

A.D. 533

Calendar

OF

"The Times of the Gentiles."

PART II., Comprising:

THE RISE, CULMINATION, AND DECAY OF THE PAPAL AND MOHAMMEDAN POWERS.

1. The birth of Mohammed, and the accession of Gregory the Great, towards the end of the sixth century, mark the commencement of the second part of the Times of the Gentiles. Of the second of these events, Archbishop Trench says in his "Mediæval Church History" (p. 14): "My conviction is that we should articulate history more justly, if we affirmed that as ancient history it closed, and as mediæval history it began, with *the Pontificate of Gregory the Great.* In him, the last of the

---

Edict and letters of the Emperor Justinian, constituting the Bishop of Rome head of all the Churches of Christendom :

"Imp. Justinian. A. Constantinopolitis.

"Cum Salvatorem et Dominum omnium Jesum Christum verum Deum nostrum colamus per omnia, studemus etiam (quatenus datum est humanæ menti assequi) imitari ejus condescensionem seu demissionem. Etenim cum quosdam invenerimus morbo atque insaniâ detentos impiorum Nestorii et Eutychetis, Dei et sanctæ catholicæ et apostolicæ ecclesiæ hostium, nempe qui detrectabant sanctam gloriosam semper Virginem Mariam Theotocon sive Deiparam appellare propriè et secundum veritatem : illos festinavimus quæ sit recta Christianorum fides edocere. Nam hi incurabiles cùm sint, celantes errorem suum passim circumeunt (sicut didicimus) et simpliciorum animos exturbant et scandalizant, ea astruentes quæ sunt sanctæ catholicæ ecclesiæ contraria. Necessarium igitur esse putavimus, tam hæreticorum vaniloquia et mendacia dissipare, quàm omnibus insinuare, quomodo aut sentiat sancta Dei et catholica et

Latin fathers, *the first*, in our modern sense of the word, *of the Popes*, we bid adieu to the old Greek and Roman culture and literature and habits of thought, as the predominant and ruling forces of the world. The ancient world still lives on, . . . but *another order of things is shaping itself, and Gregory the Great, standing at the meeting place of the old and new, does more than any other to set the Church forward upon the new lines on which henceforth it must travel to constitute* a LATIN CHRISTIAN-

apostolica ecclesia, aut prædicent sanctissimi ejus sacerdotes; quos et nos sequuti, manifesta constituimus ea quæ fidei nostræ sunt ; non quidem innovantes fidem (quod absit) sed coarguantes corum insaniam qui eadem cum impiis hæreticis sentiunt. Quod quidem et nos in nostri imperii primordiis pridem satagentes cunctis fecimus manifestum."

" In the remainder of the edict, the Emperor gives a statement of his own faith, and denounces anathemas against Nestorius, Eutyches, and Apollinarius, and their followers. The edict is dated on the ides of March, 533. The same edict was addressed to twelve other cities of the empire, among which were Jerusalem, Cæsarea, and Ephesus."

" Upon the promulgation of this edict, Justinian addressed an epistle to the Pope, as the acknowledged head of all the holy churches, which was transmitted by the hands of Demetrius and Hypatius, two bishops. From this epistle I quote the following extracts :—"

" Victor Justinianus, pius, felix, inclytus, triumphator, semper Augustus, Joanni sanctissimo Archiepiscopo almæ Urbis Romæ et Patriarchæ.

" Reddentes honorem apostolicæ sedi, et vestræ sanctitati (quod semper nobis in voto et fuit et est), et ut decet patrem honorantes vestram beatitudi-nem, omnia quæ ad ecclesiarum statum pertinent festinavimus ad notitiam deferre vestræ sanctitatis ; quoniam semper nobis fuit magnum studium, unitatem vestræ apostolicæ sedis, et statum sanctarum Dei ecclesiarum custodire, qui hactenus obtinet, et incommotè permanet, nulla intercedente contrarietate. Ideoque omnes sacerdotes universi Orientalis tractus et subjicere et unire sedi vestræ sanctitatis properavimus. In præsenti ergo quæ commota sunt (quamvis manifesta et indubitata sint et secundum apostolicæ

ITY, *with distinctive features of its own, such as broadly separate it from Greek.*"

The accession of this pontiff, and the birth of Mohammed, the founder of the great system of false religion in the East, are separated from the era of Nabonassar by 1335 *calendar,* and 1335 *solar* years.

1335 calendar years are 1316 solar : from the era of Nabonassar, B.C. 747, to the birth of Mohammed, A.D. 570, is this period.

---

vestræ sedis doctrinam ab omnibus semper sacerdotibus firme custodita et prædicata) necessarium duximus, ut ad notitiam vestræ sanctitatis perveniant. Nec enim patimur quicquam, quod ad ecclesiarum statum pertinet, quamvis manifestum et indubitatum sit, quod movetur, ut non etiam vestræ innotescat sanctitati quæ caput est omnium sanctarum ecclesiarum. Per omnia enim (ut dictum est) properamus honorem et auctoritatem crescere vestræ sedis."

"The epistle next states the circumstance of certain men having maintained heretical doctrines respecting the person of Christ, and it then contains a statement of the faith of the Church and of the Emperor himself on this point, and it concludes as follows :—"

"Suscipimus autem sancta quatuor concilia : id est, trecentorum decem et octo sanctorum patrum, qui in Nicæna urbe congregati sunt : et centum quinquaginta sanctorum patrum qui in hac regia urbe convenerunt : et sanctorum patrum qui in Epheso primo congregati sunt, et sanctorum patrum qui in Chalcedone convenerunt: sicut vestra apostolica sedes docet atque prædicat. Omnes ergo sacerdotes sequentes doctrinam apostolicæ sedis vestræ ita credunt et confitentur et prædicant.

"Unde properavimus hoc ad notitiam deferre vestræ sanctitatis per Hypatium et Demetrium, beatissimos episcopos, ut nec vestram sanctitatem lateat, quæ et a quibusdam paucis monachis male et Judaice secundum Nestorii perfidiam denegata sunt. Petimus ergo vestrum paternum affectum ; ut vestris ad nos destinatis literis, et ad sanctissimum episcopum hujus almæ urbis, et patriarcham vestrum fratrem (quoniam et ipse per eosdem scripsit ad vestram sanctitatem, festinans' in omnibus sedem sequi apostolicam beatitudinis vestræ), manifestum nobis faciatis, quod omnes qui prædicta recte confitentur, suscipit vestra sanctitas, et eorum qui

From the era of Nabonassar, 1335 solar years terminate in
A.D. 589,—the year before the accession of Gregory the Great.
If the prophetic period of 1335 *years should prove to begin
with this point, and to be reckoned in solar years, the whole
extent of the Times of the Gentiles will be* 1335 *years doubled,
and the accession of Gregory the Great will be its* BISECTION.

2. The edicts of Justinian and Phocas, constituting the Bishop
of Rome head of all the Churches of Christendom, are
the limits of the 74-5 years interval which comprises

Judaice ausi sint rectam denegare fidem, condemnat perfidiam. Plus enim
ita circa vos omnium amor, et vestræ sedis crescet auctoritas ; et quæ ad
vos est unitas sanctarum ecclesiarum inturbata servabitur, quando per vos
didicerint omnes beatissimi episcopi corum, quæ ad vos relata sunt,
sinceram vestræ sanctitatis doctrinam. Petimus autem vestram beatitudinem
orare pro nobis, et Dei nobis adquirere providentiam."

" The above epistle was dated at least as early as the 25th
of March, 533 ; for in his letter to the Archbishop of Constantinople, which bears that date, the Emperor mentions his
having already written to the Pope."

" The reply of Pope John to the above memorable epistle is
dated the 24th March, 534; and the following are extracts
from it · "

" Gloriosissimo et clementissimo filio Justiniano Augusto,
" Johannes Episcopus Urbis Romæ.

" Inter claras sapientiæ ac mansuetudinis vestræ laudes, Christianissime
principum, puriore luce tanquam aliquod sydus irradiat, quod amore fidei,
quod charitatis studio edocti ecclesiasticis disciplinis, Romanæ sedis rever-
entiam conservatis, et ci cuncta subjicitis, et ad ejus deducitis unitatem, ad
cujus auctorem, hoc est apostolorum primum, Domino loquente præ-
ceptum est, *Pasce oves meas :* Quam esse omnium vere ecclesiarum caput,
et patrum regulæ et principum statuta declarant, et pietatis vestræ rever-
endissimi testantur affatus."

✳   ✳   ✳   ✳   ✳

" Proinde serenitatis vestræ apices, per Hypatium atque Demetrium,
sanctissimos viros, fratres et coepiscopos meos, reverentia consueta suscepi-
mus : quorum etiam relatione comperimus, quod fidelibus populis propo-

"SEVEN TIMES" WITH THE ADDED 75 YEARS;

Reckoned
I, from Nabonassar , 2, from Nebuchadnezzar

Nabonassar Era	B.C. 747	
Capt. Israel		

Nebuchadnezzar   B.C. 598
Capt. Judah.

I Empire Babylonian

75 Y.
75 Y. } 150 Y.

II Empire Persian

III Empire Grecian

IV Empire Roman

END West Rom. Emp.   Aug. 22 476 ....1260 Lunar
1260 Solar .... 2520 Solar Y.

Gregory the Great.   589-590 ....1335 Sol   Bisection?

Vitalian. Lateinos.   663 ....1260 Sol Nebr................ } 2520 Solar Y

Papal and Mohammedan Powers.

Louis XVI. F Revol.	1774	... 2520 Solar.
Napoleon	1804	
	1848-9 ...2520 + 75 Y	
Pius IX {	1878-9	
	?	

Val. Era

30 Y.
45 Y. } 75 Y.
2520 Lunar Y.

30 Y.
45 Y. } 75 Y. ?

nearly the whole of the reign of Justinian, together with the period and pontificate of Gregory the Great, and those of Boniface III.,—*the era of the establishment of the Papacy.*

3. The commencing point in the Mohammedan calendar is the so-called flight of Mohammed, or his reception at Medina as Prophet and Prince, A.D. 622.

This date, called the era of the Hegira, is the new moon of July 16, A.D. 622.

4. Reckoning from the 74-5 years interval of the *establishment*

---

suistis edictum amore fidei pro submovenda hæreticorum intentione, secundum apostolicam doctrinam, fratrum et cöepiscoporum nostrorum interveniente consensu. Quod, quia apostolicæ doctrinæ convenit, nostra auctoritate confirmamus."

" Upon the same occasion Justinian also addressed a letter to the Patriarch of Constantinople, of which I shall give the first paragraph."

" Idem imperat. Epiphanio sanctissimo et beatissimo Archiepiscopo Regiæ hujus Urbis et Œcumenico Patriarchæ.

" Cognoscere volentes tuam sanctitatem ea omnia quæ ad ecclesiasticum spectant statum : necessarium duximus, hisce ad eam uti divinis compendiis, ac per ea manifesta eidem facere, quæ jam moveri cœpta sunt, quanquam et illa eandem cognoscere sumus persuasi. Cum itaque comperissemus quosdam alienos a sancta, catholica, et apostolica ecclesia, impiorum Nestorii et Eutychetis sequutos deceptionem, divinum antehac promulgavimus edictum (quod et tua novit sanctitas) per quod hæreticorum furores reprehendimus, ita ut nullo quovis omnino modo immutaverimus, immutemus aut prætergressi simus eum, qui nunc usque, coadjuvante Deo, servatus est, ecclesiasticum statum (quemadmodum et tua novit sanctitas) sed in omnibus servato statu unitatis sanctissimarum ecclesiarum cum ipso S. S. Papa veteris Romæ, ad quem similia hisce perscripsimus. Nec enim patimur ut quicquam eorum, quæ ad ecclesiasticum spectant statum, non etiam ad ejusdem referatur beatitudinem : quum ea sit caput omnium sanctissimorum Dei sacerdotum ; vel eo maxime quod, quoties in eis locis hæretici pullularunt, et sententia et recto judicio illius venerabilis sedis coerciti sunt."

" The above documents are to be found at full length in the volume of the civil law (Codicis lib. I. tit. i.), and by being of Papal power, 1260 years from its commencement and close, in *lunar, calendar,* and *solar* forms, extend to the overthrow of Papal power in the French Revolution, and *the bursting of its after waves,* the Revolutions of 1830, 1848–9, and 1868–70 ; including the double overthrow of the temporal power in the Pontificate of Pius IX.

From the accession of Gregory the Great, and from the subsequent decree of Phocas, 1260 *solar* and 1260 *calendar* years meet in the crisis of 1848–9,—the revolution era of the rise of *the Second French Republic*; thence to 1870, is the period of the

---

published in that collection, they obtained the stamp of public and legislative authority as the laws of the empire. In these documents we find the Emperor publishing a rule of faith to his subjects of the Eastern Empire, and addressing the Pope of Rome on the occasion, as *the acknowledged head of all the churches* (not the Western churches only), and requesting the approbation of what he had done. We see the Pope, in reply, giving the sanction of his authority *as the acknowledged head of the Church,* to the religious edict of Justinian."—*Cuninghame on the Seals and Trumpets of the Apocalypse and the prophetical period of 1260 years,* p. 222–227.

THE DECREE OF PHOCAS is thus referred to by Diaconus

" Hic (Phocas) rogante Papa Bonefacio, statuit sedem Romanæ ecclesiæ, ut caput esset omnium ecclesiarum ; quia ecclesia Constantinopolitana primam se omnium ecclesiarum scribebat" (Paulus Diaconus, "De Gestis Romanorum ad Eutropii Historiam Additus," lib. xvii.).

(Diaconus refers to it in the same terms in his work "De Gestis Longobardorum.")

The following is from Anastasius, "Historia Ecclesiastica et de Vitis Pontificum," P. ii. p. 44, c. 3 :—

" Bonefacius III., Anno Christi, 606 ; Phocæ Imp., 4.

" Bonefacius, natione Romanus, ex patre Joanne Cabaudioce, sedet men‧ ses octo, dies viginti octo. Hic obtinuit apud Phocam Principem, ut sedes apostolica beati Petri apostoli caput esset omnium ecclesiarum, id est, ecclesia Romana, quia ecclesia Constantinopolitana primam se omnium ecclesiarum scribebat."

third Napoleon, linked in his rise and fall with the restoration and destruction of the Papal temporal power.

5. From the Hegira era, 1260 Mohammedan or lunar years extend to 1844-5, a year signalised by the Mohammedan decree granting religious toleration.

The accession of Pope Boniface III. is stated in the Calendar as Feb. 18, 607, from Clinton's "Fasti Romani"; also the statement that he presided 8 m. 24 d., and died 10th Nov., 607. The see remained vacant after the death of Boniface III. from Nov. 11, 607, to 24th Aug., 608, or 9 m. 14 d.

Calendar of "The Times of the Gentiles."

PART II.

From the Rise to the Fall of the PAPAL and MOHAMMEDAN POWERS.

"TIME, TIMES, AND AN HALF TIME."

Eastern Roman Emperors.	Bishops of Rome.	Kings of France.	Mohammedan Caliphs.

FINAL DIVISION OF THE ROMAN EMPIRE BETWEEN ARCADIUS AND HONORIUS, A.D. 395.

EARLIER TRUMPETS, Rev. viii. DESTRUCTION OF ROM (N EMPIRE.)

Arcadius, accession, Jan. 17, 395. Alaric commences his ravages in Greece early in 395.

CHRYSOSTOM.

(Lunar eclipse, June 11, 401, total, Rome.)
(Lunar eclipse, Dec. 6, 12h. 15 m, 401, tota Rome.)
(Lunar eclipse, June 1, 8h. 43 m., 402, Rome.)
(Lunar eclipse, Nov. 10, 20h. 33m., 402, Rome.

INNOCENT I.

Required all the Western Churches to conform to the customs of the Church o Rome, 416.

Theodosius II., May

BONASSAR.
AR. | SOLAR.   A.D.

77 | 1142

35 | 11 9

91 11

00

Attila, king of Huns : The "age of God."

LEO THE SAINT.
Marcianus, Aug. 25.
Leo the Thracian, Feb. 7.
HILARY.
SIMPLICIUS.

Odoacer, king of ... (Rev. viii.). Ove... how the last of the Western Roma Emperors.

Leo Junicr II. and Zeno, Feb. 9.

END OF WESTERN ROMAN EMPIRE, 22nd Augus A.D. 476.
1260 LUNAR YEARS FROM ERA OF NABONASSAR.

MEROVI NGI NS.
Clovis (the Great), Founder of Frenc Mona ...
Early ... of "*Middle Ages.*'—Hallam
Solar eclipse, Jun. 13, 9 h. 53 m, 484, ...iople

FELIX II.
Excommunicated the Emperor Zeno, together with the Patriarchs o Co stantinople and Alexandria, A.D. 484.

Anastasius I., April 11.
The Sile itary.

GELASIUS. ...piled the MASS.
AN ...SIUS.
SYMMACHUS.
BABYLONIAN ... completed, 50 4.

12 3		
12 9		
1260	1 22	
1266	1228	481
1268	1230	483
1276	1238	491
1277	1239	492
1281	1243	496
1284	1245	498

HORMISDAS.

Wit ... the ... cation of he E. Emperor and Patriarch in terms involving *the supremacy of the Roman Pontiff,* A.D. 519.

Justin the Thracian, July 9.

JOHN I.

FELIX III.

Introduced extreme unction as a sacramen

... I., April 1.

BONIFACE II.

JOHN II.

DECREE of the Emperor Justinian constituting THE BISHOP OF ... "HEAD OF ALL THE HOLY CHURCHES, AND OF ALL THE HLY PRIESTS OF GOD" M ..h, A.D. 533 (see Decree, pp. 607-8).

FROM THIS ... here ex end—

1260 LUNAR exrs to A.D. 1755, per od o: ou ck of INFIDEL TY (the first vial: Rev. xvi.).

1260 CR YEARS to .B. 1774, cession o Louis XVI, the com-cat of ERA OF FRENCH REVOLUTION; and termination of 2520 so ar years "seven times") from he accession of Nabonassar—beginning of kingdom of ; gB.

1260 SOLAR YEARS to A.D. 1793; execu ion of Lou s XVI, and o Queen Marie Antoinette, and REIGN OF TERROR.

AGAPETUS.

	PAPAL	JUSTINIAN.	
297	1258		511
300	1261		514
304	1265		518
309	1270		523
312	1273		526
313	1274		527
316	1277		530
320	1280		533
320	1280		533
22.	1282		535

SYLVERIUS.
Son of Pope Hormisdas.

VIGILIUS.
Banished, but restored.

PELAGIUS I.

Clotare I.

JOHN III.
Great ornamenter o churches. *Charibert.*

COLUMBA, Celtic Missonary.

Justin II., Nov. 14.

Chilperic.

MOHAMMED born at Mecca, 570. (1335 CALENDAR YEARS. Mohammed died, 632, aged 63,—Mohammedan reckoning is by *lunar years.*)

FROM THE ERA OF NABONASSAR TO THE BIRTH OF MOHAMMED 1335 CALENDAR YEARS.

BENEDICT I.
Burial, 31st July, 578.

PELAGIUS II.
Died of the Plague, 8th Feb, 590.

Tiberius II. Sept. 26.
COLUMBANUS, Celtic Missionary.

Mauritius, Aug, 13.
The Cappadocian, killed by Phocas, 602.

Co are il.

TERMINATION OF 1335 SOLAR YEARS FROM THE ERA OF NABONASSAR.
(A.D. 589 = 1335 *complete,* and 1336 *current* years.)

1323	1283	536	4
1324	1284	537	5
1342	1302	555	23
1345	1305	558	26
1347	1307	560	28
1348	1308	561	29
1353	1312	565	33
1355	1314	567	35
1357	1317	570	38
1362	1321	5	42
1366	1325	578	46
1366	1325	578	46
1370	1329	582	50
1372	1331	584	52
1376	1335	589	57
1377	1336		

3	133	5	58
1	1349	0	7
3	13 1	604	7
5	1	60	75

GRY THE GREAT.

...ain, Sept. 3, 9. STANDS AT MEET NG PLACE OF ANCIENT AND MEDIÆVAL HISTORY. Did ...re han ...ny ...ber "to set the Church forward upon the new lines on ...hich henceforth it ...ust travel to constitute A LATIN CHRIST AN ...F" ...ied 13 y. ...h. 10 d. Funeral, 12th ...th, o4.

PHOCAS, ...V. 23.

A centurion—rebels against the Emperor Mauritius is ...roclaimed and crowned, Nov. 23, and ...hn slays ...Ms, four of his sons, and his ...hr Petrus, on Nov. 27, o6. Tortures and beheads ...a, ...two Maurice, and her daughter, June, 605.

SABINIANUS.

Said to have introduced ...ith b..ls; ...ded 13th Sept 64 (after an interval of 6 m. 1 d.); ...pd Episcopate to Feb. 21 6. See of ...e then vacant 11 m. 26 d., to 17th Feb., 6...

POPES.

BONIFACE III.

Accession, Feb. 18, 607; pres ded 8 m. 24 d.; died, 10th ...M, 6...

DECREE of the Emperor ...us conceding to Boniface III. the ...EADSHIP ...VER ...LL THE CHURCHES OF CHRISTENDOM :—

Hic rogante Papa Bonefacio statuit (...rim Romanæ et Apostolicæ ...tic ...pu esse omnum ...desi m, quia eccl ...a ...onstantinopolitana primam se ...onium ecclesiarum scribebat" (Pau us Diaconus, " De ...tis Longobardorum," lib. 4, c. 36).

So ...so Anastasius, "Historia Ecclesiastica et de Vitis Ponti ...fim," P. ii., c. 3.

...d by the PILLAR OF PHOCAS AT ...ME, bearing inscription and date, "Die prima Mensis August. I ...d. Und. ac Pietatis ejus ...ho ...into. Pro innumerabilibus · ...tis ejus Beneficiis."

FROM THE ...ME OF THE DECREE OF ... ... , A.D. 607, ...re ...end -

National Assembly divest the Pope of all temporal ..., 8 h Feb., 1849.

160 SOLAR YEARS o A.D. 1866— Overthrow of Austria, Spain, ..., and Papal kingdom in Italy. ...l defeat o Aust... by Prussia. Battle of Sadowa, 3rd July, 1866.

Invitation o the Pope to all Catholic bishops to mee at ..., to ce e- ...te the 18t cen enary of the ...m o Peter and Pau , 8th Dec., 1866.

99 ...ps and ...ds o priests ...en at the Pope's al ocution, 26th June, 1867.

...surrection at ... French troops enter ..., and ...ss it, 30th Oct., 1867.

Œcumenical Council ...ned a ..., 8th Dec., 1869.

PAL INFALLI ...TY DECREED, 8TH JULY, 1870.

F anco-German War; and

TERMINATION OF PAPAL TEMPORAL POWER, 187

(1260 SOLAR YEARS ...OM THE DEATH OF 1 ...B.

BONIFACE IV. elected, 25th Aug., 608.
The , PTHEON at ...e (built by M. Agrippa, B.C. 25, as a ...le for ...le and all the gods) dedicated to the V GIN M RY and ALL THE MARTYRS, A.D. 608.

...nistration, t ...m , and cruel y o ...us produce universa ...ny. He is given up to Heraclius and beheaded ..., ... 5, 610.

55   608   6

A.D.	PAPAL.		Eastern Roman Emperors	Pope	Kings of France.	Mohammedan Caliphs.
	SOLAR.	SOLAR.				
610	78		**Heraclius, Oct. 5.** Reigns 610–641. Terms in decline of Eastern Empire of Rome. ' From he tic of his, the Byzantine theatre is contracted and darkened" i th, " Decline & Fall," p. 845). **DEUSDEDIT. BONIFACE V.** F FTH TRUMPET, Rev. ix. THE LOCUST WOE ON APOSTATE EASTERN CHRISTENDOM.			**MOHAMMED** declares hiself at the age of 40, 610. Flight o Med from Ma to Medina : red as a Prophe and Fr.

ERA OF HÉGIRA BV oN, July 16, 622.

Termi us a quo of Man CALENDAR.

(1) From the daw of Jehoiakim (thro e of Judah), by Nebuchadnezzar, B.C. 602, to the era of Hégira 1260 LUNAR YEARS.

(2) Frm new mon of 5th month, July 16, IC. 457, date of Ezra's reaching Jerusalem to restore it, a cycle of 22 jubilees (great j lue si- ur cle) to the Hégira.

MOHAMMEDAN CALENDAR.

H ra. LU AR. 1

HÉGIRA 1260 NAD

which is he ermination of 2300 years from B.C. 457, EDICT OF ARTAXERXES. and beginning of the seventy weeks."

(Lunar eclipse, Feb. 11 h. 2 m., otal, 622, Constantinople.)

HONORIUS I.

MOHAMMED dies at the age o 63, 8th June, 632. Expedition into Syria delayed a month by his death.

Dagobert.

ABUBEKER.
Succeeded day of Mohammed's death. In following month Osama, by his command, leads army of Saracens into *Syria*. Take Damascus, 23rd Aug., 634. Abubek dies same day.

OMAR I.
Battle of Yermouk; overthrows Roman army and determines fate of Syria : con-

1 7	625	93	9	7 11
1375	628	96	2 6	
1379	632	100		
13 1 6 4	102	28	13	

ONASSAR.	.D.	PAPAL		E. H.				
R. SOLAR.		SOLAR.	SOLAR. Phocas	LUNAR. Moham medan.				
7 1384	637	⟨⟩ 105	31	16				

Eastern Roman Emperors.	Popes.	Kings of France.	Mohammedan Caliphs.

CAPTURE OF JERUSALEM BY THE SARACENS.

Baalbec   ied by t e Sa   ns, 20th Ju., 36. Abu Obei dh hav ng received orders at close of 636 o besiege Jerusalem, sent did first wih 5000   en.   I ly quote the   erse from the Koran (ch. v. 24). "O   ⟨⟩!   ter ye into the holy land hich God hath   ided for   ⟨p⟩" ELIA (i. Jerusalem) holds ot fir   mhs   (her). Saracens suffer fom cold (Ockley, "Hist. Saracens," p. 207). OMAR sent for to whom the Patriarch Sophronius surrenders the ci y. (Hegira 16; A.D. 637.) OMAR divides Syria into two parts; commits as ern part to   i h, and   turn to   id; ad sends Amrou to invade Egypt. Cæsarea besieged in   wr of 637–8. It surrenders in 7th   yr of Hegira, 5th of   a's reign, July 638. After this al the   br   wns in Syria surrendered. Conques compl ted in 638.

MOSQUE OF   OR ERECTED ON SITE OF TEMPLE.

From the date of NEBUCHADNEZZAR's   URNING THE TEMPLE, B.C. 587, 5 m. 10d., to the setting up of the MOHAMMEDAN DESOLAT ON in J   n, A.D. 63   the   end

160 LUNAR YEARS.

From   R's   ture of Jerusalem, A.D. 637   ttre ex nd 160 LUNAR YEARS to   A. 1860.   Man   ms- sacre of 3300 K ristians at   t   his (9th Ju, 860), followed by English and French In ervention ; 4000 French rops   ded at Beyrou   and Aug   Lord Dufferin, British   om ss oner in Syria,   thes Damas- cus, 6 h Sept., 1860.

beginning of the 1260 h   ...   year from the summer of A.D. 63'.

1260 SOLAR YEARS o A.D. 1897.

C ovis II., 638.

SEVERINUS.
.OHN.

Saracens i   Egypt, 6.. Take Alex-
hia, 6..

DECLINE OF EASTERN ROMAN EMPIRE.

Cons antine L, Feb.
o My 24, 103 days.

Herac eonas.
8 ..

Constans II.
.., 668.

THEODORUS.

Pursue   in Persia, 642.

OTHMAN.

Saracens penetrate Ro-
man Africa, 647; con-
quer   ..., 648;   ..
.te conquest of Persia;
651, and of Rhodes, 653.

MARTIN I.
EUGENIUS.

ALI.

C o are III.

VITALIANUS.

HASSAN.

30	1387	640	108
30	1387	640	108
31	1388	641	109
31	1388	641	109
32	1389	642	110
34	1391	644	112
39	1396	649	117
45	1402	655	123
46	1403	656	124
47	1404	657	125
52	1408	661	129

NABONASSAR.		A.D.	PAPAL.			E. H.
VAR.	SOLAR.		SOLAR. Justinian	SOLAR. Phocas.		LUNAR. Mohammedan.
52	1408	661	129	55		41
54	1410	663	131	57		43

Eastern Roman Emperors.

Constantine IV.
Pogonatus.

Popes.

Pope VITALIAN enjoins the EXCLUSIVE USE OF THE LATIN TONGUE in the offices of DIVINE WORSHIP throughout Christendom, A.D. 663, and thus completes the development of the LATIN or ROMAN CHURCH. LATEINOS, LATIN (numerical value of letters = 666), suggested by Irenæus in the second cen ury as solution of "the number of the Beast" (Rev. xiii. 18).

From the complete overthrow of Jerusalem by the BABYLONIAN POWER, he captivity of Jehoiachin, and of "all Jerusalem." in the 8th year of Nebuchadnezzar, B.C. 598, there ex end—

260 SOLAR YEARS to A.D. 663, the date of completion of the captivity of the Chu ch by the MODERN BABYLON, "Babylon the Great."

A.D. 663 thus bisects the period of "seven times" (2520 solar years) extendi g from Babylonian overthrow of Jerusalem, B.C. 598, to A.D. 1923.

From A.D. 663 extend—

260 unar years to A.D. 1886;
260 calendar years o A.D. 1905;
260 solar years to A.D. 1923.

Kings of France.

Ch lderic II.
Th err .

Mohammedan Caliphs.

OMMIADES, 661–750.
MOAWIYAH.

Saracens nvade Sicily, 669.
Founded Cairoan, 670.
Saracens besiege Consta

YEZID I.

MOAWIYAH II.
ABDALLAH.
MERWAN I.
ABDULMELEK.

C ovis III.

Childebert III.

Saracens conquer menia, 693.

Solar eclipse, Oct. 4, 23 h. 54 m, 693, Constantino

S orm and des Carthage 6 8.

DOMNUS.
AGATHON.
Persecution of PAULICIANS.
LEO II.
Instituted ho y water.

BENEDICT II.

JOHN V.

Anti-popes—
PASCAL, 687.
THEODORE, 687.

CONON.
SERGIUS.

Justinian II.
Expelled, 695.

Leon ius
Tiberius III. Absimar. Beheaded, 705.

JOHN VI.

Justiniar II. restored : killed, 711.

65
65
66

67
68
72

76
79

82
86

1473
1474 1430
1475 1431
1475 14 1
1476 1432

1477 14 3
1478 14 4
1483 14 8

1487 1442
1490 1445

1493 1448
1497 1452

S S

NABONASSAR		A.D.	PAPAL	Eastern Roman Emperors.	Popes.	Kings of France.	Mohammedan Caliphs.
LUNAR.	A		SOLAR Julian				
1497	14				JOHN VII.		WALID I.
1500	14				SISINNIUS.		Saracens overcome the Berbers and all N. Africa, ?. Land in Spain 7o.
1500	14				20 days.		
					CONSTANTINE.		
					...m of kissing the Pope's toe introduced, 708.		
1503	14 8			1 · His Bardanes.		FIRST INVASION OF EUROPE BY THE CALIPHS.	
				Assassina d, 713.		SPAIN IN THE POWER OF THE SARACENS, 712.	
1503	1458					Dagobert III.	
1505	1460			Anastasius II.	GREGORY II.		
1507	1462					Chilperic II.	SOLIMAN.
1507				Theodosius III.			
1508				Retires into a monastery. BEDE, historian.		eclipse, Jan. 13, 7 h., total, 716, Constantinople.	
					WINFRED, apostle of Germany.		
1509				Leo III.			OMAR II.
				The		Solar eclipse, June 3, 1 h. 15 m., total, 718, (&c.)	
1512							YEZID II.
1516						Thierry IV.	HASHAN.
1524					GREGORY III.		...EL overcom the SARACENS a ... MOHAMMEDANS ...es ed n ...ir ...se of 1 ...t

Childeric II

WALID II.
YEZID III.
5 months.
IB / ...
3 months.
MERWAN II.

ABBASSIDES.
Caliphs, 750-1258.

SAFFAH.

CARLOVING ANS.

ALMANSOR.
...phs of
...m 755.

STEPHEN II. & III. Pen,
Son of Carles Martel.
Ep n onfers ho EXARCHATE and
PENTAPOLIS upon S. Peter (the
Pope), 756.

ORIGIN OF THE POPE'S TEMPORAL SOVEREIGNTY.

From this date to the fall of the Pope's temporal sovereignty, in 1870, here
aro 1114 years, or *two five cycles* (557 egrs is an pie cycle).
In the interval from its on Era to this point the Nabonassar year falls bak
364 d ag, *i.e.* 12 ... ed, or a solar egr.

Anti-pope—
PAUL I. THEOPHYLACTUS.
CONSTANTINE, called Anti-pope.

Saracens build Bag ad.
CALIPHS OF RAGDAD.
TERMINATION of FIVE
...is of lunar
...gs, or Mohamme-
dan years, fom the
E. of Illégira (R.
ix. 5).

...				44
45	149	149		750
				52
47	150			754
49	503			56
50	194		225	5
61	1514		235	6
			151	
			161	

ABONASSAR YEAR SOLAR	A.D.	PAR. LUNAR	PAR. SOLAR	E.H. LUNAR Mohammedan	Eastern Roman Emperors	Popes	Kings of France	Mohammedan Caliphs
62	1515		768	36 · 162 · 151		STEPHEN IV.	*Charlemage.*	E.E. Son of æq, EMPEROR OF THE E.E. Compels the æqe he conquers to embrace Christianity. Payment of tithes first made compulsory by a law o Charlemagne.
66	1519	240 ·	772	; · 155		ADRIAN I. Sanctioned i æg. Caused money to be ·and wi h his name 80.		ı ħr eclipse, Nov. 22, 14h. 37m, 774. Rc.
69	1522	243 · 169	775	158	Leo IV.			AL MAHDI.
74	1527	248 · 174	780	164	Constantine VI.			AL HADI.
79	1532	253 · 179	785	169			ates of temporal possessions o he Pes increased by Charlemagne, 787.	HAROUN AL RASCHID. *Sends the keys of Jerusalem to Charlemagne,* 800.
80	1533	254 · 180	786	170			(So an eclipse, Sept. 14, 20 h. 43 m, 787. Gen.i lp.) Seven h Gel Gencil (Nicæa) established the religious adoration of es, 787. From A.D. 607 to 787 are ten eclipse cycles; from 767 to 1868-9 are sixty eclipse cycles: together sixty eclipse cycles. IC,	King of Mercia and East Anglia; to atone for having murdered his son-in-law Ethelbert, i imposes an annual tax of one enny on each family in his dominions, to be paid to the Roman See. This, in 792, with a similar donation of Ina, king of West Saxons, in 725, lays foundation of PETER'S PENCE.

181	265		1592	1 44	**Irene.**	...ed and banished, 802.
186	270	**797**	1597	1 49	**Nis I.** [Pius I.]	...led by ...he Bulgarians, 18.
194	2 7	**802**	1604	1 56	**St...ius.** Reigned only a few days.	**AL AMIN.**
196	2 9	**809**	1606	1 58	**Michael I.** Res...to a ... say, 813	
198	281	**811**	1608	1 60	**Leo V.** The Armenian. Assassinated, 20.	Solar ec...pse, May 14, 2 h. 13 m., 812, Constantinop **AL MA...**
199	282	**813**	1609	1 61	ou s — Le débonnaire.	
201	284	**814**	1611	1 63	**STEPHEN V.**	
202	285	**816**	1612	1 64	**PASCAL I.**	
20	288	**817**	1615	1 67	**...e II.** The Stammerer.	
	2 2	**820**	1619	1 71	**EUGENIUS II.** *Anti-pope* ZIZIMUS.	
	29	**824**	1623	1 74	**VALENTINE.**	
	29	**827**	1623	1 74	**GREGORY IV.** *END OF SAXON HEPTARCHY.* *ANGLO-SAXON LINE.*—Egbert.	
		827	1625	1 76	**Theophilus.**	
			1629	1 80	**Michae... I.** The So... Assassinated, 867.	**AL MOTASSIM**
			1636		*Charles the Bald.*	
			1638		**SERGIUS II.**	**AL WATHEK.**
			1640			

1 Hr eclipse, an. 15, 9 h. ...8, Ron

FORMOSUS. Solar eclipse, Aug. 7. [2]	1689	1638	891
BONIFACE VI. Deposed.	1690	1639	892
STEPHEN VII. Dishonoured the corpse of Pope Formosus. Strangled by the people.	1694	1643	896
Anti-pope—	1694	1643	896
ROMANUS. SERGIUS. *Charles th*			
THEODORUS II. Governed 20 days.	1696	1645	898
JOHN IX.	1696	1645	898
BENEDICT IV.	1696	1645	898
LEO V. Expelled; died in prison.	1698	1647	900
CHRISTOPHER. Several Popes made by the infamous Maro	1701	1650	903
SERGIUS III. Disgraced by vices.	1701	1650	903
	1702	1651	904
ANASTASIUS III.			
	1706	1655	908
Alexander. Constantine X. Porphyrogenitus.	1709	1658	911
	1709	1658	911
LANDONIUS.	1709	1658	911
JOHN X. Stifled by Guy of Tuscany.	1711	1660	913
	1712	1661	914
Romanus I.	1711	1666	919

EDWARD. The Elder, 900.

NABONASSAR LUNAR.	NABONASSAR SOLAR.	A.D.	PAPAL SOLAR. Justinian.	PAPAL SOLAR. Phocas.	E. H. LUNAR. Mohammedan.	Eastern Roman Emperors.	Popes.	Kings of France.	Mohammedan Caliphs.
1722	1670	923	391	317	311			*Rudolph.*	
						ATHELSTAN, 925.			
1727	16 5	928	396	322	316		LEO VI.		
1728	16 6	929	397	323	31		STEPHEN VIII.		
1730	16 8	931	399	325	319		JOHN XI.		
							Son of Marozia ; mprisoned in Castle of S Angelo, where he died.		
1731	1679	932	400	326	320				AL KAHER.
1733	1681	934	402	328	322				AL RADHI.
1735	1683	936	404	330	324		LEO VII.	*ouis V.*	
						Athe stane's victory over DANES, 937.	STEPHEN IX.	D'outremer.	
							Of ferocious character.		
1738		939	407	333	328				
1739		940	408			EDMUND I., 940.			AL MOTAKI.
		942	410				MARINUS II.		
		944	412			Constantine X.			AL MOSTAKFI.
		945	413				AGAPETUS II.		AL MOTI.
		946	414			EDRED, 946.			
						DUNSTAN promotes Monachism and celibacy o clergy, 952.		*Lothaire.*	
						EDWY, 955.	JOHN XII.		

1763		
1764	LEO VIII.	
1765	BENEDICT V.	
1769	JOHN XIII.	

Phocas. Assassinated, 969.

John Zimisces.
Removes a great part of the Paulicians o Philippopolis, in Thrace.
(Solar eclipse, May 7, 1 h. 38 m, 9 o, Constan nople.)

AL TAI.

1772   BENEDICT VI.
Murdered in prison.

Anti-pope——

1774   DOMNUS II.   BONIFACE VII.
1775   BENEDICT VII.

EDWARD II., the Martyr, 975.

Basil II. and
Constantine XI.

1776   23

ETHELRED II., the Unready, 978.

1783   1 30   JOHN XIV.
Imprisoned by Boniface VII.

1785   1 32   JOHN XV.
1786   1

ouis V.

CAPETIANS.
Hugh Capet.

1788   1 4   Solar eclipse, May 28, 6 h. 4 m, 9 o, Constantinople.)
Solar eclipse, Oct. 21, 4 ; m, 990, Constantinople.)

AL KADER.

1792   1 38   Firs instance of canonization o a sain (U ric, Bishop of Augsburg) by the Pope in a Lateran Counci , 99

Nabonassar L. MAR.	Papal SOLAR. SOLAR sun	Eastern Roman Emperors.	Popes.	Kings of France.	Moh und Caliphs.
1797			GREGORY V. *Anti-pope*—JOHN XVI, 10 un hs. Expelled by the emperor and ; hdusly sud.		
1797					
1800			SILVESTER II. *Robert II., th* ℣. The first who suggested the idea of a CRUSADE. All ons ued to ray for souls in PURGATORY, by the authority of the Pope.		
1804			JOHN XV. Six months.		
1805			JOHN XVIII. Al.		
1810			SERGIUS IV.		
1813			(Lunar ecli pe, March 18, h. 41 m., 10, M *Anti-pope*—GREGORY. BENEDICT VIII., Ironside, 1016. EDMUND II., Ironside, 1016. CANUTE THE DNE, Sole Mh, of.		
1826			JOHN XIX. Elevated by bribery.		
1830			Romanus III. Poisoned, 1034.		
1833			BENEDICT IX. Raised to the Papal See at the age o en ng, for my. Life pı and scandalous. Expelled for ud.	Henry I.	AL KAIM.

1843	1 88	1041		
1844	1 89	1042	433	Leo V. Expelled, 40.
			434	...one XII. EDWARD III., the Confessor 40. SAXON LINE RESTORED.
1846			436	Anti-pope— GREGORY VI. SILVESTER III. Deposed. 3
1848			438	CLEMENT II. Three rival Popes ...ed by Counc l o Sutry. Capital punishment for ...ry so-called
1850			440	DAMASUS II.
1851			441	LEO IX. BERAGER I ...ing ...ed doubts on ...A ...ded by Leo in a Council at ..., 1050. Treatise of Scot... The first Pope who kept AN ARMY.
1857			446	Theodora.
1858			447	VICTOR II.
1859			448	Michael VI.
1860			449	Isaac Comnenus. STEPHEN X. BENEDICT X., 1058. Anti-pope— Resigns, 1059.
1862			451	Constantine XIII. NICHOLAS II. Ducas. Increased temporal
1863			452	Philip I., Anti-pope—
1864			453	ALEXANDER II. HONORIUS II., 1066. HAROLD II., 1066.

MBR. SOLAR	A.D.	PAPAL. SOLAR. hi.	PAPAL. SOLAR.	E. H. LUNAR. Mohammedan.	Eastern Roman Emperors.	Popes.	Kings of France.	Mohammedan Caliphs.
1815	1068	536	462	46	Romanus IV., Diogenes.			
1818	1071	539	465	464	Michael VII.	*Anti-pope—* CLEMENT III., &c.		
					ttes as Bp o Ephesus, 1078.			
1820	0 3		467	466				

GREGORY VII. or HILDEBRAND.

HILDEBRAND establishes *a Papal Theocracy.* HE CLAIMS ABSOLUTE AND UNLIMITED DOMINION OVER ALL THE STATES OF ROME, AS SUCCESSOR OF ST. PETER AND VICAR OF CHRIST UPON EARTH."

says is ahead of a CRUSADE; projects the arming of all Christendom against the SARACENS (the idea first suggested by Bpe Silvester, 999); obliges Henry IV., emperor of ...y, to stand barefoot at the gate of the Castle o ... a the days, in the depth of ... er, o implore his pardon, ...

I. From the accession of Gregory I. o the accession of ...gry VII.—483 years, or sixty-nine weeks of years—era of rise of Papal ...

II. From the accession o Gregory VII. o the establishment of the Reformation by the Religious office of u ...sburg,—also sixty-nine weeks of ys.

From the Nativity, B.C. 6, o the accession o Gregory VII., o 8 ..., or 22 jubilees; the great jubilee ...

VICTOR III.
WLLAM II., 1087.
URBAN II.
AL MORTADER.

F RST CRUSADE; carnal and premature attempt to "cleanse the Sanctuary."

From the Cleansing of the Sanc uary by Judas Maccabeus, B.C. 165, after its profanation by Antiochus Epiphanes (the preliminary "little horn") to the First Crusade, A.D. 096, here is an interval of 1260 SOLAR YEARS.

JERUSALEM taken by the Crusaders, July 15, 1099 (anniversary of Hégira). From the IIégira terminus, July 5–16, 622, 477 solar years to this date or 490+1 lunar, i.e. "seventy weeks' of LUNAR YEARS.

KINGDOM OF JERUSALEM FOUNDED by Godfrey of Bouillon, A.D 1099.

PASCAL II.

VAUDOIS. "The noble Lesson" written, A.D. 1100. Their confession of faith and treatise on Antichrist, A.D. 1120. Pierre de Bruis, after labouring twenty years for Christ, burned in Languedoc, A.D. 1126.

HENRY I., 1100.

Louis VI., the Fat.

(Solar eclipse, March 1, 19h., 1 3, Jerusalem)

Anti-pope—

GELASIUS II. GREGORY VIII. AL MOSTARSHED.

Retired to a monastery.

CA_LISTUS II.

John II.

ORDER of Knight Templars instituted, 1120.

HONORIUS II.

Laity forbidden by Counci of Toulouse to read he O d or New Testamen excepting he Psalter, and t a only in Latin, 1129.

03	18 6	1099	
12	1855	1108	6
23	1865	1118	86
24	1866	1119	8
29	1871	1124	92

| | Emperors. | Popes. | Kings of | Caliph |

A rotated chronological table. Column headers (left to right): LUNAR, SOLAR, (Lunar/Solar years), SOLAR Justinian, SOLAR Phocas, LUNAR Mohammedan, Emperors, Popes, Kings of, Caliph.

LUNAR	SOLAR		SOLAR Justinian.	SOLAR Phocas.	LUNAR Mohammedan.	Emperors.	Popes.	Kings of	Caliph
1935	1877		598	524	24			*Anti-pope—* ANACLETUS, 1130.	
							INNOCENT II.	...introduced ...ng the ...rs by Mgr Johannes.	AL RASCHID.
1940	1882		603	529	30	STEPHEN, 1135.			AL MOKTAFI.
1941	1883		604	530	31			*Louis VI .,* the ...	
1942	1884		605	531	32		*Anti-pope—*VICTOR III., 1138.		
							...of the SEVEN SACRAMENTS established by the Schoolmen.		
1948	1890		611	537	8	Manuel Comnenus. CELESTIN II.			
						ADORATION OF THE HOST.			
1949	1891	1145	612	538	39	LUCIUS II.			
1950	1892		613	539	40	EUGENIUS III.		Conrad and Louis VII., 1147,	quoted
						SECOND ... the Empero... by BERNARD of ...			
1959	190	1153	621	547	48	ANASTASIUS IV.			
1960	1901	1154	622	548	49	ADRIAN IV.			
						HOUSE OF PLANTA..., ..., 1154-1399.		Struggle ... between the Ghibilines (...ipial party o...	Lasts near...y a century,
						HENRY II., 1154.		staufen) and the ...hs (papal faction).	
								and carries ... o Papacy to its h ight.	
9 5	1906	1159	627	55	55	ALEXANDER III.		*Anti-popes—* VICTOR IV, 1159.	
						Thomas à Becket.		PASCAL III., ...64.	
								CALLISTUS III., 1163.	
								INNOCENT III., 1178.	
1966	1907	1160	628	55	55				AL MOSTANJED.

1 ... est of IRELAND, 11 2.

PETER Mo and ... men o Lyons, 1170.

RISE OF WALDENSES. Persecuted from 117

E communicated by Council of Verona, 1184.

...se errors and corruptions of the ...

"LUX LUCET IN TENEBR S.

Mo preached—

1. That the Pope is Anti hist.

2. Tha the Mass is an abominati n.

3. Tha the Host is an id.

Tha purga ory is a fab e.

Philip II.
Augustus.

A xius II.
Killed 83.

LUCIUS III.

Andronicus I.
Killed 118

Isaac II. Angelus. URBAN III,
Dethrcned, 95.

GREGORY VIII.

CLEMENT III.

R CHARD I., 1189; defeats SALADIN, 1192.

F ve HUN red I ws, ged in York Gt c, c ea h other s thro

avo d the fuy of the rb.

CELESTIN III.

Alexius III.
The Tyrant, elled by the La ns, 1203.

576	1986 1927 8
577	1987 1928 1 81
579	1990 1930 1183
581	1992 1932 1 85
583	1994 1934 1187
583	194 1934 1187
587	1998 1938 11 1
591	2002 1942 11 5

PAPAL. SOLAR.	E. H. SOLAR. LUNAR.	Eastern Roman Emperors.	Popes.	Kings of Fra ce.	Mohammedan Caliphs.

"WAR W TH THE SA NTS" BY PAPAL ROME.

"It was given unto him to make war with the sain s and to overcome hm" (Rev. xiii. 7).

INNOCENT III.

BN, 11 9. King Ho. The Persecutor of the Albigenses.

SYSTEMAT C WHOLESALE SLAUGHTER OF THE SAINTS BEGINS under INN CT III., whose accession is in the 66th year from rise of Papacy at IUSTINIAN'S EDI T.

THE FOURTH GE, 202.

Isac II., Angelus.

Restored; wd, 104.

LATIN EMPIRE established in the East, 1204–26

Church of Constantinople subjec to See of Rome.

Baldwin I. NORMANDY ost to England, 14. EWS imprisoned and inhu- mly butchered by King John, 104.

Act of KNEELING at the ELEVATION OF THE HOST enjoined a Co ga, 1204, and mde an universal law in 1217.

Henry.

EARLY FOUNDATION OF I QUISITI S, 06.

Rise of FRANCISCANS, 1207.

BISHOP OF ARTZ dies o extermina e ho WALDENSES.

ALBIGE ES MURDEROUSLY PERSECUTED for 108, in Languedoc, Provence, and Catalonia. n BEZIERS every soul massacred. S mn de Mon ford, of infamous ry. Tou ouse. ders

6 2 8

6 4 60

Courtenay.

SUPERSTITION ON AT TS HE HG. THE FIFTH CRUSADE, 1217.

Robert of ... ay.

auis VIII, the ...

AL ZAHER.

uais X,, the Saint. AL MOSTASER.

GREGORY IX.

R SE OF THE INQUISITION ; COUNC L OF TOULOUSE, 1229.

John de Brienne.

SIXTH ..., 1228.

DECREE of Gregory, granting full persecuting ... er to the Dominica
Friars, April 12, 1233.

THE DOMINICANS " ... lps ... Bw tatis ' The 630th ...
t e Hég ra, or *bisection* of the 1260 ... nt eyrs ... tinat ig in 1844-5.

Baldwin II.   The ... Ons, persecuted n the south of France, take refug
Expelled, 6z.   in the ... rps ... the light of the gospel had 1 og bec
preserved.   THE SRAEL OF THE ALPS."

CELESTIN IV.   AL MOSTASEM.
INNOCENT IV.   CARMELITES, a ... nd cant order.
BONAVENTURA   p es worship of he Virgin My.
SEVENTH CRUSADE, 1248.

ALEXANDER IV.
Established Inquisition in ... Ee.

GREEK EMPIRE RESTORED, 6z.

Michael VIII, URBAN IV.
PALÆOLOGUS.

CLEMENT IV.
COINCIDENCE OF THE SOLAR PERIGEE WITH THE W NTE
SOLST CE A.D. 26

203
203

203
204

2045

2049 1988
2052 190

652   2063 2001

659   2070 2008

663   2074 2012
665   2076 2014

T T

LUNAR.	SOLAR	SOLAR	SOLAR Justinian	A.D.	SOLAR	R.	Emperors.	Popes.	Caliphs
2077	2015	62	736	1268		666	The 668 h gar o the **gh.**	CONTEST between the House of Hohenstaufen and the Po erminates in fav ar of th latter, 1268.	
								THE PAPAL DOMINION AT ITS UTMOST HEIGHT, 1268.	
								Statute that NO JEW should enjoy a freehold, 1269.	
								EHTH (AND LAST) **Che**, **IG**, under Louis o Fra and Prince afterwards King) Edward o E gland. Res of **Che**, and en egrs t **ic.**	
								Philip III., the Bo d.	
2079	2017	664	738	1270		665	EDWARD I., 1272.	GREGORY X.	
2080	2018	66	739	1271		90			
086	2023		744	2 6		675		INNOCENT **V.**	
086	2023		744	2 6		675		ADRIAN V.	
2085	2023		744	12 6		675		JOHN XX.	
2087	2024		745	12 7		676		NICHOLAS III.	
								267 J ws, accused of clipping coin hanged and quartered 12 8.	
			749	281		680	**Andronicus.** Resigns 328.	MARTIN IV.	
			750	1282		681			
			753	1285		684		HONORIUS IV.	*Philip IV.,* the Fair.
			6	1288		687		NICHOLAS IV.	
						693		**J** EWS BANISHED from ENGLAND, **9a.**	
						693		CELESTIN V.	
								BONIFACE VIII.	
								Proclaimed that "God had set him o er kings and kingdoms."	

DEVICE *THE CRESCENT;*

The sign of aggressive ISLAM.

THE OTTOMAN TURKS stream westward from the OTHMAN or OSMAN.

UPPER EUPHRATES led by ERTOGHRUL, th ... Name ... the "bone breaker."

father of OTHMAN.

LOLLARDS, 13 o.

BENEDICT XI.
Said to have been po ... nd.

CLEMENT V.
Removed Papal sea form ... o AVIGNON.

Louis X.

John I.
Lived but eight days.

Philip V., the ...

JOHN XXII.
Pursues persecu on begun by Innocent III.

Charles IV., the Fa r.

WICKLIFFE, b. ...

ORCHAN.
Took the ti e "SUL-
TAN." Trained Chris-
t'an ... (the
prisoners) to form a
body-guard for hi-
self, ... of
the anissaries.

HOUSE OF VALOIS.

Philip VI., o ... his.
The Fortunate.

Andronicus III,

John V., PALÆOLOGUS.
Excluded, 1347.

o9	2046	1299	767	693
113	2050	1303	771	697
115	2 5o	1305	773	699
125	2061	1314	782	708
126	2062	1315	783	7o9
127	2063	1316	784	710
132	2068	1321	789	715
137	2073	1326	794	720
139	2075	1328	796	722
142	2078	1331	799	7 5

| NABONASSAR | | A.D. | PAPAL | | E.II. | Eastern Roman Emperors. | Popes. | Kings of France. | Ottoma |
LUNAR.	SOLAR.		SOLAR. Justinian.	SOLAR. Phocas.	LUNAR. M. ad.				
2145	2081	1334	802	728	735		BENEDICT XII.		
2154	2089	1342	810	736	743		CLEMENT VI.		
							Urges forward the persecution of the Vaudois.		
2159	2094	1347	815	741	748	John VI., CANTACUZENE.			
						Usurps, 47.			
						Expelled, 1354.		John II.	
2163	98	1351	8:9	745	752				
2164	99	1352	8:0	746	753		INNOCENT VI.		
2166	01	1354	822	748	755	John V., PALÆOLOGUS.			
						Restored.			
						WICKLIFFE publishes his "Last Age o he Church." 1356.			
2172	2107	13 0	828	754	761	Controversy with the Oxford 360.			MURAD
2174	2109	13 2	830	756	764		URBAN V.	Charles V., the Wise.	
2176	2111	13 4	832	758	766		GREGORY XI.		
2182	2117	13 0	838	764	772	W kl ng, on his return from Rome, dec ares his conviction t is ANTICHRIST, 1374.			
						RICHARD II., 1377.			

SCHISM OF THE WEST.

URBAN VI., CLEMENT VII., 1378.
Cruel.

Charles VI., the Bc   ...

J[ ] [ ]E OF [ ]HE propagates Wickliffe's teachings.

Interregnum.

SOLYMAN.

INNOCENT VII.

GREGORY XII.

Gregory and Benedict [ ]use to [ ] [ ] [ ]ore he [ ]ncil of [ ], whic[h] appoints a *third* Pope, Alexander V. Each of [t]he three Popes has hi[s] adherents, and ea[c]h excommunicates the o[ ].

ALEXANDER V.

Died, supposed by poison.

JOHN XXIII.

Deposed.

A fresh Bull against HUSS. Place o[f] his res[ ] [ ]nce laid under interdict, 1 13.

LOLLARDS cruelly [e]xecuted.

Martyrdom of SIR JOHN OLDCASTLE and LORD COBHAM, 416.

MARTIN V., CLEMENT VIII., 1424.

AMURATH II.

Char[l]es VII., the Victorious.

JOAN OF ARC 1429.

John **VI.,** PALÆOLOGUS.

HENRY VI., 1430.

EUGENIUS IV, FELIX V., 1439.

General [Cou]ncil of [B]a[ ], 1431.

END OF THE SCHISM.

INVENTION OF THE [AR]T OF PR[I]NTNG.

NICHOLAS V.

2215	2149	1402	8[ ]0	796	805
2216	2150	1403	871	797	806
2217	2151	1404	872	798	80
2220	2153	1406	8[ ]4	800	809
2223	2156	1409	877	803	812
2224	2157	1410	878	804	813
2227	2160	1413	881	807	816
2231	2164	1417	885	811	820
2235	2168	1421	889	815	824
2236	2169	1422	8o	816	825
2239	2172	1425	893	819	828
2245	2178	1431	899	825	835
2262	21 4	447	9 5	841	851

		1448	96		852	**Constan ine XIV** PALÆOLOGUS LAST EM EOR OF THE EAST.
		1451	919		855	MOHAMMED II.
						EUPHRATEAN OF OM AN WOE. Rev. ix. 13–21. Period, "a day, a th, and a yr" = 1 + 30 + 360, or 391 eyrs; terminates in the Ott man Edict of Tolerati n, M. 21 (1 Nisan), 1844. — Bk Cont pl 1453. By his com mand, *St. Sophia*, th polis of the Eas ern Kh, was tr formed into a *mosqu*
						TI E LAST OF THE CÆSARS, falls in the Storming of Cons antinop e by the OTTOMAN My 29, 1453, "buried under a tmn of he slain" Gb, Decline and Fall of th Roman Empire, ch. 58, p. 5.
2268	2200	1453	921	847	857	**END OF EASTERN ROMAN EMPIRE.**
						END o English govern ment in F ae, 1454.
2270	2202	1455	923	849	859	CALIXTUS III.
						Ch uch of the BOHE MN (and MVIAN) Brethren UN TAS FRATRUM forme from the remnant of the HSS TES 1457.
2273	2205	1458	926	852	862	PIUS II.
2276	2208	1461	929	855	866	EDWARD IV. *Louis XI*
2279	2211	1464	932	858	869	PAUL II.
2286	2218	1471	939	865	876	SIXTUS IV.
2297	2228	1481	949	875	886	INQUISITION esbl ied in Spain. Firs Aut ba-fé, 148 — BAJAZET II.
						BONAVENTURA cad, 1482.
2299	2230	1483	951	877	888	EDWARD V., 1483, murdered in 5. *Charles VIII.*
2300	2231	1484	952	878	889	INNOCENT VIII.

RICHARD III., 484.

Iunt [...] as a CRUSADE against the WALDENSES, in
of [...] lge [...] Bull), 1487. (G en o Pra-di-torre.

Zw [...] E, d. 484.

HOUSE OF TUDOR.

HENRY VII., 1485.

ALEXANDER VI.

Or [...] k Borgia ; a mons er o wickedness ; [...] a feast by drinking of a [...] wl he hd prepared for thr.

EWS banished [...] m Spain, Portugal, ad [...] ffice 492-4 ; i [...] d by hem as [...] t a [...] nity as
the Roman [...] in of J[...] n.

[...] S [...] RS [...] AR E, 492.

[...], b. 97.

A O DE [...] A [...] o rs passage to INDIA by he [...], 198.

SAVONAROLA, [...] nd [...] En, for preaching necessity of [...] M in he [...] d to
th by the [...] r of Be [...] er V ; [...] d ad [...] th. [...] h

ouis XII.

PIUS III.

JULIUS II.

Began the [...] c on of ST. [...] s [...] H a ROME.

JOHN KNOX, b. 1505.

[...] Y VIII., 1509.

LUTHER [...] OES [...] O [...] E, 1510.

LATERAN [...] G, 1512, reverses all he [...] ts o [...] the   SELIM I.
[...] cils of [...] stance nd Bas e.

LEO X.

His [...] t o i du gences for crime [...] ip ta es the

R SE OF [...] Y, 1514.

Francis

2308	2239	1492	96	86	89
2314	2245	49	966	892	94
2319	2250	50	971	897	909
2319	2250	50	971	897	99
2327	22	7	15		
2329	22	9			
2330	22	0			
2332					

THE REFORMATION.

ERA OF THE "LITTLE BOOK OPEN" (Rev. x.)

LUTHER *publishes his ninety-five theses*, Oct. 31, 1517.

MELANCHTHON, Professor of Greek at Wittenberg, 1518.

LUTHER publishes his treatise on "The Babylonian Captivity of the Church," 1520; denounces the Papacy as the KINGDOM OF BABYLON and ANTICHRIST.

SOLYMAN I. The Magnificent.

HENRY VIII, having written a defence of the Seven Sacraments" against Martin Luther, receives from Pope Leo X. the title of DEFENDER OF THE FAITH, 1521. (By a Bull thus dated, given at St. Peter's, in Rome, the fifth of the Ides of October, in the year of our Lord's Incarnation 1521, and in the ninth year of our Papacy.")

LUTHER before the Diet of Worms, 1521.

ERA ...

IGNATIUS LOYOLA.

ADRIAN VI.

CLEMENT VII.

TYNDAL's English translation of the New Testament, 1526.

DIET OF ... draws up Confession, 1530. Nov. 28.

FALL OF WOLSEY, 1530, d. Nov. 28.

of ... Francis ... led by The infamous Baron D'Oppède.

PAUL III.

The English Parliament ABROGATES THE PAPAL SUPREMACY in England and recognises ... THE KING, 1534. Oath of supremacy imposed.

2337					
		988			
2338	2682	1521	989	915	927
2339	2269	1522	990	916	928
2340	270	1523	991	917	92
2351	2281	1534	1002	928	941

publis ed, 1534.

From A.D. 312, date of the ⸺rsion of CONSTANTINE and o the rise o the ⸺AL CHURCH, the ERA of INDICTIONS (Papal ERA), o this brogaa tion of Fpa ⸺cy and publication o the Scrip ⸺es, in 1 34, the interval is

1260 LUNAR YEARS.

CALVIN's INSTITUTES published, 1535.

SOCIETY OF JESUS established by Paul III. LOYOLA first ⸺al o the ⸺l, 59.

FIRST SESSION OF COUNCIL OF TRENT, 1545.

(Anti-Reformation Thunders.)

DEATH OF LUTHER, 15 6.

EDWARD VI., 547.   *Henry II.*

Book o Common Pra gr aut?orized, 1548.

JULIUS III.

M⸺, Aessi n, 6th July, 1553. RESTORES POPERY. V OLENT PAPAL ⸺RSECU-T ONS in EN AND. ⸺Y and LAT ⸺ER burn at Oxford, ⸺8, 1555. ⸺en-y-two sacrificed at the stake ⸺ne ⸺err. , ⸺R suffers at Oxford, M h 21, 1556.

MARCELLUS II.

COMPLETE ESTABLISHMENT OF THE REFORMAT ON by the RELIGIOUS PEACE OF AUGSBURG, confirming the Protes ant Churches of Germany in all heir rights and ⸺is, in entire INDEPENDENCE OF THE POPE, Sept. 25, A.D. 1555.

From A.D. 313, the dat of the DECREE OF TOLERATI ⸺s, by the Emperors Constantine ⸺d Licinius,—the Ed ct o ⸺Mn, 13th Jan., 313,—the

1547	1015	941	94
1550	1018	944	7
1555	1023	9 9	9 2

| NABONASSAR | | A.D. | PAPAL | | E. H |
AR.	SOLAR.		SOLAR. Justinian.	SOLAR. Phocas.	LI NA Moh n.-d.
73	2302	**1555**	1023	949	962
77	2306	**1559**	1027	953	96
78	2307	**1560**	1028	954	9 8
81	2310	**1563**	1031	957	9 1

Popes.	Kings of France.	Ottoman Emperors.

Termination of Roman a[P]an Persecuti[on]s,—to the Establishment [of th]e Reformation at the [off]ice of A[ug]sburg, the interval is **1260 CALENDAR YEARS.**

Preliminary a[b]using of the spiritual Sanctuary 2300 y[ea]rs from the ise of the kingdom of BABYLON at the era of Nabonassar.

PAUL IV.

EL[IZA]BETH, 1558. Protestant Church of England re-establi[shed].

· **PIUS IV.**

Francis II.

Knox mightily helps forward the R[ef]orma[t]ion in Scotland, 1559.

Sl[au]ghter of the Protestant population of Calabria, 1560.

Ch[arle]s IX.

Martyrdom of Louis [Rab]el in the presence of the Pope, at [R]ome, 9th Sept., 1560.

Dea[t]h of Mel[anch]th[o]n, 1560.

Publicati[on] of Thir[ty]-[e]ight Articles, 1563.

Close of the Council of Trent 4th Dec., 1563.

End of the "[SEV]EN THUNDERS" (Papal) responding [t]o the lion-like v[oi]ce of the REFORMAT[ION]. The [SEV]EN AN-[GE]LIC [OAT]H Rev. x.).

Wars with the Huguenot[s] begin, 1562.

Secret [Tr]ibunal of the H[ol]y OFFICE in Spain (Inquisition) in full operation. Prolonged [t]ortures and auto-da-fés.

PIUS V.

HIRTY-N NE RTI ES ap ed as he rul e Church o England, 1571.

Birth o Kep er, 1571.

GREGOR" XIII.

Dea h o Knox, æt. 67, 1572.

MASSACRE OF FRENCH PROTESTANTS, ON ST. BARTHOLOMEW'S DAY Aug. 24, 1572.

SIXTY THOUSAND PROTESTANTS SLAUGHTERED IN FRANCE in the course of thirty days.

REJ CINGS AND PUBLIC THANKSGIVINGS AT ROME.

The TE DEUM sung, and a MEDAL struck by Pope Gregory XIII. to commemorate the SLAUGHTER, with inscription STRAGES HUGONOTORUM."

From A.D. 312, the ERA OF INDICTIONS (Papal) and beginning of Imperial Roman Church, to this slaughter of the "Wit sæcs in 1572, there elapsed 260 SOLAR YEARS (Rev. xi.).

Dea h o Pen ecos March 30, 1574, æt. 25.

Henry III. Fifth Reli gus War in France.

AMURATH III. Had his five brothers.

EDICT OF PACIFI CON WITH THE PROTESTANTS, 8th May, 1575.

Hry of Navarre abjures the Romish faith, and places half at the head of the Hugue ts, 1576. Formation of the Catholic Association called the " Hly League" headed by the king, 15 6, foll wl by the Sixth Religious War.

JANSENIST May, 1579; ntly renewed.

PAPAL REFORMATION OF TI E AM, 582.

SIXTUS V.

Seventh Reli gus War in France, 1584.

ROW OF THE SPANISH ARMADA, July, 1588.

966	9 0			
2321	1042	968	982	1574
2322	1043	969	983	1575
2332	1053	9"9	993	1585

| NABONASSAR. | | | PAPAL. | | E. H. |
LUNAR.	SO	R.	SOLAR. Justinian	SOLAR.	LUNAR.
2408	2336	1589	1057	983	997
2409	2337	1590	1058	984	999
2409	2337	1590	1058	984	999
2410	2338	1591	1059	985	1000
2411	2339	1592	1060	986	1001
2414	2342	1595	1063	989	1004

Popes.

URBAN VII.
GREGORY XIV.
INNOCENT IX.
CLEMENT VIII.

LEO XI.

Kings of France.

HOUSE OF BOURBON.

H[en]ry IV., the Great.
King o[f] Navarre.

Ed[i]ct of Nantes, by which Henry V. gives religious liberty to the Huguenots, April 13, 1598.

HOUSE OF STUART.

James England and Scotland united as The K[i]ngdom of Great Br[i]tain.

[Powd]er Plot detected, 5th [No]v, 1605. [Ba]y [Wa]rs on, 1609.

Louis XIII.

Authorized Vers[i]on o[f] the Eng[l]ish Bible, 1611.

Ottoman Emperors.

MOHAMMED III.
Strangled all his bro-
th[ers], and drowned
his father's [wives].

AHMED I.

MUSTAPHA I.
Deposed by the Janis-
saries.

AMURATH IV.

ed ; strangled.

URBAN VIII.

CHARLES I, 1625. Order of Sisters of Charity founded, 34.
20,000 Protestants ꞏꞏ in Magdeburg, 1631.
Diabolica ꞏꞏ es of Count Tilly in Saxony.

IBRAHIM.
Strangled by the Janis saries.

ꞏꞏ sh CONSP ꞏꞏ N IRELAND.
ꞏꞏRE OF 40,000 PROTESTANTS, 2 rd Oct., 1641.
REVOLUTION n England, 1 46.

ou s X, V.

INNOCENT X.

C v L War conti ꞏꞏ es. Battle of Naseby, June 14, 645.
Peace of WESTPHALIA; end of THIRTY YEARS' War, 648.

MAHOMET IV.

ꞏꞏ fns basis for Settl ꞏꞏ ent of Europe.
COMMONWEALTH, 1649–1653.
ꞏꞏe JEWS, after having ꞏꞏ en abished ꞏꞏ om England for 370 ꞏꞏ ears, are permitted to turn by CROMWELL, 1 69.
OL VER CROMWELL, PROTECTOR, 16.h ꞏꞏ eB, 1653.

ALEXANDER VII.

R CHARD CROMWELL, PROTECTOR, 1658–. 6.
HOUSE OF STUART restored.
CHARLES II., 1 66.
OHN BUNYA ꞏ ipr so ed twelve years n Bedford ai for preach ng the gospel ꞏꞏ t the Ac aga nst nventicles ꞏꞏ d on he Restoration). Writes "The Pil g m's Progress" and the "Holy War."
The G ca Plague n London, 1665 ; estimated ꞏꞏ rtali y, 1 0.

2443			
2461			
2464	1111	1037	1643
2465	1112	1038	1644
1469	1116	10 2	1648
2474	2400	1121	104	1653
2476	2402	1123	1049	1655

The Grea Fi eo London, Sept. 2-3, 66.

CLEMENT IX.

WILL AM ℞N imprisoned in the Τ rvies No Cross, no Crown," 6α

CLEMENT X.
INNOCENT XI.

TIIE SCOTTISII oℛrs defea C averhouse at Drumclog, June 1, 1679.

CAMERON killed, July 23.

Nationa Council of France, 1682. Four propositi n*.
Bossue

DRAGONNADES.

Hving ǿn conveted to Romanism in 1663, becomes a ℞pal instrument in England.

EℝR TIIE GREAT, Rus ia, 1682.

JAMES II. Feb. 6, 1685.

REVOCATION OF THE EDICT OF Tℵs, 22d Oct., 1685. Cruel and deadly Papal spcution in France; 400,000 Protestants flee fom tℏr cntry and take refuge in England, Holland, Prussia, Switzerland, and ℳerica. Followed by the war of the 1 ℰs, or ℂMISARD ℳR.

SOLYMAN II.

ARNAUD ꞌ ℳpl ꞌ ℏes the glorious return ("la Rentrée Glorieuse") of the eᴎed ℳis to their ℳe ℏ. They se uℏ, Aug. 16, 1689, and ₰ℓd afte despera e nine months' strugg e.

33	16 7	3	1078
92	16 0	1138	1081
98	16 6	1144	987
91	16 9	1147	1090
24 2	11		1 96
59	℞	1155	1081	098
10	1688	1156	1082	00

to es o e he ...cy of the CHURCH OF ROME.

R ...D BAXTER. JOHN ...

WILLIAM, ...NCE OF ORANGE is called by the English nation to ...ts ...ee, July, 1688. Lands at Torbay, Nov. 5. Joined by a large military force; ...ed to London, ...Q. 20, 1C83.

ALEXANDER VIII.

WILLIAM and MARY pl...ced upon the THRONE, Feb. 13, 1689.

JAMES II. lands at Kinsale, 12th M...h, 1 89, welcomed w...th transports by the Romanists. Civil War.

S...ege and n ...e defence of LONDONDERRY, 105 d...ys. Garrison d...ed from 7000 effective men to about 3000. Deli...; ...e, 28th July, 1689. Browning. Walker.

Louis XIV. s...ds a French ...rmy o help J...MES II. and the Papal ...n, which lands in Ireland, March 14, 1 69.

WI...LIAM sets out for Ireland, June 4. James defeated in ...he Battle of the BOYNE, July 1, 1 69. Drogheda taken. Siege o Limerick.

INNOCENT XII.

D...ppe ...rd, Jul...r2, 1694. Havre de ...; ...G. Dunkirk. William takes Nam...r, Sept. 2, 1695.

PEACE OF RYSWICK, 15th Sept., 1697, a ...pce be...ween Great Britain, the United ...his, France, Spain, and the Emperor Leopold I.; ratified by William III. at Loo, 15th Sep...., and by ...he German Empire, Oct. 22. End of as...guinary confli...ts, and FULL ESTABLISHMENT IN ENGLAND OF CIVIL ...ND RELIGI...US LIBERTY.

MUSTAPHA II.

Deposed.

1	24	6	1689	1157	1083	1011
3				1159	1085	1103
7	2438		1691	1163	1089	1107
	2442		1695			

| ABONASSAR. | | A.D. | PAPAL. | | E.H. |
NAR.	SOLAR.		SOLAR. Justinian.	SOLAR. Phocas.	LUNAR. Mohammedan.
19	2444	1697	1165	1091	1109
20	2445	1698	1166	1092	1110

Popes.	Kings of France.	Ottoman Emperors.

THANKSG[I]V[I]NG DAY, [A.D.] 2, 697. New ca[t]hedral o[f] ST. PAUL'S [used] for Divine [Service] on the d[a]y of thanksgiving for the peace o[f] Ryswick.

Soc[i]ety for [Prom]o[t]ing Christian Know[l]edge founded.

Orphan H[ou]se at H[al]le founded.

Un[ive]r[sit]y o[f] Halle (founded [i]n [16]94 b[ecom]es the fountain [he]ad o[f] Scriptural theology in [German]y. Spe[n]er, Franke. Introduction o[f] a [NEW] E[R]A of [evan]g[e]listic and missionary zeal.

The [year] 1698, following the [t]ermination o[f] the English Pro[testan] Revolution is THE 16TH LUNAR YEAR [FROM] THE END OF THE WESTERN ROMAN EMP[I]RE, A.D. 476, AND THE 2520TH LUNAR YEAR FROM THE ERA OF NABONASSAR, THE BEGINNING OF THE KINGDOM OF BABYLON.

(As "*seven times*" *lunar* [i]s [dated] f[ro]m the Era of Nabonassar to *the English Revolution*, so "*seven times*" *solar* [is dated] f[ro]m that era to *the French Revolution*,— [and] but widely different Papal overthrows.)

CLEMENT XI.

E[ ] [aims] to establish the [Pa]pal dominion in its former extent.

SOCIETY for the Propagation o[f] the [Gospel] in [Fore]g[n] Parts [fo]nd, 1701.

ANNE, 1 70[2].

JOHN [We]y born, 1703.

HOUSE OF BRUNSWICK.

GEORGE I, 1714.

AHMED III.

Deposed, and died in [ ].

0	24	4	1727		

No Zinzendorf. Church of the United Brethren established a Herrnhut, 1727.

GEE II., 1727.

Death of Newton, March 20, 1727.

53	2477	1198	1124	1143	30
55	2478	1199	112	1144	31

CLEMENT XII.　　　　MAHMOOD I.

Whitefield and ☙ey commence their ☙s, 17.1.
Whitefield in ☙a, 1738.
First Methodist Society, 1739.

64	2487	1208	1134	11 3	1740

BENEDICT XIV.

Widespread ☙ Evangelisation o Engl nd, 1746.
Statute o naturalise Jews in En gld passed, 1753, and ☙led in 1754.

THIRD WOE. ERA OF THE SEVEN VIALS (Rev. xi. 14, xv., xvi., xvii., xviii.). From the middle of the eighteenth century.

78	2501	1222	1148	1168	1754
7	2502	1223	1149	1169	1755

LOUIS XVI, b. ☙t 23, 1754.　　OSMAN III.

Voltaire by his writings deluging France with Infidelity.

☙e Antoi ☙e afterwards ☙n) b. ☙v., 1 55, on the same ☙y hat the great Earthquake destroys L sbon. Jesu ts ☙d from ☙ort in Spain and Portugal.

Rousseau publishes "Discours sur l'origine et les Fondements de l'Inigalité parmi les Hommes," in 1 55, Diderot and D'Alembert ☙ng at that time the ☙ fidel "Encycl pédie."

General ☙k of ☙tinental Infidel ty The First Vial There fell a noisome and grievous sore upon the men wh ch had the mark of the Beast" Rev. xvi. 2

From the *Rise of the Papal Power* act al with the DECREE of the Emperor JUSTINIAN, March, A.D. 533, constituting the BISHOP OF ROME "HEAD OF ALL THE HOLY CHURCHES," to the First Vial, A.D. 1755, there elapsed

160 LUNAR ·ARs (expired in Sept, 1755).

MUSTAPHA III.
Died Jan. 2, 1774.

I. 1260 LUNAR.
Justinian.

CLEMENT XIII.

GE III., 1760.

BONAPARTE, b. 5th Feb, 1768.

CLEMENT XIV.

Ganganelli app essed the Jesuits by famous brief "Dominus ac Pr noster," 1773. From this me his life n de miserable by constant fear; he died the foll ing year, Sept. 22, 1774 (su pp l to have bn poisoned).

ERA OF RETRI UTI B. **PIUS VII.**
Feb. 15, 1775.

ABDUL AHMED, or **AMID I.**
Conquered by the Rus-ns. Compelled to sign the humiliating Peace of Kain dji, 21st July, 1774.

ouis XVI

Appalling da h of the corrupt and profligate Louis XV., My 10, 1774.

Accession on same day of Louis XVI. and Me Antoinette. Come ht of the REIGN act al with he REVOLUTION.

F RST GREAT TERM NATION OF "SEVEN T MES, SOLAR.

F om the accession of Nabonassa to he accession of Lo is XVI. (or from he beginning of t he re gn conne ed with the rise of Pagan Babylon to

I	2504	1757	1225	1151	1171
2	2505	1758	1 26	1152	1172
4	25 16	1769	1237	1163	1183
9	2520	1774	1242	1163	1188
0	2521				

the beginning of the reign connected with the fall of ... (Babylon), the ee
... els an ... tal of

2520 SOLAR YEARS SEVEN TIMES" SOLAR.

From the rise of Papal Power through the DECREE OF JUSTIN N, March, A.D. 533, to he accession of Pius VI, Feb. 15, 1775, the Pope whose temporal governmen was ... down in he ... diluti n, the int e- ... is

60 CALENDAR ...,

... Times, and a half Ti me," ... or prophetic.

II. 1260 CALENDAR. Justinian.

THE FRENCH REVOLUTION commences with the destruction of SELIM III. ...d by mis-saries. the Bastile, 14th July, 1789.

Decree of National Assembly against the Priests; ..., oo exil d, 26th Aug., 97. Massacre in Paris, Sep. 2-5, 1792 (including oo priests).

EXECUTION OF LOUIS XVI, 21st Jan., 1793.

WAR IN LA VENDEE. MARCH. " ...s." Drowning victims en masse. Legion of Marat. 18,000 perish in Nantes ln, by the guill ia. The ri er Loire choked with ...; 30,000 victims (..., Hist. of Europe," vol. ii., ch. 12

REIGN OF ..., PARIS, May, 1793.

The Queen Marie ...ette ...ed, Oct. 16, 1793.

...H P OF THE ...SS OF REASON, ...h Nv., 1793.

| 1 | 2536 | 1789 | 1183 | 19 |
| 3 | 2540 | 1793 | 1187
 1263/1261 | 1208 |

Kings of Fra ce.	Ottoman E. perors.	Popes.

Adoption o [New] REPUBL[ican] [CALENDAR], 24th Nov., 1793.

TERMINATION OF TIME, TIMES, AND HALF A TIME."

From the rise of Papal [?] con[nec]ted with the DECREE OF JUSTINIAN, March, 533, to he centra [year] of the [Fren]ch Revolution, 1793;

260 SOLAR YEARS.

THE POPE DETHRONED BY BONAPARTE.
ROME SEIZED by th French Repub[lic] chin [?] Berthier, Feb., 1798.
THE [POPE] [LED] FROM THE VATI[CAN], a[n]d [carrie]ed led from [Rome]; fi[n]ds asylum in a [convent] in [Tusca]ny. Spoliation o [pictures], [stat]uents, and rich collections in Rome.

Proclamation of a ROMAN REPUBLIC, March 20, 1798 (preceded by enormous and unscrupulous plunder of Papal treasures in Nort[h] [Ital]y an[d] [fina]l [?].
From the [siege] o[f] [Samaria] by Shalmanezer, king of Assyria (commencement of Captivity of the [Te]n Tribes) to the *ruin of the Papa[l] government*, M[arch],
1798, the interval is

2520 [LUN]AR [YE]ARS, or "SEVEN TIMES."

NEW ERA in the REVOLUTION. PIUS VI. dies at [?], 29th Aug., 1799.
[Counci]l o[f] Five Hundred [expe]led by BONAPARTE, [who] is [held] FIRST [?]
10th N[ov]., 1799 (1 [anni]versary of the wo[r]ship of the Goddess of Reason).
PIUS VII.
[Dated] [Mth] 13.

N[apo]leo[n] s march a[cr]oss the A[l]ps, [a]nd defeat o[f] the A[us]t rians.

III. 1260 SOLAR.
Justinian.

BONASSAR. AR. SOLAR.	A.D.	ANAL. SOLAR. Jun.	SOLAR Mas.	E.H. LUNAR. M. da.
4 25 5	1798	1266	1192	121
2546	1799			
25 7	1800			

1804 — ʋeᴉ times and *thirty* ʋɡ.

S tting o the great Sanhedrim of aᴸs, convened by Napo en, 18th Sept., 1806.

GREAT SER ES OF N ' ᴹᴼNIC CONQUESTS.

THE FOURTH ᴹᴸ.

MUSTAPHA IV.
ᴃd, and with late ᴛ ᴂn Selim murdered.

MAHMOOD II.

Society for promoting Christianity among ᴛhe J ᴇws fᴬᴮed 1808.

Overthrow of Napoleon by the allied ᴛᴇ. His abdicat on, April 5, and ᴹᴬl to Elba.

Louis XVIII., 3rd ᴸaʋ.

The Pope re-establ isᴛs the INQUISITION and the JESUITS, 7th ᴬᴜ.

Napoleon's ᴇᴬᴘᴇ ᴛᴏrm ᴇlba. French ᴬᴹy deserts to him in a body. Complete ᴬᴮo, 18th June, 1815. Napoleon ᴪ ᴂᴸd and final defeat in the Battle of ᴬᴮo to St. Helena. ᴛᴇ⅄ War of Independence, 1821.

GEORGE IV., 1820.

L beration of ᴛᴳ, 27th J ᴬn., ᴛᴆ. Horrible ᴪᴬᴇ at SCIO, 2 ᴛd April, 1822. 40,000 of the ᴛmbitants ᴜᴳᴸᴛ-ered by the ᴈᴇ.

LEO XII.

Charles X.

A ᴬᴪsacre of Janisᴪᴂes at ᴛᴳntiᴬnople, June 14–16, 1826.

2	4	1807			
2	5	1808	1276	1202	
2	1	1814	1282	1208	
2	62	18 5	1283	1209	
25	69	1822	1290	1216	1238
570		1823	1291	1217	1239
571		1824	1292	1218	1240

Turkish fleet destroyed in the battle of Navarino, 20th Oct., 1827.

War with Russia, 1828.

PIUS VIII.

WILLAM IV., 1830.

REVOLUTION IN PARIS commences with Barricades, 27th July; conflicts between the populace (ultimately aided by the National Guard) and the army, 28th-30th July. Flight of the French Ministry, 31st July. Abdication of Charles X., 2nd Aug., 1830.

From the Papal Decree of Phocas, A.D. 607, to the Revolution of 1830, the interval is 160 LUNAR YEARS.

Louis Phillippe.

I. 1260 LUNAR.
Phocas.

GREGORY XVI.

Bill for JEWISH EMANCIPATION in England passes on second reading, 17th May, 1836. SIR MOSES MONTEFIORE called Sheriff of London, and knighted by the Queen, 9th Nov., 1837. The first Jew on whom this honour has been conferred.

ABDUL MEJED.

Persecution of Jews at Damascus, 840.

Mission to the East under Sir Moses Montefiore, 1840-1.

DECREE OF RELIGIOUS TOLERATION wrung from the OTTOMAN Government, dated 21st March (1st Nisan 1844. 1 Iyar run, Mar. 20.

IN THE 260TH YEAR OF THE HEGIRA.

5	2	1829	1297	1223	1245
56	2	1830	1298	124	1246
58	2	1831	199	1225	124
56	86	1839	13 7	1233	12
7	91	1844	1312	1238	12 0

dy, a [m]h, and a [wa]r," Rev. ix.), after the rise of the Ott[n] Empire, as dated from the capture of Constanti[ple], and end of the Eastern [Ro]man Empire.

PIUS IX., 16th [June].

[...]TION. Barricades thrown up; Tuileries ransacked; prisons opened; frightful disorders committed. Louis Philippe abd[...] [...], 24th Feb. A REPU[BLIC] [...] DE VILLE, 26TH FEB. Perpetual banishment of Louis Philippe and his family decreed, 26th May. Ele[...] of Louis Napoleo[n] [t]o National Assembly, 13th June. Rise of [Re]d Republi[c]ans, and [...] with t[...] [...]. 300 Barri[...], 23rd June. Paris in a state of siege, 25th June. National losses—30,000,000 [fcs], 16,000 persons killed and woun[ded], and 8000 prisoners [taken]. LOUIS NAPOLEON proclaimed Presi[dent] of the French Rep[ublic], 20th [De]. This [...] [...] out at Paris, 23rd [Feb]., and "before the 5th of [...] [every] [country] lying between the Atlantic and the Vistula had in a greater or less degree [been re...] [said]" On March 15, a little more th[an] a fortnight a[fter] the [fall] of Louis Phili[ppe], a constitution was proclaimed at Rome. The POPE [fled] to Ga[eta], where an asylum had [been provi]d[ed] for him by the King of Naples, 24th Nov 1848.

The POPE FORMALLY DE[POSED] FROM HIS [TEM...] [...]L AUTHORITY, and a REPUBLIC P[...], 8th Feb., [...]

[F]rom the Pope-ex[alting] DECREE OF PHOCAS, A. 607, to the [Re]vol[u]tion of 1848, and [De]position of the [Po]pe, 8th Feb., 1849, the interval is 1260 CALENDAR [...].

From the Nabonassar era of the rise of the kingdom of BABYLON, Feb. 26, B.C. 747, to the [year] extending from Feb. 26, 1848, to [A.D.] 8, 48, the [...] of th[...] oveth [...]w of P[ap]al [...]er, there is an interval of 2 20 [...]R YEARS, AND 75 YEARS—OR "SEVEN TIMES," AND SEVENTY-F[I]VE YEARS.

II. 1260 CALENDAR.
Phocas.

3	2593	1846	1314		
5	2595	1848	1316		
6	2596	1849	1317	1243	1265

Popes.	Kings of France.	Otto an Emperors.

The first "Grea Exhibition' opened. NAPOLEON'S COUP D'ETAT, 2nd Dec., 1851. Sanguinary conflicts in Paris; t rops · Assembly dissolved. 83 members of the Legisla ive ly banished. 575 ps, for resistance to the coup d'etat, d to Havre for transportation to ye. The inscription, Liberty, Equality, Fraternity," erased throughout n.

The Prince P es den declared EMPEROR. Assumes the title of N o eon III.

Vi EMMANUEL. Insurrection in ho Papal S t, 8th Sept. Sardinians enter, 11th Sept. Defeat of the Papal troops at Castel Fidardo, 18th Sep' Take Ancona, Sept. 17 29. Victor Emmanuel takes command of th ny, and rs the king dm of Naples, 15th . Garibaldi defeats the Neapolitans at th Volt ro, and greets Victor Emmanuel as King of Italy," 26th Oct. Victor Emmanue rs es as king, 7th Nov.

SYRIAN . Massacre of istians by the zes, 29th May, to 1st July. Mohammedans massacre Christians at Damascus; ut 3300 sla n, 9th July. English and French ts int , 3rd Aug. 4000 French rs land at t, 22nd . Lord Dufferin, the Bri ish iss oner in Syria, arrives at Damascus, 6th Sept.

From the Mohammedan Capture of Jerusalem, A.D. 637, to the Syrian Massacres, followed by European intervention, in 1860, there are 1260 lunar years.

BONASSAR.		A.D.	SOLAR. Justinian	SOLAR.	E.H. LUNAR. Mohammedan.
YR.	SOLAR.				
8	2598	1851	1319	1245	1268
9	2599	1852	1320	1246	1269
7	2 67	1860	1328	1254	1277

14	1867	1335	
	1261	1284	
2615 su	1868	1336 1262	1285

Vict ... in ... ies o: battles. Total defea of the Austrians at Sadowa, rd July.

VENETIA. Massac e o Pro es an s a Barletta, in Italy, 19th M. Bill for su-pn of Monas enes and ... ation of Property passed, 7th July.

War ... led by Italy against Au , 18th June. Austrians retire from Peschiera, Mantua, Verona, and Venice, O. 9-17. Plebiscitum in Venetia for annexation to I., 21st Oct. (... bu unanimous).

The Iron Crown presented to the King at Turin, 4th Nov. Invitation from the Pe to all Catholic bishops to meet at Rome to cel bea e the 18th centenary of the ... of Peter and al, 8th ... ber.

Parliament opened by the King, who decl as hat "Italy is now restor ... o herself," 15th ... do.

Law prohibiting Protes an worship, ... repl a Embass es, n ... enfor ... 31st ...

Mry evolt and a "reig of terror" in Spain, June to Sept.

599 ... ips and this of priests at the ... cution delivered by the Pope on the 6th June.

25 ... yrs ... on the 29th Ju e.

Attempted insurrection in ... , aided by Gari Bd, 26th Oc Repressed by French tro ps, O. 30-Nov. 2-3.

Pub ... in of the Pope's ncyclical letter, moning the Œcumenical Council at R.e fo the 8th ... 86, Sept. 13.

... l Insurrect on in Sp ... Begins n flee; 8 h Sept.; joined by city and garrison of ..., 19th Sep Accepted by nearly all Spain, Sept. 19-30. The Queen flies, Sep 29- o. Dep sition of Queen at Madrid, 29th Sept. Ministers resign, 20th Sept.

resuits ard ot dr reli gus ... laws xpelling the J ws abrogated; freedom of reli gus ... owsl p dec ed Oct. 12-13.

Popes.   Kings of France.   Ottoman Emperor

Twenty-firs General Council opened at   Rome, 8th Dec.

ŒCUMENICAL COUNCIL. First Œcumenical Council summoned by encyclical
let et of Pope Pius IX., 8th Sept., 1868 ; met, 8th Dec., 1869. Present—
6 Archbishop Princes, 49 in all, 11 Patriarchs, 680 Archbishops and
Bishops, 28 Abbots, 29 heads of Orders : 803 in all. Held four public
sessions, and between ninety and one hundred congregations. New canons
issued, 24th April, 1870. INFALLIBILITY OF THE POPE, as head of
the Church, affirmed by 547 placets against 2 non-placets, decreed and promulgated, 18th July, 1870. Council closed, 11th Nov.

FRANCE. Declaration to declare war against Prussia, July 15. Declaration signed,
July 17. Delivered at Berlin, July 19, on the day after that signalised by the
act of Papal infallibility.

Day of general fast battle in Prussia, 27th July. French was chief command of army
at Metz, July 28–9 ; Saarbruck, 30th July. Crown Prince passes the Lauter, the valley of
France, and defeats the French at Wissemburg and Worg, 4th ; and Weissenburg, Defeats Mac-
feated the Mac. at Woerth, August 6, Forbach, August 6. Battle of Strasburg, Aug. 14. The defeated the M. ; Metz, August 18. tis to the Emperor Sedan, 1st Sept. Capitulation of
San ; the Emperor tis to the King, 2nd Sept. Revolution at Paris, and proclamation
of Republic, 4th Sept. Seven French (about 300,000 men) approaching Metz, 13th Sept.
Siege of Paris begun, 15th Sept. July 1 revived, 19th Sept. Versailles surrenders, 19th
Sept. 1 Metz on 0 Metz, 27th Sept. is captured, 11th Oct. Soissons surrenders,
6th Oct. Marshal Bazaine surrenders Metz and his army, including 3 marshals, 66 generals,
60 officers, 173,000 men, including the Imperial Guard 27th Oct. Phalsburg and, 12th
Dec. Tours taken, 21st Dec. Sortie of Trochu fru ed, 19th Jan., 71. Capitulation of
Paris, 28th Jan. French loss about 350,000 in Jan. German loss : killed, 17,570 ; died of wals
een July, 10,707 ; total killed and wild, 127,867. German troops enter Paris, March 1–3,
1871 Treaty of Peace May 10. Ratified by the National Assembly, 18th May.

Rome and its provinces incorporated with the Italian kingdom by Royal Decree, 9th Q. 1870.

A.D. 1866-70.

III. 1260 SOLAR.
Phocas.

A.D. 866, THE 1260TH SOLAR YEAR FROM THAT OF THE DECREE OF THE EMPEROR PHOCAS ... to Boniface III. THE EM-SHIP OVER ALL THE CHURCIES OF CHRISTENDOM, A.D. 67.

From the death of ... 60 solar years terminate in 1870.

"TIME, ..., AND AN HALF ..."

END OF PAPAL TEMPORAL POWER.

TURKISH ATROCITES AND MASSACRES. At Batak, Bazardjik, ... sixty-five t ... and villages in the surrounding district, and in the districts of Roptchus and Phili ...; towns and villages ... ; men and chil ... cruelly slaughtered ; men violated and slaugh ted ; monasteries and churches destroyed ; 15, 00 ... ; disfigured corpses in putrefying heaps.

("The ... question of all is not what was suffered in a ... district at a given date, but ... the ... and habitual condition of the subject ..., who, ... fifteen generations of ... have ... in servitude to the Turk."—Rt. Hn. W. E. Gds ..., "Lessons in Massacre," p. 73.)

CONFERENCE of Plenipotentiaries in Constantinople, Jan. Tu ... rejects their proposals. Ambassadors recall ...

THE EMPEROR OF RUSSIA ... WAR AGAINST ..., AR L 2 ... my immediately ... es ... Pruth.

Pl ... assault on, Sept. 11 ; ...

63	1876	1 70	1293	
2624	1877	1 71	1294	

	Popes.	Kings of France.	Otto an Emperors.

Æ. 7, probably the las of the popes wielding temporal sovignty.

DEATH OF POPE P US X.,

LEO XIII.

Cárdinal Pecci, Feb. 20.

Term nat on o Russian War by the Trity o San St ; ¢ph, N ar.

By his trea y a lge portion of ARMENIA Turkey in Asia) was ced d o Russ a, ho DOBRUDJA was lost to Turkey; the dpte independence of RUM.AN A was recogn sed ; the limits of SERVIA and MENE GRO were extended, and BUL-GAR A was ted into an aut i mus Christian principality. The provi sins of h s daty were luly modified a the Berlin Confer en, which div ded he pvince of Bulgaria, refusing independence to tht portion of it south of the Balkans. The signature of the Treaty of Berlin was preceded by th ANGLO-TURKISH CONVENT D, 1 nct wh ch, n re urn for the c ssi n of Cyprus o England, this un ry 1 nat ok o defend the Turkish possess ons in Asia agains Russian aggress on, tho Por e 1 jug necessary fms subject to Brit h approval.

Berlin Conference, first session, June 13. S gna ure o Trea y o Berlin, July 1

SEASSAR. SOLAR.	A.D.	PAPAL.		E. H.
		SOLAR. Justinian.	SEL Ed.	LUNAR. Mohammedan.
2625	1878	1346	1272	1295

REMARKS ON THE CALENDAR.

I. The character, magnitude, and multiplicity of the events constituting the rise, course, decline, and fall of the four great Pagan empires of antiquity, render *the fact that their joint duration* was, as shown in the calendar, *limited to the exact bisection of "seven times,"* or the period of "TIME, TIMES, AND A HALF TIME," one of the profoundest interest and importance.

The chronological fact thus discovered is marvellous in itself and in that which it implies.

The hand of God in history, and the inspiration of prophecy, are clearly attested by this marvellous relation between celestial revolutions and chronological periods, which presents also irresistible confirmation of the *year-day* interpretation of the 1260 "days" of prophecy,—the assigned duration of the second and more important portion of the "Times of the Gentiles."

II. Measuring thus the duration of the four empires by lunar years, we reach some important facts respecting *the separate duration of each of these empires,* and *the joint duration of the second and third.*

1. THE BABYLONIAN. The overthrow of Babylon by Cyrus, B.C. 538, took place in the 210th solar year from the era of Nabonassar ; the duration of that empire was therefore *seven prophetic months of solar years*—one-twelfth of "seven times."

2. THE PERSIAN. Reckoning the four empires as *successive,* the Persian dates from the capture of Babylon by Cyrus, B.C. 538, and terminates with the conquest of Persia by

Alexander, B.C. 334, a duration of 204 solar or 210 lunar years, *seven prophetic months of years in lunar form.*

3. THE GRECIAN. From the Grecian conquest of the Persian empire, B.C. 334, to the Roman conquest of Syria and overthrow of Antiochus IX., *the last of the Seleucidæ,* B.C. 65, followed and completed by the capture of Jerusalem, B.C. 63, the year Augustus Cæsar was born, there elapsed 271 solar or 280 lunar years ; that is, *forty weeks of lunar years.*

(210 years is the twelfth, and 280 years the ninth, of 2520 years, or "seven times.") Connecting the last two measures we observe that the *thirty weeks* of lunar years of the Persian, together with the *forty weeks* of lunar years of the Grecian, make together SEVENTY WEEKS OF LUNAR YEARS.

Thus from the capture of Babylon by Cyrus to the capture of Jerusalem by Pompey, the interval was "seventy weeks"; in other words, from the *Cyrus* or *Persian* era of Jewish restoration, to the *Augustus* or *Roman* era of "Messiah the Prince," was "seventy weeks" of lunar years ; and it should be remembered that the entire duration of the four empires is measured by lunar years.

Here again we recognise the hand of God in history. It was revealed to Daniel that "seventy weeks" or 490 years should extend from a Persian edict of Jewish restoration to Messiah the Prince, and such a period did extend from the edict of Artaxerxes to the accomplishment of our Lord's atoning work, followed, as foretold, by the Roman destruction of the city and temple of Jerusalem ; and here, in harmony with this foretold and accomplished fact, we find that the interval which reached from *the beginning of the Persian empire,* an empire marked in its very outset by Jewish restoration, *to the beginning of the Roman empire,* as reckoned from the subversion of the Grecian Seleucidæ, and the Roman conquest of

Syria and capture of Jerusalem,—that this interval, embracing the entire duration of the second and third of the four great empires, viewed as such, was also 490 years, or "seventy weeks" of lunar years.

4. THE ROMAN. As the Persian and Grecian kingdoms occupied 490 of the 1260 years duration of the four empires, the joint duration of the first and last, the Babylonian and Roman was limited to 770 lunar years. Had the Babylonian just *equalled* the Persian, 210 lunar years, the Roman would have exactly doubled the Grecian, 280 lunar years (for $280 \times 2 = 560 + 210 = 770$). As the Babylonian was 210 solar or 217 lunar, 553 lunar remain for the Roman empire, or 79 instead of 80 weeks of lunar years.

Thus then, viewed as successive the Babylonian and Persian empires endured respectively for seven months of solar, and seven months of lunar years; the Grecian for forty weeks of lunar years, and the Roman for double that period, less one such week.

III. As to the period now reached in the Calendar, the year A.D. 1879. We *know* that the latter half of the Times of the Gentiles is in Dan. xii. lengthened by two additions of 30 and 45 years, making the 1260 into 1335 years. We assume that the former half may have been similarly lengthened, and as a matter of history we see that while 1260 lunar years comprised exactly the duration of the four great Pagan empires, 1335 solar led to the accession of Gregory the Great, the commencement of Latin Christianity. This point seems to be the bisection of the entire "Times of the Gentiles" as measured from its extreme termini, and comprising two periods of 1335 years. From this point 1260 years terminated in the revolution era 1848-9 (which was also 2520 *lunar* years from Nebuchadnezzar's overthrow of Judah), but 1335 years do not terminate until the yet future year, 1923. That is, not only the main period but the added 30 years have already elapsed, and we are now entering on the final 45. The year Feb. 1878-9 was the 2625th from the era of Nabonassar (*i.e.* 1335 + 1260 + 30). It witnessed the death of the last Pope wielding temporal sovereignty, Pius IX.; the overthrow of Turkish power by Russia, and the establishment of a British protectorate over Turkey in Asia. We have long passed the termination of the 2520 years as reckoned from Nabonassar, and we are within 45 years of their termination as reckoned from Nebuchadnezzar, their *latest* commencing point. If the added 75 years are *included* (as seems probable, and from the nature of the case almost *certain*) in this latest form of the period, then we have already entered on the brief final fraction of the prophetic times; they *may*, of course, be supplementary to it, when the end of the age would be by so much the more distant. Time only can declare.

"THEREFORE BE YE ALSO READY, FOR IN SUCH AN HOUR AS YE THINK NOT THE SON OF MAN COMETH."

APPENDIX B.

—⊸◇⊶—

AUTHORS CONSULTED IN THE PREPARATION OF THIS WORK.

WORKS ON ROMANISM.

ABOUT, E.—The Roman Question. Translated from the French. London : W. Jeffs.

ALEXANDER, WM. LINDSAY.—Anglo-Catholicism not Apostolical : an Enquiry into the Scriptural Authority of the leading Doctrines advocated in the "Tracts for the Times." Longmans.

APOSTASY.—The Great Apostasy ; or, the Church of Rome proved to be *not* the Church of Christ. London : Hamilton, Adams & Co.

ARTHUR, WM., M.A.—The Pope, the Kings, and the People. 2 vols. London : Nisbet.

BARLEE, ELLEN.—The Bible in Rome, with a record of Protestant Missions established since 1873. London : Hatchards.

BARROW, ISAAC, D.D.—A Treatise of the Pope's Supremacy.

BAXTER, RICHARD.—A Key for Catholics, to open the Juggling of the Jesuits, and to satisfy all who are truly willing to understand whether the cause of the Roman or Reformed Churches be of God. London · Hamilton, Adams & Co.

BERTRAM.—The Book of Bertram the Priest, concerning the Body and Blood of Christ in the Sacrament. Written by the command of the Emperor Charles the Bald, in the 9th century. Translated into English in 1549.

BUCKLEY, THEODORE ALOIS.—The Catechism of the Council of Trent. Translated into English. London : Routledge.

BURNET, GILBERT, D.D.—Letter from the Assembly General of the Clergy of France to the Protestants, inviting them to return to their Communion. Translated and examined by Gilbert Burnet, D.D. 1683.

CATHOLIC REGISTRY.—Battersby's Registry for the Catholic World, with the complete Ordo. The Registry contains lists of the bishops, priests, and parishes of the three kingdoms, and Continental, Asiatic, African, American, Oceanican, and Colonial Registries. London : Richardson.

CAYETANO, EL PADRE. Explicacion de la doctrina Christiana segun el metodo con que la enseñan los padres de las escuelas pias. Valladolid. 1802.

CHILLINGWORTH.—Religion of Protestants, a safe Way to Salvation, with his ten Tracts against Popery. London : Thomas Tegg.

CLARK, THE REV. JNO. A.—Rome, its Wonders and its Worship. London : Samuel Bagster & Sons.

CLEMENT XIV.—Letters of Pope Clement XIV. (Ganganelli), to which are prefixed Anecdotes of his Life. Translated from the French, 1777.

COURT OF ROME.—The History of Monastical Conventions and Military Institutions, with a Survey of the Court of Rome ; or, a Description of the Court of Rome, in all the great Offices, and Officers ecclesiastical and civil dependant thereon ; also the Ceremonies of the Consistories, Conclave, and those that have been used in the creation of Cardinals, the election of the High Bishop or Pope, etc. 1686.

COVERDALE, MILES.—The Letters of the Martyrs: collected and published in 1564 : with Introductory Remarks by the Rev. Edward Bickersteth. London : Shaw.

CUNINGHAME, WM.—The Apostasy of the Church of Rome and the Identity of the Papal Power with the Man of Sin and Son of Perdition. London : Hatchard.

DUFF, ALEXANDER, D.D.— The Jesuits : their Origin and Order, Morality and Practices, Suppression and Restoration. Edinburgh : Johnstone & Hunter.

DUPIN, L. E.—The History of the Church. In 4 vols. Translated from the French.

ELLIOTT, REV. CHARLES, D.D.—Delineation of Roman Catholicism, drawn from the authentic and acknowledged Standards of the Church of Rome; namely, her Creeds, Decisions of Councils, Papal Bulls, Roman Catholic Writers, the Records of History, etc. London: Mason.

FAULIS, HENRY, B.D., FELLOW OF LINCOLN COLLEGE, OXFORD.—The History of Romish Treasons and Usurpations, together with a particular Account of many gross Corruptions and Impostures in the Church of Rome. 1671.

FLEMING, ROBERT.—The Rise and Fall of Rome Papal. Reprinted from the first edition in 1701. London : Houlston & Stoneman.

FOYE, REV. M. W., M.A. OXON.—Romish Rites, Offices, and Legends; or, Authorized Superstitions and Idolatries of the Church of Rome ; containing the greater portion of the Roman Pontifical, the Ordinary of the Mass ; the principal Festivals and Offices of the Blessed Virgin Mary, copious Selections from the Services, Hymns and Legends of the Roman Breviary, and the Canonization of the Saints, etc., with the Latin text and translations. Published by the British Society for Promoting the Religious Principles of the Reformation.

FREE THOUGHTS.—Free Thoughts on the Toleration of Popery, deduced from a Review of its Principles and History, with respect to Liberty and the Interests of Princes and Nations. Edinburgh : Donaldson.

GAVAZZI, ALESSANDRO.—My Recollections of the last four Popes, and of Rome in their times. An answer to Dr. Wiseman. London : Partridge & Co.

GIBBINGS, RICHARD, A.B.—An exact Reprint of the Roman Expurgatorius : the only Vatican Index of this kind ever published. London : Rivington.

HALL, JOSEPH, D.D., BISHOP OF EXETER AND NORWICH.—The Peace of Rome : whereto is prefixed a serious Dissuasive from Popery. Oxford : D. A. Talboys.

HALL, NEWMAN, B.A.—The Land of the Forum and the Vatican. London : Nisbet.

HENRY VIII., KING OF ENGLAND, FRANCE, AND IRELAND.—Assertio Septem Sacramentorum : or, a Defence of the Seven Sacraments, against Martin Luther. To which are adjoined, His Epistle to the Pope. The Oration of Mr. John Clark (Orator to His Majesty) on the delivery of this book to his Holiness, and the Pope's Answer to the Oration, as also, the Pope's Bull, by which his Holiness was pleased to bestow upon that King (for composing that book) that most illustrious, splendid, and most Christian-like title of Defender of the Faith. Faithfully translated into English from the original Latin Edition. By T. W. Gent. 1766.

HOMILIES.—Homily appointed to be read in Churches in the time of Queen Elizabeth against the peril of Idolatry.

HUGHES.—The " Man of Sin ;" or, a Discourse of Popery, wherein the numerous and monstrous Abominations, in Doctrines and Practices, of the Romish Church are by their own hands exposed so to open light that the very blind may see them, and Antichrist in capital letters engraven on them. By no Roman but a Reformed Catholic. 1677.

INQUISITION.—Artes de la Inquisizion Española ; primer traduczion Castellana de la obra Escrita en Latin. Por el Español Raimundo Gonzalez de Montes. Printed by A. B. B. Wiffen. Woburn.

INQUISITION.—Authentic Memoirs concerning the Portuguese Inquisition, never before published. London : Murray. 1769.

JANUS.—The Pope and the Council. Translated from the German. Rivingtons.

LUTHER, MARTIN.—The Pope Confounded and his Kingdom Exposed. Translated by the Rev. Henry Cole. London : J. Nisbet & Co.

McGHEE, Rev. Robert J., A.B.—The Complete Notes of the Doway Bible and Rhemish Testament. Extracted from the quarto editions of 1816 and 1818, published under the patronage of the Roman Catholic Bishops and Priests of Ireland, as the Authorized Interpretation of the Church, and the Infallible Guide to Everlasting Life. London: Hatchard.

MacWALTER, J. G.—The Irish Reformation Movement, a History of the Irish Church. London: Seeleys.

MAISTRE, Count Joseph de.—Letters to a Russian Gentleman, on the Spanish Inquisition. Translated by the Rev. Æneas M'D. Dawson. London : C. Dolman.

MANUAL, The Ursuline.—Richard Coyne, Dublin.

MANUAL DE PIÉTÉ.—A l'usage des élèves du Sacré Cœur. Lecoffre fils et Cie., Paris.

MEAGHER, A.—(Originally a priest in the Church of Rome.)—Paganism and Romanism Compared. London : Seeleys.

MEDE.—Apostasy of the Latter Times, with an Introduction by Rev. T. R. Birks. London: W. H. Dalton.

MENDHAM, Rev. Joseph, M.A., M.E.H.S.—An Index of Books Prohibited by command of Pope Gregory XVI. London : Duncan.

MICHELSON, Dr. Edwd. H.—Modern Jesuitism ; or, the Movements and Vicissitudes of the Jesuits in the Nineteenth Century, in Russia, England, Belgium, France, and Switzerland, etc. London : Darton.

MIDDLETON, Dr.—Popery Unmasked, being the substance of Dr. Middleton's celebrated Letter from Rome : demonstrating an exact Conformity between Popery and Paganism. 1744.

MORE, H., D.D.—Inquiry into the Mystery of Iniquity. 1664.

O'SULLIVAN, Rev. Mortimer.—The Apostasy Predicted by St. Paul. London : Longman, Brown & Co.

O'SULLIVAN, Rev. Mortimer.—Romanism as it Rules in Ireland. By Rev. M. O'Sullivan and Rev. Robert J. McGhee, A.B. 2 vols. London : Hatchard & Co.

PAPAL POWER ; or, an Historical Essay on the Temporal Power of the Popes, the Abuse of their Spiritual Authority, and the Wars they have Declared against Sovereigns ; containing very Extraordinary Documents of the Roman Court, never before published. Translated from the French. 2 vols. London : Hatchard.

PAPIST, A, Misrepresented and Represented ; or, a Twofold Character of Popery. Containing a sum of the Superstitions, Idolatries, Cruelties, Treacheries, etc., of Popery. Published 1685.

PERCY, Hon. J. W.—Romanism as it exists at Rome, exhibited in various Inscriptions and other Documents in the Churches and other Ecclesiastical places in that city. Seeley, Burnside & Seeley. 1847.

PHILPOT, Js. M.A.—The Advance of Popery in this country, viewed under both its Religious and Political Aspect. London : J. Gadsby.

PIUS V.—The Life and Pontificate of St. Pius V., by Rev. Joseph Mendham, M.A. London : Duncan.

POOLE, MATTHEW.—Dialogue between a Popish Priest and an English Protestant. London : Baisler.

POULTER, J. J.—A Course of Lectures on the Rise, Progress, Present Aspect, Papal Development, and Tendencies of Puseyism. London : Ward & Co.

POYNDER, JNO.—Popery in alliance with Heathenism. London : Hatchard.

PROTESTANT, THE.—A Series of Essays on the Principal Points of Controversy between the Church of Rome and the Reformed. Four vols. Glasgow : Blackie.

RANKE, LEOPOLD.—History of the Popes, their Church and State, and especially of their Conflicts with Protestantism in the sixteenth and seventeenth centuries. Translated by E. Foster. London : Bohn.

ROGERS, JOHN.—Anti-Popery ; or Popery Unreasonable, Unscriptural, and Novel, with a Chronological Map, showing the post-apostolic and modern origin of Popery. London : Simpkin & Marshall.

ROME, CHURCH OF.—A Report on " the Books and Documents on the Papacy," deposited in the University Library, Cambridge, the Bodleian Library, Oxford, and the Library of Trinity College, Dublin, entitled The Church of Rome ; her present Moral Theology, Scriptural Instruction, and Canon law. London : Partridge.

RULE, W. H., D.D.—History of the Inquisition, in every country where its Tribunals have been Established, from the twelfth century to the present time. 1868. London : Wesleyan Conference Office.

RYCAUT, PAUL.—Lives of the Popes, to the reign of Sextus IV. 1685.

SEYMOUR, REV. M. H., M.A.—Mornings among the Jesuits at Rome. London : Seeleys.

SHOBERL, F.—Persecutions of Popery : historical Narratives of the most remarkable Persecutions occasioned by the Intolerance of the Church of Rome. London : Bentley. 2 vols.

STANFORD, C. S.—A Handbook to the Romish Controversy : being a Refutation in detail of the Creed of Pope Pius IV. London : Seeleys.

STEELE, SIR RICHARD.—An Account of the State of the Roman Catholic Religion throughout the World. Written for the use of Pope Innocent XI., by Monsignor Cerri, Secretary of the Congregation de Propaganda Fide. 1715. Translated into English from the Italian.

STILLINGFLEET, EDWARD, D.D.—A Discourse concerning the Idolatry practised in the Church of Rome. London. 1671.

TRENT, COUNCIL OF.—The Canons and Decrees of the Council of Trent, by Theodore Alois Buckley, B.A. London : Routledge.

URWICK, WILLIAM.—The Triple Crown; or, the Power, Course, and Doom of the Papacy. London : Simpkin & Marshall.

WHITBY, DANIEL, D.D.—A Discourse concerning the Idolatry of the Church of Rome. London. 1674.

WILLET, ANDREW, D.D.—Synopsis Papismi; or, a general View of the Papacy. Published by the British Society for Promoting the Religious Principles of the Reformation. Ten vols.

WORDSWORTH, CHR. (Canon of Westminster).—Letters to M. Gondin, on the destructive Character of the Church of Rome, both in Religion and Polity. London: Rivington. 1848.

WYLIE, REV. J. A., LL.D.—The Road to Rome viâ Oxford ; or, Ritualism identical with Romanism. London : Partridge and Co.

WYLIE, REV. J. A., LL.D.—The Papacy ; its History, Dogmas, Genius, and Prospects : being the Evangelical Alliance prize Essay on Popery. London : Hamilton, Adams & Co.

WORKS ON PROPHECY.

ABDIEL.—Essays on the Advent and Kingdom of Christ and the Events connected therewith. By the Rev. J. W. Brooks, M.A. London : Simpkin & Marshall.

ADDIS, ALFRED, B.A.—The Theory of Prophecy : as it respects more particularly Civil Establishments of Christianity, the Nicene Heresy of Antichrist, and the Doctrine of the Millennium. London : Hurst.

BARNES, REV. A.—Notes explanatory and practical, on the Book of Daniel. London : Routledge.

BAXTER, ROBERT.—Prophecy the Key of Providence. London : Seeley, J. & H.

BEN EZRA, JUAN JOSAFAT.—The Coming of Messiah in Glory and Majesty. London : Simpkin & Marshall.

BICHENO, J., M.A.—The Fulfilment of Prophecy farther illustrated by the Signs of the Times. London : Ogles, Duncan & Co. 1817.

BICKERSTETH, REV. EDWARD.—A Practical Guide to the Prophecies. London : Seeleys.

BICKERSTETH, REV. E.—The Restoration of the Jews to their own Land in connection with their future Conversion and the final Blessedness of our earth. London : Seeley & Co.

BICKERSTETH, REV. E.—The Divine Warning to the Church, at this time, of our Enemies, Dangers, and Duties, and as to our Future Prospects. London : Seeley & Co.

BIRKS, REV. T. R.—The Mystery of Providence; or, the Prophetic History of the Decline and Fall of the Roman Empire. An Historical Exposition of Rev. viii., ix. London : Nisbet.

BIRKS, REV. T. R.—First Elements of Sacred Prophecy : including an Examination of several recent Expositions, and of the Year-day theory. London : Painter.

BIRKS, REV. T. R.—Commentary on the Book of Isaiah, critical, historical, and prophetical ; including a revised English Translation. London : Rivington.

BIRKS, REV. T. R.—The four prophetic Empires and the Kingdom of Messiah ; being an Exposition of the first two Visions of Daniel. London : Seeley.

BIRKS, REV. T. R.—The two later Visions of Daniel : historically explained. London : Seeley.

BONAR, REV. A. A.—Redemption Drawing Nigh. A Defence of the Premillennial Advent. London : Nisbet.

BONAR, REV. HORATIUS.—Prophetical Landmarks. Containing data for helping to determine the question of Christ's Pre-millennial Advent. London : Nisbet.

BONAR, REV. HORATIUS.—The Coming and Kingdom of the Lord Jesus Christ, being an examination of the work of the Rev. D. Brown, on the Second Coming of the Lord. London : Nisbet.

BOSANQUET, J. W.—Messiah the Prince ; or, the Inspiration of the Prophecies of Daniel. Containing remarks on the views of Dr. Pusey, Mr. Desprez, and Dr. Williams, concerning the Book of Daniel ; a rectified system of Scripture dates, throwing light on the Prophecy of the seventy weeks ; a treatise on the Sabbatical Years and Jubilees ; and a compendium of sacred and secular chronology. London · Longmans, Green & Co.

BRIGHTMAN, THOMAS.—A Revelation of the Revelation ; that is, the Revelation of St. John opened clearly with a logicall Resolution and Exposition. Wherein the sense is cleared, out of the Scripture ; the event also of thinges foretold is discussed out of the Church Historyes. 1615.

BROOKS, REV. J. W.—Elements of Prophetical Interpretation. London : Seeley.

BROWN, REV. DAVID.—Christ's Second Coming, will it be Pre-millennial? London : Hamilton & Adams.

BURDER, HENRY F., D.D.—Notes on the Prophecies of the Apocalypse. London : Ward & Co.

CHAUNCEY, W. S.—Dissertations on Unaccomplished Prophecy. London : Nisbet.

CLARKE, J. ALGERNON.—A Compendium of Scripture Prediction, with special reference to the Duration and Doom of the Papal Antichrist, the Judgments of the Great Day of God Almighty, and the Dawn of Millennial Glory. London : Nisbet.

CLARKE, J. E —Dissertation on the Dragon, Beast, and False Prophet of the Apocalypse. 1814.

CLOGHER, LORD BISHOP OF.—A Dissertation on Prophecy, wherein the Coherence and Connexion of the Prophecies in both the Old and New Testament are fully considered. 1749.

CUMMING, Rev. J., D.D.—The Fall of Babylon Foreshadowed in her Teaching, in History, and in Prophecy. London : Bentley.

CUMMING, REV. J., D.D.—The Last Warning Cry. London : Nisbet.

CUMMING, REV. J., D.D.—Lectures for the Times ; or, Illustrations and Refutations of the Errors of Romanism and Tractarianism. London ∙ Hall & Co.

CUMMING, REV. J., D.D.—Apocalyptic Sketches ; or, Lectures on the Seven Churches of Asia Minor. London : Arthur Hall.

CUMMING, REV. J., D.D.—The Millennial Rest ; or, the World as it will be. London : Bentley.

CUMMING, REV. J., D.D.—Apocalyptic Sketches ; or, Lectures on the Book of Revelation. First and second series. London : Hall.

CUMMING, REV. J., D.D.—Lectures on the Book of Daniel. London : Hall.

CUNINGHAME, WM.—On the Jubilean Chronology, with a brief account of the discoveries of M. L. de Cheseaux as to the Great Astronomical Cycles. 1834.

CUNINGHAME, WM.—The Season of the End. London : 1841.

CUNINGHAME, WM.—The Fulness of the Times. London : 1837.

CUNINGHAME, WM.—The Certain Truth, the Science, and the Authority of the Scriptural Chronology. London : Seeleys.

CUNINGHAME, WM.—A Dissertation on the Seals and Trumpets of the Apocalypse, and the Prophetical Period of 1260 years. Hatchard. 1813.

DAUBUZ, CHARLES, M.A.—A Perpetual Commentary on the Revelation of St. John. 1720.

DAUBUZ, CHARLES, M.A.—A Symbolical Dictionary, in which, agreeably to the Nature and Principles of the Symbolical Character and Language of the Eastern Nations in the first ages of the World, the general Signification of the Prophetic Symbols, especially those of the Apocalypse, is laid down and proved from the most Ancient Authorities, sacred and profane. London : Nisbet.

DENNY, SIR E.—Companion to a Prophetical Chart, entitled "The Feasts of the Lord." London : Broom.

DUFFIELD, GEO.—Millenarianism Defended ; a reply to Prof. Stuart. New York : Newman.

DUFFIELD, GEO.—Dissertations on the Prophecies relative to the Second Coming of Jesus Christ. New York : Newman.

ELLIOTT, REV. E. B., A.M.—Horæ Apocalypticæ ; or, a Commentary on the Apocalypse, Critical and Historical ; including also an Examination of the chief Prophecies of Daniel. Illustrated by an Apocalyptic Chart, and engravings from Medals and other extant Monuments of antiquity. 4 vols. London : Seeley.

ELLIOTT, REV. E. B., M.A.—The Destinies and Perils of the Church, as Predicted in Scripture. London : Seeley.

FABER, G. S., B.D.—The Sacred Calendar of Prophecy ; or, a Dissertation on the Prophecies which treat of the grand period of "Seven Times," and especially of its second moiety, or the latter Three Times and a Half. 3 vols. London : Painter.

FABER, G. S., B.D.—A Dissertation on the Prophecies that have been fulfilled, are now fulfilling, or will hereafter be fulfilled, relative to the great period of 1260 years ; the Papal and Mohammedan Apostasies. 1808.

FABER, G. S., B.D.—A General and connected View of the Prophecies relative to the Conversion, Restoration, Union, and Future Glory of the Houses of Judah and Israel. London : Rivington. 2 vols.

FRERE, J. H.—A Combined View of the Prophecies. Hatchard.

GOSSE, PHILIP HENRY, F.R.S.—The Prophetic Times.

HABERSHON, MATTHEW.—An Historical Exposition of the Prophecies of the Revelation of St. John ; showing their connection with and confirmation of those of Daniel, and of the Old Testament in general ; particularly in the most important aspect on the present times. 2 vols. London : Nisbet.

HABERSHON, MATTHEW.—An Historical Dissertation on the Prophetic Scriptures of the Old Testament, chiefly those of a Chronological character ; showing their aspect on the Present Times, and on the Destinies of the Jewish nation. London : Nisbet.

HOARE, REV. E.—Rome, Turkey, and Jerusalem. London : Hatchard.

HOLLINGSWORTH, REV. A. G. H., M.A.—The Holy Land Restored ; or, an Examination of the Prophetic Evidence for the Restitution of Palestine to the Jews. London : Seeley.

HOLMES, REV. J. D., A.M.—The Fulfilment of the Revelation of St. John Displayed. 1819.

HURD, RICHARD, D.D.—An Introduction to the Study of the Prophecies concerning the Christian Church ; and in particular concerning the Church of Papal Rome. London : Rickerby.

INVESTIGATOR.—Investigator and Expositor of Prophecy. By Rev. J. W. Brooks. 5 vols. London : Simpkin, Marshall & Co.

IRVING, REV. EDWARD, A.M.—Babylon and Infidelity Foredoomed of God. A Discourse on the prophecies of Daniel and the Apocalypse which relate to these Latter Times, and until the Second Advent. London : Hamilton, Adams & Co.

ISRAEL, GOD'S DEALINGS WITH. Being Lectures delivered during Lent, 1850, at St. George's, Bloomsbury. London : Nisbet.

KEITH, ALEX., D.D.—The Signs of the Times, as denoted by the Fulfilment of Historical Predictions, traced down from the Babylonish Captivity to the present time. London : Longman & Co.

KEITH, ALEX., D.D.—The Harmony of Prophecy; or, Scriptural Illustrations of the Apocalypse. Longman & Co.

KEITH, ALEX., D.D.—The History and Destiny of the World and of the Church, according to Scripture. London : Nelson & Co.

KEITH, ALEX., D.D.—The Land of Israel, according to the Covenant with Abraham, with Isaac, and with Jacob. London, Longman & Co.

KIMCHI, RABBI DAVID.—Commentary upon the Prophecies of Zechariah. Translated from the Hebrew. London : Jas. Duncan.

MANCHESTER, DUKE OF.—The Finished Mystery. To which is added an examination of Mr. Brown on the Second Advent. London: Hatchard.

MANCHESTER, DUKE OF.—The Times of Daniel, Chronological and Prophetical, examined with relation to the Point of Contact between Sacred and Profane Chronology. London : Darling.

MEDE, JOSEPH, B.D.—The Works of Joseph Mede, in five books. 1648.

MEDE, JOSEPH, B.D.—Clavis Apocalyptica ex innatis et insitis Visionum Characteribus Eruta et Demonstrata.

MILLENNIAL KINGDOM, THE.—Lectures delivered during Lent, 1852, at St. George's, Bloomsbury, by Twelve Clergymen of the Church of England. London : Shaw.

NEWTON, SIR ISAAC.—Observations upon the Prophecies of Daniel and the Apocalypse of S. John. 1733.

NEWTON, THOMAS, D.D.—Dissertations on the Prophecies. London · Blake. 1830.

PITCAIRN, REV. DAVID.—Zion's King : the Second Psalm expounded in the light of History and Prophecy. London : Jackson.

SEISS, J. A., A.M.—The Last Times. An earnest Discussion of momentous themes. Baltimore : Kurtz, 1856.

SHERLOCK, DR. THOMAS.—The Use and Intent of Prophecy in the Several Ages of the World. London : Simpkin, Marshall & Co.

SIMPSON, REV. DAVID, M.A.—A Key to the Prophecies ; or, a Concise View of the Predictions contained in the Old and New Testaments, which have been fulfilled, are now fulfilling, or are yet to be fulfilled in the latter ages of the world. London : Baynes, 1809.

STUART, MOSES.—A Commentary on the Apocalypse. London : Tegg.

TREGELLES, S. P., LL.D.—The Hope of Christ's Second Coming : How is it taught in Scripture? and Why? London : Houlston & Co.

URWICK, WILLIAM, D.D.—The Second Advent of Christ, the blessed Hope of the Church. London : Simpkin, Marshall & Co.

VIALS, THE LAST.—A series of Essays upon the subject of the Second Advent. London : Seeleys.

VITRINGA, CAMPEGIO.—Anakrisis Apocalypsios Joannis Apostoli qua in veras interpretandæ ejus hypotheses diligenter inquiritur ; ex usdem Interpretatio facta, certis Historiarum Monumentis confirmatur atque illustratur. 1695.

WARLEIGH, REV. HY. SMITH.—Ezekiel's Temple. London : Shaw.

WOOD, REV. WALTER, A.M.—The Last Things. An examination of the doctrine of Scripture concerning the Resurrection, the Second Coming of Christ, and the Millennium ; with special reference to the second edition of the Rev. David Brown's work on the Second Advent. London : Nisbet.

WOODHOUSE, JNO. CHAPPEL, D.D.—Annotations on the Apocalypse. London : Hatchard.

WORDSWORTH, CHR., D.D.—The Apocalypse, or Book of Revelation : the original Greek text, with MSS. collations ; an English Translation and Harmony, with notes. London : Rivington.

WYLIE, REV. J. A., LL.D.—The Seventh Vial ; or, the Past and Present of Papal Europe, as shown in the Apocalypse. London : Hamilton, Adams & Co.

FUTURIST.

BONAR, ANDREW, ESQ., OF LEAMINGTON.—The Development of Antichrist. London : Partridge & Co.

BURGH, REV. WILLIAM, A.B.—An Exposition of the Book of Revelation. London : Bagster.

DARBY, JNO. NELSON.—Notes on the Book of Revelation. London : Groombridge.

HUCHEDÉ, P., PRÉTRE.—Histoire de L'Antéchrist, ou exposé des événements certains et probable qui concernent sa personne, son règne, sa fin, et son temps, d'après l'écriture et la tradition. Par P. Huchedé, prétre, professeur de Théologie au grand séminaire de Laval. Paris : F. Bouquerel.

KELLY, W.—Six Lectures. London : Broom.

KELSALL, HY., M.D., R.N.—A Comparison of Prophetic Scripture with reference to the Antichrist, as to his person, actings, and future manifestations. London : Nisbet.

MAITLAND, CHARLES.—The Apostle's School of Prophetic Interpretation: with its History down to the present time. London : Longmans.

MOLYNEUX, REV. CAPEL, B.A.—The World to Come. Lectures delivered in the Lock Chapel, in Lent, 1853. London : Partridge.

MOLYNEUX, REV. CAPEL, B.A.—Israel's Future. Lectures delivered in the Lock Chapel, in Lent, 1852.

NEWTON, BENJAMIN WILLS.—Thoughts on the Apocalypse. London: Houlston & Son.

NEWTON, BENJAMIN WILLS.—Aids to Prophetic Enquiry. First, second, and third series. London : Houlston.

TODD, JAMES HENTHORN, B.D., M.R.I.A.—Discourses on the Prophecies relating to Antichrist in the writings of Daniel and St. John. London : Rivington.

TREGELLES, S.P., LL.D.—Remarks on the Prophetic Visions in the Book of Daniel. London : Bagster.

TROTTER, W.—Plain Papers on Prophetic and other subjects. London : Morrish.

HISTORICAL WORKS.

ALISON, SIR ARCHIBALD, BART.—History of Europe from the commencement of the French Revolution in 1789, to the Restoration of the Bourbons in 1815. London: Blackwood.

ALLNUTT, H.—Historical Diary of the War between France and Germany, 1870. London : Estates Gazette Office.

BEATTIE, W., M.D.—The Waldenses ; or, Protestant Valleys of Piedmont and Dauphiny. London : Geo. Virtue.

BLANC, Louis.—Histoire de la Revolution de 1848. Paris : Lacroix, 1871.

BLAQUIERE, EDW.—An Historical Review of the Spanish Revolution. London : Whittaker.

BROOKS, REV. J. W.—The History of the Hebrew Nation. London : Seeley.

BROWNE, H., M.A.—Ordo Sæclorum. A Treatise on the Chronology of the Holy Scriptures. London : Parker.

BUNGENER, J. F.—History of the Council of Trent. London : Hamilton, Adams & Co.

BURNET, GILBERT, D.D.—The History of the Reformation of the Church of England. 4 vols. London : Scott & Co.

CHESEAUX, LOYS DE.—Abrége Chronologique. 1786-9.

CLINTON, H. F., Esq., M.A.—An Epitome of the Civil and Literary Chronology of Rome and Constantinople, from the Death of Augustus to the death of Heraclius. Oxford : University Press.

CLINTON, H. F., M.A.—Fasti Hellenici. The Civil and Literary Chronology of Greece. Oxford : University Press.

COTTON, H., D.C.L.—The Five Books of Maccabees. Oxford : University Press.

CREASY, SIR EDWARD S., M.A.—History of the Ottoman Turks : from the beginning of their Empire to the present time. London : Bentley.

CUNINGHAME, WILLIAM.—The Chronology of Israel and the Jews from the Exodus to the Destruction of Jerusalem by the Romans. London : Nisbet.

DA COSTA, DR. ISAAC.—Israel and the Gentiles. Contributions to the History of the Jews from the earliest times to the present day. London : Nisbet.

D'AUBIGNÉ, J. H. MERLE.—History of the Reformation of the Sixteenth Century. London : Hamilton, Adams & Co.

CRAIG, REV. J.—History of the Protestant Church in Hungary, from the beginning of the Reformation to 1850. London: Nisbet.

EUSEBIUS.—The Greek Ecclesiastical Historians of the first Six Centuries of the Christian era. 6 vols. London: Bagster.

EUSTACE, J. CHETWODE.—A Classical Tour through Italy. 1818.

FOXE, JOHN.—The Acts and Monuments of the Christian Martyrs. By John Foxe. London : Seeley.

FINN, JAMES.—Sephardim ; or, the History of the Jews in Spain and Portugal. London: Rivington.

GARDNER, REV. JAMES, M.D. and A.M.—The Faiths of the World. London : Fullarton.

GERVINUS, B. G. G.—An Introduction to the History of the Nineteenth Century. London : Ward, Lock & Co.

GIBBON, EDW., Esq.—History of the Decline and Fall of the Roman Empire. London : Westley.

GIBBON, EDW.—History of the Crusades. London: Warne.

GLADSTONE, RT. HON. W. E., M.P.—Bulgarian Horrors and the Question of the East. London : John Murray.

HALES, REV. W., D.D.—Analysis of Chronology. London : Rivingtons.

HALLAM, HENRY, LL.D.—View of the State of Europe during the Middle Ages. London : Alexander Murray.

HUGONOTS.—The Protestant Reformation in France ; or, History of the Hugonots. 2 vols. London : Bentley.

JESUITS.—Regulæ Societatis Jesu. Auctoritate Septimæ Congregationis Generalis auctæ. Romæ, in Collegio Romano eiusdem Societatis. Anno Domini M.D.C. xvi. Superiorum permissu.

JOINVILLE, LORD JNO. DE.—Chronicles of the Crusaders ; being Contemporary Narratives of the Crusade of Richard Cœur de Lion, by Richard of Devizes and Geoffrey de Uinsauf ; and of the Crusade of Saint Louis.

JOSEPHUS, FLAVIUS.—The Works of Flavius Josephus. London : Tegg.

KINGLAKE, A. W.—The Invasion of the Crimea : its Origin, and an account of its Progress down to the death of Lord Raglan. London : Blackwood.

KRASINSKI, COUNT V.—Historical Sketch of the Rise, Progress, and Decline of the Reformation of Poland. 2 vols. London : Hatchard.

LARDNER, REV. D., LL.D. etc.—The Cabinet Cyclopædia : Outlines of History. London : Longman.

LAVELEYE, EMILE DE.—De D'Avenir des Peuples Catholiques. Paris : Germer, Bailliere.

LAYARD, AUSTEN H., M.P.—Discoveries in the Ruins of Nineveh and Babylon. London : Juo. Murray.

MACLEAR, REV. G. F., B.D.—Apostles of Mediæval Europe. London : Macmillan.

MACLEAR, REV. G. F., B.D.—A History of Christian Missions during the Middle Ages. London : Macmillan.

MAUNDER, SAMUEL.—The Treasury of History. London : Longmans.

McCRIE, REV. T.—Sketches of Scottish Church History : embracing the period from the Reformation to the Revolution. London : Johnstone.

McCRIE, THOS., D.D.—History of the Progress and Suppression of the Reformation in Spain in the Sixteenth Century. London : Cadell.

MIGNET, F. A.—History of the French Revolution. London : Davie Bogue.

MILMAN, H. H., D.D.—History of the Jews. London : Murray.

MILMAN, H. H., D.D., Dean of St. Paul's.—History of Latin Christianity. In nine vols. London : Murray, 1872.

MILNES, REV. T., M.A. The Turkish Empire : the Sultans, the Territory, and the People. London : Religious Tract Society.

MILNES, JOSEPH.—The History of the Church of Christ, from the days of the Apostles to the close of the eighteenth century. London : Chadwick.

MONASTIER, ANTOINE.—A History of the Vaudois Church from its origin, and of the Vaudois of Piedmont to the present day. London : Religious Tract Society.

MOSHEIM, JNO. LAWRENCE, D.D.—An Ecclesiastical History, from the birth of Christ to the beginning of the eighteenth century. 2 vols. London : Tegg.

NEANDER, DR. A.—General History of the Christian Religion and Church. London : Bohn.

OCKLEY, SIMON, B.D.—The History of the Saracens : comprising the lives of Mohammed and his successors, to the death of Abdalmelik, the eleventh Caliph, with an account of their most remarkable Battles, Sieges, Revolts, etc., collected from authentic sources, especially Arabic MSS. London : Bohn.

OSBURN, WM. (Junr.).—Egypt : her Testimony to the Truth. London : Bagster.

PRIDEAUX, HUMPHREY, D.D.—The Old and New Testament Connected in the History of the Jews and Neighbouring Nations, from the declension of the Kingdoms of Israel and Judah to the time of Christ. London : Baynes.

READ, HOLLIS, A.M.—The Hand of God in History. London : Nelson.

RECORDS.—Records of the Past : being an English translation of the Assyrian and Egyptian Monuments. London : Bagster.

REFORMATION.—The Reformation and Anti-Reformation in Bohemia.
(From the German.) 2 vols. London : Houlston.

REID, DANIEL.—The Law of History, being a supplement to, and com-
plement of, "The Divine Footsteps in Human History." London :
Blackwood.

RIDDLE, J. E., M.A.—Ecclesiastical Chronology ; or, Annals of the Christian Church from its foundation to the present time. London : Longman.

ROBERTSON, WM., D.D.—The History of the Reign of the Emperor
Charles V., with a view of the Progress of Society in Europe, from
the subversion of the Roman Empire to the beginning of the sixteenth
century. London : Rivingtons.

ROLLIN, M.—The Ancient History of the Egyptians, Carthaginians, Assyrians, Babylonians, Medes and Persians, Grecians, and Macedonians.
London : Tegg.

ROSSE, WILLOUGHBY.—An Index of Dates. London : Bohn.

ROSSE, WILLOUGHBY.—Blair's Chronological Tables, revised and enlarged. London : Bohn.

SALE, GEORGE.—The Koran. London : Wm. Tegg.

SCOTT, JNO., M.A.—Calvin and the Swiss Reformation. London : Seeley.

SISMONDI, J. C. L. DE.—Fall of the Roman Empire. 2 vols. London :
Longman, Rees & Co.

SISMONDI, J. C. L. DE.—A History of the Italian Republics, being a
view of the origin, progress, and fall of Italian Freedom. London :
Longman, Rees & Co.

SISMONDI, J. C. L. DE.—History of the Crusades against the Albigenses,
in the Thirteenth Century. London : Wightman & Cramp.

SMEDLEY, REV. EDWARD, M.A.—History of the Reformed Religion in
France. 3 vols. London : Rivingtons.

SPANHEIM, FREDK., D.D.—Ecclesiastical Annals. London : Rivington.

STANLEY, ARTHUR PENRHYN, D.D.—Lectures on the History of the
Eastern Church. London : John Murray.

TEMPLE, SIR JOHN, KNT.—The Irish Rebellion ; or, an History of the
attempts of the Irish Papists to extirpate the Protestants in the kingdom of Ireland, together with the barbarous Cruelties and bloody
Massacres which ensued thereupon. Written from his own observations, and authentic depositions of other eye-witnesses, by Sir John
Temple, Knt., Master of the Rolls, and one of his Majesty's most
honourable Privy Council, at that time in Ireland. White, Cochrane
& Co. London. 1812.

THIERS, M. A.—The History of the French Revolution. London : Whittaker & Co.

"TIMES, THE."—A Reprint from *The Times*. The annual summaries for a quarter of a century. Printed at *The Times* Office.

"THE TIMES" Register of Events, for 1877, and 1878. Printed at *The Times* Office.

TRENCH, RICHARD C., D.D., Archbp. of Dublin.—Lectures on Medieval Church History. London: Macmillan, 1877.

TREVOR, REV. GEORGE, M.A., Canon of York.—Rome : From the Fall of the Western Empire. London : Religious Tract Society, 1868.

TROLLOPE, T. ADOLPHUS.—The Papal Conclaves, as they were and as they are. London : Chapman & Hall, 1876.

URWICK, W.—Ecumenical Councils. London : Simpkin & Co.

USHER, JAMES, D.D.—The Annals of the Old and New Testament, with the Synchronismus of heathen story to the Destruction of Hierusalem by the Romanes.

VALDENSES.—Authentic Details of the Valdenses, in Piedmont, and other countries; with abridged translations of "L'historie des Vaudois," par Bresse, and "La Rentrée Glorieuse," d'Henri Arnaud, with the ancient Valdensian Catechism. London · Hatchard.

ASTRONOMICAL WORKS.

AIREY, SIR G. B.—Ipswich Lectures. London. 1849.

ANNALES DE L'OBSERVATOIRE DE PARIS.—Publiées par U. J. Le Verrier, Directeur de l'Observatoire. Paris : Gauthier-Villars, Quai des Grands-Augustins, 55.

ARAGO, M.—Popular Lectures on Astronomy. London : Routledge.

BARLOW, PETER.—New Mechanical Tables, containing the Factors, Squares, Cubes, Square Roots, Reciprocals, and Hyperbolic Logarithms of all numbers from 1 to 10,000. London : Robinson.

BARLOW, PETER.—The Theory of Numbers. London : Johnson. 1811.

BONNYCASTLE, JOHN.—An Introduction to Astronomy, by John Bonnycastle, of the Royal Military Academy, Woolwich. London : Johnson, 1811.

BRINKLEY, JOHN, D.D.—Elements of Plane Astronomy. Dublin : Hodges & Smith.

CHAMBERS, GEORGE F., F.R.A.S.—A Handbook of Descriptive Astronomy. Third edition. Oxford : Clarendon Press.

DE CHESEAUX, LOYS.—Mémoires Posthumes. Correspondant de l'Académie Royale des Sciences de Paris, Associé étranger de celle de Gottingue ; sur divers sujets d'Astronomie et de mathématiques, avec de nouvelles tables exactes des moyens mouvements du soleil et de la lune. A Lausanne : Antoine Chapuis, Imprimeur. 1754.

DUNKIN, EDWIN.—The Midnight Sky. By Edward Dunkin, of the Royal Observatory, Greenwich, and F.R.A.S., London. London : Religious Tract Society.

FERGUSON, JAMES, F.R.S.—Astronomy Explained upon Sir Isaac Newton's Principles, with Notes, etc. By David Brewster, LL.D. London : Whittaker.

GILBRAITH, WILLIAM, M.A.—Mathematical and Astronomical Tables. London : Simpkin & Marshall.

GRANT, ROBERT, F.R.A.S.—History of Physical Astronomy from the Earliest Ages to the Middle of the Nineteenth Century. London : Bohn.

GUILLEMIN, A.—The Heavens. Translated by J. N. Lockyer. London : 1865.

HERSCHEL, SIR JNO. F. W., BART.—Popular Lectures on Scientific Subjects. London : Strahan.

HERSCHEL, SIR JNO. F. W., BART.—Outlines of Astronomy. London : Longmans, Green & Co.

HIND, J. RUSSELL.—The Solar System. London : Orr & Co.

HIND, J. RUSSELL.—An Introduction to Astronomy. London : Bohn.

HUMBOLDT, A. VON.—Cosmos. Translated by E. C. Otté. London. 1849-58.

HYMERS, J., B.D.—The Elements of the Theory of Astronomy.

LAPLACE, P. S. DE.—Traité de Mécanique Céleste. 5 vols. 1798-1827.

LAPLACE, P. S. DE.—Mécanique Céleste. Translated, with Commentary, by N. Bowditch. 4 vols. Boston, U.S. 1829-39.

LAPLACE, P. S. DE.—Elementary Illustrations of the Celestial Mechanics of Laplace. London : Murray.

LAPLACE.—The System of the World. 2 vols. Translated by J. Pond. London. 1809.

LARDNER, DIONYSIUS, D.C.L.—Handbook of Astronomy. 2 vols. London : Walton & Maberley.

LARDNER, DIONYSIUS, D.C.L.—Natural Philosophy, with a Preliminary Discourse by J. F. W. Herschel, Esq., M.A. London : Longmans.

LE VERRIER.—Mémoires des Variations Séculaires des Elements des Orbites. Paris. 1845.

LINDSAY, JAMES BOWMAN.—The Chrono-Astrolabe ; containing a full set of Astronomic Tables, with rules and examples for the Calculation of Eclipses and other Celestial Phenomena ; comprising also Plane and Spherical Trigonometry, and the most copious list of ancient Eclipses ever published ; connected with these, the dates of ancient events are exactly determined, and the authenticity of Hebrew, Greek, Roman, and Chinese writings is demonstrated. London : Bohn.

LLOYD, H., D.D., D.C.L.—A Treatise on Magnetism, General and Terrestrial. London : Longmans.

LOOMIS, E.—Practical Astronomy. New York. 1855.

MITCHELL, O. M., A.M.—The Orbs of Heaven; or, the Planetary and Stellar Worlds. London : Routledge.

MOON, THE.—The Moon, considered as a Planet, a World, and a Satellite. By James Nasmyth and J. Carpenter, F.R.A.S. London : Murray.

NAUTICAL ALMANAC.—Nautical Almanac and Astronomical Ephemeris.

NICHOL, J. P.—The Architecture of the Heavens. London : Parker.

OLMSTED, D.—Mechanism of the Heavens. Edinburgh.

POWELL, REV. BADEN, M.A., F.R.A.S.—Historical View of the Progress of the Physical and Mathematical Sciences, from the earliest ages to the present times. London : Longman, Rees & Co.

PRIOR, W. H.—Lectures on Astronomy. London : Longman, Rees & Co.

PROCTOR, RICHARD A.—A Star Atlas, drawn by Richard A. Proctor, B.A., F.R.A.S. London : Longman, Rees & Co.

PROCTOR, RICHARD A.—Other Worlds than Ours: the Plurality of Worlds studied under the light of recent Scientific Researches. London : Longmans.

PROCTOR, RICHARD A.—The Sun : Ruler, Fire, Light, and Life of the Planetary System. London : Longmans.

PROCTOR, RICHARD A.—The Universe and the Coming Transits, presenting Researches into and new views respecting the Constitution of the Heavens ; together with an investigation of the coming Transits of Venus. London : Longmans, Green & Co.

REGISTER.—The Astronomical Register. London : Potter.

ROSSER, W. H.—The Stars, how to Know them and how to Use them. London : Imray.

SMYTH, CAPTAIN W. H., R.N.—A Cycle of Celestial Objects. London : J. W. Parker, West Strand.

SMYTH, C.P., F.R.S.S. L. & E. (Astronomer Royal for Scotland.)—Our Inheritance in the Great Pyramid. London : Strahan.

SOMERVILLE, MRS.—Mechanism of the Heavens. London : John Murray.

WHEWELL, WILLIAM, M.A.—Astronomy and General Physics, considered with reference to Natural Theology. London : Pickering.

WORKS ON PHYSICS.

AGASSIZ, LOUIS.—Principles of Zoology : touching the Structure, Development, Distribution, and Natural Arrangement of the races of Animals, living and extinct. Boston : Gould, Kendall & Lincoln.

CARPENTER, WILLIAM B., M.D. — Principles of Human Physiology. London : Churchill.

CHESEAUX, LOYS DE.—Discours Philosophique. 1762.

HARRIS, SIR W. SNOW.—Rudimentary Magnetism : being a concise Exposition of the general Principles of Magnetical Science and the purposes to which it has been applied. London : Lockwood.

HAY, D. R.—The Natural Principles and Analogy of the Harmony of Form. 1842.

HAY, D. R.—Principles of Beauty in Colouring Systematized. London. 1845.

HUMBOLDT, ALEXANDER VON.—Aspects of Nature in different Lands and different Climates, with Scientific Elucidations. 2 vols. London : Longman, Brown & Co.

INSECTS.—The Transformations of Insects. By R. Martin Duncan, F.R.S. London : Cassell, Petter & Galpin.

KIRBY, WILLIAM, M.A., F.R. & L.S.—An Introduction to Entomology. London : Longman, Rees & Co.

LINDLEY, JOHN, PH. D., F.R.S.—An introduction to Botany. 2 vols. London : Longman, Brown & Co.

"LANCET, THE."—*The Lancet* for years 1842-3 and 1843-4. London : Churchill.

McCOSH, REV. JAMES.—Typical Forms and Special Ends in Creation. London : Hamilton, Adams & Co.

"MEDICAL REVIEW."—*The British and Foreign Medical Review.* London: John Churchill.

MILNER, REV. THOMAS. A Universal Geography. In four parts : Historical, Mathematical, Physical, and Political. London : Religious Tract Society.

PAGE, DAVID, LL.D., F.G.S.—Advanced Text-book of Physical Geography.

POUCHET, F.A., M.D.—The Universe. London : Blackie.

QUÉTELET, L. A. J.—Recherches sur la Réproduction et la Mortalité de l'Homme. 1832.

QUÉTELET, L. A. J.—Facts, Laws, and Phenomena of Natural Philosophy. 1835.

QUÉTELET, L. A. J.—Physique Sociale. Essai sur le Développement des Facultés de l'Homme. 2 vols.

QUÉTELET, L. A. J.—Recherches sur le Penchant au Crime aux différents ages.

SMITH, JOHN PYE, D.D., F.R.S., F.G.S.—On the Relation between the Holy Scripture, and some parts of Geological Science. London : Jackson.

SOMERVILLE, MRS. M.—On the connection of the Physical Sciences.

STRABO.—The Geography of Strabo. 3 vols. London : Bohn.

WAGNER, RUDOLPH, M.D.—Elements of the Comparative Anatomy of the Vertebrate Animals. London : Longman, Brown & Co.

APPENDIX C.

East London Institute,

FOR HOME AND FOREIGN MISSIONS.

HARLEY HOUSE, BOW, E.,

AND

HULME CLIFF COLLEGE, CURBAR, DERBYSHIRE.

Hon. Director: H. GRATTAN GUINNESS.
ASSISTED BY TUTORS AND LECTURERS.

Treasurer: STEVENSON A. BLACKWOOD, Esq.

Bankers: LONDON AND SOUTH WESTERN BANK, BOW BRANCH.

THIS INSTITUTE was founded under a deep and pressing sense of the claims of the heathen, and of the need of a practical Training Home, where Christian young men, of any evangelical denomination, gifted for God's service, and sincerely desirous to devote themselves to it, might be received and tested, instructed in the truth, and exercised in various branches of evangelistic labour, and when sufficiently prepared, helped to go forth as missionaries to any country or sphere to which God might providentially open their way.

The need for, and the benefit of, such an Institute may be judged from the facts, that during the six years which have elapsed since its commencement, about ONE THOUSAND CHRISTIAN YOUNG MEN have applied to be admitted, that about two hundred of these have been received, and that of these more than one hundred are already labouring successfully in the gospel, either in the Home or the Foreign field.

The students have been of various nationalities; not only English,

Scotch, and Irish, but French, German, Italian, Spanish, Swedish, Danish, Russian, Bulgarian, Syrian, Egyptian, Caffre, Negro, Hindoo, Parsee, Koordish, Jewish, etc., and they have been of various evangelical denominations; while those of them who have gone forth as missionaries are now connected with equally various societies, as a glance at the accompanying list will show.

The training given is not only intellectual but PRACTICAL; several Mission Halls, and a Mission Cutter for work among seamen, are attached to the Institute, and the Derbyshire branch has a small farm. There are about a thousand children taught in the Sunday-schools of the Institute.

The Biblical instruction is designed to give a clear grasp of the fundamental truths and evidences of Christianity. In addition to the ordinary branches of an English education, the students are instructed in the Greek of the New Testament, in history and science. Those of them who are preparing to become medical missionaries, attend the school of medicine at the London Hospital.

With hardly an exception, the students received into the Institute are not in a position to contribute towards the expenses of their own support and training, so that this work involves to the Director a very heavy financial responsibility. It is carried on in humble dependence on God, whose kingdom it seeks to extend on earth, and it has, so far, been sustained, in answer to prayer, by his Almighty power through the liberality of his people.

It involves considerable outlay, though the services of Director and Secretary are entirely gratuitous, the ordinary expenses being at the rate of about £50 a year for each of the seventy students in training, and a considerable sum besides being expended directly in missions. Annual reports, with regularly audited accounts are published, and may be obtained on application to the HON. SECRETARY, Mrs. H. GRATTAN GUINNESS, HARLEY HOUSE, BOW, E., together with the periodical of the Institute, entitled "THE REGIONS BEYOND."

The author earnestly hopes that every reader of the foregoing volume— who believes with him, that the time is short, and that the last command of our quickly coming Saviour, "Go ye into all the world, and preach the gospel to every creature," ought to be obeyed far more widely and fully than it is,—WILL ENDEAVOUR TO THE UTMOST OF HIS OR HER POWER TO HELP FORWARD MISSIONARY WORK. LET THOSE WHO CAN GO,

GO, AND LET THOSE WHO CAN GIVE, GIVE, THAT THE UTTERMOST
PARTS OF THE EARTH MAY, WHILE YET THERE IS TIME, LEARN THE
SALVATION OF GOD !

Communications from earnest Christian young men wishing to become
missionaries, and free-will offerings towards the funds of the Institute, from
those who wish to aid missions to the heathen, may be addressed to

H. GRATTAN GUINNESS,

Harley House, Bow, London, E.

The following are some of the Stations occupied by Missionaries who have been Students in the Institute.

In Europe.

ENGLAND.

1. W. B.	Bible Carriage.	Itinerant	N. of England.
2. E. M .	Evangelist . . .	,,	England.
3. W. B. .	Missionary to Germans .	Whitechapel .	London.
4. F. B. .	Bible Carriage . .	Itinerant	N. of England.
5. C. B. .	Home Mission . .	Sheffield	Yorkshire.
6. D. C. .	Gaelic Mission . .	Hebrides	Scotland.
7. W. C. .	Episcopal Minister .	.	Isle of Man.
8. F. E. C.	Evangelist .	Devizes	Wiltshire.
9. H. D. .	Town Missionary .	Hertford	Herts.
10. W. D. .	City Missionary . .	Stepney	London.
11. W. F. .	Village Pastor . . .	Milford .	Surrey.
12. T. H.	Army Scripture Reader .	Plymouth	Devonshire.
13. J. K.	Village Pastor . . .	Watlington	Oxfordshire.
14. J. P. .	Master of Children's Home	Hackney	London.
15. T. E. R.	Home Missionary	Sheffield	Yorkshire.
16 R. H. S.	Colportage .	.	Yorkshire.
17. W. S. .	Assistant Pastor	Bury .	Lancashire.
18. G. T. .	Pastor . .	Stratford	London.
19. J. W. .	Village Pastor .	Urchfont	Wiltshire.

FRANCE.

20. L. D.	Missionary . .	Mentone	S. of France.
21. A. M.	Ecole préparatoire .	Batignolles	Paris.
2. E. S.	Mr. McCall's Mission	.	Paris.
23. R. S.	Gospel Mission .	Several Halls	Marseilles.

SPAIN.

24. E. L. .	Missionary	Figueras	N.E. of Spain.
25. S M. .	,,	Leon .	N. of Spain.
26. F. P. .	,, .	Figueras	N.E. of Spain.

PORTUGAL.

27. M. M.	Missionary	Lisbon.

ITALY.

28. G. M. .	Missionary .	Turin	N of Italy.

BULGARIA.

29. D. V.	Missionary	Bulgaria.

In Asia.

CHINA.

30. J. A.	China Inland Mission	Wu-chang (previously in Bhamo, Burmah).	
31. J. A.	Scottish Bible Society	Hankow (itinerations in province of Hunan).	
32. F. B.	China Inland Mission	Kiu-chau (itinerations in province of Gan-hwui).	
33. J. C.	,, ,,	has traversed China from Shanghai to Burmah, now in S.W. China.	
34. S. C. .	,, ,,	Chung-king .	Province of Szchuen.
35. A. C. .	,, ,,	I-chang .	Province of Hupeh.
36. A. C. D.	,, ,,	Ta-tung .	Province of Gan-hwui.
37. A. W. D.	,, ,,	Kiu-chau .	Province of Chekiang.
38. J. F. .	,, ,,		
39. J. H.	United Methodist Free Church	Tientsin .	Province of Chili.
40. J. M.	China Inland Mission .	Yang-chaw .	Province of Kiangsu.
41. J. M.	British and Foreign Bible Soc.	Foochow (extensive itinerations in various provinces).	
42. G. N.	China Inland Mission	Chung-king (itinerations in province of Szchuen).	
43. G. P.	,, ,,	(Itinerations in the provinces of Shensi and Kansuh).	
44. J. H. R.	,, ,,	Chung-king .	Province of Szchuen.
45. S. S. .	,, ,,	Hangchau .	Province of Chehkiang.
46. H. T. .	,, ,,	Kiu-chau (extensive itinerations in the province of Honan).	
47. A. W. .	,, ,,	Tai-chau .	Province of Kiangsu.
48. Miss E. B.	,, ,,	Nankin .	Province of Kiangsu.

INDIA

49. J. C. .	Baptist Missionary Society	.	Madras.
50. M. M. .	Mission to Parsees, etc. .	.	Bombay.
51. J. N. .	Mission to English in India	.	Saharampore.
52. H. P. .	Mission to Santhals .	. Jamtara	Bengal.

SIBERIA.

53. J. J. T.   Bible Colportage, across southern Siberia, from Perm to Irkutsk.

SYRIA.

54. F. W. C.	Mission to Arabs .	. Damascus (itinerations in the Hauran).	
55. P. W. .	Missionary . . .	. . . Port Said.	
56. G. Z. .	Mission to the Druzes	. Itat .	. Mountains of Lebanon.

ARMENIA.

57. Dr. K. .	Medical Missionary .	. Tokat	Turkey in Asia.

EGYPT.

58. A. H.

In Africa.

WEST COAST.

59. D. C. .	Wesleyan Missionary Society .	. . .	Ashantee.
60. H. C. .	Livingstone Inland Mission	Cardiff Station	Congo.
61. C. J. .	,, ,,	,, ,,	,,
62. C. A. M'K.	Wesleyan Missionary Society	Bathurst . .	Gambia.
63. J. N. .	Native Agent	Cameroon Mountains	Guinea.
64. G. P. .	Livingstone Inland Mission	near Falls of Yellala	Congo.
65. H. R. .	,, ,,	,, ,, ,,	,,
66. — T. (dec.)	,, ,,	,, ,, ,,	,,
67. G. V. .	,, ,,	,, ,,	,,
68. S. Z. .	Mr. D. Mackenzie's Expedition	Cape Juby . .	Western Sahara

SOUTH AFRICA.

69. S. A. .	B.Y.M.F.M. Society	Ikwesi Lamaci	Kaffraria.
70. J. A. .	Missionary	Dysseldorp	Cape Colony.
71. E. C. .	,,	Ixopo .	Kaffraria.
72. W. K. .	Evangelist	.	Cape Colony.
73. R. L. .	Missionary	Oudshoorn	,, ,,
74. J. N. .	Evangelist	Cape Town	,, ,,
75. M. S. .	Native Agent	Lovedale .	,, ,,
76. U. S. .	,, ,,	,, ,	,, ,,

EAST AFRICA.

77. E. C. H.	London Missionary Society.	Ujiji . . ,	Lake Tanganyka.
78. A. R.	Free Church Mission. .	Livingstonia . .	Lake Nyassa.
79. W. S. .	. . . . . .	Ribe . . .	Zanzibar & Gallas.

In America.

MANITOBA.

80. W. H. .	Evangelist	Itinerant.
81. W. S. .	,,	,,

CAPE BRETON.

82. D. M'D.	Gaelic Missionary.

UNITED STATES.

83. J. B. .	Evangelist	Itinerant.
84. D. H. .	,,	,,
85. B. N. .	,,	Texas.
86. W. N. . .	,,	Itinerant.

JAMAICA.

87. G. C. .	Missionary	Stacey Ville.
88. J. J. .	,,	Bethany.
89. W. H. .	,,	Bamboo.
90. G. H. .	,,	
91. A. J. K.	Pastor	
92. J. W. M.	U. M. F. C. Mission	Kingston.
93. H. T. (dec.)	Evangelist . .	Itinerant.
94. F. T. .	,,	
95. G. W.	,,	

BRAZIL.

96. W. B. (dec.)	Missionary . .	Pernambuco .	Brazil.
97 J. F. .	Scottish Bible Society	,,	,,
98. L. Da S.	,, ,, ,,	,,	,,

ARGENTINE REPUBLIC.

99. F. F. .	. . . .	S. America.

In Australia.

100. F. M. .	Evangelist . . .	Itinerant .	Queensland.
101. A. N. .	Episcopal Minister.		
102. A. R. .	Methodist Evangelist	,,	S. Australia.
103. J. S. .	Evangelist	,,	,,

In New Zealand.

104. D. M'L.	Presbyterian Pastor . . .	. .	Auckland (N. Island).
105. W. S. .	Baptist Pastor . . .	Greendale	Canterbury (S. Island).

Butler & Tanner, The Selwood Printing Works, Frome, and London.

Made in the USA
Middletown, DE
19 August 2024

59461699R00413